# Political Campaign Communication

# COMMUNICATION, MEDIA, AND POLITICS

## Series Editor: Robert E. Denton, Jr., Virginia Tech

This series features a range of work dealing with the role and function of communication in the realm of politics, broadly defined. Including general academic books and texts for use in graduate and advanced undergraduate courses, the series encompasses humanistic, critical, historical, and empirical studies in political communication in the United States. Primary subject areas include campaigns and elections, media, and political institutions. *Communication, Media, and Politics* books will be of interest to students, teachers, and scholars of political communication from the disciplines of communication, rhetorical studies, political science, journalism, and political sociology.

# Political Campaign Communication

## Principles and Practices

*Ninth Edition*

Robert E. Denton, Jr.
*Virginia Tech*

Judith S. Trent
*University of Cincinnati*

Robert V. Friedenberg
*Miami University of Ohio*

ROWMAN & LITTLEFIELD
*Lanham • Boulder • New York • London*

To Rachel L. Holloway, and
to the memory of Jimmie Douglas Trent and
Aaron and Florence Friedenberg

Executive Editor: Elizabeth Swayze
Assistant Editor: Megan Manzano
Senior Marketing Manager: Kim Lyons

Credits and acknowledgments for material borrowed from other sources, and reproduced
with permission, appear on the appropriate page within the text.

Published by Rowman & Littlefield
An imprint of The Rowman & Littlefield Publishing Group, Inc.
4501 Forbes Boulevard, Suite 200, Lanham, Maryland 20706
www.rowman.com

6 Tinworth Street, London SE11 5AL, United Kingdom

British Library Cataloguing in Publication Information Available

**Library of Congress Cataloging-in-Publication Data**

Names: Denton, Robert E., Jr., author. | Trent, Judith S., author. | Friedenberg, Robert V.,
    author.
Title: Political campaign communication : principles and practices / Robert E. Denton, Jr.,
    Virginia Tech, Judith S. Trent, University of Cincinnati, Robert V. Friedenberg, Miami
    University of Ohio.
Description: Ninth Edition. | Lanham : ROWMAN & LITTLEFIELD, [2019] |
    Series: Communication, Media, and Politics | Previous edition: 2016. | Includes
    bibliographical references and index.
Identifiers: LCCN 2019006404 (print) | LCCN 2019009648 (ebook) | ISBN 9781538112618
    (electronic) | ISBN 9781538112601 (paper : alk. paper)
Subjects: LCSH: Political campaigns. | Communication in politics.
Classification: LCC JF1001 (ebook) | LCC JF1001 .T73 2019 (print) | DDC 324.7/3—dc23
LC record available at https://lccn.loc.gov/2019006404

$\infty$™ The paper used in this publication meets the minimum requirements of
American National Standard for Information Sciences—Permanence of Paper
for Printed Library Materials, ANSI/NISO Z39.48-1992.

# Contents

# Preface

If there is any one theme to this book—and its eight preceding editions—it is that using the principles and practices of speech communication to examine elective politics contributes appreciably to our knowledge and understanding of the electoral process. It is, and always has been, written from a speech-communication perspective. While we certainly draw on other disciplines and acknowledge the merit of much of the material they contribute to the study of election campaigns, we argue that communication is the epistemological base of political campaigns. We have been extremely gratified by the reception that our first eight editions received and hope you will continue to value this new, ninth edition.

We view political campaigns as communication phenomena, and in the following pages, we examine those communication principles and practices central to election campaigns across America's rich electoral history. Our goal is to offer readers a realistic understanding of the strategic and tactical communication choices candidates and their managers must make as they wage the campaign. We attempt to balance historical examples with contemporary ones throughout the entire text.

In this ninth edition, we have added chapters on ethical considerations of political campaign communication and the practice of contemporary journalism in today's campaigns. We have also added a dedicated chapter on political campaign communication in the 2016 presidential election. We expanded the material in campaign use and tactics of social media and new platforms and communication technologies. All the chapters have been updated to include the 2016 presidential elections.

In 1982, Judith Trent and Robert Friedenberg approached me about a potential project for my Praeger Series in Political Communication. Their idea of the book grew out of frustration at not having books or textbooks available for classes in political communication with an emphasis on elements and theories of communication. Of course, there was a tremendous need for such a volume for the growing subdisciplinary field of political communication. While it might make them uncomfortable, of course I was well aware of their scholarship and considered them as mentors in my own research and career. I was honored that they wanted the volume in my new series. It was, without question, the first book-length study of election campaigns focusing on the principles and practices of speech communication. Needless to say, the volume was most successful and became a mainstay of the discipline. With a change of editorial policy at Praeger, the fifth edition became part of the new series of Communication, Media, and Politics with Rowman & Littlefield. I had the high privilege of joining Judith Trent and Robert Friedenberg for the seventh and eighth editions. As I now take the lead for this edition, it remains true to the vision, mission, and scope of earlier volumes. The collective ideas and historical materials of my colleagues remain. Thus, the volume is still very much a collective endeavor.

Over the years we acknowledged many people for their aid in producing this book. Particularly helpful were our colleagues, students, staffs, and libraries at our home institutions, the University of Cincinnati, Miami (Ohio) University, and Virginia Tech. We also acknowledge all the impressive scholarship by our academic colleagues. Without their work, this volume would not be possible. The staff at Rowman & Littlefield has always been uniformly helpful and pleasant.

Finally, and most important, Judith Trent always enjoyed the love and support of her husband, Jimmie Douglas Trent, and Bob Friedenberg the wonderful support he received throughout the writing of every edition of this book from his wife, Emmy.

I, Robert Denton, remain genuinely humbled by the opportunity to continue the legacy of the authors of a classic and seminal work in political communication. I would like to thank my colleagues in the Department of Communication at Virginia Tech. As now a continuing and long-term administrator, I thank my colleagues for their continued collegiality and encouragement, as well as for their recognizing the importance of maintaining an active research agenda. Thanks also to Robert Sumirchrast, dean of the Pamplin College of Business, and Rosemary Blieszner, dean of the College of Liberal Arts and Human Sciences, for they, too, understand the importance of the "right mix" that makes the job of department head a privilege and a pleasure. Finally, as always, countless thanks to my wonderful wife, Rachel, a true blessing, friend, colleague, and partner in my life, and also to my now grown sons, Bobby and Chris, and their own wonderful spouses, Christen and Sarah. The boys and Rachel have always been tolerant of the countless hours in the study, perhaps too tolerant and too many hours. Together these five, plus our precious dog Abby, enrich and fulfill every moment of my life.

# 1

⊷

# Communication and Political Campaigns

## *A Prologue*

Criticizing our electoral system has become a favorite pastime in the United States. Campaigns? Too long, too expensive, too negative, and way too partisan. Candidates? Dishonest, overly focused on presenting an image, self-centered, and able to speak only in sound bites. Voters? Don't trust government *or* politicians, are bored with the entire electoral process, and often don't bother to vote. But despite these and other complaints, elections—and the political campaigns that are a part of them—are vital to us in at least three different but complementary senses.

## IMPORTANCE OF POLITICAL CAMPAIGNS

Elections allow us the freedom to actively participate in selecting our leaders. They are the core of democracy. Nowhere in the world are more people more freely engaged in active, responsible participation in the choice of leadership than in the United States. Whether the election will determine the occupants of two seats on the city council or one chair in the Oval Office of the White House, the political election campaign is an essential element of a democratic system.

Elections provide us with the opportunity to determine how our own interests can best be served. We may, for example, try to decide which board of education candidate does not favor increasing our property taxes. We might also ask whether the Republican candidate for governor sees the need to create jobs as the state's top priority or whether the Democratic challenger running for Congress supports increasing money for education and public transportation. Once we feel enough questions have been answered, we must decide how actively to participate in the campaign. Will we try to ignore it? Will we work for the candidate or political party we favor? Will we vote? Any decision contributes to our self-development and expression and to our democratic form of government.

Not only do elections give opportunities for quiet decision making or overt participation in determining who will govern; they also provide the legitimacy with which to govern. The winners of elections receive a general acceptance of their right to power. No matter how large or small the margin of victory, the candidate who receives the necessary votes has been granted legitimacy quite distinct from power. Any election can give the winner power. Only a democratic election will provide the sense of "rightness" or even "genuineness" necessary to govern or be governed. Although disputed by some in 2000 or 2016, we may no longer "like" the president for whom we voted two years ago, but we recognize that he or she has a legitimate claim to the office until the next election. The president, like all other candidates we elect, can only be "overthrown" as a consequence of the next election.

Thus, in pragmatic ways, our electoral system is important to us. No less significant are the symbolic aspects of election campaigns. The past is composed not only of historical "fact" but of what is "made" of history. It is, in the largest sense, the collective memory—the national myth—that unites us as a people. Not only do elections provide leaders and grant them authority to govern, but they also add to our memory or image of the electoral process and thus give proof that the system is a good one. The fact that we have elections, that leaders are not overthrown by revolution, that citizens freely discuss and participate in the selection process, or that the Constitution "worked" during the Watergate crisis of the 1970s, the impeachment process of the 1990s, and the challenge of ballots in 2000 grants support for the belief that the American Dream is real and that this country really is destined to be the mighty keeper of liberty. All the fanfare and excitement of the political campaign—be it bands and parades, buttons and billboards, speeches and rallies, television ads and heated debates, or internet chat rooms and social media—are important for the reinforcement provided about the rightness of what we do and the way we do it.

Now, all of this is to tell you that the subject matter of this book is worthwhile. Although aspects of our electoral system may need repair from time to time, the process and the product are worth the effort. While the value of elections has remained constant, the manner in which they are conducted has changed enormously in recent years. As a matter of fact, the political campaign has undergone such a radical transformation that those principles and practices accepted by practitioners and theorists even a decade ago are in many respects largely irrelevant today. With each election cycle there are new strategies and tactics of execution. Thus, before we can describe and analyze any of the dimensions of campaign communication in the chapters that follow, we must examine those changes that, to the greatest extent, constitute the essence of the new politics. Four of them will be discussed in the following order: (1) the decline in the influence of political parties, (2) electoral financing legislation, (3) political action committees, and (4) technological advancements.

## CHANGES IN THE POLITICAL CAMPAIGN

The legendary party bosses once determined who would run for political office. In national and state politics, these people were often called kingmakers, who from the sanctity of the so-called smoke-filled rooms at nominating conventions handpicked "their" candidate to be the party nominee. In local politics, especially in the large cities, party bosses, through a system that combined the disposition of jobs with political favors, support, and even protection, controlled the votes, the party, and thus the selection of all candidates.

## Decline of Political Parties

Undoubtedly, the most significant change in presidential politics occurred when, in 1976, the reform rules adopted by the Democratic Party and, to a lesser extent, the Republican Party forced changes in state laws regarding delegate selection. Under party rules adopted before the 1976 campaign, the caucus convention procedure was wide open for participation by everyone, and any candidate who could inspire a following had a chance to win delegates. By changing the process of delegate selection, political reformers aided in reshaping the presidential nominating system. In 1968, there were only fifteen primaries, in which less than 40 percent of the delegates were chosen. In 1976, however, 77 percent of the delegates at the Democratic Convention had come from thirty primary states, reducing the strength of delegates from caucus states to 704 of the 3,008 delegates. In 2012 there were seventy-eight primaries and caucuses. These led to the election of 2,286 delegates to the Republican National Convention and 5,554 delegates to the Democratic National Convention.

Clearly, then, the reform rules changed the nature of the presidential nominating system by transferring power from party officials to citizens who voted in state primary elections. The result is that the change in rules and the proliferation of primaries have weakened political parties, the traditional vehicle for building coalitions and forging consensus. In the past, candidates had to work their way up through party ranks and appeal to party bosses, but, since 1960, successful candidates at all levels have often ignored the party regulars, built their own organizations, and taken their campaigns directly to the people. Perhaps the epitome of this was the candidacy of Donald Trump in 2016. As presidential chronicler and political journalist Theodore H. White reflected, "The old bosses are long gone and with them the old parties. In their place has grown a new breed of young professionals whose working skills in the new politics would make the old boys look like stumblebums."[1]

While for our purposes it is unnecessary to trace the fall of the political bosses from "kingmaker" to "stumblebum," it is important to realize that citizens feel little allegiance to political parties. Each year since the mid-1960s, fewer and fewer voters identify themselves as Republicans or Democrats, while more people than ever call themselves Independents. In 1964, approximately 24 percent of the population eligible to vote labeled themselves as Independents. On Election Day 2008, Independents comprised 33 percent of voting Americans, compared with 36 percent Democrats and 26 percent Republicans. By 2012, Independent affiliation grew to 36 percent, with Democrats at 33 percent and Republicans at 25 percent. By 2016, Independent voters increased to 39 percent, with Democrats at 32 percent and Republicans at 23 percent.[2] Obviously, candidates at all levels cannot simply rely on partisan votes to win an election.

## Finance Reforms

The decline in party identification and influence is not the only element that has altered the nature of the election campaign. Closely related are the reforms in financing that, although initially affecting only presidential candidates, have had some effect at all levels.

The Federal Election Campaign Act of 1974 and the amendment to it in 1976 changed much of the character of presidential campaigning, particularly in the early portion of the electoral cycle. The act provided for voluntary income tax donations, and the U.S. Treasury used the money to provide matching grants to presidential candidates who had raised $5,000 in amounts of $250 or less from citizens in at least twenty states. The maximum any individual could give a candidate was $1,000. But the Supreme Court ruled in 1976 that this ceiling could not prevent individuals or committees from spending unlimited amounts of money in support of a candidate so long as the effort was separate from the candidate's campaign, without any consultation or coordination. Suddenly, running for president became a possibility for people who were not wealthy. In fact, in the three elections that immediately followed passage of the act, thirty-six people were serious enough as presidential contenders to have qualified for federal matching funds. Two of the thirty-six candidates who qualified, Marion G. (Pat) Robertson in 1988 and John Connally in 1980, refused to use the funds, thereby freeing their campaigns from having to impose spending limits during the primary elections. In the 1996 presidential campaign, two Republican hopefuls, Malcolm S. (Steve) Forbes, Jr., and Maurice (Morry) Manning Taylor, Jr., spent their own money on their campaigns, as did Independent candidate H. Ross Perot. And during the presidential primaries in 2000, the front-running Republican hopeful, Texas governor George W. Bush, did not accept federal matching funds during the early stages of the election cycle. However, the biggest change happened in the 2008 cycle, when Arizona senator John McCain accepted federal funds but the Democratic candidate, Illinois senator Barack Obama, did not accept federal matching funds throughout the entire campaign, breaking fund-raising records with $750 million.[3] The Supreme Court's decision in 2010 in *Citizens United v. Federal Election Commission* changed the dynamics of campaign fund-raising once again. It empowered the influence of corporations, unions, and wealthy individuals. The 2012 presidential campaign made history. For the first time since 1972, neither candidate accepted public funds for the primary or general election. With the ability to raise unlimited funds and garner support from special interest groups, the 2012 contest was America's first one-billion-dollar presidential campaign.

Campaign finance was both a practical and political issue in 2016. Cayce Myers notes that Trump from the beginning criticized the role of special interest campaign money. He was very critical of the Supreme Court's ruling in *Citizens United v. FEC*. However, the joint fund-raising committees for both Trump and Clinton once again raised more than $1 billion. Super PACs alone contributed another $300 million.[4] Myers thinks that now, in essence, public financing of elections is over. "Both Clinton and Trump opted out of public funding, and it is difficult to imagine a successful campaign agreeing to limit its fund-raising abilities, especially if their opponent chooses to refuse funding. Similarly, it seems that

Super PACs are not necessarily producing the type of results that detractors anticipated. While they certainly play a role in campaigns, they have not produced a reality where the best-financed candidate is the automatic victor."[5] Advertising has become a major factor in rising campaign costs. During the 2012 presidential contest, both the Obama and Romney campaigns spent more than $1 billion in political advertising alone. The 2016 presidential campaign was unique when, for the first time, expenditures for television political advertising did not exceed the previous election. In fact, broadcast TV was down 20 percent and cable and digital up. Overall nearly $10 billion was spent on advertising in 2016. For the first time, digital advertising reached over $1 billion, coming in at $1.4 billion spent, up from just $159 million in 2012.[6]

Thus, for many who run even for mayor, governor, and Congress, the ability to raise money has been the most important effect of the reforms. It has widened the electoral process by bypassing the political parties. Candidates run their own campaigns and frequently hire their own professionals to raise funds—often completely independent of party support or discipline. In turn, raising money has become more challenging because individual voters who view themselves as political independents are contributing to specific candidates and causes and not to political parties. Thus, two factors—the decline of the influence of political parties and campaign finance legislation—have worked together to change contemporary political campaigns.

### Political Action Committees

There is, however, a third and related element that has also altered the way in which campaigns are waged—political action committees (PACs) or single-issue groups. Pressure groups have existed since the founding of the republic. Over the years, the efforts of some of these groups have brought about important changes, such as the abolitionists who helped eliminate slavery and the suffragists who helped give women the right to vote. However, in recent years, pressure groups have become so powerful and so numerous that their efforts to influence legislation and elections have had a dramatic impact on electoral politics. Their campaigns for or against proposed legislation have often served to fragment the political system, and their efforts to affect the election of specific candidates have contributed to the declining influence of political parties.

Although by definition the single-issue or pressure groups are small, they have nonetheless become increasingly powerful. By the 1980 election, pollsters estimated that one in four voters was willing to vote against politicians for their position on a single issue, and the issues themselves affected 10 to 15 percent of the general electorate. While the issues around which the groups coalesce vary all the way from import quotas to environmental control, it is the so-called emotional or passionate issues such as abortion, gun control, prayer or public displays of religion, immigration, and sexual orientation that attract the most attention and motivate groups to spring into action quickly if they feel that a proposed bill or even an individual legislator threatens their interests. They concentrate on the grass roots, pressuring city councils and state legislators, while simultaneously bombarding members of Congress with telephone calls, emails, letters, and personal visits;

heckling during public appearances; or letting them know that, without support for the issue, the PAC will work to defeat them in the next election.

In 1950, there were fewer than two thousand lobbyists in Washington. However, by the 1978 elections, pressure groups had proliferated to such an extent that fifteen thousand lobbyists were based just on Capitol Hill to work for the interests of more than five hundred corporate lobbies, with sixty-one working on Japan's interests, fifty-three minority group lobbies, thirty-four social welfare lobbies, thirty-three women's lobbies, thirty-one lobbies for environmental interests, twenty-one lobbies for religious interests, fifteen lobbies for the aging, ten for Israel, six for population control, and twelve for gun-related issues.[7] In 2000, there were 12,537 registered lobbyists in the United States. By 2008 there were more than 14,000, and in 2012 the precise number was lower but they spent the most ever on lobbying efforts: $3.31 billion.[8] However, in reality, thousands of individuals "influence" legislation without ever registering as an official "lobbyist." Thus, the true number of citizens who fulfill the role of "strategic policy consultants" adds thousands to the number of "real" lobbyists.

In 2012 there were more than 4,600 groups registered as PACs.[9] Corporations establish most of these PACs. Using computerized mailing lists that identify supporters, many PACs have been able to raise large sums of money that have been spent not only to lobby for their specific issue but also to defeat legislators who have not supported them and to elect others who have. The PACs' ability to do this is directly related to the election law reforms we have already discussed. However, as already mentioned, the 2010 and 2012 election cycles were impacted by the January 2010 ruling of the U.S. Supreme Court on the *Citizens United v. Federal Election Commission* case. In addition to the large amount of money now available for campaigns, candidates could still receive tens of thousands of dollars in so-called soft money from dozens of corporate PACs. By 2015, gearing up for the pending presidential context, there were more than 7,000 PACs. The majority, over 4,000, were "nonconnected," and corporate related were 1,738.[10]

Just as the PACs work toward specific candidates' success, they can work for their defeat as well. Perhaps the most interesting development regarding PACs and presidential politics occurred in 2004 with the appearance and breathtaking efficiency of organizations that became known as 527s. One such group, MoveOn.org, was created by Joan Blades and Wes Boyd in 1998 at the time of the President Clinton impeachment movement. Frustrated with the partisan politics in Washington, Blades and Boyd started the liberal MoveOn as an online petition to stop what they saw as a "ridiculous waste of our nation's focus" on the impeachment hearings.[11] During the 2004 presidential campaign, MoveOn maintained its liberal origins by focusing on raising money from individual citizens for the purpose of defeating the right wing and electing moderates and progressives. As of 2004, MoveOn.org raised $11 million for eighty-one candidates from more than three hundred thousand donors.[12] Since 2004, MoveOn has helped to "bring ordinary people back into politics" by "building electronic advocacy groups" as a way of democratic participation.[13] It provides an outlet for more than two million online participants. In 2004, there were not only politically liberal 527s but many conservative ones as well. For example, the group Progress for America spent more than $35 million to reelect Bush.[14]

Thus, it would make little sense to discuss contemporary political campaigns without acknowledging the effect of political action committees. They have become an important element because they breach party lines and make uncompromising, all-or-nothing demands on legislators and candidates. They care little for party loyalties, legislative voting records, or a candidate's overall philosophy or platform. They view every legislative roll call and every election as a major test of their cause. And, as we just noted, their zealotry allows them to be highly successful in raising money. With each election cycle, they now contribute hundreds of millions of dollars of influence. Thus, although the primary source of funds for political elections remains private citizens, the large-scale entrance of single-issue groups into the electoral process has contributed mightily to the changed nature of the electoral process for many statewide and national elections.

## Technology

Perhaps the most obvious transformation in political campaigns has been in technology. Although the additions of radio in the 1920s and television in the 1950s brought with them a number of alterations to U.S. political campaigns, as technological advancements, they were only the beginning. Today, campaigns from the county to the national level rely on technologies that had hardly been envisioned in a campaign as recently as a decade ago. In so doing, their nature as well as the people who run them have changed. Campaigns need all types of specialists: media, finance, speechwriters, pollsters, and managers, to name a few. Candidates select key consultants very carefully. Especially at the national level, the bigger the name of the consultant, the more serious a contender the candidate is considered to be.

Not only have the media consultants taken over the modern political campaign, but they are also assisted by other specialists—in media advertising, in public opinion polling, in direct-mail fund-raising, in street and telephone canvassing, and even in ethnic analysis. Now social media and analytics experts are essential staff members to campaigns. Thus, the sophisticated use of modern technology has brought significant alterations to political campaign communication.

For decades, technology has had an influence: in 1952 when Dwight Eisenhower first brought television commercial spots to presidential campaigns; in 1960 when John Kennedy became the first presidential candidate to use his own polling specialist; in 1972 when George McGovern pioneered mass direct-mail fund-raising; in 1984 when Ronald Reagan used satellite transmissions to appear at fundraisers and rallies; in 1992 when Bill Clinton was first to use the internet; or even in the 2008 presidential campaign when Barack Obama harnessed social networks such as Facebook to connect with the public. Regardless of the particular technology involved, the result is the same. Technology has changed the way candidates run for office.

Technology played a significant role in most presidential election campaigns, but by the 2000–2008 election cycles, the use of both old and new technology was even more intensified. Talk television and radio, which first played a prominent role in national political campaigns in 1992 and 1996, had become a fixture by 2004–2008.

New technological advances helped candidates and parties reach large numbers of people in short periods. Some of the most innovative technological campaigning occurred on the internet. With the escalating cost of campaigning, the internet has been increasingly utilized because it is cost effective and has high visibility, creating public awareness and support for presidential candidates and their platforms. It also is an effective way to raise campaign money. For example, in the 2000 presidential campaign Ralph Nader, the candidate of the Green Party, relied on the web for fund-raising. He collected $7 million in a year, but Senator John McCain raised $6 million "in a few months, using the Internet during his primary."[15] However, in the 2004 and especially the 2008 cycle, presidential hopefuls raised more funding than at any time in presidential campaign history. In fact, Obama's half-a-billion-dollar online fund-raising surpassed previous online fund-raising records by millions.[16]

Indeed, the internet's potential began to be realized in the 2000 campaign when a variety of online services were developed by the candidates, parties, news media, and groups of all kinds. By campaign 2008, for example, the websites of many candidates used features such as online voter registration, online volunteer sign-up, online fund-raising, and video biographies. Not only did the websites use these features, but also candidates frequently referred voters to their campaign websites in speeches.

In addition to the widespread use of candidates' websites, blogs began to have an impact in the 2004 and 2008 presidential campaigns, as well as in the 2006 and 2010 midterm elections. Political blogs were pioneered with the first major liberal blog of MyDD in 2001.[17] Since then, blogs have been responsible for giving unknown candidates a start and helping to ignite political movements around the country. This type of campaigning is now called "netroots" and is growing faster every year, with more and more blogs being created by more and more bloggers and larger numbers of people interacting through them.[18] And since 2008, social networking sites such as Facebook, MySpace, and Twitter have pushed online campaigning to a new level. In 2008 Barack Obama's Facebook page counted more than three million "friends," and by 2010 he had more than thirteen million "friends."[19] Just before the 2016 election, Trump had over twenty-two million followers across Facebook, Twitter, Instagram, and Reddit accounts. Clinton had fourteen million across the same accounts.[20] Trump dominated the followers and supporters across social media in 2016.

In short, advances in technology, as well as the advent of the single-issue groups, the election law reforms, and the decline in the influence of political parties, have combined to transform the nature and manner of our electoral system. Whether we like it or not, one significant result of these changes has been that we can scarcely avoid taking part in the campaign process. Those who choose not to participate directly become involved at some level, even if it is only to explain to friends why they are refusing to respond to a candidate's telephone survey or why they are turning off the television to avoid political programs and advertisements. "We must actively choose not to be active; hence we are participating symbolically even if not actually" because the political campaign is ubiquitous.[21]

Somebody is always seeking elective office, and the "somebodies" are no longer strangers but your neighbor, the clerk in the store, or the mother of your best friend. The modern campaign knows no season. It seems that as one ends another begins. Candidates start running for office months and even years in advance of the primary election. Thus, campaigns are now an unavoidable part of our environment, forcing us to become consumers of political communication.

## COMMUNICATION AND POLITICAL CAMPAIGNS

The major argument of this book is that political election campaigns are campaigns of communication. Certainly, numerous forms or combinations of economic, sociological, psychological, and historical features are crucial to or reflective of the electoral process. However, the core of each campaign is communication. This is not to argue that a variety of economic and situational needs, power relationships, and a whole host of additional elements and demands do not affect the campaign process or outcome, but rather to say that all of these other factors become important in the electoral system principally through the offices of communication. Communication occupies the area between the goals or aspirations of the candidate and the behavior of the electorate, just as it serves as the bridge between the dreams or hopes of the voter and the actions of the candidate. It is through communication that a political campaign begins. Individuals verbally announce their intention to run, and posters and billboards nonverbally announce that election time has begun. During the campaign, candidates and their staffs debate, appear on television, answer call-in questions on radio and television talk shows, prepare and present messages for media commercials, take part in parades and rallies, wear funny hats, submit to media interviews, write letters and position papers, produce web content, and speak at all forms of public gatherings. They kiss babies, shake hands at factory gates and supermarkets, prepare and distribute literature, produce campaign videotapes and email newsletters, wear campaign buttons, and establish phone banks to solicit money, workers, and votes. In addition, countless hours are spent during the campaign trying to raise enough money to buy radio and television time or computerized lists of voters. All of this effort is for the single purpose of communicating with the electorate, the media, and each other. And when the time comes, it is through communication that the campaign draws to a close. Candidates verbally concede defeat or extol victory, and the posters and billboards are taken down, announcing nonverbally that one campaign is over, even as another begins.

Hence, communication is the means by which the campaign begins, proceeds, and concludes. It is, as we suggested, the epistemological base. Without it, there is no political campaign. It is, therefore, not enough to approach the study of political campaign communication by analyzing the demographic characteristics or the attitudes of the electorate, although the information provided by such work is significant for our overall understanding of the phenomenon. It is also not enough to examine political campaign communication by studying only psychological construct theory or even the relationship and effect of the mass media on the campaign, although each explains much about the contemporary electoral process. What is needed is a study that provides a communication perspective of a communication event or series of events—the political election campaign. Campaigns are exercises in the creation, re-creation, and transmission of significant symbols through communication. Communication activities are the vehicles for action—both real and perceived. Thus, as we attempt to make sense of our environment, our current state of existence, political bits are elements of our voting choice, worldview, or legislative desires. As voters, we must arrange these bits into a cognitive pattern that constitutes our mosaic of a candidate, issue, or situation. Campaigns, then, are great sources of potential information and contain, however difficult to identify or measure, elements that impact decision making. Although you will find references to the works of political scientists, historians, and psychologists, as well as political journalists, we have drawn primarily on the work generated by scholars in communication.

Robert E. Denton, Jr., and Gary C. Woodward identify four characteristics of political communication. Political communication tends to have a short-term orientation. Especially in terms of campaigns, there is a beginning and an ending on Election Day. In terms of issues and policies, there tends to be a "season" of discourse surrounding issues with resulting legislation. In addition, it is communication based on objectives. The communication is directive and persuasive to alter some belief, attitude, or value leading to a behavior (voting, candidate support, issue motivation, etc.). As will become clear, today as never before, political communication is largely mediated. We come to know candidates, issues, positions, and arguments through the mass media largely defined. Finally, because political communication is based upon objectives, the communication is audience centered. This latter can be said of all communication, but political communication is strategic, crafted and targeted to specific audiences. In general, Denton and Woodward conceive of political communication as "a practical, process-centered, decision-oriented activity."[22]

### Essential Elements of Political Campaigns

Robert E. Denton, Jr., and Mary E. Stuckey developed a communication model of political campaigns. The model explores the interaction of key elements over the four stages of a political campaign. Denton and Stuckey identified six elements crucial to understanding a campaign from a communication perspective: the strategic environment, organization, finance, public opinion polls, candidate image, and media. They argue that each of the elements functions independently as well as interactively influencing the communication strategies and tactics of a campaign.[23]

*1* The strategic environment is the broad context of the campaign. There are numerous political concerns that influence the strategic environment. They include party identification, nomination rules, opponents, incumbency, voter behavior, and attitudes of core constituent groups. Social dimensions of the strategic environment include the various issues of the day as well as perhaps unexpected events, such as scandal, weather event, tragedy, or crisis. Thus, the social and political contexts influence campaign strategic decisions.

*2* The organization is critical in all aspects of a political campaign. Campaigns have become highly specialized and complete events involving large staffs of individuals. The organization includes all the strategists, advisors, specialists, and management personnel.

**3** Campaign finance, some would argue, has become the lifeblood of electoral politics. Money certainly does not guarantee electoral victory, but money does influence the viability of all campaigns. Today, campaign fund-raising has become a cottage industry to include all the PACs and private organizations that contribute funds.

**4** Public opinion polls are another important and essential element of political campaigns. Polls provide information on voter attitudes, message creation, campaign strategy, and status of the contest. Beyond campaign polls, media and special interest polls influence electoral races. Campaigns must react to those polls that may influence voter support and views of the campaign.

**5** Candidate image includes personal traits, job performance, job experience, personal history, and issue positions. Some candidates certainly try to "fit" voter notions of what is most desirable. Campaigns want to portray their candidate in specified ways: strong leader, competent, compassionate, right experience, and so on. Interestingly, once an image is set in voters' minds, it is often hard to reset. In terms of candidate image, it is just as important to control through events, media, debates, and all activities as it is to attempt to create an image. Research continues to demonstrate that many voters will decide their vote based on "likability" and "connection" with candidates rather than just on issues.

**6** Finally, media is an obvious element of consideration. Campaigns are essentially media campaigns. Most voters only come to know candidates and elected officials based on what they see or hear in the media. Today, social media continues to play an increasing role in political campaigns at all levels. In fact, recently Jennifer Stromer-Galley noted that given the new communication technologies, the element of citizen involvement should be added to the list. "The internet age has opened up new opportunities for citizens to be more directly harnessed by political campaigns."[24] Digital technologies provide voters new ways to get involved with campaigns in terms of organizing events, messaging, and especially mobilizing support.

Thus, these six elements (and the additional one of citizen involvement) are essential to all phases of a campaign and their roles, impact, and functions change across the phases. Some of the elements become "dominant" or more important in some phases than others. For example, during the pre-primary or surfacing phase, the dominant elements are finance, polls, and organization. Fund-raising and establishing the campaign organization are critical. In this phase, polls provide legitimacy for a candidate entering a race and provide early information in developing a campaign theme, issues, and image. In the primary phase of campaigns, the dominant elements are media, strategic environment, and campaign organization. Candidate media and news media begin to provide assessment of campaigns and candidates. Candidates must respond, virtually daily, to issues and topics in the strategic environment. Some aspects and issues are predictable but must adapt to current events and headlines of the day. The decisions and actions by the campaign staff and organization are critical in this phase. In many ways this is the most active and strategic part of the campaign for the organization and staff. Campaign staffs must decide which contests to challenge, how to address opponents, and how to stay on message. In the convention phase, once again, the organization is key. The campaign organization, if successful, plans the convention, orchestrates speakers, frames themes, and stages for the national media. The media, broadly defined, remain dominant in this phase, perhaps more external than internal to the campaign. The general election phase is the shortest yet most intense phase of the electoral contest. Here the elements of strategic environment, media, and organization are key.

Thus, by examining the elements in each phase of a campaign, one can detect the communication strategies and tactics utilized by candidates. This approach also recognizes the dynamic nature of campaigns, noting how the roles and impact of the elements change across the phases.

In exploring such theoretical concerns as agenda setting, uses and gratifications, targeting, gatekeeping, information diffusion, positioning and repositioning, functionalism, and legitimizing, or even in analyzing the pragmatic details of planning, organizing, and presenting speeches, television ads, debates, or fundraising appeals, we have been guided by one question: what ought we to study as political campaign communication? Our answers are contained in the subject areas we examine in the following chapters.

## ORGANIZATION AND PREVIEW OF CHAPTERS

This book has two parts. Chapters 2 through 6 analyze important principles and theoretical concerns of political campaign communication, while chapters 7 through 14 examine the crucial practices of contemporary political campaign communication. Although this distinction is designed to help you better understand the phenomenon, in the real world of political campaigns, principles and practices blend. As you read the section on principles, keep in mind that, in political campaigns, principles often generate practices, and practices often generate principles. For example, in chapter 2 when we discuss the principles involved in an individual's surfacing as a viable candidate, principles cannot be presented meaningfully without examining the practices of many individuals who have surfaced. In turn, those practices have subsequently generated many of the principles. Similarly, in chapter 7 when we discuss the practices of political speechwriters, we cannot readily examine them without developing some of the principles that speechwriters utilize. Thus, artificial as the distinction is, it does provide us with a pedagogically useful organizational framework from which to view political campaign communication.

Following this introductory chapter, the next four chapters focus on principles of political campaign communication. *Political communication* is a broad term. It has been used to describe the communication involved in winning elections, governing a nation, reporting on governmental activity, gathering and determining public opinion, lobbying, and socializing people into a nation. We have deliberately chosen to narrow the term and focus not on political communication but rather on political campaign communication. We do not deny the validity of studying other forms of political communication. However, in a democratic society, to govern one must first win an election. To report on governmental activity, there must first be an elected government about which to report. To lobby, there must first be elected officials to be persuaded. To gather and determine public opinion about candidates and their progress, there must first be a campaign. And to socialize people so that they accept cultural norms, elected officials must first help set the norms. In other words, we believe that political campaign communication is the root of all other forms of political communication. Undoubtedly, for this reason political campaign communication has been the focus of far more scholarly and popular journalistic inquiry than any other form of political communication. In addition, the number of elaborately planned and professionally implemented campaigns is growing each election year. Thus, it is particularly appropriate to limit our examination of political communication to political campaigns.

Chapter 2 examines the four stages of a political campaign, discussing the many pragmatic and symbolic functions provided by communicative acts to the electorate, the candidates, and the media.

Chapter 3 analyzes the communicative strategies and styles that incumbents and challengers have used in U.S. elections from 1789 to the present. In addition, a third style, one popularized by the two campaigns of Ronald Reagan and the 2000 campaign of Al Gore, is examined.

Chapter 4 presents an examination of the means or channels used in contemporary political campaigns. Theoretical approaches used to study the effect of mass media on political campaigns are discussed.

Chapter 5 considers the communicative types and functions of televised political advertising. In addition, the way in which women appear to use televised attack advertising in their campaigns is examined.

Chapter 6 discusses ethical considerations of political campaign communication. It does so from a citizen and democracy value perspective. We do not provide a list of dos and don'ts. Rather, we provide a theoretical perspective and areas of concern.

At the conclusion of these five chapters, many of the principles associated with political campaign communication will have been explored. We hope that, by the end of part I, our readers will have an appreciation of the theoretical basis of campaign communication from the vantage point of a consumer, but we also hope that campaign communication principles will be understood from the vantage point of the user, one actively involved in campaigning for public office. We are aware that readers majoring in such fields as speech communication, mass communication, political science, and public relations may anticipate being involved in political campaigns professionally. Many other readers may also participate in campaigns, if not professionally, at least as highly interested citizens concerned with their communities. We believe that part I can provide a valuable understanding of the principles of campaign communication from any vantage point that readers choose to follow in the future. Part II focuses on the practices of political campaign communication. In this section, we will discuss five of the most common communication events in contemporary political campaigns.

Chapter 7 examines public speaking in campaigns. It explains how political candidates decide where and when to speak, how they develop speeches, and how they utilize speechwriters and surrogate speakers.

Chapter 8 also focuses on public speaking in political campaigns. But whereas chapter 7 concentrates on the normal day-to-day public speaking that character-izes campaigns, chapter 8 examines forms of speeches that occur in most cam-paigns, are unique unto themselves, and are not day-to-day occurrences. Portions of the chapter deal with announcement speeches, press conferences, speeches of apologia, and acceptance speeches. Each of these forms takes place in virtually ev-ery campaign. The purposes and strategies involved in each genre are presented.

Chapter 9 deals with political debates. Debates are often the most anticipated and most publicized communication activity engaged in by candidates. The chapter presents a history of political debating and then discusses the factors that motivate candidates to accept or reject the opportunity to debate, the strategies that are used, and the effect of political debates.

Chapter 10 examines interpersonal communication in political campaigns. Five interpersonal communication situations, typical of all campaigns, are analyzed in light of current interpersonal communication theory.

Chapter 11 discusses the advantages and disadvantages of a variety of media used for political advertising in campaigns. It also discusses the key players in political advertising, the consultants.

Chapter 12 examines political campaigning in the age of the internet and social media. Social media are now an essential element of all campaigns with dedicated staff. Spending continues to increase across platforms and specific sites are emerg-ing as the primary sources of news and information about campaigns.

Chapter 13 looks at the role and practice of journalism in contemporary political campaigns. We examine the transition from providing information and coverage of campaigns to the growing influence of bias and impact of "fake news."

Finally, chapter 14 summarizes the political campaign communication in the 2016 presidential campaign. All the elements, strategies, and tactics discussed throughout the earlier chapters are reviewed in greater detail as part of the his-toric 2016 election.

We find the study of political campaign communication to be fascinating and believe that some of our enthusiasm for the subject is apparent in the following pages. We hope readers come away from this book not only better informed but also with renewed understanding and interest in a political system that, although abused and attacked in recent years, does not depend on coercion or force but derives its strength from the fact that it relies on human communication, largely as manifested in political campaigns, as a major means of decision making.

## NOTES

1. Theodore H. White, "The Search for President," *Boston Globe*, February 24, 1980, A1.

2. "5 facts about America's Political Independents," Pew Research Center, July 5, 2016, accessed September 19, 2018, http://www.pewresearch.org/fact-tank/2016/07/05/5 -facts-about-americas-political-independents.

3. "Party Identification," *Huffington Post*, January 21, 2015, accessed January 25, 2015, elections.huffingtonpost.com/pollster/party-identification.

4. Cayce Myers, "Campaign Finance and Its Impact in the 2016 Presidential Campaign," in *The 2016 US Presidential Campaign: Political Communication and Practice*, ed. Robert E. Denton, Jr. (Cham, Switzerland: Palgrave Macmillan, 2017), 276.

5. Ibid., 277.

6. Kate Kaye, "Data-Driven Targeting Creates Huge 2016 Political Ad Shift," *Ad Age*, January 3, 2017, accessed September 19, 2018, https://adage.com/article/media/2016-political-broadcast-tv-spend-20-cable-52/307346.

7. "Single Issue Politics," *Newsweek*, November 6, 1978, 49.

8. "Lobbying Database," OpenSecrets.Org, January 22, 2015, accessed January 24, 2015, www.opensecrets.org/lobby.

9. Ibid.

10. "Number of Political Action Committees in the United States in 2015 by Committee Type," *Statista*, July 2015, accessed September 19, 2018, https://www.statista.com/statistics/198140/number-of-us-political-action-committees-by-committee-type.

11. www.MoveOn.org/about.

12. Ibid.

13. Ibid.

14. Holly Bailey, "Politics," *Newsweek*, February 20, 2006, 10.

15. L. Patrick Devlin, "Contrasts in Presidential Campaign Commercials of 2000," *American Behavioral Scientist* 44, no. 12 (August 2001): 2338–69.

16. Jose Antonio Vargas, "Obama Raised Half a Billion Dollars Online," *Washington Post*, November 20, 2008, 3.

17. David Weigel, "Blogging Down the Money Trail," *Campaigns and Elections*, October/November 2005, 19–22.

18. Ibid.

19. Facebook.com (accessed January 22, 2011).

20. John Allen Hendricks and Dan Schill, "The Social Media Election of 2016," in *The 2016 US Presidential Campaign: Political Communication and Practice*, ed. Robert E. Denton, Jr. (Cham, Switzerland: Palgrave Macmillan, 2017), 124.

21. Bruce E. Gronbeck, "The Functions of Presidential Campaigning," *Communication Monographs* 45 (1978): 271.

22. Robert E. Denton, Jr., and Gary C. Woodward, *Political Communication in America*, 3rd ed. (Westport, CT: Praeger, 1998), 6.

23. Robert E. Denton, Jr., and Mary E. Stuckey, "A Communication Model of Presidential Campaigns: A 1992 Overview," in *The 1992 Presidential Campaign: A Communication Perspective*, ed. Robert E. Denton, Jr. (Westport, CT: Praeger), 1994, 1–18.

24. Jennifer Stromer-Galley, *Presidential Campaigning in the Internet Age* (New York: Oxford University Press, 2014), 13.

# 2

# Communicative Functions
# of Political Campaigns

One of the ways to examine political campaigns is to analyze their communicative functions—that is, to investigate what functions the various forms or acts of campaign communication provide to the electorate and to the candidates themselves.[1] Many of these functions are instrumental or pragmatic in that they make specific tangible contributions. Others are consummatory or symbolic in nature; they fulfill ritualistic expectations or requirements. Both are discussed in this chapter.

The modern political campaign passes through relatively discrete stages, which can be categorized as pre-primary, primary, convention, and general election. This chapter is organized and divided analogous to the campaign itself; the different functions are discussed in terms of these four specific stages. It is important to remember that each stage, although discrete, has a direct relationship to and bearing on all that follow. Thus, the functions of each stage affect the entire campaign.

## FIRST POLITICAL STAGE: SURFACING

Although the first or pre-primary stage has been called the "winnowing period,"[2] we have labeled it *surfacing* because this term more completely conceptualizes those communication activities that occur. *Surfacing* was originally labeled and defined as "the series of predictable and specifically timed rhetorical transactions which serve consummatory and instrumental functions during the pre-primary phase of the campaign."[3] It would be difficult to set an exact time limit on the first stage because it can vary from candidate to candidate and election to election. Political hopefuls must assess their visibility and credibility as well as determine their financial backing and organizational strength. Predictable rhetorical activities (the verbal and nonverbal communication acts) during the surfacing stage include building a political organization in each city, district, state, or region (depending on the geographic scope encompassed by the office being sought);

speaking to many different kinds of public gatherings in an attempt to capture attention (media attention for state and national campaigns); conducting public opinion polls to assess visibility or to determine potential issues for which stances will later have to be devised; putting together an organizational structure and campaign blueprint; and raising money. These activities take time whether an individual is running for mayor or for president.

If surfacing takes months for city council and gubernatorial candidates, it appears to take even longer for presidential contenders. As in every presidential election cycle since 1976, the 2016 campaign started shortly after Obama's victory in 2012. One could argue that the 2016 presidential campaign began in 2013 when Secretary of State Hillary Clinton resigned, positioning herself for the next election. She raised millions of dollars—and her profile—through speaking engagements across the country; this also allowed her to begin sharing issue messages. The number of those expressing interest for the Republicans was at a historic high with more than a dozen serious contenders. Beginning in March and continuing until the Iowa caucus, an assortment of hopefuls campaigned across the country (especially in Iowa and New Hampshire), hosting television shows and writing books and newspaper columns about themselves in terms of their accomplishments and goals for the country while they bemoaned the president's policies. Although numerous of the "soon-to-announce" contenders were appearing at all manner of events and "nonevents" in Iowa and New Hampshire, the vast majority did not "own up" to their potential candidacy. Whether it was wishful thinking, overwhelming desire, or less than artful advice from political consultants, there were seventeen announced contenders for the Republican nomination and another five Democrats who either thought about or "were reputed" to be thinking about running who by 2015 appeared in the televised primary debates.

In 2016, the very big difference from most presidential elections was that there was not an incumbent president. While incumbency may not represent political "magic," most Americans "treat incumbency advantage as axiomatic."[4] Incumbents have significant advantages, both symbolically and pragmatically. In fact, not only do incumbent governors and members of Congress generally prevail against their challengers, "during the twentieth century, only five presidents lost their reelection bids; in the total history of our country 75 percent of incumbent presidents have been reelected."[5]

Not only do we know what is typically demanded of the candidate during the first stage, but we also have some idea of the characteristic functions served by the communication acts of the surfacing period. Although these can vary with the level of office sought (just as the time period does), we have observed seven functions that appear to be important in all political campaigns.

## Demonstrating Fitness for Office

The first function is to provide an indication of a candidate's fitness for office—the "caliber" of the individual. During the campaign, especially the earliest portions when public images of potential candidates are beginning to be formed, the electorate draws inferences from campaign actions about how a particular contender would behave as mayor, governor, or even president.

The electorate does not want elected officials who are viewed as dishonest, dull, unjust, immoral, corrupt, incompetent, or slick—or even those who are the brunt of television hosts' late-night jokes. In other words, U.S. voters historically have some preconceptions about people who run for public office. Generally, successful candidates will be perceived as trustworthy, intelligent, or competent enough to do the job; compassionate; articulate; poised; and honorable. The higher the office, the more judgmental voters become. For example, voters expect those candidates who run for or serve as our chief executive to be of "presidential timber"—to possess special qualities not always found to the same degree in all people. And although there is not a one-to-one relationship between the two, campaign actions are taken as symbolic of actions as president. We do not want presidents who hit their heads on helicopter doors (Obama), fall down steps (Ford), mispronounce words (G. W. Bush), or are attacked by "killer rabbits" (Carter). These are behaviors that cause a candidate to be characterized as "clumsy," "dumb," or a "loser." Furthermore, everything a candidate says or does is scrutinized by the media and public. Does the would-be president order a hot dog? Beer? Ice cream? Such actions show how they relate to the general public. However, in 2016 then Republican candidate John Kasich, who was running for the nomination, on a campaign stop was "caught" eating a slice of pizza with a knife and fork. It made the news, showed up in editorials and articles, and he was ridiculed on the late-night programs.

As a matter of fact, perhaps conditioned by the negative perceptions of Ford's and Carter's actions, voters' assessments of many of the 1988, 1992, 1996, and 2000 presidential hopefuls were sometimes harsh. For example, in 1988, before his confrontation with CBS News anchor Dan Rather, then vice president George H. W. Bush was perceived (in spite of his valor in World War II) as being a "wimp, a tinny-voiced preppy" who didn't possess the toughness to be president.[6] In 1992, Senator Tom Harkin came to be viewed (in spite of his championing of the poor, various ethnic groups, and laborers) as mean to the people around him, especially those who waited on him. In 1996, former vice president J. Danforth (Dan) Quayle was perceived to lack the intelligence to be president. Also in 1996, Republican presidential hopeful Phil Gramm was considered nasty, negative, and "charismatically challenged."[7] During the 2000 surfacing period, Malcolm (Steve) Forbes, Jr., tried a second time to appeal to Republican primary voters, but all he got for his efforts were statements such as "he looks like a geek" or "he looks like a turtle."[8] And for the 2010 election cycle, even Republicans were inclined to use Mississippi governor Haley Barbour's description of himself as a "fat redneck with an accent."[9]

In 2016, from the beginning of his candidacy, many found the public comments and tweets of Donald Trump disturbing, unkind, and problematic, to say the least. Some labeled him racist, sexist, and xenophobic, among other things. Trump's defenders said he was "authentic," "said what people were thinking," and "was not politically correct." Certainly, in modern times, no presidential candidate won with such high personal negative ratings or disapprovals.

Potential presidents are not supposed to be considered wimps or mean people, but neither should reference to them produce laughter. This was the problem with the general perception of Dan Quayle during his vice presidential campaigns and as an early presidential hopeful in the 2000 election. Few other national political figures have been the brunt of so many "dumb" jokes—jokes that were frequently the result of his own misstatements. Among the many infamous Quayle quotes is one made during a speech to the United Negro College Fund when he said, "What a waste it is to lose one's mind or not to have a mind is very wasteful."[10] What he meant to say, of course, is that "a mind is a terrible thing to waste." Whatever the ultimate judgment, certainly one function of the pre-primary period is to provide an indication of a candidate's fitness for office.

Humor, of course, long a part of presidential politics, has seldom been demonstrated more than during the 2008 presidential campaign. There were frequent jabs at front-runners John McCain and Barack Obama from late-night talk show hosts Jay Leno and David Letterman. In addition, the television show *Saturday Night Live* created its "versions" of the contenders, ridiculing them on live television with actors who looked and spoke like the four presidential and vice presidential candidates. And just as George W. Bush was mocked for his mangling of words in 2000 and 2004 (specifically his term *strategery*) and Al Gore for his concept of "the lock box" in 2000 (in reference to his assurance that nothing would happen to Social Security funding if he became president), in 2008 late-night humor regarding potential candidates continued. The most cutting humor was directed toward former Alaska governor and 2008 Republican vice presidential candidate Sarah Palin. Not only did Palin receive a large share of late-night comic attention, but also former *Saturday Night Live* cast member and head writer Tina Fey returned to mimic the governor. In addition to the skits, Palin and Hillary Clinton made appearances on the show with their look-alikes. And one week, Republican presidential candidate Senator John McCain even hosted a show.

From a candidate perspective, one should avoid sarcasm and most jokes will offend someone, a group, or a segment of the electorate. However, self-deprecating humor can be beneficial to a candidate demonstrating a "common touch" and "likability."

## Initiating Political Rituals

A second communication function of the surfacing stage is that it initiates the ritualistic activities important to our political system. In his book *The Symbolic Uses of Politics*, social scientist Murray Edelman discusses the idea of U.S. political campaigns as traditional, rule-governed rituals and then describes rituals as a kind of motor activity that involves its participants symbolically in a common enterprise.[11] While each stage of the campaign demands certain rituals, none is more clearly defined than the activities surrounding the pre-primary announcement speech.

When candidates decide to enter the political arena formally, they must perform certain protocols because they are expected. For example, a press conference is called, the candidate is surrounded by family and friends while announcing the decision to run for office, and then the candidate embarks immediately on a campaign swing through the district, state, or nation. The candidate may only be announcing a campaign for the mayor's office, but there are expectations concerning how it is done. However, to capture the full flavor of the announcement ritual, we need to examine it at the presidential level.

Senator Robert Dole went home to Russell, Kansas, and delivered his announcement address on April 10, 1995. Amid a shower of balloons, he positioned himself as seasoned and experienced, yet someone who was able to change and keep up with the times. Then Texas governor George W. Bush gave a speech on June 12, 1999, in Cedar Springs, Iowa, in which he said he would later announce that he would be a candidate for the Republican presidential nomination. Barack Obama returned to the Springfield, Illinois, State House and in the shadow of Abraham Lincoln formally announced his bid for the Democratic presidential nomination. In 2012, Mitt Romney announced his candidacy on a farm in New Hampshire, the home of the first primary. A big flag was hanging from an old barn and Romney spoke from the bed of a hay wagon. He wore dark slacks and an open shirt. Attendees were served Ann Romney's chili.[12]

Hillary Clinton announced her candidacy on a Sunday afternoon with the release of a two-minute video. The first minute and half were images featuring several personal stories. Near the end of the video Clinton appeared standing outside a suburban home and simply stated, "I'm getting ready to do something too. I'm running for president."[13] Donald Trump made his announcement at his signature retail and lavish apartment building Trump Tower. Trump made a dramatic entrance with his wife riding down the magnificent escalator. He covered many topics in his forty-five-minute announcement speech, some considered controversial, to say the least. He concluded the announcement with, "So, ladies and gentlemen, I am officially running for president of the United States, and we are going to make our country great again."[14]

Thus far in discussing the pre-primary period, we have been focusing on what has been termed "consummatory functions of campaigning." These functions are essentially symbolic in nature—functions that seem to be rooted more deeply in the heart or soul than in the mind of the electorate. In other words, as communication scholar Bruce E. Gronbeck has written, "campaigning creates second-level or metapolitical images, personae, myths, associations, and social-psychological reactions which may even be detached or at least distinct from particular candidates, issues, and offices."[15] Thus, communication during the first stage plays two symbolic but important roles: it provides an indication of a candidate's fitness for office, and it initiates the ritual we have come to expect in political campaigns. However, there are five additional contributions provided by the communication acts and symbols during the surfacing period. These functions are related to the pragmatic aspects of the campaign and have thus been labeled "instrumental."

## Learning about a Candidate

The first of these instrumental functions is that the electorate begins to have some knowledge about a candidate's goals, potential programs, or initial stands on issues. During the surfacing period, in an attempt to determine whether and with whom their campaign has any appeal, candidates must speak at countless neighborhood coffees, potluck dinners, and service club meetings. During these appearances, they often have to answer questions about why they are running for office and state their positions on specific issues important to those attending the gathering. Answers may at first be sketchy, but as the frequency of the speaking occasions and the perceived receptivity of the audiences increase, so does the candidate's confidence. Statements about political goals and aspirations as well as positions on issues become refined. What was in the beginning somewhat tentative now becomes more definite as the candidate proceeds to formulate statements of philosophy apparently acceptable to most potential constituents.

In recent presidential cycles, the major party contenders not only attended rallies and "town hall" meetings to introduce their candidacies but also published best-selling memoirs. For example, Senator Barack Obama wrote two best-selling memoirs, *Dreams from My Father* and *The Audacity of Hope*. Both books helped to educate millions of readers about the senator and created media buzz and public support about his presidential bid. More recently, 2016 presidential hopefuls continued to publish pre-campaign volumes: Hillary Clinton's memoir of her tenure as secretary of state, *Hard Choices*, released in 2014; Senator Marco Rubio's *American Dreams: Restoring Economic Opportunity for Everyone* in 2015; Arkansas governor Mike Huckabee's *God, Guns, Grits, and Gravy*, published in 2015; and Jeb Bush's *Reply All: A Governor's Story 1999–2007*, also out in 2015. Thus, a good signal that someone intends to run for the presidency is if they publish a book prior to the election year.

## Developing Voter Expectations of a Candidate's Style

Closely related is the second instrumental function: voter expectation regarding a candidate's administrative and personal style begins to be established. For example, candidates who have well-organized and disciplined staffs provide some knowledge about the kind of administration they might have if they are elected. Even in a campaign for a seat on the local school board, those candidates who from the beginning appear to be operating from a precise plan or blueprint with regard to where and when they will canvass the district, distribute literature, or speak at neighborhood coffees provide voters with information regarding the level of organization and efficiency it might be reasonable to expect if and when they are elected to the school board.

For those candidates not currently holding an elective office, the kind of organization they were able to put together to plan and manage their campaigns in the early voting states; their skill, or lack thereof, in fund-raising; and their creativity and use of the newest technology have much to say about their potential administrative style, if not their administrative skills. For those candidates already in office, voters can determine administrative style from current style. In the early months of the 2012 campaign, administrative style varied from hopeful to hopeful, but there were cases in which the message did not help candidacies. For example, in June 2011, the Gingrich campaign imploded—about fifteen staff members quit, including his entire Iowa organization (partly because he and his wife suddenly went on a week's vacation instead of campaigning in the state) and in December, although his New Hampshire headquarters had been open for a month, the telephone system was not hooked up and the offices were empty.

On the other hand, the Mitt Romney campaign conveyed a very different message. While a case can easily be made that shortly after bowing out of the 2008 Republican race, the former Massachusetts governor began campaigning for the

2012 nomination, the fact is that the message conveyed in the early stage was one of organization, support of fellow Republicans, and skill in fund-raising. In 2009, Romney founded a political action committee, Free and Strong America, which he used to fund-raise for Republican incumbents across the country who were seeking reelection in 2010 (he raised almost six million dollars by August 2010); sold his homes in Utah and Boston and moved to New Hampshire; retained some of his staff members from 2008 (including his traveling press aide); kept in contact with a network of other high-profile associates who were ready to go back to work for him; set up state-level political action committees in Iowa, New Hampshire, and South Carolina; and in a number of media interviews talked about the ways in which he believed his party needed to take a fresh approach to government regulations in regard to economic problems nationally and internationally.

Donald Trump made many and frequent changes to his campaign staff. Corey Lewandowski was the campaign's first real campaign manager. As the campaign moved closer to the convention, Paul Manafort became the campaign manager and pushed more policy speeches, using professional speechwriters and the use of teleprompters in an attempt to keep Trump on message. In August 2016, Trump initiated another major change, bringing in Steve Bannon as chief executive officer and promoting campaign pollster Kellyanne Conway to the role of campaign manager.[16]

Thus, in terms of the second function, there was little or no comparison in terms of the way the Romney campaign was administered and the early campaigns of his opponents. Perhaps because of lessons learned by the former governor in the 2008 presidential cycle, he and his staff understood and were prepared and indeed did build not only a foundation on which a national campaign could go forward but also the image of a candidate who knew how to administer and lead.

### Determining Main Campaign Issues

The third instrumental function of surfacing is that it aids in determining what the dominant theme or issues of the campaign will be. The early candidates set the rhetorical agenda for the campaign. As they crisscross the country, state, congressional district, or even city, they begin to come to grips with the issues on people's minds and begin to address themselves to those issues. In national or statewide elections, the media repeat a candidate's statements and thus aid in translating the problems and positions into national or state issues. In local campaigns, candidates often determine the problems by word of mouth rather than the media.

Naturally, if an incumbent is running for reelection, they tout their record of accomplishments across various areas and issues to demonstrate a successful record. In 2016, as the early wannabes of both parties (those who had formally announced and those who had not) traveled the country, especially in Iowa, New Hampshire, and South Carolina, they began to develop some sensitivity to those issues and problems that were on voters' minds and began talking about their solutions to problems that seemed to be compatible, especially with candidate and party core constituencies. *Newsweek* and the *New York Times* tracked the topics candidates presented during the surfacing stage of the campaign. Not surprisingly, Democratic candidates and Republican candidates focused on different issues and topics. For

Democratic candidates, the discussions focused on income inequality, Wall Street's influence, education, criminal justice, race, women's rights, energy, and the environment. In contrast, Republican candidates talked about excessive government, the Constitution, the legacy of Ronald Reagan, religious liberty, gay marriage, immigration, military power, Israel, North Korea, and China.[17] What is important to note is that the party candidates had very different rhetorical agendas and issues of focus. From a micro level, some of the issues and concerns may well vary in importance in different regions of the country or groups of constituents.

Thus, the surfacing stage is important because the rhetorical agenda begins to be established. If these early concerns are widespread enough, they can become the dominant issues in succeeding stages of the campaign. And those candidates who surface early help determine what will be the agenda.

## Selecting Serious Contenders

The first stage is also important because it begins the process of selecting front-runners or separating the serious contenders from the not so serious. Becoming a serious candidate during the surfacing period involves obtaining visibility. Even in small races, just as in state or national contests, obtaining visibility requires persuading the media that one is a viable enough candidate to deserve attention.

Almost from the beginning, at least in state and national contests, the media strongly influence who will be considered a major candidate. Generally, the media tend to provide more exposure to one candidate of each party early in the surfacing process. In 2008, a good deal of early media attention was given to New York senator Hillary Rodham Clinton largely because of her active role as first lady from 1992 to 2000. In addition, perhaps because he "never really stopped running for President after his loss to George W. Bush in the South Carolina 2000 Republican primary," John McCain also received a lot of early media attention.[18]

In 2016, Donald Trump led all candidates, with 213,000 mentions (43 percent of Republican coverage). Unexpected is that most of Trump's surfacing coverage came from MSNBC (34 percent) and CNN (27 percent) and interestingly, Fox News provided only 17 percent. But most of Trump's coverage was negative. However, although coverage of Trump's tweets was rarely positive, this coverage made his campaign the centerpiece of the national conversation. Clinton received 74 percent of the Democrats' coverage, with 143,000 mentions. Jeb Bush was third, with 80,000 mentions and Bernie Sanders fourth, with 42,000 mentions.[19]

Visibility during the surfacing period is often the initial reaction of the media to a candidate's past or present self. This has been illustrated numerous times when people who have achieved national recognition in the nonpolitical arena have decided to run for public office and the media have, in a relatively short period of time, turned them into serious candidates. Consider the cases of Senator John Glenn (one of the first U.S. astronauts); Senator Bill Bradley (a former All American and All Pro basketball player and a Rhodes scholar); California mayors Clint Eastwood and Sonny Bono (a famous actor and singer, respectively); governor of California and U.S. president Ronald Reagan (a movie actor and television host); governor of California Arnold Schwarzenegger (a bodybuilder who became a movie star); and, of course, now with Donald Trump.

Who candidates are and their current position also aid in determining initial visibility. For example, George H. W. Bush, Al Gore, and Robert Dole were considered leading contenders during the early stages of the 1988 and 2000 presidential campaigns because of their respective positions as vice presidents and Senate minority leader. In 2016, Jeb Bush, former governor of Florida, was thought to be an early favorite among Republican candidates because of his job as governor, but also as brother to President George W. Bush and son of George H. W. Bush.

The capability of some jobs to generate visibility was also demonstrated by two people who held powerful positions outside the federal government during the surfacing period of 2008. In fact, former New York mayor (during the events of September 11, 2001) Rudy Giuliani and former Massachusetts governor Mitt Romney, who came to fame through his work with the 2002 Salt Lake City Winter Olympic Games, received so much media attention that they were considered front-runners long before any caucus or primary.

A second run for the presidential nomination can foster high visibility, as exemplified by Mitt Romney in 2012. This was also true for Arizona senator John McCain's campaign during the 2008 presidential election. As a Vietnam War military hero and as a major contender in the 2000 presidential primary, he had national visibility that few other contenders could match. In campaign 2000, Al Gore, as the sitting vice president, had unlimited national visibility, was strongly favored by opinion polls, and was therefore, almost automatically, declared the leading Democratic candidate. Similarly, George W. Bush rapidly achieved national visibility due, in part, to being the son of a former U.S. president, being governor of a major state, and his success in raising more money earlier than any of the other contenders in the 2000 presidential primary.

Quite apart from persuading the media that one is a front-runner based on roles and present positions, a candidate may also emerge from the surfacing period as a possible leading contender by successful grassroots organizing and fund-raising. Acquiring sufficient money to generate the momentum necessary to do well in the primary stage has always been and continues to be important for local, state, and congressional candidates. But with the advent of the campaign-financing laws, motivating enough support to raise the money to qualify for federal matching funds has become crucial to presidential contenders. In addition, the growing roles of Super PACs that will provide millions of dollars usually have very specific issue position expectations. In 2016 the top fundraisers during the surfacing phase were Clinton at $76 million and Bernie Sanders at $41 million. Republicans followed the Democrat hopefuls, with Ben Carson raising $31 million, Ted Cruz $26 million, and Jeb Bush $24 million.[20] Donald Trump utilized his own funds and raised only $5 million. Self-financing his campaign allowed him to speak his mind, ignoring the policy litmus tests of major PACs.

Becoming a front-runner because of early grassroots organizing and successful fund-raising helps explain the initial successes of presidential contenders such as Jimmy Carter in 1976, Michael Dukakis in 1988, Bill Clinton in 1992, George W. Bush in 2000, and Barack Obama in 2008. Not one of them had been considered a serious candidate by the media prior to the first or second competition. Each used the surfacing period to gather the strength necessary to do well in the first contests

(Iowa and New Hampshire) and thus forced the media to acknowledge them as serious presidential candidates. On the other hand, not using the surfacing period to become a front-runner through grassroots organizing and fund-raising in the early primary/caucus stages helps explain the initial losses experienced by numerous contenders who did not last beyond the first two or three primaries.

### Establishing Candidate-Media Relationships

The final communicative function of the surfacing stage is that the media and the candidates get to know one another. While this function is often not vital for local campaigns, it can be important in congressional and state races, and it is absolutely crucial in presidential campaigns. In these contests we can most completely understand the significance of the function to the entire campaign.

At each stage of the campaign, the relationships between candidates and the media who cover them are vital not only to the candidate but to the individual media representative. The candidate needs the visibility that only the media can provide, and the media need information that only access to the candidate or immediate campaign staff can provide. It is not, especially in the pre-primary period, an adversarial relationship (the exception, of course, being Donald Trump in 2016). The candidate needs the media and the media needs the access to the candidate.

Relationships can be established during the surfacing stage because there are few media representatives assigned to cover a specific candidate and because the candidate has a skeleton traveling staff—perhaps only the campaign director. Contact is informal; candidates and staff are accessible. It is a time for finding out details and learning enough about one another to know who can be counted on when or if the candidate's campaign begins to gather momentum. Conditions change from the first stage to the second, and it is the surfacing period that allows media and candidate to get to know one another. The importance of the relationship is, first, that it provides the opportunity for local media–candidate interaction, which is not always available after candidates find that they can get national exposure and, second, that it gives both candidate and national media representatives a contact to be used later. In other words, the reporter soon discovers who on the staff will have the "real" story or lead, and the candidate's people know not only whom they can trust but which reporter has the best chance of getting stories in print or on the air.

Similarly, candidates themselves frequently try to establish relationships with a few of the major political journalists. It is rather common for candidates to have favorite reporters, those who tend to provide more favorable coverage or share similar views on issues. Some candidates actually seek "off-the-record" advice from key reporters. There is more frequency of informal contact in the early stage of campaigns.

These, then, are the necessary functions served by communicative acts during the first political stage. The period is crucial because of the functions it provides. Candidates who announce late and thus do not participate in surfacing activities or those who fail to use the period wisely have little success and frequently do not even advance to the second stage.

## SECOND POLITICAL STAGE: PRIMARIES

Primary elections are, at any level, "America's most original contribution to the art of democracy."[21] Under the primary system, voters who make up the political party determine who the party's candidates will be. Although the system varies from state to state, generally, primaries provide for a full-fledged intraparty election with the purpose of choosing a single candidate from each party to run in the general election. Direct primary elections, unlike the presidential primary, normally have a degree of finality in that the winning candidate is automatically placed on the November ballot. But in instances in which a number of candidates are competing for the same office, it is often necessary to have a second or runoff primary because one candidate usually does not capture a majority of votes in the first election. In the case of the presidential primary, even after all the state elections have been held, the party nominees still have not been chosen. The national nominating convention (the third political stage) officially selects the candidate. Thus, in presidential campaigns, primary elections are only one phase of the nominating process, not the final act or choice.

There are almost as many variations of primaries as there are states. For example, Wisconsin for many years had what was known as the "most pure" of the open primaries because voters could vote in any primary (it was not necessary to be preregistered and vote as a Republican or as a Democrat and vote only in that party's primary) and have their vote remain secret. Registration took place on primary day, and crossover voting was the norm. Connecticut, on the other extreme, only began holding full-fledged presidential preference primaries in the 1980s. For many years, the state allowed party leaders to choose its statewide candidates without fighting it out in primary elections.

Not only are there different forms of state primaries; some states do not even hold direct primaries but operate under the caucus system to determine nominees. To further complicate the process, the political parties within one state may vary in terms of their selection procedure. For example, in 1980 Michigan Republicans stayed with the direct primary, while Michigan Democrats switched to a caucus system after they were unsuccessful in their efforts to get the legislature to change the state's law to prevent or inhibit crossover voting. By the time of the 1988 presidential election, however, it was the Michigan Republicans who changed the process.

New Hampshire's constitution requires their primary to be the first in the nation. The rationale is, although New Hampshire is a small state, being first with a primary would provide the state high impact and influence in the candidate nomination process. Many states jockey for an early primary date so they also may influence candidate party nominations.

Iowa remains one of the two best-known caucuses or primaries because since 1976 it has so frequently been the first real presidential testing ground for candidates of both political parties. In 1996, the Iowa caucus began the night of February 12, in living rooms, schools, church basements, and firehouses. Democrats and Republicans gathered by precinct to elect delegates to county conventions who in turn chose delegates to state conventions and finally to the national conventions. The whole process took until June. In 1992, the Iowa caucus played little or no role in the presidential campaign because Iowa's senior senator, Tom Harkin, was pretty much assured the backing of the Iowa Democratic Party.

However, in 1996 and again in 2000 and 2004, the Iowa caucus resumed some of its former importance in the process because the contenders who ultimately began to lead the pack had done well in Iowa. In fact, Senator John Kerry's unexpected win in Iowa made him the front-runner for the remainder of the primary stage, while Howard Dean, the former governor of Vermont, who had been leading in the pre-caucus polls, ended up in third place and for all intents and purposes (especially after the so-called Dean Scream) suspended much of his presidential bid. And, in 2008, although Senator Hillary Clinton had been expected to win Iowa's Democratic caucus, the unanticipated victory of Illinois senator Barack Obama may well have changed the course of the campaign. Although Romney came in second in Iowa (and South Carolina) in 2012, his feedback from voters was obviously positive in that instead of leaving the race, he went on to win New Hampshire, a majority of the February and March primaries, and, obviously, the Republican nomination.

Timing and precedence have given the Iowa caucuses inordinate importance. Although local and state nominees are not selected at the precinct level and although proportionately fewer national nominating convention delegates for either party come from Iowa, the candidates who won the precinct caucuses in 1976 through 2004 received enormous publicity boosts from the national media. With each national nomination battle, all eyes of the media and pundits are on the Iowa Caucus. In 2016, Hillary Clinton just edged out Bernie Sanders for the Democrats and Ted Cruz prevailed over Donald Trump and Marco Rubio. Since 1972, only about half of all eventual presidential nominees have won the caucuses. According to Craig Smith, no candidate coming in fifth place or lower has been nominated by either party. As a result, candidates try to finish at least in the top four in the Iowa Caucus. Smith observes, "nominations cannot be won in Iowa, but candidates' future prospects can be severely damaged by poor performances in Iowa."[22]

Many professional politicians and party leaders hate the primary stage of a campaign because a genuine primary is a fight within the family of the party—a fight that can turn nasty as different factions within the family compete to secure a place on the November ballot for their candidate. In addition, primaries can exhaust candidates, leaving them physically, emotionally, and financially drained just before the most important battle. Charges and counter-charges of candidates and their staffs often provide the opposition party with ammunition they can use during the general election campaign. Moreover, beginning with the presidential primaries of 1980, another problem developed when the unit rule forced changes in strategy and thus made the presidential primary system even more detested by party leaders than it had been. Under the new rules, there could be no winner-take-all victory anywhere. Every state and every congressional district were forced to divide their delegates in proportion to the votes the candidates had won, and then candidates would "own" the delegate chosen in their name. In practical terms, it meant that no state was worth a candidate's full attention, yet no state could really be ignored. Each candidate had to campaign everywhere in each primary because, even in losing the state, the candidate could still get a substantial share of the delegates.

Finally, primaries use a lot of money—funds not only from contributors who might have been generous for the later campaign, but money that can be a drain on state and national resources in terms of matching funds. One reason inordinate funds are spent on this stage of presidential campaigns is that there are so many primaries and they last so long. In 1996, for example, there were forty-three primaries and sixteen caucuses (not including the Alaska Republican Straw Ballot Caucus). They began on February 6 in Louisiana and did not conclude until June 14, when voters in New Mexico went to the polls. While the 1996 schedule was as drawn out as those of the previous six, it is important to note that the earliest major contests, Iowa and New Hampshire, frequently have more influence in selecting the eventual nominees than larger states simply because their caucus and primary are traditionally first. In 1996, much to the consternation of many Republican Party loyalists, Louisiana grabbed the lead as the first contest. However, not all candidates participated, for fear of upsetting party traditionalists.

Despite their size, Iowa and New Hampshire have frequently been able to exert an inordinate amount of influence because candidates have used the win to focus national attention on their campaign and build a momentum that has granted them front-runner status from the media. The idea is that the national surge of publicity provides a substantial "bounce" toward the nomination so that later, when states with large numbers of delegates go to the polls, the race is effectively over.

In the 2000 primaries, excessive front-loading continued. This included, for the first time, states such as California with the greatest number of delegates. In fact, although there were a total of eighty-nine caucuses and primaries (counting contests of both the Republican and Democratic Parties), and although they stretched from January 24 through June 6, the Super Tuesday contests accounted for nearly one-third of the 2,066 delegates to the Republican Convention and 4,338 to the Democratic Convention. Thus, when Bush and Gore won on Super Tuesday, March 7, 2000, the race for the nomination of both parties was effectively over, even though the primaries of a number of states, including eight states defined as the "Interior West," were ignored because their primaries occurred after Super Tuesday. Thus, issues important to those states and their citizens had not been a part of the presidential contenders' dialogue.

However, the 2004 and 2008 front-loading exacerbated the process. In 2004, Terry McAuliffe, then chair of the Democratic National Committee (DNC), and his allies on the committee "quietly engineered a reworking of the primary and caucus schedule that all but guaranteed the fastest-starting and fastest-finishing nominating process in American political history."[23] Rule changes implemented by the DNC moved the Iowa caucus forward to January 17 and the New Hampshire primary forward to January 27, created another "retail" primary in South Carolina, and thus moved the whole process forward by at least a month to have the party's candidate confirmed by the beginning of March.[24] "With compression of the caucus/primary stage, McAuliffe envisioned a period of time between March and the Democratic National Convention in July when the Democratic and Republican nominees would be 'mano-a-mano' and, in his view, the sitting president would not have as much of an opportunity to upstage the Democratic candidate."[25] In an effort to do this, McAuliffe sought to change the Democratic caucus/primary schedule to avoid any lull between events. He had seen the Republican Party gain an advantage in 2000, by holding six primaries between February 1 and March 7, while the Democrats held none. McAuliffe believed that this primary/caucus schedule had severely disadvantaged the Democratic Party in 2000 by forcing them out of the political spotlight for so long a period.[26] Under "his watch" that would not happen again. Interestingly, though, with the new schedule the 2008 process broke all the records—with no incumbent president or incumbent vice presidential candidate, there were nearly one hundred primaries and caucuses. In 2012, the focus was on the Republicans. They continued the long season of primaries starting on January 3 and ending on June 26. They held more than fifty-five primaries and caucuses. In 2016, thirty-nine states held primaries for one or both of the parties. The remaining states used caucuses or conventions to select nominee delegates to the national convention.

Yet, for all the problems with this second political stage, there are five functions that the communication acts and symbols of the period provide. While we do not want to suggest that primaries (particularly the presidential primary system) need no revision, we do believe that these five functions are important to the entire political campaign process. The first relates directly to the candidates and the final four to the electorate.

## A Source of Feedback for Candidates

For candidates, the primary season is a source of feedback from the voters about their campaigns, the organization they have put together, the competence of staffs, fund-raising efforts, and physical stamina—in other words, their strengths and weaknesses as campaigners. During the surfacing period, the candidates' only measures of how they are doing are the comments of the media and, in some cases, the results of polls. But the primaries provide direct feedback from the voters and thus a chance for repositioning in terms of stands on issues, themes, images, and overall campaign strategies. Obviously, for those candidates who have only one primary in which to compete (most local, state, and congressional contenders), either the feedback is of no use (except as it may account for defeat) or it is used to plan for the general election. For presidential candidates, the early contests are direct sources of feedback that can be used immediately as preparations are made for campaigning in subsequent states.

There are times, of course, when repositioning does not work, as was the case in 1984 when John Glenn attempted to reposition his image from astronaut during the Iowa caucus to experienced statesman during the New Hampshire primary. But there are other times when it does. One of the most dramatic was the repositioning of Ronald Reagan's image and campaign strategy during the 1980 primaries. As conceived originally by then campaign manager John Sears, Reagan's 1980 quest for the presidency was to be a regal campaign, one in which Reagan would slowly but surely win the delegates necessary to assure the nomination. The front-runner campaign conceptualized by Sears would be characterized by an "above-the-battle" posture in which Reagan would campaign leisurely in each state by making only one or two appearances in any one day, not appear on forums or debates with his Republican rivals, honor his own already-famous "eleventh commandment" ("Thou shall not speak ill of other Republicans"), and be assisted with a well-planned and well-financed media campaign.

The strategy was tested in Iowa, the center of Reagan's so-called rural heartland. A week before the caucuses, Iowa newspapers talked about Reagan's failure to campaign in the state or even to appear with each of the other Republican candidates in the nationally televised forum sponsored by the *Des Moines Register*. Reagan's absence was noted throughout Iowa at countless fund-raising dinners or, as they are termed by politicians and the press, "cattle shows," where each of his Republican opponents made appearances and speeches. In fact, at some of these party functions, there were not even any signs of a Reagan campaign in the state—no campaign buttons, no posters, no candidate. By the time of the caucus, Reagan had spent only forty-one hours in the state, had avoided discussing the issues, and had made only one televised speech. It had been, as one newspaper headline proclaimed, a campaign that was "Invisible to Many." In defending this strategy, Sears said that "as a front-runner, Reagan could set the pace for the campaign, decide whether to give an event like the forum the prominence of his presence, and that the job of the other candidates was to make Reagan turn around and confront them."[27] In contrast, one Republican, George Bush, had spent a full fifty-nine days campaigning in Iowa and had thoroughly extended his campaign organization throughout Iowa months in advance of the caucus. On January 21, it was clear that the effort had paid off when Bush upset front-runner Reagan and finished first among the Republican candidates.

Although we do not know Reagan's immediate private reaction to his Iowa upset, we do know that he must have accepted the caucus result as instructive feedback about his campaign strategy or image. By the following week, a "new" Reagan was campaigning in New Hampshire. "This" Reagan was talking about issues, riding a press bus, speaking at rallies throughout the state, appearing at all multicandidate Republican gatherings, participating in (in fact, pursuing vigorously) all opportunities to debate his Republican rivals, and using an expanded media campaign to present his view to New Englanders. Perhaps the clearest indication that Reagan had used feedback from Iowa Republicans to reposition his campaign strategy and thus his image came on Election Day in New Hampshire, when he fired his press secretary, his operations director, and his manager, John Sears.

The effort to reposition or recast Bill Clinton's image was undertaken to solve the governor's "character" or "trust" problem and to put him in a better position to reach a national audience. It was called "The Manhattan Project."[28] Beginning with the Gennifer Flowers allegation of a twelve-year extramarital affair with Clinton and the Vietnam draft deferment issues during the New Hampshire through April primaries, the governor continually had to defend his character. During the New York primary, for example, Jerry Brown, his last remaining competitor, portrayed Clinton as morally and fiscally irresponsible[29] and a hypocrite who sought black support but played golf at a whites-only club in Arkansas,[30] and referred to him as the "prince of sleaze."[31] It was also during the New York primary when the governor admitted that he had smoked (but never inhaled) marijuana while a student in England.

Although Clinton won New York and the other important April primaries and was assured the nomination, public opinion polls indicated that his negative rating had shot to 41 percent, that he was generally thought of as less trustworthy and less honest than President Bush, and that people had little understanding of him and why he felt he should be president.[32] Thus, with the May and June primaries as well as the convention and general election still to come, Clinton's campaign staff knew it was important that they begin to let Americans know more about the governor as a man: his values, what he stood for, what he had done in Arkansas, and his disadvantaged childhood.

Consequently, they revised and made more specific the ideas in his basic stump speech and extended the campaign media reach to include not only the morning and evening television talk shows but MTV, where Clinton could advance his own themes in response to "soft" questions and directly answer viewers' questions.[33] While doubts regarding the governor's character remained throughout the general election and into his presidency, clearly the attempt to reposition his image during the final two months of the primary period was successful. Public opinion polls indicated that Clinton's negative rating had begun to drop and he was moving ahead of both Ross Perot and President Bush.

Following his inauguration and the success of Republicans in the congressional elections of 1994 and early 1995, President Clinton again appeared to have little popular support. In fact, by summer 1994, polls showed his approval ratings to be dangerously low. In an effort to increase his credibility and viability, the president took steps to reposition or recast himself. For example, he studied Ronald Reagan videotapes with the idea of changing aspects of his rhetorical style, he merged his administration with his 1996 reelection effort, and he hired political advisor Richard Morris. Morris devised a three-prong strategy that came to be known as the Morris "triangulation" strategy. The president's position on issues moved so far to the center that Republicans (particularly the Republican presidential nominee) had little ideological space. For example, Clinton discussed the need for leadership through a "dynamic center" and proposed tax cut initiatives he termed a "middle class bill of rights."[34] The second prong of the strategy began in July 1995, when Morris aired commercials in twenty key electoral states that attacked Republican congressional leadership (Bob Dole and Newt Gingrich) and the Republican Party for cutting programs important to large segments of the American electorate, such as Medicare. By fall 1995, the ads had aired in 30 percent of the nation's media markets.

Also, during the surfacing period, Clinton began implementing the third part of the strategy, using popular, and thus safe, issues as talking points. For example, during his weekly radio addresses and on weekend trips to New Hampshire, he talked about the need for greater corporate responsibility, less violence in Hollywood, school uniforms, and drug use. The triangulation strategy was successful; the president's public approval polls went up, often ten to fifteen points, in primary states such as Pennsylvania, Florida, Michigan, Illinois, and Ohio.

## A Source of Information for Voters

Important also are the functions provided to the electorate. Just as the primary campaign is valuable in giving candidates the feedback necessary for repositioning, so, too, can it offer voters the information necessary for cognitive adjustment or readjustment.

Images are rather easily acquired by voters during primaries. As candidates crisscross the city or the state speaking at all types of political receptions, coffees, rallies, or fund-raising events, voters have the opportunity to see and hear potential mayors, governors, or presidents. They can witness for themselves the candidate's habitual patterns of thinking and acting. They need no longer rely solely on earlier, perhaps inaccurate, accounts of a candidate's style or position on issues. A candidate for mayor does look and sound capable of coping with the city's striking sanitation and transportation workers. The Republican candidate for governor does have a plan for enticing major industry into the state. The non-incumbent candidate for city council is unable to answer a simple question about zoning ordinances. And the presidential candidate uses so many "ahs," "ums," and "huhs" that it is impossible to understand responses to questions.

Thus, as the candidates seek all possible arenas of political talk during the primary stage of the campaign, voters can see on a firsthand basis just how candidates handle themselves verbally and nonverbally. The information they receive aids in determining or readjusting their opinions. As a matter of fact, political scientist Thomas E. Patterson has found that these early impressions gained during the primary stage tend to remain throughout the campaign.[35] From speeches and answers to audience questions, voters begin to have some information regarding the candidate's beliefs, attitudes, and value orientations. The process that allows voters to create notions of candidate beliefs, attitudes, and values is what one communication theorist, Samuel L. Becker, has called a "mosaic model of communication," learning bits of information and then arranging those "bits" into a new or reinforced cognitive pattern.[36]

### Citizen Involvement in the Political Process

The third function of the primary period is that it involves many citizens in the democratic process. Involvement in the political process can take a number of different forms. For example, a person can engage in *overt* political action by participating in such activities as raising money for candidates, preparing placards, canvassing door to door for a party or for a candidate, attending a rally or a neighborhood coffee or petition drive, distributing literature, licking envelopes, or voting.

While there are, of course, many other activities possible for those engaging in overt political action, involvement can also be at the *social interaction* level. By this we mean simply that politics gives people a variety of topics or issues for discussion at work, parties, or any place where people interact with one another. Involvement may be no more than talking with friends about whether a particular candidate is pro-choice or believes in "right to life," but social interaction is one form of involvement in the political process.

A third form of involvement is *parasocial* interaction. This is interaction not with other people but with the messages provided by radio, television, newspapers, the candidate's website, brochures, and so on. In other words, it is arguing or agreeing with a negative political ad when it comes on your television set or with a candidate's speech that you read in their literature or in the evening newspaper.

Finally, involvement can be a matter of *self-reflection*—an examination of your ideas or perceptions of economic or social priorities in light of the position or platform of a given candidate.[37] Although the other political stages of the campaign do encourage forms of overt political action, social or parasocial interaction, and self-reflection, it is increasingly becoming the primary period where involvement is most intense because the sheer number of candidates and the attention given to the primaries by the media demand it.

Why are citizens becoming involved in the primary stage of the campaign? Although there are no certain answers, participation has undoubtedly been strengthened for three important reasons. First, with the increased number of primaries, the public is growing more accustomed to them and the major changes they have contributed to the process of selecting a president over the past decade. People have discovered that presidential primaries are exciting, almost like a carnival, as ten or twelve presidential hopefuls, each with family, large contingents of Secret Service, and hundreds of national media representatives descend on a state for three or four weeks during the winter or spring every fourth year.

Perhaps one reason for the excitement generated by the primaries is the direct personal contact with a potential president. Primary campaigning allows the candidate to meet individual voters. It is unlike the general election when the candidate is remote and isolated and appears to exist only for the national media. The primaries, like the surfacing stage, are a time for interpersonal communication as candidates and citizens interact at dozens of small group gatherings throughout an individual state.

A second reason for increased involvement may be that a larger number of presidential candidates are actively campaigning and spending extraordinary sums of money in the primary states. For example, in Iowa the major candidates in 1988 spent record amounts on television and radio advertising, with most media budgets running to six figures. Not surprisingly, money spent by the leading candidates in their advertising campaigns continued to escalate throughout the first decade of the twenty-first century. For example, although in 2000 George W. Bush spent $28 million on the advertising portion of his campaign,[38] in 2008 Barack Obama spent more than $250 million on television advertising alone.[39] In 2012, Obama spent $69 million while Mitt Romney spent $93 million.[40] The combined amount spent on advertising during the 2016 primaries was much less, but differed greatly among the candidates. Donald Trump spent only $31 million compared to Hillary Clinton's $122 million.

Another explanation for the high levels of involvement in the second stage of the campaign is media coverage. The national media have also discovered the glamour, the excitement, the "gamelike" stakes of the presidential primary. Accordingly, each of the television networks' evening news programs devotes substantial amounts of time to covering the candidates in Iowa, New Hampshire, Florida, or wherever the primary or caucus happens to be that week. In addition to regular news features, the primaries are highlighted by special programs such as the Tuesday night telecasts of primary election returns and interview programs such as *Meet the Press*. The media create "winners" and "losers," even though the "winner" may have won by only a few percentage points or maybe did not win at all, but did so much better than was expected or came so close to the "front-runner" that he is declared by the television commentators to have "won" the election. As Patterson argues, the media treat primary elections much as they do the general election—there must be a winner. Each primary is only incidentally treated as part of a larger nominating system.

In 2016, there was a record number of primary voters for Republicans and the second highest number of participants for Democrats. In total, more than sixty million citizens voted in the presidential primaries in 2016.

## Promises Made in Personalized Settings

There is, however, a fourth and closely related function of the primary period. As candidates campaign, regardless of what level of office is sought, they often make promises about what they will do if elected. Some promise little; others promise everything from lower taxes to increased morality, but few actually deliver once they take office. We believe that one of the important communication functions of primary campaigning is related to these promises made by candidates during the heat of the campaign.

As already observed, one characteristic of primary campaigns is that they are normally more personalized than the general election stage. That is, voters have more of an opportunity for direct interaction with candidates. Campaigning is personally oriented as candidates attend countless events at which the relatively small number of people present familiarize them with the problems important primarily to their specific neighborhood, city, or state. The voters try to elicit promises of help and assistance from the candidates if they are elected. Once the promise is given, we believe that there is more likelihood of promises being kept after the election because of the physical proximity in which they were articulated and the fact that they are given to a specific individual or small groups of individuals, not an amorphous large audience or an impersonal camera.

## Determination of the True Front-Runners

Finally, we suggest a fifth function performed by the primary stage of the campaign. The voters have a chance to determine the "real" front-runners or leading contenders for the nomination. Throughout the surfacing period, the media label candidates as "possible winner" or "dark horse" or "a favorite" or even "front-runner." With the primary, voters have the opportunity to go over and above the media and actually select the nominees or at least give true meaning to the term *front-runner*. While we would not deny that the influence of the media has extended over the years in the self-fulfilling prophecy of their labels, there have still been a considerable number of instances when the voters, not the media, have determined the serious candidates.

Perhaps the 2008 campaign most quickly determined who would be the leading Republican and Democratic candidates. Barack Obama raised a significant amount of money and won the Iowa caucus, while Hillary Clinton campaigned vigorously and won the New Hampshire primary. Republican primary candidate

John McCain, who rapidly became the favored nominee for his party, pulled away from all other candidates in Iowa and New Hampshire.

However, consider the 2012 Republican nomination race, when virtually every Republican wannabe (no matter how little known they were nationally / regionally) was labeled in this way by the media as soon as they let it be known that they were considering entering the race. For example, the first announced Republican, former Minnesota governor Tim Pawlenty, while never called anything like a "front-runner" by the national media, was nonetheless referred to as the "growing choice among the conservative intelligentsia," "a credible candidate for the nomination," someone who "resonates well with mainstream GOP," and as "the real deal and authentic." Herman Cain was initially referred to by the media as "one of the two leading contenders for the GOP presidential nomination," the candidate who is "surging in the polls nationally and in key primary states, and lifting voters from their seats with rousing sermon-style oratory," "Tea Party favorite," the "center of attention," and in a "front-runner position." Jon Huntsman was termed the "coolest Republican in the race," the one who "looks presidential," the contender who will "blow you away with his speaking," "a man of many titles," and the candidate who "refuses to pander to the know-nothings." Michele Bachmann was called the "fresh face," "the perfect Tea Party rewrite of *Mr. Smith Goes to Washington*," "rock star," "strong fundraiser," "clever," and "maybe unstoppable." And Rick Perry was initially referred to as "shaking up the Republican field," "the second coming of Ronald Reagan," "a potent candidate," "a formidable candidate," "a candidate with swagger," and "someone who can unite disparate elements of the Republican coalition."

However, despite the initial media labeling of some of the 2012 early Republican hopefuls, voters in Iowa, New Hampshire, and South Carolina never responded to any of them (with the exception of Jon Huntsman, who won one delegate in New Hampshire). It is the primaries—the second stage of the early campaign—that determine who are the real front-runners and who are not.

These, then, are the communication functions of the primary stage of the campaign. They are significant because the second stage is vital to our political system. The primary campaigns allow the people to determine who the candidates will be. During the primaries, the decision making is taken from the hands of political parties and media and given to the voters. The communication functions are crucial to the process.

## THIRD POLITICAL STAGE: NOMINATING CONVENTIONS

Although a majority of citizens regularly tell pollsters that they would prefer some other method for nominating presidential candidates, the national party conventions remain as they have since their inception: the bodies that make official presidential and vice presidential nominations for the Republican and Democratic parties. However, just as the first two political stages of the modern campaign have changed, so has the third. Where instrumental or pragmatic communicative functions were once the primary reason for holding party conventions, now the symbolic or ritualistic functions are, in most instances, the chief purposes. In other words, the convention stage is an important and distinct period in the four-step process because of the symbolic functions it provides.

From the time that the anti-Masons held the first national nominating convention in Baltimore in 1832 until the Democratic Convention in 1972, nominating conventions could be viewed as deliberative bodies—assemblies faced with difficult and important decisions to make in a few days. In addition to participating in the "required" political rituals of the day, delegates made decisions that often determined the success or failure of their political party during the coming election. The conventions served important pragmatic or instrumental functions in that the presidential and vice presidential nominees were selected, the platforms were determined, and even the tone or "battle posture" for the general election campaigns was established. In short, the convention met to make party decisions. For many years, decisions were made and the conventions were controlled by bosses and special interests. Some of those conventions nominated candidates of top quality such as Abraham Lincoln and Woodrow Wilson, and other conventions tapped candidates of dubious quality such as Franklin Pierce and Warren Harding. Whatever the caliber of the candidates nominated or the platform written, it is important to remember that the nominating conventions actually made party decisions; in other words, they served instrumental functions.

However, beginning in 1952 and strengthened by action taken for the 1972 Democratic Convention, at least three significant changes have occurred, thus shifting the communicative functions of conventions from instrumental to symbolic. While they have been discussed earlier, their impact on the third stage of the campaign has been so enormous that they should be understood with regard to the nominating conventions.

The first change was the introduction of television to the campaign. Although television did not bring the sights and sounds of the presidential contest to millions of people until the 1952 campaign, nonprint media had been involved in the nominating conventions for many years. In 1912, movies and phonograph records captured Woodrow Wilson's acceptance speech; in 1924, the acceptance speech of presidential nominee John Davis was broadcast over a network of fifteen radio stations; and by 1928, the influence of the medium was so pervasive that the time and date of Alfred Smith's acceptance speech were determined by the network of the 104 radio stations that were to broadcast the speech.

However, when television was first used during the 1952 primary campaigns, it contributed to the growth of public interest. Turnout jumped from less than five million primary voters in 1948 to almost thirteen million in 1952. The new medium brought a different dimension first to the primaries and then to the conventions by dramatizing suspense, conflict, and excitement, as well as projecting a visual image of the candidates that had never before been possible. Television gave the public a sense of involvement in the conventions, and as many delegates and reporters covering the convention soon discovered, the television viewer could see more and know more of what was going on than could the persons who were on the floor of the convention hall.[41] During the 1952 campaign, there were 108 television stations on the air and, as one study of the election showed, the impact of the new medium was significant:

The public went out of its way to watch the campaign on television. Only about 40 percent of the homes in the U.S. have television sets, but some 53 percent of the population saw TV programs on the campaign—a reflection of "television visiting." On the other hand, the campaign news and other material in newspapers, magazines and on the radio did not reach all of their respective audiences: more than 80 percent of the population take daily newspapers and have radios and more than 60 percent regularly read magazines, but in each case the number following the campaign in these media was smaller than the total audience. . . . In the nation as a whole, television, though available to only a minority of the people, led the other media in the number of persons who rated it most informative.[42]

As important as television's influence was in 1952, it can be seen as a mere shadow of what it was to become in all stages of subsequent campaigns, including the nominating conventions. In fact, by 1976, when electorate interest in that year's presidential contest was studied, it was discovered that television coverage of the conventions boosted voter interest and attention to the campaign, especially among those who were not strong political partisans.[43] Perhaps in response to electorate interest, coverage of the 1980 conventions was increased to the point that media representatives outnumbered delegates by four and five to one at the Republican and Democratic conventions. In fact, according to the *New York Times*, the Democratic Convention included 3,381 delegates and 11,500 reporters, editors, camera operators, and broadcasters. And although the public appeared as bored with the 1980 conventions as it had been interested in those of 1976 (network ratings showed a sharp drop in the number of people watching the 1980 conventions as compared with four years earlier), the presence of television has, nonetheless, continued to increase. For example, the number of channels has drastically increased with new electronic technologies. Compared to the earlier coverage by the three networks (ABC, CBS, and NBC), the 1992 campaign was covered by five networks (ABC, NBC, CBS, PBS, and Fox), 1,500 television stations, and two cable networks. In 1996, coverage once again increased when the number of journalists at the Republican Convention climbed to more than fifteen thousand, or seven journalists for each delegate. The 1996 campaign was also the first time that one of the political parties televised its own convention. Republicans donated $1.3 million to Pat Robertson's cable Family Channel to air their sessions, and they arranged for their own commentators. In spite of this increased coverage, however, viewership of the 1996 conventions was down nearly 40 percent from those of 1992.[44] In the 2004 campaign, network coverage of the conventions reached an all-time low with the major networks of CBS, NBC, and ABC showing only three hours of coverage for each convention[45]—in other words, they showed one hour, 10:00–11:00 p.m., for three nights. Network coverage affected the schedule of events at the conventions, with organizers putting their major speakers, including the keynote address and the nomination acceptance speech, during that hour.

However, a host of cable news networks covered the events, including CNN, Fox News, C-Span, and even Comedy Central. The cable networks gave viewers who wanted it another opportunity to get information and watch parts of the conventions the major networks did not cover.

Interestingly, however, coverage of the 2008 nominating conventions became "must-see TV."[46] In fact, it has been determined that nearly two-thirds of all

American households, or 120 million people, watched at least one of the conventions, while almost 40 percent of households watched both conventions.[47] Otherwise there continues to be a constant decline in convention viewership, even coverage of just an hour or so a night. Viewership similar to the 2008 conventions was in 1992 in the contest between Bill Clinton and then President George H. W. Bush.[48]

In 2012, slightly more than thirty million viewed Romney's acceptance speech, down 23 percent from McCain's thirty-nine million viewership. In contrast more than thirty-five million watched Obama's acceptance speech, slightly down from 2008.[49] However, social media played a large role for the first time in convention coverage. Both parties, in addition to numerous news organizations, offered live streaming of the conventions online. Google created dedicated convention pages.

The Republican Convention YouTube channel received three million views. President Obama's convention acceptance speech was the biggest political moment ever on Twitter. His address initiated fifty-three thousand tweets per minute.[50]

There seems to be some stable viewership in recent conventions. In 2016, Republicans averaged twenty-five million viewers over the three nights of the convention, with thirty-five million viewers watching Trump's acceptance speech. Democrats, following the Republican convention, averaged thirty million viewers over the three nights, with thirty-three million watching Clinton's acceptance speech and becoming the first woman nominated for the presidency by either party.[51]

Since 1952, the presence of television has restructured convention programming so that the party's "important" events occur during "prime time." To make certain that this happens, the convention chair often ignores the activities of the delegates on the convention floor and rushes through any official party business to make certain that those events planned to give the party the most favorable image (e.g., ecumenical prayers, civic greetings, performances by show business personalities, keynote and acceptance speeches, and controlled and planned "spontaneous" demonstrations for candidates) will be seen during the hours in which most people watch television. Whether this strategy fails (as, for example, it did in 1972 when George McGovern's acceptance speech began hours after most people had gone to bed or in 1980 when Congressman Morris Udall's keynote address started as the delegates were leaving Madison Square Garden for the night) or is successful, the convention proceedings become ritual with little or no pragmatic value.

Another effect of the presence of television has been that convention participants have become almost more aware of media presence than of convention business and thus alter their behavior and interaction. As one critic of the 1980 Democratic Convention noted: "The omni-present camera eye contributed to the funny hat, placard, banner and button syndromes. . . . At times, the television camera introduced an almost schizophrenic atmosphere as speakers addressed themselves to an un-listening, often chaotic arena audience, while really hoping that their individual performance would coincide with network coverage."[52]

The last and undoubtedly most significant effect has been that television covers only those events it decides are important, thereby altering the shape, structure, and activities of the convention. The networks will cover some speakers, not others; follow some floor issue debates, not others. In short, they are very selective in what they cover. The networks are quick to do various interviews on the convention floor while business is being conducted. And sometimes they show introductory videos, but not always. For example, in 1980 an eighteen-minute film introducing President Reagan was carefully inserted into the convention schedule to assure airtime. However, only NBC and CNN showed the film in full. Thus, we believe communication analyst Gary Gumpert is correct when he writes that television has helped render the nominating conventions little more than "a series of arranged and controlled visual and auditory images."[53]

The second factor that has had a profound influence in changing the nature of the third political stage has been the reliance on primaries as the vehicle for selecting delegates to the national party conventions. As we discussed in the first chapter, the proliferation of primaries has contributed to the decline of the political parties, but now we want to emphasize that it has also changed the role of the national nominating convention from decision maker to "legitimizer." Perhaps this statement is explained best by taking a brief glance at the history of the presidential primary.

The presidential primary is a "uniquely American institution born, after decades of agitation, in the early twentieth century."[54] In the post–Civil War era, the party organizations in many states and cities came under the control of often corrupt political machines dominated by or allied with public utilities, railroads, and others who manipulated the convention system to suit their ends. In an effort to reform the system, the Populists and later the Progressives advocated the substitution of direct primary elections for party-nominating conventions. By 1917, all but four states had adopted the direct primary method of nomination for some or all offices filled by statewide election. However, the extension of primary elections from the local, state, and congressional levels to presidential politics was much more difficult.

In 1904, Florida held the first primary election for the choice of delegates to a national party convention, and by 1916, presidential primaries were held in twenty-two states amid speculation that within a few years the national convention would be only an ornament for making official those decisions already arrived at by the electorate. However, turnout remained low, and there was little popular interest in them until the 1952 campaign, when the entrance of television into the primary elections renewed voter enthusiasm, and then again in 1956, when Senator Estes Kefauver became the first candidate to use the New Hampshire primary to call attention to his campaign. Although the outcomes did not determine the parties' ultimate choices, they generated more interest than they had at any time since 1912.

Twenty years after the 1952 campaign, a major incentive for the adoption of presidential primaries was provided when the Democratic Party's Commission on Party Structure and Delegate Selection to the Democratic National Committee, popularly known as the McGovern-Fraser Commission, sought to stop some of the injustices apparent to many liberals at the 1968 convention. The commission prepared eighteen guidelines intended to ensure that the state Democratic Parties' procedures for selecting delegates to the 1972 convention were open, fair, and timely. At least four other commissions followed McGovern-Fraser in the intervening years, and the guidelines have become so complex (to make certain that there is enough representation of minorities and women) that the state parties have found that they can best comply with them, and not disturb traditional ways of conducting other party business, by adopting a presidential primary law. Thus, the number of presidential primaries has proliferated. As primaries grew, so did the number of delegates pledged to a specific candidate, and since 1972 everyone has known before the conventions begin who the candidates would be (except in 1976 at the Republican Convention when Ford and Reagan fought down to the wire). The conventions no longer determine the candidates. Voters in those states holding presidential primaries have decided who will be nominated. The conventions meet to legitimize the earlier selection.

The third factor that has influenced the changing nature of the convention stage has been the emergence of campaign specialists who, with the consent of the candidates for whom they work, determine important aspects of the convention that were once the domain of delegate and party leaders. The consultants have planned the candidate's strategies through the first two stages for the precise purpose of winning the nomination. With the nomination secured before the convention even begins, the specialists now turn to "putting on the best show" possible, or what theorists Larry David Smith and Dan Nimmo describe as the orchestration of "cordial concurrence,"[55] for the television-viewing audience.

The party platform is negotiated in advance of the convention, with the staff of the candidate certain to be the nominee controlling the deliberations. If a spirited debate concerning a specific issue would enhance the "television show" or if, in the spirit of compromise, it becomes important to give the losing candidate and his supporters the chance to air a minority position, portions of the party's platform will be discussed during the convention itself. More often, such debates are done during the day and certainly not in "prime time" for television coverage.

In other words, all real decisions regarding the convention are made by the candidate, based on the advice of consultants. The candidate, not the party leaders, determines the platform, the issues to be debated, the songs to be played, the identity of those who will speak from the podium during prime time, the name of the keynote speaker or speakers, and the content and length of the "spontaneous" demonstration. Because of the influence generated by television coverage, presidential primaries, and campaign specialists, the overall function of the national nominating convention to the campaign has been altered. Gone is the once powerful role of decision maker. In its place is a new function. The primary significance of the modern nominating convention is symbolic-ritualistic—and as such, it serves four important communication functions, discussed next.

### Reaffirming and Legitimizing the Electoral Process

The first function, and one of the most significant, is that convention rituals provide an opportunity for the legitimation and reaffirmation of the "rightness" of the American way or dream. The various communication acts and symbols of conventions (keynote speeches, nomination speeches, debates, demonstrations, state-by-state roll call balloting, official "greetings" from past party heroes, patriotic music, buttons, hats, placards, as well as nomination acceptance speeches) serve to renew our faith that U.S. citizens share not only a glorious tradition but a grand and proud future. In a sense, each convention can be viewed as a huge political rally where the candidate shares the spotlight with the democratic system that made success possible. When, for example, the presidential and vice presidential nominees make their triumphant entrance to the speaker's platform the last night of the convention, their appearance reinforces the belief that citizens are bound together in a noble tradition. There have been instances when nominees have acknowledged the reciprocity of the relationship during the nomination acceptance speech.

Certainly, conventions function to legitimize the selection of the candidates, the platform, and the unity of the party and its leaders. But in the largest sense, the communication rituals celebrate what is good about our system, and thus about ourselves. Convention sessions, for example, open and close with prayers (we are a spiritual and godly people). During the convention, former heroes are acknowledged (we have a sense of our roots), and countless speakers evoke selected elements of the American Dream (we believe that the United States is destined to become a mighty empire of liberty where everyone can share in the prosperity of society). On the final night, the selected candidates articulate their visions of a grand and more noble country (we value the traditions of reform and progress), while national songs provide periodic emotional climaxes (we have pride in and deep-seated feelings about our country).[56] The convention rituals are, in short, a kind of emotional/spiritual/patriotic catharsis in which we can, if necessary, lament current shortcomings within the party or the country while remaining proud of and faithful to our legacy.

In writing about conventions as legitimation rituals, one communication scholar found that typically the ritual has three steps: (1) it begins with a statement and demonstration of theme (traditionally the responsibility of keynote speakers); (2) it progresses to a clustering or gathering of stereotypical character types who are given convention time for speeches or "greetings" to the delegates (the hero or heroine, the also-rans or those who fought the good fight but lost in a noble cause and are now vindicated through history, and leaders representing the right and left and all divergent interest groups within the party); (3) it culminates in the anointing of the nominee who symbolizes and enacts the convention's theme.

## Legitimizing the Party Nominees

Not only do the communicative acts of the convention serve to reaffirm our general commitment to the electoral process, but there is a second and closely related function. The convention provides legitimation for the party's nominees. When the struggle for nomination is long and intense (as it has been for presidential nominees since 1972) or when the selection has gone to a relative newcomer (as it did when the Democrats nominated Jimmy Carter in 1976, Michael Dukakis in1988, Bill Clinton in 1992, Barack Obama in 2008, and Donald Trump in 2016) or even when the convention nominates nontraditional candidates (as the Democrats did with Geraldine Ferraro on the ticket as the vice presidential nominee in 1984 and as the Republicans did in 2008 in nominating Sarah Palin and, once again, Donald Trump in 2016), the ritual of the convention confirms or legitimizes the candidate as the party's nominee as a possible governor, senator, or even president of the

United States. A person may have won primary after primary, but not until the convention delegates affirm selection through their votes at the convention can the candidate become the nominee.

With the act of confirmation comes added prestige and respect. The person is no longer just a candidate, but the nominee of a political party—something of an American icon. For example, in 2004, Senator Kerry was presented as heroic and dedicated. With the first words of his acceptance speech, he reminded Americans of the expectations and fulsome responsibilities of the American presidency when he walked to the podium and saluted, saying, "I'm John Kerry and I'm reporting for duty." Democratic speaker and former Georgia senator Max Cleland, in introducing the Massachusetts senator, referred to Kerry's war record, giving an account of his experience serving with Kerry in Vietnam, saying that he was a "living testimony to his [Kerry's] leadership, his courage under fire, and his willingness to risk his life for his fellow Americans."[57] Incumbent Republican candidate President Bush was presented as a leader holding to his principles and not giving in to opinion polls or politics. Bush's leadership was presented as "rooted in the timeless values that have made America a unique and exalted nation: respect for individual rights; a deep commitment to freedom; [and] a desire to serve as a living example of the power of democracy."[58] In addition, the choice to hold the Republican Convention in New York City further helped to legitimize Bush, by referring to his work to rebuild and lead New York and the nation following the September 11, 2001, attacks.

### Demonstrating Party Unity

The third function provided by the convention stage is that the party has a chance to show its unity. Whether the cohesion is more apparent than real, the convention is the time when wounds from the primary campaigns can be addressed and healed. Perhaps the importance of a unified party to the success of the approaching campaign can be understood by examining instances when the convention ritual has failed to produce cohesiveness.

In 1964, the Republican Convention that nominated Barry Goldwater appeared to repudiate Republicans whose political philosophies were more liberal than those of the conservatives who dominated the convention. The governor of New York, Nelson Rockefeller, who had been a contender for the nomination, was booed and not given the opportunity to finish a speech. When Goldwater included an endorsement of extremism in his acceptance speech, many liberals walked out of the convention. The Republican Party remained divided throughout the campaign, and Goldwater lost the election by one of the largest margins in the history of presidential politics. Similarly, in 1968 and again in 1972, the Democratic National Convention failed to unify and come together to support either Hubert Humphrey or George McGovern. Humphrey was tormented throughout the 1968 general election campaign by those in the Democratic Party who felt his nomination was a betrayal of party principle and a disfranchisement for liberals. McGovern, on the other hand, was never able to unify the traditional or "old-line" party leaders with his more youthful and/or liberal insurgents. In each case, the

Democrats remained divided throughout the convention and general election campaign and lost in November.

Thus, even when there are tensions below the surface, the political parties strive for the appearance of unity during their conventions. The Republicans and the Democrats in 1988 attempted to evoke images of unity in the closing moments of their conventions. Although the race for the 1988 Democratic nomination was filled with bitterness, particularly because of Jesse Jackson's feeling that neither the party nor the Dukakis staff was giving him the central role he felt he deserved, the victorious Michael Dukakis had Jackson join him at the speaker's podium after he had delivered his acceptance speech. Others who had been opponents during the primary and caucus elections followed Jackson to the podium. In 1988, George H. W. Bush was joined at the podium following his address by those who had been opponents during the primary and caucus elections to sing "God Bless America."

At the 2004 Republican and Democratic National Conventions, the appearance of party unity was again a predominant theme. The Democrats talked about equality, economic prosperity, and the protection of traditional American values. Republicans, meeting in New York City, emphasized the strength and vision of their nominee, President George W. Bush, who had brought back New York City after the tragedy of the September 11, 2001, attacks. The Republicans also talked about how America was continuing to move in the right direction.

And at the 2008 Democratic and Republican National Conventions, party themes did not differ substantially from those of previous years. The Republicans celebrated McCain's heroism as a prisoner of war, his experience in the Senate, and his "maverick" qualities, while the Democrats celebrated the values of diversity and new beginnings. In 2012, according to Rachel Holloway, Romney called for a "united America" to unleash the economy, to uphold constitutional rights, to care for the poor and the sick, to honor and respect the elderly, and to give a helping hand to those in need. He said that he would work "to restore America, to lift our eyes to a better future. That future is our destiny. That future is out there. It is waiting for us. Our children deserve it, our nation depends upon it, the peace and freedom of the world require it. And with your help we will deliver it."[59]

In 2016, both parties had fences to mend and internal splits among supporters. Among Republicans, there were those who wanted a brokered convention, hoping that Trump would receive few enough votes on first ballot to open up the possible selection among other candidates. Indeed, several of Trump's opponents spoke in support of Trump. Democrats, on the other hand, wanted to assure Bernie Sanders's supporters that Clinton would acknowledge and embrace some of his issues and positions. On the first night of the Democrat convention there was a video tribute to Bernie Sanders, who followed with an endorsement of Clinton from the convention podium.

## Introducing the Candidate's Campaign Themes and Issues

The fourth communication function served by nominating conventions is that they provide the public introduction of the candidate's rhetorical agenda for the general election campaign. Whether Republican or Democrat, the acceptance speeches of the nominees have frequently signaled the issues on which they plan to campaign (typically through the introduction of a specific slogan) and/or have announced an overall campaign style/plan they intend to follow (sometimes accomplished via a direct challenge to the opposition).

Franklin Roosevelt initiated the process of the nominee speaking to the delegates in person when in 1932 he flew from Albany, New York, to the Democratic Convention in Chicago. During his acceptance speech, he introduced the phrase the "New Deal," which became the slogan for his campaign and subsequent administration. In 1948, Harry Truman not only announced that the central issue in his campaign would be the "do-nothing Congress" but also explained that he was going to keep Congress in session during the summer to try to get some legislation from them. In 1960, Richard Nixon announced his intention to take the campaign to all fifty states, while John Kennedy introduced the "New Frontier" as the slogan/theme for those issues important to his campaign. In 1976, while accepting the Republican nomination, President Ford announced his intention to debate, challenging his opponent to a face-to-face confrontation when he said, "This year the issues are on our side. I'm ready—I'm eager to go before the American People and debate the real issues face-to-face with Jimmy Carter."[60] In 1988, George H. W. Bush cited five major issues to draw a sharp distinction between his conservative agenda and Michael Dukakis's liberal agenda.[61] In 1992, Clinton defined the "New Covenant": "A solemn agreement between the people and their government based not simply on what each of us can take but what all of us must give to make America work again."[62] In 1996, Robert Dole advocated a revival of the nation's "old values" of family, duty, truth, and honor; and in 2000, George W. Bush talked about restoring dignity to the office of the president and Al Gore argued for "the people, not the powerful."

In 2004, both the Democratic and Republican conventions presented the major issues and themes of the campaign in a complex and multilayered process throughout the four-day events. For Democrats, the theme was "American Unity" and to reinforce the idea of Kerry as a fearless and courageous leader. Like the Democrats, unity was a theme at the Republican Convention, only this time it was that America "should be unified against terror and terrorists."[63] Arizona senator John McCain emphasized this in his convention speech, saying about the September 11 attacks, "We were not different races. We were not poor or rich. We were not Democrat or Republican, liberal or conservative. We were not two countries. We were Americans." McCain also stressed that national security and defense were the "greatest responsibility of the government."[64]

The 2008 Democratic nominating convention was certainly historic. Although the Democratic Convention and Senator Obama's acceptance speech had many themes, one of the most important was the nomination's historic nature—he was the first African American to be nominated for the presidency—and he delivered his speech off the convention site and at the Mile High Stadium's Invesco Field with seventy-five thousand people in attendance. Republicans had to postpone the start of their convention because of Hurricane Katrina's landfall. One of the most dominant themes was the introduction of the vice presidential nominee, Alaska governor Sarah Palin, and her family. Not only was Governor Palin the first woman to be designated by Republicans as a vice presidential nominee, but she was also virtually unknown by most delegates attending the nominating convention and rapidly became the center of media focus and attention.

In 2012, Republicans claimed that President Obama and the Democrats were a threat to the "American Dream" due to Obama's failed policies and unfulfilled promises. "They responded to what they called a disappointed and disillusioned electorate with a message focused on promoting freedom of choice and self-determination through creating opportunity for individuals to rise to a better life through their effort and God-given abilities."[65] The Republicans also needed to counter the perceptions of being uncaring and less empathetic to the economic struggles of the middle class and only committed to the "one percent" of wealthy Americans. "In contrast to opportunity created through governmental action, Republicans reiterated the American narrative in which ordinary people do extraordinary things because of the opportunity created through the free enterprise system."[66] Democrats attacked the Republican vision of the "American Dream." In contrast to Republican policies, Democrats wanted to create opportunities for all Americans. "They argued that Republican policies create inequity and less opportunity, creating a greater divide between the wealthy and the middle and lower classes."[67] Democrats also argued "to vote for Romney would be to abandon commitments, to turn away from progress, and to renege on a promise *they* made in 2008."[68]

The theme for the Republican convention of 2016 was Trump's now infamous "Make America Great Again." Each evening was a sub-theme: "Make America Safe Again," "Make America Work Again," "Make America First Again," and "Make America One Again." In his acceptance speech, as an outsider, he alone could fix the economy, strengthen our position in the world, tackle terrorism and destroy ISIS, and protect our borders. The theme of the Democrat convention was "Stronger Together." Every message was counter to Trump's statements, character, issue positions, and prescribed policies, often using clips of his own words during the primary campaign. Clinton contrasted her vision of America with the negative one of Trump.

These, then, are the communication functions served by the third political stage of the campaign. As we have pointed out throughout our discussion of this stage, though the nominating convention serves only ritualistic functions, it is no less critical to the overall campaign than are the other stages. In fact, as we suggested earlier, a campaign that fails to get the most out of the ritual demanded during the nominating convention will proceed to the fourth stage with a potentially fatal handicap.

## FOURTH POLITICAL STAGE: THE GENERAL ELECTION

"Electing time"[69] means speeches, parades, debates, bumper stickers, media commercials, band playing, doorbell ringing, posters, billboards, polling, sound bites, town hall meetings, direct-mail fund-raising, call-in talk shows, and countless television spots. As we have discussed throughout this chapter, these acts and symbols are no longer reserved exclusively for the last stage, although they remain a significant and expected part. It is almost as if all has been in readiness—a type of dress rehearsal for this final and most important scene. Certainly, candidates may have been appearing and speaking at all manner of gatherings for many months. Thirty- and sixty-second television spots may have been interfering with television viewing since the primaries. Citizens may have even voted for their candidate in a primary or watched a part of one of the conventions on television. However, once the final stage begins, the campaign communication is at once more intense and less interpersonal, but more direct and certainly more important because the candidate who emerges will be the new mayor, governor, legislator, or president. It is precisely because of the importance of the general election stage that we must discuss briefly three communicative functions, which, although not unique to this stage, are nonetheless reflective of it.

### Gaining Information

The first function is cognitive. The electorate voluntarily seeks or involuntarily learns of information about some feature of the election and/or the candidates. News regarding the campaign is so widespread during the fourth stage that additional or restructured information may be gained from something as simple as talking with a friend, watching the evening news, reading a newspaper or magazine, or through social media, tweets, websites, and countless posts. Because so much information permeates the environment during the general election, the majority of the electorate possesses at least minimal knowledge about the election.

In recent years, people have been acquiring political knowledge from yet another source: the public opinion polls of the media. While syndicated polls during election years have been a regular feature of the press since the inception of modern public opinion polling in 1936, by the 1970s, news organizations began to serve as their own polling agencies. News-gathering organizations were not simply printing or broadcasting the findings of others; they were creating news on their own initiative with their own polls—often extending opinion soundings down to the local level.

The impact of this development is reflected in the results of a 1979 study by the National Research Council, which showed that, in two parallel surveys conducted during the heat of the 1976 campaign, only 16 percent of those interviewed failed to recall hearing something "in the news or in talking with friends" about "polls showing how candidates for office are doing."[70] Twenty years later, by the time of the general election stage of the 1996 campaign, virtually every major news organization was conducting some poll each week, thus providing a constant stream of information regarding the election. The challenges of polling in today's media and technology environment will discussed later, but polls of all types continue to drive headlines across media.

### Legitimizing the Political System

Communicative acts also serve a second function. The general election assigns legitimacy, the idea that the campaign process itself provides further proof that the system works.

In discussing the ritualistic functions of the nominating conventions, we discovered the importance of legitimation in affirming the candidate as the party's choice and the electoral system as superior. Legitimation is also an important function of the general election. As people stand in line to greet a candidate, put up posters for "their" candidate for city council, attend a rally, watch the presidential candidates debate, discuss with a friend the merits of one of the mayoral candidates, vote, or engage in any of the participatory activities typical of the final stage of the campaign, they symbolically reinforce the values for which the activities stand.[71] Thus, campaigning becomes a self-justifying activity that perpetuates two primal U.S. myths, according to Bruce Gronbeck:

> Acquiescence—providing a paradigmatic, "fail-safe" rationale for choosing leaders and fostering programs with particularly "American" bents, making it difficult for anyone to object to the process (for if you do, the system's ideological web reaches out, telling you to seek the desired change by participating—running for office, pressuring the parties, voicing your opinions in public forums); and, Quiescence—reasserting the values associated with campaigning and its outcomes (free-and-open decision-making, public accountability, habitual and even mandatory modes of campaigning, the two-party system), in order to remind a citizenry that it is "happy" and "content" with its electoral system; emphasizing the mores and ceremonial rituals associated with elections which make the country "devil-proof," invincible to attacks from within or without.[72]

Since the presidential campaign of 2000 that ended in a ruling by the Supreme Court, there have been calls to reevaluate the electoral system to include the Electoral College, ballot security, voter fraud, and other issues challenging electoral results. Electoral process questions were raised once again after the 2016 presidential election. Trust in our electoral process is critical to governance and democracy.

## Meeting Campaign Expectations

Finally, the third stage of the political campaign contributes to fulfilling our expectations regarding campaign rituals. We expect candidates to address themselves to society's problems; we expect debates, rallies, door-to-door volunteers, bumper stickers, buttons, continuous election specials and advertisements over radio and television, polls, and all manner of drama, excitement, and even pageantry. In other words, we have any number of expectations regarding political campaigns. While the previous stages also function to fulfill our "demands," the directness, intensity, and finality of the fourth stage emphasize our pleasure or displeasure with the way in which a particular election has or has not met our pragmatic or ritualistic expectations. If during the general election stage the candidates fail to address those issues of paramount importance to us, fail to debate each other, or even fail to provide for us any of the excitement or drama we normally expect, we may feel cheated. It is, in short, the climax of a political season—a time for decision and participation. It is electing time.

## CONCLUSIONS

With the changes in election campaigns in recent years, countless proposals have been made to modify or alter each of the four political stages. While many of the suggestions might well prove beneficial, we hope that the reader can now better appreciate that our system is far from purposeless. The various verbal and non-verbal acts of communication provide a full range of instrumental and consummatory functions for the candidate and the electorate in each political stage. While some of the functions are perhaps more significant than others, taken together, they are justification enough for the routines and rituals that in this country constitute the political election campaign.

# NOTES

1. Bruce E. Gronbeck, "The Functions of Presidential Campaigning," *Communication Monographs* 45 (November 1978): 268–80.

2. Donald R. Matthews, "Winnowing: The New Media and the 1976 Presidential Nominations," in *Race for the Presidency*, ed. James David Barber (Englewood Cliffs, NJ: Prentice Hall, 1978), 55–78.

3. Judith S. Trent, "Presidential Surfacing: The Ritualistic and Crucial First Act," *Communication Monographs* 45 (November 1978): 282.

4. Mark S. Mellman, "The Real Value of Incumbency," *The Hill*, June 5, 2013, 1.

5. Judith S. Trent, "The Early Presidential Campaign of 2012 and the Grand Old Party 'Wannabes,'" in *Studies of Communication in the 2012 Presidential Campaign*, ed. Robert E. Denton, Jr. (Lanham, MD: Rowman & Littlefield, 2014), 1.

6. Michael Oreskes, "President Bush: He's a New Man Now, Thanks to the Press," *New York Times*, January 22, 1989.

7. Judith S. Trent, "The Beginning and the Early End," in *The 1996 Presidential Campaign: A Communication Perspective*, ed. Robert E. Denton, Jr. (Westport, CT: Praeger, 1998), 56.

8. Carey Goldberg, "Remember Homely Abe, Forbes Says," *New York Times*, January 30, 2000, 20.

9. Sean J. Miller, "Barbour Pushed to Run," *The Hill*, July 13, 2010, 8.

10. Jacob Weisberg, "Making Sure Black Minds Are Never Wasted," *Los Angeles Times*, November 15, 1992, 3.

11. Murray Edelman, *The Symbolic Uses of Politics* (Urbana: University of Illinois Press, 1964).

12. Dan Balz, *Collision 2012* (New York: Viking, 2013), 98.

13. Amy Chozick, "Hillary Clinton Announces 2016 Presidential Bid," *New York Times*, April 12, 2015, accessed September 28, 2018, https://www.nytimes.com/2015/04/13/us/politics/hillary-clinton-2016-presidential-campaign.html.

14. Jeremy Diamond, "Donald Trump Jumps In: The Donald's Latest White House Run Is Officially On," *CNN Politics*, June 17, 2015, accessed September 29, 2018, https://www.cnn.com/2015/06/16/politics/donald-trump-2016-announcement-elections/index.html.

15. Gronbeck, "Functions of Presidential Campaigning," 271.

16. "Donald Trump Presidential Campaign Key Staff and Advisors, 2016," Ballotpedia.org, accessed September 29, 2018, https://ballotpedia.org/Donald_Trump_presidential_campaign_key_staff_and_advisors,_2016.

17. Craig Allen Smith, "Setting the Stage: Three Dimensions of Surfacing for 2016," in *The 2016 US Presidential Campaign: Political Communication and Practice*, ed. Robert E. Denton, Jr. (Cham, Switzerland: Palgrave Macmillan, 2017).

18. Judith S. Trent, "The Early Presidential Campaign of 2008: The Good, the Historical, but Rarely the Bad," in *The 2008 Presidential Campaign: A Communication Perspective*, ed. Robert E. Denton, Jr. (Lanham, MD: Rowman & Littlefield, 2009), 6.

19. Gdelt, "Presidential Campaign 2016: Television News Tracker," gdeltproject.org, accessed February 10, 2016, http://television.gdeltproject.org/cgi-bin/iatv_campaign2016/iatv_campaign2016.

20. Federal Election Commission, "2016 Presidential Campaign Finance," accessed February 6, 2016, http://www.fec.gov/disclosurep/pnational.do.

21. William R. Keech and Donald R. Matthews, *The Party's Choice* (Washington, DC: Brookings Institution, 1976), 91.

22. Smith, "Setting the Stage," 19.

23. John Nichols, "Racing into 2004: The Primaries Are in Full Swing," *Nation*, February 17, 2003, 16–17.

24. Judith S. Trent, "Surfacing in 2004: The Democrats Emerge," in *The 2004 Presidential Campaign: A Communication Perspective*, ed. Robert E. Denton, Jr. (Lanham, MD: Rowman & Littlefield, 2005).

25. Ibid.

26. William G. Mayer, ed., *The Making of the Presidential Candidates 2004* (Lanham, MD: Rowman & Littlefield, 2004).

27. Adam Clymer, "Reagan's Fortunes in Iowa Caucuses Appear to Hang on His Organization," *New York Times*, January 13, 1980, A13.

28. Peter Goldman and Thomas Mathews, "Manhattan Project: 1992," *Newsweek*, Special Election Issue, November/December 1992, 40–41.

29. Jeffrey Schmalz, "Brown, in New York, Assails Clinton with a New Ferocity," *New York Times*, March 23, 1992, A1.

30. Gwen Ifill, "Bruised Clinton Tries to Regain New York Poise," *New York Times*, April 5, 1992, A1.

31. Ibid.

32. Goldman and Mathews, "Manhattan Project: 1992," 40–41.

33. Trent, "Surfacing in 2004," 24.

34. Trent, "Beginning and the Early End," 61.

35. In studying the effects of the media on the 1976 presidential campaign, Patterson found that, even in the final stages of the campaign, intense partisanship and overtly partisan media communication did not override early impressions. In fact, in 80 percent of the cases Patterson analyzed, he found that any single impression of a candidate held during the general election was related more closely to earlier impressions of the candidate than to partisanship. Those people who thought favorably of a candidate's background, personality, leadership, or positions before the conventions also thought favorably about the candidate in these areas after the conventions, regardless of partisan leanings. See Thomas E. Patterson, *The Mass Media Election: How Americans Choose Their President* (New York: Praeger, 1980), 133–52.

36. Samuel L. Becker, "Rhetorical Studies for the Contemporary World," in *The Prospect of Rhetoric: Report of the National Developmental Project*, ed. Lloyd F. Bitzer and Edwin Black (Englewood Cliffs, NJ: Prentice Hall, 1971), 21–43.

37. Gronbeck talks about five classes of consummatory effects in "Functions of Presidential Campaigning," 272. See also Jay G. Blumer and Elihu Katz, eds., *The Uses of Mass Communication* (Beverly Hills, CA: Sage, 1974). For further discussion of the uses and gratifications perspective, see Jay G. Blumer, "The Role of Theory in Uses and Gratifications Studies," *Communication Research* 6 (January 1979): 9–36.

38. L. Patrick Devlin, "Contrasts in Presidential Campaign Commercials of 2000," *American Behavioral Scientist* 44, no. 12 (August 2001): 2340.

39. Lynda Lee Kaid, "Videostyle in the 2008 Presidential Advertising," in *The 2008 Presidential Campaign: A Communication Perspective*, ed. Robert E. Denton, Jr. (Lanham, MD: Rowman & Littlefield, 2009), 209.

40. "The 2012 Money Race: Compare the Candidates," *New York Times*, November 26, 2016, accessed September 29, 2018, https://www.nytimes.com/elections/2012/campaign-finance.html.

41. David B. Valley, "Significant Characteristics of Democratic Presidential Nomination Acceptance Speeches," *Central States Speech Journal* 25 (Spring 1974): 56–62.

42. Samuel L. Becker and Elmer W. Lower, "Broadcasting in Presidential Campaigns," in *The Great Debates*, ed. Sidney Kraus (Bloomington: Indiana University Press, 1962), 25–55.

43. Ibid.

44. Robert E. Denton, Jr., "Communication Variables and Dynamics of the 1996 Presidential Campaign," in *The 1996 Presidential Campaign: A Communication Perspective*, ed. Robert E. Denton, Jr. (Westport, CT: Praeger, 1998), 52.

45. Rachel L. Holloway, "Political Conventions of 2004: A Study in Character and Contrast," in *The 2004 Presidential Campaign*, ed. Robert E. Denton, Jr. (Lanham, MD: Rowman & Littlefield, 2005), 29–73.

46. Rachel L. Holloway, "The 2008 Presidential Nominating Conventions: Fighting for Change," in *The 2008 Presidential Campaign: A Communication Perspective*, ed. Robert E. Denton, Jr. (Lanham, MD: Rowman & Littlefield, 2009), 18.

47. Ibid.

48. Beth Fouhy, "Republican Convention Ratings Plummet from 2008," *Huffington Post*, September 3, 2012, accessed February 1, 2015, www.huffingtonpost.com/2012/09/04/republican-convention-ratings_n_1852535.html.

49. Nichola Groom, "Obama Draws Biggest Convention TV Audience, Twitter Record," Reuters, September 7, 2012, accessed February 1, 2015, www.reuters.com/article/2012/09/07/us-usa-campaign-media-idUSBRE88619220120907.

50. Ibid.

51. Tom Huddleston, Jr., "More People Watched Donald Trump's RNC Speech Than Hillary Clinton's," *Fortune Magazine*, July 29, 2016, accessed September 29, 2018, http://fortune.com/2016/07/29/rnc-dnc-tv-ratings.

52. Gary Gumpert, "The Critic in Search of a Convention or Diogenes in Madison Square Garden," *Exetasis* 6 (October 1980): 5.

53. Ibid.

54. Keech and Matthews, *Party's Choice*, 92.

55. Robert E. Denton, Jr., ed., *The 1992 Presidential Campaign: A Communication Perspective* (Westport, CT: Praeger, 1994), 87.

56. Kurt W. Ritter, "American Political Rhetoric and the Jeremiad Tradition: Presidential Nomination Acceptance Addresses, 1960–1976," *Central States Speech Journal* 31 (Fall 1980): 153–71.

57. Mary E. Stuckey, "One Nation (Pretty Darn) Divisible: National Identity in the 2004 Conventions," *Rhetoric and Public Affairs* 8, no. 4 (Winter 2005): 639–56.

58. Ibid.

59. Rachel L. Holloway, "The 2012 Presidential-Nominating Convention and the American Dream: Narrative Unity and Political Division," in *The 2012 Presidential Campaign: A Communication Perspective*, ed. Robert E. Denton, Jr. (Lanham, MD: Rowman & Littlefield, 2013), 12.

60. When Ford issued his challenge to Carter, he was trailing badly in the polls and needed something to give a boost to his campaign. As Bitzer and Rueter point out, Ford chose a prime moment at the convention to announce his intention to debate. In his speech accepting the nomination, Ford was aggressive and confident, and when he challenged Carter to a debate, the convention audience gave sustained applause. See Lloyd Bitzer and Theodore Rueter, *Carter vs. Ford: The Counterfeit Debates of 1976* (Madison: University of Wisconsin Press, 1980).

61. George Bush, "Acceptance Address, Republican National Convention, August 18, 1988," *New York Times*, August 19, 1988, A14.

62. "Clinton/Gore: 'New Covenant' for a New Generation," *Daily Report Card*, July 17, 1992, accessed May 3, 1999, web.lexis.nexis.com/universe.

63. Holloway, "Political Conventions of 2004," 29–73.

64. Ibid.

65. Holloway, "2012 Presidential-Nominating Convention," 8.

66. Ibid., 9.

67. Ibid., 17.

68. Ibid.

69. This phrase is borrowed from Edwin Black, "Electing Time," *Quarterly Journal of Speech* 58 (April 1973): 125–29.

70. Albert E. Gollin, "Exploring the Liaison between Polling and the Press," *Public Opinion Quarterly* 44 (Winter 1980): 451.

71. Gronbeck, "Functions of Presidential Campaigning," 272.

72. Ibid., 273.

# 3

⟰

# Communicative Styles and Strategies of Political Campaigns

One of the central imperatives of political campaign communication is the whole notion of the manner in which incumbents seek reelection and their challengers seek to replace them—in other words, the style and strategies used by candidates as they campaign. Campaign styles have undergone significant changes over the years. There have been, for example, elections when candidates campaigned by staying home and saying nothing. There have been others when the contenders "swung around the circle" on anything from trains to jets to riverboats to buses in an effort to draw attention to themselves and to be seen and heard by as many voters as possible. And we can each recall instances of campaigns that have been waged primarily by means of the mass media. In short, there has been no one way in which local, state, or national contenders have gone about the task of getting our vote. Strategies have been as varied and sometimes outrageous as those who have used them. Perhaps because of this, there has been relatively little systematic investigation or analysis of the communicative strategies and styles that have been, and continue to be, used by all manner of incumbents and challengers.

Thus, the subject of this chapter is the exploration of campaign styles. While it may be that readers are more interested in contemporary examples, the present is better understood when viewed from the perspective of the past. For this reason, examples from nineteenth- and early-twentieth-century campaigns have been incorporated, thereby providing a more complete catalog of the communication strategies important to all who have sought and those who will seek elective office. The strategies and tactics of the 2016 presidential campaign are presented in chapter 14.

Understanding of the material in this chapter is enhanced by an examination of three preliminary considerations that are important to the way in which candidates campaign. A consideration of the term *style* is first. Second is a discussion of political image and its role in developing campaign styles. Third is an exploration of the relationship of technological advancements to styles of campaigning.

# PRELIMINARY CONSIDERATIONS

## Style

For many years style has been studied by scholars who are interested in the cus-
toms and rules governing the use of language, including the choice of words (figures of speech) and the way the words are arranged (syntactical patterns) in oral
and written communication. Although controversy over its meaning occurred
historically because some believed style was divorced from content and was only
a frill or ornamentation, the conception of style as the peculiar manner in which
people express themselves by means of language has been generally accepted. In
other words, style traditionally has been the province of those concerned with
the correctness, beauty, or even workability of language—the investigation or
analysis of the words and arrangements a speaker or writer chooses in preparing
a message. Thus, one of the elements to be considered in the analysis of campaign
style is the language that political candidates use as they campaign.

More recently, however, communication theorists have argued that style
should not be limited to the language but ought to be considered a quality per-
vading all elements of an individual's communication. Barry Brummett defines
style as "a complex system of actions, objects, and behaviors that is used to form
messages that announce who we are, who we want to be, and who we want to be
considered akin to. It is therefore also a system of communication with rhetorical
influence on others. And as such, style is a means by which power and advantage
is negotiated, distributed, and struggled over in society."[1] Considered in this way,
style would include each of the nonverbal aspects of communication—physical
behavior, sound of the voice, body shape and movement, appearance, clothing,
and choice of settings—that operate as symbols to create the meanings we infer
from the transaction. In written messages, a number of symbols (in addition to
language) create meaning, such as the quality, texture, size, and color of the paper
and whether it is handwritten or typed for one particular person or printed and
prepared for distribution to many. Thus, in election campaigns, style can be seen
as a blend of what candidates say—in speeches, news conferences, websites, talk
show interviews, advertisements, brochures, and so on—as well as their nonverbal political acts or behavior, such as kissing babies, wearing funny hats, shaking
hands at rallies, waving at crowds from the motorcade, and their facial expressions and gestures while answering a question. It is what Bruce Gronbeck terms a
question of "leadership style"—a combination of habitual modes of thought and
action on which individuals perceive or judge a candidate.[2] What does any of this
have to do with our analysis of campaign styles and strategies? In this chapter,
style is a manner of campaigning that can be recognized by the characteristics
defining it and giving it form. We have termed these characteristics "communication strategies" and the styles "incumbency," "challenger," and the combined
"incumbent/challenger." Certainly, in describing each of the styles we have been
concerned with the traditional dimension of language; but as you have seen in
the first two chapters, we believe strongly that political campaign communication
is much more than just "talk." Thus, as the styles are explored, it will become
obvious that many of the characteristics deal with nonverbal political behaviors
as well as verbal.

## Image and Campaign Style

Imagery plays an important role in the consideration of style. All candidates, whether they campaign using the strategies of incumbency or those of the challenger, must do and say whatever it is that will enhance voter perception of them. They are concerned, in other words, about their image.

Although widespread awareness regarding the significance of image creation to the political campaign did not occur until the early 1970s, it had been used for years. The first major image campaign took place in the presidential campaign of 1840 when the Whigs, after searching for a candidate they thought could defeat Martin Van Buren, found no one. So, they invented a national hero, gave him a slogan, said he was champion of the ordinary citizen as well as a giant of the frontier, and elected a president.[3] When William Henry Harrison was "discovered" by the Whigs, he was sixty-seven years old, serving as clerk of courts of Hamilton County, Ohio, a long-retired army officer, and had spent twelve years in Congress and three years as ambassador to Colombia.

While military and legislative experience must be considered reasonable credentials for a presidential challenger, Harrison's career had been distinctly undistinguished. The Whigs, however, billed Harrison as a legendary Indian fighter and maintained that he was known widely and fondly as "Old Tippecanoe." The Whig campaign ignored all issues, except those relating to the personality of their candidate, and gave image creation and "hype" a permanent place in presidential politics. When Democrats suggested that the aging Harrison might be content to spend his declining days in a log cabin "studying moral philosophy"—provided he had a barrel of hard cider at his side—the Whigs cleverly turned the attack into a reinforcement of Harrison's contrived image as a "common man."[4] From then on, every Whig rally sported cider barrels and miniature log cabins, and songs were written and sung celebrating Harrison's humble tastes (the idea being that if logs and liquor were good enough for the people, they were also good enough for the president).

Image campaigns did not end with the elevation of Old Tippecanoe to the presidency. Instead, the place of imagery became entrenched in elective politics, especially in the area of campaign style, where specific strategies must be created and utilized to keep alive the perception of an incumbent or a challenger. The Harrison campaign's visual symbol of the log cabin represents what has come to be called "image" advertising in politics. As political analyst Wilcomb E. Washburn argues, "The modern-day equivalent would be the 30-second television spot commercial."[5] The importance of imagery is evidenced each time we see yet another television commercial of a candidate surrounded by family, talking earnestly with a senior citizen, walking through a peanut field, or standing in front of a sea of flags. Television commercials that present candidates in such situations are clearly designed to build or maintain certain perceptions of the candidate. Are the candidates in coat and tie, or plaid shirt with rolled-up sleeves?

Political images, however, are more complex than simply the strategies devised to present a candidate to voters. Images should also be considered in terms of the impression voters have—what they believe to be true or untrue, desirable or undesirable about the candidates and the campaign. As Kenneth

E. Boulding wrote in his classic book *The Image*, each of us possesses a store of subjective knowledge about the world, a collection of ideas we believe to be true. This knowledge constitutes our image.[6] While in recent years the work of a number of researchers has served to broaden the perspective by which scholars as well as practitioners view image, nonetheless, it is generally understood that the strategies candidates use to construct a public persona constitute an important area of political communication inquiry.

We believe, however, that despite the importance of a candidate's role in the creation of a public perception, it is only part of the equation. As voters we evaluate candidate behaviors and attributes to create or confirm an "image" of a candidate. In other words, beliefs that voters have about candidates are based on the interaction or interdependence of what candidates do and the evaluative responses voters have to it: a "transaction between a candidate and voter."[7] The view of image as a transaction, however, raises questions of balance or proportion between the strategies used by a candidate to create an image and the ideas already believed by the voter. Is one more important to the creation of persona than the other? Is one more likely to influence voter behavior than the other? Generally, researchers believe that one dimension does not necessarily play a more pivotal role than the other. People have some preconceived ideas regarding what a candidate's personal characteristics and behavior should be, and these ideas are continually measured against the reality of what an actual candidate says and does during the campaign. Donald Trump is a multibillionaire with advanced degrees and a lavish lifestyle. Yet, middle-class voters and blue-collar workers related to his message of "telling it like it is" and relating to their economic challenges and situation. In this way, voters define the campaign for themselves—sorting through competing or contradictory messages.

However, there are circumstances in which the balance between the idealized and actual can be disrupted. For example, the context in which the campaign occurs can become the dominating force—the Vietnam War during the 1972 election, the war on terror in 2004, and the sinking American economy in 2008. In each instance, the images of the candidates were framed by an all-consuming event that in some instances overshadowed the candidates' strategies to build an image and in others overcame voters' preconceptions of the "ideal" candidate.

It is also possible that a single and dramatic campaign event can tip the scale one way or the other. During the surfacing period of the 1988 presidential campaign, Senator Gary Hart's alleged relationship with a Miami model, his challenge to the media to prove the relationship, the public accusation by reporters from the *Miami Herald*, and the subsequent intensity of national media attention completely overwhelmed anything else Hart said or did. No image strategies the senator might have utilized could have competed with public preconceptions about the way in which candidates who would be president should behave and the contrast of this with Hart's alleged behavior. And in 1984 when Geraldine Ferraro was nominated by the Democratic Party for vice president, we believe that there was very little the congresswoman could have said or done to have created a public persona favorable enough to refute the preconceptions of some Americans regarding the personal characteristics or attributes vice presidents are expected to possess. She, in fact, like Republican Alaska governor Sarah Palin in 2008, did not look or sound like—she did not resemble—a vice presidential nominee. Thus, for some voters the fact of Ferraro's and Palin's gender created an imbalance between imaging determinants. The same could be argued for the Hillary Clinton campaign in 2016. The issue and challenges of gender are discussed in chapter 14.

Even though imbalance regarding the way in which people organize their thoughts about politics can occur, nonetheless, a consistent finding after years of research indicates that we share a lot of beliefs about the personal qualities candidates ought to possess—especially presidential candidates. Moreover, these characteristics are strongly associated with voting preferences and, in most cases, dominate ideas (cognitions) about the candidates and the campaign.[8] These personal qualities or attributes tend to cluster around such leadership characteristics as competency, experience, trustworthiness, ability to be calm, cautiousness, decisiveness, and boldness[9] and closely related personality characteristics such as strength, honesty, fairness, open-mindedness, reliability, energy, and physical attractiveness.[10] Whether or not a candidate exists who embodies all of these attributes is almost immaterial in that we use the characteristics as a basis of comparison—a standard—by which to judge the acceptability of the flesh-and-blood women and men actually seeking our votes. As voters, we may ask ourselves whether the candidate campaigns as an incumbent should or whether the challenger fulfills our expectations.

Viewed from this perspective, the reason for two common campaign activities becomes clear. First, one of the most crucial tasks facing candidates, especially during the surfacing stage, is to determine just what attributes voters believe are ideal for the office sought. Second, campaign activities in later stages are designed to attempt to illustrate that the candidate possesses these qualities.

Although we know that voter assessment of a candidate's image is a significant factor in voting behavior (far more important, for example, than party identification) and that voters have a mental picture of an ideal candidate that they use as a gauge in evaluating actual candidates, it is less clear whether these characteristics vary among candidates and across election levels. In other words, are all candidates competing in the same race judged by the same preconceived attributes, and are the dimensions of "idealness" the same for candidates running for local offices as they are for those campaigning for president? While scholars studying the political campaigns of the 1970s into the twenty-first century have provided few absolutes, some evidence indicates that the relative importance of particular clusters of characteristics has remained fairly constant from one presidential election to another. For example, in a study spanning eight New Hampshire presidential primary cycles, Judith Trent and colleagues found that most characteristics voters believe important for presidential candidates to possess remain constant: honesty, ability to identify the nation's problems and propose solutions to them, and highest moral integrity. Of the seventeen characteristics measured over the campaigns, fourteen varied greatly. In 2016, the five most important attributes were "talk about nation's problems," "honest," "have solutions to problems facing the country," "comfortable talking about national security," and "compassionate about people's needs."[11] There were party affiliation differences among the importance of candidate characteristics. Democrats wanted "experienced in elective office," "compassionate about people's needs," "elect a woman as president or vice president," and "elect a person of color as president or vice president."[12] For Republicans, the characteristics were "physically energetic and aggressive leader," "talk about personal religious beliefs," "comfortable talking about national security," and "has military experience."[13]

At this point, it is uncertain whether questions regarding preconceived image characteristics are important in local races, where the attributes and idiosyncrasies of the candidates, as well as their positions on the relevant issues, are well known. However, in a study in 1998 of one of the image characteristics, physical attractiveness, in which subjects were told that the pictures they viewed were of candidates in local and congressional races, Jimmie Trent and co-researchers found that physical attractiveness on initial candidate selection was an asset. In every case, across race, gender, and age, subjects preferred the most physically attractive candidates.[14] In 2014, a study found people rated candidates of their own political party as more attractive than those of the opposing party.[15]

Obviously, further research is needed before we can say with any degree of certainty that voter expectations either do or do not vary across candidates and across election levels. One thing, however, is clear. The creation and maintenance of image, long a part of political campaigns, plays a dominant role because voters have a whole series of impressions regarding the behavior of those who seek elective office that they compare with a personal vision of an ideal candidate. And although other factors are important to the consideration of campaign style, it may well be that the extent to which a candidate is able to achieve these idealized expectations is the extent to which success can be achieved on Election Day.

## Technology and Campaign Style

During the earliest period of our electoral system, the style of political campaigning was, at least in part, defined by the limits of our transportation system. This is one of the reasons that there were no national political campaigns as we think of them today. While it is true that in 1789 and again in 1792 George Washington had no opposition, it would have been difficult for him to conduct a national campaign even had it been necessary. Travel was difficult, uncomfortable, and time-consuming. Even in 1800, when the Jeffersonian Democratic-Republicans launched the first activity that could be called a presidential campaign, it was not a national or even a regional effort. The rallies, parades, and leaflets were not nationally planned but the work of individual county and state political committees. The national road system, begun in Maryland in 1808, was the chief east-west artery, and it did not reach even the Ohio border until 1817. Commercial water travel started in 1807, but it took many days to go just from Pittsburgh to New York City. Therefore, the presidential election of 1824 was the first one in which any real mass campaigning took place. Friends of the three candidates (John Quincy Adams, Henry Clay, and Andrew Jackson) traveled within their own and neighboring states to campaign for the presidential contenders.

Although the Baltimore and Ohio Railroad began in 1829, it was 1853 before the tracks reached the Mississippi River and 1869 before the transcontinental railroad system was completed near Ogden, Utah. By 1854, although the transportation system had improved, it still took thirty hours to travel from Indianapolis to

Cleveland by rail and twenty-four hours from Chicago to St. Louis. Thus, it is small wonder that 1840 was the first time a political party conducted a national campaign by sending speakers to all twenty-six existing states or that 1860 was the first time a presidential candidate traveled throughout the north campaigning for his own election. Moreover, it was not until 1896, after railroads serviced most of the nation and automobile production had begun, that a presidential challenger, William Jennings Bryan, was able to "whirl" through twenty-one states, give six hundred speeches, and be seen by five million people.

Developments in the transportation network continued to affect the style of political campaigning. For example, the beginning of air travel in the 1920s allowed Franklin Roosevelt to fly to Chicago to accept the Democratic presidential nomination in 1932, just as the initiation of commercial jet service in 1959 afforded Richard Nixon and John Kennedy the opportunity to conduct "jet-stop" campaigns in 1960.

However, by the middle of the nineteenth century, a second factor had become important to the development of campaign style. With the invention of the telegraph in 1835, a communication network was able to transcend the networks of transportation because messages were able to move at the speed of electrical impulses rather than the speed of humans, horses, boats, or trains.[16] Moreover, the emergence of the telephone in 1876, wireless telegraph and the motion picture camera in 1895, commercial radio in 1920, and motion pictures with sound in 1927 allowed the public to "bypass the written word and extend communication senses and capabilities directly."[17] Communication scholar Frederick Williams has written that "speech and images could now span distances, be preserved in time, and be multiplied almost infinitely."[18]

Even the first advances in the communication network began to influence political campaigning. For example, one of the primary issues of the 1848 presidential campaign was the almost two-year war with Mexico. The Whigs selected one of the war's heroes, General Zachary Taylor, as their candidate. The principal reason the war could become important to the campaign was that the initiation of commercial telegraph service in 1844 and the subsequent founding of the Associated Press Wire Service had provided far more rapid news dissemination than the country had ever known. Citizens were aware of specific battles and vigorously applauded each victory over the Mexicans. In other words, the telegraph was able to inject the war into the campaign with an immediacy not known before.

By the campaign of 1884, the telegraph had so unified the nation's communication system that, as James G. Blaine unwittingly discovered, even one election eve gaffe could be telegraphed across the country and influence election returns. The day before the election, a Republican clergyman denounced the Democratic candidate, Grover Cleveland, by saying that his party was the party of "Rum, Romanism, and Rebellion." Republican candidate Blaine failed to disavow the statement and therefore lost the support of Irish Catholic voters. Another thousand votes in New York, a stronghold of Irish Catholics, would have elected him.

Although each early communication development had some influence on political campaigning, certainly the most dramatic were the changes brought about by radio. Beginning in 1921, when President Warren Harding first used the new medium to talk to the public, the radio became the nation's most important means of political communication. It remained so until the widespread use of television in 1952.[19] Radio had a direct effect on campaign style because it made the personal appearances of candidates less necessary by providing an option. For the first time, candidates (even unknown ones) could become public personalities without campaigning around the country. In 1924, William McAdoo, a contender for the Democratic presidential nomination, hoped to establish a radio station powerful enough to reach all parts of the country so that he would not have to travel around the nation making speeches.[20] Although McAdoo never put his plan into action, losing the nomination to John W. Davis, subsequent candidates did. In 1928, Republican contender Herbert Hoover undertook only a few public appearances. Rather, he made seven radio speeches the focal point of his campaign. In 1936, 1940, and 1944, incumbent Franklin Roosevelt used radio extensively so that he could reach the entire nation without traveling.[21] Thus, the early achievements in electronic media had a profound effect on the manner of political campaigning.

Although many innovations have occurred, those that have had some direct effect on campaign style include the beginning of scheduled television broadcasts in 1941, the first electronic computer in 1942, the beginning of color television in 1951, the introduction of portable video recorders in 1968, the widespread use of microelectronic chips in 1970, the perfected development of fiber-optic signal transmission in 1975, the popularity of home computers in 1980, the use of cable television in 1984, the widespread use of videocassettes and satellite transmissions in 1988,[22] the use of online computer networks and bulletin boards in 1992, the use of candidate listservs and online home pages in 1996, the increased interactivity of candidates' websites with voters in 2000, and the widespread use of social media websites such as Facebook in 2008. By 2012, mobile devices allowed constant contact with voters pushing messages, images, and appeals to create, reinforce, and maintain the desired candidate images. In 2016, social media and dozens of applications ("apps") raised funds, activated key constituencies, and drove election agenda and media coverage.

In the largest sense, television, as radio had done earlier, increased the number of campaign strategies available because candidates no longer had to be dependent on extensive national speaking tours to become well known to the public. A few nationwide television speeches, a series of well-executed and well-placed advertising spots, an appearance on one of the news/issues programs such as *Meet the Press*, campaign coverage on the evening network news broadcasts, and several appearances on the popular talk shows guaranteed public awareness. In addition, television, unlike radio, enhanced campaign swings by showing parts of them in evening news broadcasts. Although the candidate might go to one state or region of the country to campaign in person, millions of people across the country participated in the rally or parade by watching the pageantry from their own living rooms. Not only did a television campaign provide candidates with more exposure, but it also allowed for more flexibility in the management of physical and financial resources. Perhaps the essence of the mass media strategy of the late 1960s and the 1970s is explained best in a memorandum written by H. R. Haldeman (and interpreted by Theodore White), in which he outlined the plan for Richard Nixon's 1968 presidential campaign:

Americans no longer gather in the streets to hear candidates; they gather at their television sets or where media assemble their attention. A candidate cannot storm the nation; at most he can see and let his voice be heard by no more than a million or two people in a Presidential year (the reach of the individual campaigner doesn't add up to diddly-squat in votes). One minute or thirty seconds on the evening news shows of Messrs. Cronkite or Huntley/Brinkley will reach more people than ten months of barnstorming. One important favorable Washington column is worth more than two dozen press releases or position papers. News magazines like *Time* or *Newsweek*, picture magazines like *Life* and *Look* are media giants worth a hundred outdoor rallies. Therefore, the candidate must not waste time storming the country, personally pleading for votes—no matter what he does, he can appear in newsprint or on television only once a day. . . . The importance of old-style outdoor campaigning now lies less in what the candidate tells the people than in what he learns from them with the important secondary value that outdoor exertions do provide the vital raw stuff for television cameras.[23]

Although 1968 was not the first time television had been used extensively in a campaign, it was the first time that a presidential candidate had planned his entire candidacy around the medium. Richard Nixon not only used technology to help him win an election but added an important dimension to campaign style—one that extended, in fact, to 1992 when Ross Perot became the nation's first true mass media presidential contender. Perot bypassed political parties, primaries, and traditional campaigning. Instead, he relied exclusively on television and computer technology.

In a similar fashion, the computer has made a profound impact on the manner of political campaigning since the 1980s. Its speed in information processing and its ability to allow web-based interaction between the candidates and voters since the 2000 election, as well as its ability to automate many of our methods of information analysis, have provided candidates with an invaluable resource in such traditional tasks as identifying and communicating with specific publics or raising funds.

But just as important as the past are the possibilities for the future—some of which have already been experienced in the campaigns of the 1990s and 2000s. Contemporary communication technologies continue to change the nature of campaigns by allowing voters to interact with the candidate instantaneously, anywhere. In other words, instead of a candidate simply stating a position on an issue to a mass audience during a television speech, debate, or interview, today's candidates can ask a question and invite comments. Large numbers of viewers can respond immediately to candidates with the use of cell phone apps or websites. This rapid and somewhat personal interaction allows candidates the opportunity to reposition their ideas and encourages voters to modify or change their beliefs regarding the candidate.[24] In fact, "the digital revolution" had, by 2008, made enormous changes in the process of campaigning for elective office. As Bruce Gronbeck has written, "There were communication systems designed to reach citizens directly. Added to traditional buttons, bumper stickers, yard signs, leaflets, direct mailings, and radio-television ads were computer-based communications,"[25] like email listservs, websites, and podcasts.

In fact, as Gronbeck has written, the digital revolution had, by 2008, made enormous changes in the process of campaigns for elective offices. Incumbents and challengers alike can have the benefits of person-to-person campaigning without ever leaving the campaign trail. In addition, the determination of public opinion on a given issue is no longer subject to the intervention of a third party (e.g., pollsters or the press). Mass media campaigning has, in effect, become true two-way communication.

Since 1992, the major television networks have reduced their coverage of presidential campaigns. There are fewer total number of stories provided, mostly just a daily update of status of the races. The reduction in network coverage paved the way for a new kind of presidential campaign coverage in the 1990s and 2000s, one in which nontraditional popular culture media grew in importance. For candidates, the popular media formats presented opportunities not experienced in the past. For example, talk show hosts or citizens who called in asked questions that were much "softer" than those typically asked by the national media. Moreover, there were rarely follow-up questions, and even when there were, no established journalist was there to push the candidate on evasions, contradictions, or half-truths.[26]

In presidential elections since 1992, small media operations on occasion have set the agenda for major network news by printing a sensationalized story—for example, the tabloid allegations of Paula Jones that, while governor of Arkansas, Bill Clinton made unwanted sexual advances toward her, or the report from a Maine television station during the last five days of the 2000 campaign that, when George W. Bush was thirty, he had been arrested while driving in Maine and had pleaded guilty to a misdemeanor charge of driving while intoxicated. In 2004, both Republican and Democratic candidates had a brush with the tabloids. President Bush went under fire for his military record while Senator Kerry, according to the tabloids, did not appear to be the military hero he claimed to be. Such stories provoked candidate response and thus made coverage of the story "necessary" for the mainstream news media. By the 2008 early campaign, such mainstream news coverage of "interesting" versus "important" stories; the obvious partisanship of cable news networks such as Fox News, CNN, and MSNBC; and the increased dominance of popular culture media had contributed to a growing public skepticism about the trustworthiness of the press.

One more difference regarding the use of media, which began in 1996 and continued in all the subsequent election campaigns, was that candidates came to recognize the potential of the local news stations. Beginning with New Hampshire, candidates did many of their satellite interviews with the anchors and reporters of local stations rather than with network commentators and journalists. They were able to do so because the networks could no longer control all of the pictures taken by their camera crews. For years, CBS, NBC, and ABC had refused to distribute pictures of national news events to their local stations until such pictures had first appeared in network newscasts. With the arrival of CNN, and later the Fox Network and MSNBC, this policy began to change. To make a profit, the cable networks started selling their pictures to local stations throughout the world.

Other technologies that have made an impact on political campaigning include the use of video websites such as YouTube, as well as podcasts. Campaigns create YouTube videos of the candidates on the campaign trail and giving major speeches. The practice of distributing campaign videos to provide primarily biographic information and to aid in fund-raising started with George H. W. Bush's 1980 effort in the Republican primaries and continued unabated into the 2012 election cycle. Each of the presidential hopefuls must produce videos designed to introduce themselves to voters in the early primary and caucus states and to serve as vehicles for fund-raising.

The internet is another technological innovation that is having a major influence on the way in which candidates seek our votes. And because it has become such an important new means of campaigning, we discuss it in detail in chapter 12. Although it is impossible to know just what impact new technologies will ultimately have on political campaigns in the future, as we have seen before, innovations in transportation and communication have an infinite capacity to alter the strategies that candidates use to seek political office. As such, they are an important consideration in any examination of campaign style.

## STYLES AND STRATEGIES OF CAMPAIGNS

Essentially, campaign styles are sets of communication strategies employed at times by all candidates, whether they run for president, mayor, governor, or legislator. Moreover, those who hold office may campaign in the manner of those who do not, just as those who challenge may adopt strategies of incumbency. Thus, those candidates who are incumbents are not restricted to a specific set of incumbency strategies any more than challengers are confined to a particular set of challenger strategies. In fact, candidates frequently combine strategies of one style with strategies of another so that there are times during one contest where an individual contender may assume a rhetorical posture normally associated with incumbency campaigning and at other times may appear to be campaigning as a challenger. This combination may well be a result of the seasonless electoral process discussed in the first and second chapters. As candidates extend the length of the campaign, no one style is likely to remain appropriate for the duration. New events, as well as changes in conditions, force modification in the manner of pursuit. While in February an attack on the incumbent's economic policy might be appropriate, by August the situation may be different enough to make attack an inappropriate strategy. As such, it would be misleading to try to analyze style by examining the practice of only one candidate or one campaign. Styles (incumbency, challenger, and incumbent/challenger) are a product of whatever candidates and their staffs believe is needed at a particular time within the context of their particular campaign. Therefore, the best way to understand them is to determine the composition of each—that is, to catalog their strategies.

### Incumbency Style

Incumbency campaigning in the United States is at least as old as the first presidential incumbent, George Washington, who ran for reelection in 1792. Its various strategies have been used by almost all who have sought election to any level of government. Given its longevity and frequent use, one might assume it would have been defined long ago and its characteristics carefully delineated. While that is not the case, incumbency has been considered a "symbolic resource"[27] and the "Rose Garden Strategy."[28] Although each idea is useful in attempting to understand what it is that candidates do and say when they appear to be "running as an incumbent," each is nonetheless incomplete. Incumbency campaigning is a blend of both symbolic and pragmatic communication strategies designed to make any candidate appear both as good enough for the office sought and as possessing the office (an assumed incumbency stance). This is not an easy task. We know that image creation and maintenance take significant amounts of skill, time, and money.

But developing a credible incumbency style is well worth the effort. The results of countless elections indicate that incumbents tend to win. For example, during the twentieth century, only five presidents have lost their reelection bids; in the total history of our country 75 percent of incumbent presidents have been reelected.

Given this kind of success, it is not surprising that political scientist R. F. Fenno has suggested that incumbency is "a resource to be employed, an opportunity to be exploited."[29] The 2000 election stood out as yet another incredible year for incumbents. In the 2000 election cycle, 403 incumbents of the House of Representatives sought reelection, and all but nine won. In other words, incumbents enjoyed a 98 percent "success rate."[30] In 2004, incumbents once again had a high success rate, including in the presidential election, with the win of the incumbent president, George W. Bush. In total, the 2004 election equaled that of 2000 with 98 percent of all incumbents winning their reelection bids. In 2008, there was some reversal, particularly because neither presidential ticket was composed of incumbents. In the 2010 midterm, fifty-three members of Congress lost their seats, but still 87 percent of incumbents won their reelection bids. In the presidential year of 2012, 90 percent of House representatives and 91 percent of U.S. senators were reelected.[31] Despite a congressional approval rating of just 11 percent in 2014, 96 percent of incumbents won reelection.[32] The rate was even higher in 2016, at 97 percent.[33]

With this understanding, we now consider the specific strategies that candidates employ when they seek the advantages of incumbency. The first four are symbolic in nature; the remaining eleven are pragmatic or instrumental.

## Symbolic Strategies

In exploring the symbolic characteristics of incumbency campaigning, we are, in essence, discussing presidential candidates because there is no other elective office for which the public has the same kind of feelings. In one sense the presidency can be thought of as a focus of impressions and beliefs that exist in our minds—a kind of "collage of images, hopes, habits, and intentions shared by the nation who legitimizes the office and reacts to its occupants."[34] Viewed from a related perspective, when we speak of the presidency, we are dealing with the myth of the office, the image we have possessed since childhood of the one institution that stands for truth, honor, justice, and integrity. We have a conception of an individual and an office that in ennobling each other, ennoble us. Perhaps Theodore White described it best when he wrote:

> Somewhere in American life there is at least one man who stands for law, the President. That faith surmounts all daily cynicism, all evidence or suspicion of wrong-doing by

lesser leaders, all corruptions, all vulgarities, all the ugly compromises of daily striving and ambition. That faith holds that all men are created equal before the law and protected by it; and that no matter how the faith may be betrayed elsewhere, at one particular point—the Presidency—justice will be done beyond prejudice, beyond rancor, beyond the possibilities of a fix.[35]

People may debate the character, quality, and personality of the men who have filled the office, and public opinion polls may indicate dissatisfaction with the performance of an incumbent, but the presidency is, for most citizens, an idealized institution, headed by a single visible individual through whom it is possible to grasp a "cognitive handle" or an understanding of "political goings on."[36] In this context, then, the identity of a particular president is irrelevant; the concern is the office itself and the symbolic role it can play in a campaign.

*Symbolic Trappings of the Office*

The first strategy is the use of symbolic trappings to transmit the absolute strength and importance of the office. The presidency stands for power, and therefore incumbents take on the persona of the powerful. They are surrounded by large numbers of carefully trained and "important-looking" bodyguards who appear to anticipate their every move; their song (played when they enter or leave a public ceremony) is "Hail to the Chief"; incumbents are addressed by title, never by name; when they travel, a whole contingent of Secret Service, media reporters, technicians, and lesser governmental officials accompany them in a caravan of planes and limousines; their home, although the property of "the people," is heavily guarded and off limits to all who have no official business to conduct with them or their staff; incumbents can be in instant communication with the leader of any other country; they serve as commander in chief of all armed services; incumbents can command nationwide media time; and they are always close to a small black bag, the contents of which provide them the capability to blow up the world.

Thus, it is little wonder that those who have campaigned against a president have objected to the continual and conscious use of devices that remind voters that they are seeing and hearing "the president," as opposed to "just another politician." For example, during the 1984 campaign, President Reagan changed the location of his televised press conferences. He stood before an open doorway in the East Room of the White House that reveals a long, elegant corridor. The cameras recorded a majestic setting and a stately exit that dramatized the importance of the office, and it served to remind the audience that they were listening to the president of the United States. During the Bill Clinton years and the George W. Bush years, countless bills were signed into law in the Rose Garden of the White House with the president surrounded by admirers, legislators, and media. Presidents travel to events on Air Force One, with challengers often on much smaller, rented jets. And although Donald Trump's campaign plane was smaller than Air Force One, his personal jet was a Boeing 757 airliner converted to a "private jet." It cost $100 million and he called the aircraft "T-Bird." He had owned the aircraft since 2011 but customized it to red/white/blue with the name "Trump" on both sides.[37]

## Legitimacy of the Office

The second strategy involves not so much what incumbents do—that is, the use of specific tangible symbols to remind voters of their power—but an intangible tool that only they possess and about which their challengers cannot even object. The presidency stands for legitimacy, and therefore the person who holds the office is perceived as the natural and logical leader. No matter who the incumbent may be (or regardless of the incumbent's current rating in the public opinion polls), the president is accorded a kind of sociopolitical legitimacy—a public trust. As one theorist has argued, we place our faith and trust in the hands of our leaders because they project an image that seduces us into participating in the comforting illusion that, through rigid adherence to the constituted ideals of the society, they can guide us through whatever possible troubles the future might present.[38] Moreover, their position provides automatic legitimacy during a campaign in that they, unlike any of their opponents, are from the beginning considered legitimate candidates for the job.

## Competency and the Office

The third strategy is also an intangible tool that comes with the office. The presidency stands for competency; therefore, the person who holds the office can easily convey that impression. To trust in the president's competence is to accept the incumbent as a symbol "that problems can be solved without a basic restructuring of social institutions and without the threat a radical reordering poses both to the contented and to the anxious."[39] Thus, when we attribute a sense of competency to the president, it provides us with reassurance that all can be right. We want to believe that the person who is president is capable (after all, we elected the president in the first place).

In fact, our feelings about the office itself are so strong that, whatever a specific president has done with regard to individual issues, a large number of people will always be supportive. For example, each year since World War II, every president has been ranked by U.S. citizens as one of the ten most admired persons in the world.[40] In 2017, Barack Obama retained the title of "Most Admired Man" in America, but by a narrow margin of 17 percent to Donald Trump's 14 percent.[41] Perhaps a reason for this is, as Murray Edelman suggests, that "public issues fade from attention after a period in the limelight even when they are not 'solved' because they cannot remain dramatic and exciting for long and the media then have economic and psychological reasons to softpedal them."[42] Goodwill is retained, for whatever reasons or in whatever manner. Our point is simply that any president possesses a sense of competency that none of his rivals can share. It is, of course, a distinct advantage of the office.

## Charisma and the Office

The final symbolic strategy, like the first three, is dependent on the ability of the office to transfer its persona to the incumbent. However, this one is not an intangible resource in that it has had deliberate use since presidents began barnstorming the country for their own elections. The presidency stands for excitement, a kind of patriotic glamour, and therefore the person who holds the office takes on these characteristics. In no other way is the mystique of the presidency more visible than it is during a presidential campaign visit almost anywhere in the country. When the president comes to town (advance and security personnel have already been there for at least a week), roads are blocked, airports are closed, children are dismissed from school, bands play, television cameras and reporters are everywhere, and hundreds or thousands of people converge along the streets or at the airport to greet the president; the very sight of the magnificent Air Force One produces a sense of awe, and for a while, we are participants in a warm and patriotic festival. It matters little whether we plan to vote for the incumbent; regardless of how dull and unimaginative the president may have been before living in the White House, once there, the office itself envelops the president in its aura or charisma.

Although campaign tours were not undertaken by incumbents (at least during the election period) until Herbert Hoover paved the way, their symbolic power has not been lost on any of the presidents who have succeeded him. The reasons for their trips have been as varied as have been their modes of transportation. For example, in 1948, Harry Truman whistle-stopped his way across thirty-two thousand miles to blame what he termed the "do-nothing, good-for-nothing 80th Congress" for the nation's problems. In 1956, Dwight Eisenhower, despite two international crises, felt that he had to undertake an extensive tour through the southern states to blunt his opponent's charges that he was too old and too sick to be president. In 1964, Lyndon Johnson barnstormed his way across the country, in part because he felt a psychological need to be "out with the people" and experience their warmth and acceptance of him. In 1976, Jimmy Carter boarded the paddle-wheel riverboat *Delta Queen* and traveled the Ohio and Mississippi rivers, campaigning at each stop, in an almost frantic effort to restore his popularity with voters. In 1984, Ronald Reagan whistle-stopped through several states riding the same presidential caboose Harry Truman rode in 1948. In 1992, more than two thousand people turned out to shake hands with George H. W. Bush at a mall in Concord, New Hampshire, and to hear him explain why he should be reelected despite a depressed economy. In 1996, Bill Clinton's fourteen-bus caravan was greeted by a crowd of twenty-five thousand in Paducah, Kentucky, during a week-long trip that Clinton stated allowed him "to see the people I've been working for for four years."[43] In 2000, the sitting vice president and Democratic nominee, Al Gore, and his vice presidential nominee, Senator Joseph Lieberman, departed on a boat trip down the Mississippi River after the Democratic National Convention. The purpose of their trip was to get a post-convention public opinion and media coverage boost by taking their campaign and new partnership to towns in Wisconsin, Iowa, and Missouri. Their trip emulated the Bush and Quayle boat trip to New Orleans after the 1988 Republican National Convention. In 2004, Bush and Cheney did not tour together after the convention. Instead, President Bush met with then Iraqi prime minister Iyad Allawi while Vice President Cheney spoke at campaign rallies and roundtable discussions around the Midwest. And in 2008, in perhaps the most dramatic and publicized campaign trip on record, the Democratic nominee (a two-year veteran of the U.S. Senate), Barack Obama, traveled to European capitals to conduct rallies and meet with several heads of states. After the Democratic convention in 2016, Hillary Clinton and Tim Kaine launched a bus tour of hitting the key battleground states of Pennsylvania and Ohio. In contrast, Donald Trump and Mike Pence went their separate ways to cover more states. Pence alone went to Nevada, Arizona, Colorado, North Carolina, and Virginia.

For the most part, other incumbents have used campaign trips for the same reasons. They have known that the glamour and excitement, the drama and pageantry of a presidential visit will, even if just briefly, transfer the charisma of the office to them. As such, the trips are well worth the effort.

## Pragmatic Strategies

In turning to the pragmatic strategies of incumbency, it is important to note that they are more universal than are their symbolic counterparts because they can be and have been employed by candidates who are neither presidents nor, in some cases, even incumbents. Certainly, some strategies depend on the legitimate power that holding an office provides, but others have been used by candidates who only borrow the mantle or style of the incumbent.

Strategies that are examined in this section are the following:

- Creating pseudoevents to attract and control media attention
- Making appointments to state and federal jobs as well as appointments to state and national party committees
- Creating special city, state, or national task forces to investigate areas of public concern
- Appropriating federal funds/grants
- Consulting or negotiating with world leaders
- Manipulating the economy or other important domestic issues
- Receiving endorsements by party and other important leaders
- Emphasizing accomplishments
- Creating and maintaining an "above the political trenches" posture
- Depending on surrogates for the campaign trail
- Interpreting and intensifying a foreign policy problem so that it becomes an international crisis

### Creating Pseudoevents

As the use of public relations experts and publicists has increased in political campaigns, so, too, has the frequency of hyped or manufactured news. Essentially, pseudoevents are defined as occurrences that differ from "real" events in that they are planned, planted, or incited for the primary purpose of being reported or reproduced.[44] While all candidates use pseudoevents to try to capture media attention, incumbents have more success because they are in a better position to create them. For example, a governor or state senator may be featured on the evening television and radio news throughout the state because of an announced "major" initiative in attracting a specific corporation to the state and thus creating new jobs. A member of Congress may receive headlines from appointment to a special committee or commission created by the president. Moreover, incumbents have many opportunities for participation in ceremonial occasions—events that are sure to bring the local media. The ceremonies can be as different as the ground-breaking for a new government building or the announcement that a special day has been set aside to honor the city's firefighters. But each can be hyped enough to guarantee publicity for the candidate.

In 1996, the Clinton administration was successful in drawing favorable and widely publicized coverage of presidential initiatives—initiatives that had been discussed frequently by Republican candidates. Shortly after the 1994 election when the Democrats lost control of Congress, the president and his staff identi-fied issues that congressional Republicans had championed and began writing their own legislative proposals. Some of the proposals received daily media coverage. For example, within a two-day period, Clinton's announcements of initiatives to help schools and to track the illegal sale of guns made the front pages of *USA Today* and the *New York Times*, respectively. A month earlier, ABC reported on the president's announcement of a program to combat infectious diseases and his intention to "restate his belief" that cigarettes are addictive. The wide publicity received criticism from Senator Dole, whose campaign released a statement that Clinton and his aides were "getting away with refried beans and in some cases very thin gruel, and getting coverage that makes it seem like a full platter of policy."[45]

Clinton, in other words, used the media exposure his incumbency guaranteed to seize the rhetorical agenda for the 1996 presidential campaign. However, his heir apparent in campaign 2000, Vice President Gore, threw away most of the incumbency strategies to which he was entitled because of his fear of being as-sociated too closely with the scandals surrounding President Clinton. He, in fact, never even accepted the president's offer to speak for him in any state, including Arkansas, Tennessee, and Florida—places where Clinton was popular and states whose Electoral College votes Gore and Lieberman eventually lost.

In 2003, President Bush staged a speech declaring the end of the active phase of the Iraq war on the USS *Abraham Lincoln*. The president flew onto the carrier in a Navy plane wearing a pilot's jumpsuit, with a helmet under his arm. The event was covered by all media outlets and showcased how an incumbent president can use his office to draw attention to himself. As we have discussed previously, in 2008 neither candidate was an incumbent.

In short, incumbents have at their disposal the ability to create pseudoevents that not only generate media exposure but allow some measure of control over the coverage.

### Making Appointments to Jobs and Committees

One of the most common yet powerful incumbency strategies revolves around the ability to appoint personal or political friends—or potential friends—to lo-cal, state, and federal jobs or to give them key positions on party committees. Although patronage has been condemned by reformers in both political parties, it continues largely because it is so advantageous to everyone concerned. First, it allows candidates (and is not limited to incumbents in that all contenders can hold out the "promise" of appointment) to reward those who have helped them in the past. Second, it creates potential friends or at least puts people in a position of gratitude. Third, and undoubtedly most significant, it places supporters in key positions that may well be important in later stages of the campaign or even in subsequent elections. As such, few candidates, from county commissioner to governor to president, have failed to use this strategy.

### Creating Special Task Forces

Modern candidates understand the need not only to determine which issues are of concern to the voters in their city, district, or state, but to speak to those concerns. One way to do this is to announce the formation of a special task force whose purpose is to investigate the issue/problem and make recommendations to the candidate regarding steps or actions to be taken in the future. The strategy is employed by incumbents and those who are not incumbents because the act of forming the task force is all that is really required to create the illusion that the candidate is concerned about the problem.

For example, during his first term, President George W. Bush formed a task force, headed by Vice President Dick Cheney, with the purpose of developing a national energy policy. He also created a drug importation task force and forces on education, Social Security, national security, and domestic surveillance in the fight against terrorism.

Early in the 2012 presidential election year, Obama created a task force to generate concrete proposals to reform firearm laws. Under the leadership of Vice President Biden, the task force was to produce legislation that would be presented to Congress.[46]

Within a month of his inauguration, Donald Trump formed a Task Force on Crime Reduction and Public Safety. Under the Department of Justice, the task force was to develop "strategies to reduce crime, including, in particular, illegal immigration, drug trafficking and violent crime," with a report due within the year.[47]

The primary advantage of the strategy is that the candidate is perceived as a person who understands and cares about those issues important to a particular constituency. However, a second benefit is that the candidate is in the position to postpone taking a stand on a controversial issue—one that might create as many enemies as supporters. Thus, every election year seems to bring a plethora of specially created task forces composed of concerned community/state/national citizens who investigate topics as varied as mental health facilities and taxes for a new sewer system.

### Appropriating Funds/Grants

Absolutely no incumbency strategy is less subtle or more powerful than appropriating special grants to "cooperative" (politically supportive) public officials for their cities and states. It is reserved only for incumbents (in that the strategy does not include promises for the future) and is viewed best at the presidential level, although it is certainly done at the state and local levels as well.

Although every modern president since Franklin Roosevelt has had a prodigious amount of discretionary money to distribute in the form of federal grants, by the election of 1980, the amount totaled $80 billion. Like his predecessors, Jimmy Carter was determined to use it to aid him in the primaries—especially the early contests when the campaign of Edward Kennedy was still viewed as a threat. The money was employed to reward those public officials who announced their preference for the president, to gain a public endorsement where there had not been one, or to punish those who denied or withdrew support. For example, prior to the Illinois primary, Jane Byrne, mayor of Chicago, was told by the White House that U.S. Air Force facilities at O'Hare Field would be relocated to allow Chicago to expand its major airport. However, after the mayor announced her support of Senator Kennedy over the president, the secretary of transportation said that the cabinet had "lost confidence in Mayor Byrne, and would look for opportunities to deny transportation funds to Chicago and its mayor."[48] Thus, the Carter White House went into the 1980 campaign determined to "grease" its way through the primaries. Florida (in advance of the Democratic straw primary) received a $1.1 billion loan guarantee to an electric cooperative, $29.9 billion in grants for public housing in various counties, and $31 million for housing projects for the elderly throughout the state. Prior to its primary, New Hampshire received funds for such projects as a four-lane highway from Manchester to Portsmouth and a special commuter train from Concord to Boston.[49]

In 1992, President Bush made extensive use of his power to allocate funds. For example, government contracts were granted in states where jobs were affected. And after Hurricane Andrew swept through Florida, massive federal resources were promised to the disaster area. In 1996, President Clinton generously used his power to allocate funds. For example, federal funds were provided to enlarge local police forces throughout the country. And after Massachusetts suffered severe flooding from the "Great Rain of '96," it was immediately announced that funds would be made available by the government to those counties hit hardest.

In the first term of George W. Bush's presidency, he allocated funds for several new programs and added funds for the continuation or extension of others. In 2002, Bush controversially asked for federal grant money for faith-based organizations (FBOs). Later in his first term, the president also supplied money for special education state grants, making money available for education and related services for three-to-five-year-old children with disabilities. The 2003 budget included funds for the extension of the AmeriCorps program, funded early childhood care and education, and provided over $100 million for the Department of Homeland Security.

Is the appropriation of funds a successful incumbency strategy? While it is impossible to claim the effect of any one element in a phenomenon as complex as a primary election, President Carter soundly defeated Kennedy in New Hampshire and virtually annihilated him in the Florida and Illinois primaries. On the other hand, the emergency federal funds President Bush promised to Florida ultimately worked against him because Florida citizens said it was too little and arrived too late.

*Consulting with World Leaders*

While at first glance consultation with world leaders may appear to be a strategy possible only for presidential incumbents, the fact is that this strategy is employed by any number of governors and members of Congress as they attempt to build their credentials for reelection. Governors extend invitations to athletic teams or artists and may even negotiate with foreign business corporations and governments about the prospect of building a major factory in their state. Members of Congress take frequent junkets overseas in the effort to illustrate their power and importance to voters in their districts or states.

In addition to its use by incumbents, the strategy is employed by challengers who must also build credentials and convey a sense of their individual importance. Moreover, its use may be even more crucial for them because they do not possess the real authority or power of the incumbent. Thus, a meeting with foreign governmental leaders grants at least a sense of legitimacy because it illustrates acknowledgment and a kind of acceptance into an important and official group of leaders. For example, in 1992, challenger Bill Clinton met Russian president Boris Yeltsin to assure him of his support for the multibillion-dollar aid package for Russia that was then pending in Congress. Following the meeting, the governor described how the half-hour chat with the Russian leader was a meeting of the minds.[50] In 1998, in anticipation of the Iowa caucus for presidential campaign 2000, Republican hopeful Malcolm (Steve) Forbes, Jr., brought former British prime minister Margaret Thatcher to Iowa to campaign by his side. In 2000, Elizabeth Dole, who was campaigning for the Republican nomination, had many international contacts, thanks to her husband's acquaintances during his years as Senate majority leader and as the 1996 Republican presidential nominee and her own years as president of the American Red Cross. In fact, to help demonstrate her international credentials, she traveled to Macedonia to hear "firsthand," she said, about the problems confronting the refugees. In 2004, President George W. Bush frequently invited the media as he visited with other world leaders, particularly Russian president Vladimir Putin, Afghanistan president Hamid Karzai, and British prime minister Tony Blair. The alliance between Bush and Blair was particularly well documented with time spent together along with their wives. Each also verbalized support for the other during reelection campaigns. And in the 2008 campaign, Democratic candidate Barack Obama's trip to meet and interact with European leaders was clearly an effort to establish the credentials of the nonincumbent, relatively inexperienced candidate. Mitt Romney also made several trips overseas to meet world leaders in 2012. On one trip he met with Prime Minister David Cameron and top leaders of the Labour and Liberal Democratic parties.[51] During the 2016 presidential campaign, Donald Trump met with the prime minister of Israel, Benjamin Netanyahu, Egyptian president Abdel Fattah al-Sisi, and Mexican president Enrique Peña Nieto.[52]

While significant to congressional and gubernatorial candidates, a trip abroad—especially to Russia, China, or the Middle East—is virtually a prerequisite for potential presidential contenders, particularly those whose previous experiences have not included "official" foreign travel and consultation with government officials. At the very least, it allows them to work their trips into their discourse with such phrases as "in my meeting with the prime minister, I was told that . . ." But even more important, the strategy provides those candidates who have absolutely no foreign policy experience the appearance of seeming to be a part of or involved in international affairs. As such, it is a useful strategy of the incumbency style.

*Manipulating Important Domestic Issues*

As a number of these strategies illustrate, incumbents have considerable power, which is, of course, one of the reasons they are difficult to defeat and challengers are so eager to assume their campaign style. However, the manipulation or management of important issues is one strategy that can be assumed only by the incumbent.

For example, throughout the years, the economy has been a primary area of presidential management. One way this has been done is timing economic benefits to specific groups within the electorate to ensure their vote in the election. Political scientist Frank Kessler has pointed to the following Social Security incident during the 1972 presidential campaign as a case in point:

> Checks went out in October 1972, one month before the elections, with the following memo enclosed and personally approved by President Nixon to each of the 24.7 million Social Security recipients: "Your social security payment has been increased by 20% starting with this month's check by a new statute enacted by Congress and signed into law by President Richard Nixon on July 1, 1972. The President also signed into law a provision which will allow your social security benefits to increase automatically as the cost of living goes up."[53]

In using this strategy, presidents have not limited themselves to economic manipulation; other issues have been managed. For example, President George H. W. Bush took a number of actions designed to win voter approval in 1992, including supporting the sale of F-15 fighters to Saudi Arabia in time to announce it to defense workers in Missouri,[54] signing a bill making carjacking a federal crime,[55] announcing to farmers a complicated plan for using corn-based ethanol fuel as an antidote for urban smog,[56] vetoing a bill that would regulate cable prices—saying that it benefited special interests rather than the public[57]—and retooling training programs that he said could be paid for without new taxes. And in 1996, in an effort to boost his campaign, President Clinton vetoed a bill that would have outlawed some late-term abortions,[58] signed legislation aimed at preventing gay marriages,[59] transferred U.S. Border Patrol agents from Texas to California (although illegal immigration is a major problem in both states),[60] vetoed bills that would place new limits on the ability of Americans to pursue civil court claims,[61] and signed a bill that increased the minimum wage.[62] In 2003, President George W. Bush signed the Medicare Prescription Drug Modernization Act, the Partial Birth Abortion Ban Act, and the Patriot Act II, among others, in order to show voters that he was moving forward with his agenda. In his first four weeks in office, Trump signed thirteen executive orders. Literally within hours after inauguration, he signed an executive order seeking to reverse the Affordable Care Act, better known as Obamacare. Within a week he issued executive orders to strip federal grant money to "sanctuary cities" and to enhance border security by directing the federal government to build a wall along the U.S. and Mexico border. Trump signed more executive orders in his first hundred days than any contemporary president, more than fifty in his first year alone.[63]

*Receiving Endorsements from Other Leaders*

Although the growth of primaries has reduced their importance, endorsements are an attempt to identify and link the candidate with already established, highly respected, and generally acknowledged leaders. The idea is that endorsement by respected leaders signifies that the candidate is already part of their group and should therefore also be thought of as a leader—in other words, credibility by association. Obviously, this perception can be crucial for a nonincumbent who wishes to adopt the incumbency style. It is, of course, equally significant for the incumbent because continued acceptance by other governmental or political leaders is one way of advancing the perception of a successful term of office. Similarly, candidates hope they receive no endorsements from individuals or groups who are not perceived positively by large segments of society because negative association is also possible.

### Emphasizing Accomplishments

One of those strategies forming the core of the incumbency style is emphasizing accomplishments. Candidates must be able to demonstrate tangible accomplishments during their term of office if they are incumbents or in some related aspect of public service if they only assume the style. This is, of course, the reason that incumbents go to great lengths to list for voters all that they have done while in office.

The strategy is simple as long as the deeds exist. The difficulty occurs when there have been few accomplishments or when major problems have arisen that overshadow positive contributions (taxes are higher than they were before the incumbent took office; inflation is worse; unemployment has not been reduced). When this happens, the strategy becomes more complex in that the incumbent must either deny that the current problems are important ones (normally an impossible task for even the most persuasive) or blame them on someone else—even on uncontrollable forces. Blaming someone, scapegoating, is the path normally chosen. Examples are as numerous as candidates. State legislators blame the governor, governors blame the federal government (especially Congress), presidents blame Congress, and, surprisingly enough, members of Congress often blame other congressional members.

The practice of casting blame elsewhere is certainly not a new variation of the accomplishment strategy. However, its most interesting use is by members of Congress, especially in the House of Representatives. Popular perceptions of Congress are not high and hit historic lows in the single digits starting in 2013, seldom over 15 percent. In fact, surveys on congressional job approval and disapproval ratings have shown a trend of disapproval for decades. However, despite these feelings, congressional incumbents win the overwhelming majority of their elections, as noted above. One of the reasons for this paradox is that, when individual representatives seek reelection, they disassociate themselves or even "run against" the institution of which they are a member. They talk about their accomplishments rather than those of Congress, and as two political communication scholars have noted, they play up the negative "myths" (Congress is a kind of shadowy process in which sinister figures operate) while projecting themselves as hardworking and honest people who work against evil.[64] In this way, then, even when genuine accomplishments may be few, scapegoating makes the strategy possible.

*Creating an Image of Being Above the Political Trenches*

Another strategy at the center of incumbency style is the technique in which candidates try to create the image that they are somehow removed from politics. Essentially, the strategy is composed of any combination of the following three tactics (each designed to create the impression that the contender is a statesman rather than a politician):

- Appearing to be aloof from the hurly-burly of political battle—the office has sought them, so they run because of a sense of love of country and duty
- Failing to acknowledge publicly the existence of any opponent—candidates may have opponents, but statesmen do not
- Sustaining political silence (absolutely refrain from any personal campaign trips or confrontations with opponents, including not answering any charges or attacks or discussing partisan issues)[65]

While contemporary candidates use portions of this strategy, it has been around for a long time. In fact, its progenitor was George Washington. He did not have to create a nonpolitical or statesman image because he was not a politician and he had been reluctant to become president. In spite of this, for candidates who were to follow (at least presidential candidates), he bequeathed a legacy of "being above politics," in a sense, conveying the attitude that being political would some-how "dirty" the office. Thus, for many years, the public picked presidents without ever seeing or hearing what their ideas or policies were—at least during the time in which they were candidates. With only two exceptions,[66] no major party candidates, even after formal nomination, personally solicited votes. They were not expected to (even after transportation networks improved) because the prevailing attitude was that the office must seek the person; that is, the appearance of modest reluctance—of being above politics—had to be maintained.

Stephen Douglas was the first to break the taboo in 1860 when he undertook announced campaign speaking tours around the country on behalf of his own candidacy. Although other Democratic candidates followed his example, none became president until Woodrow Wilson was elected in 1912. Republicans remembered Washington's example longer and eschewed mass campaigning (campaign speaking tours around the country on behalf of their own candidacy) until the 1932 campaign, when an incumbent was faced with a problem of such magnitude that he felt he had to travel the United States explaining why he should not be blamed for the Great Depression.

Thus, this strategy has a long history, and its use, in combination with the next two strategies, continues to play a central role in the development and maintenance of incumbency style.

*Using Surrogates on the Campaign Trail*

This strategy is closely related to the last one in that it is possible for candidates to assume an above-politics posture because others are overtly campaigning for them while they stay home being nonpolitical. While the strategy is employed by a wide spectrum of candidates, the sophisticated use by presidential incumbents since the 1970s allows us to see most clearly the technique at work.

In the 2004 presidential campaign, for example, both the incumbent Bush and the challenger Kerry used surrogates in their campaigns. For the first time in his political career, Bush's twenty-something twin daughters, Jenna and Barbara, traveled around the country focusing on college campuses and young voters in an effort to gain votes for their father. The twins also spoke on their father's behalf at the Republican National Convention in New York City. As well as his daughters, President Bush's parents, the former president George H. W. Bush and first lady Barbara, also campaigned for their son. Like Bush's family, Kerry's children and stepchildren campaigned across the country, and like the Bush twins, the Kerry sons and daughters focused on young voters and college campuses. And while surrogates were certainly a part of the presidential campaign of 2008, for the most part they were part of each candidate's "political" rather than "relational" family. In 2012, Romney's sons Tagg and Matt were active participants in the campaign with travel scheduling equal to their father's. Four of Trump's children actively campaigned for him during the entire 2016 campaign. They also spoke at the Republican National Convention. Firstborn son Donald Trump, Jr., and daughter Ivanka were the most notable and made many media appearances on behalf of their father.

*Interpreting or Intensifying Foreign Policy Problems into International Crises*

Although variations of the strategy of interpreting or intensifying foreign policy problems into international crises are employed by incumbents at all levels, it is most completely studied as used by presidents. Its purpose is simple: to create enough of a crisis so that voters (either because of patriotism or not wanting to change leaders at the time of an emergency) will be motivated to rally around the president. There have been many instances when the technique has been successful. In 1964, when U.S. ships in the Gulf of Tonkin were fired upon, President Johnson interrupted his "campaigning" to go on television, where he pledged that the United States would take rigorous defensive measures. In 1975, when a U.S. merchant ship, the *Mayaguez*, was captured by Cambodian forces, President Ford (who was about to make official his bid for reelection) used the situation to build his leadership or command credentials by ordering marines to bomb Cambodia until the *Mayaguez* crew was released. However, one of the most adept uses of the strategy occurred in the surfacing and primary stages of the 1980 campaign when President Jimmy Carter (who had two genuine foreign policy problems with the seizure of the U.S. embassy in Iran and the Soviet advances into Afghanistan) combined the use of surrogates, a nonpolitical image, and international crises to promote his renomination campaign.

Prior to the Iowa caucus and continuing through the Maine and New Hampshire primaries, Carter pledged that he would not personally campaign until the hostages in Tehran were released. Later, when the Soviets marched into Afghanistan, the president reinforced his earlier vow when he announced that, because "this is the most serious crisis since the last World War," he would be unable to leave the White House to campaign in person for reelection. In addition, when other candidates (notably Senator Edward Kennedy and Governor Jerry Brown) questioned the administration's handling of the "crisis," the president completed the strategy by suggesting that attacks on his policy were "damaging to our country and to the establishment of our principles and the maintenance of them, and the achievement of our goals to keep the peace and to get our hostages released."[67]

Until the very last round of the primaries, the president stuck to his pledge. He emerged only rarely from the White House or Camp David and left most comments on politics to his surrogates. Carter's use of incumbency strategies was eminently successful. While giving the appearance that he was too busy trying to solve the international crises to campaign for reelection, he was defeating his opponents in the Democratic primary elections.

Twenty-four years later, President George W. Bush's most prominent strategy was reminding Americans of the tragedies that occurred on September 11, and his "all-out" response to it. Not only were there references to 9/11 in the president's speeches around the country, but also his reelection campaign built TV commercials that showcased the president's leadership in responding to the fall of the World Trade Center in New York City.

### Summary

These, then, are the strategies that constitute the incumbency style. There are, as we have seen, many of them—each somewhat different from, although often dependent on, the others and each potentially effective in the hands of candidates who understand and appreciate their power. Perhaps what is most startling about them is the extent to which they work. Normally, it takes enormous amounts of money, organization, and skill to defeat even somewhat inept incumbents. They have at their command not only the strategies we have examined but also whatever privileges the office itself provides—including public awareness (visibility) and the opportunity to perform various popular and noncontroversial services for constituents. These strategies have repeatedly enabled incumbents to win reelections overwhelmingly and to win by larger margins than victorious nonincumbents. As we have said before, given all the benefits, it is no wonder that candidates who are not incumbents often assume elements of the style.

### Disadvantages to Incumbency Campaigning

But under what conditions can incumbents lose? In other words, are there burdens of the style as well as benefits? It seems to us that incumbency campaigning has at least four major disadvantages. First, and maybe most important, incumbents must run (at least in part) on their record. While they may cast blame elsewhere or minimize the scope or significance of problem areas within their administration, an effective challenger can make certain that the record of the incumbent (and shortcomings can be found in virtually all records) forms the core of the campaign rhetoric. The incumbent can be kept in a position of having to justify and explain—answering rather than charging, defending rather than attacking. Being forced to run on one's record can be a severe handicap, particularly in the hands of a skilled challenger.

The second and related burden faced by many incumbents is simply that the public may blame them for all problems—whether or not they were at fault. Incumbents are in the public eye, and if the city sanitation workers refuse to pick up the garbage for a week or if the public transportation system is shut down because of weather, an accident, or striking employees, the incumbents are held accountable. At the very least, the question of competency or job effectiveness is raised in the public mind, waiting perhaps for the skilled challenger to capitalize on it.

The third disadvantage, although quite different from the first two, can be equally troublesome. The challenger is free to campaign, but incumbents must at least give the appearance of doing the job for which they have been elected. As campaign seasons become longer, this becomes more difficult. Incumbents often find it unnerving to go about the day-to-day task of administering a city, state, or nation while their opponents spend countless hours out on the hustings—garnering media attention with attacks against them and their policies. If they respond by indulging in overt campaigning, they are criticized for not doing their job. If they ignore it, they may well be accused of having no defense and being afraid to go out and face voters. In other words, it is a real "damned if you do and damned if you don't" situation.

Finally, because incumbents are at the center of media/public attention far more than their opponents, expectations are great regarding their "front-runner" status. If those expectations are not met, the incumbent is in trouble. Nowhere has this been more thoroughly illustrated than in presidential primary campaigns. Even when incumbents win, if they fail to meet some preconceived percentage set by the media or even by their own staffs, they have, at least in terms of media publicity, lost.

Thus, there are some burdens. Even the incumbency style does not guarantee election. With this in mind, we will now contrast the strategies of the incumbent style with those of the challenger, knowing that in each there are burdens as well as benefits.

## Challenger Style

Challenger campaigning is not easy because the style demands a two-step process, the implementation of which requires not only a good deal of deliberate planning but also equal portions of skill and luck. The style can be defined as a series of communication strategies designed to persuade voters that change is needed and that the challenger is the best person to bring about the change. While the kind of change can vary all the way from shifts in a whole economic system to personality characteristics desired in the officeholder, challengers must convince the electorate that some kind of alteration is necessary to stand any chance for success.

However, the second part of the process is equally important; the voters must also be persuaded that the challenger is the candidate most likely to produce more desirable conditions or policies. Therefore, the complexity of the style is increased because not only must those who challenge call for change, but they also must simultaneously demonstrate their own capability in bringing about that change. As if all of this were not difficult enough, it is entirely possible that the success of the challenger may ultimately depend on the skill of the incumbent—whether the incumbent makes a major mistake in campaign strategy or becomes a victim of prevailing conditions. Thus, it is no understatement to maintain that the task facing most challengers is formidable.

Despite the potential hazards or burdens, advocating change—the challenger campaign style—is not new. In fact, it probably got its start in the presidential campaign of 1800 when Jeffersonians distributed leaflets that asked, "Is it not time for a change?" Whenever it began, it has been used by many candidates who have sought elective office. Moreover, elements of the style have even been employed by incumbents such as Harry Truman and Gerald Ford, who felt it would be more beneficial to their candidacies to call for a change in Congress than only try to explain the present problems.

The strategies examined in this section include the following:

- Attacking the record of opponents
- Taking the offensive position on issues
- Calling for a change
- Emphasizing optimism for the future
- Speaking to traditional values rather than calling for value changes
- Appearing to represent the philosophical center of the political party
- Delegating personal or harsh attacks in an effort to control demagogic rhetoric

### Attacking the Record

Just as running on the record of their accomplishments is a central strategy of incumbency, attacking that same record is a prime characteristic of the challenger style. In fact, the ability to criticize freely (and often in exaggerated terms) may well be one of the most important benefits the challenger possesses.[68] When there is no incumbent, candidates attack the record of the current administration (if they do not represent the same political party) or even an opponent's record in a previous position. Whatever becomes the focus of criticism, the object is to attack—to create doubt in voters' minds regarding the incumbent's/opponent's ability—to stimulate public awareness of any problems that exist or to foster a sense of dissatisfaction and even unhappiness with the state of affairs generally.

In 1996, Senator Dole attacked President Clinton on a number of issues and tried to convince voters that problems existed that demanded attention. For example, Dole attacked Clinton's campaign for accepting large financial contributions from foreign business interests.[69] He also demanded that President Clinton forgo future pardons connected with Whitewater, the failed land deal in which Clinton had been accused of wrongdoing.[70] The problem for Dole was twofold. First, the president's campaign responded immediately by counterattacking; and second, voters appeared to have little interest in his attacks on the president. In the 2000 campaign, Vice President Gore (who, in his role as the sitting vice president, could have run as an incumbent but chose to attack as though he were the challenger) called Governor Bush's proposals a "risky scheme."[71] Not to be "outdone" by the attacks of his rival, Bush during his nomination acceptance address attacked the vice president by joking that if Gore had been around when Edison was testing the lightbulb he would have called it a "risky anti-candle scheme."[72] In 2004

Senator Kerry continually challenged President George W. Bush on his lack of an overall plan for Iraq as well as charging that the president had no plan for the health care system. Senator McCain frequently mentioned Senator Obama's lack of experience in most of the domestic and international issues important to the electorate during the 2008 campaign. And in 2012, Romney attacked the Obama administration over its "failed" economic and foreign policies.

Interestingly, attack is so much a part of the challenger style that it frequently occurs even when the predominant public perception of the incumbent is that a credible job has been done. In this instance, the challenger may minimize the importance of the accomplishments, credit them to someone or something else (often another branch or level of government that happens to be controlled by their own party), never mention the accomplishments, or point out that in the years ahead accomplishments will be viewed as problems. By whatever means various challengers go about it, their ability to attack existing records or policies is a crucial tool and integral to the overall style.

*Taking the Offensive Position on Issues*

Essentially, this strategy involves nothing more than taking the offensive position on issues important to the campaign—probing, questioning, challenging, attacking, but never presenting concrete solutions for problems. It is the incumbent who has to defend unworkable solutions to unsolvable problems; the challenger can limit rhetoric to developing problems, keeping the incumbent in a position where all actions have to be defended.[73] In a sense, it is part of a challenger's expected role—to criticize, attack, point out needs—generally guiding voters to begin thinking that the incumbent has been ineffective. Challengers are not expected to solve problems (they have had no chance as officeholders to do so). This is, of course, a major advantage (one of the relative few), and those who abandon it often lose the election. In fact, the more detailed that challengers become in offering solutions, the more material they provide to be attacked themselves. In other words, when they drop the offensive, they have essentially traded places with incumbents, thus compounding their difficulties because, unlike incumbents, they lack the tools to solve problems. Thus, the strategy is simply to talk about what is wrong without suggesting any precise ways in which conditions can be righted.

History is replete with examples of successful challengers who used this strategy and won. In 1932, Franklin Roosevelt never divulged the contents of his "New Deal"; in 1952, Dwight Eisenhower never suggested how he would deal with the Korean conflict except to promise that he would personally go there and look it over; in 1960, John Kennedy never shared the details of the "New Frontier"; in 1968, Richard Nixon only said he had a plan regarding the war in Vietnam but never provided any clues regarding it; in 1976, Jimmy Carter seldom offered solutions more substantive than his love and admiration for the people; in 1980, Ronald Reagan never explained just how his supply-side economics would do all he claimed for it; and in 1992, Bill Clinton presented the necessity for economic reform, health care reform, and welfare reform without providing clear details of the solutions he advocated. In 2000, George W. Bush never really explained how he could cut taxes while simultaneously maintaining the surplus in the federal budget. In 2004, John Kerry and his running mate, John Edwards, continually attacked the president's tax cuts, which they argued only helped America's most wealthy and called for an end to "the two Americas." And in 2008, the Democratic challenger, Barack Obama, was successful in "consistently presenting and developing his overall economic theme that the current problems were a result of Bush administrative policies supported by Senator McCain."[74] In retrospect, it is unlikely that most of these challengers even knew how they might solve all the problems they discussed once they were elected. Whether they did or did not, solutions were not offered, and the candidates managed to keep their offensive position on the issues while forcing their opponents to defend, justify, and offer plans.

Conversely, in 1964 and again in 1972, two challengers never seemed to understand the essential nature of the strategy. Barry Goldwater and George McGovern thought they had to present specific proposals on topics as varied as welfare and the way to fight wars. As the details of their plans became known, they were subjected to intensive analysis, debated, refuted by opponents and media, and finally rejected as absurd. Goldwater and McGovern not only lost their credibility as serious presidential candidates but lost an important advantage. Taking and keeping the right to attack without proposing solutions is a major challenger strategy that only the foolish abandon.

### Calling for a Change

From the beginning of each campaign season, it becomes clear that many candidates announce that they are "willing" to run for office because they believe that a change is necessary. Whether it involves specific programs and policies, philosophical assumptions regarding the nature of government, or even modification in administrative style, calling for a change has become the dominant characteristic of those who challenge.

This strategy has been employed in various ways. For example, John Kennedy talked about the need to "get the country moving again"—a stylistic and substantive change from a passive attitude to aggressive, take-charge action. Jimmy Carter urged a moralistic change—a return to honest, decent, and compassionate government. Ronald Reagan argued for economic as well as philosophical change, while Edward Kennedy gave, as his only reason for an intraparty challenge, the need for a change in the manner and style of presidential leadership. Perhaps one of the most specific uses of the strategy was exemplified by Senator John Glenn, who in the early months of the surfacing stage of the 1984 presidential campaign called for a change of direction in budgeting for basic research and technological development as well as a dramatic overhaul of the Social Security system. Conversely, the failure of Michael Dukakis to call for a change in 1988 was one of the reasons for his defeat. According to John Sasso, the chief strategist for Dukakis's presidential campaign, "the failure to establish a clear campaign theme and a compelling case for political change" was a mistake on their part.[75] In 1992, Clinton integrated talk of reform into his overall call for change. In June 1992 he told an audience, "When I got into this race, the President was at an historic high point in popularity. But I was convinced then and I am convinced now that this country needs profound change."[76] In 1996,

Bob Dole asserted that the nation needed material, or economic, as well as moral change. In 2000, the Republican nominees George W. Bush and Dick Cheney asserted that the American military had been allowed to decline because funding to the Department of Defense had not increased significantly during the Clinton years. In 2004, Senators Kerry and Edwards argued that changes were needed in our managing of Iraq. In 2008, Senators Obama and Biden criticized President Bush and Senator McCain, arguing that the wars in Iraq and Afghanistan should be ended in sixteen months. And in 2012, Romney observed,

> This country we love is in peril. And, my friends, is why we are here today. . . . Barack Obama has failed America. When he took office, the economy was in recession. He made it worse. And he made it last longer. Three years later, over 16 million Americans are out of work or have just quit looking. Millions more are underemployed. Three years later, unemployment is still above 8%, a figure he said his stimulus would keep from happening. Three years later, foreclosures are still at record levels. Three years later the prices of homes continue to fall. Three years later, our national debt has grown nearly as large as our entire economy. Families are buried under higher prices for food and higher prices for gasoline. It breaks my heart to see what's happening to this country.[77]

Thus, regardless of how it is employed, the essence of challenger style must revolve around seeking change. If a change from existing conditions, incumbents, or administrations is unnecessary, then so, too, are challengers.

### Emphasizing Optimism for the Future

While most candidates, regardless of the level of office sought, traditionally spend some time during the campaign talking about their vision or their optimism for the future, the strategy is particularly important for those who would challenge the status quo. After all, if existing conditions are so bad, can they ever be better? Thus, the task of the challenger is not only to attack but to hold out the promise of a better tomorrow—a day when wrongs will be righted, when justice will prevail, and when health, wealth, and happiness will be more than just vague illusions. In other words, challengers must assume a "rhetoric of optimism" as opposed to a "rhetoric of despair."[78] This is not to suggest that candidates who employ the strategy dismiss the nation's needs from their discourse; rather, it is a question of emphasis. For example, in 1932, Franklin Roosevelt obviously acknowledged the problems caused by the economic depression, but the central focus of his campaign was hope for the future. John Kennedy talked about problems, but his emphasis was on the country's potential to get moving again; Ronald Reagan pledged that he would lead a crusade to make the United States great again; the commitment of George H. W. Bush to the spirit of volunteerism as a substitute for federal government programs was embodied in the phrases, first used in his nomination acceptance speech, a "kinder, gentler nation" and "a thousand points of light"; the focus of Bill Clinton's rhetoric was the creation of a government that efficiently works for people for a change; in 2008 Barack Obama's phrase was "Yes, we can"; in 2012 Mitt Romney's slogan was "Believe in America"; and in 2016 we had the infamous "Make America

Great Again" slogan of Donald Trump. In short, a part of the challenger style is reliance on the positive—emphasizing hope and faith in the future, an optimism that the nation's tomorrow will, in fact, be better than today.

### Speaking to Traditional Values

Speaking to traditional values, the overall challenger style being dominated by a call for redirection or change does not mean a redefinition of values. In fact, it is just the opposite. Successful challengers must reinforce majority values instead of attempting to forge new ones. In other words, they must have some understanding of the way in which people view themselves and their society—some understanding of the current tenets of the American Dream. In 1992, Bill Clinton used the challenger strategy of speaking to traditional values as both a defensive and an offensive weapon. For example, he defended against direct attacks from Bush by saying, "I think the implication he has made that somehow Democrats are godless is deeply offensive to me . . . and to a lot of us who cherish our religious convictions and also respect America's tradition of religious diversity."[79]

While this strategy has been understood by challengers such as Richard Nixon, Jimmy Carter, Ronald Reagan, George H. W. Bush, and Donald Trump, it may be more interesting to explain it by the example of one who did not. In 1972, before suffering the worst defeat in the history of presidential politics, Democratic challenger George McGovern seemed to have little comprehension of what most citizens wanted. He talked about massive or radical changes in welfare and tax reform, military spending and inflation, school busing, amnesty for those who had left the country rather than participate in the Vietnam War, and the need for more civil rights legislation. What McGovern failed to understand was that most citizens "were tired of social reforms, tired of the 'good-cause' people; that the majority preferred to live their own lives privately, unplagued by moralities, or war, or riots, or violence."[80] Middle-class citizens viewed McGovern as a candidate of an elitist upper class whose values they did not understand except to know that they angered and frightened them. Through his failure to speak to the dreams or visions of the electorate, McGovern abandoned an important strategy of the challenger style.

### Appearing to Represent the Philosophical Center

Throughout our political history, successful challengers have been ideological representatives from the mainstream of the major parties, or they have tried to appear as though they were. While some may have been, on one or two issues, a bit to the right or left of the majority of the party, they have not been representatives of the outer or fringe groups. In most campaigns, the fringe groups eventually have compromised and supported their party's candidate, even though that candidate may have been more conservative or liberal than they would have preferred. In the presidential campaign of 1980 and even in 1984, Ronald Reagan, who had long been the champion of the ultraconservatives within the GOP, attempted to position himself closer to the ideological Republican middle once he had secured the nomination. In 1988, George H. W. Bush used the same strategy by repositioning himself on such issues as abortion. In 1996, Bill Clinton modified his stand on so many domestic issues that it was difficult, and frequently impossible, for his opponent to claim even traditional Republican positions. And in 2000, George W. Bush steadily moved to the philosophical center after his victories in the Super Tuesday primaries all but finalized his selection as the Republican nominee.

The two classic exceptions in contemporary presidential politics have been Barry Goldwater and George McGovern, each of whom, as the candidate of groups to the right and left of the centers of their two parties, did not try to reposition himself in the center of his respective party. Instead, each attempted to reform the ideological majority around the ideological minority. In so doing, they failed to employ a traditional challenger strategy.

While Goldwater and McGovern did not attempt to occupy a more central ideological ground, two nominees during the 1980s were blocked from using the strategy by their opponents. In 1984, Ronald Reagan was able to position Walter Mondale as a candidate of the extreme Democratic Left because of the former vice president's stand on increased taxes, social welfare issues, and defense spending, and because of the endorsement of him by groups such as the National Organization for Women and the Gay Liberation Movement. Similarly, in 1988, George H. W. Bush, who for much of his political career had been perceived by conservative Republicans as too liberal, repositioned himself in the center and branded Michael Dukakis as a liberal even among Democrats. A liberal, according to the Bush definition, was someone who, like Governor Dukakis, was opposed to children saying the Pledge of Allegiance in school, was so soft on crime he let convicted murderers out of prison on weekend furloughs, and who did not support defense initiatives such as the MX missile—in other words, someone who was outside the mainstream of traditional American values. The label proved disastrous for Dukakis because the governor failed to reposition himself or to redefine the vice president's interpretation of a liberal.

In 1992, Bill Clinton did not allow himself to be defined by his opponents. From the surfacing period onward, he positioned himself as a "new kind of Democrat." In fact, he was one of the founding members of the Democratic Leadership Council—a group of Democrats recognized for its conservative to moderate position on many issues. However, in 1996, Republican challenger Bob Dole had a singular inability to define himself. In fact, it was his very lack of definition that allowed the incumbent and his fellow Democrats to maintain the hold on the ideological center and force Dole to the conservative Right, a position that he did not always fit.

Of course now in a post-2016 environment, the ideological and political "middle" is very narrow indeed. The social fragmentation and polarization are near historic levels. The tribal nature of both parties today really does make it difficult to identify "the middle." Campaigns are less likely to target "independents" as they are fragmented constituent groups. The 2020 elections will signal whether the current segmentation prevails.

## Delegating Personal or Harsh Attacks

Although attack remains a central imperative of the challenger style, successful candidates (particularly in statewide or national races) do not themselves indulge in demagogic rhetoric. While smear tactics and political hatchet work have been a part of elective politics for years, wise challengers have left harsh or vitriolic language to running mates, surrogate speakers, or their television advertising and printed materials. The reason for delegating this kind of attack is, at least in part, related to the symbolic nature of the campaign itself. As we have mentioned earlier, campaigns are a symbolic representation of how candidates might behave if elected—a kind of vignette from which voters are able to transfer campaign performance into performance as officeholders. Thus, the challenger who likens the incumbent to Adolf Hitler, asserts that the president behaves like a reformed drunk, or argues that the incumbent is ignorant of foreign policy—as did George McGovern in 1972, Edward Kennedy in 1980, and Walter Mondale in 1984—is unwise.

Historically, demagogy is never viewed as an asset and normally backfires for the challenger who employs it. In 1988, Michael Dukakis was attacked as being soft on defense, soft on crime, and soft on patriotism. However, George H. W. Bush was smart enough to leave direct attacks on his opponent to others and to his television advertising campaign. In 1992, Clinton attacked the policies of the president and his administration but was careful to show no disrespect to President Bush, even after the president referred to Clinton as a "bozo." However, in 1996, Bob Dole attacked President Clinton's personal character. Not only were Dole's attacks ineffective—the president retained his double-digit lead in the polls—but the strategy actually persuaded some voters to oppose Dole and support Clinton because they thought personal attacks were "in bad taste and removed from the issues of being the president."[81] In 2000, George W. Bush, while never actually mentioning the Clinton–Monica Lewinsky scandal or the subsequent impeachment of the president, nonetheless made Dole's argument more tactfully by focusing on how he would uphold the dignity of the presidency and his own family values. In 2004, John Kerry, while attempting to show no disrespect for President Bush and the office of the president, nonetheless attacked or frequently talked about the president's failed economic policies; and in 2008, Senator Obama's major lines of argument revolved around the country's economic problems. Interestingly, in 2012, Romney nearly always complimented President Obama as a "good man" and "great parent" who simply supported wrong policies that failed to pull America out of the recession.

Once again, the 2016 presidential campaign of Donald Trump countered traditional wisdom. He never hesitated to attack opponents directly and personally. Devising nicknames, especially for his opponents, was certainly a new rhetorical strategy never seen before in presidential campaigning. Although perhaps juvenile, the nicknames went a long way in providing memorable descriptions of opponents and helped to destroy all of them. The nicknames included Lyin' Ted Cruz, Little Marco Rubio, and Low-Energy Jeb Bush of his own party and for Democrats Crooked Hillary Clinton, Crazy Bernie Sanders, and Pocahontas Elizabeth Warren. Some labeled such nicknames as a form of bullying.

*Summary*

These, then, are the strategies that constitute the challenger style. While there are fewer of them than there are incumbency strategies, they can also be powerful when used correctly. However, those who employ them, just as those who employ their counterparts, must understand the importance of image creation and maintenance. For example, it does little good if a candidate attacks the record of the incumbent but does so using demagogic language or leaves no outlet for the promise of a better tomorrow. Similarly, those who fail to understand the necessity of appearing to represent the values of the majority of the electorate as they call for a change in the course or direction of present policies will have little success. In short, challenger campaigning is difficult primarily because being a challenger is not nearly as advantageous as being an incumbent. Challengers win but not as often. Challengers have some advantages over incumbents but not very many. In the final analysis, challengers may be only as successful as incumbents are incompetent to employ the symbolic and pragmatic strategies their office provides.

### Incumbent/Challenger: A Merger of Styles

As discussed earlier, the incumbent and challenger strategies are not absolute categories. Those candidates who are incumbents are not restricted to a specific set of incumbency strategies any more than challengers are confined to a particular set of challenger strategies. While the rhetoric of most candidates typically reflects their actual position in the race, there are instances wherein aspects of incumbency and challenger styles have been combined. It is not uncommon, for example, for challengers to assume the mantle of incumbency whenever and wherever possible; its advantages are well documented. Those who challenge must try to emphasize whatever accomplishments they have had in public life and appear to be acquainted with other leaders, and have a clear need to use whatever means available to them to gain the attention of the media. Similarly, events may, from time to time, compel incumbents to borrow strategies more frequently associated with the challenger. While we consider it unlikely that any incumbent would ever find it advantageous to drop completely the symbolic strategies or to call for a change, an incumbent may well emphasize ideological centrality or rely on surrogate speakers for overt/direct personal attacks on opponents. Such rhetorical borrowing between categories, perhaps in response to changing conditions, is only part of what we mean by the incumbent/challenger style.

The most prominent characteristics of the combined style are abandonment of the essential purpose or thrust of incumbent or challenger rhetoric and abandonment of the responsibilities each has. If the challenger does not attack or at least question the policies and actions of the incumbent, no real campaign dialogue occurs. In a similar vein, if the incumbent will not acknowledge problems, defend current policies or programs, or even suggest/offer a future course of action, no real dialogue can occur. Although there is little question that occasionally incumbent presidents or vice presidents running for reelection have used strategies of incumbency as well as those of a challenger, perhaps the best way to understand the incumbent/challenger style is through two extended examples, one from 1984 and one from 2000. In 1984, we had two challengers, one of whom was president of the United States. Beginning with his nomination acceptance speech, Ronald Reagan's rhetoric was heavily centered around two staples of the challenger style: attacking the policies of the opposition (in this case going back to the Carter-Mondale administration) while taking the offensive position on issues and emphasizing optimism for the future. Incumbency strategies were only to enhance his campaign as a challenger. While Reagan was not the first sitting president to try to campaign for reelection in this manner, he was the first one since Harry Truman to do so successfully.

Part of Reagan's success as an "incumbent challenger" was his ability figuratively to step out of office at crucial moments and reflect on problems—"posing as a commentator who happened to live on Pennsylvania Avenue"—never admitting that he, as the result of election, was currently more responsible than any other single individual for the federal government.[82] But there was another part to the strategy: painting the portrait of a future at once so uplifting and patriotic that all problems of the moment were dwarfed by it.

Americans are by nature optimists. We believe in people—especially heroes— and in happy endings. Successful candidates have long known that optimism is the way to the hearts of the American electorate. "At the worst of times, Franklin Roosevelt uplifted with a smile, while years later, Jimmy Carter guaranteed his defeat by telling us that we were suffering from malaise."[83] What was so effective about Reagan's use of cheer was his own appearance of amiability and his understanding of the political fact that Americans want to hear good news, as well as the way he managed to distance himself from responsibility when things went wrong. "It was as if he was a king who reigned but did not rule—a constitutional monarch whose performance was a symbol to his people while politicians did the dirty work of governing."[84] In 1984, he campaigned for reelection as a critic of federal budget deficits even while he had created the largest deficit in history.

In short, Reagan offered voters, just as he had in 1980 when he had actually been a challenger, a picture of a future that did not include hard choices or sacrifices he might ask them to make after the election. However, a strategy of optimism is possible only if a candidate has managed to avoid the defensive position on issues. This was the second overt use of the challenger style employed by the incumbent president.

Throughout the campaign, it was as if there were two challengers—both attacking, probing, questioning, but the incumbent/challenger never defending his policies. In fact, by seizing the offensive on issues, the president reduced his opponent to the most disadvantageous challenger posture, suggesting solutions for problems. Reagan did not have to make allowances for solving problems because he did not acknowledge the existence of problems. Unwilling to accept the issues presented by Mondale as problems, let alone acknowledge any responsibility for them, the president simply smiled and said that the trend is the thing and, every day in every way, things are getting better. When Mondale charged that the nuclear arms race had heated up between Washington and Moscow and that U.S.–Soviet relations were strained, the president responded by ignoring the issue and talked about America standing tall and looking to the 1980s with courage, confidence, and hope. Finally, in an absolute measure of desperation, Mondale outlined solutions—such as the inevitable raising of taxes to deal with the national deficit. When time after time Mondale tried to push Reagan on exactly what he was going to do about the deficit, the president only responded that it was a little scary to have a deficit of a $180 billion and that, even if he had "inherited the wreckage from the Democrats," he was willing to work with them to repair the problem.

From the beginning, it appeared that the challenger and the incumbent had reversed roles. The incumbent ran against "big spending demons in Washington" and "puzzle-palaces on the Potomac," and whenever he left the White House, he talked about what a pleasure it was to be out of Washington. The challenger sought to tie the incumbent to problems the country faced, and when there was no response, he created his own solutions. The Reagan staff had reasoned that it was unnecessary to speak to the specific issues raised by Mondale. They had determined before the campaign even began that the reelection effort would be concentrated on the president's leadership and the problems resulting from the Carter-Mondale past, without defending current programs or proposing any new or specific programs for the future.[85] They believed their strategy would be successful because Reagan had been on the political stage for thirty years. His views were well known by the American people. As the press secretary for his reelection campaign, James Lake, said, "It would be foolish of us to let Ronald Reagan respond to Mr. Mondale . . . people don't care. They get his message. They see him on television and read the newspaper."[86] Thus, the incumbent outlined scenes and evoked symbols, leaving details—particularly unpleasant details—for later. Patriotic slogans, such as "America is back," "America stands tall," "America is too great for small dreams," or "the opportunity society," combined with the persona of the incumbent himself and his stage-managed appearances, drove the 1984 presidential campaign into what one political commentator called a "collage of manufactured happiness as in an infinitely extended television commercial."[87]

Similarly, during the presidential campaign of 2000, Vice President Al Gore chose to ignore many of the incumbent's rhetorical strategies (which as the sitting vice president were "rightfully" his) and to adopt, instead, the rhetorical posture of a challenger. From the beginning (when announcing his candidacy; in debating his only Democratic rival, Bill Bradley; during the primaries; in his nomination acceptance speech; and right through the general election), the vice president made it clear that he was "his own man." Given, however, that the country was at peace and experiencing sustained economic prosperity, it would have been reasonable (and rhetorically advantageous) for Gore to have used incumbency strategies—especially during the general election campaign when his opponent had no experience in many areas typically deemed important for presidents. It is not that the vice president seldom postured himself as an incumbent; it is that he eschewed some of those strategies that could have been important to his candidacy. For example, he failed to discuss any foreign policy experience he had had as vice president, including meeting or consulting with foreign leaders, being a member of the administration's national security team, or even being part of the administration that had achieved some progress with the Middle East peace process. In addition to not assuming the rhetorical posture of an incumbent in foreign policy issues, the vice president failed to maximize the administration's accomplishments in domestic policy issues important to the electorate. He sounded like the challenger, not the incumbent, for example, when he talked about reduced crime, welfare reform, or the turn from a national deficit to a national surplus. Instead of taking his share of the credit, he argued that "things were not good enough," "we need to do more and better," or "you ain't seen nothing yet." The point we make is simply this: by assuming an incumbent/challenger style, Vice President Gore threw out the rhetorical advantages of incumbency, which may ultimately have cost him votes in a historically close election. While in 1984 President Reagan was successful in combining incumbent and challenger strategies, Vice President Gore was not. Clearly it remains a "tricky" rhetorical strategy for which there is no guarantee for success.[88]

## CONCLUSIONS

In this chapter, we have examined an important yet frequently overlooked element of elective politics—campaign style. In so doing, we considered style as sets of communication strategies that are employed by all candidates and noted the relationship of image and advancements in transportation and communication to their creation and maintenance.

The incumbency style was defined as a blend of symbolic and pragmatic communication strategies designed to make voters perceive candidates not only as good enough for the office sought, but as if they already possess the office. Fifteen different yet complementary strategies were examined. Similarly, we analyzed the challenger style, defining it as a series of communication strategies designed to persuade voters that change is needed and that the candidate is the best person to bring about change. Seven different yet complementary strategies were discussed.

Finally, we considered the incumbent/challenger style and noted that the combination of strategies that constitute it, at least as illustrated during the 1984 and 2000 presidential campaigns, can play a major role in the creation of empty political rhetoric.

## NOTES

1. Barry Brummett, *A Rhetoric of Style* (Carbondale: Southern Illinois University Press, 2008), xi.

2. Bruce E. Gronbeck, "The Functions of Presidential Campaigning," *Communication Monographs* 45 (November 1978): 268–80.

3. Robert V. Friedenberg, *Notable Speeches in Contemporary Presidential Campaigns* (Westport, CT: Praeger, 2002), 1–14.

4. Ibid.

5. Quoted in Kathleen Hall Jamieson, *Packaging the Presidency: A History and Criticism of Presidential Campaign Advertising* (New York: Oxford University Press, 1984), 12.

6. Kenneth E. Boulding, *The Image* (Ann Arbor: University of Michigan Press, 1961), 6.

7. G. R. Pike, "Toward a Transactional Model of Political Images: Collective Images of the Candidates in the 1984 Elections," paper presented at the International Communication Association Convention, Honolulu, 1985. Quoted in Susan A. Hellweg, George N. Dionisopoulos, and Drew E. Kugler, "Political Candidate Image: A State-of-the-Art Review," *Progress in Communication Sciences* (1989) 9, 43–78.

8. Arthur H. Miller, Martin P. Wattenberg, and Oksana Malanchuk, "Schematic Assessments of Presidential Candidates," *American Political Science Review* 80 (June 1986): 521–40.

9. Dan Nimmo and Michael W. Mansfield, "Change and Persistence in Candidate Images: Presidential Debates across 1976, 1980, and 1984," paper presented at the Speech Communication Association Convention, Chicago, 1986.

10. Hellweg et al., "Political Candidate Image," especially 44–53.

11. Judith Trent et al., "The Consistent Attributes of the Ideal Presidential Candidate in an Increasingly Divided Electorate," *American Behavioral Scientist* 61, no. 3 (March 2017): 293.

12. Ibid., 287.

13. Ibid., 289.

14. Jimmie D. Trent, Judith S. Trent, Paul A. Mongeau, and Gay E. Gauder, "Facial Attractiveness and Initial Choice among Political Candidates: The Effect of Sex, Race, Political Preference, and Position," paper presented at the International Communication Association, Rome, 1998.

15. Becca Stanek, "Study Shows How Politics Affects Physical Attraction—And Why It Matters," MIC.com, October 16, 2014, accessed October 18, 2018, https://mic .com/articles/101592/study-shows-how-politics-affects-physical-attraction-and-why-it -matters#.9dJU4EaIn.

16. Frederick Williams, *The Communications Revolution* (Beverly Hills, CA: Sage, 1982), 37.

17. Frederick Williams, *The New Communications*, 2nd ed. (Belmont, CA: Wadsworth, 1989).

18. Ibid.

19. Edgar E. Willis, "Radio and Presidential Campaigning," *Central States Speech Journal* 20 (Fall 1969): 187.

20. Ibid., 191.

21. Ibid.

22. Michael McCurry, "The New Electronic Politics," *Campaigns and Elections*, March/ April 1989, 23–32. See also Williams, *Communications Revolution*, especially 17–39.

23. Theodore H. White, *The Making of the President, 1968* (New York: Atheneum, 1969), 154.

24. For a discussion of the potential of what he terms "push-button government," see Williams, *Communications Revolution*, 183–99.

25. Bruce E. Gronbeck, "The Web, Campaign 07–08, and Engaged Citizens: Political, Social, and Moral Consequences," in *The 2008 Presidential Campaign: A Communication Perspective*, ed. Robert E. Denton, Jr. (Lanham, MD: Rowman & Littlefield, 2009), 231.

26. Thomas Rosenstiel, *Strange Bedfellows* (New York: Hyperion, 1993), 170.

27. W. Lance Bennett, "The Ritualistic and Pragmatic Bases of Political Campaign Discourse," *Quarterly Journal of Speech* 64 (October 1977): 228.

28. Keith V. Erickson and Wallace V. Schmidt, "Presidential Political Silence: Rhetoric and the Rose Garden Strategy," *Southern Speech Communication Journal* 46 (Summer 1982): 402–21.

29. R. F. Fenno, Jr., *Home Style: House Members in Their Districts* (Boston: Little, Brown, 1978), 211.

30. Michael Nelson, *The Elections of 2000* (Washington, DC: Congressional Quarterly Press, 2001), 198.

31. Charlie Mahtesian, "2012 Reelection Rate: 90 Percent," *Politico*, December 13, 2012, accessed February 6, 2015, www.politico.com/blogs/charlie-mahtesian/2012/12/reelec tion-rate-percent-151898.html.

32. "Congress Has 11% Approval Ratings, but 96% Incumbent Reelection Rate, Meme Says," *Tampa Bay Times*, November 11, 2014, accessed February 6, 2015, www.politifact .com/truth-o-meter/statements/2014/nov/11/facebook-posts/congress-has-11-approval -ratings-96-incumbent-re-e.

33. Kyle Kondik and Geoffrey Skelley, "Incumbent Reelection Rates Higher Than Average in 2016," *Rasmussen Reports*, December 15, 2016, accessed October 18, 2018, http://

www.rasmussenreports.com/public_content/political_commentary/commentary_by_kyle_kondik/incumbent_reelection_rates_higher_than_average_in_2016.

34. Robert E. Denton, Jr., *The Symbolic Dimensions of the American Presidency* (Prospect Heights, IL: Waveland, 1982), 58.

35. Theodore H. White, *Breach of Faith* (New York: Atheneum, 1975), 322.

36. Dan D. Nimmo, *Popular Images of Politics* (Englewood Cliffs, NJ: Prentice Hall, 1974), 92.

37. Benjamin Zhang, "Check Out Donald Trump's $100 Million Personal Boeing Airliner," *Business Insider*, November 8, 2016, accessed October 18, 2018, https://www.businessinsider.com/donald-trump-boeing-757-airliner-trump-force-one-private-jet-2016-11.

38. John Louis Lucaites, "Rhetoric and the Problem of Legitimacy," in *Dimensions of Argument: Proceedings of the Second Summer Conference on Argumentation*, ed. George Ziegelmueller and Jack Rhodes (Annandale, VA: Speech Communication Association, 1982), 799–807.

39. Murray Edelman, "The Politics of Persuasion," in *Choosing the President*, ed. James David Barber (Englewood Cliffs, NJ: Prentice Hall, 1974), 171.

40. Denton, *Symbolic Dimensions*, 61.

41. Jeffrey M. Jones, "Barack Obama, Hillary Clinton Retain Most Admired Titles," Gallup, December 27, 2017, accessed October 18, 2018, https://news.gallup.com/poll/224672/barack-obama-hillary-clinton-retain-admired-titles.aspx.

42. Edelman, "Politics of Persuasion," 171.

43. Al Cross and James Malone, "Clinton Reaches Out to Heartland," *Courier-Journal*, August 31, 1996, 01A.

44. William R. Brown, "Television and the Democratic National Convention of 1968," *Quarterly Journal of Speech* 55 (October 1969): 241. For a more extensive treatment of pseudo-events, see Daniel J. Boorstin's classic *The Image* (New York: Atheneum, 1980). Originally, the book was published under the title *The Image, or What Happened to the American Dream* in 1961.

45. Howard Kurtz, "White House News Leaks of Questionable Significance Unleash Publicity Deluge," *Washington Post*, July 14, 1996, A16.

46. Ewen MacAskill, "Obama Puts Gun Control Center Stage as Biden Appointed to Lead Task Force," *Guardian*, December 14, 2012, accessed February 6, 2015, www.theguardian.com/world/2012/dec/19/obama-gun-control-biden-task-force.

47. Laura Jarrett, "Trump Signs Three New Executive Orders on Crime Reduction," CNN, February 10, 2017, accessed October 17, 2018, https://www.cnn.com/2017/02/09/politics/trump-executive-orders-crime-reduction/index.html.

48. Theodore H. White, *America in Search of Itself* (New York: Harper & Row, 1982), 296.

49. Ibid., 295.

50. "Clinton Becomes Yeltsin Fan after Early Morning Chat," *New York Times*, January 24, 1992, A24.

51. Kevin Liptak, "Romney Foreign Swing Underway as Candidate Meets with British Leaders," CNN, July 26, 2012, accessed February 6, 2015, politicalticker.blogs.cnn.com/2012/07/26/romney-foreign-swing-underway-as-candidate-meets-with-british-leaders.

52. "Donald Trump Presidential Campaign, 2016/Foreign Affairs," Ballotpedia.org, accessed October 17, 2018, https://ballotpedia.org/Donald_Trump_presidential_campaign,_2016/Foreign_affairs.

53. Frank Kessler, *The Dilemmas of Presidential Leadership: Of Caretakers and Kings* (Englewood Cliffs, NJ: Prentice Hall, 1982), 313–14.

54. Ann Devroy, "The Bush Campaign, Shake and Bakered," *Washington Post*, September 21–27, 1992, 11.

55. Andrew Rosenthal, "As Polls Shift, Bush Grabs Even Small Chance of Surge," *New York Times*, October 26, 1992, A12.

56. Rae Tyson, "Farmers Rally 'Round Bush Ethanol Plan," *USA Today*, October 2, 1992, A4.

57. Edmund L. Andrews, "Bush Rejects Bill That Would Limit Rates on Cable TV," *New York Times*, October 4, 1992, A1, A17.

58. Howard Kurtz, "Ad on Christian Radio Touts Clinton's Stands," *Washington Post*, October 15, 1996, A09.

59. Ibid.

60. George Kuempel, "Bush Criticizes Federal Transfer of Border Agents to California," *Dallas Morning News*, October 17, 1996, 32A.

61. Greg Gordon, "Tracking the Money; Cash, Campaigns—and Votes," *Star Tribune*, October 1, 1996.

62. Steve Barrett, "Couple Helps Make History," *Pittsburgh Post-Gazette*, November 3, 1996, W-3.

63. Avalon Zoppo et al., "Here's the Full List of Donald Trump's Executive Orders," NBC News, October 17, 2017, accessed October 18, 2018, https://www.nbcnews.com/politics/white-house/here-s-full-list-donald-trump-s-executive-orders-n720796.

64. Dan Nimmo and James E. Combs, *Subliminal Politics: Myths and Mythmakers in America* (Englewood Cliffs, NJ: Prentice Hall, 1980), 78.

65. Barry Brummett, "Towards a Theory of Silence as a Political Strategy," *Quarterly Journal of Speech* 66 (October 1980): 289–303.

66. William Henry Harrison in 1840 and General Winfield Scott in 1852 made, at the insistence of their managers, some speeches on their own behalf.

67. Ellen Reid Gold and Judith S. Trent, "Campaigning for President in New Hampshire: 1980," *Exetasis* 6 (April 1980): 7.

68. Nelson W. Polsby and Aaron Wildavsky, *Presidential Elections* (New York: Scribner's, 1976), 165.

69. David Jackson, "Campaign Financing under Attack," *Dallas Morning News*, October 24, 1996, 1A.

70. Jere Hester, "Irancon Figure Hits Dole," *Daily News* (New York), October 16, 1996, 18.

71. Remarks from the 2000 GOP Convention.

72. Ibid.

73. Judith S. Trent and Jimmie D. Trent, "The Rhetoric of the Challenger: George Stanley McGovern," *Central States Speech Journal* 25 (Spring 1974): 16.

74. Robert E. Friedenberg, "The 2008 Presidential Debates," in *The 2008 Presidential Campaign: A Communication Perspective*, ed. Robert E. Denton, Jr. (Lanham, MD: Rowman & Littlefield, 2009), 71.

75. David S. Broder, "The Lessons of Defeat," *Washington Post National Weekly Edition*, February 6–12, 1989.

76. Robin Toner, "Clinton Wins a Majority for Nomination but Perot's Appeal Is Strong in 2 Parties," *New York Times*, June 3, 1992, A1.

77. All subsequent quotes from Romney's announcement address come from Mitt Romney, "Remarks Announcing Candidacy for President in Stratham, New Hampshire," American Presidency Project, accessed October 10, 2014, www.presidency.ucsb.edu/ws/index.php?pid=90456.

78. Trent and Trent, "The Rhetoric of the Challenger," 17.

79. Bill Nichols, "Clinton Agonized, the Challenger Counterattacks," *USA Today*, August 24, 1992, A5.

80. Ibid.

81. "Dole's New Attack Style Leaves Bad Taste with Some Voters," *Arizona Republic*, October 20, 1996, A25.

82. Francis X. Clines, "Friend and Foe Cite Reagan's 'Masterful' Use of Incumbency," *New York Times*, September 18, 1983, E5.

83. Anthony Lewis, "Dr. Pangloss Speaks," *New York Times*, October 14, 1984, E19.

84. Ibid.

85. Jane Mayer and Doyle McManus, *Landslide* (Boston: Houghton Mifflin, 1988).

86. Howell Raines, "Reagan Appears to Succeed by Avoiding Specific Issues," *New York Times*, September 22, 1984, 14.

87. David Hoffman, "Accentuate the Positive, Put Off the Negative," *Washington Post National Weekly Edition*, March 26, 1984, 13.

88. For an excellent discussion of Vice President Al Gore's use and misuse of the incumbent/challenger style, see Craig Allen Smith and Neil Mansharamani, "Challenger and Incumbent Reversal in the 2000 Election," in *The 2000 Presidential Campaign: A Communication Perspective*, ed. Robert E. Denton, Jr. (Westport, CT: Praeger, 2002), 91–116.

# 4

⤜❦⤛

# Communicative Mass Channels of Political Campaigning

No other nation in the world consumes so much mass communication. Today in America, there are 1,286 daily newspapers,[1] 7,890 television stations, and 32,975 radio stations.[2] There are more than 118 million TV households where, on average, adults watch more than thirty-two hours of television programming per week and listen to radio thirteen hours per week.[3] There is also the proliferation of digital-only news outlets increasingly accessed more via mobile devices than by desktop. Despite this growth, television continues to play a major role in American culture. There are 47.8 million cable subscribers, 31 million satellite subscribers, and 4 million new internet-delivered pay-TV services subscribers.[4]

Of course, with increasing internet access and high-speed service, many are enjoying video content through sites such as YouTube, Netflix, or Hulu, not to mention the ability to enjoy content across smartphones, tablets, and other devices. In other words, television is a dominant force in the lives and environments of most of the public, a fact that was first called to our attention by political communication scholars Dan D. Nimmo and James E. Combs. In their book *Mediated Political Realities*, they claim that, consistently since 1963, Americans have named television as their primary and most believable news medium.[5] Today, of course, social media has become a popular and prominent part of many American lives, with 214 million Facebook users, 67 million Twitter users, and billions of tweets already sent.[6]

As we discussed in an earlier chapter and will discuss more in depth later, the widespread growth of the internet and the increase in the number of Americans who have access to and use the internet daily is another significant element in the utilization of mass media. Overall, 89 percent of American adults accessed the internet in 2018. In terms of young adults ages eighteen to twenty-nine, not surprisingly, the figure is 98 percent. Among those over sixty-five years old, 66 percent are online.[7]

Not only is U.S. mass media consumption unequaled, but in no other nation is it so inextricably linked to the electoral process. Mass communication has become the center stage for all major political events. For example, blogging, websites of 527s, campaign websites, daily newspapers, and weekly magazines keep political people and issues in our minds as they frequently report the result of the latest poll taken to measure how individuals feel about the president, governors, members of Congress, candidates, and specific issues and controversies. Radio programming is punctuated with five- and ten-minute news reports regarding some aspects of politics or with ten-, thirty-, and sixty-second spot advertisements for candidates and local "vital" issues. Moreover, by the 1992 presidential campaign, radio political talk and call-in shows had reached a zenith in popularity all over the nation and remain a major force in political campaign persuasion.

Even with the rapid acceleration of bloggers and online websites, television and television news programs still have most dramatically linked us to large-scale political campaign events such as presidential debates. Television brought Ronald Reagan to national political attention in 1964 as he delivered one of history's most financially successful speeches, just as twenty-eight years later, Texas billionaire H. Ross Perot announced on CNN's *Larry King Live* that he would run for president if citizens would be willing to gather enough petition signatures to place his name on the ballot in all fifty states. In 1998, the public watched as the results of the Minnesota gubernatorial election made clear that Jesse "The Body" Ventura, a former professional wrestler (well known to many because of his televised wrestling matches), had defeated Republican and Democratic opponents to become that state's new highest elected official, and watched once again in 2002 as Ventura declared he would not run for reelection. By 2006 it seemed as though any number of potential presidential contenders from both political parties were announcing on Sunday morning news talk shows that they were planning to run for their party's presidential nomination. Today every potential candidate and campaign has full social media units "pushing" daily messages. In short, the mass media have had a profound impact on the electoral process by connecting citizens and candidates.

In spite of this, the extent of the influence of mass communication on political behavior remains uncertain. Although media effects are one of the most studied areas in the social sciences, after more than eighty years of intense research, there are relatively few absolutes, largely because the findings of one generation of scholars are frequently challenged by the next.

The purpose of this chapter is to sort through the major theories, perspectives, hypotheses, and models that have been advanced regarding the media's relationship to political behavior and attempt to draw at least some general conclusions. In so doing, it may be helpful to understand that, for some scholars, the "theories" are not theories at all, because they are not all unambiguous, deductive, and interrelated structures from which empirically ascertained and consistent laws or general principles have been derived. For our purposes in this chapter, however, theories come in various packages. Although most have been empirically derived, not all are unambiguously and deductively determined. Moreover, if we insisted that the theories presented here must account for or predict general principles, there would be relatively little to discuss. Few of the perspectives or hypotheses have provided the consistency needed for determining general laws or principles. In other words, when it comes to the question of the role of media in determining political behavior, there is no one grand theory. There are a number of partial theories, or what (in another context) communication scholar Frank E. X. Dance refers to as particularistic theoretical bits and pieces,[8] but no single theoretical development that can account for or predict related phenomena. For this reason we discuss some of the major perspectives and approaches that have generated research. Whether multi-theoretical conceptualizations are desirable or undesirable, the fact is that more than eight decades of research have frequently led to conclusions that contrast with one another. This is one element to which we pay special attention as we proceed through the various theoretic approaches.

We define *mass* in a standard way as consisting of people representing all social, religious, and ethnic groups, from all regions of the country. Moreover, they are anonymous (do not necessarily know one another) and therefore act not in concert but spontaneously as individuals. We use the terms *mass channels* and *mass media* interchangeably to refer to the primary means of mass communication (radio, television, the internet, newspapers, and magazines). While we would not deny the existence of other modes of mass communication such as books, music, and motion pictures in the political campaign any more than we would refuse to recognize forms of "mini-communication" such as posters, billboards, and campaign literature, they are simply not as important. The major perspectives have been generated from studies of radio, television, newspapers, and magazines. Now, studies about the use and influence of social media and the web are growing exponentially.

It is also important to understand that the focus of this chapter is not candidates and the campaign process but *voters* and the campaign process. The principles that are analyzed center on the effect of mass communication on the political behavior of citizens. As such, we are concerned with the way researchers have answered such questions as these: (1) To what extent do the media influence cognitions and behavior? (2) What are the primary mass communication models that have guided research? (3) What have been the effects of the media on the electoral process itself? (4) How do people use the media in the political process?

Finally, we approach the chapter from a historic perspective. We think it is important for students interested in contemporary political campaigns to understand the history of media and associated theory. That knowledge will inform current and future use of media for campaign purposes. As noted in the first chapter, the overwhelming majority of political communication is, in fact, mediated. We experience politics, broadly defined, through mass media.

As noted, the chapter is organized chronologically in that the general conceptualizations from early and contemporary research compose separate sections. Within each, major studies are examined, and any specific hypotheses or models that have been derived from them are discussed. The conclusion focuses on a summary of principles regarding the influence of the media that are most important in understanding the nature of political campaign communication.

## EARLY STUDIES

The media's influence on political behavior has been a subject of scholarly investigation since the 1920s. Although readers might question the need to be aware of anything other than the most recent research findings, many of the early studies have been of tremendous importance. In fact, their impact has been so profound, they are considered "classics," and the conclusions they articulated as well as the methods they employed influenced all who followed. Thus, we discuss each of the major perspectives as well as the general models or hypotheses that were derived from them during the more than thirty-year period in which they dominated mass communication research.

## Hypodermic Effect

The assumption that the press is a powerful force in shaping public opinion has been around for centuries. In 1529, fifty years after the printing press had been introduced in England, King Henry VIII seized control of the printing industry. Licensed printers held their patents only if what they printed pleased him.[9] In the mid-1600s, the Puritan establishment in the Massachusetts Bay Colony maintained strict control over printing because they feared that a free press might threaten the government and promote religious heresies.[10] In 1722, the founder and editor of a Boston newspaper, the *New England Courant*, was jailed for three weeks because of his attacks on the government.[11] Years later, the press was thought to have been a powerful force in creating revolutionary fervor in the United States, in providing passion and visibility to the abolitionist movement, and in provoking Congress to go to war with Spain.

However, it was not until the 1920s and 1930s that researchers actually tried to determine the power of mass communication in shaping values and behaviors of citizens. The motivation to learn more about the ways in which media could influence the public was provided, in large measure, by Adolf Hitler's propaganda machine, which seemed to have captured the minds of the German people through movies and staged rallies, and by the use of the radio by Benito Mussolini in Italy and Father Charles Coughlin in the United States to stir public support and sentiment for the fascists. The Information and Education Branch of the U.S. Army began recruiting social scientists to study the influence of media persuasion. As researchers analyzed the effects of propaganda films such as *The Battle of Britain* or the pro-German magazine *The Galilean*, they confirmed what had been assumed for centuries. The media really were powerful; they had the strength not only to change people's attitudes but to alter their behavior. And because citizens were often helpless to resist the persuasion of propaganda, they were easily "bamboozled." Moreover, according to the researchers, these effects occurred in all people because, despite individual attributes and characteristics, individuals responded in the same way when they received similar messages. Audiences were like mobs; there were no individual minds but only a group consciousness. Messages went directly from the media to the individual, where they were immediately assimilated. "Messages were literally conceived of as being 'injected' into the mind where they were 'stored' in the form of changes in feelings and attitudes. Eventually such feelings or attitudes produced the behavior desired by the message source."[12] This is, essentially, what researchers called the *hypodermic effect*, or the *hypodermic needle model*.

Although it may be difficult for us to subscribe to specific aspects of the hypodermic model, it must be viewed in terms of the context in which it was developed. The 1920s through the early 1940s was a time of worldwide social, political, and economic unrest, passion, and violence. Economic depression, the rise of fascism and Hitler, and the domination of the Nazis throughout much of Europe suggested irrational yet somehow controlled mass group behavior. It seemed entirely likely that powerful propaganda devices were manipulating people's minds. In the view of many who were studying it, the "mass media loomed as agents of evil aiming at the total destruction of democratic society. First the newspaper and later the radio were feared as powerful weapons able to rubber-stamp ideas upon the minds of defenseless readers and listeners."[13] By the late 1930s, the hypodermic effect was accepted widely enough (even by those social scientists not involved in the government propaganda research program) to be applied specifically to the electoral process. One of the first systematic attempts to determine the political impact of the press was undertaken in 1937. Harold F. Gosnell studied the relationship of social and economic characteristics and newspaper-reading habits to election returns in several Chicago neighborhoods and found that the endorsements of newspapers could influence the way readers voted.[14] Thus, social scientists were provided with additional proof of the seemingly unlimited power of the media to persuade.

### Limited Effects or the Social Influence Model

Although the work of many of the army's psychologists and sociologists who were studying the effects of propaganda continued to reflect the hypodermic thesis, by the early 1940s, the findings of some researchers began to challenge the idea that the media were so potent that they mesmerized the public. One of the most important challenges occurred when three social scientists from Columbia University's Bureau of Applied Social Research—Paul F. Lazarsfeld, Bernard Berelson, and Hazel Gaudet—studied the 1940 presidential campaign and discovered (much to their surprise) that campaign propaganda had little impact on the way the electorate had voted. This study and others that followed began to build a competing explanation for media influence that was in stark contrast to the presumption that people were unable to control their own destinies or the destiny of the nation. It was, of course, a much more comforting thought than the hypodermic thesis because it provided reassurance that in the United States individual rationality and society's sense of order could not be overthrown because of the seizure or control of the media by a demagogue or someone who had gone insane.

The 1940 study began to form what became known as the *social influence model*. Twenty years later, mass communication scholar Joseph Klapper, in summarizing the conclusions of the work done on the impact of the media during the 1940s and 1950s, concluded that media effects are limited and, even in cases where they do occur, are mediated by other factors.[15] He coined the term *limited effects model*, a label that obviously stands in direct contrast with the earlier hypodermic perspective.

To understand this shift, it may be best to take a closer look at those studies that are regarded as the classics and that collectively influenced generations of mass communication scholars and their view of media and politics. The first study by Lazarsfeld, Berelson, and Gaudet was conducted in Erie County, Ohio, a section of northern Ohio fairly equally divided between a city and farmland. Lazarsfeld and his colleagues wanted to measure the repercussions of campaign press coverage during a presidential election. At the outset they divided potential political effects into three categories: first, they believed the media could arouse public interest in the campaign and encourage voters to seek out more information about the candidates and issues; second, they reasoned that the press could reinforce existing political beliefs to make them stronger and more resistant to change; and third, they hypothesized that the media were powerful enough to convert attitudes, changing voters from supporting one candidate or party to supporting the opposition.

From May to November, a member of the research team interviewed someone each month in every twentieth house or apartment in the county. In total, six hundred people were questioned about political parties, candidates, issues, and the news. Interviewers kept carefully structured records of each talk, and from these records Lazarsfeld and his colleagues were able to reconstruct how Erie County residents made their decision between Franklin Roosevelt and Wendell Willkie. The results were published four years later in a book called *The People's Choice*.[16] Although Lazarsfeld and his colleagues believed that their research would confirm the prevailing thesis that the media were capable of controlling individual thought processes, they instead found that very few people changed their vote in response to the campaign propaganda and that those who changed did not attribute their conversion to media information. Specifically, they learned the following:

- People who read or listened to a substantial amount of campaign media coverage were likely to become more interested in the election.
- Their interest and activation were selective in that they tended to seek out stories that were consistent with prior political attitudes.

Those relative few who did change their minds did so not because of attending to the media directly but by the filtering of information to them from people in the community whom they respected. Such people were perceived to be highly active, highly informed, interested in politics, and therefore more likely than others to read or listen to media coverage of the campaign. These individuals were labeled "opinion leaders."

In the largest sense, the results of the Erie County study were not as important as the two explanations that Lazarsfeld and his colleagues offered for their findings. The explanations formed the cornerstone of the social influence theory. The researchers maintained that, if a message presented by the media conflicts with group norms, it will be rejected. "Since groups have opinion leaders who transmit mass media information to individuals who do not attend to the media, these leaders influence whatever opinion change takes place in the followers; media messages do not have direct impact."[17] The second explanation given for their findings was that people are selective in those campaign messages to which they attend. They only listen to or read messages that are most consistent with their own beliefs, attitudes, and values. In other words, voters use the content of the media to support or reinforce the voting conclusions they would have reached because of their social predispositions. (Today, of course, we know that this "effect" is very strong.) Interestingly, the concept of selective exposure was based on an analysis of only 122 persons who by August had not yet decided for which candidate they would vote. While 54 percent of those people with a Republican predisposition exposed themselves to Republican material and 61 percent with a Democratic predisposition exposed themselves to Democratic material, 35 percent of the Republicans and 22 percent of the Democrats did expose themselves to material from the other party—material that presumably was inconsistent with prior beliefs or social predispositions.

These percentages were never explained, and the concept of selective exposure became a widely accepted phenomenon not only for the sociologically oriented voter studies but also by psychologists who eventually incorporated it into a series of studies regarding involuntary and voluntary exposure to information to reduce psychological dissonance.[18] The second of the classic studies conducted by the Columbia group was also staged in a single location. In 1948, Lazarsfeld, Berelson, and William McPhee went to Elmira, New York, to determine voter behavior during the presidential campaign. The Elmira results, published in 1954 in *Voting*, supported the Erie County findings that campaign press coverage converted few voters and that information was disseminated from opinion leaders.

The third single-location study was mounted in Decatur, Illinois, and was reported by Elihu Katz and Lazarsfeld in the book *Personal Influence*. The researchers interviewed eight hundred women regarding "four arenas of everyday decision: marketing, fashions, public affairs, and movie-going" and for each arena asked respondents "not only about themselves and their own behavior but about other people as well—people who influence them, and people for whom they are influential."[19] Essentially, the results of the Decatur study confirmed the social influence model, although they also produced a more precise conceptualization of "the two-step flow of communication." The idea that had been hypothesized from the Erie County data suggested that "ideas often flow from radio and print to the opinion leaders and from them to active sections of the population."[20] However, in Decatur, the Columbia group wanted to compare the media behavior of opinion leaders and non-leaders "to see whether the leaders tend to be the more exposed, and the more responsive group when it comes to influence stemming from the mass media."[21] They discovered that the women they studied were willing to admit that they were influenced by other women, that leadership varied by topic, that leaders for each topic had different social and psychological characteristics, and that no single leader exercised control over the political beliefs of others. However, their most important finding, in terms of media impact on the electoral process, was that "opinion leaders were not more likely than followers to attribute influence upon their beliefs or opinions to the mass media."[22] Thus, as a result of the third Columbia study, the role of the media was reduced even further in the minds of most social scientists. It appeared as if no group sizable enough to be measured was persuaded by media messages during a political campaign.

In 1952, another group of researchers began examining voters' behavior. Using the 1952 presidential election as their base, the University of Michigan Survey

Research Center, or SRC (now called the Center for Political Studies, Institute for Social Research at the University of Michigan), soon replaced the Columbia group as the dominant research force in large-scale voting studies. Methodologically as well as conceptually, the work of the Michigan group represented a major shift in the effort to examine voters and their behavior.[23] For example, the SRC relied on panels of potential voters based on national probability samples rather than a single community. In focusing on national behaviors, they moved away from sociological explanations (the emphasis on traditions, structure, composition, and the sociological nature of major institutions within single communities), which the Lazarsfeld group had presumed were the reasons for voters' predispositions. Instead, the Michigan researchers sought cognitive and attitudinal reasons for voting decisions. They asked citizens to indicate their party affiliation (the Columbia group had studied parties only in terms of social predispositions that led voters to choose one candidate over another). Thus, with party identification as a key factor in explaining voters' attitudes and evaluation of candidates, the idea of interpersonal communication and the two-step flow conceptualization as the primary means of information diffusion was relegated to a "relatively unimportant position in the SRC model."[24] However, in one important respect, the early SRC studies did not differ from their Columbia counterparts. Despite the fact that in 1952 television played a role in the presidential primaries, in the nominating conventions, and in the general advertising campaigns of at least one of the candidates, the Michigan researchers concluded that the impact of the mass media on the electoral process was minimal.[25] In fact, in *The American Voter* (a book based on the data collected in 1952 and 1956), the researchers indicated that it was party identification and not television that was the important factor in the development of political cognitions, attitudes, and behavior.[26]

Finally, in 1963, undoubtedly in an attempt to revitalize a theory that was being challenged by many, Lazarsfeld and his colleagues described a modification of the two-step flow. In the new conceptualization, information from the media was relayed from one opinion leader to another before it was passed on to followers. The revision became known as the "multistep flow," and because more people were added to the transmission process, the persuasive power of the media was viewed as even less significant than it had been before. Moreover, not only did information travel from opinion leader to opinion leader; any one of these people could act as a "gatekeeper" and thereby prevent a follower from even being exposed to part of the information. Thus, opinion leaders not only functioned as conveyers of information among each other and finally to their respective "audiences" but also determined just what information would be transmitted.

Although Lazarsfeld discussed gatekeeping in relationship to the multistep flow in 1963, the idea was not new. As early as 1950, one study had examined the selection and rejection of messages by gatekeepers. One of the key findings confirmed in many studies that followed was that when media gatekeepers made decisions, they did not have the audience in mind.[27] Essentially, a *gatekeeper* is any person in the news-gathering process with authority to make decisions affecting the flow of information to the public. "The image is precisely that of a turnstile gatekeeper at a sporting event—he examines the qualifications of each person in line, and decides whether or not to let him in. The difference is that what gets let in or left out is not a person, but a piece of news."[28] One of the reasons the gatekeeping function has received so much attention is that there are a variety of people in the media who must make decisions regarding the presentation of information and news. Examples include telegraph and wire service editors, reporters, film editors, headline writers, radio and television producers, news program anchors and commentators, and even other media (small newspapers and radio and television stations frequently take their news from the larger and more established media). Thus, given the wide spectrum of people who daily determine which of the many possible news items the public will be presented with, it is little wonder that gatekeeping has been the subject of scholarly investigation as well as public consternation. Undoubtedly one of the most famous attacks against media gatekeepers was leveled in 1969 by Vice President Spiro Agnew. One of the broad areas of his criticism concerned the similarities of the various media decision makers. In an address before the Midwest Regional Republican Committee in Des Moines, Iowa, Agnew charged:

> A small group of men, numbering perhaps no more than a dozen "anchormen," commentators and executive producers, settle upon the 20 minutes or so of film and commentary that is to reach the public. . . . We do know that, to a man, these commentators and producers live and work in the geographical and intellectual confines of Washington, D.C. or New York City—the latter of which James Reston terms the "most unrepresentative community in the entire United States." . . . We can deduce that these men thus read the same newspapers, and draw their political and social views from the same sources. . . . The upshot of all this controversy is that a narrow and distorted picture of America often emerges from the televised news.[29]

Whether or not Agnew's charges were true, they did provoke public discussion as well as a good deal of media response. In addition, gatekeeping continued to be a subject of scholarly investigation throughout the 1960s and 1970s.[30] Even today there are claims of a liberal media bias in the "mainstream media." In summarizing the major ideas advanced by the early studies of media influence, it is tempting to conclude that, despite the label of some of them as classics, almost four decades of investigation has had little relationship to contemporary theory. Researchers went from one extreme to the other; first media propaganda was the harbinger of all that was evil, and then it had little impact at all. Effects were seen primarily on a one-dimensional level—persuasion. The informational or cognitive function was largely ignored because of the dominance of selective exposure, a concept with little empirical validation then that is clearly inadequate now.[31] Moreover, investigators were so intent on confirming the basic tenets of the social influence model that they ignored media effect in such important areas as voter turnout, political activation, and information seeking. The studies were conducted at a time in which home television sets were far less plentiful than they are today, and so the medium was viewed as having little direct influence on political behavior. Radio and newspapers were important only in their role as reinforcers rather than opinion formers, thus suggesting that voters were limited perceptually by their past.

However, in spite of all this, the early studies remain an important part of our media research heritage for at least four reasons. First, they pointed the way toward research methodologies that were more sophisticated than those that had been used. Moreover, the Columbia studies were the last massive single-community analysis for many years. And the Michigan studies of the national electorate continue to provide the most authoritative source of election data available. Second, the social influence model did rescue social scientists from the mass media hysteria symbolized by the hypodermic thesis. Third, although the Columbia studies may have carried the sociological explanation of voters' behavior to the extreme, they did begin the path toward the study of mass media and interpersonal relationships, obviously an important area of political campaign communication. Finally, the limited effects theory served as a catalyst for later scholars who would challenge the idea that the mass media had little impact on voters' behavior or the electoral process. Indeed, the sheer attempt to disprove the theory may well have led to the multi-perspectivism that characterizes contemporary mass communication research.

## CONTEMPORARY STUDIES

Just as the hypodermic thesis reflected society's turmoil and the social influence model depicted a quiet, reflective people not swayed by campaign propaganda, the mass media research of the 1960s and 1970s was a product or at least representative of its time. If the 1950s are described by such words as *quiet*, *inactive*, or *dull*, the following years can be characterized as disquieting, tumultuous, and wild. While the federal bureaucracy grew in size and influence, so did citizen involvement in public affairs. Beginning with the civil rights struggle, which brought local groups together to form national organizations, a number of large-scale political and social movements appeared on the national scene. Each of them demanded new social and economic legislation to ensure equality and to guarantee their rights as citizens to help formulate national and international policy. However, each of them also needed various forms of mass communication not only to recruit, organize, and maintain their movements, but to publicize their demands by drastic and frequently passionate actions.

The changes in society and the escalation of the social movements corresponded to alterations in the mass media system. It, too, was growing, largely because of the widespread use of television. More people owned television sets, and it was beginning to replace interpersonal conversations and meetings as a leisure time activity.[32] Television was becoming the most revolutionary branch of journalism. While in the 1950s television news was typically read by one person seated in front of a wall map, during the next twenty years it became a drama featuring live coverage of national and international events. The sit-ins and marches of the social movements, the urban riots and burning of U.S. cities, the funeral of a young president and the assassination of his alleged killer, and the bloody battles of the war in Vietnam all contributed to the transformation of U.S. news gathering and of those social scientists who studied it.[33] It was in this atmosphere that many mass communication scholars began to question the basic tenets of the social influence model. Although they had no one holistic theory with which to replace it, maintaining that the media had little influence on or played no major role in the electoral process appeared a direct denial of what was happening all around them. A few researchers looked to the reigning paradigm for new explanations. For example, one study in 1962 indicated that uninvolved voters are susceptible to attitude change if any new information reaches them,[34] and another showed that, under certain conditions, it is possible for large audiences to get information directly from the media without the intervention of an opinion leader, suggesting that mass communication does not always work in a two-step flow.[35] However, the most important break with the social influence model occurred when social scientists Jay G. Blumler and Denis McQuail discovered in a study of the 1964 British parliamentary election that "regular viewers of television news developed significantly different perceptions of the Liberal and Conservative parties."[36]

Clearly, it was possible for media to do more than simply reinforce the status quo. Beginning roughly about the time that the work of Blumler and McQuail appeared to suggest a new perspective for viewing media influence in politics, other theories or quasi-theories were being articulated. In the remainder of this section, we discuss the basic assumptions or tenets of four of the most important approaches undertaken during the 1960s and 1970s and reexamined, reformulated, or extended during the 1980s through the early 2000s.

### Diffusion of Information

One of the approaches that bridges the gap between the limited effects model and the contemporary conceptualizations is the diffusion of information perspective. It is related to the research that characterizes social influence theory largely because it was initiated in that era and because it acknowledges the importance of interpersonal communication to the dissemination of information. However, it differs from that theory in at least two important respects. First, diffusion research maintains that, under certain conditions, media transmission of information will have a direct impact on individuals and can produce changes in their knowledge or even their behavior. Interpersonal communication occurs after the mass media transmit information about news events and is therefore only a response to media reports.[37] The second way in which diffusion research is distinct from social influence is that it does not study attitude changes in voting behavior during political campaigns but focuses instead on the influence of the mass media on the acquisition of political cognitions. In other words, diffusion research is concerned with such topics as knowledge of campaign issues, candidates, and general public affairs. It is also used to investigate possible stages of information dissemination, how specific groups within society become aware of particular political matters, what factors contribute to the acceptance or rejection of political ideas, and what conditions mediate the flow of information about events.

Although diffusion has been defined in a variety of ways, generally conceptualizations of it in communication research capitalize on the idea of movement— the spread of adoption of new ideas (innovations) through time and space from one individual or group of people to another. Although diffusion research and the resulting diffusion model have roots in the physical sciences, it is employed by a number of disciplines within the social sciences. In the area of our interest, much of the early important work was done by Everett Rogers. In his 1961 book

*Diffusion of Innovations* and in his later work with Floyd Shoemaker, Rogers discovered a multistage process of innovation diffusion. The four stages are (1) information or knowledge, (2) persuasion, (3) decision or adoption, and (4) confirmation or reevaluation. In essence, new information is transmitted through society (or from person to person) in a particular sequential pattern. While it can be argued that these stages will not always be either separate or sequential under some conditions for some people, according to Rogers and Shoemaker, the media are important primarily in the first or information stage, where an interest in, awareness of, and understanding of the innovation can be created. Interpersonal communication is important during the last three stages as people seek confirmation or interpretation of the information they have received from the mass media.[38] To support the view that the media were the predominant sources of information about political news events, early diffusion research in political communication was designed to measure the extent to which messages were transmitted. For example, it was discovered that the media informed most people about the death of Senator Robert Taft, President Eisenhower's decision to seek reelection, the dropping of Senator Thomas Eagleton as the Democratic vice presidential candidate, and the assassination of John Kennedy.[39]

Largely, the diffusion research even during the 1970s continued to be concentrated on the extent and veridicality of information flow. Thus, researchers appeared to be more interested in the attention arousal and information-seeking characteristics of the first stage of the process than in the later adoption or persuasion stages.[40] In fact, after reviewing the diffusion approach to political communication studies published during the 1970s, Robert L. Savage reported that, with the exception of news dissemination studies, very little use had been made of it. He urged scholars to investigate such questions as these: Are diffusing messages causes or effects of human actions? What latent and/or dysfunctional consequences follow from existing diffusion patterns? He appeared to doubt that political communication scholars had used the approach for all relevant forms of political information.[41]

In a similar vein, mass communication scholar Steven H. Chaffee acknowledged that the diffusion approach had not yet lived up to its potential when he called for research that would lead to the development of a universal scheme for categorizing different types of diffusion items according to the type of communication that transmits them and the type of person most receptive to them, and determining the way in which items are relevant from the perspective of the political system.[42]

And authors Sidney Kraus and Dennis Davis suggested that the diffusion model be supplemented by stipulating specific patterns of media use and perception to understand better the conditions that mediate the flow of information.[43] Unfortunately, those researchers who continued to use the diffusion perspective during the 1980s rarely broadened or extended the scope of the topics investigated or the ways in which human behavior was affected—especially political behavior. Studies continued to focus on crisis news events (e.g., the shootings of President Reagan and Pope John Paul II in 1981), the relative roles of interpersonal and mass communication in the dissemination process (which one is the primary source of information and under what conditions for what people), and the rate at which information is diffused through the population.[44]

In short, the model was never really expanded as some political and mass communication scholars hoped that it would be.

Thus, while the diffusion of information perspective helped redirect the focus of media/political research away from the unidimensional thrust of the social influence model, its potential has yet to be realized.

## Uses and Gratifications

A crucial assumption of the uses and gratifications perspective is that a wide range of motives exists for using the mass media and that individuals' media requirements are dictated by such factors as their social roles, situations, or personalities. In other words, media audiences should not be thought of as huge collectivities who watch television shows, attend movies, and read newspapers and magazines for the same reasons.[45] In one sense, the uses and gratifications perspective is similar to some of the other research approaches discussed in this chapter in that there is really no single theory. We do not mean to imply that the perspective is theoretical but simply that numerous theoretical bits and pieces compose the perspective. However, as one of its principal advocates, Jay G. Blumler, has argued, the various theories about the phenomena "share a common field of concern, an elementary set of concepts indispensable for intelligibly carving up that terrain, and an identification of certain wider features of the mass communication process with which such core phenomena are presumed to be connected."[46]

Although a diverse range of research has been conducted under the uses and gratifications paradigm, essentially it has been concerned with determining those uses people make of the mass media in the circumstances of their own lives as well as the gratifications they seek and receive from such consumption. To an extent, part of the popularity of the approach is that it has served as a means of integrating ideas of massive effects (the hypodermic thesis) with limited effects (the social influence model) to form a middle-ground position where the audience is viewed as active, thinking receivers who are neither susceptible to all persuasive media messages nor impervious to them. In fact, it has been argued that it is in this role as an integrative component in an effects model "that the uses and gratifications perspective offers its greatest promise to the study of political communication."[47] Not only, however, is the approach used for its bridge between the effects models, but it also has the additional benefit of allowing researchers to study more than just effects—to get at the functions mass media may provide during a political campaign. While some of these functions may be obvious (we read a newspaper account of a candidate's speech to gain more information about the candidate and the campaign), others may be latent (we watch a television commercial about a candidate so that we have enough information about the campaign to maintain our social status as an informed citizen). Thus, the functions served by the media during a campaign are not necessarily what they appear to be. Information or cognitive gain may serve many important purposes for the individual, and the uses/gratifications perspective provides a way to examine them.

Although the uses and gratifications paradigm began to be especially popular during the 1970s, research conducted under its label goes back as far as the beginning of World War II, when studies were published that dealt with the use of radio for entertainment purposes. Similarly, during the following two decades, when commercial television became important, the approach was used to generate data regarding entertainment programming. It was not until the landmark Blumler and McQuail study, published in 1969, that the perspective came into major use in examining political campaigns. In fact, it was this investigation of the 1964 British election that really spelled out the basic assumptions for researchers in political communication. Other studies followed, and in 1974, Blumler and Katz summarized much of the research the perspective had stimulated in *The Uses of Mass Communication*.

Research done with the uses and gratifications paradigm in the 1990s and early 2000s studied new communication technologies such as electronic mail and the internet to better understand people's need for and uses of these new venues. The overwhelming conclusion from these studies indicates that computer communication is similar to traditional mass and interpersonal channels of communication. According to authors Andrew Flanagin and Miriam Metzger, internet information-retrieving and information-giving capabilities are similar to those of television, newspapers, books, and magazines, and internet conversation capabilities and email are similar to telephone usage.[48] Interestingly, what scholars appear to be concluding is that the new communication technologies are equal in communication capabilities to traditional media because "new media are transitioning toward the roles of more traditional ones due to their capacity to improve or augment the capabilities of existing technologies."[49] In other words, "It appears that technologies meet needs and not that needs meet technologies."[50] Although multiple studies have been conducted under the uses and gratifications paradigm, there remains not only the lack of one unified theory, but there is still some disagreement about such basic tenets of the perspective as the meaning of an "active audience" and if media gratifications differ in any important way from one set of ideological beliefs to another or from one culture to another—or, the relationship of social structure to the understanding individual citizens bring to political messages/events. The question of the sociocultural bases on which or through which the meanings of political messages are constructed and responded to was not clear in the original categorical scheme used by Blumler and McQuail.

The five types of gratification orientations to political television programming employed in their study of the British national election were: using the political content of the media for vote guidance, reinforcement of decisions already made, general surveillance of the political environment, excitement, and anticipation of using the information in future interpersonal communication situations. The three types of avoidance were feelings of political alienation, partisanship, and relaxation.[51] However, in more recent years, some researchers—including Blumler—have emphasized the importance of the social structure, or the culture, in arriving at any understanding of the meaning people give to messages (or their motivation to use or avoid media). For example, in 1985, Blumler and his colleagues reported that they "never meant to talk about abstracted individuals, but about people in social situations that give rise to their needs. The individual is part of a social structure and his or her choices are less free and less random than a vulgar gratificationism would presume."[52] Whether or not Blumler and McQuail simply assumed the role of sociocultural influence in their gratification and avoidance categories without specifically discussing it, it is not as important as the fact that in recent years researchers have begun to more clearly acknowledge the role played by social structure.

The second area of disagreement within the uses and gratification research is closely related to the first. Not only must the social determinants of the audience's media needs and expectations be considered, but so, too, must the idea or definition of an active audience be considered. As at least one theorist has argued:

> If the uses and gratifications paradigm is truly to come to grips with the nature of the audience's media experience, it will have to give up the optimistic and simplistic notion that an active audience implies a powerful audience. It must be recognized that the concept of an active audience, as traditionally explicated in the literature, may in fact obscure the powerlessness of the audience. Certain audience media expectations are never voiced because they are perceived as inappropriate or as so unlikely as to make their articulation sound foolish or naïve. . . . Other expectations, for some individuals, when expressed, may be significantly modified or tempered due to the sense of powerlessness they feel with respect to the political and social system. . . . In-depth probing of individuals' media expectations may reveal more about the assumptions these individuals hold regarding their locations in the social and political system than about any true media needs. In-depth analysis of the meaning of a commonly expressed media expectation such as diversion may reveal the use of standard media fare not so much for polite relaxation but for opportunities to ridicule a presentation of reality which does not correspond to one's experience as opposed to mediated life.[53]

Thus, while the uses and gratifications perspective has been the focal point of a good deal of research, and although the paradigm itself has served a useful function by illustrating that people pay attention to the political content of the media, it is interesting to note that Denis McQuail argued in 1997 that the research emanating from the uses and gratifications theories has produced little in regard to predicting or explaining media choice. He wrote that connections between attitudes toward the media and media behavior are difficult to document because the "typologies of 'motives' often fail to match patterns of actual selection or use and it is hard to find a logical and consistent relation among the three sequentially ordered factors of liking/preference; actual choosing; and subsequent evaluation."[54] In general, he described uses and gratifications as an approach that "overestimates the rationality and activity of audience use behavior. Most actual audiences also turn out to be composed of people with varied, overlapping and not always consistent expectations and subjective motives."[55] Although the perspective continues to spark research (particularly in terms of its utility in studying the uses and gratifications of the World Wide Web),[56] we believe it may only reach its potential when researchers who employ it give full attention to the social bases of message construction and response.

## Elaboration Likelihood Model

Elaboration Likelihood Model (ELM) is a theory of message processing.[57] ELM may be looked at as a mass media theory that explains how receivers perceive messages and then make attitudinal changes. Elaboration is the engagement of issue-relevant thinking. If the receiver pays close attention to a message, the receiver will carefully look at all issues and variables in the argument. However, other receivers do not put forth the effort for every persuasive topic, thus showing little elaboration. Two possible routes can be taken: central route or peripheral route to persuasion. The central route is concerned with core issues of the argument and attitudes expressed are persistent and resistant to change. The peripheral route is an expression of automatic response without the effort of understanding all the information that should be considered in the argument.

There are four reasons for the choice that is made: motivation, ability, recipient variables, and message variables. Receivers either have strong motivation to pursue an argument or they do not, due to mood, lack of concern, or lack of knowledge. Distraction or the receiver's knowledge of the issues will determine the ability of the receiver to elaborate. Recipient variables are reflections of the receiver's education level, intelligence, or the amount of understanding of the issues within an argument. Last, message variables can strengthen or weaken a receiver's position due to factors such as the number of people who endorse a message, the message's personal relevance, or the existence of an attached stigma.

## Agenda-Setting Hypothesis

Undoubtedly, the most popular contemporary approach for studying the relationship of media and politics is the agenda-setting hypothesis. It has generated and continues to generate more research than any of the others. It clearly separates the persuasive and informational communicative functions of the media. It comes closer than any of the other approaches to reaffirming the early basic assumption that the media do have a great deal of influence on politics; the media may not always dominate, but they do have a significant impact on what we think about (our focus of attention). Finally, the perspective is important for another reason. The most frequent site for agenda-setting research has been election campaigns, which has clearly not been the case with the diffusion of information, uses and gratifications, or ELM perspectives.

The underlying assumption of agenda setting was first articulated by a political scientist, Bernard C. Cohen, in 1963. Cohen argued that the press may not be successful in telling its readers what to think, but "it is stunningly successful in telling its readers what to think about. . . . The editor may believe he is only printing the things that people want to read, but he is thereby putting a claim on their attention, powerfully determining what they will be thinking about, and talking about, until the next wave laps their shore."[58] Just two years later, empirical verification of Cohen's ideas began to appear. In a study of the 1964 presidential campaign, researcher Jack McLeod found that the stories from two newspapers revealed clear differences in their reports of two issues in the campaign, federal spending policies and control of nuclear weapons. Specifically, the study revealed that respondents who read the paper that provided a good deal of coverage to nuclear control (the Democratic issue) ranked it higher in importance than they did the economic issue. Correspondingly, those who read the paper that focused on spending policies (the Republican issue) ranked it higher in importance than they did nuclear control.[59]

In 1972, Maxwell E. McCombs and Donald L. Shaw explored the power of the press to set the agenda by studying the 1968 presidential campaign. Specifically, they hypothesized that "the mass media set the agenda for each political campaign, influencing the salience of attitudes toward the political issues."[60] Before the election, the researchers interviewed one hundred people in five precincts in Chapel Hill, North Carolina, who had not yet decided whether they were going to vote for Hubert Humphrey, Richard Nixon, or George Wallace. The undecided voters were the only people interviewed on the presumption that they would be the most receptive to campaign information. McCombs and Shaw compared what voters said were the key issues in the campaign with the amount of space devoted to those issues in the particular medium used by the voters. They found a strong relationship between the emphasis given by the medium to specific campaign issues and the judgment of voters relating to the salience and importance of those issues.

A third study, this time a national one conducted from 1964 to 1970, compared what people identified as the most important problems facing the United States (according to data from Gallup polls) with listings of the content of news magazines. The researcher, G. Ray Funkhouser, concluded that "the average person takes the media's word for what the 'issues' are, whether or not he personally has any involvement or interest in them."[61] In these three studies and many others that followed them during the 1970s, the agenda-setting functions of the mass media gained wide acceptance from social scientists. In part, the perspective was well received because it did not suggest that media have the all-powerful attributes envisioned by the hypodermic thesis. Instead, the theme from the corpus of work undertaken was that the media set public priorities just by paying attention to some issues while ignoring others. They determine which issues are important and, in this way, play a significant role in structuring our social reality. In other words, people not only learn about issues through the media but learn how much importance to give them because of the emphasis placed on them by the mass media.

Throughout the 1970s and 1980s, the perspective remained important because it illustrated "how significant communication variables" could be "operationalized and linked to concrete political processes such as election campaigns."[62] It stimulated a good deal of research (although few consistent conclusions) on such important areas as the distinct agenda-setting roles of newspapers and television, the differences between the intrapersonal agenda (operationalized in most studies in terms of what each individual considers personally most important) and the interpersonal agenda (what each individual talks about most often with others), and the length of time required for agenda-setting effects to manifest themselves in the public agenda.[63] Moreover, the approach continued to be employed in the 1990s to study, for example, public opinion during the Gulf War[64] and the relationship between public opinion in the United States about foreign countries and their visibility in our television news programs.[65]

In 1982, however, perhaps in part because the campaign of 1980 and the subsequent election of Ronald Reagan reemphasized that television had become "the single greatest mediator of political outcomes in both every day and campaign arenas,"[66] agenda-setting research was extended, by some researchers, to include evaluation. Thus, not only did the media tell us what issues to think about, but they told us what to think about them, too. Evaluation was a major extension of the original formulation and, for those who subscribed to it, helped place in perspective the apparent power of such campaign tools as televised political advertising (the subject of the next chapter) during the political campaigns of the decade. Among other things, these researchers argued that news stories suggest not only the importance of the subject matter but the contextual cues or frames by which to evaluate the subject matter.[67] In one study, it was found that, when the media concentrate on a particular news story, not only do program viewers become convinced that the subject is important, but through this process they become "'primed' to evaluate the president, in part, by his apparent success in dealing with this issue."[68] The researchers Shanto Iyengar and Donald Kinder also sought to assess the influence of priming in elections. They found that the issues over which voters appear most concerned as they prepare to cast their ballots for president or for the U.S. House of Representatives are shaped by whatever issues have most recently been the subject of television news.[69]

In a related study, published in 1983, scholars Gladys Engel Lang and Kurt Lang argued that Watergate never really became an issue in the 1972 presidential campaign (in spite of the extensive coverage of it) because it was cast as a partisan issue, just another example of election-year politics.[70] The assertions of candidate George McGovern were "balanced" by denials from the Nixon White House. The Langs found that most people did not pay much attention to Watergate until Judge John Sirica was "presented by the media as a credible and presumably objective spokesperson for the cover-up scenario. Subsequently, the press abandoned its practice of balancing Watergate stories and printed news that was more or less exclusively supportive of the cover-up narrative."[71] They termed the "framing" and "balancing" media activities as agenda building.

The framing or balancing studied by the Langs in regard to Watergate and the 1972 presidential election was also the subject of a 1991 book by Shanto Iyengar titled *Is Anyone Responsible? How Television Frames Political Issues*. In this book, Iyengar develops the idea that television news frames issues in different ways, each of which affects public opinion. There are, for example, *issue-specific* news frames, which pertain to specific topics or news events, and *generic* news frames, which are applied to various news topics, including those over time and cultural contexts.[72] Generic frames include *episodic framing*, which is commonly used as event-based news reports, and *thematic framing*, which provides a broader perspective by placing an issue or event in a context or as part of a trend or public debate.[73] *Conflict* frames, which refer to tensions between individuals, institutions, or countries, focus on differing points of view and also fall under the generic frame umbrella. *Economic consequence* frames follow suit and are recognized as monetary profit and loss.[74] Although framing has become important in understanding the influence of the media, it is important to note that less educated individuals and those who do not possess strong ties to political parties tend to receive negative consequences of exposure to frames due to a lack of understanding and learning about the issues and strategies of political campaigns and coverage.

Framing or balancing research continued throughout the 1990s and into the early 2000s. For example, building on Iyengar's work, Joseph N. Cappella and Kathleen Hall Jamieson in 1997 studied the "game" or "strategy frame" in which journalists "tell stories" that emphasize who is ahead and behind, and what strategies and tactics are necessary for the candidate to get ahead or stay ahead.[75]

Without much question, the agenda-setting perspective has generated more research than the other approaches we have discussed. Its growing volume is documented by a steady rate of publication and by its application in a variety of social science disciplines,[76] especially in political campaigns and advertising. Perhaps one of the reasons the perspective appears destined to retain its "popularity" among researchers is the more contemporary extensions emanating from it. One of the most intriguing of these extensions is the idea of agenda setting as "a process by which multiple actors construct shared meaning about the campaign."[77] In other words, "the actual agenda of the campaign results from the interaction of social actors; each actor is constrained by the others and by the flow of actual political events."[78] Summing up research in this area, Guido H. Stempel III states that one must look at the interaction among members of the media, news sources, and consumers of the news: "Agenda setting raises the question of which of the three sets the agenda—the media, the politicians, or the public. Research has established that each does so in certain circumstances."[79]

## Reconceptualization of the Classics

Although not a complete perspective like information diffusion, uses and gratifications, or agenda setting, we nonetheless include in this section a brief summary of the major tenets of the 1976 study that, while modeled after those of the Columbia Bureau of Applied Social Research, came to opposite conclusions. We believe that one of the reasons the study is important is that it laid a foundation for research during the 1980s and 1990s that explored the relationship between the media and political campaigns.

In an effort to provide a body of knowledge that would "contribute to an understanding of election coverage and the American voter,"[80] Thomas E. Patterson implemented the "most comprehensive panel survey ever conducted for the study of change during a presidential campaign."[81] The study and its results were described in the book *The Mass Media Election*. Although the Patterson investigation resembles the earlier work of Lazarsfeld and Berelson, there are major differences that are important to our consideration of political campaign communication in two respects. The first concerns the overall design of the study, and the second relates to the conclusions. We will begin by comparing designs.

In each of the Columbia studies, respondents were interviewed a number of times to determine whether their attitudes were changing as the presidential campaigns were proceeding. Panel surveys were the single source of data for findings. Moreover, each of the Columbia studies interviewed six hundred to eight hundred potential voters, and each was conducted in a single community. By contrast, the design of the 1976 study was more comprehensive. First, more people were interviewed (1,236). Second, they were interviewed in seven waves (five face-to-face interviews and two over the telephone), which were timed to correspond with each of the important intervals and stages in the campaign (just before the New Hampshire primary, after the early primaries, after the final primaries, after the conventions, before the general election, after the first and second presidential debates, and after the election). Third, respondents represented two communities that had substantially different populations and media (Erie, Pennsylvania, and Los Angeles, California). Finally, data collected from repeated interviews represented only one of the sources of evidence. The other was a content analysis of election-year political news stories that appeared on evening newscasts of the three major television networks, two news magazines, two national newspapers, and two local newspapers (one in each of the selected cities). The content analysis was conducted from January until after the general election in November; the interviews began in February and also concluded when the election was over. In short, the Patterson study was not only a more ambitious undertaking than any of the Columbia efforts had been; it was the largest project attempted in the intervening years—years in which research regarding the influence of mass communication was beginning to illustrate that the media were not passive entities in the political process.

As we discussed earlier, the primary conclusion derived from the Lazarsfeld/ Berelson work was that the media did not play a major role in determining voters' attitudes during a presidential campaign. In fact, media messages were far less important than the messages relayed through interpersonal communication channels. Political opinions were determined by party and social affiliations, and therefore, if the media were not absolutely powerless, they were of minor importance in influencing how people voted.

However, in reporting the results of his 1976 investigation, Patterson argued that the presidential campaign is essentially a mass media campaign. He felt that, for the "large majority of voters, the campaign has little reality apart from its media version."[82] In other words, far from being an unimportant factor, media are a significant part of the campaign process itself. In fact, virtually each of the conclusions from the 1976 study contradicted those articulated by the Columbia researchers. Among the conclusions Patterson discussed, the following three are particularly important for us:

- Although the media do not change attitudes, they do influence because people rely on them for information, thereby placing media in a position to influence perceptions.
- The stories that voters read in newspapers and watch on television "affect what they perceive to be the important events, critical issues, and serious contenders: [media] will affect what they learn about the candidates' personalities and issue positions."[83]
- Thus, the power of the press "rests largely on its ability to select what will be covered and to decide the context in which these events will be placed."[84]

Therefore, the Patterson investigation of the ways in which the media influenced voters in 1976 is important. First, it firmly dispelled the long-term myths created by the Columbia studies; second, it provided the comprehensive data necessary to begin updating and solidifying our knowledge of the ways in which voters, candidates, and the mass media interact with each other in contemporary political campaigns. In fact, thirteen years after the publication of *The Mass Media Election*, Patterson was even more convinced of the media's power in election campaigns. In *Out of Order*, published in 1993, Patterson's thesis is that the news media have become the "chief intermediary between voter and candidate."[85] In support of Patterson's thesis, David Barker and Adam B. Lawrence used the direct effects model to examine "the relationship between political news reception and candidate preference in the 2000 presidential primary races."[86] They studied the relationship between media favoritism and candidate preference. Their study found that listening to talk radio was a major predictor in which candidate was preferred. Barker and Lawrence found that listening to Rush Limbaugh was associated with choosing George W. Bush over John McCain as a candidate for president among Republican voters, even though the mainstream media favored McCain.

## CONCLUSIONS

As we have seen, beliefs regarding the political influence and power of the mass media have come nearly full circle during the almost seventy years researchers have been studying them. First, it was believed that the media were all powerful. Then their power was seen as limited and of secondary or minor importance. In each instance, conclusions were frequently based on insubstantial evidence but gained prominence because they reinforced the dominant attitudes and context of the time in which they were articulated. The effective use of propaganda in the 1930s and the early 1940s convinced researchers that the power of the media was massive. Indeed, the media were virtually unlimited in the ways they could change attitudes and produce behavior modification or conformity, whereas in the 1950s, the opposite viewpoint was held because, in the context of those years, it seemed difficult to subscribe to the belief that U.S. citizens could be reduced to puppets who would follow the ravings of any demagogue. Moreover, it must be remembered that, when the classic Columbia studies were undertaken (during the 1940 and 1948 presidential elections), television was not yet a real factor in politics or in the environment of voters. However, by the 1960 presidential campaign, television was on its way to becoming a political force. Both candidates were using the medium for spot commercials, and their precedent-setting debates broke all previously established viewing records. When more than a hundred million people watched the debates and subsequently talked about their perceptions and reactions to the candidates, it became increasingly difficult for social scientists to deny that media, particularly television, had any impact.

Thus, as the context/environment changed, some researchers began to question the limited effects model just as twenty years earlier they had challenged the validity of the hypodermic thesis. Eventually, most conceded that the media possessed some influence—even if it did not create massive changes in voting behavior. Some acknowledged the media's ability in the transmission and diffusion of information regarding candidates, issues, or the campaign itself. Other researchers suggested that people use the media for a variety of political reasons: for information, entertainment, increasing the range of topics for social exchange and acceptability, meeting expectations of peer groups, or intrapersonal communication. And there were those who argued that the media are important because of their power to determine what information or news would be presented. Thus, by the middle of the 1970s, many social scientists had begun to believe that media influence in the electoral process could not be ignored.

Finally, in 1976, a study was undertaken that provided enough data to confirm many of the trends evident since 1960. But the pendulum continued to swing. During the 1980s and 1990s, when every election year appeared to bring with it an ever-increasing reliance on television to frame candidates' rhetorical and visual messages, some worried about the omnipotence of the media. Thus, when we asserted at other points in this chapter that beliefs regarding the influence of the media had come full circle, we were not exaggerating. But do these perspectives from mass media research contribute to the understanding of campaign communication? We think they can and suggest seven principles of campaign communication that can be drawn from them.

The first of these principles is that the most important effect of media influence is seldom direct persuasion but providing information that affects perception and may ultimately persuade. Persuasion theorists have consistently determined that a "one-shot" persuasive effort or message does not change attitudes—at least, it does not change attitudes from one extreme to the other. There may be behavior modification or conformity when conditions include threat, punishment, or even reward, but not internalized attitude change. And it is naïve to assume that it is any different in the context of a political campaign. Instead, persuasive information about a candidate, about the issues for which the candidate stands, and even negative information regarding the candidate's opponent will affect perception and thus help draw attention to the candidate and campaign and may even influence later perception. Therefore, we conclude that the media are important to and powerful in a political campaign, not in necessarily changing votes because of a single message, but in drawing attention to candidates and thereby providing information for a full range of attitude formulations (including reinforcement, reformulation, and repositioning).

The second principle is simply that the contemporary candidate needs the mass media, in part because voters have expectations regarding the media's role in providing information about the candidate and the campaign. Citizens rely on newspapers, newscasts, websites, and televised political advertising to tell them about candidates, issues, and the campaign itself. Moreover, candidates have found that they can efficiently reach potential voters only through the mass media. And with the proliferation of cable channels, narrowcasting provides candidates with special challenges and opportunities in regard to communicating their messages to voters via the mass media.

The third principle is that the media have tremendous power in determining which news events, which candidates, and which issues are to be covered in any given day. Thus, a candidate's campaign must be focused, in large measure, on those sorts of issues, photographic opportunities, and events that will draw media attention and provide "sound bites" for the evening television newscasts. Whether these are pseudoevents or real, pseudoissues or real, modern candidates do those things that will "play" to the media—that will call attention to themselves and their campaigns. Perhaps more important, because of the media, candidates do not do some things and do not discuss some issues. Often what they fail to do is just as important as what they do.

The fourth principle may be less obvious. Although candidates attempt to use the media for their own purposes, they are not always able to control them. While a candidate can send a press release, its use is not guaranteed. Although an appearance at the state fair is planned, there is no assurance that the event will be used in the evening newscasts. It may well be that election coverage will focus on an opponent or on yesterday's gaffe. Moreover, media have the power to penetrate even the most expertly contrived image—the newspaper reporter catches the wording of the answer to a question, or the television camera records unplanned nonverbal behavior. Our point is simply that candidates may spend most of their campaign resources on the many avenues of the mass media, they may depend on them to present persuasive information regarding their candidacies, but, except for their own advertisements, they cannot control the media.

The fifth principle is that mass media influence is important to our knowledge and appreciation of the electoral process itself. The media allow us to witness political events; they teach and instruct, thereby adding to our expectations about the democratic process. Most of the crucial events of at least recent presidential elections have occurred on television. Indeed, it is the medium through which the candidates become known to the public through such formats as ads and appearances on talk shows and news programs. While this may increase or decrease our liking for particular candidates, issues, or campaigns, it does provide a sense of involvement as we affirm (or deny) our role as citizens.

The sixth principle regards how the mass media, primarily television and the internet, changed the way in which candidates campaign for office. As we noted in an earlier chapter, we greet candidates in the living rooms of our homes via the television screen rather than at a political rally. Moreover, the candidates' television advertising and appearances on television talk shows and town meetings, as well as their websites, are the electronic-age equivalent of the whistle-stop tours.

Finally, we believe that the influence or power of the media has contributed mightily to the many changes in the electoral process. For example, the surfacing and primary stages of the campaign have become more important to the outcome, receive more precise and planned attention by candidates, and generate more excitement and enthusiasm from the public than before television entered the political arena. This has happened because the media treat these preliminary events in much the same manner as they treat the later stages. In fact, because of high media involvement, the first two stages have replaced the attention-getting power of the nominating conventions and the general election, and they have also seized much of their legitimate power.

In the largest sense, we conclude this chapter as we began it—convinced that the mass media (especially television) have a tremendous impact on political campaign communication.

## NOTES

1. "Number of Daily Newspapers in the United States from 1970 to 2016," Statista, 2018, accessed October 26, 2018, https://www.statista.com/statistics/183408/number-of-us-daily-newspapers-since-1975.

2. Michael Balderston, "Total Number of U.S. TV Stations Continues Decline," TVTechnology, October 4, 2017, accessed October 26, 2018, https://www.tvtechnology.com/news/total-number-of-us-tv-stations-continues-decline.

3. "Frequently Asked Questions about Broadcasting," National Association of Broadcasters, 2017, accessed October 26, 2018, https://www.nab.org/documents/resources/broadcastfaq.asp.

4. "Major Pay-TV Providers Lost about 305,000 Subscribers in 1Q 2018," Leichtman Research Group, May 17, 2018, accessed October 26, 2018, https://www.leichtmanresearch.com/major-pay-tv-providers-lost-about-305000-subscribers-in-1q-2018.

5. Dan D. Nimmo and James E. Combs, *Mediated Political Realities*, 2nd ed. (New York: Longman, 1990), 25.

6. "Number of Facebook Users by Age in the U.S.," Statista, 2018, accessed October 26, 2018, https://www.statista.com/statistics/398136/us-facebook-user-age-groups.

7. "Share of Adults in the US Who Use the Internet in 2018," Statista, 2018, accessed October 26, 2018, https://www.statista.com/statistics/266587/percentage-of-internet-users-by-age-groups-in-the-us.

8. Frank E. X. Dance, "Human Communication Theory: A Highly Selective Review and Two Commentaries," in *Communication Yearbook II*, ed. Brent D. Ruben (New Brunswick, NJ: Transaction, 1978), 7–22.

9. Peter M. Sandman, David M. Rubin, and David B. Sachsman, *Media* (Englewood Cliffs, NJ: Prentice Hall, 1972), 20.

10. Ibid., 23.

11. Ibid.

12. Sidney Kraus and Dennis Davis, *The Effects of Mass Communication on Political Behavior* (University Park: Pennsylvania State University Press, 1976), 117.

13. Elihu Katz and Paul F. Lazarsfeld, *Personal Influence* (New York: Free Press, 1955), 16.

14. Harold F. Gosnell, *Machine Politics: Chicago Model* (Chicago: University of Chicago Press, 1937).

15. Garrett J. O'Keefe, "Political Campaigns and Mass Communication Research," in *Political Communication: Issues and Strategies for Research*, ed. Steven H. Chaffee (Beverly Hills, CA: Sage, 1975), 133.

16. David Blomquist, *Elections and the Mass Media* (Washington, DC: American Political Science Association, 1981), 4–6.

17. Kraus and Davis, *Effects of Mass Communication*, 117.

18. For a discussion of the methodological difficulties of the selective exposure concept, see, for example, Lee B. Becker, Maxwell E. McCombs, and Jack M. McLeod, "The Development of Political Cognitions," in *Political Communication: Issues and Strategies for Research*, ed. Steven H. Chaffee (Beverly Hills, CA: Sage, 1975), 28–31; Kraus and Davis, *Effects of Mass Communication*, 51–54; and David Sears and Jonathan Freedman, "Selective Exposure to Information: A Critical Review," *Public Opinion Quarterly* 31 (Summer 1967): 194–213.

19. Katz and Lazarsfeld, *Personal Influence*, 138.

20. Ibid., 309.

21. Ibid.

22. Kraus and Davis, *Effects of Mass Communication*, 120.

23. Becker et al., "Development of Political Cognitions," 32.

24. Ibid., 33.

25. Kraus and Davis, *Effects of Mass Communication*, 53.

26. Angus Campbell et al., *The American Voter: An Abridgment* (New York: Wiley, 1964).

27. David M. White, "The 'Gate Keeper': A Case Study in the Selection of News," *Journalism Quarterly* 27 (Fall 1950): 383–90.

28. Sandman et al., *Media*, 103.

29. Ibid., 109.

30. See, for example, Lewis Donohew, "Newspaper Gatekeepers and Forces in the News Channel," *Public Opinion Quarterly* 31 (Spring 1967): 62–66; Jean S. Kerrick, "Balance and

the Writer's Attitude in News Stories and Editorials," *Journalism Quarterly* 41 (Spring 1964): 207–15; and G. A. Donohue, P. J. Tichenor, and C. N. Olien, "Gatekeeping: Mass Media Systems and Information Control," in *Current Perspectives in Mass Communication Research,* ed. F. G. Kline and P. J. Tichenor (Beverly Hills, CA: Sage, 1972).

31. Studies in the late 1960s and in the 1970s have consistently indicated that voters use the media for purposes other than reinforcement of their views. Moreover, other studies have shown that there are cases wherein voters prefer messages that contradict their views. Finally, with the decline of party affiliation, there is reason to believe that voters are not holding on to preconceived political beliefs but enter a campaign season with a willingness to be persuaded on issues. Steven H. Chaffee and Michael Petrick call the concept of selective exposure "too simplistic." See their book *Using the Mass Media* (New York: McGraw-Hill, 1975), 141.

32. Kraus and Davis, *Effects of Mass Communication,* 123.

33. Blomquist, *Elections and the Mass Media,* 7.

34. Ibid.

35. Ibid.

36. Ibid., 8. See also Jay G. Blumler and Denis McQuail, *Television in Politics* (Chicago: University of Chicago Press, 1969).

37. Kraus and Davis, *Effects of Mass Communication,* 126.

38. Ibid., 128.

39. Ibid., 127.

40. Robert L. Savage, "The Diffusion of Information Approach," in *Handbook of Political Communication,* ed. Dan D. Nimmo and Keith R. Sanders (Beverly Hills, CA: Sage, 1981), 104–7.

41. Ibid.

42. Steven H. Chaffee, "The Diffusion of Political Information," in *Political Communication: Issues and Strategies for Research,* ed. Steven H. Chaffee (Beverly Hills, CA: Sage, 1975), 125.

43. Kraus and Davis, *Effects of Mass Communication,* 130.

44. See, for example, Walter Gantz, "The Diffusion of News about the Attempted Reagan Assassination," *Journal of Communication* 33 (Winter 1983): 56–66; Charles R. Bantz, Sandra G. Petronio, and David L. Rarick, "News Diffusion after the Reagan Shooting," *Quarterly Journal of Speech* 69 (August 1983): 317–27; and Ruth Ann Weaver-Tarisey, Barbara Sweeney, and Thomas Steinfatt, "Communication during Assassination Attempts: Diffusion of Information in Attacks on President Reagan and the Pope," *Southern Speech Communication Journal* 49 (Spring 1989): 258–76.

45. Jay G. Blumler, "The Role of Theory in Uses and Gratifications Studies," *Communication Research* 6 (January 1979): 21.

46. Ibid., 11–12.

47. Jack M. McLeod and Lee B. Becker, "The Uses and Gratifications Approach," in *Handbook of Political Communication,* ed. Dan D. Nimmo and Keith R. Sanders (Beverly Hills, CA: Sage, 1981), 71.

48. Andrew J. Flanagin and Miriam J. Metzger, "Internet Use in the Contemporary Media Environment," *Human Communication Research* 27, no. 1 (January 2001): 171.

49. Ibid.

50. Ibid., 174.

51. Ibid., 87.

52. David L. Swanson and Dan D. Nimmo, eds., *New Directions in Political Communication Research: A Resource Book* (Newbury Park, CA: Sage, 1990), 18.

53. Carl R. Bybee, "Uses and Gratifications Research and the Study of Social Change," in *Political Communication Research: Approaches, Studies, Assessments,* ed. David L. Paletz (Norwood, NJ: Ablex, 1987), 209–10.

54. Denis McQuail, *Audience Analysis* (Thousand Oaks, CA: Sage, 1997), 73.

55. Ibid.

56. Diane F. Witmer and Chutatip Taweesuk, "Flow or Function? Examining Uses and Gratifications of the World Wide Web by Mexican and U.S. Communicators," paper presented at the National Communication Association and International Communication Association Conference, July 15–18, 1998, Rome.

57. Richard E. Petty and John T. Cacioppo, "Epilog: A General Framework for Understanding Attitude Change Processes," in *Attitudes and Persuasion: Classic and Contemporary Approaches*, ed. Richard E. Petty and John T. Cacioppo (Dubuque, IA: W. C. Brown, 1981), 255–67.

58. Bernard C. Cohen, *The Press and Foreign Policy* (Princeton, NJ: Princeton University Press, 1963), 13.

59. Kraus and Davis, *Effects of Mass Communication*, 216.

60. Maxwell E. McCombs and Donald L. Shaw, "The Agenda-Setting Function of Mass Media," *Public Opinion Quarterly* 36 (Summer 1972): 177.

61. G. Ray Funkhouser, "Trends in Media Coverage of the Issues of the '60s," *Journalism Quarterly* 50 (Autumn 1973): 538.

62. Kraus and Davis, *Effects of Mass Communication*, 214.

63. Maxwell E. McCombs, "The Agenda-Setting Approach," in *Handbook of Political Communication*, ed. Dan D. Nimmo and Keith R. Sanders (Beverly Hills, CA: Sage, 1981), 127–30.

64. John Mueller, *Policy and Opinion in the Gulf War* (Chicago: University of Chicago Press, 1994), 130.

65. Holli A. Semetko, "TV News and U.S. Public Opinion about Foreign Countries," *International Journal of Public Opinion Research* 4, no. 2 (Summer 1992): 126–47.

66. Bruce E. Gronbeck, "Popular Culture, Media, and Political Communication," in *New Directions in Political Communication Research*, ed. David L. Swanson and Dan D. Nimmo (Newbury Park, CA: Sage, 1990), 85.

67. Anne Johnston, "Trends in Political Communication: A Selective Review of Research in the 1980s," in *New Directions in Political Communication Research*, ed. David L. Swanson and Dan D. Nimmo (Newbury Park, CA: Sage, 1990), 336–38.

68. Ibid., 337.

69. Shanto Iyengar and Donald R. Kinder, *News That Matters* (Chicago: University of Chicago Press, 1987), 110.

70. Gladys Engel Lang and Kurt Lang, "The Media and Watergate," in *Media Power in Politics*, 2nd ed., ed. Doris A. Graber (Washington, DC: Congressional Quarterly Press, 1990), 255–62.

71. Dennis K. Davis, "Development of Research on News and Politics," in *New Directions in Political Communication Research*, ed. David L. Swanson and Dan D. Nimmo (Newbury Park, CA: Sage, 1990), 171.

72. Shanto Iyengar, *Is Anyone Responsible? How Television Frames Political Issues* (Chicago: University of Chicago Press, 1991), 18.

73. Claes H. De Vreese, Jochen Peter, and Holli A. Semetko, "Framing Politics at the Launch of the Euro: A Cross-National Comparative Study of Frames in the News," *Political Communication* 18 (2001): 108.

74. De Vreese et al., "Framing Politics at the Launch of the Euro," 109–10.

75. Regina G. Lawrence, "Game-Framing the Issues: Tracking the Strategy Frame in Public Policy News," *Political Communication* 17 (2000): 93.

76. Maxwell E. McCombs and Donald L. Shaw, "The Evolution of Agenda-Setting Research: Twenty-five Years in the Marketplace of Ideas," *Journal of Communication* 43, no. 2 (1993): 59.

77. Russell J. Dalton, Paul Allen Beck, Robert Huckfeldt, and William Koetzle, "A Test of Media-Centered Agenda Setting: Newspaper Content and Public Interests in a Presidential Election," *Political Communication* 15 (1998): 465.

78. Ibid.

79. Guido H. Stempel III, *Media and Politics in America* (Santa Barbara, CA: ABC Clio, 2003), 55.

80. Thomas E. Patterson, *The Mass Media Election: How Americans Choose Their President* (New York: Praeger, 1980), 8.

81. Ibid., viii.

82. Ibid., 3.

83. Ibid., 95.

84. Ibid., 53.

85. Thomas E. Patterson, *Out of Order* (New York: Knopf, 1993).

86. David Barker and Adam B. Lawrence, "Media Favoritism and Presidential Nominations: Reviving the Direct Effects Model," *Political Communication* 23 (January–March 2006): 41–59.

# 5

❧

# Communicative Types
# and Functions of Televised
# Political Advertising

During the electoral campaigns of the 1980s and continuing through the 1990s and 2000s, it became increasingly apparent that political advertising on television is a central communication strategy for the growing numbers of those who seek our vote. The 1980s brought the television advertising attempts of all manner of candidates to our attention. Whether running for a seat in the U.S. Senate or for a chair on the Cincinnati city council, it seemed that every candidate was using television spot advertising. Political ads came to dominate whatever portion of public attention is reserved for things political. In fact, by 1990, during the first election of the new decade, there was at least as much discussion about the number and nature of the ads being used as there was about the candidates themselves. Voter or journalist, consultant or scholar, the central focus was television advertising. Criticism of the ads and their prominent role in the campaigns of 1988 through the 1990s was broad based. However, attention centered around what appeared to be a growing reliance on negative as opposed to positive ads; replacement of campaign dialogue with television commercials; the extraordinary cost of the spots; fear that the ads, especially those that were negative, determined electoral results; and the idea that television advertising had "turned off" the public.

According to Erika Fowler and colleagues, television is still the primary medium for campaigns to share messages with citizens and voters.[1] Even today, with the increasing availability of "television on demand" through services such as Hulu, televised political advertising occupies a pivotal position within a candidate's campaign. Thus, in this chapter, we take a brief look at the development of television advertising in presidential politics, explore the principles underlying various types of political commercials, and then discuss some of the most important communicative functions they perform during the campaign. In so doing, we examine the use of one kind of commercial, the attack or condemnation spot, by candidates who are women. We will conclude our discussion by reviewing the major question that has developed around the use of attack advertising. Because in chapter 11 we examine all forms of media advertising, for now our consideration is limited to the ads candidates use on television.

## HISTORICAL DEVELOPMENT

Most observers claim that the first political ad was aired in 1950 by Connecticut senator William Benton. His background was in advertising.[2] Televised political spots entered presidential politics in 1952 when the Republican nominee, General Dwight D. Eisenhower, filmed forty commercials that were titled "Eisenhower Answers America." Although the twenty-eight ads that were aired in forty states revolutionized the way in which presidential candidates went about the job of getting elected, in terms of narrative and cinematography, the Eisenhower spots were rather "primitive" compared to those today. The format for all the spots was exactly the same: A male voice announced, "Eisenhower Answers America." A regular citizen or "person on the street" (actually a line of people waiting to get into Radio City Music Hall in New York City) would ask Eisenhower a question, and the general would respond with a one- or two-sentence answer that implied that it was time for a change. For example, "a man on the street" would say, "General, the Democrats are telling me I've never had it so good." Eisenhower would respond, "Can that be true when America is billions in debt, when prices have doubled, when taxes break our backs, and we are still fighting in Korea? It's tragic and it's time for a change."

However, the 1952 spots brought the techniques used at the time in persuading Americans to buy commercial products to the front door of the White House. One of the most interesting aspects of the application of "Madison Avenue" strategy to the 1952 campaign was that it was unnecessary. Eisenhower, a genuine American hero, was, according to a 1952 Roper poll, the most admired living American. Although Eisenhower used the ads, his opponent, Illinois governor Adlai Stevenson, rejected the idea of appearing in spot commercials—at least during the 1952 campaign.

By 1956, when Governor Stevenson was again the Democratic nominee for president, he changed his mind about participating in spots—largely because the experts in both political parties believed television advertising had become a necessary part of the campaign effort. In fact, as political communication scholar Kathleen Hall Jamieson has written, "The major innovation of the '56 campaign was its increasing reliance on the five minute spot."[3] The ads in 1956 and the ones that followed in 1960 frequently consisted of the candidate talking directly to the television audience (the "talking head" ads) or those that made it seem as if "the viewing audience was eavesdropping on the candidate as he addressed a rally."[4]

In spite of relatively minimal production techniques, by the time of the 1960 campaign, it was clear that, with the technology of television editing, ads could provide additional arguments for or against a candidate simply by juxtaposing a still photograph of the candidate, a name, or even part of a speech with specific visuals to create a whole range of image messages. Some of the images were positive (American flags, the Liberty Bell, waving fields of grain), others were negative (deserted factories, foreign demonstrators throwing rocks at cars, farmers standing in front of empty grain bins), but all were examples of arguments by visual association. As Jamieson notes in her chronology of the evolution of American political advertising, arguments by visual association (positive and negative) were used in the presidential campaigns of 1964 and again in 1968. It was in the latter campaign between Democrat Hubert Humphrey and Republican Richard Nixon that color ads were used. Argument by positive association also characterized the Ford and Carter campaigns of 1976, and it remained a staple of political advertising through the early campaigns of the 1980s.[5] Although ads that utilized negative visual images were used from at least the 1964 campaign forward, frequently those spots that directly attacked the opponent did not picture the candidate or the opponent. Attacks were left to running mates, other surrogates, or unnamed, unknown voiceovers.

Without question, the best known of the negative concept ads aired only once (because of the legal and ethical questions it raised), and it never even mentioned the opponent's name. Nonetheless, the "Daisy Girl" ad so effectively cemented perception of the Republican nominee, Senator Barry Goldwater, as a warmonger—a man who could not be entrusted with our nation's security—that he was never able to rid himself of the negative image. The force of the ad was its ability to engage viewers' emotions and associate their negative response with Goldwater.

In many instances, ads were targeted to appeal to voters in the opposition political party. For example, in 1964, several of Lyndon Johnson's spots openly called to Republicans "worried" about voting for Goldwater to join him. And in 1972, Richard Nixon used negative association or concept ads whose airtime was paid for by an organization called Democrats for Nixon.

Jamieson argues that, in 1976, two new types of attack ads replaced the association, or concept, type—personal witness and neutral reporter. These ads featured ordinary Americans (not actors) expressing their beliefs about the opposing candidate (personal witness), or they presented a list of factual statements and invited people to make a judgment call (neutral reporter). As such, they appeared less harsh than the concept ads and somewhat removed or apart from the candidate.

In 1980, the personal witness or "man in the street" ads were used once again. In addition, longer ads, in the style of the documentary (a spot designed to present a candidate's accomplishments), were utilized—especially by Ronald Reagan. But in the 1984 election, and again in 1988, the negative visual association or concept ad returned in such force that each was, at some point, termed the "year of the negative campaign."

Another element that has undergone change from one campaign year to another is the preferred length of commercials. There have been half-hour speeches or biographies; four- or five-minute documentaries or other special appeals squeezed between evening entertainment programs or right before or after the late-night news; and twenty-, thirty-, and sixty-second segments. Thus, over the years, sandwiched between programs and product commercials, political ads have taken a variety of time frames. However, during the 1980s, thirty-second spots became dominant—largely because research had documented that they were just as effective as longer spots in getting the message across. For the most part, campaigns have come to reserve longer ads, such as the five-minute documentaries or biographies, for specific functions such as introducing a new candidate, raising money, or conveying an election eve message.

Thus, since television's entrance into the presidential campaign arena, the form and style of televised political spots have, from election to election, undergone change. In some instances, stylistic changes were temporary and disappeared just four years later. In other cases, revisions or reformulations were more permanent. Over the years, however, political ads have reflected two patterns with some regularity. While neither is surprising, each is important enough to our understanding of televised ads as a critical tool of the campaign to spend some time discussing them. First, the style or form political ads take is frequently a reflection of the larger society of which they are a part. For example, in the two campaigns of the 1950s and even in 1960, the spots were neither hard-hitting nor very specific (particularly those in which the candidates themselves appeared), largely because Americans did not yet equate the techniques and manipulations of Madison Avenue advertising and public relations with their presidential candidates, and the candidates themselves were concerned that they not appear too "political" as opposed to "presidential." Between 1964 and 1972, we believe that the harshness of the negative associations used in commercials must be seen within the context of the national anguish created by the escalating war in Vietnam and the civil rights movement. In the campaigns of 1976 and 1980, the number of positive ads and the "feel good" mood that was their theme, as well as the indirect and less attack-oriented negative spots, must be viewed as a reflection of public distrust and disillusionment with politics and politicians in the aftermath of Vietnam and Watergate. And the reemergence of strident and graphically explicit negative association or concept spots in 1984 and 1988 may well have occurred because the campaigns did not generate any major issues or themes. From the surfacing through the general election stage, the focus was the character and image of the candidates rather than the identification and discussion of "burning issues" facing the electorate. Since 2000, the volume of political advertising has grown each election cycle and the advertising has become much more negative.[6]

Not only, however, have political spots reflected broad societal problems/attitudes/preoccupations, but they have also reflected the prevailing philosophical and stylistic "schools of thought" operant in commercial or product-oriented advertising. While we would hesitate to contend that the process never works the other way—that is, particular strategies are used first in the political world and then by Madison Avenue—in general, those political consultants who work in most of the statewide to national races apply techniques that have been found successful in commercial advertising. Author Montague Kern wrote that during the 1980s the "world of political advertising absorbed its commercial counterpart and became as one."[7] Kern argues that political spots in the campaigns of the 1980s were like their commercial counterparts in that they evoked feelings or experience, relied heavily on visual and aural effects, developed messages in which the candidate and a single issue were blended, and frequently attempted to associate a candidate with an affect-laden symbol that already had meaning for us.[8] And as the campaigns of the 1980s became the campaigns of the 1990s, there were no discernible differences in the ads. The attempt to develop spots that provoke strong feelings continued through the 1996 presidential campaign.

In a study of presidential advertising in the 1992 campaign, researcher Lynda Lee Kaid found that emotional appeals were used in 52.6 percent of the ads produced for the Perot campaign and 46.2 percent of the ads produced for the Clinton campaign, and 56.3 percent of the spots produced for the Bush reelection campaign contained fear appeals.[9] Similarly, Kaid's study of presidential advertising in the 1996 campaign found that 63 percent of Dole's and 84 percent of Clinton's general election ads contained emotional appeals.[10] In the 2000 campaign, Kaid discovered that 26 percent of Bush's and 47 percent of Gore's general election ads utilized emotional appeals. Both candidates also used fear appeals. Bush used 9 percent, whereas Gore put a stronger emphasis on this style of ad at 56 percent.[11] In 2004, television advertising took yet another turn as the internet became a vehicle for the candidate's spots. As Kaid discovered, more than $1.7 million was spent by George W. Bush and John Kerry on internet ads.[12] In addition, the Republican and Democratic parties spent more than $600,000 on internet ads for their candidates.[13] Moreover, Kaid cataloged five types of internet ads, including (1) websites as political advertisements, (2) web ads that were originally available in other media, (3) appeals for fund-raising, (4) original web ads, and (5) blog ads.[14] In the 2008 campaign, once again records were shattered; whereas in 2004 John Kerry, the Democratic nominee, spent about $146.6 million on general election television ads, Barack Obama spent "at least $250 million" four years later.[15] The trend continued in 2012 with a total of $580 million spent to support Obama and $470 million spent to support Mitt Romney. Much of the spending was by independent *Super PACs*, organizations established to support a candidate or array of issues and special interests.[16] Discussion of the advertising in the 2016 campaign is in chapter 14.

Over the past couple of election cycles, political advertising continues to evolve. First, given the new campaign finance rulings and law, most ads are now sponsored not by candidate campaigns, but by special and corporate interest groups. In addition, even with ad placement in traditional media of television, radio, and print, there continues to be increasing sophistication in targeting viewers. Finally, technology changes and new social media and communication platforms increase citizen access to political messages and provide additional targeting opportunities for campaigns.[17]

Although we do not intend to trace the historical development of commercial advertising, the ways in which its methods and techniques have been used by a variety of candidates become obvious in the next sections as we explore the types and functions of televised political ads and the questions and controversies they have generated.

## TYPES AND FUNCTIONS OF POLITICAL ADS

As the number of televised spots used during election campaigns has increased, so, too, has the number of people writing or talking about them. Whether the report of a practitioner or the analysis of a scholar, all seem to have contributed a name to describe the ads they have studied or those they have used. For example, in their book *The Spot*, Edwin Diamond and Stephen Bates argue that political advertising goes through four phases and thus produces four types of ads. Phase

1 brings ID Spots (ads that are biographical and are intended to introduce or identify the candidate—provide a sense of the candidate in the surfacing or primary stages of the campaign). Phase 2 produces Argument Spots (ads that identify the candidate's causes, ideas, and concerns—what the candidate stands for). Phase 3 is the time for Attack Spots (ads that are direct and personal attacks meant to reduce the credibility of the opposing candidate—create doubt, stir fear, exploit anxiety, or motivate ridicule). Phase 4 produces Visionary Spots (ads that are used as the campaign draws to a close to provide a reflective/thoughtful/dignified view of the candidate—create the impression that the candidate has the leadership ability and the vision to move the country/state/city forward).[18]

There are numerous functions of political ads: to create interest in a candidate; to build name recognition; to create, soften, or redefine an image; to stimulate citizen participation; to provide motivation for candidate support; to reinforce support; to influence the undecided; to identify key issues and frame questions for public debate; to demonstrate the talents of the candidate; and to provide entertainment. The content, approach, and thrust of an ad are based upon several considerations. A few of these are the strengths and weaknesses of the candidates; the strengths and weaknesses of the opponent; availability of funds; the nature of news coverage of the candidate; public information and views of the candidate; and the general artistic and aesthetic inclinations of the consultant.

Although there are numerous specific advertising formats and strategies, there are four basic political advertising messages. Positive messages are those designed to promote the positive attributes of the candidate and to link the candidate to voters in a positive way. Such efforts range from rather basic biographical spots to more myth-evoking, "product of the American Dream" spots. Negative messages are specifically designed to attack the opponent. They may focus on the personal weaknesses, voting record, or prior public behavior of the candidate. Comparative messages are still designed to attack the opponent but tend to focus on issue positions. The most effective comparison ads give the appearance of providing a two-sided argument, but the presentation is always slanted to favor the candidate sponsoring the ad. Some comparisons are implied, thus never specifically referring to the opposition. Audience interpretation favors the candidate sponsoring the ad. Finally, there are response messages designed to directly answer challenger charges, allegations, and attacks.

In his analysis of presidential television commercials used from 1952 through 1984, L. Patrick Devlin describes spots in terms of categories such as talking head ads, negative ads (those spots that tear down the opponent), cinema verité ads (those in which the candidate is filmed in a real-life setting interacting with people), documentary ads (spots that present the accomplishments of the candidate), man-in-the-street ads (those in which real people talk positively about the candidate or negatively about the opponent), testimonial ads (spots in which prominent people speak on behalf of the candidate), and independent ads (those that are sponsored by organizations separate from the candidate).[19] Montague Kern contributes two additional types of spots from her book, *30-Second Politics: Political Advertising in the Eighties.* She defines *platform ads* as those that present a candidate's commitment to a position or oppose the opponent's position and *slogan ads* as those that contain no policy statement, why statement, or any answer.[20]

In a study of political advertising and its meaning in American elections, Richard Joslyn identifies four different perspectives or approaches by which the contemporary election can be understood, and he argues that, within each perspective, specific kinds of appeals are used in television commercials. After examining 506 of these commercials, he found that the most prevalent type of appeal is one he labeled "benevolent leader." Benevolent leader ads, according to Joslyn, focus on a candidate's personality traits rather than programmatic actions, policy positions, or political values and "attempt to accomplish a correspondence between the role expectations for a public office and the persona of the candidate."[21] For example, the benevolent leader ads might focus on such traits as the candidate's courage, honesty, strength of character, sense of fairness and justice, or compassion. The ads can be in the form of biographies or documentaries in which the candidate is shown in situations wherein the traits discussed are evident, in testimonials in which a prominent person discusses a specific characteristic of the candidate, or even in a man-on-the-street format in which several people are featured as they remark on the candidate's virtues. Whatever form the benevolent leader ad might take, its focus is the candidate's personality or character strengths.

Not only have scholars offered a classification scheme for the variety of televised commercials, but some have suggested that negative ads can be divided by specific types. As mentioned earlier in this chapter, Kathleen Hall Jamieson suggests three kinds of negative spots that she terms *concept ads* (those that juxtapose unrelated visual images to suggest false inferences), *personal witness ads* (which feature regular citizens giving unscripted negative opinions about the opponent), and *neutral reporter ads* (those in which a series of informational statements is made and then the voter is invited to make a judgment or draw a conclusion about the opponent).[22] In 1985, and again in 1994, Bruce E. Gronbeck identified negative ads as *implicative* (those that operate by innuendo without attacking directly), *comparative* (ads which juxtapose the opponent's record or positions on issues with those of the candidate), and *assault* (those directly assaulting the character, motivations, associates, or actions of an opponent).[23]

Although this summary is certainly not exhaustive, it may help you appreciate the complexity of trying to understand and distinguish among the types of televised commercials that have been used since 1952. However, we have no real desire to contribute either to the proliferation of ad types or to the difficulty of describing contemporary political advertising. Rather, our goal is to reduce ambiguity by classifying spots according to their primary rhetorical purpose. Within each category, we subdivide only in terms of videostyle factors (verbal content, nonverbal content, film/video production techniques)[24] that appear to have characteristics significant enough to distinguish one from another. In some cases, you will see that at least one component of videostyle (usually film/video production techniques) overlaps from category to category, although the overall purpose of the ad is unchanged. You will also note that what we term *videostyle factors* other theorists have classified as types of ads.

We suggest that the only important reason to categorize types of political commercials is to gain some understanding of their rhetorical purpose. While candidates use ads to fulfill a variety of functions (which we discuss shortly), they have three primary rhetorical purposes: to praise the candidate, to condemn the opponent, or to respond to charges. Although from time to time these purposes may overlap, essentially ads can be understood in terms of their primary rhetorical purpose. Thus, we characterize televised political commercials and the communicative functions they perform in the following manner.

## Ads Extolling the Candidate's Virtues

The videostyle factors available to be used in ads whose overall purpose is to praise the candidate are virtually unlimited. Over the years, techniques such as testimony, documentary, talking head, cinema verité, man-on-the-street, slogan, platform, or benevolent leader have all been used. And although some election years and the campaigns of some candidates have made extensive use of a particular videostyle (e.g., in 1980, 41 percent of the Reagan campaign's television commercials were documentaries),[25] most campaigns that have the financial resources to do so use a variety of videostyles to promote the virtues/strengths of their candidate. It is important, however, that the videostyle not detract from the ad's primary objective—extolling the candidate and ignoring the opponent.

The communicative functions performed by ads of this nature are as varied as the videostyles. Moreover, they are critical for both incumbents and challengers, although the extent to which they are used may vary in relationship to other conditions. For example, if the candidate is a relatively unknown challenger running against an entrenched incumbent, it is critically important that the campaign tell the candidate's "story" or, in other words, provide information on her background, accomplishments, positions on issues, strengths of character and personality, family, and associates—define her. And television commercials can perform this function better and more rapidly than most other campaign tools available to the candidate and her staff.

While there are countless examples of challengers running at all levels who have had some success in using commercials of this type to "define" themselves to the electorate, ones who did *not* come readily to mind. In the 1988 presidential campaign, for example, challenger Michael Dukakis did not move rapidly enough after the Democratic National Convention to tell the public who he was, what he stood for, what he had accomplished, and why he should be president. Consequently, the first series of ads aired by the Bush campaign immediately following the Republican National Convention provided the missing definition of Dukakis. The problem for the Democratic nominee was, of course, that the Republican definition was not very flattering.

Interestingly, the same thing happened to George H. W. Bush in 1992. In an examination of ads used in the presidential campaign, communication researcher L. Patrick Devlin argues that "the Bush Ad team was unable to emphasize a positive futuristic message."[26] Early in the campaign, there were only negative messages. When they began the positive ads, it was too late. In his study of the 1996 presidential campaign ads, Devlin reports that Bob Dole's efforts to define his character were also flawed. For example, Dole's biographic video included a good deal of black-and-white footage of Dole's war experiences, but it omitted any references to his thirty-five years in Congress. While his military accomplishments did make voters aware of the senator's service to his country during World War II, they did

not convince them that he was "the right person to be president." In addition, instead of focusing on a single theme or strategy, Dole's ads communicated multiple
messages about Dole as a person. As a result, the Dole camp fell behind and never
caught up with Clinton's lead.[27] However, by the 2000 campaign, Republicans had
learned about the value of positive messages. In fact, the Bush campaign used only
seventeen negative ads throughout the campaign, while the Gore campaign used
seventy-one.[28] Obama was most successful in both of his presidential campaigns
in defining the opposition, particularly Romney. Over the summer of 2012, the
Obama campaign spent a great deal on advertising portraying Romney as rich and
out of touch (focusing on Bain Capital's closure of businesses) and as a candidate
who flip-flopped on critical issues such as abortion.

A second important function performed by these ads includes using commercials to develop and explain the candidate's stand or position on issues. Not
only has television become the primary source of information, but political commercials have become a significant source of voter information about all aspects
of the campaign. As research has demonstrated, voters can learn more about a
candidate's position or stand on an issue from a commercial than they can by
watching the evening newscasts.[29] Moreover, ads have a cumulative effect in
that their frequent repetition during the course of a campaign helps voters learn
just where the candidate stands on a given issue. During the 1996 campaign,
Clinton made significant use of issue ads, especially during the general election
stage when 90 percent of the commercials were issue focused. Among the issues
emphasized were education, Medicare/elderly problems, the economy, crime,
and children's concerns.[30] In 2000, both presidential candidates used a number
of issues ads; Bush frequently focused on education, while Gore often explained
his position on education as well as on the environment. And in 2004, President
Bush focused on the threat of terrorism while Senator Kerry explained his position on taxes for the country's richest citizens. In 2008, the two presidential candidates spent much of their time talking about the economy. And again in 2012,
economic topics (jobs, taxes, government spending) dominated the presidential
ads, followed by health care and energy.[31]

Additional and related functions performed by spots that extol the candidate's
virtues include reinforcing the positive feelings of supporters and partisans (just
watching the ad may strengthen conviction of the rightness of one's cause or
choice of candidates), redefining or softening the candidate's image (in 1968,
Richard Nixon's earlier image as one of "life's losers" was redefined to "statesman," in part, by his television commercials, and in 1976 Gerald Ford's image as
a well-intentioned "buffoon" was redefined to "president" by the genius of the
campaign's "I'm Feeling Good about America" spots), raising money (in 1984,
Democrats used a special five-minute commercial about Walter Mondale so that
they could raise money from supporters to air future ads), presenting statistical or
"factual" information on issues (in 1992, Ross Perot's use of sixty-second "crawls"
made him appear knowledgeable and straightforward on issues important to the
campaign),[32] and focusing on shared public values (a component of Bill Clinton's
ad strategy in 1996 was that "public values beat private character"—the attempt
to divert attention away from character to the public values the president believed
he shared with voters, such as banning cigarette ads and protecting education and

the environment).[33] In short, ads whose purpose is to praise the candidate can fulfill functions important to the success of the campaign.

## Ads Condemning/Attacking/Questioning the Opponent

Just as a wide variety of videostyle factors can be used in ads that emphasize the virtues of the candidate, so, too, can a number of different techniques be utilized in spots that focus on the opponent. For example, contemporary campaigns have used techniques such as personal witness, comparison, negative association or concept, talking head, assaultive, or cinema verité. Although the videostyle factors can vary and, therefore, alter the directness and strength of the attack, the primary purpose cannot. These are ads designed to place the opponent in an unfavorable light or in an uncomfortable position. They focus on the shortcomings (real or imagined) of the opponent rather than the attributes of the candidate. In the largest sense, the purpose of this kind of ad—no matter the variability of techniques employed—is to increase the opponent's "negatives." They are most successful when they motivate voters to "vote against" the opponent. As such, they have received a good deal of attention from the public, as well as from journalists and scholars.

In most national and state campaigns, especially now with outside and special interest groups generating ads, the vast majority of the ads are "attack" or "negative" in nature. Most voters are fine with negative or attack ads as long as the attacks seem fair and legitimate. However, personal attacks on candidates or family members or name calling will anger voters. Thus, evidence suggests that strong attack ads can both mobilize or demobilize voters in favor of one candidate over another.[34]

Candidate position in the polls influences the use of negative or attack ads. Candidates behind in the polls usually attack the most. The further behind one is in a campaign, the more attacks or negative ads used. If an incumbent falls behind, the attacks will be more personal on issues of character or competence than on policy.[35]

Incumbents are more immune to attacks than challengers. They tend to have greater credibility with voters. It is usually best not to respond to attacks as an incumbent unless the campaign experiences slippage in the polls or favorable ratings.[36]

Since the introduction of televised ads whose purpose was to attack the opponent, a wide variety of formats and strategies has been employed. Some commercials have utilized humor and ridicule, others have linked the opponent with unpopular issues or negatively perceived people (guilt by association), some have fastened labels on their opponents and then defined those labels negatively, many have relied on fear appeals, and others have sought to create suspicion or anxiety about the opponent's beliefs or previous actions. At times, viewers are directed to make up their own minds; that is, the attack or condemnation is implied. For example, the records of the candidate and opponent are compared, and the opponent appears to have no positive attributes. But direct charges or conclusionary statements are not made. In other instances, the attack is direct and overt. For example, either in the narrative or by use of visual or aural symbols, viewers are told of the opponent's shortcomings. Clearly, depending on the videostyle and, of course, the intent, the commercials in this category can vary a good deal. Montague Kern has given names to two of the hardest-hitting spots and distinguished between them in terms of what we think of as their videostyle strategies—primarily format and production techniques. She calls them "soft-sell" ads that make "heavy use of lighter entertainment values, humor, self-deprecation, storytelling, or the unexpected turn of events"; and "hard-sell," those that utilize "dark colors and threatening voices" and create "harsh reality advertising."[37]

Without question, the heavy use of emotionally laden attack or condemnation spots continued through the 1988 presidential election into the campaigns of the 1990s. In fact, during the 1992 presidential campaign, candidates Bush and Clinton established an advertising record: 56 percent of the Bush ads were negative, 69 percent of the Clinton spots were negative, and each had "a 50/50 positive to negative ad buying ratio."[38] It was "a new high in negative advertising by two presidential candidates."[39]

But the trend continued in the 1996 general election campaign, which was considered "the most negative campaign in the history of presidential elections." According to Kaid, 71 percent of President Clinton's ads were categorized as negative, as were 61 percent of Senator Dole's. What's more, simply looking for the inclusion of a negative attack of some kind (as opposed to categorizing the entire ad as negative) showed that 85 percent of Clinton's ads contained a negative attack and 76 percent of Dole's ads had a negative component. In total, 81 percent of all 1996 general election campaign ads contained a negative attack.[40]

In campaign 2000, as noted earlier, the emphasis on negative ads changed, at least for the Republican candidate, George W. Bush, who used far fewer negative ads than did his Democratic opponent, Al Gore. But, in 2004, perhaps one of the most profound changes in presidential campaign ads occurred, when the 527 organizations began flooding the airwaves with some of the most negative ads since the 1964 "Daisy Girl" ad.

When the 2004 election was over, many scholars and journalists believed that it had been the worst the country had ever experienced because of the harshness, fear appeals, lying, and distortion in the attack spots sponsored by many of the 527 organizations. In fact, according to Kaid, both Bush and Kerry spent more time and money on commercials criticizing each other than they did talking about their own virtues.[41] Most interesting, however, was the candidates' use of fear appeals. Although Kaid found that President Bush was significantly more likely than Senator Kerry to try to frighten the American voter, the senator also used fear appeals—especially regarding the loss of manufacturing jobs in the country and low wages for American workers.

In 2008, 66 percent of Obama's general election ads were negative compared to 55 percent for McCain.[42] The negativity of presidential campaigns continued in 2012. Indeed, 75 percent of all the ads were negative.[43] Romney's 2012 campaign produced only 36 percent of the total Republican ads, and Obama 66 percent of Democrat ads. On the Republican side, 92 percent of all pro-Republican ads included some form of attack.[44] We have arrived at the unfortunate norm that despite the talk of running "an issues campaign," most ads are attack and negative.

For the most part, the communicative functions of attack ads are straightforward. If the candidate uses them early enough in the campaign and if they are aired frequently, they can set the rhetorical agenda for the opponent, who must respond in some fashion. Perhaps the best example of attack ads that seized the agenda were those used by a college professor, Paul Wellstone, in his successful 1990 campaign for the seat of the Minnesota incumbent, Senator Rudy Boschwitz. In a series of spots designed to paint Boschwitz as an out-of-touch, "inside-the-Beltway politician" who was concerned only with his image, Wellstone simultaneously made himself a credible candidate and taught Minnesota voters to "read Boschwitz's polished TV blitz as cynical imagemaking."[45] The spots were simple in terms of production—just the candidate and a camera. In one of the early commercials, "Looking for Rudy," Wellstone was seen "searching" for his "invisible" opponent. First, he looked at Boschwitz's St. Paul Senate office where he asked to borrow a pen to leave his telephone number for the senator (one of the ideas being conveyed was the "rich" Boschwitz campaign versus the "bare-bones" Wellstone effort), and then he "searched" at the Boschwitz Minneapolis headquarters and was told by two big men in suits "that we don't like strangers walking around here."

To some extent, the late Senator Wellstone's commercials had an even greater impact than they might have had in other campaign years. Not only did they attract attention because they were different from those used by other candidates, but the press effort to scrutinize political messages resulted in media discussion of the ads and, consequently, of Wellstone's issues.

A second function of attack ads is that they may well cause a defensive posture—even in a challenger—and therefore reduce the time, thought, and money that can be allocated to presenting a positive image. Similarly, and perhaps most apparent in recent campaigns, the use of attack or condemnation ads (if the charges against the opponent take hold in the public mind) can make, by comparison, even a mediocre candidate look better than the opponent. In the parlance of the consultants, candidates attempt to reduce their negatives and build their positives by increasing their opponents' negatives. The use of attack spots can also aid candidates by contributing to the perception of them as strong or decisive. This, for example, was clearly part of the 1996 strategy designed to allow Bill Clinton to run the most negative advertising campaign in the history of presidential elections yet be perceived by voters as less negative than Bob Dole. In the 2000 election, the Republican National Committee (RNC) was accused of sponsoring an ad that used subliminal messages, now infamously known as the "RATS" ad. This spot flashed at high speed the letters *r, a, t,* and *s* from the word *bureaucrats* and accused Vice President Gore of allowing bureaucrats to lessen the effectiveness of health-care plans. When the ad was played at normal speed, the letters were not visible; but in slow motion, the message, which was declared unintentional by the RNC, became more obvious.[46] However, the results of a study conducted by Lynda Lee Kaid indicated that this subliminal message made no difference in how voters reacted to the spot,[47] as we have already discussed, primarily because of the rise of negative attack ads and fear appeal ads used not only by the two political parties and candidates but also by the proliferation of independent groups (527s) whose total goal was destruction of one of the candidates.

Finally, employment of attack ads can function to divert public attention away from those issues that might threaten the incumbent or prove embarrassing for the challenger. In other words, they can serve to keep the focus of the campaign on areas of strength, avoiding areas of vulnerability. Clearly, many of these functions can block or prevent meaningful campaign dialogue.

### Ads Responding to Attacks or Innuendos

Until recently, little has been written about this final category of televised advertising, but, as is the case with the other two types, a wide variety of videostyles can be and has been employed by candidates as they attempt to answer charges or attacks that have been leveled against them. The only "rule" or "law" that appears to be consistent in regard to these ads is that they must occur and occur very rapidly, as well as repeatedly, after the initial attack. In fact, most media consultants believe that some response to a televised attack spot must be aired as soon as possible after the initial attack because people are influenced by them (many are disposed to believe the worst about politicians anyway). Some theorists believe that the only instance in which a candidate can get away without responding to an attack is when the attack has been made by a weak candidate (someone with "low name recognition, no prior electoral experience, inadequate funding").[48]

While a response commercial may take a variety of forms, the most frequently used are those that employ a refutation strategy (a direct rebuttal to the attack), a counterattack strategy (instead of refuting the charge, the candidate launches an attack on the character/issue positions/motives/actions of the attacker), or a humor/ridicule/absurdity strategy. For example, Senator John Melcher used a "Talking Cows" ad in 1982 to respond to charges that he was too liberal for Montana (Melcher was one of the incumbents whom the National Conservative Political Action Committee [NCPAC] had targeted for defeat). In one response, cows were talking and warned voters about outsiders in Montana who "have come to Montana to 'badmouth Doc Melcher'" and how the "cow pasture was full of material like NCPAC's."[49] There have been a number of successful response spots, and with each election campaign their use becomes more frequent—growing, obviously, in direct proportion to the increasing use of attack spots.

In subsequent elections, response ads not only became more plentiful, but they were on the air more rapidly than they had ever been in the past. Consultants frequently created and broadcast them within six hours, hastening the process by beaming the ads off satellites and sending them to television stations in specifically targeted areas. In fact, "satelliting" became a campaign buzzword. One of the reasons for focusing on a rapid response is that consultants fear the attack ads of the opponent will control the dialogue or even set the dialogue for the campaign. Although speeches given by candidates or written position papers were once the framework for dialogue, in recent years, the framework has frequently been the attack and response spots.

In the 1992 presidential campaign, one researcher described Bill Clinton's strategy as "to let no charge stay unanswered, to let no accusation remain in the news without being refuted by Clinton, his campaign spokesman, or his ads."[50] In the 1996 presidential election, response ads were once again a major category of Clinton ads. As the president's media producer stated, "It was our strategy to be reactive. In fact, we wanted these attacks because we wanted to rebut them so that people would grow increasingly comfortable with voting for the president."[51] In 2012, Obama attacked Romney beginning in spring and throughout the summer. Romney failed to respond. Obama's early "air war" enhanced his support and made Romney an unacceptable alternative. By fall, there were fewer persuadable voters for Romney.[52]

Without question, the most important communicative functions of response ads revolve around attempting to contain damage resulting from the attack. Specifically, the candidate's response must function to deflect attention away from the subject of the attack/charge and onto the candidate's own safe ground. Similarly, the ad should ideally function to put the candidate back in an offensive or "one-up" position. Candidates who must continually assume a defensive position rarely win the election.

One thesis regarding the strategy and defense of attack advertising is offered by Michael Pfau and Henry C. Kenski in their book *Attack Politics: Strategy and Defense*. They argue that the most effective strategy candidates can use is to preempt attacks before opponents use them, "thus militating their effectiveness." Specifically, Pfau and Kenski contend that one kind of preemption, inoculation message strategy, is most effective because it not only anticipates and responds to an opponent's attack before it is initiated, but it strengthens resistance to accepting or believing future attacks by exposing the voter to a "weak dose" of the attack. The "weak dose" is strong enough "to stimulate defenses but not strong enough to overwhelm him."[53]

Whether future candidates will take the advice of Pfau and Kenski in the use of response ads is difficult to forecast. In sum, we have attempted to present a complete yet uncomplicated view of the types of political commercials used by a wide variety of candidates in the television portion of their campaigns.

## FINAL QUESTIONS: HOW EFFECTIVE IS TELEVISION ADVERTISING AND DO TELEVISED ATTACK ADS WORK?

Most researchers agree that political advertising influences citizens, but measuring the effect and influence is challenging. Early research suggests that while political advertising does provide increased knowledge of campaigns and issues, its primary influence was reinforcement of individual predispositions. Individuals tend to attune only to candidates they favor or messages that confirm their existing beliefs, attitudes, and values. Thus, the predominant findings suggest that campaigns have "minimal effects" in terms of converting individuals over the course of a campaign.[54] More recent research suggests a theory of "conditional effects," suggesting that campaigns and political messages may influence some people depending upon their situation, personal characteristics, or social environmental factors.[55] However, it does appear that those who are less interested in politics ("political novices") are more prone to be influenced by campaigns and messages than those who are well informed and follow politics in general.[56] In sum, political advertising and campaigns do have some influence and can impact elections.

Questions and concerns about the use of televised attack advertising in political campaigns have risen almost as dramatically in the past two decades as has the employment of the genre itself. Out of all the dialogue, whether from journalists, consultants, political communication scholars, or even the public, we believe one important question emerges that has not yet been specifically addressed in this chapter: do televised attack ads work? Although areas of uncertainty remain, we believe that the bulk of the information available indicates that the answer to the question is yes. But an explanation is clearly in order.

The fact that since the 1984 election there has been a fairly consistent increase in the use of attack advertising by candidates at all levels suggests to us that political consultants who at least influence, if not make, the strategic choices in a campaign believe they are effective. Although consultants acknowledge the existence of some risks in using the option, clearly the frequency of their choice to "go negative" suggests more advantages than disadvantages.

One of the most discussed disadvantages in employing attack ads is that they will "turn voters off" or away from the election itself. However, although only a third of those eligible to vote actually do, there is really no direct evidence to indicate that people are ignoring their voting responsibilities because candidates employ attack advertising. In fact, the results of a 1990 study conducted, at least in part, to test the effect of attack advertising on the political process indicated that there is no real evidence that negative advertising has any effect on voter involvement. In fact, based on their findings, the researchers observed, "Perhaps negative advertising turns off some voters, yet motivates others to vote."[57]

Research suggests that negative ads increase cognitive understanding of issues[58] and influence evaluations of opponents.[59] Attacks on an opponent's issue positions are more effective than personal attacks,[60] and ads that attack the opponent but also provide a positive comparison are more effective and acceptable.[61]

Amy Jasperson and David Fan found that negative ads are four times more powerful in terms of effects than positive ads.[62] The second concern regards what researchers and practitioners call the backlash effect.[63] Because consultants and candidates fear such an effect, attack ads are frequently sponsored by a group that is technically not a part of the campaign, frequently a political action committee.[64] However, in many of the campaigns since 1984, consultants and candidates appear to have decided that the risk of backlash is acceptable because of the research that indicates that "over time voters tend to forget the origins of political messages while retaining their content."[65]

Despite the potential risks, most consultants believe that the advantages of using attack ads outweigh the disadvantages, and the preponderance of research suggests that voters are more influenced by attack ads than by nonattack ads, that they pay more attention to them, recall them more accurately, and remember them longer.[66] Thus, we conclude that there is one very good reason for the increased use of attack commercials: they work.

## CONCLUSIONS

In this chapter, we have examined the most common element in political campaigning today: televised advertising commercials. In so doing, we have briefly discussed their historical development in presidential politics and defined three types of commercials in terms of the overall communication functions they perform in contemporary campaigns. Finally, despite the general public's distaste for attack or negative ads, research suggests that they are effective in some ways. Today, most television political ads are negative in nature.

## NOTES

1. Erika Fowler, Michael Franz, and Travis Ridout, *Political Advertising in the United States* (Boulder, CO: Westview Press, 2016), xiv.

2. Ibid., 7.

3. Kathleen Hall Jamieson, *Packaging the Presidency: A History and Criticism of Presidential Campaign Advertising* (New York: Oxford University Press, 1984), 97.

4. Kathleen Hall Jamieson, "The Evolution of Political Advertising in America," in *New Perspectives on Political Advertising*, ed. Lynda Lee Kaid, Dan D. Nimmo, and Keith R. Sanders (Carbondale: Southern Illinois University Press, 1986), 15.

5. Ibid., 17.

6. Fowler, Franz, and Ridout, *Political Advertising*, 61.

7. Montague Kern, *30-Second Politics: Political Advertising in the Eighties* (New York: Praeger, 1989), 23–24.

8. Ibid.

9. Lynda Lee Kaid, "Political Advertising in the 1992 Campaign," in *The 1992 Presidential Campaign: A Communication Perspective*, ed. Robert E. Denton, Jr. (Westport, CT: Praeger, 1994), 118.

10. Lynda Lee Kaid, "Videostyle and the Effects of the 1996 Presidential Campaign Advertising," in *The 1996 Presidential Campaign*, ed. Robert E. Denton, Jr. (Westport, CT: Praeger, 1998), 149.

11. L. L. Kaid and A. Johnston, *Videostyles in Presidential Campaigns* (Westport, CT: Praeger, 2001).

12. Lynda Kaid, "Political Web Wars: The Use of the Internet for Political Advertising," in *The Internet Election: Perspectives on the Web in Campaign 2004*, ed. Andrew Paul Williams and John C. Tedesco (Lanham, MD: Rowman & Littlefield, 2006), 67–82.

13. Ibid.

14. Ibid.

15. Lynda L. Kaid, "Videostyle in the 2008 Presidential Advertising," in *The 2008 Presidential Campaign: A Communication Perspective*, ed. Robert E. Denton, Jr. (Lanham, MD: Rowman & Littlefield, 2009), 210.

16. John Tedesco and Scott Dunn, "Political Advertising in the 2012 US Presidential Election," in *The 2012 Presidential Campaign: A Communication Perspective*, ed. Robert E. Denton, Jr. (Lanham, MD: Rowman & Littlefield, 2013), 78.

17. Fowler, Franz, and Ridout, *Political Advertising*, xiv.

18. Edwin Diamond and Stephen Bates, *The Spot: The Rise of Political Advertising on Television*, 3rd ed. (Cambridge, MA: MIT Press, 1992), 293–345.

19. L. Patrick Devlin, "An Analysis of Presidential Television Commercials, 1952–1984," in *New Perspectives on Political Advertising*, ed. Lynda Lee Kaid, Dan D. Nimmo, and Keith R. Sanders (Carbondale: Southern Illinois University Press, 1986), 21–54.

20. Kern, *30-Second Politics*, 51–54.

21. Richard Joslyn, "Political Advertising and the Meaning of Elections," in *New Perspectives on Political Advertising*, ed. Lynda Lee Kaid, Dan D. Nimmo, and Keith R. Sanders (Carbondale: Southern Illinois University Press, 1986), 139–83.

22. Jamieson, "Evolution of Political Advertising," 17–19.

23. Arthur H. Miller and Bruce E. Gronbeck, eds., *Presidential Campaigns and American Self Images* (Boulder, CO: Westview Press, 1994), 67.

24. Lynda Lee Kaid and Dorothy K. Davidson, "Elements of Videostyle: Candidate Presentation through Television Advertising," in *New Perspectives on Political Advertising*, ed. Lynda Lee Kaid, Dan D. Nimmo, and Keith R. Sanders (Carbondale: Southern Illinois University Press, 1986), 184–209.

25. Devlin, "An Analysis of Presidential Television Commercials, 1952–1984," 32.

26. L. Patrick Devlin, "Contrasts in Presidential Campaign Commercials of 1992," *American Behavioral Scientist* 37 (November/December 1993): 282.

27. L. Patrick Devlin, "Contrasts in Presidential Campaign Commercials of 1996," *American Behavioral Scientist* 40 (August 1997): 1067.

28. John C. Tedesco and Lynda Lee Kaid, "Style and Effects of the Bush and Gore Spots," in *The Millennium Election: Communication in the 2000 Campaign*, ed. Lynda Lee Kaid, Dianne Bystrom, and Mitchell McKinney (Lanham, MD: Rowman & Littlefield, 2003).

29. Devlin, "Contrasts in Presidential Campaign Commercials of 1992," 283.

30. Kaid, "Videostyle and the Effects of the 1996 Presidential Campaign Advertising," 149 and 151.

31. Tedesco and Dunn, "Political Advertising in the 2012 US Presidential Election," 81.

32. Devlin, "Contrasts in Presidential Campaign Commercials of 1992," 288.

33. Devlin, "Contrasts in Presidential Campaign Commercials of 1996," 1060.

34. Fowler, Franz, and Ridout, *Political Advertising*, 177.

35. Jason Johnson, *Political Consultants and Campaigns: One Day Sale* (Boulder, CO: Westview Press, 2012), 134.

36. Ibid., 135.

37. Kern, *30-Second Politics*, 94.

38. Devlin, "Contrasts in Presidential Campaign Commercials of 1992," 287.

39. Ibid.

40. Kaid, "Videostyle and the Effects of the 1996 Presidential Campaign Advertising," 148–49.

41. Lynda Lee Kaid, "Videostyle in the 2004 Presidential Advertising," in *The 2004 Presidential Campaign: A Communication Perspective*, ed. Robert E. Denton, Jr. (Lanham, MD: Rowman & Littlefield, 2005), 205, 283–300.

42. Kaid, "Videostyle in the 2008 Presidential Advertising," 216.

43. "2012 Obama vs Romney," *The Living Room Candidate*, accessed February 21, 2015, www.livingroomcandidate.org/commercials/2012.

44. Tedesco and Dunn, "Political Advertising in the 2012 US Presidential Campaign," 80, 92.

45. Charles Trueheart, "The Incumbent Slayer from Minnesota," *Washington Post National Weekly Edition*, November 26–December 2, 1990, 10.

46. Lynda Lee Kaid, "TechnoDistortions and Effects of the 2000 Political Advertising," *American Behavioral Scientist* 44, no. 12 (August 2001): 2371.

47. Ibid.

48. Michael Pfau and Henry C. Kenski, *Attack Politics* (Westport, CT: Praeger, 1990), 36.

49. Ibid., 22.

50. Devlin, "Contrasts in Presidential Campaign Commercials of 1992," 275.

51. Devlin, "Contrasts in Presidential Campaign Commercials of 1996," 1063.

52. Hank C. Kenski and Kate M. Kenski, "Explaining the Vote in the Election of 2012: Obama's Reelection," in *The 2012 Presidential Campaign: A Communication Perspective*, ed. Robert E. Denton, Jr. (Lanham, MD: Rowman & Littlefield, 2013), 187.

53. Pfau and Kenski, *Attack Politics*, xiv.

54. Fowler, Franz, and Ridout, *Political Advertising*, 138–39.

55. Ibid., 139.

56. Ibid., 140.

57. Gina M. Garramone, Charles K. Atkin, Bruce E. Pinkleton, and Richard T. Cole, "Effects of Negative Political Advertising on the Political Process," *Journal of Broadcasting and Electronic Media* 34 (Summer 1990): 308.

58. Craig Brians and M. W. Wattenberg, "Campaign Issue Knowledge and Salience: Comparing Reception from TV Commercials, TV News, and Newspapers," *American Journal of Political Science* 40 (1996): 172–93.

59. Spencer Tinkham and Ruth Ann Weaver-Lariscy, "A Diagnostic Approach to Assessing the Impact of Negative Political Television Commercials," *Journal of Broadcasting and Electronic Media* 37 (1993): 377–99.

60. Kenneth L. Fridkin and Patrick J. Kenney, "Do Negative Messages Work? The Impact of Negativity on Citizens' Evaluations of Candidates," *American Politics Research* 32 (2004): 570–605.

61. Patrick Meirick, "Cognitive Responses to Negative and Comparative Political Advertising," *Journal of Advertising* 31, no. 1 (2002): 49–62.

62. Amy Jasperson and David P. Fan, "An Aggregate Examination of the Backlash Effect in Political Advertising: The Case of the 1996 U.S. Senate Race in Minnesota," *Journal of Advertising* 31, no. 1 (2002): 1–12.

63. Gina M. Garramone, "Voter Responses to Negative Political Ads," *Journalism Quarterly* 61 (Summer 1984): 250–59. Also see Gina M. Garramone, "Effects of Negative Political Advertising: The Roles of Sponsor and Rebuttal," *Journal of Broadcasting and Electronic Media* 29 (Spring 1985): 147–59; Lynda Lee Kaid and John Boydston, "An Experimental Study of the Effectiveness of Negative Political Advertisements," *Communication Quarterly* 35 (Spring 1987): 193–201.

64. Garramone, "Effects of Negative Political Advertising."

65. Pfau and Kenski, *Attack Politics*, 158.

66. Ibid., 4.

# 6

*≈*

# Ethical Considerations of Political Campaign Communication

For most Americans, to link the terms *ethics* and *politics* is either naïve or comical. The concept of "political campaign communication ethics" may well be considered an oxymoron. However, those of us in the disciplines of rhetoric and communication studies recognize the essential ethical dimensions of all human communication.[1] Richard Johannesen, Kathleen Valde, and Karen Whedbee posit that ethical issues are inherent in any instance of communication "to the degree that the communication can be judged on a right-wrong dimension, that it involves possible significant influence on other humans, and that the communicator consciously chooses specific ends sought and communicative means to achieve those ends."[2]

Since the beginning of time, humans have expressed a concern for ethics. Plato's *Republic* is essentially a work of political ethics, as is Aristotle's *Nicomachean Ethics*. For both Plato and Aristotle, the good person was a conscientious citizen contributing to the city-state. The notion of civic virtue implies a citizenry that is informed, active, selfless, enlightened, and, above all, just. For Aristotle, a rhetor's character or ethos was the most important element in public discourse. Quintilian argued that a good orator was a "good man speaking well." St. Augustine very clearly described the responsibility to communicate honestly. "It is evident that speech was given to man, not that man might therewith deceive one another, but that one man might make known his thoughts to another. To use speech, then, for the purposes of deception, and not for its appointed end, is a sin."[3] We have choices in what we say and how we say it.

Communication ethics are requisite for social relationships and trust. Sissela Bok argues, "there must be a minimal degree of trust in communication for language and action to be more than stabs in the dark. This is why some level of truthfulness has always been seen as essential to human society, no matter how deficient the observance of other moral principles."[4] She cautions that trust in some degree of veracity is a foundation for relationships among human beings; without it, institutions would collapse. More than forty years ago philosopher Jack

Odell recognized and proclaimed, "a society without ethics is a society doomed to extinction. . . . Ethical principles are necessary preconditions for the existence of a social community. Without ethical principles, it would be impossible for human beings to live in harmony and without fear, despair, hopelessness, anxiety, apprehension, and uncertainty."[5]

Historically, there has always been great skepticism about the practice of politics and, above all, about politicians. In many public opinion polls, politicians rank below car salespeople and attorneys as the most dishonest profession. In recent years, Congress has reached single digits in approval among the public. Traditionally, communication is thought to be the primary means through which a nation forges a common identity, a common purpose, and a common resolve. At the very heart of democracy is public communication. The quality of that public communication directly impacts the quality of our democracy and society at large.

Americans place great faith in the ability of citizens to make rational and reasonable decisions in life. We also believe strongly in the guarantees of the First Amendment: freedom of speech and freedom of the press. These values and practices place a special burden on those who communicate with others in any context or intent. With freedom comes responsibility of the communicator for the form and content of our communication behavior. The notion of the responsible (and hence ethical) communicator lies in the very nature or characteristics of a Democratic form of government. Related to the notion of responsibility is that of accountability. Because citizens delegate authority to those who hold office, politicians must answer to the public for all actions and deeds. Especially in a democracy, accurate information is critical for citizens to make informed judgments and evaluations of elected officials. Incomplete or inaccurate information can lead to bad public decisions. Also, vital to the concept of democracy is the concept of a free marketplace of ideas. Diversity of thought and respect for dissent are hallmarks of the values of freedom and justice. When multiple viewpoints are heard and expressed, the common good prevails over private interests. Finally, related to the above notion of the marketplace of ideas, we enjoy a process of collective deliberation on disputes about issues and fundamental values. National and public debate determines the collective wisdom and hence the will of the people.

Is there a relationship between government and cultural values? Is there a relationship between the current divisions, polarizations, and coarseness of our culture and the general distrust and cynicism toward government? We certainly think so. According to public opinion polls, many Americans have lost confidence in their government and trust in elected officials and politicians. Government and the political process are viewed as dominated by special interests rather than notions of the "common good" for all Americans. Citizens feel caught in the crossfire of self-interested politicians, special interest groups, and large corporations.

A democratic government is a reflection of its citizens. And the values of the citizens will be reflected in the behaviors of elected officials and government. Our body politic is fractured in many ways. If we want moral leaders, then we need to be moral. If we want leaders to act in the common interest of all Americans, then we need to be less self-centered and more other focused. If all interest is self-interest, then our "social contract" with one another is in danger and democracy as a form of government becomes virtually impossible.

## AGE OF CITIZEN MISTRUST, POLARIZATION, AND CYNICISM

Much of today's rise in public alienation is fed by incessant scandal and our mistrust has created political habits and institutions that now continue to produce ever more mistrust and cynicism. We continue to lose good people in public service. Much has changed in the intervening millennia. Life today is more individualistic; we are concerned with self-actualization, "success," comfort, convenience, acquisition of material, and the pursuit of happiness. For nearly three decades, there have been increasing numbers of studies, polls, and news articles lamenting the decline of ethical behavior in America.

The fragmented nature of society today makes defining ethical behavior more difficult. We separate our world into personal, business, political, and religious realms. We approach each realm with a different set of behaviors. The segmentation can be an excuse to ignore ethical behavior appropriate in one context if we're operating in a different realm. We might find lying to our spouse completely unacceptable but could soften the stance on lying if talking to a supervisor. Deception and fraud abound in society across all occupations and socioeconomic groups. Individuals from the fields of entertainment, business, politics, and others too numerous to list are frequently in the news as a consequence of acts of deception. These examples don't remove the responsibility of conducting ourselves in an ethical manner, but they offer abundant rationales if we're looking for excuses.

There has been an obvious continual decline of the public's trust in government. Since 1958, the University of Michigan's Survey Research Center has tracked how much the public trusts the government in Washington to "do what is right." This annual survey confirms the suspicions that Americans are losing confidence in their government. In 1958, 78 percent of the public said they could trust government all or most of the time. The numbers stayed at that level until the second year of Lyndon Johnson's administration, dropping to 69 percent. By 1976, the number had fallen to 35 percent. During the Reagan years, the numbers were in the low 40s. However, by the 1992 presidential campaign, only about 23 percent thought the government could be trusted to do what's right all or most of the time. During Bill Clinton's first term, the number was on average about 20 percent and during his second term about 30 percent of Americans could trust government to do what is right. Interestingly, George W. Bush was the first president since Richard Nixon during whose term trust in government surpassed 50 percent. But that was short lived, with a steady decline back to 24 percent. Even with the hope and optimism of the Barack Obama presidency, trust in government hovered in the mid- to low 20 percent.[6] Donald Trump finished his first year of the presidency with 20 percent trust in government.[7]

When Gallup breaks down confidence in government by branch of government, all the executive branches are at or near historic lows. Congress went from 24 percent in 2000 to just 7 percent approval in 2015. Those who have a great deal or quite a lot of confidence in the Supreme Court went from 47 percent in 2000 to 30 percent in 2015. In terms of the presidency, confidence has fallen from 42 percent in 2000 to 29 percent in 2015.[8] Confidence in all branches of government improved in 2016, but was still within historic low ranges.[9]

America's general angst against government and politicians continues. Since 2010 to date, on average 65 percent of Americans think the country is heading in the wrong direction.[10] In fact, since 1972 Americans have generally believed that America is on the "wrong track." During the Reagan administration from 1984 to 1986, nearly 60 percent of Americans thought the nation was on the right track, as well as in the final years of the Clinton administration and post–9/11, but that positive feeling only lasted for seven months.[11] According to Gallup, only 54 percent of citizens are proud to be an American, down from 70 percent in 2003. Only 43 percent of those under thirty indicate that they are proud to be an American.[12]

Since 1966 the Harris Poll has measured how alienated Americans feel. They have formed an Alienation Index. In 2015 the Poll Alienation Index was an incredible 70 and in 2016 the rating was 80, highest in in the history of the poll. The index of 70 compares to 67 in 2013, 63 in 2011, 52 in 2010, and 53 in 2009. More specifically, in 2016, 82 percent of Americans believed that "the people running the country don't really care what happens to you," which is down from 85 percent in 2015; 78 percent believed "the rich are getting richer and the poor are getting poorer"; 70 percent believed that most people in power "try to take advantage of people like you"; 68 percent believed that "what you think doesn't count very much anymore"; and 40 percent believed that "they are left out of things going on around them."[13]

Finally, numerous studies and surveys report the highest levels of political polarization in terms of beliefs, values, and ideology in American history. Over two decades the national divide grew over issues of race, income, gender, morality, and even geographical divides across the nation. According to the Pew Center for Research, political polarization is the defining feature of the early twenty-first century. In a year-long study, they found that Republicans and Democrats are further apart from an ideological perspective than ever before in recent history. This polarization is both political and personal. The number of Americans who consistently express liberal or conservative views has doubled over the last twenty years from 10 percent to 21 percent. This means that Republicans are more conservative than 94 percent of Democrats and Democrats are 92 percent more liberal than Republicans, compared to 70 percent and 64 percent, respectively, twenty years ago. Unfavorable opinions of the opposite party have also gone up, with 43 percent of Republicans revealing "very unfavorable" views of the Democratic Party and 38 percent of Democrats having "very unfavorable" views of Republicans. In both cases, the percentage has more than doubled in the past twenty years. The studies also show that "consistent conservatives" (63 percent) and "consistent liberals" (49 percent) mainly interact with people and friends of similar viewpoints. Finally, the center has gotten smaller and even so-called moderates tend to be more passionate on specific issues such as immigration, gun control, or health care policy.[14]

Another indication of the polarization of politics in America is revealed in media usage. Evidence suggests that Americans tend to select their source of news based upon perceptions of philosophical and ideological leanings within the news broadcasts. Examples across the media abound but it is safe to speculate that Fox News enjoys more conservative viewers and Republicans whereas CNN attracts more liberals and Democrats. Also, liberals tend to watch the mainstream network news while conservatives listen to talk radio. Thus, the Pew Research Center found that the most consistent ideological views on the right and left expose themselves to media distinct from each other. Even in terms of social media, when on Facebook folks are more likely to hear opinions similar to their own and are more likely to have friends who share their worldview and more likely to "block" or "unfriend" someone on social media because of political views.[15]

As public cynicism and distrust toward government and politics grow, there are parallel concerns about the ever-increasing coarseness and rudeness of our culture. According to Michael Josephson of the Josephson Institute of Ethics, "we have become desensitized to the enormous significance of lying. The effects are all destructive, generally lowering the level of trust in anything we read or hear."[16] The cumulative effect is to give everyone permission to lie because, most certainly, the powerful do so.

Jennifer Lawless and Richard Fox argue that today's young Americans have grown up during a time of political turmoil, division, and deep partisanship. They have come to know politics through "spectacle." Consequently, many young Americans "see politics as pointless and unpleasant. They see political leaders as corrupt and selfish. They have no interest in entering the political arena."[17]

Thus, for nearly three decades, only about a third of Americans generally trust government. Government and the political processes are viewed as dominated by special interests rather than notions of the "common good" for all Americans. Many citizens feel caught between the crossfire of self-interested politicians, special interest groups, and large corporations. Divisions have grown across issues of race, gender, income, and the very role of government in American life. Increasingly, Americans find campaigns too intense, personal, and negative. Independent voters are the fasting growing segment and partisans view the opposition with distain. Most Americans no longer believe promises undertaken in the heat of campaigns. For many voters, it becomes a matter of who will do less damage while in office, the lesser of two evils.

## A "PHILOSOPHY" OF POLITICAL CAMPAIGN ETHICS

As already noted, freedom of speech is a fundamental value of democracy. With that freedom comes responsibility—responsibility for the form and content of our communication behavior. Thus, at the heart of democracy, and certainly politics, is public communication. The quality of that public communication directly impacts the quality of our democracy and society at large.

The notion of ethics is about values, judgment, and conduct. Values frame the content of ethical considerations, judgment becomes the principles and rules one uses in conduct or behavior. From this perspective, ethics refers to standards of conduct based on moral duties and virtues derived from principles of right and wrong. There are behavioral dimensions to ethics involving the ability to discern right from wrong and a commitment to do what is right, good, and appropriate. Thus, it is important to note the action dimension to ethics. It implies more than words; it involves active compliance with rules or standards of behavior.

Society collectively forms the expectations for behavior. Ethical principles are the rules of conduct derived from a culture's ethical values. For example, honesty is a value. From this value, we form many principles such as to be truthful, don't mislead, don't cheat, and others. Sometimes principles become laws to ensure social compliance. Some might argue that government has overstepped its boundaries in trying to legislate morals. However, those who see a decline of morals may well advocate even more laws to regulate behavior.

Louis Day makes the case that all societies need a system of ethics for social stability. According to him, "ethics is the foundation of our advanced civilization, a cornerstone that provides some stability to society's moral expectations."[18] A system of ethics serves as a moral gatekeeper by identifying and ranking the norms and morals of a society. A system of ethics also helps societies resolve conflicts and establishes rules and laws for behavior. Finally, a system of ethics helps clarify competing values and new social dilemmas.

Along with the need for a system of ethics for social stability, Celeste Condit argues for the need for public morality. For her, public morality is "constructed by collectivities through their public discourse in a process of reflexive reproduction that utilizes the capacity of discourse simultaneously to create, extend, and apply moral concepts."[19] The public and the individual interact to produce morality. More specifically, "it is through the arguments of individuals about enactment of particular moral rulings that the collective moral code is built."[20] The process of constructing public morality "fulfills the human urge for goodness, creativity, and perfection."[21]

Aristotle recommended that a true student of politics must study "virtue above all things."[22] Moral virtues, such as those of "courage, moderation, and justice" dispose us toward good behavior. Moral virtue, for Aristotle, comes about as a result of habit. Thus, repeated "good" acts develop facilities for acting rightly in the future. From this classical perspective, the "good life" is the morally good life, and political authority is responsible for creating an environment for citizens, and hence the state, to develop themselves morally.[23]

Rabindra Kanungo and Manuel Mendonca categorize virtues into four groups. The moral virtues consist of honesty, truthfulness, decency, courage, and justice. Intellectual virtues are thoughtfulness, strength of mind, and curiosity. Communal virtues include neighborliness, charity, self-support, helpfulness, cooperativeness, and respect for others. Political virtues are commitment to the common good, respect for law, and responsible participation.[24] It is the concerns with political virtues that must guide political campaign communication.

Collins and Skover distinguish the principles of political discourse characterized by rational decision making, civic participation, meaningful dissent, and self-realization from contemporary political speech characterized by entertainment, passivity, pleasure, and self-gratification. Note that for them, political discourse is conducted within the framework of traditional American political values of freedom, but also in terms of equality, mutual respect, and opportunity for all voices and sides to be heard. For them, we are on the border of equating "amusement with enlightenment, fantasy with fact, and the base with the elevated."[25]

Before we consider political campaign ethics, we wish to address the importance of ethical and moral leaders. We believe that leaders are important. They do more than initiate policy. Leaders inspire and motivate us as individuals and as a nation. In our opinion, all elected leaders are and should be role models. Collectively, elected officials at all levels reflect the values, hopes, and aspirations of the nation.

Today, as never before, we need to select moral leaders. We recognize that the use of the word *moral* may be problematic for some. However, for reasons that will become clear, we think the word is most appropriate in considering the role of public service and leadership. At the very least, we should select leaders of character and integrity. We should actively seek those who reflect the very best of personal values. Our expectations should exceed those of the private sector. Elected officials are more than managers. Moral leadership is more than words.

There were strong public expectations of moral public leadership in the eighteenth and nineteenth centuries. People were elected because of their past and often heroic behavior. Public service was viewed as a trust, an obligation, and an honor. By the twentieth century, management skills took priority over character. The rise of the professional politician replaced the genuine public servant. Elected office became a prize, less an opportunity to "do good." Personal power rather than genuine public service became a primary motive. Politics became largely a game and less a method or channel of service.

Robert Putnam popularized the notion of "moral capital."[26] As citizens, we make moral judgments about people, places, and institutions. When our judgments are positive, they inspire trust, belief, and allegiance that politically may in turn produce willing acquiescence, obedience, loyalty, support, action, and even sacrifice.

It is important for politicians to be seen to serve and to stand for something apart from their own self-interests. In short, they must establish a moral grounding. "This they do," according to Putnam, "by avowing their service to some set of fundamental values, principles and goals that find a resonant response in significant numbers of people. When such people judge the agent or institution to be both faithful and effective in serving those values and goals, they are likely to bestow some quantum of respect and approval that is of great political benefit to the receiver. This quantum is the agent's moral capital."[27]

Moral capital is different from mere popularity. Popularity may be based in part on moral judgment or appraisals but is more often based on other sources of attraction. Popularity may be bought, but moral capital cannot.

Leadership is essentially about relationships, and at the heart of any relationship is trust. For two decades, Kouzes and Posner have surveyed the general public to identify the characteristics of most admired leaders. Although they differ in order from year to year, only four characteristics continuously receive the most votes: honest, forward-looking, inspiring, and competent.[28] Note that trust emerges as the single most important characteristic. People want to know their leaders are truthful, ethical, and principled.

Mutual trust is the foundation of democratic self-rule. John Locke viewed the special relationship between citizens and the executive as a fiduciary trust.[29] The government as trustee incurs an obligation to act for the public good. In giving our support and trust to a leader, we the citizens bestow legitimacy upon the government and leader. Trust is given in exchange for a vote. Elections determine the object of trust, but then it must be earned through deeds, words, and legislative actions. In general, the public cedes power to make decisions based on implicit and explicit understandings. It is assumed that politicians will act in the public interest, not self-interest. It is assumed that leaders will be honest with the American people, and provide debate and information to support decisions and actions. Finally, it is assumed that elected officials will use the powers of the office in reasonable, responsible, and competent ways.

Studies have also shown that ethical conduct by leaders increases ethical conduct by followers.[30] Ethical behavior by leaders may excite admiration but also invite imitation. With ethical leadership, public cynicism decreases and public trust increases. However, Kouzes and Posner argue that over time, when we lose respect for our leaders, we lose respect for ourselves.[31] In many ways, as Edmund Burke noted, great leaders "are the landmarks and guideposts of the state."[32] When guideposts misdirect, citizens who follow their leaders begin to wallow and become lost. Indeed, the public's confidence and trust provide the context in which elected leaders initiate policy, respond to challenges, and in general govern. The more trust and confidence the public has in a president, for example, the more latitude the president has to take action and shape policy. Thus, once again, we see that trust is the bond that holds a democracy together: trust in government, in public institutions, in social and private relationships, and among each other.

## CAMPAIGNS AND ETHICS

When it comes to considerations of ethical communication from a political perspective, Karl Wallace identifies four values that are essential to our political system. The first is the "habit of search" requiring communicators to ensure that they have sufficient and adequate information about the topic or issue discussed. Second is the "habit of justice" in presenting information and opinion fairly. The third value addresses the issue of motivation. For Wallace, it is important to "prefer public to private motivations." One is communicating for the public good, thus avoiding bias, prejudice, or falsehoods. The final value is the "habit of respect for dissent," being tolerant of the expression of counter or opposing views and opinions.[33]

Persuasion is an essential tool of communication, and hence, politics and campaigns. As a tool, the process of persuasion can be used by both good and bad people for equally good or bad purposes. No one strategy or tactic is good or bad. Strategies and tactics of persuasion are just that. It is the motives of persuaders that determine if the use of specific strategies is good or bad. How and why they are used provides a context for judgment. Craig Smith makes a distinction between strategy and ethics related to political campaign communication. "Every rhetorical effort varies with respect to ethics (from low to high) and strategy (from low to high); neither variable predicts the other."[34] For example, most academics and politicians complain about the use of overtly emotional rather than more rational or logical appeals. However, one could argue that to use a strong emotional or fear appeal in producing a teenage anti–drunk driving ad may well be appropriate.

To address the notion of campaign ethics is a very difficult and challenging task. In actuality, most of us do not experience campaigns firsthand, even in local elections. Political campaigns are mediated events. We experience campaigns, the candidates, and the issues through media portrayals from a variety of sources and across a variety of media platforms. How we form political attitudes and candidate images of competence, leadership, and character depends largely on the sources we attune for information, mediums viewed, and messages attended. Seldom does one message determine preference, unless one is a single-issue voter. The process of years of political socialization, years of media exposure, conditions specific responses during campaigns. Given the complexity of the media's role in electoral politics, it is difficult to trace all the strands of campaign ethics.

To further complicate considerations of campaign ethics, there are many players involved in campaigns: candidates, consultants, reporters, editors, special interest groups, and others. There are certainly no uniform considerations of ethics or motivations among all the players, although it is important to note that each has some role in determining how candidates are portrayed or presented and in the strategies of campaigns.

In addition, there are numerous and varied media and candidate activities involved in campaigns, from simple bumper stickers and brochures to political advertising, to two-minute news packages, to the talking-head political shows, to the constantly increasing number of candidate debates, to name only a few. Thus, as is one of the themes of this chapter, the ethical concerns or decisions lie not in the "machinery" of campaigns but in the people who use the media, strategies, and tactics. While this rationale is perhaps rather obvious and simplistic, it is at the core of understanding ethical dimensions of campaigns from all participants to include citizens. Of course, intentionality is a variable of ethics, but so is capability or access. For example, many scholars have targeted television as a medium over the years as the source of numerous social and political ills: reduced voter turnout, decline of political parties, decline of political participation, reduction of issue discussion to sound bites, automatic reelection of incumbents, increased use of symbolic rather than problem-solving strategies of leadership, and an increase of general public distrust and cynicism. Are these concerns the results of the medium itself, the content, access, control, or socialization (i.e., how we *use* a medium)?

Finally, there really is no single set of standards, criteria, or behavior that defines political campaign ethics, despite the proliferation of individual codes of ethics for professional groups and consultants. Everyone, from consultants to candidates to citizens, would argue for the necessity to tell the truth in political ads. However, as already noted and will be mentioned below, do ads generally tell the "whole truth and nothing but the truth?" While what is said may be true, what is *not* said could be more useful in voter decision making. By practice, political ads only tell part of any story or political claim.

A number of years ago, Bruce Gronbeck developed a model to assess ethical issues of presidential campaigns.[35] He views campaigns as corporate rhetorical ventures in which it is becoming increasingly difficult to place blame on individuals. Gronbeck argues that in order to make ethical assessments, citizens reduce campaigns to comprehensible dramas where they examine the action (motives),

**Table 6.1.   Ethical Pivots**

| Moral Vantages | Motives | Character | Competence |
|---|---|---|---|
| Message Makers | Are candidates' motives acceptable? | Are candidates' characterological styles acceptable? | Have candidates demonstrated political competence? |
| Message Consumers | What political motives do sets of voters find acceptable? | What characterological styles do sets of voters find acceptable? | What measures of competence are used by particular sets of voters? |
| Messages | Are candidates' motives expressed in acceptable ways? | Are candidates' characterological styles depicted in acceptable ways? | Are candidates illustrating their political competence in messages and responses to opponents' messages? |
| Situations | What motives are acceptable in various situations? | What characterological styles are expected in various situations? | Do candidates read various political situations competently? |

people (character), and thoughts (competence as politicians) of the candidates. These dramas can be assessed from four moral vantage points: message makers, message consumers, the messages themselves, and situation expectations. In constructing a 3 × 4 matrix (see table 6.1), Gronbeck generates twelve questions voters should ask in assessing the ethical dimensions of presidential candidates.

## AREAS OF ETHICAL CONCERNS IN POLITICAL CAMPAIGN COMMUNICATION

It should be obvious by now that any ethical concerns of political campaigns reside with us as citizens, candidates, operatives, elected officials, and professional communicators. And considerations of ethics are essential in democratic forms of government. Thus, there are ethical concerns at every phase, component, and practice of political campaign communication. Indeed, entire volumes could be written addressing all the various areas and abuses of political campaign communication. Here, we will note two broad areas of concern: news media and political advertising.

### News Media and Journalism

It has already been noted that political campaigns are primarily mediated events. The single greatest area of debate and concern is the news media and journalism. For over two decades there has been growing concern about the practice of journalism in America. Criticisms range from allegations of bias and distortion to outright lying. The attack upon the press reached new levels during the 2016 presidential campaign, as noted in chapter 14. The so-called mainstream media became a target of the Trump campaign during the election, which continued into his presidency.

From a historical perspective, most of the concerns center on several broad themes. First, there is concern about how the media cover people, places, and events. Some argue that the coverage is largely irrelevant to the average citizen. Journalists tend to ask questions for themselves rather than questions that reflect the interests of citizens. The questions tend to be hostile and technical and attempt to trap or catch the interviewee in a misstatement. The news media provide far more coverage on people than events, sensational behaviors rather than the routine, and superficial overviews rather than in-depth analyses that may well inform voters on issue positions. Certainly, the last couple of national elections have seen the rise of tabloid journalism where drama is created, seeking emotional reactions rather than focusing on audience education and reporting. Some news outlets started paying sources for exclusive interviews or accepting limitations to questions that a journalist can ask. As audience viewing eroded for the traditional outlets, even more attention to the values of drama and entertainment were used in presenting the news.

Another major concern of media critics is the negativity of the press that has contributed to public alienation from the political process. Since the 1970s, journalists have increasingly put more negative presentations of events and spin on issues. Since Watergate, news coverage in general became more negative. This is also true for coverage of presidential campaigns. With the exception of the 2008 presidential campaign with Barack Obama, all other candidates since 1982 actually received more negative tone in coverage than positive.[36] The trends continue after the elections, especially for Republican presidents. For example, in the 2016 presidential race, 77 percent of media coverage for Donald Trump and 64 percent for Hillary Clinton was negative.[37] The Shorenstein Center on Media, Politics, and Public Policy found that 93 percent of media coverage of Donald Trump's first one hundred days in office was negative in tone—a historic record.[38]

Related are the constant and continual claims of media bias. For more than thirty years academics, media professionals, and partisan pundits have proclaimed allegations of media bias. Literally for decades, conservative politicians, pundits, and talk show celebrities complained about what they perceived as the liberal bias of the mainstream media and most cable news organizations. Indeed, Brant Bozell founded the Media Research Center in 1987 to "bring balance and responsibility to the news media" and to systematically document "the extent of media bias."[39] However, in the early 2000s, academics and pundits found no bias and a few proclaiming conservative biases.[40]

From a more technical perspective, much of the criticism of contemporary journalism focuses on the coverage of politics and political campaigns. Joseph Cappella and Kathleen Jamieson argue that the contemporary journalistic culture and its focus on strategy, conflict, and motives encourage public cynicism.[41] Specifically, they claim that voters exposed to news framed in terms of campaign strategy report higher levels of cynicism than those who saw it framed in the more traditional problem-solution story formats. Campaign strategy coverage is composed of several characteristics: winning and losing are the central concerns; the language of war, games, and competition dominates; stories with performers, critics, and audience hold attention; performance, style, and perception of the candidate are central features; and an overabundance exists of reporting based on polls, those generated by the media outlets. In 2004, 48 percent of the network news stories focused on campaign strategies, tactics, and projected winners or losers.[42] In 2008, 59 percent focused on strategy/tactics, horse race, and campaign conduct.[43] Interestingly, in 2012, the broad horse race coverage was down from 2008, with 38 percent focused on strategy/tactics and horse race stories.[44] And for 2016, 42 percent focused just on horse race, with another 24 percent on other "non-policy" topics and issues.[45]

Another interesting development, first recognized by Richard Davis and Diana Owen, was the rise of an elite corps of "celebrity journalists" that increasingly became integral parts of news stories and events.[46] They enjoy celebrity status in terms of pay, perks, fan clubs, and huge speaker fees; they have their own "star system" and compete for airtime. Accompanying this trend is the rise of interpretive content of news; each story has a slant to fit a particular news theme, program, or even network. Stories are also shorter to accommodate more human-interest segments (non-breaking stories that focus on the personal experiences of people not in the public spotlight). Equally alarming is the now routine trend of individuals moving from political jobs to the newsroom and back. These partisan pundits "masquerade as reporters on newscasts and talk shows."[47] There is no expectation or pretense of objectivity or independence. Some "celebrity" journalists appear in movies as well as in product commercials. They often blur the line between what is real and who to believe.

Today, partisan and ideological media are a fact of life. Such outlets across platforms well outnumber the more historic and traditional media. According to Matthew Levendusky, most studies show that those watching highly partisan programming that echoes and mirrors their own political beliefs and views actually become more extreme because viewers are not exposed to counterarguments or information. In addition, viewers of partisan media come to have less respect for those of the opposition, seeing them as less legitimate and as untrustworthy. Finally, such viewers are less willing to compromise on issues or policy or even to consider appeals from the other side. Thus, Levendusky concludes that partisan media of today make citizens more polarized and divided; less trusting of the other side; and less willing to compromise and shape how citizens participate (or not) in the electoral process.[48] Kevin Arceneaux and Martin Johnson go one step further. They argue that cable news talk shows "erode viewers' trust in political institutions."[49]

Interestingly, in the late 1980s and early 1990s, scholars discovered what is now called "the hostile media effect" or "hostile media bias" among news consumers in general. No matter what is written, reported, or stated, viewers interpret the content as "hostile" to their personal views and perspective. As citizens, we see what we want to see and hear what we want to hear.

If one goes back to the foundational principles of journalism, there are several general ethical considerations for journalists. Story selection should be based on newsworthiness or importance to a large number of people and not on whether the story fits a particular perspective, worldview, or drama consideration. Likewise, source selection should involve careful evaluation of information and reliability rather than selecting only sources that mirror the opinions of a preferred position. Fact selection and arrangement must report all perspectives in a balanced manner. Because we know that words and language impact perceptions and meaning, language selection should be devoid of bias or emotion. Finally, timing and context are important. Journalists should provide the proper context for story, facts, and opinions for balanced, fair reporting.

From a communication perspective, we want to conclude by recognizing that news gathering is a human communication endeavor. "News" is selected, created, and communicated by people. News is much more than just facts. It is a story and an argument that reveals how journalists perceive reality and the symbols they use to describe that reality to the audience. News stories influence how readers and viewers perceive reality. As consumers of news, we need to recognize that news presentations contain very persuasive messages (verbally and visually). News and the truth are not the same thing. News reporting is just one version of the facts—a created sequence. Some aspects are magnified; others are downplayed.

## Political Advertising

Concerns about the impact and influence of political advertising in campaigns have been around since the 1960s. Because ads are largely protected as freedom of speech, regulation of content is virtually nonexistent. It is up to viewers to evaluate the messages. Most of the research has focused on attack ads. Scholars have found that attack or negative political ads influence voters because they are more compelling, more memorable, and more believable than positive ads.[50] However, Stephen Ansolabehere and Shanto Iyengar find that the heavy reliance on negative political ads results in lower voter turnout and general public cynicism. "Attack advertisements resonate with the popular beliefs that government fails, that elected officials are out of touch and quite corrupt, and that voting is a hollow act. The end result: lower turnout and lower trust in government, regardless of which party rules."[51]

Larry Powell and Joseph Cowart identify four broad areas of concern about attack or negative advertising. First, there are fairness issues. Such ads focus on a single negative factor, mostly personal in nature, while disregarding an opponent's entire career and life. They oversimplify issues and candidate views. Second, there are concerns about appropriateness. Because they tend to make personal attacks, they do not contribute to issue and political debate. The authors also question the general effectiveness of attack ads. While they may have some effect, they are more likely to feed feelings of cynicism and may even suppress voting by those turned off by the electoral process. Similarly, they express great concern about the impact of negative advertising on the political system in general. They undercut the electoral process by polarizing the electorate and reduce voter turnout.[52] Even if the sources of allegations are disclosed, the references are on the screen for just seconds and often out of context.

Interestingly, Richard Fox and Jennifer Ramos found that ads on the internet are actually more positive and less deceptive than those on television. On television, the ads target a wide range of audiences to include supporters, independents, and even those of the opposition. On the internet, the target is primarily supporters and thus there is less need for deception.[53]

In addition to the failure to disclose the source of communication, other common concerns include heavy reliance upon emotion (especially negative emotions such as fear), the lack of providing adequate or complete information, and the ambiguity and/or inconsistency of messages. Visual impressions may lead viewers to "see what they want to see." All ads deal with shades or degrees of truth and deception. Becoming an informed, educated, and critical voter is one's best safeguard against unethical political advertising.

## CONCLUSIONS

The purpose of this chapter was not to provide a comprehensive list of "dos and don'ts." Rather, the purpose was to engage in a philosophical discussion of ethics in general within a democratic form of government. Inherent in persuasive communication are concerns for ethics. Messages can inform or confuse, be accurate or mislead, unite or divide. A casual reading of the polls and sentiments of Americans over the last decade speaks to a nation that is polarized and fragmented based on issues of race, income, age, gender, ideology, and even geography. Our culture has become more coarse. Trust in democratic institutions and leaders is at all-time lows. However, arguably, our nation has survived greater challenges of revolution, civil war, depression, world wars, and civil rights battles.

Ethical considerations of political campaign communication are important because political elections provide the foundations for self-rule and government. A government is only as good, decent, and moral as its citizens. Individual integrity, responsibility, and accountability are the best check on government abuse. The collective social values of citizens become the conditions necessary for the existence of political authority. The government that encompasses and expresses our collective values ensures the respect and voluntary compliance of all citizens. Political authority rests on the assumption that it exists to promote the good of those who accept it and that the common good will prevail rather than the self-interests of those in authority.

Civic responsibility, accountability, and initiative should once again become touchstones of social life. Working toward the common good promotes the development of self-control, moral reasoning, and a generalized respect for others. Such an approach to social life helps citizens recognize the values behind laws enacted to guarantee that everyone's rights are protected. Democracy makes government accessible and accountable to ordinary citizens. We need leaders whose characters clearly demonstrate that they possess the moral authority necessary for governing. In order to elect better leaders, we must become better citizens, friends, and neighbors.

We too often overlook the fact that democratic life carries equal responsibilities for citizens. As is true with most things in life, we often get what we deserve. The polity must share the praise or blame that it heaps on its leaders. Indifferent audiences are a greater danger than uninformed ones. The greatest threat to democracy is neglect of the public forum. We need to return to a civic culture, one based on communication and persuasion, active citizen participation, and a high level of information.

As with all democracies, the greatest threat is internal, not external. We must stem the growing tide toward political cynicism and despair. As a nation, we must find common themes and values that transcend our ever-deepening cultural differences. We must all be able to identify, to articulate, and to appreciate the core values of America. We need to reaffirm ourselves to our national civic values, those principles embodied in the Declaration of Independence, the Constitution, and the Bill of Rights that bring us together as a people. The ideals of freedom, equality, democracy, and justice provide the basis for building community and trust in America today. We need some common understanding of what is acceptable, what is fundamentally right and wrong, good and bad. Thus, ethical political campaign communication is not based on a specific set of rules, standards, or dogma, but in accordance with the basic principles of democracy.

## NOTES

1. Robert E. Denton, Jr., has been writing about ethics of political communication for nearly forty years. The sentiments, arguments, and some materials come from the following works: Robert E. Denton, Jr., and Ben Voth, *Social Fragmentation and the Decline of Democracy in America: The End of the Social Contract* (New York: Palgrave Macmillan, 2016); Robert E. Denton, Jr., ed., *Studies of Identity in the 2008 Presidential Campaign* (Lanham, MD: Lexington Books, 2010); Robert E. Denton, Jr., and Jim Kuypers, *Politics and Communication in America: Campaigns, Media, and Governing in the 21st Century* (Prospect Heights, IL: Waveland Press, 2008); Robert E. Denton, Jr., *Moral Leadership and the American Presidency: Leadership in the 21st Century* (Lanham, MD: Rowman & Littlefield [Trade hardback], 2005); Robert E. Denton, Jr., and Rachel L. Holloway, eds., *Images, Scandal, and Communication Strategies of the Clinton Presidency* (Westport, CT: Praeger, 2003); Robert E. Denton, Jr., ed., *Political Communication Ethics: An Oxymoron?* (Westport, CT: Praeger, 2000); Gary Woodward and Robert E. Denton, Jr., *Persuasion and Influence in American Life* (Prospect Heights, IL: Waveland Press, 1–7 editions, 1987–2014); Robert E. Denton, Jr., ed., *Ethical Dimensions of Political Communication* (New York: Praeger, 1991); Robert E. Denton, Jr., "The Challenges and Limitations of Identity Politics in a Democracy," in *Studies of Identity in the 2008 Presidential Campaign*, ed. Robert E. Denton, Jr. (Lanham, MD: Lexington Books, 2010), 200–15; Robert E. Denton, Jr., "Ethical Dimensions of the Media in Campaigns: The Form and Content of Political Communication," in *Shades of Gray: Perspectives on Campaign Ethics*, ed. Candice Nelson et al. (Washington, DC: Brookings Institute Press, 2002), 185–214; Robert E. Denton, Jr., "Dangers of 'Teledemocracy': How the Medium of Television Undermines American Democracy," in *Political Communication Ethics: An Oxymoron?* ed. Robert E. Denton, Jr. (Westport, CT: Praeger, 2000), 91–124; Robert E. Denton, Jr., "Constitutional Authority and Public Morality," in *The Moral Authority of Government*, ed. Moorhead Kennedy (News Brunswick, NJ: Transaction Publishers, 2000), 108–113.

2. Richard Johannesen, Kathleen Valde, and Karen Whedbee, *Ethics in Human Communication*, 6th ed. (Long Grove, IL: Waveland Press, 2008), 2.

3. Quoted in Sissela Bok, *Lying: Moral Choice in Public and Private Life* (New York: Vintage Books, 1989), 32.

4. Ibid., 18.

5. As quoted in John Merrill and Jack Odell, *Philosophy and Journalism* (New York: Longman, 1983), 2, 95.

6. "Public Trust in Government: 1958 to 2014," Pew Research Center, accessed July 20, 2015, http://www.people-press.org/2014/06/26/section-2-views-of-the-nation-the -constitution-and-government/#trust.

7. "Public Trust in Government Remains Near Historic Lows as Partisan Attitudes Shift," Pew Research Center, May 3, 2017, accessed December 22, 2017, http://www

.people-press.org/2017/05/03/public-trust-in-government-remains-near-historic-lows-as-partisan-attitudes-shift.

8. "Americans Losing Confidence in All Branches of U.S. Gov't," Gallup, June 30, 2015, accessed August 12, 2015, http://www.gallup.com/poll/171992/americans-losing-confidence-branches-gov.aspx.

9. "Americans' Confidence in Government Takes Positive Turn," Gallup, September 19, 2016, accessed January 1, 2018, http://news.gallup.com/poll/195635/americans-confidence-government-takes-positive-turn.aspx.

10. "Right Direction or Wrong Track?" Rasmussen Reports, August 10, 2015, accessed August 12, 2015, http://www.rasmussenreports.com/public_content/politics/mood_of_america/right_direction_or_wrong_track.

11. Dean Obeidallah, "We've Been on the Wrong Track since 1972," *Daily Beast*, November 7, 2014, accessed August 12, 2015, http://www.thedailybeast.com/articles/2014/11/07/we-ve-been-on-the-wrong-track-since-1972.html.

12. "Smaller Majority 'Extremely Proud' to Be an American," Gallup, July 2, 2015, accessed August 14, 2015, http://www.gallup.com/poll/183911/smaller-majority-extremely-proud-american.aspx?version=print.

13. "Americans' Sense of Alienation Remains at Record High," Harris Polling, July 28, 2016, accessed January 1, 2017, http://www.theharrispoll.com/politics/Americans-Alienation-Remains-Record-High.html#.

14. "7 Things to Know about Polarization in America," Pew Research Center, June 12, 2014, accessed August 12, 2015, http://www.pewresearch.org/fact-tank/2014/06/12/7-things-to-know-about-polarization-in-america.

15. "Political Polarization & Media Habits," Pew Research Center, October 21, 2014, accessed August 11, 2015, http://www.journalism.org/2014/10/21/political-polarization-media-habits.

16. Karen S. Peterson, "High-Profile Fibs Feed Public Cynicism," *USA Today*, July 5, 2001, accessed August 23, 2015, http://www.usatoday.com/news/health/2001-07-05-lying.htm.

17. Jennifer Lawless and Richard Fox, *Running from Office* (New York: Oxford University Press, 2015), 4.

18. Louis Day, *Ethics in Media Communications: Cases and Controversies*, 5th ed. (Belmont, CA: Wadsworth, 2006), 19.

19. Celeste Michelle Condit, "Crafting Virtue: The Rhetorical Construction of Public Morality," in *Contemporary Rhetorical Theory*, ed. John Lucaites, Celeste Condit, and Sally Caudill (New York: Guilford Press, 1999), 320.

20. Ibid., 321.

21. Ronald Collins and David Skover, *The Death of Discourse*, 2nd ed. (Boulder, CO: Westview Press, 2005), 203.

22. Aristotle, *Nicomachean Ethics* I.13: 1102–1103.

23. Richard Regan, *The Moral Dimensions of Politics* (New York: Oxford University Press, 1986), 14–18.

24. Rabindra Kanungo and Manuel Mendonca, *Ethical Dimensions of Leadership* (Thousand Oaks, CA: Sage, 1996).

25. Collins and Skover, *Death of Discourse*, 203.

26. Robert Putnam, *Making Democracy Work: Civic Traditions in Modern Italy* (Princeton, NJ: Princeton University Press, 1993).

27. Ibid., 10.

28. James Kouzes and Barry Posner, *Leadership Challenge*, 6th ed. (San Francisco: Jossey-Bass, 2017), 31.

29. John Locke, *Two Treatises of Government* (Stilwell, KS: Digireads.com, 2015).

30. William Hitt, *Ethics and Leadership* (Columbus, OH: Battelle Press, 1990), 3–4.

31. Kouzes and Posner, *Leadership Challenge*, 28.

32. Ibid.

33. Johannesen, Valde, and Whedbee, *Ethics in Human Communication*, 22.

34. Craig Allen Smith, *Presidential Campaign Communication*, 2nd ed. (Cambridge: Polity, 2015), 89.

35. Bruce E. Gronbeck, "Ethical Pivots and Moral Vantages in American Presidential Campaign Dramas," in Robert E. Denton, Jr., *Ethical Dimensions of Political Communication* (Westport, CT: Prager, 1991), 49–68, and updated in "The Ethical Performances of Candidates in American Presidential Campaign Dramas," in *Political Communication Ethics: An Oxymoron?* ed. Robert E. Denton, Jr. (Westport, CT: Prager, 2000), 1–23.

36. Center for Media and Public Affairs, see various studies for each election from 1987 to 2010 at http://www.cmpa.com/studies.htm, and subsequent years studies at Media Research Center (https://www.mrc.org) as well as Pew Research Center (http://www.pewresearch.org).

37. "News Coverage of the 2016 General Election: How the Press Failed the Voters," Shorenstein Center on Media, Politics and Public Policy, December 7, 2017, accessed January 7, 2018, https://shorensteincenter.org/news-coverage-2016-general-election.

38. "News Coverage of Donald Trump's First 100 Days," Shorenstein Center on Media, Politics and Public Policy, May 18, 2017, accessed January 7, 2018, https://shorensteincenter.org/news-coverage-donald-trumps-first-100-days.

39. Brant Bozell, *Weapons of Mass Distortion: The Coming Meltdown of the Liberal Media* (New York: Crown Forum, 2004), 1.

40. For example, see publications such as Eric Alterman's *What Liberal Media?* (2003); Joe Conason's *Big Lies: The Right-Wing Propaganda Machine and How It Distorts the Truth* (2003); and Al Franken's *Lies and the Lying Liars Who Tell Them* (2005).

41. Joseph Cappella and Kathleen H. Jamieson, *The Spiral of Cynicism: The Press and the Public Good* (New York: Oxford University Press, 1997), 31, 33, 96.

42. Center for Media and Public Affairs, "Network News Flip-Flops on Candidates," Press Release, November 22, 2004, accessed January 18, 2006, http://www.cmpa.com/documents/04.11.19.Flip.Flop.Release.pdf.

43. Center for Media and Public Affairs, "Campaign Watch 2008: Final," accessed June 27, 2012, http://www.cmpa.com/pdf/media_monitor_jan_2009.pdf.

44. "Winning the Media Campaign 2012," Pew Research Center, November 2, 2012, accessed January 7, 2018, http://www.journalism.org/2012/11/02/winning-media-campaign-2012.

45. "News Coverage of the 2016 General Election."

46. Richard Davis and Diana Owen, *New Media and American Politics* (New York: Oxford University Press, 1998), 189–209.

47. Jim Squires, "The Impossibility of Fairness," *Media Studies Journal* 12, no. 2 (1998): 66–71.

48. Matthew Levendusky, *How Partisan Media Polarize America* (Chicago: University of Chicago Press, 2013), 4, 5.

49. Kevin Arceneaux and Martin Johnson, *Changing Minds or Changing Channels?* (Chicago: University of Chicago Press, 2013), 127.

50. Michael Pfau and Henry Kenski, *Attack Politics* (New York: Praeger, 1990), xiii.

51. Stephen Ansolabehere and Shanto Iyengar, *Going Negative* (New York: Free Press, 1995), 148.

52. Larry Powell and Joseph Cowart, *Political Campaign Communication: Inside and Out*, 2nd ed. (Boston: Pearson, 2013), 256–57.

53. Richard Fox and Jennifer Ramos, *iPolitics* (New York: Cambridge University Press, 2012), 116–17.

# 7

# Public Speaking in Political Campaigns

Politics, in general, is primarily a communication activity. For William Sweeney, "a political campaign is fundamentally a communications exercise about
choices between the aspirants for public office and the audience of voters."[1] Campaigns are exercises in the creation, re-creation, and transmission of significant
symbols through communication. Communication activities are the vehicles for
action—both real and perceived.

This chapter focuses on what is perhaps the most fundamental communication
practice in any campaign, public speaking. In the first section, we examine the
factors that enter into a candidate's decision to speak. Decisions on where and
when to speak and what to say to a given audience should not be made randomly
but should be the result of considerable thought and planning on the part of candidates and their staffs. In the second section, we inspect the use of two types of
stock speeches. Virtually all candidates utilize some type of stock speech to help
them meet the massive speaking demands typically placed on them. In the third
section, we discuss the practice of political speechwriting. Candidates are using
speechwriters more today than ever before; any examination of public speaking
practices in political campaigns must consider the use of speechwriters. Similarly,
many candidates today are making extensive use of advocates or surrogates.
These "substitutes" for the candidate may be heard in person by as many people,
if not more, as those who actually hear the candidate. Hence, any examination of
public speaking practices in contemporary campaigns that does not consider the
use of surrogate speakers would be less than complete.

## THE DECISION TO SPEAK

Perhaps the most important resource available to any campaign is the time of
the candidate. That time must be used wisely. Decisions to use the candidates'
time for public speeches are made out of self-interest; the candidates attempt

to influence the maximum number of voters. Hence, it is vital that candidates and their staffs do an effective job of analyzing voter audiences to best utilize the candidates' time. Essentially candidates face two tasks: first, to determine whom they should address and, second, to determine what messages should be presented to those they address.

## Audiences

Since 1946 when Jacob Javits, then running for a seat in the House of Representatives, employed the Elmo Roper Organization to take opinion polls of his constituency to better determine what issues he should develop in his campaign,[2] political campaigns have increasingly relied on two tools to assist them in analyzing audiences. The first is studies of past voter statistics. The second is the public opinion poll. Recently, particularly in well-financed campaigns, candidates have also made use of focus groups to help develop their messages. As we have seen in earlier chapters, these tools have blossomed in recent years because of improvements in computer technology.

Local and national candidates make use of past voter statistics to analyze audiences. Yet these statistics play a more vital role in the campaigns of local candidates than they do in the campaigns of national or major statewide contenders. Indeed, there is no more valuable campaign aid to the local candidate than accurate voter statistics. Although voter statistics may serve many potential purposes, their chief function is to pinpoint, on a precinct-by-precinct basis, where candidates should be concentrating their efforts. This knowledge enables candidates to determine what speaking invitations should be accepted and in what areas of the district their staffs should attempt to arrange speaking opportunities and otherwise concentrate.

Although the same principles apply for national figures and local figures, in practicality major national or statewide figures are rarely able to aim their speeches or campaign materials to a specific precinct as can the local candidate dealing with a smaller constituency. Local and statewide politics are retail politics. This means it's about direct voter contact. It's about meeting voters, talking to voters, and shaking as many hands as possible. The more local the race, the more retail the expectation. Direct voter contact is invaluable for several reasons. First, direct contact with a candidate makes the voter more committed to the candidate and engaged in the campaign. Second, it allows for two-way communication and interaction. Voters can express concerns and ask questions, thus making them feel important while generating interest in the candidacy and campaign. Face-to-face contact also humanizes the candidate, allowing a firsthand observation and evaluation. Studies also show that people are more likely to vote for a candidate they meet in person, regardless of party or even issue positions.[3]

Thus, local candidates, far more than counterparts seeking national or statewide office, must know precisely, down to the precinct, the nature of the constituency. Because their constituencies are smaller, in many instances the local candidate can knock on every door in the district, or at least on every door in those precincts that are deemed most valuable. When statewide or national candidates spend time walking door to door, they are doing so largely for the media coverage they expect to receive.

Local candidates, however, will not receive the media exposure of candidates for more prominent office. Rather, their walks in the district can put them face to face with a large percentage of their constituency. The act is real rather than symbolic. To be effective, the local candidate must know in which areas of the district to walk, speak, get out the vote, and otherwise campaign. Accurate voter statistics are an acute concern for local candidates, who can meet a substantial portion of their constituency, who can express their concern for voter problems face to face, and whose limited financial resources must be used with maximum effect.

Typically, candidates direct their efforts primarily toward precincts where their party traditionally runs well, those where elections are likely to be close, and those where ticket-splitting commonly takes place. It is in these areas that candidates should concentrate most of their speaking efforts. That may even mean actively soliciting speaking engagements in these areas when none are forthcoming. It means consistently giving preference to those regions when simultaneous speaking opportunities arise in two or more sections of the district. Local candidates can think in precinct terms. National and statewide candidates use the same process but must think more in media market and electoral vote terms. Thus, utilizing past voter records and computers to help analyze the data, state and local political organizations will often provide candidates with a precinct-by-precinct breakdown of their district.

Yes, local candidates address diverse audiences. However, they also need to distinguish between the primary audience and secondary audiences. One may be speaking before the local Chamber of Commerce but reporters, "trailers," and others also share those remarks publicly to additional audiences. Remember how Mitt Romney's "47 percent" remark in 2012 in reference to the percentage of those who "are dependent on government" and will naturally vote for Obama made headlines when made public. Although that is a national example, it is true for local races as well.

National and statewide candidates operate on the same premises. They, too, target about 70 percent of their constituency. Typically, presidential candidates target states and media markets within states rather than precincts and choose to speak and campaign accordingly.[4]

In recent presidential campaigns, both the Republican and Democratic candidates have targeted ten to fourteen states and directed most of their campaign efforts, including speaking, to those states.

## Messages

The second primary tool of audience analysis is the public opinion poll. Polls help candidates develop their messages. But polls are utilized differently by local and major candidates. Accurate voter statistics down to the precinct level are of acute concern to the local candidate but often of lesser concern to the major candidate. However, the public opinion poll is of more concern to major candidates but often of lesser concern to the local candidate. Typically, the explanation for this different emphasis on the use of polls involves two distinctions between local and major candidates. First, the major candidate can normally afford a polling service and may also be helped by national polls such as those of the national television networks and national newspaper chains. Candidates for Congress and statewide and national offices all utilize polling services. Most state legislative candidates and contenders for local offices in larger urban districts also use polls.

Since the 1970s, pollsters relied upon phone interviews for collecting data. As technology improved, they used "random digit dialing" to identify individuals and families to canvass. Of course, within a decade or so, more and more individuals refused to answer the phone, blocked calls, and used voicemail more; thus, random digit dialing became problematic. In the early 2000s, pollsters relied upon "clustered random sampling from voter registration lists" to comprise samples.[5]

By 2015, over 90 percent of American adults of voting age owned cell phones. In increasing numbers, younger Americans used cell phones only. The use of cell phones increased problems for pollsters. Federal law prohibited automated calling of cell phones, questionnaires were too long for users, and most were unwilling to respond to poll requests. As a result, there were questions of polling accuracy, bias, and non-representativeness of younger voters.[6]

Online surveys began being used nationwide in the 1990s. Results were less than predictive, with average variation of nearly 9 percent. However, there are some advantages to online surveys. They are less expensive than traditional polling methods, provide for more interactivity, can accommodate longer questionnaires, and can be compiled in real time.[7]

While speaking about polls, credibility of the entire industry took a hit with the miscalculations of the presidential predictions of 2016. All polls, and hence pundits, declared with great certainty that Hillary Clinton would prevail over Donald Trump. A committee of the American Association for Public Opinion Research reviewed the polls of the 2016 presidential race. Without question, pre-election polls predicted a high likelihood of Clinton winning the White House. Most of the polling favored her with 71 to 99 percent certainty. Upon review, the national polls were generally accurate, reflecting a 3 percent popular vote preference when Clinton did win the popular vote by two points. At the state level, polls showed a more competitive and even uncertain contest. The report notes that "eight states with more than a third of the electoral voters needed to win the presidency had polls showing a lead of three points or less."[8] The reasons that the polls underestimated support for Trump include change in vote preference during the final week of the campaign favoring Trump; overrepresentation of college graduates in the polls relative to their actual vote; Trump supporters who participated in pre-election polls did not reveal their choice; and from 2016 there was heavier Republican voting in traditional Republican counties. The review committee also noted that there was no partisan favoritism reflected in the polls. Over the course of recent elections, polls have missed the same "surge" equally among the parties. Finally, in terms of primaries, the polls were very accurate in predicting results.[9]

In considering issues, most congressional candidates identify with valence issues such as good schools, strong economy, job growth, safe streets, and national security; these issues and positions possess universal agreement. Candidates avoid more controversial or wedge issues. Challengers will often make one issue the centerpiece of their campaign. Economic issues drive congressional races, whether positive, such as low inflation and good jobs, or negative, such as high unemployment and increased taxes. In general terms, Democrats tend to discuss economic issues in terms of fairness, Republicans in terms of growth and opportunity. Political reform is a mainstay of both parties.[10]

Candidates for lesser local offices, such as sheriff, county or city recorder, clerk, or engineer, particularly in less populated communities, often cannot afford polling services. Many polling consultants themselves suggest that a campaign that is budgeted at $100,000 or less probably should think twice about using a poll. Typically, even the most basic benchmark polls will cost thousands of dollars. In smaller campaigns it is more important to preserve funds for the campaign to adequately communicate with the public.

Second, even if the local candidate could afford polls, the essentially administrative nature, rather than policy-making nature, of most local offices tends to minimize the distinctions between the viewpoints of local candidates. Issues of policy, which sharply divide candidates for major office, often are not at stake in local elections. This is not to say that there is no opportunity for policy making at the local level. Rather, it is to suggest that while major campaigns almost invariably involve clashes over policy issues, many local campaigns are waged for positions with comparatively few policy-making responsibilities. For example, county sheriffs and recorders are not primarily engaged in making policy. Rather, they are primarily engaged in enforcing and carrying out policies set by legislatures, city councils, and similar policy-making agencies. Hence, there is often little distinction between candidates based on issues and less need for polls.

Issue polls are designed to determine what concerns are uppermost in the minds of voters. They serve major candidates as a topoi, or topics, system. In addition to suggesting topics upon which to speak, they indicate voter opinions or beliefs. As we have noted earlier, candidates rely on polling services when they develop positions on issues.

Typically, the candidate's polls will be able to rank issues of concern among specific constituencies such as older voters, women voters, or middle-income voters. The degree to which the polling data are broken down and analyzed depends on the candidate's needs and the finances available. A national campaign will break down the polling data extensively, determining, for example, what issues are of concern on such bases as geography, income, race, religion, and party. As candidates speak, they can vary their subject matter to ensure that they are addressing the major concerns of the groups to whom they are speaking.

Polls also provide candidates with indirect feedback on messages. Candidates often reposition their stands on issues because of that feedback. In recent years political campaigns have begun to make use of a tool that was pioneered by advertising researchers, the focus group. In 1988, George H. W. Bush's campaign team used focus groups to help them identify weaknesses in the background and statements of their opponent, Massachusetts governor Michael Dukakis.[11] A focus group brings together a group of eight to twenty voters. A skilled questioner leads them through a series of questions that the campaign seeks to answer. Focus groups provide "qualitative" insight into issues and attitudes held by the participants. The facilitator's job is to encourage discussion to reveal useful insight and information. The material is usually used to pretest television ads and gauge audience responses to certain campaign themes and appeals.[12]

In 2012, the Obama campaign launched an "ethnography" project. They recruited one hundred people specifically between the ages of thirty-five and sixty-five and with household incomes between $40,000 and $100,000. They identified themselves as independents or weak partisans. The group was also largely undecided. The campaign asked the participants to fill out a journal twice a week responding to eight to ten questions on a variety of topics. They also conducted nine focus groups within this group. The sessions allowed the campaign to explore more deeply the responses provided in the journals. By the summer of 2012, the research division of the campaign generated a forty-five-page summary document of their findings. These findings provided the message strategy for the campaign. Obama's message needed to be forward-looking rather than emphasizing what he had done. The campaign needed to focus on the contrast between the parties on the values and visions for the future. Focus group research also revealed that there was major dissatisfaction with the economy, in general people had not given up on Obama as president, and they were wondering whether he was able to handle the challenges.[13]

Focus groups have two virtues. First, they are typically less expensive than polls. Moreover, they provide, from a small group, an indication of the depth and nuance of potential messages. However, particularly when combined with polling, they can help campaigns in message development.[14]

## Competency and Format

Obviously, most candidates need to feel comfortable in front of an audience. Often, even local candidates have extensive prior public speaking experience. If prospective candidates are apprehensive about the speaking demands of their races, they might well prepare by seeking the advice of competent professionals. Many candidates utilize the services of speech coaches who specialize in training political speakers. Students of speech communication will be familiar with much of the advice offered by such individuals. Additionally, the Republican and Democratic National Committees, as well as many state and local party committees, provide speech training in their candidates' schools.

If candidates are uncomfortable with some speaking formats, they and their staffs might attempt to place them in formats where they do not feel uncomfortable. If, for example, they are uneasy delivering formal speeches, perhaps their formal speeches could be kept brief and be followed by extensive question-and-answer periods. The type of training and formats utilized by candidates varies on an individual basis but should not be ignored. A frank and realistic assessment of the candidate's speaking abilities, no less than assessments about where and when to talk and what to talk about, must enter into the candidate's decisions to speak.

## Campaign Messages

Campaign messages are based on four things. First is the candidate's strengths and weaknesses, including personal history, experience, competence, knowledge, and so on. A candidate's background and experiences may enhance credibility among voters as well as emphasize commonality with members of the public. The second element in message creation for a campaign is the candidate's ideology and political beliefs. Political ideology frames issues and presentations. The third element is the political environment. Major issues change; each election presents different factors and events that influence messaging strategies. Are the economic times good or bad or is the nation at war? The task for consultants is to create messages true to ideological considerations of the candidate and the issues of the time.[15]

Some political operatives create a "SWOT" box for campaigns to "visualize what they stand for, where the opposition stands, and how to properly target messages."[16] SWOT stands for identifying strengths, weaknesses, opportunities, and threats. Key points to consider for message development include what you say about yourself, what you say about your opponents, what your opponents say about you, and what your opponents say about themselves.[17]

According to Jason Johnson, marketing and messaging strategies come down to several very simple concepts: change versus status quo, old versus new, idealism versus pragmatism, and fear versus security. These become the "umbrella" campaign theme to position issues.[18]

Message consistency is essential and most important for candidates during a campaign. No matter how contentious or unpleasant it gets, candidates must stay on message during the worst of times. If the message points are indeed targeted to core constituency groups, one needs to remain on message at every opportunity.[19]

In general, campaign messages should be brief, memorable, positive, and consistent. The key messages should be communicated through all the channels of communication from speeches, social media, direct mail, newsletters, and even yard signs. Campaign veteran Josh Womack suggests that especially at the local level, candidates should sell hope and integrity. This builds trust with voters.[20]

## Incumbent/Challenger Strategies

In terms of campaigns, incumbents project a personal home style that is more about relationships than about issues or policy positions. On display is demonstrating a sense of identification with constituents, mutual trust, and continual accessibility. This style of campaigning stresses that the way issues are addressed is more important than the issues themselves.[21] For this reason, polls generally show that citizens do not like Congress as an institution but love their own congressperson. A standard tactic of incumbents is to completely ignore the opposition; don't mention their names, refuse to debate (or perhaps only once), and never agree to joint appearances. If the challenger grows in strength, the incumbent will attack the inexperience, lack of qualifications, and general naïveté of the challenger. Naturally, it is routine for incumbent campaigns to make frequent references to things done for the district and the value of experience and seniority in Washington.

The main objective of challengers is to convince voters that they are qualified to serve in office. Some take advantage of scandal, individual political failings such as excessive junketing, or lack of attention to district concerns. They most often attempt to demonstrate that incumbents are simply out of touch with district needs and the citizens.[22] Not surprisingly, challengers portray themselves as caring, hardworking, and bringing common sense and experience to the job. The incumbent is part of "that mess in Washington" and is clearly "out of touch" with the people, needs, and values of the district.

There are five major defining messages that campaigns use against opponents. The first and most common is that the opponent is out of touch. This message strategy works well against incumbents and challengers alike. Another defining message of opponents is incompetence. The opponent has failed to accomplish campaign promises or to adequately represent constituencies. As noted above, most incumbents define their challengers as inexperienced and lacking the knowledge or experience to fill the post. Similar to the charge of the incumbent being out of touch, long-term incumbents may be portrayed as too old, too long in office—it's time for a change. Finally, the most direct and harsh portrayal is defining an opponent as corrupt. Usually, this tactic is used when the opponent has been involved in some public scandal or questionable behavior.[23]

## THE SPEECH

Though candidates make hundreds, in some cases thousands, of speeches in the course of a campaign, those speeches always seem new and appropriate for each audience. Nevertheless, candidates typically draw upon a well-prepared message repeatedly during the campaign. This material is often called the candidate's "stock speech" and typically takes two forms. A module approach to stock speeches is the approach most frequently used by candidates, such as major national and statewide candidates, who address diverse audiences often interested in a wide variety of topics.

A second type of stock speech, used more by candidates for lower-level offices, especially administrative offices that do not involve a wide variety of topics and policies, are variations of the "Why I Am Running" speech. The demand to speak is also one of the principal reasons used by candidates to justify the use of speechwriters. In this section, we will examine the use of both types of stock speeches, and in the next section we will examine the practices of political speechwriters.

### Need and Justification

Speechmaking is fundamental to political campaigning. The politician cannot reasonably expect to campaign without continually facing audiences. Even the candidate for city council in a small community must constantly speak. Typically, such a candidate is called upon to make several major speeches during the campaign at such events as the local League of Women Voters "Meet the Candidates Night" or at the Rotary Club's monthly meeting. Moreover, these candidates must be continually speaking, often three or more times an evening throughout the final weeks of the campaign, to smaller groups of citizens. Campaign coffees, teas, church socials, and similar activities crowd the calendars of most candidates. It is not unusual for local candidates to find themselves confronting the prospect of a hundred or more speeches during the last four to six weeks of a campaign. Similarly, as we will see in the next section, candidates for more important local, state, and federal offices face situations where they must speak thirty or more times a week. Because of these demands, most candidates make use of a stock speech and, if possible, the services of speechwriters.

## Stock Speeches: Utilizing Speech Modules

Although the phrase "stock speech" has entered the vocabulary of most politically aware citizens, it is a misnomer. We tend to think of it as a speech that is delivered repeatedly with little change. However, candidates do not give an identical speech time after time, irrespective of the audience, occasion, or the actions of their opponents. Rather, they adapt to these factors.

How do the candidates adapt, given the heavy demands on time? The first commonly used approach is to make use of speech modules. A speech module is a single unit of a speech. Typically, candidates will have a speech unit, or module, on each of the ten to twenty issues on which they most frequently speak. Each module is an independent unit that can be delivered as a two-to-seven-minute speech on the issue. The length of each can be varied simply by adding or subtracting examples, statistics, illustrations, or other support material. Perhaps the first candidate of the modern era of political campaigning to use speech modules was John F. Kennedy. During the early phase of his 1960 campaign for the presidency, he observed that he had broken up his ideas into "sections" and that he knew those sections "pretty well and so I can easily piece them together into a speech aimed at the problems of a specific area."[24]

Typically, the organization of each module or "section" is similar and will be readily recognized by many students of public speaking. Each module opens with some attention-gaining device, and then candidates quickly move to a discussion of a problem. Having sketched the problem, they present their policies as an appropriate solution to the problem. If more time is available, they might then vividly describe or visualize what would happen if they are elected and their policies carried out. Thus, the typical speech module is designed to (1) gain attention, (2) describe a problem, (3) present a solution, and (4) visualize the solution.[25] The first three of these steps are characteristic of virtually every speech module that the candidate presents. The final step may not be necessary. It may be implicit from the discussion of the problem and the solution and hence not warrant explicit treatment.

## Speech-Like Opportunities and Modular Speech

One of the principal advantages of developing a basic speech through modules is that the modules can be used by the candidate in many speech-like situations. Often candidates desire to appear on interview shows such as *Meet the Press* or talk shows such as *Hannity*. With the recent proliferation of all-news cable stations such as the Fox News Channel, MSNBC, CNBC, and similar channels, the opportunities for such appearances have increased dramatically for major candidates. Candidates operating on a limited budget are especially attracted to free media. Moreover, almost every media market has local radio and television talk shows. Hence, these decisions are not unique to national contenders.

If candidates have already prepared speech modules on most major topics, they are likely to do well on these shows. The module, which can be varied in length, lends itself to use in these formats. Candidates can accept such invitations with a minimum of preparation and be confident that they are unlikely to be caught ill prepared. Moreover, they can be certain that their remarks will be consistent with those they have made throughout the campaign.

Occasionally, if a module is done especially well, it can also be turned into an effective commercial or used for other purposes. Since the module can stand alone and its length can be varied by the addition or deletion of support material such as statistics and examples, it is easy to adapt to a commercial. Often media advisors wish to show their candidate in "the real world," talking to "real people." The speech module lets them do just that. Virtually every Republican presidential candidate since Richard Nixon in 1968 has made use of modules excerpted from their acceptance address in precisely this fashion.[26]

## Stock Speeches: The Basic Stump Speech

The stump speech is the one used by candidates most of the time. A few themes may vary with attention to context and audiences. However, the key issues and selling points largely remain the same. The topics are usually generated by survey and poll results.[27]

Usually, local stump speeches follow a general outline. First is the simple "intro" containing "I am . . . " and "I am running for . . . ," for example. Second is a local shout-out such as "I grew up here" or "I always enjoy visiting . . . ," or "what makes this place special is . . . " Next, the candidate should always recognize family members who are present, or if absent, express gratitude for their support. It is also important to recognize local officials and high-profile supporters. As a prelude to the sharing of issue positions, one should provide a little personal history or highlight résumé and work experience.[28]

According to long-term speechwriter Robert Lehrman, political speech material should be persuasive, likable, upbeat, understandable to "average folks," quotable, and able to be used again and again.[29] For him, the basic stump speech should adhere to the following outline:[30]

*Introduction*

   Opening joke, usually a hit on the other side
   Acknowledgments recognizing local dignitaries and sponsors
   Attention-getter addressing common concern
   Praise for the specific group assembled
   Statement of purpose

*Body*

   Record of accomplishment
   Problems and failures of the other side
   Transition to solutions, building up proposed alternatives
   Solutions

*Conclusion*

    Reflective section
    Inspirational example or vision of success
    Lessons learned
    Call to action
    Clincher

## Stock Speeches: The "Why I Am Running" Speech

Another form of the stock speech is the "Why I Am Running" speeches of varying lengths. Political consultant and commentator Ron Faucheux suggests that many candidates can meet most of their speaking demands by preparing three speeches. He recommends that the first be about two minutes in length, the second should be about five minutes in length, and the third should be about twenty minutes in length. In each speech, candidates should explain, in as much detail as the time allows, why they are running.[31]

Based on sound research on the demographic makeup of the district, the prevalent beliefs in the district, the distinctions between the candidate and the opponent, and any other pertinent information, Faucheux advises candidates to develop "a sentence or short paragraph that summarizes the reason why the voters should elect you, keeping in mind your strengths, the opposition's weaknesses, and your points of inoculation."[32] This short statement is, in effect, the essence of the candidate's message throughout the campaign. Once crafted, it should be repeated consistently throughout the campaign. Depending on the audience and time available, a candidate could elaborate upon virtually any part of their justification for running. One could discuss plans for health care, for education, for jobs and the economy, for pension reform, for immigration reform, and so on.

Once a candidate has developed a concise answer to "Why I Am Running," Faucheux offers several questions that can be used to evaluate and amend the answer.[33] First, Faucheux suggests asking, "From a geographic, ethnic, partisan, social, and demographic perspective, will this message appeal to the groups necessary for my winning coalition?" In 2008 and 2012 Obama mentioned key Democratic issues, including health care, a decades-old goal of Democrats; education, a major concern of the teacher unions, who are a major constituent group of the Democratic Party; jobs, wages, and pensions, all of which are concerns of organized labor, yet another major constituent group of the Democratic Party. For environmentalists, largely Democratic in their political leanings, Obama expressed concern for global warming and would seek to end the war in Iraq. Obama's message was aimed at assembling a broad enough coalition to win the election.

Second, Faucheux suggests that the "Why I Am Running" speech should "zero in" on both your strengths and your opposition's weaknesses. It should take full advantage of mirror opposites if they exist. Republicans are philosophically disposed toward a smaller federal government and allowing citizens to solve problems without the "interference"—Democrats would say "help"—of government. Most of Obama's "Why I Am Running" speech reflected his desire to provide government solutions to health care, the schools, the economy, and global warming, all of which are mirror opposites of the Republican tickets that would resolve these issues through the private sector or state and local governments.

Third, Faucheux suggests that the "Why I Am Running" speech should be unique. It should not be so broad that other candidates could use essentially the same speech. Aspects of candidate life history, experiences, and personal stories help to make the speech unique and fitting. Fourth, Faucheux suggests that the "Why I Am Running" speech should be "big enough." This means substantial in terms of issues discussed.

Finally, Faucheux suggests that candidates should ask whether their "Why I Am Running" speech would "inoculate" them on points where they are weak and subject to attack. The speech provides an opportunity to explain any weaknesses or obvious attacks by the opposition. If an incumbent, it allows the candidate to justify past actions.

## Stock Speeches: Issue Speeches

In terms of developing strategy for policy and issues, there are several considerations. Basically, there are policy positions and issue expectations "owned" by the party. Issue distinctions are usually clear. Then, through polling and research, there are issues that voters care about that must be addressed. If polls reflect that the economy is the number one issue among voters, then campaigns must develop issue positions relative to job creation, and so on. Finally, there are issues that campaigns hope to "prime" voters to pay attention to. This is one way a campaign may come to "own" a new issue. Also in the mix are attempts to frame issues targeted to independents, undecideds, and swing voters.[34]

According to Powell and Cowart, an issue speech attempts to define a candidate's position on an issue, to frame the issue to the advantage of the speaker, and to generate positive news coverage for the candidate. Locations of issue speeches are very important and often relate to the issue itself. For example, a speech revealing a new tax policy might be given at a Chamber of Commerce meeting or a speech on increasing the minimum wage at a fast-food restaurant.[35] They suggest the following format:[36]

State the held premise about the issue (taxes need to be cut or minimum wage needs to be increased).
Link the issue to the position taken.
Support the argument with candidate's record on the issue and with specific proposals to deal with the issue.
Appeal for support and action relevant to the issue.

## Political Speechwriting

The use of speechwriters by political figures dates to ancient Greece and Rome when men such as Julius Caesar and Nero received aid in preparing their speeches. In the United States, the use of speechwriters has been a feature of our politics since our nation's inception. George Washington had at least four different speechwriters, including Alexander Hamilton. Amos Kendell, a former editor of the *Kentucky Argus* newspaper and a close personal confidant of Andrew Jackson, was called by one of Jackson's critics "the President's thinking machine, and his writing machine, ay, and his lying machine."[37]

Abraham Lincoln frequently called upon his secretary of state, William Seward, for advice on public speeches. Lincoln's successor, Andrew Johnson, had grown up on the frontier and did not learn to read and write until meeting and courting his wife, a teacher. Not surprisingly, he too sought a speechwriter. This rough-hewn president found his man in George Bancroft, perhaps the most erudite and distinguished historian of the day.

Although both presidents Calvin Coolidge and Herbert Hoover made use of the same speechwriter,[38] it was not until the administration of President Franklin Delano Roosevelt that the public at large became fully aware of the pervasive use of speechwriters by political figures. Roosevelt used a variety of individuals to provide him with aid in preparing speeches. Typically, Roosevelt drew upon subject matter experts, often cabinet members, and stylists, such as authors Robert Sherwood and John Steinbeck. Among the most famous individuals to have ever been a speechwriter was President Dwight David Eisenhower who, early in his military career, served as a speechwriter for General Douglas MacArthur.[39] While the press on occasion reported on the use of speechwriters, it was not until Richard Nixon that an American president publicly acknowledged that individuals in his employ were in fact employed primarily to help write speeches.[40]

## Justification and Implications of Political Speechwriting

Since Roosevelt, the public has been aware that political figures often use speechwriters. Today no national or statewide campaign is run without them. The vast majority of candidates running for Congress utilize speechwriters, as do many candidates running for lesser office. Incumbents, whether presidents, members of Congress, mayors, state representatives, or town council members, almost invariably delegate some of their speechwriting chores to paid staff members. The staff member's title may be "assistant to" or "press secretary," but part of the job responsibility is speechwriting. Similarly, challenger candidates normally hire a "wordsmith" to help with speeches, press releases, and similar tasks right after hiring a campaign manager.

Although the public has accepted leaders who make use of speechwriters, somehow we remain vaguely troubled by the thought that those who aspire to lead us often do so by mouthing the words of others. Traditionally, there have been two basic justifications for using speechwriters.

First, candidates face such extensive demands on their time that it is impossible to fulfill those demands without speechwriters. In 1948, while governing the nation and running for reelection, President Harry Truman delivered seventy-three speeches in one fifteen-day period.[41] In 1952, during the final months of the campaign, the Republican and Democratic presidential and vice presidential candidates delivered a combined total of nearly one thousand speeches.[42] In 1960 John Kennedy delivered sixty-four speeches in the last seven days of the campaign.[43]

The speaking demands on more contemporary candidates continue to grow. In recent presidential campaigns, it is not unusual for candidates to be exhausted and hoarse from their extensive speaking efforts.[44] These demands are not unique to presidential candidates. In 1954 Orville Freeman, running for governor of Minnesota, found himself facing more than 120 speaking situations for which he felt the need for advance preparation.[45] This number does not include the countless situations in which he spoke with little preparation. In 1970 Nelson Rockefeller delivered more than three hundred speeches in his campaign for the governorship of New York.[46] A survey of candidates for Congress indicates that they spoke approximately four times a day.[47]

Thus, candidates at all levels simply cannot prepare for the many speeches they must make while simultaneously fulfilling other responsibilities as candidate, breadwinner, and family member without the help of a speechwriter. This justification is a compelling one. Although the public is aware of speechwriters and understands the time demands that justify their use, it remains slightly troubled by the practice of one person writing the words of another. A second reason candidates use speechwriters is that they believe the writer will produce a good speech. Speechwriters possess unique skills. If their skills can be marshaled on behalf of the candidate, the result will be a stronger speech and, to that extent, an increased likelihood of election. But this justification raises troubling questions.

One critic has suggested that "the essential question is how much borrowing is ethical."[48] There is, he suggests, a continuum of help that one can provide to a speaker. On one end of the continuum, few people would find anything wrong if a candidate had a spouse or an aide listen to the rehearsal of a speech or perhaps review drafts of a speech, in each instance making occasional suggestions to improve the language or organization. On the other end, most people might object to finding that speeches were written entirely by speechwriters who did not consult with the candidates, who in turn had no idea about what they were going to say until the moment they started to deliver the speeches that had been written for them. Where on this continuum does one draw the line between honest and dishonest borrowing and collaboration? This is an especially vexing question when candidates are using speeches to present themselves as competent to serve in a leadership position in their community, city, state, or nation.

Communication scholar Ernest Bormann finds that the point on the continuum where one must draw the line is "where the speech changes character. The language becomes different from what it would have been had the speaker prepared the speech for himself with some aid in gathering information and some advice from friends and associates about parts that he should consider revising. At some point the ideas are different, structure of the speech is different, the nuances of meaning change from what they would have been had this speech really been 'his own.'"[49] When this happens, the speech cannot achieve what should be one of its chief goals, portraying the speaker accurately to the audience, and the public clearly has reason to be troubled.

Thus, voters accept the use of speechwriters. However, we remain vaguely troubled because the speechwriter is a skilled artisan who produces a polished product, and this too causes the candidate to hire him. To the extent that the speech reflects the writer and not the speaker, the public has cause for concern.

The very nature of political speechwriting prevents us from knowing how often "the speech changes character," becoming more a creation of the speechwriter than of the candidate. However, an examination of the job demands imposed upon the political speechwriter suggests that this is probably not as frequent an occurrence as many may think. Fortunately for free societies, the demands of political speechwriting coincide with the needs of the public.

## Job Demands

A veteran of more than twenty-five years of political speechwriting for a wide variety of Democratic candidates, Josef Berger, claims that the most important part of a speechwriter's work is "to know his man, to know his man's ideas, not only his general philosophy and background but his thoughts on the issues that he's talking about if he's clear enough on them."[50] Similarly, virtually every political speechwriter who has commented on the job reaffirms the absolutely critical importance of knowing the candidate for whom they are writing because they seek to create a speech that is essentially that of the candidate, accurately portraying the candidate to the audience. Speechwriters must be thoroughly acquainted with the candidate's value system. Speechwriters must not present what they believe is the best justification for the candidate's policy—rather, they must put forward the candidate's justification for a policy.

William F. Gavin, a veteran political speechwriter who served on the staff of Representative Robert Michel when Michel was minority leader of the U.S. House of Representatives, has observed that a speechwriter should never "think he is writing speeches for himself. If you are doing that, then you're in the wrong business," he comments.[51]

Moreover, speechwriters must use language with which the candidate will feel comfortable, language that is an accurate reflection of the candidate. Jon Favreau, President Barack Obama's principal speechwriter during the campaign and the head of the speechwriting office in Obama's White House, worked very closely with Obama. Speaking about major speeches, Favreau claimed, "What I do is sit with him for half an hour. He talks and I type everything he says. I reshape it. I write. He writes. He reshapes it. That's how we get a finished product."[52] Clearly Favreau and Obama were so comfortable with each other that the final speech was in effect a collaboration between the two men.

Thus, the primary demand placed on speechwriters is to gain an intimate familiarity with the candidates for whom they are working. That familiarity should include a thorough knowledge of the candidate's position on major questions, value systems, and the way the candidate thinks through questions and makes decisions, as well as the candidate's manner of using language.

This information will enable the writer to produce a speech that accurately reflects the candidate. The speechwriter owes that to the public so that it might fairly judge the candidate. But what we often forget is that the speechwriter owes it to the candidate as well.

If the speechwriter does not accurately portray the candidate, the speech is likely to be a failure for several practical reasons. First, the candidate may choose to stray from the speech or ignore it altogether. In either case, the speechwriter will probably be fired for writing a speech with which the candidate felt uncomfortable or that he or she could not use. Second, if the candidate does choose to use a speech that is an inaccurate portrayal, there will likely be trouble in delivery. Unfamiliar with the basic lines of argument, the evidence, and the language, the candidate cannot be expected to present the case well. Third, candidates are likely to experience discomfort and nervousness in a public situation where they are liable to make some type of error as a consequence of that discomfort. Fourth, they may repudiate parts of the speech in a question-and-answer session or in subsequent public appearances. This inconsistency could create an opening for criticism. Hence, the demands on the political speechwriter are to produce a message useful to the candidate and create a speech that is an accurate reflection of the candidate's policies, thought processes, values, and language. Three recent examinations of the speechwriter's craft by experienced practitioners stress the importance of being faithful to the candidate and suggest that perhaps the principal function of the speechwriter is to polish the language a candidate might use, while remaining faithful to the candidate's policies, thought processes, and for the most part language as well.[53] In so doing, the interests of the speechwriter and candidate coincide with the interests of the public in securing accurate information about the candidate.

In addition to knowledge of the candidate, speechwriters need at least two other types of knowledge. First, they must know the subject. Occasionally, a political figure is concerned with a specific issue and calls on someone to help with speeches because of that individual's expertise on the issue. However, most political speechwriters are generalists because most candidates need generalists.

Campaign speechwriters must be versatile. The speechwriter for a Missouri congressional candidate in a recent election was asked to write speeches in a one-month period on such topics as international terrorism, the importance of engineering technology to the St. Louis business community, abortion laws, a federally funded lock and dam project on the Missouri River, Israel and Middle East affairs, and National Fire Prevention Week. Thus, speechwriters invariably are well read, often in literature as well as politics and current events. Moreover, they know how to do research. If they do not know about the topic, they know where to learn about it.

Another type of knowledge required by the good speechwriter is information regarding the audience and occasion. Speechwriters must know which audiences in the candidate's district are essential for victory. Moreover, they must know what message or impression the candidate wishes to leave with these target audiences. Is this speech being delivered exclusively to the audience in the room? If so, what is the nature of that audience? What are their interests? Is the immediate audience of secondary importance to the audience that will be reached by press accounts of this speech? How can the interests of those two audiences and the candidate be reconciled in an appropriate speech for this particular occasion? Answering these questions and then operationalizing the answers to produce a speech demands many kinds of information. It demands knowledge of the candidate's ideas, value system, reasoning process, and use of language. It demands knowledge of the subject matter, the audience(s), and the occasion.

A final demand placed on speechwriters is the trying circumstances in which their knowledge must be utilized. As one speechwriter expressed it when commenting about the type of person hired to help, "We looked for the capacity to work under harsh and often preposterous time pressures. When a speech for a particular evening calling for a ban on leaded gasoline has been co-opted by your opponent that morning, swiftness, along with eloquence, is routinely expected of the writer in coming up with a substitute."[54]

**Speechwriting Teams**

As the previous section has indicated, the job demands of political speechwriting are formidable. These demands grow in proportion to the office contested. Although the types of knowledge we have discussed are required by every political speechwriter, they are normally felt to a greater degree by the speechwriter working for a major candidate because of such factors as the need to coordinate the candidate's speaking with the radio and television messages of the campaign, the need to respond to an opponent who is also constantly speaking and using media, and the constant interjection into the campaign of new issues. Hence, speechwriting in most major campaigns is done by speechwriting teams and characterized by a sharper division of labor than is found in the small campaign. Additionally, the team may perform functions that are not performed in other campaigns.

Firsthand accounts by members of the campaign staffs of Franklin Roosevelt, Harry Truman, Adlai Stevenson, Orville Freeman, Nelson Rockefeller, John Kennedy, Richard Nixon, Robert Michel, Gerald Ford, Hubert Humphrey, George McGovern, Jimmy Carter, Ronald Reagan, Michael Dukakis, George H. W. Bush, Bill Clinton, George W. Bush, John McCain, Barack Obama, and a wide variety of other gubernatorial, senatorial, and congressional candidates suggest that speechwriting teams exhibit similar division of labor in most larger campaigns. Craig Smith, who has been a part of several such teams and has studied many others, finds that typically speechwriting teams in larger campaigns are composed of three groups: the researchers, the stylists, and the media or public relations advisors.[55]

All these individuals should be familiar with the policies, values, and decision-making processes of the candidate. In practicality it may not be possible for each member of these teams to acquire that knowledge. Rather, key figures in each group acquire it.

The research group does basic research. Prior to the 1990s, this was a group that frequently employed college students who were familiar with library research techniques. Pre-law and law students, college debaters, or other students interested in campaigns and with good research backgrounds often got their first experience in larger campaigns as part of the research force. While that continues to happen, more and more since 1990, well-funded candidates have turned to professional opposition research firms. The information explosion of the 1990s, fueled in part by the computer explosion, has given rise to the rapid growth of consulting firms that specialize in opposition research.[56]

The second group, the stylists, is normally composed of experienced speechwriters. They are often hired based on recommendation and/or writing samples. These individuals must be able to write in an easy, conversational style with which the candidate feels comfortable. They must be sensitive to the candidate's ability to tell a story, show righteous indignation, tell a joke, or use a particular jargon or group of metaphors. President Barack Obama, according to one account, joked that his principal campaign speechwriter, then his principal White House speechwriter, Jon Favreau, "is not so much a speechwriter as a mind reader." That account claims that Favreau "is intimately familiar with Obama's 1995 autobiography and has virtually memorized Obama's Keynote Address to the Democratic Convention in 2004. He has mastered Obama's writing style—short elegant sentences—and internalized his boss's tendency toward reflection and ideological balance."[57] In preparing speeches during the second term in the White House, Favreau gathered more than a dozen of Obama's best speeches, mining them for "inspiration, memorable turns of phrase and compelling themes."[58] With intimate familiarity with the candidate and his speaking style, indeed with his way of thinking, the speechwriters use the materials presented by the researchers to produce a speech that meets high rhetorical standards and with which the candidate feels comfortable.[59]

The final group, the media and public relations consultants, are particularly concerned with the audience. More than the other groups, they tend to be familiar with survey research techniques. Their suggestions are designed to make the speeches consistent with the other messages the audience is receiving from the campaign and, given their surveys of the audience/public, to make sure that the audience favorably perceives the candidate's speeches.

Thus, the demands put on speechwriters in large campaigns do not differ greatly from the demands put on speechwriters in smaller campaigns. The basic differences are not so much in the demands of the task, but rather in the division of labor employed to accomplish the task. Additionally, since a larger campaign is providing the audience/public with a considerable number of messages, most larger campaigns involve media and public relations consultants who focus on the speech from an audience's perspective.

## Methods of Political Speechwriting

The literature of speech communication, as well as an examination of newspaper reports, biographies of the principals, and similar material, indicates that most speechwriters and speechwriting teams operate in a similar manner.[60] In this section we will examine the basic steps involved in campaign speechwriting.

First, the speechwriter(s), the candidate, and in some instances subject matter experts will confer. In this initial conference, the purpose of the speech will be agreed upon. The candidate will indicate positions and rationales, "talking through" the speech. Many speechwriters have noted that often the conference will be recorded or a stenographer will be present. If not, the speechwriter will take copious notes. The record of the candidate's remarks will constitute a first rough draft. Michael J. Gerson, who headed President George W. Bush's speechwriting team during his campaigns and in the White House, and Jon Favreau, who served a similar function in the Obama White House, both talked through major addresses with their respective principals. Both took detailed notes. Both had extremely close relationships with the individual for whom they wrote.[61]

From the very inception, the ideas of the speech are those of the candidate. The justification and reasoning within the speech are those of the candidate. Often, some of the language the candidate used in these conferences is worked into later drafts and remains intact in the final speech. Nevertheless, in many situations, speechwriters have input into the development of the ideas that the speech reflects. That input is invariably secondary to that of the candidate, but as Martin Medhurst, a scholar of presidential speechwriting, has recently observed, it is a "myth" to presume that speechwriters have no input into policy.[62]

At this point the speechwriters, armed with a clear understanding of what the candidate wants, do their research. If the campaign has a research staff, it is brought into the development of the speech. If the campaign is small, the speechwriter does the research. One of the advantages of incumbency is that incumbent office holders can often put the resources of government to work on their behalf. A speechwriter for the president might draw on the expertise of a cabinet member or someone in the appropriate department. Similarly, congressional speechwriters' efforts might be supplemented by the Legislative Reference Service of the Library of Congress, acting on a legislator's request.

At this point a draft is developed. In larger speechwriting teams, this draft is typically done by one staff member whose work may be reviewed and altered by other speechwriters. In a small operation, an equivalent process takes place as the speechwriter prepares a draft and then revises it, perhaps drawing on the suggestions of staff members or advisors who know the candidate well but have no responsibilities for speechwriting. In major campaigns it is not uncommon for the original draft to undergo five or more revisions as speechwriters revise their own work and incorporate the suggestions of others. If possible, the candidate is shown successive drafts for input.

Depending on the candidate's reaction, several actions can be taken with the version that the speechwriter believes to be close to final. Often the candidates accept it as final, normally continuing to make minor changes, primarily stylistic, during free moments up until the time of delivery. If the speech is basically sound, but the candidate has more than stylistic concerns, these may be indicated in marginal notes or in a meeting. Subsequent drafts, better conforming to the candidate's wishes, can then be developed and resubmitted. The candidate may have an objection to one section of the speech or perhaps to some aspects of organization. Frequently when reading over the speech, the candidate may be concerned that the material will run too long or too short for the allotted time. If the speech is to be delivered over the radio or on television, the media consultants will normally enter the speechwriting process during the final few drafts. Their suggestions will be geared to ensuring that the speech is appropriate for the allotted time and contains portions that can be used for brief spots on the news shows. These sound bites normally contain vivid and startling language that exemplifies the point the candidate wishes to make. In smaller campaigns, media consultants will not be available, but a conscientious speechwriter will strive to include potential sound bites in the speech in case of press coverage. Additionally, sound bites, even in smaller campaigns, might be submitted to the media in the hope they will be used.

With slight variations to accommodate their own circumstances, this process is an accurate characterization of speechwriting in the vast majority of political campaigns where speechwriters are employed.[63] Several key points result from this description.

First, throughout this process the candidate is a major writer/editor/ collaborator. The final speech is a clear reflection of the candidate. The candidate accepts responsibility for what is said. For this reason, as one speechwriter has noted, "I don't think it occurs to the general public that a speech is ghost-written. Even if someone in the audience has read somewhere that Congressman X has a ghostwriter and he knows it as the man speaks, he forgets it. He's listening to the man, and he's holding him responsible, and he's responding to him for everything that is said."[64]

Second, although the speechwriter has also contributed to the final product, the speech belongs to the person who utters it. It is the candidate, not the speechwriter, who will receive praise or blame for the speech. Thus, it is easy to understand why one experienced political speechwriter has commented that "if there is any prerequisite to ghostwriting for political figures, I suggest that it is a willingness to sublimate one's self to the figure for whom one works."[65] Although the majority of speechwriters labor in anonymity, in recent years many presidential speechwriters have breached the code of anonymity that characterized their predecessors. Emmet John Hughes and Theodore Sorensen, who wrote for presidents Eisenhower and Kennedy, respectively, were among the first presidential speechwriters to acknowledge their roles and, in so doing, make the role of presidential speechwriter more public.[66] Today, even the speechwriters for losing presidential candidates may become public figures.[67]

Third, major campaign addresses undergo many drafts. A study of members of Congress indicates that they typically draft major campaign speeches at least three times.[68] The speeches Peggy Noonan wrote for presidents Reagan and George H. W. Bush routinely underwent five or more drafts.[69] Mike Gerson spent more than two months on the key speech of the 2000 campaign, Bush's acceptance address to the Republican National Convention. That speech ultimately went through fifteen drafts, with Bush constantly making changes to the manuscripts that Gerson and aides Karl Rove and Karen Hughes provided to him.[70]

## SURROGATE SPEAKERS

Even though most candidates make use of speechwriters, speech modules, and variants on the "Why I Am Running" speech to help them meet the demands on their time, inevitably they find that they simply cannot be in two places at once. Hence, even in smaller campaigns, it is not unusual to see a surrogate or substitute speaker filling in for an absent candidate. In large national campaigns, hundreds of people serve as surrogates for the candidate, many of whom have been trained by the campaign staff.

### Selection of Surrogates

The selection of surrogate speakers is not left to chance. Candidates seek surrogates who meet certain requirements. First, they should have a proven record of competence as public speakers. In smaller campaigns, family members, lawyers, teachers, or anyone else with speaking experience may be called upon. In larger campaigns, public officials with extensive speaking experience might be used. In a governor's race, for example, members of the state legislature might serve as surrogates for their party's nominee. At the presidential level those cabinet members, members of Congress, and family members who are good speakers are often utilized as candidate surrogates.

Second, the surrogate must have a connection to the candidate. During virtually every recent presidential campaign, many members of the candidates' families served as surrogates. The most active are the spouses. During the 2008 primaries, Hillary Clinton's principal surrogate was her husband, former president Bill Clinton.[71] In 2012, Ann Romney had her own daily campaign schedule. Many thought she was a better speaker than her husband. Candidates' children also play an active campaign role, especially if more mature. Romney's five sons targeted college campuses and youth groups. Relatives are perceived as being unusually close to the candidate, as are cabinet members and legislative allies. In 2016, all of Donald Trump's grown children and their spouses blanketed the nation speaking on behalf of their father or father-in-law.

If surrogate speakers do not have an obvious connection to the candidate, they should make their connection clear to the audience early in the speech. Perhaps they grew up with the candidate, previously worked with the candidate, or have simply been longtime supporters of the candidate. In 1976 Jimmy Carter, a peanut farmer by profession, made heavy use not only of his relatives, but also of many other longtime supporters from Georgia who became known as the "Peanut Brigade." In 2004 many of Senator Kerry's most effective surrogates were men who had served with him in Vietnam.

Third, the surrogate should have some clearly identifiable connection to the audience. Since the substitute is just that, a substitute, the candidate or the staff should select a substitute who is appropriate for the audience. In local campaigns, the surrogate may be a member of the organization sponsoring the speech or a native of the geographic area. In national campaigns, the surrogate may be the cabinet member with responsibilities for the area of government that most affects the sponsoring group, as when the secretary of labor represents the president at union affairs. Again, surrogates should make clear reference to this connection early in their speeches if it is not obvious.

Clearly, whoever is speaking on the candidate's behalf is not the audience's first choice; hence, that individual may have to overcome the resentment of the audience. For this reason the speaker should be able to stress a connection to the candidate. In effect, the surrogate is saying, "I'm the next best thing," and reminding the audience that, like Hallmark cards, this candidate cares enough to send the very best.

Surrogates should have attempted to familiarize themselves with the candidate's positions. Indeed, one reason that some candidates like to use their speechwriters for surrogates is that they are uniquely adept at putting themselves in the candidate's shoes. Nevertheless, surrogate speakers should consider using two guidelines. First, particularly in smaller campaigns, surrogates should acknowledge why the candidate is not there. Most people understand the demands placed on a candidate, and a frank statement of where the candidate is will be better received than an attempt to hide the fact that the candidate has chosen to speak elsewhere. Depending on the audience being faced, most surrogates can indicate why their principal is not present in a tactful or humorous way. One rather rotund surrogate we are acquainted with often opened his after-dinner or after-luncheon addresses by saying that his candidate wanted to maintain his weight, and it was difficult to do so during the campaign when he was constantly out attending breakfast meetings, luncheons, dinners, coffees, teas, beer busts, and the like.

> So, he's out rounding up some votes tonight in _____ where they are not serving food. Since I am the one member of the staff who clearly does not have a weight problem, he sent me here to guarantee that your food would be appreciated. Well, I certainly appreciated this fine meal, and I hope that when I am finished this evening you will have a better appreciation of why _____ ought to be elected to Congress.

An introduction like this one acknowledges that the candidate is campaigning elsewhere but does so in a humorous and tactful fashion, which reduces audience resentment.

Second, surrogates should not hesitate to remind the audience that they are not the candidate. Hence, they may not know all the answers or precisely what the candidate thinks. If the surrogate is well prepared, there should not be many occasions for this to happen. However, the speaker may confront a difficult question. When this occurs, the surrogate should simply acknowledge that to be the case, rather than guess. Arrangements should then be made for the candidate or staff to respond later.

## Benefits of Surrogates

The use of surrogate speakers can provide a variety of benefits to campaigns. In some instances, the surrogate may be a more credible speaker for a given audience than the candidate. Additionally, surrogates can say things that the candidate feels uncomfortable saying. Finally, surrogates can often aid candidates in fund-raising.[72]

Surrogates who have a unique connection to the audience may, on occasion, be more effective with that audience than the candidate. During the 2008 Republican primaries, and again in 2012, Ann Romney was the only Republican candidate's wife who consistently addressed audiences on her own, without her husband at her side. Ann Romney has multiple sclerosis and often talked about how she has handled that disease and what her husband might do for those who suffer from chronic diseases such as MS. A polished speaker, she became a uniquely strong advocate for her husband when speaking to groups with interests in medical research and other health-related matters.

Frequently, candidates may wish to say something but find that it is not politically expedient. A surrogate may be able to make the statements for the candidate. For example, in the 2008 Democratic primaries, the Hillary Clinton campaign initially had difficulty in determining how to use their most valuable surrogate, her husband, former president Bill Clinton. "It took a while—for the duration of the Iowa campaign to be exact—but the Clintons have figured out the most productive way to use former president Bill Clinton in Hillary Clinton's campaign. Their division of labor is very simple: he criticizes Barack Obama while she mostly stays positive." Hence, when the Clinton campaign wished to challenge Obama's claim that he had never supported the Iraq war and point out that the Illinois senator was highly inexperienced in foreign policy, it was Bill, not Hillary, who claimed that Obama's claims were "the biggest fairy tale I've ever seen" and stressed his inexperience by calling Obama "a kid."[73] Typically, surrogates deliver the harshest criticism of the foe. It is for this reason that vice presidential candidates are often characterized as the "attack dogs" of the campaign, while the presidential candidate stays "above the fray," appearing presidential at all times.

A classic example of the desire of the presidential candidate "to stay above the fray" and let his surrogates do the "dirty work" was evident in the first 2004 political debate when moderator Jim Lehrer questioned Senator Kerry. "You've repeatedly accused President Bush—not here tonight, but elsewhere before—of not telling the truth about Iraq, essentially of lying to the American people about Iraq. Give us some examples of what you consider to be his not telling the truth." Kerry responded by claiming, "Well, I've never used the harshest word, as you did just then. And I try not to. I've been—but I'll nevertheless tell you that I think he has not been candid with the American people."[74] Clearly, Senator Kerry was attempting to distance himself from the charge that the president was a liar. Yet, repeatedly his surrogates used that term to describe the president, particularly in discussing the president's justifications for going to war in Iraq. Surrogates can call their opponents liars. Candidates, like Kerry, often prefer to suggest that their opponent lacks candor.

Finally, surrogates are often able to help candidates raise money. Many candidates feel that it is unbecoming for them to personally ask for money. Surrogates are not embarrassed or compromised because they are not asking for themselves. Commonly, during presidential campaigns, vice presidential candidates, such as Governor Sarah Palin and Senator Joseph Biden, serve as surrogates whose primary responsibility is often to raise money for the ticket. Headlining an article on three fund-raising events that Governor Palin attended on one day in Ohio, the *Los Angeles Times* claimed that "with little notice, Sarah Palin becomes a GOP fund-raising machine." Similarly, the *Chicago Sun Times*, reporting on Senator Biden's fund-raising efforts in Seattle, Washington, observed, "The estimated total haul for Biden's fund-raisers in the Emerald City this evening: a cool million bucks."[75]

In sum, the use of surrogate speakers can provide many benefits. Their primary function is to spread the candidate's messages to audiences that might otherwise not hear them. However, as Martha Kessler stresses, this is by no means the only advantage to using surrogates.[76] Indeed, the benefits of using surrogate speakers are so important in larger campaigns, where candidates cannot possibly address all the audiences that wish to hear them, that most national and many state and regional campaigns actively recruit surrogate speakers, provide them with training, and schedule them through a speaker's bureau.

## CONCLUSIONS

Although, as we have seen in chapter 4, the media have come to play an increasingly important part in contemporary political campaigns, the public speaking of candidates and their surrogates nevertheless is at the core of any campaign. In small campaigns, public speaking may be the principal form of persuasion utilized. In this chapter, we have seen that the decision to speak is not left to chance in well-managed campaigns. Rather, the campaign identifies the audiences to whom it wishes to speak and the messages it wishes to send and then arranges situations that conform to those wishes. Moreover, we have observed how candidates make use of speech modules and variants on the "Why I Am Running" speech to create a basic speech that can be used, with some adjustments, repeatedly during the campaign. Additionally, we have examined the reasons for the growing use of speechwriters, the demands placed on such individuals, and the methods they use to meet those demands. Finally, we have observed the use of surrogate speakers, focusing on the criteria for selecting such speakers, the techniques such speakers commonly employ, and the benefits surrogate speakers provide to a campaign. Despite changes that have occurred in technology and the way campaigns are managed, all candidates, whether incumbents or challengers, whether speaking at a rally, at a press conference, on television, or on the radio, utilize the ideas we have discussed in this chapter. Clearly, public speaking remains a fundamental practice of political campaigns.

## NOTES

1. William Sweeney, "The Principles of Planning," in *Campaigns and Elections*, ed. James Thurber and Candice Nelson (Boulder, CO: Westview Press, 1995), 14.

2. Jacob Javits, "How I Used a Poll in Campaigning for Congress," *Public Opinion Quarterly* 11 (Summer 1947): 222–26.

3. Daniel Burton and Michael Shea, *Campaign Craft*, 3rd ed. (Westport, CT: Praeger, 2006), 182–83.

4. See Martin Schramm, *Running for President: A Journal of the Carter Campaign* (New York: Pocket Books, 1977), 428–31, for insight into a national campaign's targeting strategies.

5. Dennis W. Johnson, *Democracy for Hire: A History of American Political Consulting* (New York: Oxford University Press, 2017), 338.

6. Ibid.

7. Ibid., 339.

8. "An Evaluation of 2016 Election Polls in the U.S.," American Association for Public Opinion Research, May 21, 2017, accessed June 21, 2018, https://www.aapor.org/Education-Resources/Reports/An-Evaluation-of-2016-Election-Polls-in-the-U-S.aspx.

9. Ibid.

10. Paul Herrnson, *Congressional Elections*, 2nd ed. (Washington, DC: Congressional Quarterly Press, 1998), 172–74.

11. Pamela Hunter, "Using Focus Groups in Campaigns: A Caution," *Campaigns and Elections* 21 (August 2000): 38.

12. Larry Powell and Joseph Cowart, *Political Campaign Communication: Inside and Out*, 2nd ed. (Boston: Pearson, 2013), 166–67.

13. Dan Balz, *Collision 2012* (New York: Viking, 2013), 52–56.

14. See Robert V. Friedenberg, *Communication Consultants in Political Campaigns: Ballot Box Warriors* (Westport, CT: Praeger, 1997), 51–54.

15. Jason Johnson, *Political Consultants and Campaigns: One Day Sale* (Boulder, CO: Westview Press, 2012), 59–62.

16. Ibid., 75.

17. Ibid.

18. Ibid., 74.

19. Ibid., 69.

20. Josh Womack, "How a Copywriter Can Be a Candidate's Best Friend," *Campaigns & Elections*, April 4, 2018, accessed July 12, 2018, https://www.campaignsandelections.com/campaign-insider/how-a-copywriter-can-be-a-candidate-s-best-friend.

21. Gary Jacobson, *The Politics of Congressional Elections*, 4th ed. (New York: Longman, 1997), 74.

22. Ibid., 70–71.

23. Johnson, *Political Consultants and Campaigns*, 74–79.

24. Kennedy is quoted in Ralph G. Martin, *A Hero For Our Time: The Intimate Story of the Kennedy Years* (New York: Macmillan, 1983), 149.

25. Organizing a persuasive message by gaining attention and then presenting a need, satisfying the need, and visualizing that satisfaction are recommendations that date at least as far back as the earliest editions of Allan Monroe's classic public speaking text, *Principles and Types of Speech Communication*, which first appeared in 1935. Yet those very terms are currently being used by political speech coaches. See Michael Shadow and Greg Peck, "Politically Speaking," *Campaigns and Elections* 12 (May 1991): 54.

26. In 1992 Democratic candidates Clinton and Gore put together a book that was little more than their speech modules. See Bill Clinton and Albert Gore, *Putting People First* (New York: Times Books, 1992).

27. Powell and Cowart, *Political Campaign Communication*, 142.

28. Josh Womack, "An Outside Perspective on the Traditional Stump Speech," *Campaigns & Elections*, May 7, 2018, accessed July 12, 2018, https://www.campaignsandelections.com/campaign-insider/an-outside-perspective-on-the-traditional-stump-speech.

29. Robert Lehrman, *The Political Speechwriter's Companion* (Washington, DC: CQ Press, 2010), 13.

30. Ibid., 297.

31. Ron Faucheux, "Public Speaking and Doing Press Interviews," presentation to Campaigns and Elections 12th Annual National Campaign Training Seminar and Trade Show, Washington, DC, June 17, 1995. Also see Ron Faucheux, "The Message," *Campaigns and Elections* 15 (May 1994): 46–49.

32. Faucheux, "The Message," 49.

33. The next few paragraphs utilize the questions that Faucheux suggests. See Faucheux, "The Message," 49.

34. Johnson, *Political Consultants and Campaigns*, 132.

35. Powell and Cowart, *Political Campaign Communication*, 143.

36. Ibid.

37. Quoted in William Norwood Brigance, "Ghostwriting before Franklin D. Roosevelt and the Radio," *Today's Speech* 4 (September 1956): 11.

38. Robert Bishop, "Bruce Barton—Presidential Stage Manager," *Journalism Quarterly* 33 (Spring 1956): 85–89.

39. Discussed in Peggy Noonan, *What I Saw at the Revolution: A Political Life in the Reagan Era* (New York: Random House, 1990), 92.

40. Bernard K. Duffy and Mark Royden Winchell, "'Speak the Speech I Pray You': The Practice and Perils of Literary and Oratorical Ghostwriting," *Southern Speech Communication Journal* 55 (Fall 1989): 105.

41. Irwin Ross, *The Loneliest Campaign* (New York: New American Library, 1968), 89.

42. Walter J. Stelkovis, "Ghostwriting: Ancient and Honorable," *Today's Speech* 2 (January 1954): 17.

43. John F. Kennedy, *The Speeches of Senator John F. Kennedy: Presidential Campaign of 1960* (Washington, DC: Government Printing Office, 1961), 840–1267.

44. Evan Thomas and the staff of *Newsweek*, "How Bush Did It," *Newsweek*, November 15, 2004, 124.

45. Donald K. Smith, "The Speech-Writing Team in a State Political Campaign," *Today's Speech* 20 (Spring 1972): 16.

46. Joseph Persico, "The Rockefeller Rhetoric: Writing Speeches for the 1970 Campaign," *Today's Speech* 20 (Spring 1972): 57.

47. Perry Sekus and Robert Friedenberg, "Public Speaking in the House of Representatives: The 97th Congress Speaks," unpublished study, Miami University, 1982, 9.

48. Ernest Bormann, "Ethics of Ghostwritten Speeches," *Quarterly Journal of Speech* 47 (October 1961): 266.

49. Ibid., 266–67.

50. Thomas Benson, "Conversations with a Ghost," *Today's Speech* 16 (November 1968): 73.

51. Quoted in Martin Medhurst and Gary X. Dreibelbis, "Building the Speechwriter-Principal Relationship: Minority Leader Robert Michel Confronts His Ghost," *Central States Speech Journal* 37 (Winter 1986): 242.

52. Richard Wolffe, "In His Candidate's Voice," *Newsweek*, January 6, 2008, accessed January 7, 2008, www.newsweek.com/id/84756/output/print.

53. James T. Snyder, former speechwriter for New York governor Mario Cuomo, offers seven suggestions for aspiring speechwriters. Three of them deal directly with language and style. See Snyder, "7 Tips for Writing a Great Campaign Speech," *Campaigns & Elections*, February 2000, 68–70. Melvin Helitzer's discussion of political speechwriting focuses on characteristics of language that facilitate good delivery. See Helitzer, "Political Speeches," in *The Practice of Political Communication*, ed. Guido H. Stempel (Englewood Cliffs, NJ: Prentice Hall, 1994), 71–88. Peggy Noonan, in perhaps the most informative recent discussion of the craft of speechwriting, stresses that political speechwriters are dealing with policy. But her discussion of her years in the Reagan White House indicates that as a speechwriter she largely followed the policy directives of others and made most of her important contributions by providing Reagan with language that helped persuade audiences to support his policies. Especially see chapter 5, "Speech! Speech!" in Noonan, *What I Saw at the Revolution*, 49–67.

54. Persico, "Rockefeller Rhetoric," 58.

55. Craig R. Smith, "Contemporary Political Speech Writing," *Southern Speech Communication Journal* 42 (Fall 1976): 52–68; Craig R. Smith, "Addendum to Contemporary Political Speech Writing," *Southern Speech Communication Journal* 43 (Winter 1977): 191–94.

56. See Friedenberg, *Communication Consultants in Political Campaigns*, 72–73.

57. Eli Saslow, "Helping to Write History," *Washington Post*, December 18, 2008, A1, accessed December 22, 2008, www.washingtonpost.com/wpdyn/content/article/2008/12/17/AR2008121703903.html.

58. Sam Stein, "Obama's Inaugural Address 'One of the Hardest Speeches I've Written,' Jon Favreau Says," *Huffington Post*, February 3, 2013.

59. On the matter of candidate comfort with the writer and the speech, see Medhurst and Dreibelbis, "Building the Speechwriter-Principal Relationship," 242.

60. The speech communication literature utilized in this section includes Robert F. Ray, "Ghostwriting in Presidential Campaigns," *Central States Speech Journal* 8 (Fall 1956): 8–11; Benson, "Conversations with a Ghost," 71–81; Persico, "Rockefeller Rhetoric," 57–62; Howard Schwartz, "Senator 'Scoop' Jackson Speaks on Speaking," *Speaker and Gavel* 5 (November 1968): 21–31; Robert Friedenberg, "The Army of Invisible Men: Ghostwriting for Congressmen and Congressional Candidates," *The Forensic* 62 (May 1977): 4–8; Sara Arendall Newell and Thomas King, "The Keynote Address of the Democratic National Convention 1972: The Evolution of a Speech," *Southern Speech Communication Journal* 39 (Summer 1974):

346–58; Smith, "Contemporary Political Speech Writing," 52–68; Smith, "Addendum," 191–94; Lois J. Einhorn, "The Ghosts Unmasked: A Review of Literature on Speechwriting," *Communication Quarterly* 30 (Winter 1981): 41–47; Medhurst and Dreibelbis, "Building the Speechwriter-Principal Relationship," 239–47; Robert V. Friedenberg, "Jesse Alexander Helms: Secular Preacher of the Religious Right," *Speaker and Gavel* 24 (Fall/Winter/Spring 1987): 60–68; Lois J. Einhorn, "The Ghosts Talk: Personal Interviews with Three Former Speechwriters," *Communication Quarterly* 36 (Spring 1988): 94–108; Duffy and Winchell, "'Speak the Speech I Pray You,'" 102–15; and Noonan, *What I Saw at the Revolution*, 68–92. The best detailed account of the composition of a George W. Bush speech does not involve a political race. However, the speechwriting process in his White House no doubt closely resembled that used during the campaign. See Dan Balz and Bob Woodward, "A Presidency Defined in One Speech," *Washington Post*, February 2, 2002, A-1, www .washingtonpost. com/wp-dyn/articles/a11062-2002Feb1.html. For Obama and McCain, see Saslow, "Helping to Write History"; Ashley Parker, "What Would Obama Say?" *New York Times*, January 20, 2008, accessed October 23, 2009, www.nytimes.com/2008/01/20/ fashion/20speechwriter.html; Wolffe, "In His Candidate's Voice"; and Michael Leahy, "McCain Chief Loyalist Has New Role," *Washington Post*, October 30, 2008, accessed April 2, 2010, www.washingtonpost.com/wp-dyn/content/article/2008/10/29.

61. Mike Allen, "For Bush's Speechwriter, Job Grows Beyond Words," *Washington Post*, October 11, 2002, A35, www.washingtonpost.com/wp-dyn/articlesa9575-2002Oct10.html.

62. See Martin J. Medhurst, "Presidential Speechwriting: Ten Myths That Plague Modern Scholarship," in *Presidential Speechwriting: From the New Deal to the Reagan Revolution and Beyond*, ed. Kurt Ritter and Martin J. Medhurst (College Station: Texas A&M University Press, 2003), 12–14.

63. An extremely brief description of the ghostwriting process, which coincides with this one, can be found in Einhorn, "Ghosts Unmasked," 42. Also see Medhurst and Dreibelbis, "Building the Speechwriter-Principal Relationship," 242–45.

64. Benson, "Conversations with a Ghost," 79–80.

65. Friedenberg, "Army of Invisible Men," 4.

66. Medhurst, "Presidential Speechwriting," 9–10.

67. Robert Shrum, a veteran Democratic political consultant and speechwriter, has worked for a host of losing Democratic presidential candidates, including John F. Kerry in 2004. Shrum is frequently interviewed and quoted. Although his presidential candidates often lose, he is acknowledged as among the finest liberal Democratic speechwriters.

68. Sekus and Friedenberg, "Public Speaking," 6.

69. Noonan, *What I Saw at the Revolution*, 74.

70. On the development of this speech, see Robert V. Friedenberg, *Notable Speeches in Contemporary Presidential Campaigns* (Westport, CT: Praeger, 2002), 234–35.

71. See, for example, "Obama Faces Off against Both Clintons," *Politico*, accessed January 21, 2008, dyn.politico.com/printstory.cfm?uuid=9A178539-3048-5C12-0080084B087E4764.

72. On the functions of surrogates, see Martha Stout Kessler, "The Role of Surrogate Speakers in the 1980 Presidential Campaign," *Quarterly Journal of Speech* 67 (May 1981): 148–50.

73. On Bill Clinton's attacks, see Fred Barnes, "The Bubba Factor," *Daily Standard*, January 20, 2008, www.weeklystandard.com/Content/Public/Articles/000/000/000/014/6271 chzc.asp?pg=1; and Noemie Emery, "The Wages of Sensitivity," *Weekly Standard*, January 28, 2008, www.weeklystandard.com/Utilities/printer_preview.asp?idArticle=14616&R=138F.

74. The quoted material in this paragraph is drawn from the text of the first presidential debate of 2004. See the text found on the site of the Commission for Presidential Debates at www.debates.org/index.php?page=september-30-2004-debate-transcript.

75. See Andrew Malcolm, "With Little Notice, Sarah Palin Becomes a GOP Fundraising Machine," *Los Angeles Times*, September 17, 2008, accessed April 8, 2010, http://latimesblogs .latimes.com/washington/2008/09/sarah-palin-mon; and Lynn Sweet, "Joe Biden at Seattle Fund Raiser Transcript Says Obama Will Be Tested," *Chicago Sun Times*, October 21, 2008, accessed April 8, 2010, blogs.suntimes.com/sweet/2008/10/joe_biden_seattle_fund_rais.

76. Kessler, "Role of Surrogate Speakers."

# 8

⁓

# Recurring Forms of Political Campaign Communication

In his classic article "The Rhetorical Situation," Lloyd Bitzer defined a rhetorical situation as "a complex of persons, events, objects and relations presenting an actual or potential exigency which can be completely or partially removed if discourse, introduced into the situation, can so constrain human decision or action as to bring about the significant modification of the exigence."[1] Bitzer's work has served as the basis for many studies of rhetoric that are based on the premise that comparable rhetorical situations produce comparable rhetorical responses.[2]

While such studies have been subject to criticism, we find that the basic premise that some rhetorical situations are relatively analogous and hence produce relatively analogous discourse is a valuable premise for the study of much political campaign communication.

In this chapter, we shall suggest that most political campaigns tend to produce several similar, comparable, or analogous situations. Moreover, these situations tend to produce similar, comparable, or analogous discourse. Four such comparable situations, found in most campaigns, are the rhetorical situations created by:

1. the need of candidates to announce formally their candidacies to the public,
2. the need of candidates to accept publicly the nomination of their party,
3. the need of candidates to seek media coverage of their views,
4. the need of candidates to make public apologies for their statements or behavior.

In this chapter, we will examine the discourse to which these situations traditionally give rise: announcement speeches, acceptance addresses, press conferences, and political apologies. We will study these recurring forms first by describing the situations that create the need or exigency for their use. Second, we will discuss the purposes that these four recurring forms of political campaign communication traditionally serve. Third, we will discuss the strategies most frequently and successfully employed by candidates delivering these four recurring forms of political campaign communication. As in other chapters, we will use contemporary and historical examples. We reserve discussions and examples from the 2016 presidential campaign for chapter 14.

## ANNOUNCEMENT SPEECHES

Candidates normally announce that they are seeking public office through a formal address to the public. However, this formal address is rarely the first act of the campaign. Rather, considerable work has preceded it. The effort in which candidates and their associates have engaged during the surfacing stage helps to shape the rhetorical situation in which the announcement address is made.[3]

### Preannouncement Situation

At least three activities typically precede any announcement address, regardless of the office being sought or the candidate who is announcing. First, an assessment must be made of the likelihood of winning. This will include an assessment of the candidate's ability to attract sufficient financial and voter support and to develop an organization capable of winning the office. The results of this analysis may enter into the announcement address itself. In any event, it gives the candidate a clearer understanding of the situation.

Second, most candidates tend to inform key individuals personally, prior to their public announcement. Typically, these are politically, financially, or personally significant individuals whom the candidate wishes to flatter. If the office being contested is statewide or national in scope, often the candidate may inform a small group of individuals personally and then send a personal letter of announcement, in advance of the candidate's public statement, to several dozen, hundred, or even thousands of others. The point is that these individuals are significant, and the candidate wishes to flatter them.[4] However, the advance announcement in person to a few key figures fulfills a second purpose. It serves as a means of providing the candidate with feedback regarding the rhetorical situation to be faced. These key, well-placed individuals may be able to help shape strategy, better understand the concerns of the constituency, or identify possible obstacles.

Finally, the announcement should conform to any preconceived expectations that the public might have about it. Hence, the third preliminary activity of the candidate is to determine public expectations about the announcement. For example, have prior candidates conditioned the public to expect that an announcement of candidacy for the office sought should be made from the state capital rather than from the candidate's home? Does the public have any expectations about what the candidate should say? Does the public have expectations about the qualifications necessary for this position, which might be mentioned in the announcement speech?

In recent years, at the presidential level, public expectations for a candidate announcement have changed to some degree. In the past, voters expected candidates to give major speeches announcing their candidacy, generating considerable press coverage. Then the candidates would campaign. Today, considerable coverage is not automatic. Moreover, the coverage is likely to center on the horse-race aspects of the coming campaign: the chances the candidate has of winning and the tactics the candidate will employ to win, rather than the message of the candidate to voters. Consequently, in recent years, at the presidential level, candidates have often revealed their intentions gradually. The public has come to expect that a serious presidential candidate will likely go through several steps before ultimately delivering an announcement speech. The presidential announcement "trek" of Mitt Romney is illustrative.

During the Christmas holiday season in 2010, all family members met to discuss whether Romney should run for the nomination for a second time. Actually, at that time ten of twelve family members "voted" no to the notion of running for president. Most of the reservations were personal about the rough and tough campaign process. There were also political concerns such as the need to raise millions of dollars, countless nights away from family, and continual personal attacks in the media.[5] One of the two favorable votes was from Ann Romney. She had become concerned about the direction Obama was taking the nation. She thought Mitt's business and government experience could right the nation. In fact, Ann had totally changed her mind about another run for the office.[6]

Just weeks before the family meeting, Romney met with his political team. He had laid the groundwork for running, "paying his dues" by campaigning for national, state, and local Republican candidates; meeting with donors; raising money; and promoting his book *No Apology*. There were about a dozen campaign professionals attending the meeting, a larger number than most campaigns. The meeting covered many topics, from potential rivals to policy concerns to a rationale for running for president.[7] He was the early favorite and was in no real rush to announce his candidacy. In fact, before he announced, a number of candidates had indicated their interest in entering the nomination race: Tim Pawlenty, Herman Cain, Newt Gingrich, John Thune, Mike Pence, Rick Santorum, and Michele Bachmann.[8]

Romney had a final meeting with his senior advisors in April 2011, just days before officially forming his exploratory committee. In the meeting, they shared a state-by-state primary strategy. They also discussed his political vulnerabilities.[9] Everything was set to announce the formation of his exploratory committee. This signals the "official" start of a campaign and allows for fundraising, hiring of staff, and establishing state-by-state campaign organizations. Romney made the announcement by video. He was casually dressed and spoke directly into the camera for only two and a half minutes. He shot the video on the campus of the University of New Hampshire. Romney focused on the loss of jobs and failed economic policies of the Obama administration. "Over 20 million Americans still can't find a job or have given up looking. . . . How has this happened in the nation that leads the world in innovation? The answer is that President Obama's policies have failed." Much of the video highlighted his career as a businessperson creating jobs in the private sector and his management experience as former governor of Massachusetts. Romney wanted to present himself in announcing the formation of his presidential exploratory committee as a "skilled—and experienced—jobs creator."[10]

On June 2, 2011, in the first presidential primary state of New Hampshire in the town of Stratham, Romney formally announced, "We know we can bring this country back. I'm Mitt Romney. I believe in America. And I am running for President of the United States."[11] But Romney's announcement "trek" was not over. As traditional, there is immediate post-announcement campaigning. Most candidates for virtually any office will attempt to underscore their seriousness of purpose by immediately following their announcement with some type of campaign event. Romney was no exception. He scheduled a town hall meeting in Manchester, New Hampshire, followed by a speech at a Faith and Freedom forum in Washington, D.C.[12]

Clearly the rhetorical situation for every announcement address differs. Yet, typically, the candidate has first to analyze prospects for the campaign, second to share the impending candidacy with a group of significant associates, and third to consider public expectations concerning the announcement address. The latter, especially for high-profile offices, often involves gradually preparing the public for the announcement of candidacy and immediately following up on the announcement with campaign activities.

## Purpose of Address

The announcement address should serve several purposes. Depending on the situation that the candidate confronts, one or more of the purposes discussed here may be minimized or underplayed, while others are stressed.

First, it clearly signals the candidate's intention to run. Second, it may serve to discourage the competition. If the announcement address alludes to the candidate's strengths, such as the ability to articulate the issues, raise money, or wage an aggressive campaign, it may discourage other potential candidates from contesting for the party nomination or the office itself. As we will see in our discussion of strategies, typically the content of the address must be accompanied with actions that successfully discourage the competition.

The third purpose that announcement addresses often serve is to indicate why the candidate is running. Candidates may want to stress what they can bring to the office that others cannot—how they can uniquely serve the public. For example, in announcing his presidential candidacy, Donald Trump observed, "Our country is in serious trouble. We don't have victories anymore. We used to have victories, but we don't have them. When was the last time anybody saw us beating. . . . The U.S. has become a dumping ground for everybody else's problems. . . . This is going to be an election that's based on competence, because people are tired of these nice people. And they're tired of being ripped off by everybody in the world. Sadly, the American dream is dead."[13] And for Trump, what makes him unique is "I don't need anybody's money. It's nice. I don't need anybody's money. . . . I'm using my own money. I'm not using the lobbyists. I'm not using donors. I don't care. I'm really rich."[14] He is running because he has "the kind of thinking our country needs. We need that thinking. We have the opposite thinking. We have losers. We have losers. We have people that don't have it. We have people that are morally corrupt. We have people that are selling this country down the drain."[15]

A fourth purpose frequently served by the announcement address is to initiate the themes of the campaign. As the candidate's first major campaign address, it is appropriate to initiate any important themes that may run throughout the campaign. In 2016, Trump addressed many themes or issues of the campaign: unemployment and jobs, immigration, health care, trade, the military, and terrorism, to name a few.[16]

Hillary Clinton posted a video on YouTube to announce her candidacy. The video begins with stories by a diverse group of people discussing changes or "something they are about to do." Clinton begins, "I'm getting ready to do something, too, I'm running for president. Americans have fought their way back from tough economic times, but the deck is still stacked in favor of those at the top. Everyday Americans need a champion, and I want to be that champion, so you can do more than just get by. You can get ahead and stay ahead because when families are strong, America is strong. So I'm hitting the road to earn your vote because it's your time. And I hope you'll join me on this journey." Interestingly, Clinton, unlike in the past, did not provide a litany of issues or themes she wanted to address. The campaign decided "to ease into presenting her ideas for alleviating the growing gap between rich and poor and for increasing wages."[17] This approach allowed Clinton to continue to generate news coverage in a more positive way while the Republican candidates challenged each other in rather heated debates.

In sum, the announcement address may serve several purposes in addition to the obvious one of officially signaling the candidate's intent to run. It may serve to discourage possible competitors, indicate why the candidate has chosen to run, and initiate major campaign themes.

## STRATEGIES OF ADDRESS

In preparing to announce their intention to run, a variety of choices confronts candidates. They must consider the timing, location, who should accompany them, speech content, and finally the way they will follow up on their announcement.

Timing the announcement speech may be difficult. Often the first candidate to announce receives more coverage and, by virtue of being first, may be perceived as being more serious, credible, or legitimate. Although an early announcement may attract media coverage, content of the coverage might well focus on the candidate's potential to win, the funds raised, and the staff that has been recruited. Obviously, by announcing early to gain coverage, the candidate runs the risk that the announcement will not be taken seriously because there are few other overt trappings of a campaign.

Timing is also vital because of the effect that it may have on others who are politically important, both other candidates and potential supporters. There is evidence to suggest, for example, that Michael Dukakis was not anxious to run for the presidency in 1988, but was forced to do so because he feared that in 1992 Massachusetts senator Edward Kennedy would be a presidential candidate.[18] By running in 1988, Dukakis could start with the support of his own home state, which could not be taken for granted if he delayed until 1992. In 2012, because Romney was ahead in the polls for the nomination among Republicans, he had less pressure to announce early. In races for lesser offices, timing of the announcement can also be important. Obviously, it may not receive the publicity that is associated with a presidential candidate's announcement, but it will be noticed and considered by other crucial decision makers in the constituency: potential opponents, potential contributors, volunteers, staff members, and supporters.

Where to deliver the announcement address is a second strategic consideration that candidates must confront. In so doing, they must consider voter expectations and tradition, as well as the issues they hope to develop in the upcoming campaign. In recent years, candidates have typically chosen to deliver their announcement addresses from (1) locations that have symbolic meaning, (2) locations that have personal meaning for the candidate, (3) locations that underscore a major theme of their campaign, or (4) locations that are likely to attract a large audience.

Trump held his announcement in the lobby of his Trump Tower retail and residential building. He made a grand and impressive entrance with his wife, riding down the very tall escalator. It was as if he were descending from above to the waiting crowd—certainly, a notable entrance staged for television and video.

Romney chose to formally announce his candidacy at Bittersweet Farm in Stratham, New Hampshire. The owners of Bittersweet Farm, Doug and Stella Scamman, are "big-time" Republicans who host many Republican rallies and events with such notables as former president George W. Bush and governors, senators, and members of Congress. The venue had a rich political history as well as being located in the all-important first primary state of New Hampshire. Romney spoke from the bed of a hay wagon wearing dark slacks and an open-collared shirt. Romney's campaign tested several styles of presentation using focus groups. The research revealed that Romney was "best" when in jeans and less scripted.[19] The appeal was that of a "common citizen candidate," not a multimillionaire. President Obama launched his 2012 election campaign with large rallies in Columbus, Ohio, and Richmond, Virginia. Both of these were key battleground states in 2008 that flipped from Republican to Democrat in the presidential election. Once again, these two states would be crucial to any reelection bid.[20]

Attracting a large audience is a fourth consideration when determining the location of the announcement address site. This is often of exceptional importance to candidates who are long shots and not very well known. Consequently, in recent years some candidates have chosen to announce their candidacies on radio and television shows where potentially large audiences can see and hear them. Local candidates may use a highly rated local show.

In 2006 and 2008 two long-shot presidential candidates used the appeal of entertainment shows to make their announcement in front of large audiences. On September 4, 2006, former Tennessee senator Fred Thompson skipped the Republican candidates' debate in New Hampshire to appear on Jay Leno's *Tonight Show* to announce his candidacy. His communications director, Todd Harris, explained Thompson's decision by observing that "it makes a lot of sense for Thompson to appear on the Leno show instead of the GOP debate because the candidate will reach everyday normal Americans who don't live in the 202 [Washington, D.C.] area code."[21] Clearly Thompson was seeking a larger audience than the few who might be attentive to a political debate or an announcement speech, two years prior to the election. Leno provided him with that large audience.

Similarly, Democratic long-shot presidential candidate Connecticut senator Chris Dodd announced his candidacy for the 2008 Democratic presidential nomination on the then-nationally syndicated radio and cable television program *Imus in the Morning*. Dodd claimed that he utilized the forum Imus provided because he had been appearing on that show for fourteen years. However, there was also a practical consideration. Dodd had first sought to appear on NBC's *Today Show*, which would have provided him a larger audience. However, the *Today Show* had already made plans to interview Secretary of State Condoleezza Rice and hence they would only provide Dodd with three minutes of airtime. Imus gave him twenty minutes. Candidates who are perceived as having little chance, such as Thompson and Dodd, have difficulty attracting large audiences, which the public expects, to an announcement address. Hence, in recent years some have chosen to make their announcement on radio and television shows, often followed up by a campaign swing through the district or, in the case of presidential candidates such as Thompson and Dodd, the early primary states.[22] A third question candidates consider when making their announcement addresses is with whom they might wish to share the spotlight. That is, who else should be present and in a prominent position? Traditionally, most candidates have announced their candidacies while surrounded by family, close friends, admirers, and supporters. However, exactly who should be invited, who should sit with the candidates, and who might also make a few brief remarks are questions that must be answered by candidates as they plan their announcement event. Often the presence of prominent individuals in the community, city, or state; supportive remarks from party leaders; and similar visible signs of support for the candidate at the very outset of the campaign can help establish credibility and discourage potential competitors for the nomination or the office itself.

In 1960 John Kennedy's staff was in close contact with Ohio governor Michael DiSalle. The Kennedy announcement was made with the full knowledge that immediately thereafter, DiSalle would be the first governor to endorse Kennedy. In doing so, DiSalle could guarantee that the large Ohio delegation to the Democratic convention was committed to Kennedy.[23] DiSalle's actions, immediately after the Kennedy announcement, made it clear to prospective challengers that the Kennedy campaign was not to be underestimated and may well, as the Kennedys hoped, have slowed down or discouraged the challenges of other possible contenders.

In contrast, as previously noted, when he announced that he would seek the 2008 presidential nomination of the Democratic Party, John Edwards was alone. The fact that he was alone might have dramatized that Edwards was alone among political leaders, or at least stood out among political leaders, because of his interest in the poor. Although Edwards selected the location of his announcement to emphasize his concern for the poor, the total lack of any of the accoutrements of an announcement event, such as the presence of family, friends, party allies, and other supporters, might equally as well have been interpreted by many as indicative of a lack of support for Edwards.

On occasion, as in John Kerry's announcement address in 2004, the candidate may wish to share the stage with individuals whose very presence may signal a major theme of the campaign. While opening his campaign in Mt. Pleasant, South Carolina, with the USS *Yorktown* looming in the background, John Kerry shared the stage with eight of his Vietnam War Swift boat crewmates and was introduced by former Georgia senator Max Cleland, a triple amputee as a result of his Vietnam War injuries.[24] The presence of these individuals reaffirmed a major Kerry campaign theme, that he was uniquely fit for leadership in a time of war. The announcement address itself is yet a fourth strategic consideration with which candidates must deal. The content of this speech is, in part, dictated by its purposes. Typically, three themes are present in most announcement addresses. Candidates announce that they are, in fact, running. Additionally, typically they explain why they are running. Finally, they also suggest the likelihood of their victory.

Unless candidates can provide some cogent reasons for running, their candidacy may end very early. Senator Edward Kennedy experienced this difficulty in 1980 when he announced his intention to run for the presidency. In his announcement speech and in the speeches and interviews that followed, he had difficulty offering cogent reasons for running. He chose to challenge an incumbent president of his own party. Yet, analysis of his positions on major issues, compared to those of President Carter, revealed very few significant differences at the outset of the campaign.[25] Kennedy's failure to offer a clear explanation of why he was running hurt his candidacy. The public expects candidates to have rational reasons for running and to share those reasons at the outset of the campaign. Candidates who fail to provide them in the announcement speech, or very shortly thereafter, tend to generate public distrust of their motives.

More typical of announcement addresses is to provide the public with reasons to elect them. For Romney in 2012, it was about his executive management experience, job creation, and specifically to repeal Obamacare. He argued that all his experiences—"starting and running businesses for 25 years, turning around the Olympics, governing a state—have helped shape who I am and how I lead." He further pledged, "I will insist that Washington learns to respect the Constitution, including the 10th Amendment. We will return responsibility and authority to the states for dozens of government programs—and that begins with a complete repeal of Obamacare." In addition, "from my first day in office my number one job will be to see that America once again is number one in job creation."

Donald Trump also highlighted his business successes and vast experience negotiating with foreign countries. Interestingly, a major part of his argument was simply that the "professional" politicians will not and cannot get things done.

> Well, you need somebody, because politicians are all talk, no action. Nothing's gonna get done. They will not bring us—believe me—to the promised land. They will not. As an example, I've been on the circuit making speeches, and I hear my fellow Republicans. And they're wonderful people. I like them. They all want me to support them. They don't know how to bring it about. They come up to my office. I'm meeting with three of them in the next week. And they don't know—"Are you running? Are you not running? Could we have your support? What do we do? How do we do it?" I like them. And I hear their speeches. And they don't talk jobs and they don't talk China . . . But you don't hear that from anybody else. You don't hear it from anybody else. And I watch the speeches. I watch the speeches of these people, and they say the sun will rise, the moon will set, all sorts of wonderful things will happen. And people are saying, "What's going on? I just want a job. Just get me a job. I don't need the rhetoric. I want a job."[26]

It is not uncommon for incumbents not to make formal announcement addresses. In fact, incumbent presidents William Jefferson Clinton and George W.

Bush simply used press releases and statements on their internet sites. Neither felt it was necessary to give an announcement address, no doubt in part because as incumbent presidents so much of what they said was widely covered. Bush did post a brief statement on his campaign website on August 18, 2003, in which he thanked visitors for their interest and encouraged their involvement in his forthcoming campaign, thus signaling that he would run.[27] There was never any doubt that both men would seek reelection in an effort to continue to advance their policies. Unlike challenger candidates, both evidently felt it unnecessary to go to the effort involved in staging a major event to announce their candidacies and both trusted that the public understood that the reason to reelect them was to continue their first-term policies. However, as noted, President Obama is a notable exception.

In announcing candidacy, most office seekers also stress the likelihood of their victory. In so doing, they often focus on their strengths and on the weaknesses of potential opponents. Implicit in this discussion is their fitness for the office. The candidate claims to be better able to manage the office, better able to represent the constituency, and of course better able to attract funds and wage an effective campaign than anyone else. President Obama offers a challenge to supporters in 2012:

> But if there is one thing that we learned in 2008, it's that nothing is more powerful than millions of voices calling for change. When enough of you knock on doors, when you pick up phones, when you talk to your friends, when you decide that it's time for a change to happen, guess what? Change happens. Change comes to America. And that's what we need again. . . . So, if you're willing to stick with me, if you are willing to fight with me, and press on with me; if you're willing to work even harder in this election than you did in the last election, I guarantee you—we will move this country forward. We'll finish what we started.

The content of the candidate's announcement address varies with the situation. However, most candidates, perhaps conditioned in part by public expectations, will formally declare their candidacy, attempt to explain why they are running, and suggest that they will win.

The strategies involved in the announcement address must also include the immediate follow-up to the address. The candidate should not simply announce that he or she is running and then seemingly disappear from public view. Rather, the timing of the address, its location, the other people invited to the announcement, and the discourse itself might all contribute to and climax in the way the candidate follows up on the announcement. For example, in recent years many cash-starved candidates, or candidates for local offices, have followed up their announcement addresses by taking a walking tour of their district or state. Such a method of following up may allow the candidate to stress key issues and begin to live up to announcement address promises. It enables the candidate to express concern for all constituencies within the district, evidencing ability to unify people. At various points in the walk, the candidate can be greeted by prominent supporters, discuss the campaign with them, and of course get extensive media coverage.

Regardless of the specific method used, a walk, follow-up mailings, the endorsement of prominent citizens, announcing staff appointments, and the like, it is sound strategy to coordinate the announcement address with some type of follow-up activity illustrating that the candidate is serious about seeking office and is already gaining support. Often within hours of making their announce-ment addresses, candidates make campaign visits to the early primary and caucus states of New Hampshire, Iowa, and South Carolina. Similarly, on the local and state level, candidates typically engage in an early flurry of campaign activity im-mediately after delivering their announcement addresses.

In sum, the announcement address is not as simple as it may at first appear. Considerable thought must be given to the timing of the address, to its location, to the other parties who may share the spotlight with the candidate, to what the candidate will actually say, and to how the candidate will immediately follow up on the announcement. The announcement address is the centerpiece of a rhe-torical situation created by the candidate's need to formally announce his or her candidacy to the public. Although the address may be the first public indication of candidacy, it should not be the first political activity the candidate attempts. Rather, considerable thought and preparation should precede the announcement speech to ensure that the candidate's campaign is opened effectively.

## ACCEPTANCE ADDRESSES

In the 1830s, national candidates nominated by the Democratic Party began to respond to their nominations with letters of acceptance. By the 1850s, Demo-cratic candidates began to respond to their nominations with informal speeches. In 1868 Horatio Seymour delivered the first formal nomination acceptance ad-dress, but like most such addresses in the latter portion of the nineteenth cen-tury, it was a perfunctory speech indicating gratitude upon receiving the nomi-nation and promising a full formal letter of acceptance. It was not until 1892, when Grover Cleveland accepted his nomination for the presidency by speaking at a large public meeting in Madison Square Garden, that acceptance addresses began to assume their current importance. Cleveland, William Jennings Bryan in 1896, and subsequent national candidates have used acceptance addresses as a means of thanking their supporters, seeking party unity, and dramatizing the issues. In 1932 Franklin Delano Roosevelt flew to the Democratic National Convention and became the first presidential candidate to accept personally his nomination at the convention.[28]

### Situation during Address

The situations faced by candidates delivering acceptance addresses have often varied, but typically they share several key characteristics. Most importantly, can-didates have successfully attained their party's nomination for office. This success may be the consequence of running in primaries throughout the nation, as it is with current presidential candidates. It may be the consequence of persuading a majority of party voters in a statewide or local primary. It may be a consequence of persuading a majority of key party officials in a local, regional, or state party caucus or committee. It may even be a consequence of default because no one else chooses to run. Regardless of how it was achieved, the important point is that candidates have obtained the nomination of their party and the legitimacy and attention accompanying that nomination.

Acceptance addresses are given to audiences as varied as the massive television audience that watches the major party presidential nomination conventions or a small group of highly partisan political activists who form the Republican, Democratic, or third-party central or executive committee for a small town. The acceptance address may be given after a long, exhausting, and bitter fight, or it may be given after a placid and uncontested nomination. Clearly the nature of the audience and the nature of the struggle preceding the nomination are situational factors that must be accounted for in the candidate's acceptance address.

A final situational factor that heavily affects acceptance addresses is the fact that they must be considered as part of what a variety of scholars have called "a legitimization ritual."[29] In full view of those who have nominated them, candidates lay claim to their nomination and attempt to justify their supporters' faith and belief. Both their nominators and the public have come to expect such a ritual. Both nominators and the public will judge the candidate's effort and begin to accord the nominee legitimacy in part based on their judgments of the candidate's success at fulfilling the demands of the acceptance address ritual.

## Purpose of Address

Acceptance addresses should satisfy four closely related purposes. First, the address is the means through which the candidate publicly assumes the role of a candidate/leader of the party. Second, the address should generate a strong positive response from the immediate audience. Third, it should serve to unify the party. Finally, it is a partisan political address, which in some instances may be the most important such address the candidate makes throughout the campaign. Hence, it should also serve as a strong persuasive message.[30]

The candidate typically spends very little time formally assuming the role as a party leader. In his 2012 acceptance address, Romney began the speech with his acceptance, "Mr. Chairman, and delegates, I accept your nomination for President of the United States." For President Obama, he accepted the nomination after acknowledging his wife, daughters, and Vice President Biden: "Michelle, I love you. The other night, I think the entire country saw just how lucky I am. Malia and Sasha, you make me so proud . . . but don't get any ideas, you're still going to class tomorrow. And Joe Biden, thank you for being the best vice president I could ever hope for. Madam Chairwoman, delegates, I accept your nomination for President of the United States."

Donald Trump, in 2016, accepted the nomination in the first sentence, "Friends, delegates and fellow Americans: I humbly and gratefully accept your nomination for the presidency of the United States."[31] Thus, typically candidates accept the nomination of their party in the opening moments of their speech. However, Hillary Clinton broke with the long-held tradition. She simply never directly accepted the nomination. Her opening was acknowledging and thanking family, friends, and foes. She then launched into an address primarily focused on challenging and attacking Donald Trump.

The immediate audience for acceptance addresses is normally composed of those individuals who have affirmed the candidate's nomination. Hence, it is imperative that they respond positively to the candidate's remarks. These individuals, be they national, state, or local party officials, should constitute a nucleus of solid and vigorous support for the candidate in the forthcoming election. A second major purpose of the acceptance address is to arouse these individuals and properly motivate them for the responsibilities that will be falling upon them as the campaign progresses. This may be particularly difficult if large numbers of them have supported other candidates for the party nomination.

The third major purpose of acceptance addresses is to reaffirm and, if necessary, reestablish party unity. If the most active members of the party, its delegates to local, state, and national nominating conventions, leave the proceedings divided and with mixed attitudes toward the candidate, the base that most candidates count on for election—their party support—is of little value. In acceptance addresses that have been delivered by candidates who won bitterly contested nominations, it is not uncommon to see major segments of the acceptance address aimed at restoring party unity.

Finally, the acceptance address is a partisan political speech. David Valley has pointed out how each new advance in communications technology has brought national presidential acceptance addresses to larger and larger audiences.[32] Similarly, at least portions of the acceptance address of state and local figures, delivered at state and local nominating proceedings, may be read or heard by a large portion of the public. Consequently, acceptance addresses present the candidate with a unique opportunity to speak not only to party partisans, but also to the general public. Valley concludes that as early as 1896, William Jennings Bryan was tailoring his acceptance address not to the immediate audience but to the hundreds of thousands of citizens who might read his speech.[33] Similarly, even state and local candidates must consider that their acceptance addresses may be carried in full, or quoted in part, by a variety of media outlets and placed on internet sites. Additionally, the campaign may choose to use segments of the address in advertisements. Through such exposure, even local acceptance addresses may acquire broad audiences, while the audiences for the acceptance addresses of national figures number in the tens of millions. Hence, acceptance addresses serve partisan political purposes.

### Strategies of Address

Campaigners have utilized a variety of strategies to satisfy the purposes associated with acceptance addresses. Traditionally, acceptance addresses are characterized by:

- simplified partisan statements
- laments about the present and celebrations about the future
- stress on the crucial nature of this election
- calls for unity
- use of biography
- use of biography to go negative

In recent years, as the importance of political parties has declined, and as decision making has shifted from nominating convention delegates to the will of party voters as expressed in primary elections, the functions of acceptance addresses have changed. As communication scholar Kurt Ritter has argued, candidates giving acceptance addresses today "face a voting public who will judge them not so much on the basis of their political party as on their personal appeal on television." As a consequence, Ritter continues, acceptance addresses "must persuade audiences who are less inclined to vote on the basis of party affiliation, and more inclined to vote on the basis of the individual candidate and his or her general orientation as liberal, moderate, or conservative."[34] Hence, Ritter suggests that acceptance addresses are now less distinct from other campaign speeches and exhibit two additional characteristics not readily apparent in such addresses earlier. First, candidates are increasingly utilizing their biographies as "important sources of material for acceptance addresses." Second, acceptance addresses are increasingly "likely to reflect a personal comparison between the leading candidates."[35]

Which of these six strategies will dominate an acceptance address is largely a function of the specific situation in which that address is being delivered. All six strategies are common in current acceptance addresses.

### Using Simplified Partisan Statements

In an attempt to attain a strong positive response from the immediate audience and deliver a frankly partisan political address to the large secondary audience, candidates often use simplified partisan statements. Such statements characteristically suggest that the nominees and their parties are necessary to solve any problems confronting the constituency and/or that the opponents and their parties will exacerbate any problems confronting the constituency. Typically, in harsh and uncompromisingly partisan language, candidates suggest that there is no real choice in this election—that their positions and party are clearly right, and their opponents are clearly wrong. Although simplified partisan statements are still common in acceptance addresses, Ritter cogently argues that as party affiliation becomes less important to voters, such statements are likely to be found less often in an acceptance address.[36] A comparison of the 1992 and 2008 acceptance addresses of the Republican and Democratic candidates suggests that Ritter is correct in arguing that simplified, harsh partisan statements are growing less important in these addresses.

In his 1992 acceptance address, George H. W. Bush reviewed the soul-searching decisions he made as commander-in-chief during the Persian Gulf conflict and then sarcastically asked, "Well, what about the leader of the Arkansas National Guard, the man who hopes to be commander in chief? Well, while I bit the bullet, he bit his nails." He spoke of Bill Clinton as a "con man" and claimed that as governor, Clinton had raised taxes "128 times and enjoyed it every time."[37] Similarly in his 1992 acceptance address Bill Clinton claimed that the Bush administration had "hijacked" government for the "privileged, private interests." He went on to claim that the Bush administration represented "forces of greed" and that the Bush administration was "brain-dead."[38] Both Bush and Clinton used harsh and uncompromising language to suggest that there was no real choice.

In contrast to the harsh partisan criticism that reached a crescendo in the acceptance addresses of the 1992 candidates, in virtually every election until 2016, the partisan criticism has been much more muted.[39] In 2012, Romney argues that it was Obama's lack of experience that led to his economic failures.

> The president has not disappointed you because he wanted to. The president has disappointed America because he hasn't led America in the right direction. He took office without the basic qualification that most Americans have, and one that was essential to the task at hand. He had almost no experience working in a business. Jobs to him are about government. . . . Every president since the Great Depression who came before the American people asking for a second term could look back at the last four years and say with satisfaction, "You're are better off than you were four years ago." Except Jimmy Carter. And except this president. . . . America has been patient. Americans have supported this president in good faith, but today the time has come, the time to turn the page.

Obama actually never criticized Romney but focused his criticism on the Republican Party: "Now, our friends at the Republican convention were more than happy to talk about everything they think is wrong with America, but they didn't have much to say about how they'd make it right. They want your vote, but they don't want you to know their plan. And that's because all they have to offer is the same prescription they've had for the last thirty years." Toward the end of the speech, there was another attack, but quite mild in comparison.

> If you reject the notion that this nation's promise is reserved for the few, your voice must be heard in this election. If you reject the notion that our government is forever beholden to the highest bidder, you need to stand up in this election. If you believe that new plants and factories can dot our landscape; that new energy can power our future; that new schools can provide ladders of opportunity to this nation of dreamers; if you believe in a country where everyone gets a fair shot, and everyone does their fair share, and everyone plays by the same rules, then I need you to vote this November.

In contrast, both Hillary Clinton and Donald Trump directly attacked each other throughout their acceptance addresses. Trump attacked Clinton as being a failure as secretary of state and in dealing with terrorism, for illegal storage of classified emails, and for being pro–unlimited immigration, weak on crime, supporting terrible trade deals, and calling for tax increases, to name only a few. Clinton attacked Trump for dividing America, evoking fear among citizens, being too boastful, cheating contractors and refusing to pay bills, misleading about "America First" when his clothing line is made in third world countries, and for being insensitive with a bad temperament, among others.

Although it might well be argued that the past reduction in partisan statements is unique to those few candidates in these particular elections, it seems more likely, as Ritter claims, that there was a growing recognition on the part of candidates that harsh partisan attacks are not likely to be well received by contemporary audiences who have less party affiliation than ever before. It will be interesting to see whether partisan attacks continue in the future or candidates return to a more muted approach.

The work of communication researchers William L. Benoit, William J. Wells, P. M. Pier, and Joseph R. Blaney also points to an interesting trend in nomination acceptance speeches. These researchers found that since 1980 the acceptance addresses of major party presidential candidates have focused far more on candidates than on parties. In the five earlier campaigns they studied (1960–1976), Benoit and his colleagues found that acceptance addresses acclaimed or attacked individual candidates almost exactly as often as they did the parties. However, since 1980, more than four times as many remarks were aimed at candidates than were aimed at parties.[40] Clearly, acceptance addresses are partisan statements, but in recent years the diminishing stature of parties and the growing candidate-centeredness of campaigns have produced a corresponding shift in the targets of that partisan rhetoric.

### Lamenting the Present while Celebrating the Future

A second strategy characteristic of acceptance addresses is that they tend to lament the present while celebrating the future. As Kurt Ritter has illustrated, challengers lament the present, claiming that incumbents have abandoned the abiding principles of the American Dream and hence have contributed to the nation's problems. Challengers offer to lead the people back to fundamental American values, thereby resolving our problems and giving rise to a bright future.[41]

While lamenting the past and celebrating the future appears to be a strategy uniquely suited to challenger nominees, Ritter points out that it is also used, with slight adaptation, by incumbents.

> The "in-party" version of the acceptance speech places the speaker at the later stages in the sequence of the rhetorical form. Instead of citing immediate difficulties, the incumbent cites the national decline immediately prior to his arrival at the White House. The incumbent typically describes the sorry state of America when he took office and then points out how he has brought the nation back to its historic purpose. . . . Each incumbent is quick to add that our work is not yet done. In fact, the opposing party threatens the restoration.[42]

Hence, this strategy of lamenting the past and celebrating the future is one that incumbents may also utilize in their acceptance addresses.

### Stressing the Crucial Nature of the Election

A third common strategy found in acceptance addresses is to stress the urgency and crucial nature of this election. In his study of presidential acceptance addresses, David Valley reports that 74 percent of all the words in the acceptance speeches of Democratic nominees he studied "have been used to discuss contemporary issues."[43] Ritter similarly concludes that "although incumbent and challenging candidates have found different lessons from the American past, they all find that their election represents a key moment in American history."[44]

In 2004, with the nation at war, both Senator Kerry and President Bush stressed the crucial nature of the election. Although Kerry made repeated references to the importance of this election, none were more forceful than his claim that "this is the most important election of our lifetime. The stakes are high. We are a nation at war; a global war on terror against an enemy unlike we've ever known before."[45]

Bush, too, acknowledged the crucial times in which we live and the importance of this election. "This election will also determine how America responds to the continuing danger of terrorism, and you know where I stand. Three days after September the 11th, I stood where Americans died, in the ruins of the Twin Towers. Workers in hardhats were shouting to me, 'Whatever it takes.' A fellow grabbed me by the arm, and he said, 'Do not let me down.' Since that day, I wake up every morning thinking about how to better protect our country. I will never relent in defending America, whatever it takes."[46]

In 2012, there was an equal sense of urgency. For Obama, the Republican agenda was too dangerous for middle America: tax cuts for the rich, budget cuts to education and Medicare, favorable loopholes for corporations. "And now, after a long and spirited primary, Republicans in Congress have found a nominee for President who has promised to rubber-stamp this agenda if he gets the chance. Ohio, I tell you what: We cannot give him that chance. Not now. Not with so much at stake. This is not just another election. This is a make-or-break moment for the middle class, and we've been through too much to turn back now."

Romney shared an equal sense of alarm. "Today we are united not only by our faith in America. We are united also by our concern for America. This country we love is in peril. And that, my friends, is why we are here today."

## Calling for Unity

A fourth strategy characteristic of acceptance addresses is to call on all audience members, immediate and secondary, to unify behind the nominee to secure victory in the upcoming general election. Calls of this sort may be exceptionally important if the nomination has been bitterly contested. In 2008, because of the highly divisive primary campaign between Senators Hillary Clinton and Barack Obama, the latter made a special point of including a passage in his acceptance address acknowledging his most tenacious primary opponent. Immediately after having accepted the nomination, less than a minute into his speech, Obama stated, "Let me express my thanks to the historic slate of candidates who accompanied me on this journey and especially the one who traveled the farthest—a champion for working Americans and an inspiration to my daughters and to yours—Hillary Rodham Clinton." Obama was trying to unify his party by graciously acknowledging Clinton.

In 2012, despite a spirited nomination race, Romney did not call for party unity. Rather, he appealed to "we as all Americans."

> The America we all know has been a story of many becoming one. Uniting to preserve liberty, uniting to build the greatest economy in the world, uniting to save the world from unspeakable darkness. . . . That united America can unleash an economy that will put Americans back to work, that will once again lead the world with innovation and productivity, and will restore every father and mother's confidence that their children's future is brighter than even the past.

Without a challenge for the nomination, it is not surprising that Obama followed the same approach to appeal to all Americans. He concluded his address with

> America, I never said this journey would be easy, and I won't promise that now. Yes, our path is harder—but it leads to a better place. Yes, our road is longer—but we travel it together. We don't turn back. We leave no one behind. We pull each other up. We draw strength from our victories, and we learn from our mistakes, but we keep our eyes fixed on that distant horizon, knowing that Providence is with us, and that we are surely blessed to be citizens of the greatest nation on earth.

Hillary Clinton made a special recognition of opponent Bernie Sanders. "And I want to thank Bernie Sanders. Bernie, your campaign inspired millions of Americans, particularly the young people who threw their hearts and souls into our primary. You've put economic and social justice issues front and center, where they belong. And to all of your supporters here and around the country, I want you to know, I've heard you. Your cause is our cause. Our country needs your ideas, energy and passion. That's the only way we can turn our progressive platform into real change for America. We wrote it together—now let's go out there and make it happen."[47]

## Using Biography

The final two strategies that are commonly utilized in acceptance addresses are outgrowths of the increasingly candidate-centered nature of campaigning. As Ritter and Wayne Fields have argued, the candidate-, rather than party-centered nature of recent campaigns is reflected in acceptance addresses by the stress recent candidates have placed on elements of their own biography.[48] Additionally, it has caused candidates to compare themselves to their opponents to a greater degree than ever before. The stress candidates have placed on elements of their biography is not surprising. It attempts to demonstrate competence. Those without prior electoral success tend to focus on business and military experiences as well as social and charitable endeavors.

## Using Biography to Go Negative

Along with the growth of personal campaigning, one of the most discussed characteristics of American campaigns in the past twenty years has been negative advertising. But candidates can "go negative" not simply in their ads but also in their speeches. Often, the biographical sections of their acceptance address are used to contrast themselves with their opponents and hence to make implicit, if not explicit, attacks on their foes. Interestingly, Obama did not attack Romney, only focusing on the Republican Party. Romney, on the other hand, did attack Obama related to two policy areas. One is the failure of the economy and jobs, in a direct comparison to his role in creating jobs in the private and government sectors. "In the richest country in the history of the world, this Obama economy has crushed the middle class. . . . Today more Americans wake up in poverty than ever before. . . . His policies have not helped create jobs. They've depressed them. . . . His plan to raise taxes on small businesses will not add jobs. It will eliminate them." The second personal attack challenges Obama's general approach to foreign policy. "On another front, every American is less secure today because he has failed to slow Iran's nuclear threat. . . . President Obama has thrown allies like Israel under the bus even as he has relaxed sanctions on Castro's Cuba. He abandoned our friends in Poland by walking away from missile defense commitments. But he is eager to give Russia's president Putin the flexibility he desires after the election."

As already noted, the attacks by Hillary Clinton and Donald Trump were among the most adversarial in recent history. It remains to be seen whether this is a new trend or a reflection of a very fragmented and polarized society.

## Summary

In sum, acceptance addresses are often among the most important speeches of a campaign. They are responses to a unique rhetorical situation that serve a variety of purposes beyond simply accepting a nomination and that may utilize at least six common strategies to fulfill those purposes.

## NEWS CONFERENCES

Candidates universally complain of their lack of media coverage. But some events or statements that occur during the campaign are perceived by candidates and their staffs as uniquely important and especially deserving of media coverage. Such occasions often cause candidates to call news conferences.

### Situation for News Conference

News conferences are normally occasioned by events or statements that the candidate feels warrant special attention. Ostensibly, they provide a means of making statements that will be passed on, through the media, to the public at large. Changing technology has impacted political press conferences. Perhaps the two most dramatic effects of technology on news conferences took place in 1954 and 1992. In 1954 Eastman Kodak perfected a new type of fast film. This film allowed press conferences to be televised without the use of high-intensity lights. Immediately following this breakthrough, President Eisenhower began delivering televised press conferences monthly. Televised press conferences soon became far more common for political figures, and campaigns could be far more flexible in selecting the time and place of the conference.[49] The manner in which candidates communicate with the public at large underwent a second substantial change in 1992. The growth of cable television created many new talk and news programs. In 1992, to a far greater extent than ever before, candidates bypassed the traditional news media and spoke directly to the public, primarily through television talk shows such as *The O'Reilly Factor, Oprah, The Daily Show, Good Morning America, Today, Tonight,* and the Sunday morning talk/interview shows. Although this was most evident in the presidential campaign, use of local television and radio shows in lower-level races was also common. In the election cycles since that time, including those of 2006, 2008, 2010, 2012, and 2016, many candidates have utilized talk shows to address voters directly. Earlier in this chapter, we saw how several candidates even used such shows to announce their candidacies. Moreover, the growth of twenty-four-hour news/talk stations on radio and cable television is providing candidates more opportunities than ever before. Hence, the traditional importance of press conferences may be diminishing, as new technology and programming formats facilitate candidates bypassing the press to speak directly to the public.

Nevertheless, although their importance may be diminishing somewhat, news conferences remain an important and reoccurring means of campaign communication. Part of that importance is derived from the fact that although the public is one audience in the news conference situation, at least four other audiences also exist: the candidates' rivals, their own staffs, political elites, and journalists. These five potential audiences exist for every news conference.[50] Moreover, on occasion, the candidate's remarks at a news conference are not meant primarily for the general public but for one or more of the other four audiences. It is through a news conference, ostensibly held for the public, that the candidate may also choose to address these other audiences.

News conferences are an exceptionally effective means of addressing an opponent. Candidates can exchange challenges, promises, or threats in private and by using third parties. But if such messages are conveyed through a news conference, they take on a different dimension. A message to one's rival, made publicly during a news conference, clearly implies a degree of commitment that the same message conveyed privately lacks. By deliberately going on public record and calling unusual attention to the message, the candidate is telling the opponent that this is no idle challenge, promise, or threat, but rather a deadly serious message. The use of a news conference, more than virtually any other form of communication, conveys that seriousness and hence is occasionally employed by candidates as a means of addressing one another.

Candidates may also use news conferences as a means of addressing their own staff. As political scientist Leon Sigal has observed, "Campaign organizations tend to combine decentralization at the bottom with inaccessibility at the top."[51] The decentralized groups of supporters at the bottom of the campaign have infrequent and short contact with the candidate. A news conference presents the candidate with a forum to which the campaign organization will no doubt be attentive. Hence, messages aimed primarily at the candidate's organization may be transmitted through the news conference.

News conferences also serve the candidate by providing a means of addressing political elites. In prior years, as discussed in chapter 1, campaign decisions were often made by relatively few individuals, often in private meetings to which the public had little access. The decline of political parties and changes in campaign financing have tended to increase the number of political elites. In the past, candidates might have used a few meetings and phone calls to put out the word that they needed money, had dramatically spurted in the last poll, or had found a new campaign issue. Today, it would be difficult to contact all those with whom a candidate might want to share this news. Hence, candidates may choose to use news conferences as a means of reaching political elites with information.

Candidates obviously use news conferences as a means of influencing journalists. Those journalists who attend the news conference constitute the immediate audience. Candidates clearly seek to influence what they disseminate and by so doing influence the four other audiences: the public, their rivals, their own staff and supporters, and political elites. Additionally, many news organizations may choose not to be represented at the news conference and fail to cover it. If candidates are in fact newsworthy at their news conferences, providing genuine news in their remarks, and if those journalists who are in attendance write articles that get good coverage in their respective outlets, the likelihood of increased media coverage of the campaign will be enhanced.

In sum, rhetorical situations in which candidates perceive the need to seek media coverage of their views for the purpose of better expressing themselves to the public, to rivals, to their own staffs, to political elites, and to journalists may frequently give rise to press conferences.

## Purposes of News Conferences

News conferences serve three basic purposes. First, they enable the candidate to get the attention of a variety of audiences. News conferences often serve this purpose better than alternatives, such as news releases. However, they should not be abused. National candidates and major regional and state candidates can often be assured of reasonable media attendance at any news conference they call, simply because of the importance of any statement being made by a potential president, senator, or governor. Incumbents also have an advantage in attracting the media, simply because news organizations routinely assign someone to cover state senators, state representatives, members of the city council, and administrative offices. Other candidates frequently have trouble getting media coverage of their campaigns. There are three reasons why properly used news conferences can increase coverage.

The first reason is novelty. The conference must be a reasonably unusual event. Candidates who are not overly newsworthy cannot expect the media to respond to daily announcements of press conferences. On the other hand, if they call conferences only a few times during the campaign, the very novelty may cause some news organizations to send representatives. Second, the conference should be called with a clear newsworthy issue in mind. As former vice presidential spokesman David Beckwith has observed, "Having a press conference is a good idea when you have something to announce or something positive to say."[52] News organizations should be made aware of what the candidate will discuss. Unless the candidate has hard news and hopefully the data to support statements, news organizations may choose to ignore the conference. But if candidates are prepared to really make news that will be of interest to the readers, listeners, and viewers of the news organizations in their area, the news conference may be well covered.

A final reason that news conferences can effectively serve to focus widespread attention on the candidate's message is that reporters consider them reliable. Reporters often express doubts about the reliability of press releases or political advertisements. But the reliability of news conferences, witnessed by many reporters, with the candidate's statements captured on both audio and videotape, cannot be doubted.

Thus, the news conference can serve as a means through which the candidate is able to reach many audiences. Even candidates whom news organizations judge to be unworthy of much attention can gain some coverage if they use news conferences properly.

A second important purpose served by news conferences is to allow candidates to focus attention on one issue or a limited number of issues. As we discussed in chapter 2, a major function of the press is to help set the campaign agenda. But the candidate also wants to help shape the agenda. By focusing remarks on one issue, the candidate is able to influence strongly what issue the media will cover. Using a press conference but focusing on the issues treated and stressed in that conference is an effective means utilized by many candidates to help set the campaign agenda.

A final purpose served by news conferences is to establish and improve relationships between the candidate and individual members of the media. The more efficiently run the conference is, the more prepared and responsive the candidate is, the easier the job of the reporter becomes. Press conferences are one means by which candidates can make the job of reporters easier and in so doing improve relationships between themselves and the media. The chief purpose of news conferences—to allow candidates to bring their views to the attention of many audiences—may be readily apparent, but we should not ignore the other purposes served by press conferences: to allow the candidate to focus attention on one or a limited number of issues, presumably selected by the candidate to be of advantage to the candidate, and to enhance candidate-press relationships.

## Strategies of News Conferences

Candidates attempt to use news conferences to their own advantage. One of the reasons they are used is to foster the illusion that the candidate is in control. C. Jack Orr has suggested that presidential news conferences can be thought of as "counterpoised situations" in which the reporters have competing obligations. They must confront the president, and they must give deference to him.[53] To a lesser extent, the same counterpoised situation exists when reporters interview any office seeker. The candidate must be shown some deference as a responsible individual running for a responsible job. Moreover, the conference is, after all, the candidate's proceeding. Yet, reporters also may seek to confront, challenge, and criticize.

The candidate's control extends beyond the deference that may be shown by reporters. The control is real. The candidate decides when and where to hold a news conference. The candidate decides what format will be used. The candidate decides who will ask questions, and of course the candidate provides the answers. Scholars who have examined news conferences, such as Robert Denton and Dan Hahn, have concluded that while the situation may appear to be one in which the press has considerable control, ultimately it is the skilled respondent who controls the news conference.[54] Candidates exercise their control by utilizing one or more of at least ten common strategies.

Since it is the candidates who call news conferences, they will do so to suit their own needs. Decisions by the candidate about the timing of news conferences are important, and determining when to call a conference is the candidate's first strategic decision. As indicated earlier, for the vast majority of candidates, excepting those at the very top of the ballot, typically the fewer conferences called, the more attention the press will extend to those that are called. Calling a news conference to deal with a topic is a clear means not only of signaling that the candidate attaches major importance to this topic, but also of increasing the treatment it receives in the media.

In addition, the candidate must consider the media that will attend and the deadlines with which they operate. Typically, candidates vary the time of day that they hold press conferences, so that they are not slighting any of the media organizations serving their constituency. However, this too is a strategic decision. The candidate, by determining the time of day to hold the conference, can play favorites with the media.

A second consideration is where to hold it. Candidates may make their conferences visually interesting to audiences and hence especially appealing to television and internet news organizations by holding them in visually appealing settings. The candidate who has promised to repair the roads and eliminate dangerous potholes might choose to hold the conference at the site of a recent fatal accident caused by poor roads. The need for a visually appealing setting should also be balanced with consideration of the accessibility of the site and the technical requirements of the media.[55]

Although George H. W. Bush held relatively few press conferences during the 1988 election, he used site selection to the utmost advantage when he attacked Michael Dukakis. For example, in his attempt to claim that Dukakis was weak on environmental issues, Bush visited the most polluted harbor in the nation, which just happened to be Boston Harbor, in Dukakis's home city. Similarly, Bush subsequently discussed the environment and pollution with the press while visiting the New Jersey coast, off which Governor Dukakis had proposed dumping sewage from Massachusetts. By selecting these sites, Bush provided the media with visually appealing settings and focused the media's attention on the weaknesses of his opponent.

Candidates should keep in mind that sometimes a site might be highly visual, lending itself to television news and the internet, but it might be difficult and time consuming to reach. Such sites may cause radio and print media representatives to feel that a news conference is hardly worth their effort. Typically, candidates seek to balance their news conference site selections. Some are held with television in mind, while others are held in the campaign headquarters or some highly accessible central location. Whatever decision is made, the candidate can use the selection of a news conference site strategically, to help fulfill overall purposes.

Candidates utilize at least five strategies to guarantee that the agenda-setting function of the media works in their favor when news organizations cover their press conferences. Perhaps the most commonly used of these strategies is to make an opening statement at the outset of the conference. Based on her studies of presidential press conferences and her experience as director of political coverage for ABC News, Carolyn Smith has suggested that opening statements are an exceptionally effective means of setting a press conference agenda if they are used at the outset of press conferences that involve reacting to a single major event or treating a single major policy.[56] Although this tactic seems commonplace today, years ago it was not frequently used. Dwight Eisenhower was the first president who regularly made opening statements at his news conferences.[57] The opening statement should be newsworthy in itself. If it is, it will generally prompt questions on the issue it treats and be the focus of most reports of the news conference. Moreover, as Catherine Collins has illustrated in her examination of press conferences, if the interviewee assumes the role of the expert, defines the topic of immediate concern, develops a perspective from which events should be viewed, utilizes data to depict the event, and warns the media that other perspectives will not be considered acceptable, the chances are greatly increased that the interviewee's perspective will be reflected clearly in media accounts of the conference.[58]

Similarly, candidates may not only present opening statements, but they may also restructure questions. In restructuring a question, candidates are again generally attempting to focus attention onto key issues, from certain perspectives, in order to make their points better.

A third strategy frequently utilized by candidates to ensure that news conferences focus on their agenda is to follow the advice of Republican political consultant and Fox News executive Roger Ailes. Ailes recommended that candidates use the formula $Q = A+1$ when responding to questions. Ailes explained that when asked a question (Q) his clients "reply briefly and directly with an answer (A). Then if it will help, add a point or points (+1) preferably from your agenda."[59]

A fourth strategy utilized to make sure candidates are able to focus the conference on their topics and from their perspective is to plant questions. This tactic became commonplace in the presidential press conferences of Eisenhower and Johnson.[60] It has since been used by many candidates for public office. Typically, a staff member approaches a reporter and suggests a question that might be asked, noting that it will no doubt produce a newsworthy response. Obviously, many reporters may not choose to be used in this fashion. But others will, perceiving the suggested question as a means of drawing attention to something that is newsworthy, which is just what the candidate also wants.

The final strategy, utilized primarily to focus the news conference, is selective recognition of reporters. Candidates recognize those who question them, but they can fail to recognize those who wish to question them. Most of the time, recognition is haphazard. But it can also be done in a deliberate fashion. A survey of the White House press corps found that "the random selection of questioners by the President" was among the most serious problems associated with White House news conferences.[61] News conferences held by candidates for lesser office will not draw the massive number of reporters that a White House news conference attracts. But any conference that draws a reasonable sample of the media is one in which a candidate might selectively recognize reporters.

Candidates normally hold news conferences when they seek extensive coverage of their views. Typically, they have a limited number of issues on which they wish to focus in the news conference and that they hope the public will learn of through the efforts of the journalists in attendance. To ensure that these topics are clearly the centerpieces of the news conference, candidates often assume the role of the expert, utilizing an opening statement that spells out their position on issues and indicates the perspective on the issue that they find satisfactory. They may also choose to restructure questions, consistently add comments from their agenda to answers (Q = A+1), plant questions, and selectively recognize reporters. All these strategies are used primarily to enable candidates to stress their issues and prevent the conference from dealing with other issues. However, as Smith points out, reporters attend press conferences to address their own agendas of what is newsworthy, not to serve as a foil for the individual holding the conference.[62]

Three final strategies can be utilized by most candidates holding news conferences. First is to prepare. Candidates differ in the manner of their preparation for news conferences. However, most attempt to anticipate and prepare responses to questions that might be asked. Presidents Truman and Kennedy typically rehearsed for news conferences by reviewing forty to seventy-five possible questions that might arise in their press conferences.[63] Most candidates follow similar procedures. They rely on their staffs to generate possible questions and then prepare responses.

Second, if the conference starts to go badly, the candidate can filibuster. Typically, press conferences are called for specific time periods. The press has deadlines and the candidate has a full schedule. Hence, if their conferences are going poorly, some candidates will take considerable time in answering questions, particularly those that they are comfortable with and deal with topics they wish to address. By so doing, they reduce the opportunity the press has for further questioning.

Finally, candidates often attempt to appear vulnerable in press conferences. Given the many controls and strategies available to candidates who utilize news conferences, it may be easy to forget that there are other actors in this situation. President Carter's television advisor noted that even though the news conference was in effect a theater in which the president called upon reporters to play their supporting roles, "it is important that the President appear vulnerable."[64] Similarly, most candidates wish to appear vulnerable in news conference situations. The desire to appear vulnerable often motivates the use of the news conference. It is one of the reasons why candidates will utilize "risky" news conferences, rather than safer press releases, internet clips, or other forms of communication with the public. The appearance that the candidate is taking a chance and is vulnerable is one that most candidates believe the public admires. The news conference situation suggests openness and honesty, as well as confidence in one's ability. Candidates are not readily able to suggest these qualities using other forms of communication.

The symbiotic relationship that exists between candidates and journalists is, perhaps, nowhere more evident than in the news conference. News conferences are called by candidates seeking widespread coverage of their views. News conferences are attended by representatives of news organizations who sense that the conference may produce newsworthy material. Both the candidate and the reporter have an interest in aiding one another. But candidates are not only desirous of creating news; they are also desirous of influencing and persuading. Hence, most candidates utilize a variety of strategies attempting to ensure that their conferences are indeed covered and that the conferences focus on those issues upon which the candidates wish to focus. Moreover, although they prepare in order not to be vulnerable and weak, they recognize that a format that suggests their vulnerability may be desirable.

## APOLOGIAS

An increasingly recurring form of speech that many candidates have recently found necessary to deliver is the apologia. In this section, we will examine the situations that create apologias and in so doing perhaps also gain an understanding of why they have been on the increase in recent years. We will also examine the major purposes of such speeches and the strategies utilized to attain those purposes.

### Situation for an Apologia

Apologias are speeches made by candidates who find it necessary to apologize for some statement or behavior. Typically, the statement or behavior implies a serious flaw in the candidate's character, one that if widely accepted by the public would prevent the candidate from winning office. In 1984 Jesse Jackson's anti-Semitic remarks, characterizing Jews as "Hymies" and New York City as "Hymietown," were not only offensive to Jews, but also suggested that Jackson could not equitably and fairly govern a racially, ethnically, and religiously diverse nation such as the United States.

Similarly, in 1992 Bill Clinton was the subject of widespread rumors that he engaged in numerous extramarital affairs while governor of Arkansas, the most infamous of which was alleged to have lasted for twelve years, with a former Little Rock newswoman turned nightclub singer, Gennifer Flowers. If such rumors and accusations proved true, Clinton, at that point just one of several candidates for the Democratic Party nomination, was in grave trouble. With relatively few people familiar with Clinton and his candidacy, charges of this sort would suggest to many that Clinton lacked the integrity, honesty, and other qualities of character desired in national leaders.

Apologias have become a feature of recent campaigns for two reasons. First, the news media seem more prone than ever before to report on the candidate's weaknesses and flaws. Gone are the days when Franklin Delano Roosevelt could dictate that he never be photographed in leg braces or while being carried by his aides. Gone are the days when the candidate's private life was not discussed. The press is far more unsparing of candidates today. Additionally, one of the legacies of Watergate has apparently been to sensitize the public to the personal integrity of candidates.

During both of his campaigns for the presidency, as well as during his administration, Bill Clinton's personal integrity came under frequent attack and his vice president, Albert Gore, suffered throughout the 2000 campaign from the perception on the part of many that he often lied. In 2004 accusations that both Senator Kerry and President Bush had at the least embellished, if not lied about, their Vietnam service permeated the presidential campaign. The 2008 presidential campaign was a clear exception to the recent rule, for neither of the major party candidates faced situations that warranted major apologias. However, on August

8, 2008, former senator John Edwards, the 2004 Democratic vice presidential candidate and a candidate for the Democratic presidential nomination in 2008, issued an apologia for having had an extramarital affair.[65] Moreover, during the 2010 primaries, such diverse candidates as South Carolina Republican gubernatorial candidate Nikki Haley, West Virginia Democratic congressman Alan Mollohan, Indiana Republican congressman Mark Souder, and Connecticut Democratic senatorial candidate Richard Blumenthal all had to deal with questions about some aspect of their personal integrity.[66]

Second only to Bill Clinton, Donald Trump's integrity was questioned throughout the entire presidential campaign of 2016. He was questioned about his statements on the campaign trail, his finances and abuse of building contractors and, of course, for his comments captured on tape for the *Access Hollywood* program. His use of apologia is discussed in chapter 14.

## Purposes of Apologia

Apologias serve to enable the candidate to explain some statement or behavior that casts doubt on the candidate's suitability for office. To accomplish this explanation, with the least amount of damage to their image, candidates often have three purposes in mind when they deliver apologias.

First, they hope to explain the behavior or statement in a positive light. In so doing, they hope to minimize damage to their character and image. If the incident that triggered the need for the apologia cannot be explained positively, the second purpose of the apologia may be considered. The candidate can at least justify behavior. Again, by so doing, the candidate hopes to minimize damage to character and image.

The final purpose of an apologia is to remove the topic from public discussion. Ellen Reid Gold has pointed out that, at least with major national figures, frequently reporters repeat the charges against a candidate so often that it is difficult for the candidate not to appear guilty.[67] Day after day, the candidate is seen denying the charge. The proliferation of media has compounded this problem. With many relatively new twenty-four-hour-a-day cable news networks, the growth of twenty-four-hour-a-day talk radio stations, and a host of new politically oriented publications, the "feeding frenzy" of the press is greater today than ever before. To the extent that an apologia can put an end to questioning and allow the campaign to move on to other issues, it has served a vital purpose.

## Strategies of Apologia

Rhetoricians have identified six strategies commonly utilized by speakers delivering apologias. Not every strategy can be used in every apologia, but all six have been used frequently.

### Control of the Apologia Setting

First, apologias are often best delivered in settings where individuals other than the candidate seem in control.[68] Many early apologias were delivered in settings where the candidate seemed to be in complete control. For example, Richard Nixon's 1952 "Checkers" address, following charges that Nixon benefited from a slush fund set up by wealthy supporters, and Ted Kennedy's 1969 "Address to the People of Massachusetts," following the incident at Chappaquiddick, in which Kennedy's car went off a bridge and a young woman died, were both made by men who had purchased air time and were in complete control of what was said. However, as Sherry Butler points out in contrasting these two addresses, by 1969 mass media viewers were "more sophisticated, less likely to place automatic belief in magic power of the television tube, more likely to question."[69] Additionally, the legacies of Vietnam, Watergate, and the Clinton scandals include voter disenchantment with less-than-honest officials. Both facts, growing voter sophistication in using media and growing voter disenchantment with public figures, have contributed to changes since the early apologia, typified by Richard Nixon's "Checkers" address.

Rather than an address such as Nixon's in which the candidate is in complete control of the setting, candidates today often deliver their apologias in settings that appear to be controlled by others. For example, among the best-known and most successful political apologias of recent years is no doubt the interview granted by Bill Clinton in response to the accusations that he had conducted a twelve-year affair with Gennifer Flowers. Significantly, Clinton's apologia was delivered on a special edition of CBS's *60 Minutes*, one of the nation's most respected investigative TV shows. Viewers no doubt were aware that Clinton and his wife were not in control of the situation as they responded to questions from correspondent Steve Kroft, who appeared to control the interview. When Bill Clinton saw the broadcast, he is reported to have been "furious," claiming that the interview was "a screw job."[70] As Clinton's appearance on *60 Minutes* illustrates, appearing in a setting where one does not have complete control involves risk. However, many contemporary candidates choose to take this risk, believing that public sophistication with media and alienation from leaders make this an acceptable risk that must be taken if their message is to be appreciated.

## Denial

A second strategy utilized by candidates delivering apologias is to simply deny the "alleged facts, sentiments, objects, or relationships" that give rise to the charge.[71] If the candidate cannot deny the substance of the charge, one can deny the intent, arguing that the statement or action has been misunderstood.[72] Kroft opened his *60 Minutes* interview by observing that Gennifer Flowers "is alleging and has described in some detail in a supermarket tabloid what she calls a twelve-year affair with you."[73] As Kroft finished his statement, Bill Clinton jumped in: "That allegation is false." He went on to suggest that although as a public figure in Little Rock he had known Flowers when she was a TV reporter in the same city, her story was a total fabrication that she no doubt made up for the payment she received from the tabloid.[74] As the interview progressed, Kroft again offered Clinton an opportunity to deny the alleged affair. "I am assuming from your answer," said Kroft, "that you are categorically denying that you ever had an affair with Gennifer Flowers." The camera showed Clinton nodding his head affirmatively as Kroft spoke and then declaring, "I said that before."

Although Clinton clearly denied having an affair with Gennifer Flowers, he did not deny the possibility of other infidelities. At one point he acknowledged, "I have caused pain in my marriage." Kroft responded by stating, "Your answer is not a denial, is it?" Clinton responded: "Of course it is not." Thus, while Clinton's denial might resolve the charges of Gennifer Flowers, he did not attempt to deny all the rumors about his infidelity. Clinton's response to the broader issue of infidelity utilized several additional strategies common to apologias.

### Bolstering

A third strategy frequently used in apologias is what B. L. Ware and Wil Linkugel characterize as "bolstering strategies." Bolstering strategies are attempts by the candidate to identify "with something viewed favorably by the audience."[75] Bill Clinton made use of bolstering when he attempted to make a virtue out of his inability to totally deny the accusations of marital infidelity. "I have acknowledged wrongdoing. I have acknowledged causing pain in my marriage. I have said things tonight and to the American people from the beginning that no American politician ever has." Repeatedly Clinton and his wife claimed that they had "leveled" with the American public and had been "candid" with the American public. Clearly Clinton was attempting to bolster his case by claiming to display character traits viewed favorably by the audience: candor and honesty. To the extent that Clinton might make his candor and honesty in dealing with charges of infidelity the focus of audience attention, rather than the infidelity itself, he was likely to bolster his case successfully.

Clinton's apologia was unusual because of the presence and statements of a second individual: his wife, Hillary. Throughout the interview the couple was seated side by side, and as one spoke, the camera, for the most part, remained focused on both. In contrast, in 2008, when he acknowledged his infidelity, John Edwards did so by issuing a three-paragraph statement and then that evening appearing by himself on ABC's *Nightline*. His wife, Elizabeth, a victim of cancer and an enormously sympathetic and admired figure, was nowhere to be found.[76]

Both Hillary Clinton's presence at her husband's side and her statements in defense of him may have fulfilled bolstering functions for the governor. Mrs. Clinton's presence and active defense of her husband suggested a solid marriage that had endured stress. Clinton observed, "My wife and I are still in love with each other; we have a stronger marriage than most people who have never had to survive the trials and tribulations of a challenging marriage. As most married Americans will acknowledge, marriage is a hard institution. But it is a better alternative to divorce that is prevalent in our society." To the extent that Americans associated the Clintons with people who had successfully resolved troublesome issues in their marriage, they bolstered their own case by identifying themselves with a second set of qualities typically admired by most Americans, the determination and ability to work through a troubled relationship rather than abandon it.

### Differentiation

A fourth strategy frequently used in political apologias is differentiation. Ware and Linkugel define differentiation strategies as "separating some fact, sentiment, object, or relationship from some larger context within which the audience presently views that attribute."[77] As Gold notes, "In political campaigns, the candidate may try not only to redefine the larger context for the audience, but to separate himself symbolically from the accusation by attacking the source."[78]

Attacks on the source have become increasingly common in political apologias. Kathryn M. Olson offers us an incisive explanation of why this tactic has become widely used, though, as she observes, it is a "strategy near last resort."[79] Olson claims that in recent years, in part because of the growing dominance of television as a news medium, the blending of journalism and entertainment, and the economic realities of the contemporary news media, journalists have faced growing tension between "objective" reporting and "adversarial" reporting. Candidates can exploit that tension to their advantage by utilizing what Olson has characterized as role-imbalance attacks. That is, candidates can suggest that journalists have crossed the line between objective reporting and treated them in a harshly adversarial fashion, thereby exacerbating, exaggerating, or otherwise inappropriately reporting the charges against the candidate.

The Clintons repeatedly utilized differentiation and role-imbalance attacks as they attempted to differentiate the questions of infidelity from the context of Clinton's fitness for office and place it within the context of the right to privacy. If the public viewed infidelity as an issue pertinent to the right of privacy, rather than one pertinent to presidential fitness, then Clinton's role-imbalanced attacks on the press were also pertinent and potentially persuasive. Olson claims that for role-imbalance attacks to succeed, the accused "must not appear totally self-serving" and hence must suggest "that the news media's role imbalance has negative implications for someone in addition to him- or herself." Clinton's strongest attempt to do this is his last remark in the interview. He claimed that "this will test the character of the press. It is not only my character that is being tested." Clearly, he was suggesting that the press coverage of him is really a test of the press's objectivity, and that both the press and the entire public will suffer if the press continues its nonobjective, imbalanced, adversarial treatment of him.

Similarly, Olson claims that for role-imbalance attacks on the press to succeed, the accused must indicate that press coverage "threatens the democratic system and/or hurts innocent individuals." Both Bill Clinton and his wife made accusations of this type during their interview. Clinton claimed that "the press has to decide if it is going to engage in a game of 'got you'" and went on to add that the excessively imbalanced adversarial attacks he had already endured made it impossible for him to defend himself. "No matter what I say," asserted Clinton, "to pretend the press will then let this die, we are kidding ourselves. This has become a virtual cottage industry." Bill Clinton portrayed the press as engaging in unfair, imbalanced adversarial reporting from which it profited. Hillary Clinton suggested that many innocent individuals, not simply the Clintons, would suffer if the press continued in this type of behavior, observing, "I think it is real dangerous in this country if we don't have some zone of privacy for everybody."

Thus, the Clintons used differentiation strategies to move questions about his infidelity out of the context of presidential fitness and into the context of the right to privacy. Placing the charges against him in the context of the right to privacy then facilitated the Clintons' use of role-imbalance attacks on the press.

## Transcendental Strategy

The fifth type of strategy found in political apologias is what Ware and Linkugel have called the transcendental strategy. This kind of strategy "cognitively joins some fact, sentiment, object, or relationship with some larger context within which the audience does not presently view that attribute."[80] Such strategies "psychologically move the audience away from the particulars of the charge at hand in a direction toward some more abstract, general view of his character."[81] The combined effect of the Clintons' strategies, if successful, would serve this purpose. That is, if the Clintons were able to get the public thinking about the courage they had in appearing on *60 Minutes*, their candor and honesty in "leveling" with the American public about the difficulties they had experienced in their marriage, their perseverance in working through the troubles of their marriage, and the press abuses of their rights to privacy, then these more abstract general issues, not Clinton's character as reflected specifically in charges of infidelity, would be the focus of attention.

## Confession

The final strategy that political figures have utilized in their apologias is to confess. If the candidate is guilty, a quick confession may put the unwinnable issue generating the apologia behind the candidate and let the campaign progress to other issues. In 1984, Jesse Jackson's attitudes toward Jews became the focal point of fourteen days' worth of news coverage about his campaign, at the very outset of the critical first primary in New Hampshire. Finally, on the fourteenth day, rejecting the advice of his staff, Jackson spoke to a Jewish audience at Temple Adath Yeshurun in Manchester, New Hampshire, confessed to making the derogatory statements that had given rise to the controversy, and observed, "However innocent and unintentional, it was insensitive and it was wrong. In part, I am to blame, and for that I am deeply distressed."[82] With that confession, Jackson was finally able to put the controversy behind him and return to other issues. Moreover, the issue never surfaced in Jackson's 1988 campaign.

Similarly, although Bill Clinton denied a long-standing affair with Gennifer Flowers, he never flatly denied having had extramarital affairs. Most Americans, including moderator Steve Kroft, interpreted his remarks about having caused "pain" in his marriage essentially as a confession of infidelity.[83] Having so confessed, there was little more that the press could pursue on this story. Moreover, combined with the other attempts discussed earlier to put the most favorable light on his extramarital affairs and combined with his criticism of the press, this confession helped cause this story to drop out of the campaign early in the Democratic primaries.

The situation Clinton faced in 1998, when he was accused of having had an affair with a twenty-two-year-old White House intern, Monica Lewinsky, was substantially more complex than the situation that typically gives rise to a campaign apologia. First, the accusations were not made in the context of a political campaign. Clinton was president at the time of the affair and much of the affair took place in the White House. Second, campaign apologias rarely involve statements or behavior that can provoke legal action. Clinton lied about his affair, which he ultimately acknowledged under oath, while testifying in the sexual harassment case brought by Paula Jones. The legal dimensions of this situation distinguish it from most occasions that give rise to campaign apologias. Third, many of the strategies associated with apologias presume that the candidate is innocent or that, at the least, there is doubt about guilt. Those strategies were essentially denied to Clinton with the presence of physical evidence of his affair in the form of Monica Lewinsky's famed semen-stained dress and his subsequent statements on August 17, 1998, acknowledging his affair.

## Summary

Apologias seem to be characterized by the use of one or more of six strategies. Increasingly, candidates are making their apologias in situations over which they do not have full control. Moreover, they are using denial, bolstering, differentiation, transcendental, and confessional strategies to carry out their apologias.

In recent years apologias have become a common, often recurring form of political speech. Contemporary stress on the character of candidates and the aggressiveness of contemporary journalists seem, in recent years, to have created far more situations calling for apologias than ever before. It is likely that apologias will be a feature of American political rhetoric for years to come.

## CONCLUSIONS

In this chapter, we have observed that most campaigns are marked by similar, comparable, or analogous situations that require a rhetorical response. The responses to four such situations take the form of announcement of candidacy speeches, nomination acceptance addresses, news conferences, and apologias. We have examined the situations that give rise to these types of presentations, the purposes of such presentations, and the major strategies employed in each type of presentation.

## NOTES

1. Lloyd Bitzer, "The Rhetorical Situation," *Philosophy and Rhetoric* 1 (January 1968): 6.

2. Karlyn Kohrs Campbell and Kathleen Hall Jamieson, "Form and Genre in Rhetorical Criticism: An Introduction," in *Form and Genre: Shaping Rhetorical Action*, ed. Karlyn Kohrs Campbell and Kathleen Hall Jamieson (Falls Church, VA: Speech Communication Association, 1977), 15.

3. Judith S. Trent, "Presidential Surfacing: The Ritualistic and Crucial First Act," *Communication Monographs* 45 (November 1978): 281–92.

4. See, for example, Hamilton Jordan, "Memo of August 4, 1974, to Jimmy Carter," in *Running for President: A Journal of the Carter Campaign*, ed. Martin Schram (New York: Pocket Books, 1977), 416.

5. Dan Balz, *Collision 2012* (New York: Viking, 2013), 87–88.

6. Mark Halperin and John Heilemann, *Double Down: Game Change 2012* (New York: Penguin Press, 2013), 105.

7. Balz, *Collision 2012*, 88–89.

8. Ibid., 91–92.

9. Ibid., 92–93.

10. Maggie Haberman, "Mitt Romney Forms Exploratory Committee," *Politico*, April 11, 2011, accessed December 24, 2014, dyn.politico.com/printstory.cfm?uuid=462061D7-974D-0760-09C48743A13AE7B4.

11. Mitt Romney, "Remarks Announcing Candidacy for President in Stratham, New Hampshire," American Presidency Project, accessed October 20, 2014, www.presidency.ucsb.edu/ws/index.php?pid=90456.

12. "Campaign for President Launches," *Huffington Post*, June 2, 2011, accessed December 27, 2014, www.huffingtonpost.com/2011/06/02/mitt-romney-2012-campaign_n_869868.html.

13. "Here's Donald Trump's Presidential Announcement Speech," *Time*, June 16, 2015, accessed November 9, 2018, http://time.com/3923128/donald-trump-announcement-speech.

14. Ibid.

15. Ibid.

16. Ibid.

17. Amy Chozick and Maggie Haberman, "Hillary Clinton to Announce 2016 Run for President on Sunday," *New York Times*, April 10, 2015, accessed November 9, 2018, https://www.nytimes.com/2015/04/11/us/politics/hillary-clinton-to-announce-2016-run-for-president-on-sunday.html.

18. Shortly before Dukakis announced his 1988 candidacy, *Boston Globe* political columnist David Nyhan claimed that Kennedy might well be ready to run for the presidency again in 1992 and that Massachusetts junior senator John Kerry was looking to 1996. If one believes this scenario, and certainly Dukakis and his advisors were aware of it, then 1988 loomed as the only year in which Dukakis could run and be assured of the unified support of the Massachusetts Democratic organization from the outset. See *The Winning of the White House*, ed. Donald Morrison (New York: Time Incorporated, 1988), 125–26.

19. Balz, *Collision 2012*, 98.

20. "Read President Obama's Full Campaign Kickoff Speech," *Los Angeles Times*, May 5, 2012, accessed October 20, 2014, articles.latimes.com/print/2012/may/05/news/la-pn-transcript-obama-campaign-kickoff-20120505.

21. Bill Sammon, "Campaign Officials Hope for Smoother Course," *Washington Examiner*, accessed September 4, 2007, www.examiner.com/printa-914917-Campaign_officials_hope_for.

22. On Dodd's announcement, see Dan Balz, "Democratic Sen. Dodd Enters Presidential Race," *Washington Post*, January 12, 2007, accessed May 23, 2007, www.washingtonpost.com/wp-dyn/content/article/2007/01/111/AR2007011100311_p.

23. Kenneth P. O'Donnell and David F. Powers, *Johnny, We Hardly Knew Ye* (New York: Pocket Books, 1977), 416.

24. On those who shared the spotlight with Kerry, see Jim Vandehei, "Kerry Opens Campaign on War Theme," accessed September 3, 2003, www.washingtonpost.com/ac2wpdyn/A13394-2003Sep2?language=printer, and William Saletan, "The Thin Man: The Mystery of John Kerry's Missing Courage," accessed September 2, 2003, slate.msn.com/toolbar.aspx?action=print&id=2087839.

25. See the Kennedy and Carter responses in *The Candidates 1980: Where They Stand* (Washington, DC: American Enterprise Institute, 1980). Also see Robert V. Friedenberg, "Why Teddy Wasn't Ready: An Examination of the Speaking of Senator Edward Moore

Kennedy during the 1980 Presidential Primaries," paper presented at the Ohio Speech Association, October 1980, 3–4.

26. "Here's Donald Trump's Presidential Announcement Speech."

27. George W. Bush, "A Charge to Keep," accessed May 22, 2004, www.georgewbush.com/News/read.aspx?ID=1947.

28. For a thorough history of Democratic acceptance addresses, see chapters 2 and 3 of David B. Valley, *A History and Analysis of Democratic Presidential Nomination Acceptance Speeches to 1968* (Lanham, MD: University Press of America, 1988). A more concise history can be found in Valley's "Significant Characteristics of Democratic Presidential Nomination Acceptance Speeches," *Central States Speech Journal* 25 (Spring 1974): 56–60.

29. Thomas B. Farrell, "Political Conventions as Legitimation Ritual," *Communication Monographs* 45 (November 1978): 293–305; Kurt W. Ritter, "American Political Rhetoric and the Jeremiad Tradition: Presidential Nomination Acceptance Addresses, 1960–1976," *Central States Speech Journal* 31 (Fall 1980): 153–71.

30. For discussions of these purposes, see Robert O. Nordvold, "Rhetoric as Ritual: Hubert H. Humphrey's Acceptance Address at the 1968 Democratic National Convention," *Today's Speech* 18 (Winter 1970): 34; Valley, "Nomination Acceptance Speeches," 60; and Ritter, "American Political Rhetoric," 155.

31. "Full Text: Donald Trump 2016 RNC Draft Speech Transcript," *Politico*, July 21, 2016, accessed November 9, 2018, https://www.politico.com/story/2016/07/full-transcript-donald-trump-nomination-acceptance-speech-at-rnc-225974.

32. Valley, "Nomination Acceptance Speeches," 61.

33. Ibid.

34. Kurt Ritter, "The 1996 Presidential Nomination Acceptance Addresses: What Do the Speeches by Dole and Clinton Tell Us about the Genre of Acceptance Speeches?" paper presented at the annual meeting of the Speech Communication Association, San Diego, November 1996, 2.

35. Ibid., 1.

36. Ibid., 1–3.

37. George H. W. Bush, "Transcript of Bush Accepting the Nomination for Another Four Years," *New York Times*, August 21, 1992, A14.

38. William Jefferson Clinton, "Acceptance Address to the 1992 Democratic National Convention: A New Covenant," in Bill Clinton and Albert Gore, *Putting People First* (New York: Times Books, 1992), 218–22.

39. See the previous three editions of this book for examples of declining partisanship in the acceptance addresses of presidential candidates in 1996–2004.

40. On this and other differences between contemporary and earlier acceptance addresses, see William L. Benoit, William J. Wells, P. M. Pier, and Joseph R. Blaney, "Acclaiming, Attacking, and Defending in Presidential Nominating Acceptance Addresses, 1960–1996," *Quarterly Journal of Speech* (August 1999): 247–67.

41. Ritter, "American Political Rhetoric," 157–64.

42. Ibid., 161–62.

43. Valley, *History and Analysis of Democratic Presidential Nomination Acceptance Speeches*, 60.

44. Ritter, "American Political Rhetoric," 162.

45. This and all subsequent quotations and references to the Kerry acceptance address are taken from the text of the address, accessed July 30, 2004, at www.washingtonpost.com/ac2wp-dyn/a256778-2004Jul20?language=printer.

46. This and all subsequent quotations and references to the Bush acceptance address are taken from the text of the address, accessed May 31, 2005, from the Weekly Compilation of Presidential Documents at frwebgate.access.gpo.gov/cgi-bin/getdoc.cgi?dbname-2004_presidential_documents.

47. "Full Text: Hillary Clinton's DNC Speech," *Politico*, July 28, 2016, accessed November 9, 2018, https://www.politico.com/story/2016/07/full-text-hillary-clintons-dnc-speech-226410.

48. Wayne Fields, *Union of Words: A History of Presidential Eloquence* (New York: Free Press, 1996), 72.

49. Rick Shenkman, "Presidency: What George W. Bush and William Howard Taft Have in Common," History News Network, accessed June 8, 2005, hnn.us/articles/221.html, 1–2.

50. This analysis of news conference audiences is adapted from Leon V. Sigal, "Newsmen and Campaigners: Organization Men Make the News," *Political Science Quarterly* 93 (Fall 1978): 466–67.

51. Ibid., 466.

52. Beckwith is quoted in the U.S. Department of State's Bureau of International Information Programs "Press Conferences," accessed June 8, 2005, usinfo.state.gov/products/pubs/pressoffice/conferences.htm.

53. C. Jack Orr, "Reporters Confront the President: Sustaining a Counterpoised Situation," *Quarterly Journal of Speech* 66 (February 1980): 17–21.

54. Most such examinations have focused on presidential news conferences, but the rationales for the conclusions, as well as the conclusions themselves, seem appropriate for most political candidates. See Robert E. Denton and Dan F. Hahn, *Presidential Communication* (New York: Praeger, 1986), 252; Michael Grossman and Martha Kumar, *Portraying the President: The White House and the News Media* (Baltimore: Johns Hopkins University Press, 1981), 243–44; Orr, "Reporters Confront the President," 31–32; and Delbert McQuire, "Democracy's Confrontation: The Presidential Press Conference," *Journalism Quarterly* 44 (Winter 1967): 638–44.

55. U.S. Department of State, "Press Conferences," 2.

56. Carolyn Smith, *Presidential Press Conferences: A Critical Approach* (New York: Praeger, 1990), 81.

57. Peter M. Sandman, David M. Rubin, and David B. Sachsman, *Media: An Introductory Analysis of American Mass Communications* (Englewood Cliffs, NJ: Prentice Hall, 1972), 344.

58. Catherine Ann Collins, "Kissinger's Press Conferences, 1972–1974: An Exploration of Form and Role Relationship on News Management," *Central States Speech Journal* 28 (Fall 1977): 190–93.

59. Roger Ailes, *You Are the Message: Secrets of the Master Communicators* (Homewood, IL: Dow Jones-Irwin, 1988), 154–55.

60. Grossman and Kumar, *Portraying the President*, 248.

61. McQuire, "Democracy's Confrontation," 640.

62. Smith, *Presidential Press Conferences*, 89. Although Smith's observations deal directly with presidential press conferences, many of her comments on agendas seem entirely appropriate for press conferences held in the course of political campaigns.

63. A. L. Lorenze, Jr., "Truman and the Press Conference," *Journalism Quarterly* 43 (Winter 1966): 673–75; and Harry P. Kerr, "The President and the Press," *Western Speech* 27 (Fall 1963): 220–21.

64. Barry Jogoda quoted in Grossman and Kumar, *Portraying the President*, 243.

65. See "Statement of Senator John Edwards," August 8, 2008, accessed April 28, 2010, firstread.msnbc.msn.com/news/2008/08/08/4435196-edwards-admits-affair-in-statement. In this apologia Edwards acknowledged the affair but continued to claim that he had not fathered the baby that resulted from his affair. Subsequently he acknowledged having fathered the child.

66. Nikki Haley was accused of having not one, but two extramarital affairs. They were disproven; she won the Republican primary and they did not surface in the general election. Representative Allan Mollohan was subject to House Ethics Committee investiga-

tions, and those investigations are widely believed to have contributed to the fourteen-year House member's loss in the Democratic primary. Representative Mark Souder acknowledged an affair with a staff member and withdrew his candidacy for reelection. Connecticut attorney general Richard Blumenthal lied and exaggerated about his military service in his campaign for the U.S. Senate. His lying and exaggerations were major issues during the Democratic primary, but nevertheless he won. The issue was of little importance in the general election, which he also won.

67. Ellen Reid Gold, "Political Apologia: The Ritual of Self Defense," *Communication Monographs* 45 (November 1978): 311–12.

68. Ibid.

69. Sherry Devereaux Butler, "The Apologia, 1971 Genre," *Southern Speech Communication Journal* 37 (Spring 1972): 283.

70. The morning after the interview broadcast Bill Clinton is reported to have claimed, "It was a screw job. They [*60 Minutes* producers/editors] lied about how long it was going to be. They lied about what was going to be discussed. They lied about what the ending would be. It couldn't have been worse if they had drawn black X's through our faces." Quoted in "How He Won: The Untold Story of Bill Clinton's Triumph," *Newsweek*, Special Election Issue, November/December 1992, 34.

71. B. L. Ware and Wil A. Linkugel, "They Spoke in Defense of Themselves: On the General Criticism of Apologia," *Quarterly Journal of Speech* 59 (October 1973): 25.

72. Gold, "Political Apologia," 308.

73. This and all other direct quotes drawn from this *60 Minutes* segment have been transcribed directly from the videotape of the *60 Minutes* broadcast of January 28, 1994.

74. Flowers was reported to have received $150,000 for her story from the *Star*.

75. Ware and Linkugel, "They Spoke in Defense of Themselves," 277.

76. Elizabeth Edwards's absence was made all the more noticeable by the introduction ABC news prepared for the *Nightline* piece, which pointed out that Edwards was speaking from his house in Chapel Hill, North Carolina.

77. Ware and Linkugel, "They Spoke in Defense of Themselves," 278.

78. Gold, "Political Apologia," 308.

79. This and all subsequent references are to Kathryn M. Olson, "Exploiting the Tension between the News Media's 'Objective' and Adversarial Roles: The Role of Imbalance Attack and Its Use of the Implied Audience," *Communication Quarterly* 42 (Winter 1994): 36–56.

80. Ware and Linkugel, "They Spoke in Defense of Themselves," 280.

81. Ibid.

82. Quoted in Jack Germond and Jules Witcover, *Wake Us When It's Over: Presidential Politics of 1984* (New York: Macmillan, 1985), 159.

83. In January 1998, giving a sworn deposition in the Paula Jones case, Bill Clinton acknowledged having had a sexual relationship on one occasion with Gennifer Flowers. Clinton's defenders observed that in 1992 he had denied a twelve-year affair and claimed that his statement made under oath did not contradict his 1992 claim.

# 9

# Debates in Political Campaigns

In the summer of 1858, one of the most remarkable local political campaigns in U.S. history was being waged on the plains of Illinois. The 1858 Illinois Senate race was remarkable for many reasons. Few races, regardless of office, bring together two such outstanding public servants as those competing for the Senate seat from Illinois in 1858. Few races, regardless of office, have had as profound an impact on our national history as did the race for the Illinois Senate seat in 1858. Few races have produced such masterpieces of campaign oratory as those produced on the plains of Illinois in the summer of 1858. For in that year, Abraham Lincoln and Stephen Douglas vied for the Senate seat from Illinois. On July 24, Lincoln challenged Douglas to a series of debates. Douglas accepted. As the front-runner in what was anticipated to be a close election, Douglas dictated the terms. He suggested seven debates and demanded the opportunity to both open and close four of the debates. Lincoln would open and close only three. Lincoln accepted, and thus ensued what the *New York Tribune* called "a mode of discussing political questions which might well be more generally adopted."[1]

Although the Lincoln-Douglas debates were the first significant political campaign debates in U.S. history, as Jamieson and Birdsell remind us, they were not the first American political campaign debates.[2] Moreover, unlike their successors, they were real debates rather than joint speeches or joint press conferences. Most authorities would agree with J. Jeffery Auer when he argues that there are five essential elements for a true debate. "A debate," claims Auer, "is (1) a confrontation, (2) in equal and adequate time, (3) of matched contestants, (4) on a stated proposition, (5) to gain an audience decision."[3] Auer points out that "each of these elements is essential if we are to have true debate. Insistence upon their recognition is more than mere pedantry, for each one has contributed to the vitality of the debate tradition."[4]

The Lincoln-Douglas debates were not followed by many others. It was not until a century later, in 1960, that we next had "Great Debates" of comparable significance. However, the 1960 presidential debates between Senator John F.

Kennedy and Vice President Richard M. Nixon gave rise to political debating as we now know it in the media age.

Yet most contemporary political debaters, including presidents Reagan, George H. W. Bush, Clinton, George W. Bush, and Obama have not engaged in political debates. Based primarily on the Kennedy-Nixon model of 1960, most contemporary political debates can be characterized as "counterfeit debates."[5] This is not to say that contemporary political debating is, like a counterfeit bill, of little value. As we will see later, contemporary political debates are extremely valuable. But in large part because of the influence of media, they involve different formats and strategies than those of the Lincoln-Douglas era.

Perhaps the counterfeit nature of contemporary political debates can best be understood by using Auer's five essentials of debate to compare the Lincoln-Douglas debates with the prototypic contemporary media political debate, that of Kennedy and Nixon in 1960.

First, the Kennedy-Nixon debate and most political debates since do not involve direct confrontation. Lincoln and Douglas confronted one another. They met on the same platform, questioned one another, and refuted one another. Indeed, the highlight of the seven debates came in the second debate, at Freeport, when Lincoln confronted Douglas with a series of four questions to set up what became known as "The Freeport Dilemma."

Lincoln claimed that Douglas had to repudiate the Supreme Court's *Dred Scott* decision (which made it illegal for voters to prohibit slavery in the territories and hence was enormously popular in the South) or repudiate his own program of popular sovereignty. As chair of the Senate Committee on Territories, Douglas had argued that each of the Western territories should be allowed to choose by popular vote if it would enter the Union free or slave. Repeatedly in the debates after Freeport, Lincoln confronted Douglas with this dilemma. Lincoln demanded that Douglas choose between a fundamental tenet of U.S. democracy—the sanctity of Supreme Court decisions—or his own proposal. If Douglas supported the *Dred Scott* decision, he was admitting that he had labored in the Senate on behalf of a policy that was illegal. If he supported popular sovereignty, he was admitting that Supreme Court decisions were not the highest law of the land and was isolating himself from the Southern wing of the Democratic Party. Lincoln confronted, questioned, followed up, and harangued Douglas. Douglas responded, claimed the dilemma was false, and argued that Lincoln ignored a third alternative.

In contrast, it was not Richard Nixon but a journalist who suggested to John Kennedy, "You are naive and at times immature." Nor was it John Kennedy but rather a journalist who suggested to Richard Nixon that his experience as vice president was as an observer and not as a participant or initiator of policy.[6] Kennedy and Nixon did not talk to each other, as did Lincoln and Douglas. Kennedy and Nixon did not question and pursue one another, nor did they respond to one another. Rather, if Kennedy, Nixon, and most political debaters since are confronted at all, it is by the media, not by one another.[7] Some of the debate formats utilized since 1960 have allowed for somewhat more direct confrontation between candidates than those of 1960.

Second, the Kennedy-Nixon debate, and most political debates since, did not involve equal and adequate time. The key, of course, is adequate time. Lincoln and Douglas dealt almost exclusively with one issue, the future of slavery in the territories. Each man spoke for one and a half hours in each of seven debates. Kennedy and Nixon each spoke for half an hour in each of four debates. The subject matter for the first Kennedy-Nixon debate was domestic affairs, for the last foreign affairs, and no restrictions whatsoever existed for the middle two debates. It is entirely fair to say that Lincoln and Douglas spent up to twenty-one hours debating one issue, while Kennedy and Nixon spent eight minutes on any one issue. Similarly, in 2012, Obama and Romney spent between five and fifteen minutes between them on each issue that the moderators introduced.[8]

Formats like those used in 2012 typically allow each candidate two minutes and thirty seconds to seven minutes and thirty seconds to deal with an issue.[9] Kennedy and Nixon, and most political debaters since, did not have adequate time to deal with major public issues.

In 2016, across the three debates, Hillary Clinton spoke an average of forty-one minutes compared to Trump's forty minutes. However, based upon percentages of time, Trump actually spoke an average of 46 percent to Clinton's 40 percent.[10]

Political debates do typically meet the third criteria for debates. The contestants are closely matched. If one contestant is vastly brighter, more fluent, more poised, more knowledgeable, and better prepared, no real debate can take place. Typically, this is not the case in political debates, where both candidates must agree to debate and hence are probably able debaters, having merit enough to secure major party nominations to the office.

However, political debates frequently do not meet the fourth criteria of debates. The Kennedy-Nixon debate and most political debates since did not involve one stated proposition. Rather, depending on format, ten or more topics are discussed in a single debate. In the first Kennedy-Nixon debate, the two men dealt with such diverse questions as who was most fit and prepared to lead the country, how each man would handle the farm subsidy programs, what policies each would advocate for reducing the federal debt, what each man would do about improving the nation's schools, what policies each would pursue with respect to medical aid to the aged and with respect to a comprehensive minimum hourly wage program. Moreover, each was asked how serious a threat to national security he believed communist subversive activity in the United States was and how he would finance public school construction. In sum, Kennedy and Nixon had less than an hour to deal with nine totally diverse topic areas. In 2012 Obama and Romney had ninety minutes to deal with six or more topics, depending on the debate format.

Finally, the Kennedy-Nixon debates did not really gain an audience decision of the issues. Debates, as Auer suggests, are "clashes of ideas, assumptions, evidence, and argument."[11] They secure from audiences a decision on the issues. In 1858 the Lincoln-Douglas debates revealed the inadequacies of Douglas's program of popular sovereignty for the territories and the inconsistency of that program with existing institutions. It was because he illustrated the inadequacies and inconsistencies of Douglas's position, while justifying and defending his own belief in restricting slavery's spread into the territories, that Lincoln emerged from the debates a national figure and Douglas's national aspirations were shattered. Those debates were a true clash of ideas, assumptions, evidence, and argument. In 1960 the Kennedy and Nixon debates did not facilitate the audience's making a decision about the issues. Contemporary political debates, which are heavily oriented toward the broadcast media audience, are not in the tradition of issue-oriented debates.

Political debating is widespread in this country. It is almost a ritualistic aspect of campaigns for one candidate to challenge the other to a debate. Yet, as we have seen, contemporary media-oriented debates, regardless of what office is sought, are vastly different from earlier political debates. Although they typically involve matched candidates, they rarely if ever entail direct confrontation, equal and adequate time, one stated proposition, and a clear decision on the issues. In the next section, we will trace how political debates evolved from the Lincoln-Douglas debates to the media-oriented debates we have today.

## HISTORY OF POLITICAL DEBATES

During the nineteenth century, debating was an important aspect of campaigning, although perhaps not as widespread as it is today. However, a few debates of local or statewide interest did take place.[12] Although Lincoln and Douglas had gained national attention, figures of comparable stature did not engage in campaign debates in the years that followed. Rather than debating their opponents, in the nineteenth century many candidates utilized surrogate debaters. This practice was especially widespread in nineteenth-century presidential elections.[13] Nevertheless, relatively few nineteenth-century debates received attention beyond their own constituencies, and none attained national prominence.[14]

By the mid-1920s, due to the growth of radio, national debates began to seem feasible. In 1924, testifying before a congressional committee investigating broadcast regulations, William Harkness, an executive of the American Telephone and Telegraph Company, made what is generally believed to be the first suggestion for broadcasting political debates.[15] At the time of Harkness's suggestion, such a broadcast probably would have been local or regional in scope, but within two years, with the birth of the National Broadcasting Company in 1926, nationwide political broadcasts became feasible. NBC's first programs were carried over a twenty-four-station hookup serving twenty-one cities from the East Coast as far west as Kansas City. Other networks soon followed.

The implication of national radio networks for political campaigns was not lost on Congress. In 1927 Congress included a section in its radio broadcast regulations dealing with political broadcasts. Those regulations were modified in 1934, and section 315 of the Communications Act of 1934 affected political broadcasts for years. This "equal time" provision required that if any licensed radio or television station allows a legally qualified candidate for any public office to use its station, it must "afford equal opportunities to all other such candidates for that office in the use of such broadcasting station."[16] This provision, designed to provide equal access to the public's airwaves to all candidates, tended to inhibit political debates. It required that if major party candidates received airtime from a station, that station would have to provide airtime to every other candidate, regardless of the extent of their following. Few broadcasters were willing to make time for the many minor party candidates, and hence little time went to any campaign activities. Although this act was modified in 1959 to ensure that broadcasters could cover the normal newsworthy activities of major political candidates without being subject to harassment by lesser candidates,[17] throughout the period 1934–1976, section 315 inhibited political debates in any race where more than two candidates were involved.

Nevertheless, political debating did not come to a complete standstill during this period. On October 17, 1936, during the presidential election between Governor Alfred Landon and President Franklin Roosevelt, Republican Senator Arthur Vandenberg of Michigan produced a "fake" debate over the CBS network by editing recordings of Roosevelt's speeches. The live Vandenberg naturally bested the edited Roosevelt. The nature of this debate was not made clear to stations until shortly before the broadcast. Of the sixty-six stations scheduled to broadcast the debate, twenty-three did so without interruption. Clearly Vandenberg had edited Roosevelt's speeches to produce a partisan one-sided program. However, perhaps more than anything that had preceded it, this program focused attention on the possibilities of nationally broadcast political debates between major figures.[18]

Four years later, in 1940, Republican Wendell Willkie opened his campaign by challenging President Roosevelt to debate. Polls found the public almost evenly divided in their response to Willkie's challenge.[19] Apparently much of the opposition stemmed from the public's perceptions of the risks that might be involved in having an incumbent president debate. Roosevelt suffered no significant political consequences in declining to debate.

In 1948 the first broadcast debate between two major presidential candidates took place. The candidates were Governor Harold Stassen of Minnesota and Governor Thomas Dewey of New York. They were seeking the Republican nomination to challenge President Harry S. Truman. In the midst of the Oregon primary, Stassen challenged Dewey to debate. Dewey accepted but specified the terms. As Dewey wished, the debate was held in private, with only a small audience of journalists. Stassen had suggested that it might be held in a ballpark with a large public audience. Dewey spoke last, as he wanted. Dewey selected the topic: that the Communist Party should be outlawed in the United States. Moreover, Dewey chose to defend the negative. The debate was broadcast nationally by all four major radio networks and was well received by audiences and political observers.[20]

Among the first suggestions that 1952 presidential candidates General Dwight David Eisenhower and Illinois governor Adlai Stevenson engage in a televised debate were those made by Michigan senator Blair Moody and Democratic media specialist J. Leonard Reinsch.[21] Both NBC and CBS immediately offered to provide the airtime, if Congress would suspend or revoke the equal time provision. However, nothing came of the network's offer, since both Eisenhower and Stevenson were reluctant to debate.[22] Not so reluctant were the two Massachusetts senatorial candidates, Henry Cabot Lodge and John F. Kennedy, who debated that year in Waltham, Massachusetts.

By 1956 virtually the entire country had access to television. Televised political programs of every sort were commonplace. Candidates at all levels—presidential, senatorial, congressional, as well as scores of local candidates—were routinely appearing on television. But with one significant exception, broadcast debates between political candidates were not seen on the nation's television screens.

In 1956 the contest for the Democratic presidential nomination became a fight between Tennessee senator Estes Kefauver and former Illinois governor Adlai Stevenson. Kefauver had become a well-known political figure in 1951 when, as chair of the Senate Crime Investigating Committee, he had presided over nationally televised hearings investigating organized crime. Kefauver challenged Stevenson to debate during the primaries. Stevenson, the Democratic nominee in 1952, had been reluctant to debate Eisenhower and was again reluctant to debate. However, after losing the Minnesota primary, Stevenson agreed to debate Kefauver in the Florida primary. The debate was televised nationally, and although it apparently helped Stevenson, he came away unimpressed with political debates.[23] As in 1952, in 1956 neither Stevenson nor Eisenhower wished to be involved in broadcast debates during the general election.

In 1960 John Kennedy was challenged to debate in the primaries by Senator Hubert Humphrey. During the West Virginia primary, both men agreed to a televised debate. Observers agreed that Kennedy did well in the debate, which was televised throughout the East Coast as well as throughout West Virginia. Perhaps this experience and his 1952 debate with Lodge contributed to Kennedy's acceptance of an NBC offer for free time during the general election if he would agree to a series of joint appearances with the Republican nominee. This offer had been made feasible by a joint resolution of Congress suspending the equal time law until after the election. Like Kennedy, Richard Nixon quickly accepted the NBC offer but noted that since the other networks had issued similar invitations, the networks should coordinate their proposals. The networks had lobbied earlier in the year to suspend the equal time law for just this opportunity. They perceived televised presidential debates as providing them with enhanced credibility as a news medium. Hence, in 1960, for the first time since 1858, the United States was absorbed by a political debate or at least a joint appearance, national in scope and significance.

Political debates at the presidential level were not held for the sixteen years following the Kennedy-Nixon debate. However, they became commonplace in campaigns for almost all other offices. In the years immediately following the Kennedy-Nixon debate, there were political debates between candidates for statewide office in Michigan, Massachusetts, Connecticut, Pennsylvania, and California. Races for lesser offices frequently included debates. For example, two short years after the Kennedy-Nixon debates, debates were held between the candidates for all six congressional seats in Connecticut.[24] Although presidential candidates frequently utilized debates during the primaries that were held after 1960, it was not until 1976 that presidential debates were held during the general election. However, unlike their presidential counterparts, local, regional, and statewide candidates made increasing use of debates during the 1960s and 1970s. One such debate, which took place between the two candidates for governor of Tennessee in 1970, led indirectly to the 1976 presidential debate between Governor Jimmy Carter and President Gerald Ford and resolution of the impediment to political debates caused by the equal time provision.

In 1970 Winfield Dunn, Republican, and John J. Hooker, Jr., his Democratic opponent for the governorship of Tennessee, decided to debate. Aiding Dunn was a University of Virginia law student, Stephen A. Sharp, who found several

Tennessee stations reluctant to carry the debates for fear that they would have to provide equal time to all other minor candidates for the governorship. Sharp's involvement in the Tennessee race caused him to prepare a law school paper on the history and interpretation of section 315. He found that political debates between major candidates might well be considered "bona fide" news events under the 1959 changes to section 315. If so, they could be reported on by stations as normal newsworthy activities, and those stations would not be subjected to providing equal time to all other candidates.

Sharp was subsequently hired by the Federal Communications Commission (FCC), where his work with section 315 became known. The FCC had previously ruled that candidate appearances not "incidental to" other news events were not newsworthy and hence not exempt from the equal opportunities requirement. Political debates by major candidates that were not incidental to any other activity were not exempt. But a political speech incidental to a rally or a dinner was exempt.

After considerable legal maneuvering by a variety of interested parties including the Aspen Program for Media and Society, the Columbia Broadcasting System, and others, the FCC ruled in 1975 that debates that were covered live and in their entirety, and not sponsored by broadcasters (and hence presumably legitimate news events that would take place with or without the press) could be covered without fear of having to provide time to all minor candidates.[25]

This 1975 FCC ruling, known as the Aspen decision, made nationally televised presidential debates feasible from the networks' standpoint. But debates do not take place without willing debaters. In 1960 Kennedy and Nixon had both been willing to debate. Republicans and Democrats in Congress, following the lead indicated by their presidential candidates, had suspended section 315. After the Aspen decision, an act of Congress was no longer necessary for presidential debates, but willing debaters were.

The League of Women Voters, responding to the Aspen decision, took it upon itself to become the sponsoring organization for presidential debates in 1976. In 1976 both major candidates perceived that political debates might well serve their own self-interest. The League set the format for the presidential debates from 1976 to 1984. In 1987 both political parties created the Commission on Presidential Debates. The commission negotiates all the details for the presidential debates to include number, format, location, moderators, and even details such as podium heights and room temperature. Prior to nominee selection, major media outlets host debates. Today, political debates are widespread at all levels.

## DECIDING WHETHER TO DEBATE

At virtually every level of politics, candidates and their advisors strategically address themselves to six questions in determining whether to engage in political debates.[26] Public expectations that serious candidates for the nation's highest office should be willing to debate their ideas have grown steadily stronger since 1976. Today, presidential candidates risk the possibility of severe backlash if they decline to debate: they would be perceived as less than open to share ideas on issues, afraid to face challengers, or violators of historical campaign practice. Candidates for other high offices, such as most statewide offices and congressional seats, also face strong public expectations that they will debate.[27]

Candidates for lesser office are not likely to face as much public aversion to their failure to debate. Consequently, since 1976 these factors have grown less important for many major office candidates, although they remain factors for consideration in most other races.

1. *Is this likely to be a close election?* Expectations about the outcome of the election are vital to the decision to engage in debates. If the election seems as though it will be close and both candidates are in doubt about the outcome, the likelihood of political debates is greatly increased. If either candidate has a strong conviction that he or she can win the election without engaging in debates, the likelihood of debates taking place is dramatically reduced.

2. *Are advantages likely to accrue to me if I debate? Will I suffer for not debating?* No candidate willingly engages in counterproductive activity. Consequently, both candidates must have good reason to expect that the debates will be advantageous to them. Conversely, as public expectations that candidates will debate have grown, especially since 1976, candidates who feel that they are unlikely to be advantaged by a debate must also consider to what degree they might suffer in the public's mind, and be handing their opponent an issue, by not debating.

3. *Am I a good debater?* Candidates do not willingly put themselves in a position where their foe will clearly appear to be stronger. Consequently, when measuring themselves against their opponent, candidates must be confident about their debate ability.

4. *Are there only two major candidates running for the office?* Typically, our political system produces two serious candidates for each office. On those occasions where a third candidate seems to have a possibility of drawing a respectable share of the vote, the likelihood of political debates taking place is reduced. Third-party candidates are not predictable. They are not bound by the same "rules" as candidates who anticipate election. Often, they speak to make a point, or to dramatize a single issue, rather than to win an election. Moreover, the presence of a third candidate provides the possibility that two candidates may "gang up" on one. These variables reduce the likelihood that political debates will take place in races where a third candidate is on the ballot and appears to have a possibility of drawing a respectable share of the vote.

5. *Do I have control of all the important variables in the debate situation?* Candidates cannot be expected to place themselves in positions where they cannot reasonably anticipate what will happen. Consequently, each candidate must feel comfortable with all the major variables in the debate situation: the dates, locations, formats, topics, and other participants (moderators and questioners). Unless candidates are satisfied with all the major variables in the debate, they are unlikely to consent to debating.

6. *Is the field clear of incumbents?* If either candidate is an incumbent seeking reelection, the probability of debate taking place is reduced, especially for lower-level races. Incumbency is a greater obstacle to political debating in lower-level races than it is in upper-level races for at least four reasons.

First, most incumbents reason that their credibility is very high by virtue of prior service. The credibility of their opponents is often an issue in the campaign. This is more apt to be true in lower-level races where challengers may be virtually unknown than in more prominent races where challengers have probably held other offices or attained prominence in their chosen fields.

Second, incumbent officeholders are frequently better able than challengers to make their views known to the public. Hence, they are reluctant to provide their opponents with a platform from which to be heard. Again, this is more apt to be true in lower-level races, where the overall press coverage of the race is not as extensive as the coverage for major races and challengers have an especially difficult time getting coverage.

Third, almost any incumbent will necessarily be placed on the defensive in a political debate. The incumbent's record will probably be a major topic of discussion. Typically, no incumbent will hand an opponent the opportunity to attack vigorously, much less in a well-publicized situation. Again, this is more apt to be true in a lower-level race. In major races challenger candidates have generally held offices and established political records that may lend themselves to attack by an incumbent. But in lower-level races challengers may not have held office in the past and may not have an established political record for an incumbent to attack.

Finally, since 1976 when President Ford became the first incumbent president to engage in a debate, the public has grown to expect candidates for major office to engage in debates. By 1984, public expectations had grown so strong that some have argued that incumbent Ronald Reagan, holding a commanding lead in all the polls, nevertheless risked debating because he felt that not to do so would create a greater problem for him than any possible error he might make in debating.[28] In recent years incumbents have come to fear that their failure or obvious reluctance to debate will be interpreted extremely negatively by the public to mean that they are weak and unable to defend their own positions and policies.[29] Candidates for lower-level offices do not generate quite the same expectations in the public and hence are unlikely to suffer as greatly if they fail to debate. Nevertheless, public expectations that candidates debate have grown to the point where almost any candidate refusing to debate is likely to suffer for doing so.

These guidelines for determining whether to engage in political debates are no longer anywhere near as important as they were in the precedent-setting presidential debates of 1960 and 1976 and many other debates of that era. By the 1980s political debates had become a common fixture in American elections. Hence, candidates were often reluctant to decline the opportunity to debate, fearing that the public would perceive them to be weak and unable to defend their own policies if they refused to debate. Today, political debates are an accepted part of our campaigns, and often potential candidates are evaluated by the likelihood of their performing well in campaign debates.[30]

In the 2000 presidential contest, Al Gore was favored over George W. Bush. The expectation was for Gore to dominate the debates. However, in the first debate, Gore was perceived as rude, constantly interrupting Bush, going over the time limits, and always having the "last word." Gore was actually irritating the audience and Bush held his own. Bush was perceived as the winner of the first debate primarily because of the optics of Gore's performance. According to Gallup polling,

Bush moved twelve points after the debate.[31] This situation is similar to the 2012 presidential debate where Romney exceeded general expectations and Obama was "flat" with low energy and lack of rebuttal to attacks. Romney's performance eliminated a seventeen-point advantage for Obama post the first debate.[32]

In 2016, Hillary Clinton did benefit slightly in post-debate polls. However, during the three weeks of debates, there were dramatic events, such as the *Access Hollywood* tape release of a comment by Trump, that also affected the poll standings.

## POLITICAL DEBATE STRATEGIES

Political debate strategies can best be understood if we recognize that they involve three stages. First are those strategies that take place prior to the debate itself. Second are those the candidate attempts to implement during the debate. Finally there are those following the debate. Each is important. A political debate can be won or lost before it takes place, as it takes place, or after it is held. In this section, we will examine political debating strategies.

### Pre-Debate Strategies

#### Lowering Public Expectations

The candidate who is perceived to have won the debate is often a function of what people expected. Hence, many candidates seek to lower public expectations of their performance. If prior expectations are low, then it may not take a strong effort on the part of the candidate to appear to have done well. Moreover, if a candidate is expected to be outclassed but does well, it may be perceived as a major victory.

Goodwin F. Berquist and James L. Golden have noted that the media tend to establish public expectations regarding the probable outcome of political debates.[33] Observing the 1980 Reagan-Carter debate, Berquist and Golden point out that prior to the debate the media alerted the public to what might take place by discussing expected candidate strategies, interviewing campaign staff, and presenting guidelines for successful debating to which the candidate might adhere.[34]

The interaction between the candidate and campaign staff on the one hand, and the media on the other, can be crucial during the pre-debate period. As the media go about their job, they will seek comments from the campaigners. Campaigners will normally tend to downplay the potential outcome of the debate. By minimizing expectations, campaigners feel they are putting themselves in the best possible position to capitalize on a strong performance and to rationalize a weak one.

The importance of minimizing expectations was made exceptionally clear in the 2000 debates between Texas governor George W. Bush and Vice President Al Gore. Almost immediately after the Commission on Presidential Debates announced its proposal for a series of debates, the Gore team accepted and posted a section on its home page called "Bush Debate Duck." Day after day, hour after hour, throughout the primaries and beyond, the Gore home page indicated how long Bush had avoided accepting Gore's offer to debate him.[35] The implication was clear. The weak debater Bush was afraid of the strong debater Gore. Gore's campaign staff was foolishly minimizing expectations of Bush.

During the early summer, Gore appeared on NBC's *Meet the Press* and CNN's *Larry King Live*. On both shows, he challenged Bush, claiming that he would be delighted to debate the Texas governor "anywhere, anytime," suggesting to the hosts of both shows that their shows would be good places for such a debate. On September 3, Bush held a press conference rejecting the first two debates recommended by the Commission. He did not care for their formats. Rather, he accepted Gore's challenge to debate him on the two television shows, and then added that he would accept the third debate recommended by the Commission. Once more, the Gore staff denigrated Bush's ability to debate.

Gore spokesman Mark Fabiani claimed, "George Bush is trying to do everything he can to avoid primetime presidential debates that will be seen on all three networks." Again, the implication was clear. The weak debater Bush was afraid of the strong debater Gore. Once more, the Gore staff was playing right into the hands of the Bush campaign, by reinforcing the perception that Bush was a weak debater and Gore a strong one. But while Gore's staff was portraying him as the Superman of presidential debates, Superman was feeling more like Clark Kent. Gore told his staff that he would never be able to win the debates. The expectations for Bush, he claimed, were just too low.[36] By the time of the first debate, Bush had effectively minimized expectations for himself, with inadvertent help from the Gore staff, and raised expectations on Gore. Gore proved correct. Expectations on him were exceedingly high, and although neither he nor Bush made serious errors in the debates, for a variety of reasons, clearly including public expectations created in part by the two campaigns, Bush was perceived to have benefited more from the debates than Gore.

In 2008, both the Obama and McCain campaigns attempted to maximize expectations of their opponent and minimize expectations of their own candidate. The Obama campaign was unusually adept at doing this. Prior to the first presidential debate, which was to focus heavily on foreign policy, Obama spokespersons, such as Nick Shapiro, told the press that "John McCain has boasted throughout the campaign about his decades of Washington foreign policy experience and what an advantage that will be for him. This debate offers him major home court advantage and anything short of a game-changing event will be a key missed opportunity for him."[37]

The Obama campaign's attempt to set high expectations for McCain was especially evident prior to the second debate, which utilized the town hall format. Senator McCain had frequently expressed his preference for town hall debates. During the Republican primaries, he did very well in debates using the town hall format. Early in the campaign McCain challenged Obama to a series of twelve such debates to be held around the country. Obama refused the challenge.[38]

Such debates differ from the more traditional presidential debates in several ways. First, they feature "ordinary people" asking questions of the candidates, rather than the press. Second, unlike more traditional presidential debates where audience reaction shots are limited, the town hall format allows the cameras to show more extensive audience responses to the answers provided by the candidates. Third, in traditional debates the candidates are trying to appear presidential as they stand behind podiums. In town hall debates candidates move around the stage and seek to present themselves as personable and likable, not necessarily presidential. The candidates are surrounded by normal citizens and questioned by normal citizens, and with the reactions of normal citizens being viewed by millions in the media audience, success in the town hall format calls for somewhat different skills than the normal presidential debate.[39]

Thus, the Obama campaign attempted to portray McCain as the master of the town hall format and minimize expectations for Obama during the second debate, which utilized this format. Obama's campaign manager David Plouffe explained their strategy.

> McCain was widely known as a master of the town hall format, having received rave reviews for his town hall performances in both the 2000 and 2008 primaries. We aggressively tried to hype this reputation and raise expectations for his performance, an effort that was helped by McCain's gambit to get us to agree to do a dozen town halls in the summer. We called him the best town hall performer in the history of American politics.[40]

Prior to the first of the 2012 presidential debates, both the Obama and Romney camps followed the traditional pattern of attempting to lower expectations on their candidate and increase them on the opponent. Typical were the remarks of Obama's campaign manager Jim Messina. As the first debate approached, Messina told reporters that "Governor Romney is a very skilled debater." In contrast, Messina continued, "Obama was long and windy." Hence, Messina concluded, "Clearly the governor has the advantage."[41] Similarly, two days before the first debate, Obama was reported as having told a campaign rally in Henderson, Nevada, that he believed that he was "just okay" at debating but that Romney was "a good debater."[42]

The Romney team was also attempting to lower expectations on their candidate. Romney's chief surrogate, vice presidential candidate Congressman Paul Ryan, claimed that "President Obama is a very, very gifted speaker. The man's been on the national stage for many years." In contrast, Ryan pointed out that "this is Mitt's first time on this kind of a stage."[43] Clearly both campaigns hoped to lower expectations for their candidate prior to the first debate.

But in 2012, the expectations game did not run true to form for all the debates. President Obama performed exceptionally poorly in the first debate. That debate was immediately followed by a surge in support for Romney. Thus, Obama had no need to try to lower expectations before the second debate. His performance in the first debate had dramatically lowered public expectations of him. A Pew poll released the day before the second debate indicated the magnitude of the shift in public perception. Prior to the first debate, independents favored Obama to win the first debate 44 percent to 28 percent. But on October 14, the day before the second debate, Pew reported that 42 percent expected Romney to win and only 31 percent expected an Obama victory. The Democratic-leaning *Huffington Post* summarized Obama's dilemma by observing that "President Barack Obama is gaining ground somewhere he might not have preferred—the battle of lowered debate expectations."[44] Indeed, Obama's fall was so great that, as the second debate between the two presidential candidates approached, the Obama team attempted to increase expectations on their candidate.

Given his poor performance in the first debate, Obama was unlikely to heighten expectations to the point where they hurt him, as did Vice President Gore's campaign in 2000. But his campaign did not want him perceived as negatively as he was after the first debate. Hence, typical of the messages they issued as the second presidential debate approached was the statement by former White House press secretary and senior Obama campaign advisor Robert Gibbs. "I think you will see somebody who will be strong, who will be passionate, who will be energetic," claimed Gibbs in anticipating how Obama would perform in the second debate. Similarly, Obama campaign aide David Axelrod promised "a more aggressive President Obama in this next debate," observing that "I think he's going to be aggressive in making the case for his view of where we should go as a country."[45]

Statements like these essentially acknowledged that Obama had done very poorly in the first debate, but with Obama's poor performance dramatically lowering public expectations, there was no longer need for the campaign to continue doing so. Rather, the campaign sought to restore confidence in the president by taking the relatively unusual step of heightening expectations on him prior to the second presidential debate.

In 2016, there was tremendous excitement about the pending debates. Everyone knew about the "rough-and-tumble" style of Donald Trump as exhibited during the Republican primary debates. There was much speculation about how Trump would confront Hillary Clinton. However, the Trump campaign proclaimed that Hillary was the professional politician and had much more experience in political debates over her career. Clinton had debated nearly forty times, including her Senate race and the two presidential races.[46] The Clinton campaign argued that with all the years on television and his winning of the primary debates, Trump would do very well as a performer. Interestingly, the Clinton campaign was concerned that the expectations were so low for Trump performing in a debate, that Clinton might be held to a higher standard of performance. Campaign members urged reporters to indeed hold both to the same standards.[47]

### Determining the Target Audience

A second pre-debate strategy is to determine the target audience clearly. Political debates typically draw the largest audiences of any single communicative event of the campaign. The candidates must determine who their target audiences are for the debate. Typically, they will be the same as the normal campaign target audiences. However, due to the unusual size of the audience, it is possible that the candidate may choose to go after a new target group of voters during a debate. The debate may be the first time that this group has been exposed to the candidate. Most practitioners would not suggest using the debate to attract massive numbers of new and different voters to the candidate. But the unusual nature of debate audiences—their size, the presence of many adherents of the opponent, the propensity of both the college educated and women to watch debates—means that the candidates must determine clearly whether they wish to maintain their campaigns' targeted audiences for the debate or whether they wish to make some changes, normally in the form of adding targeted groups.

### Devising and Rehearsing Possible Answers

Finally, with a clear conception of targeted audiences in mind, candidates must work out answers to possible questions and practice them. This is the third pre-debate strategy. The firsthand reports of many participants in political debates suggest several successful approaches to practice.[48] First, in a relaxed atmosphere, the candidate and a limited number of aides should work through possible questions and answers, consistently keeping in mind overall themes and target audiences.

Second, the candidate should practice the answers in a situation as similar to the real one as possible. For nationally televised presidential debates, this has meant simulating the television studio or auditorium to be used and often utilizing a stand-in for the opponent. In 2008 Barack Obama's advisors closely studied the 1980 Carter-Reagan debate in which Reagan scored a decisive victory. Like Reagan, the Obama campaign built an actual replica of the stage that would be used in each of the debates. The real stage dimensions, podium placements, even the carpeting of the real stages that would be used were duplicated and used in Obama's practice sessions. Reviewing their practice sessions, Obama's campaign manager David Plouffe claimed that the advice of Tom Donilon and Ron Klain, who had helped in debate preparation for several Democratic presidential candidates, to duplicate the actual stages upon which the debates would be held, "was wise counsel. The move added to Obama's comfort heading into the debates."[49]

In 2012 both President Obama and Governor Romney practiced for the second debate, the town hall debate where they were free to move about on the stage, by building replicas of the set on which they would actually debate.[50] Because the other debates involved the candidates speaking from behind podiums and seated at a table, the physical setting of the town hall debate where both candidates would be moving freely around the stage was the one where the physical movements of the candidate were of utmost concern and hence replica stages were used in practicing. The Romney replica included TV lighting, a digital timer, and video cameras all placed as they would be in the studio where the debate would take place. It even included risers where the onstage questioners would sit as well as chairs for the candidates and the moderator's desk and chair. The Romney team was particularly concerned that their candidate not be caught seated as Obama walked toward him and hovered over him. Romney was coached to immediately stand up if Obama moved toward him.[51]

Some candidates have reviewed the speeches and tapes of their opponent's past performances. In the case of opponents who have debated in the past, an examination of their past debates has proven helpful.[52] Preparing for a debate may well mean curtailing other campaign activity for several days, but given the attention normally focused on debates, this sacrifice would seem worthwhile.

In 2012 all four major party candidates for the presidency and vice presidency took time out of their campaign schedules to practice for the debates.[53] Significantly, President Obama, according to campaign aides, did not take his debate preparation seriously prior to the first debate.[54] In contrast, Governor Romney saw the debates as a potential turning point in the campaign and prepared accordingly.

Republican candidate Romney began his preparation in early July, fully thirteen weeks prior to the first debate. At that time, several sources reported that during a three-day retreat in Park City, Utah, Romney began debate preparations with six to eight campaign aides. "They sorted through a variety of topics sure to come up in the three presidential debates, like the state of the economy and the war in Afghanistan, and kicked around the best 'test responses' to questions they expected Obama and the debate moderators will toss at the ex-Massachusetts governor." Thomas DeFrank, reporting on the event for the *New York Daily News*, claimed that sources told him that several similar sessions were planned for the summer, but that actual practices at a podium and with an Obama surrogate would not happen until later in the campaign, "mainly because Romney doesn't like them all that much." Romney advisors claimed that Romney had the ability to "absorb copious amounts of information, assembling and parsing the facts, then debating the most persuasive lines of attack or defense with staffers and confidants." Once Romney had a good mastery of the facts, he started actual practices at a podium and with an Obama surrogate. Romney was late in announcing that Ohio senator Rob Portman would serve as the Obama surrogate for his practices. Portman had impersonated both Al Gore in President Bush's debate rehearsals in 2000 and Massachusetts senator John Kerry in 2004. Most importantly, he had already impersonated Obama, having done so for Senator McCain's debate practices in 2008. In 2008 Portman largely prepared himself to be a faithful replica of Obama by studying Obama's audiobooks. In 2012 he supplemented that by studying briefing material provided by the Romney campaign. The fact that Portman was on the short list of candidates Romney was considering for the vice presidential nomination likely contributed to the delay in announcing his role until late August, after the Republican convention.

Meanwhile, in mid-June President Obama's staff announced that former Democratic presidential candidate and Massachusetts senator John Kerry would play the role of Romney for the president's debate practices. Kerry was termed "an obvious choice" by Obama campaign senior strategist David Axelrod. Axelrod noted that the senator was a fine debater, had a mastery of a wide range of issues, and, perhaps most importantly, was exceedingly familiar with Romney's years as governor of Massachusetts. The Obama campaign was confident that in their debate practices, Kerry could accurately foreshadow Romney's attacks against Obama, as well as mimic Romney's speaking style and model his posture. They believed that all this would contribute to making Obama feel comfortable when he debated Romney.

However, prior to the first debate, Obama did not prepare as he had in 2008 and as he would for the two subsequent debates he had with Governor Romney. One member of Obama's inner circle claimed that the president was disdainful of Romney and did not believe he needed to practice. "President Obama made it clear he wanted to be doing anything else—anything—but debate prep. He kept breaking off whenever he got the opportunity and never really focused on the event," claimed this advisor to Obama. During his final preparation for the first debate, which took place in Las Vegas, Obama joked with a volunteer that his advisors were "keeping me indoors all the time" to practice. "It's a drag. They're making me do my homework," he joked. Perhaps significantly, the day before the first debate, Obama wasted a large portion of the afternoon visiting the nearby Hoover Dam. He did so regardless of the worries of some of his advisors, who felt that he had been distracted and detached during some of his practices with Senator John Kerry and had not practiced well.[55] During the actual first debate, he also came across as detached, perhaps distracted, and clearly was bested by Governor Romney.

Both of the vice presidential candidates also prepared for their debate by studying their opponent and practicing against a surrogate opponent. Ted Olson, a topflight Washington lawyer long active in Republican politics, who had for a time been President Bush's solicitor general, served as the Biden surrogate for Congressman Paul Ryan's debate practice. Ryan, although less experienced than Vice President Biden in political debates, was perhaps the foremost Republican expert in the House of Representatives on economic matters. Ryan, the House Budget Committee Chairman, had considerable debate experience in the House, but he had no experience in presidential or vice presidential debates. In contrast, the vice president had twice been a presidential candidate and of course had debated Governor Sarah Palin four years earlier. In addition to any individual study that he engaged in, Ryan and Olson had nine sessions of ninety minutes each in which Ryan honed his potential debate responses. Meanwhile, Vice President Biden practiced against Maryland representative Chris Van Hollen, the ranking Democrat on the House Budget Committee. Just as Republicans often turned to Ryan as their spokesperson on economic matters, Van Hollen frequently filled that role for Democrats. As the chair and ranking member of the same House committee, both men were exceedingly familiar with one another and had argued frequently in the past, making Van Hollen an excellent choice to serve as a surrogate for Ryan in Biden's practices.

In 2016, Clinton and Trump were very different in how they approached the pending debates. Clinton studied, practiced, and prepared specific responses to anticipated questions. She studied briefing books, reviewed opposition research, and rehearsed multiple times specific questions and full-length debates. One of the challenges for the Clinton team was to prepare for "multiple" Trumps. Which one should they prepare for: the bomb-thrower or a kinder and gentler person?[56] The week prior to the first debate, Clinton left the campaign trail to practice for the debate.

Trump took a very different approach. Although Trump's staff prepared briefing books, Trump did not spend much time with them, did not hold any mock debates, continued his campaign rallies, and bragged that he did not need to prep for the debates. He would meet with his informal group of advisors, former New York mayor Rudolph W. Giuliani, talk-radio host Laura Ingraham, Fox News Channel chair Roger Ailes, CEO Steve Bannon, retired general Mike Flynn, and campaign manager Kellyanne Conway. They would meet at his golf course and "test out zingers and chew over ways to refine the Republican nominee's pitch."[57]

## Debate Strategies

### *Relating Issues to an Overall Theme*

As the debate progresses, candidates must constantly respond to specific questions on the issues of the day. While those issues vary from campaign to campaign, most successful political debaters have been able to integrate the specific issues into an overall framework. For example, when senators John Kennedy and Hubert Humphrey debated in the 1960 West Virginia primary, Kennedy developed the overall thesis, just as he did months later when debating Nixon, that while the United States was a great nation, it could and should be greater. As he dealt with specific issues concerning West Virginia and the nation, he integrated many of them into his overall thesis that the United States could do better.[58]

Skilled political debaters will first present their overall theme in the introductory statement, if the opportunity to make such a statement is allowed in the debate format being used. Then they will reinforce it with answers to as many specific questions as possible. Finally, they will return to it in their concluding statement.

Both Barack Obama and, to a lesser extent, John McCain had a clear overall theme in their first debate, to which they remained consistent throughout the 2008 presidential debates. For Obama, that theme was, in his words in his very first answer, "It [the economic policy of Bush/McCain] hasn't worked. And I think the fundamentals of the economy have to be measured by whether or not the middle class is getting a fair shake."[59] Obama went on to add that he would offer an economic change to the middle class from the Bush/McCain policies. Repeatedly, throughout all the debates, Obama used answers to specific questions to reinforce this theme. Similarly, Obama consistently attempted to link McCain to Bush on foreign policy questions and suggest that the policies of Bush/McCain had not worked and that it was time for a change. Repeatedly Obama talked both to and about the "middle class," "the folks," "ordinary Americans," "the nurse, the teacher, the police officer," suggesting that Bush and McCain were more concerned about "what's good for Wall Street, but not what's good for Main Street." McCain was less successful in developing a unified theme in the first debate. On economic questions he attempted to stress that he would cut government spending while Obama would increase government spending and hence by implication taxes. On foreign policy he attempted to stress his experience and judgment, suggesting that Obama was woefully lacking in both. McCain claimed Obama's inexperience was especially evident in Obama's willingness to meet with the leaders of rogue states that have been our enemies.

In 2012 the debate formats did not provide for opening statements. Nevertheless, the candidates used the first questions and their closing statements to develop an overall theme. For example, the first debate opened with moderator Jim Lehrer asking both candidates, "What are the major differences between the two of you about how you would go about creating new jobs?"[60] President Obama answered first. He briefly tried to indicate the accomplishments of his administration over the past four years, citing achievements in the auto and housing industries, but quickly pivoted to focus on his theme. Obama's theme was that the future would be better under him than under Romney. "The question here tonight is not where we've been, but where we're going," claimed Obama as he tried to pivot to his theme. At this point he claimed that Romney wanted a tax cut "skewed towards the wealthy" and that Romney "would roll back regulations." In contrast, Obama claimed he would "invest in education and training . . . develop new sources of energy," and "change our tax code to make sure that we're helping small businesses and companies that are investing here in the United States." Consistently Obama tried to keep the debate focused on the future.

Romney used his response to present his overarching theme that the past four years had been an economic failure and that Obama would simply continue the same unsuccessful policies. "The path that we are on," claimed Romney, "has just been unsuccessful. The president has a view very similar to the view he had when he ran four years [ago], that a bigger government, spending more, taking more, regulating more—if you will, trickle-down government—would work. That's not the right answer for America."

Throughout the debate Obama continually tried to portray himself as championing a host of specific programs, all of which would contribute to job growth and a stronger American economy, while often by implication suggesting that Romney was more interested in protecting the wealthy. The key passage in his closing statement well reflects his theme.

> And everything that I've tried to do and everything that I'm now proposing for the next four years in terms of improving our education system, or developing American energy, or making sure that we're closing loopholes for companies that are shipping jobs overseas and focusing on small businesses and companies that are creating jobs here in the United States, or—closing our deficit in a responsible, balanced way that allows us to invest in our future—all those things are designed to make sure that the American people, their genius, their grit, their determination is—channeled and—and they have an opportunity to succeed. And everybody's getting a fair shot and everybody is getting a fair share. Everybody's doing a fair share and everybody's playing by the same rules.

Obama had trouble developing an overarching theme in the first debate because he was attempting to do too much. First, he was trying to defend his economic record. Second, he was focusing on the future, claiming that his policies would produce an improved economy in the next four years. And finally, he was trying to indict Romney as largely disinterested in the lower and middle classes.

In contrast, Romney used his closing statement, as he had used his first answer, to develop one simple overarching theme: that Obama's past and current economic policies had failed and would, with the addition of Obamacare, continue to fail in the future.

> There's no question in my mind that if the president were to be re-elected you'll continue to see a middle-class squeeze with incomes going down and prices going up. I'll get incomes up again. You'll see chronic unemployment. We've had 43 straight months with unemployment above 8 percent. If I'm president, I will create—help create 12 million new jobs in this country with rising incomes. If the president's re-elected, "Obamacare" will be fully installed. In my view that's going to mean a whole different way of life for people who counted on the insurance plan they had in the past. Many will lose it. You're going to see health premiums go up by some $2,500 per—per family.

Romney focused throughout the first debate on indicting Obama for having failed economic policies. Romney remained tightly focused on this overarching theme throughout the 2012 debates, even effectively using it to indict Obama's foreign policies in the last debate.

Issues serve skilled debaters by allowing them to develop an overall thesis. We know that most people forget much of what they hear in as little as twenty-four hours. Any response to an opponent or a moderator on a specific issue is liable to be forgotten by most of the audience. But by making the response to a specific issue part of a theme that is consistently repeated, issues can be used to best advantage. Strategies on specific issues, of course, cannot be generalized. They vary depending on the candidate and the situation. But developing an overall thesis, which can be presented in opening and closing statements and repeatedly reinforced by the responses to many specific issues, is a highly effective strategy employed by many political debaters.

*Developing an Image*

Issues are one of the two major concerns of the candidate during the debate. The other is image. As Robert O. Weiss has argued, in political debates "issues and images are in practical fact overlooked and . . . they intertwine in all manner of convolutions and mutually affect one another in countless ways."[61] Weiss calls this relationship the "issue-image interface."[62] Although issues and images are closely intertwined, there are several image strategies that can be employed in political debates.

The principal image strategies that can be utilized in political debating include the development of a leadership style, personification, and identification.[63] As Dan Nimmo points out, political figures can develop an activist leadership style or a passive leadership style. The activist is just that. In a debate, activists consistently refer to their actions, their initiatives, and their effect on events. Passive leaders are cautious. They do not speak of their initiatives, but rather portray themselves as reacting to events.

During the 2012 debates, both President Obama and Governor Romney attempted to portray themselves as activist leaders. In their very first answers in the first debate, both Obama and Romney spoke about what they would do, what actions they would take. The questions asked how they would create jobs. Obama briefly defended job creation during his administration and attacked Romney's perspective, claiming that Romney would change tax policies so that they were "skewed towards the wealthy." Then Obama claimed that he would invest in education and training, develop new sources of energy, and change the tax code to help small businesses. Moments later he claimed that he would "hire 100,000 new math and science teachers," "create 2 million more slots in our community colleges," and "make sure that we keep tuition low for our young people." Throughout all three debates, Obama consistently talked about what he had done and what he wished to do. He attempted to portray himself as an activist leader who would move the country forward.

Similarly, Governor Romney portrayed himself as an activist leader. Romney did so in the first debate by skillfully attacking the failures of the Obama administration and contrasting them with what he would do. He would cut taxes for middle-income Americans. He would work for energy independence, increased trade, improved training and education programs, a balanced budget, and help for small business. As he developed each of these points, he indicted the failure of the Obama administration and offered specific suggestions. For example, he pointed out that the Obama administration had cut in half the number of permits and licenses to drill for oil and natural gas on government land. Romney claimed, "If I am president, I'll double them, and also get the—the oil from offshore and Alaska. And I'll bring that pipeline in from Alaska."

Similarly, during their closing speeches at the end of their third debate, the last time either man would address such a large audience, they both attempted to portray themselves, as they had throughout the debates, as activists. The president spoke first. The activist nature of his final speech can be indicated by simply noting the subjects and verbs he used. He claimed, "I want to build . . .," "I've put forward a plan to . . .," "I want to make sure we've got . . .," "I want to control . . .," "I want to reduce . . .," "As Commander in Chief, I will . . .," "I promise you . . .," "I will fight for . . .," "I will work every single day to . . ." In a thirteen-sentence closing statement, involving many long compound and complex sentences, the president referenced himself fourteen separate times. Often, as indicated above, he did so by starting a sentence with the pronoun "I" and then following it immediately with an active verb. Obama made few references to Romney or his policies in his closing statement. Clearly his language was that of an activist.

Governor Romney also portrayed himself as an activist throughout the 2012 debates. Although clearly portraying himself as an activist leader, his approach in his closing statement of the final debate was somewhat different from Obama's. Obama had largely ignored Romney in his closing remarks, focusing on his own policies. But Romney would not ignore the president. Romney relied heavily on short declarative statements. Typically, he would indict one of the president's failures and then use a short declarative sentence to indicate what he would do. For example, "The president's path means 20 million people out of work struggling for a good job. I'll get people back to work with 12 million new jobs." In a thirty-five-sentence closing statement, Romney referenced himself eighteen times. He too was portraying himself as an activist, but he was also indicting the policies of the Obama administration.

During the 2008 debates, both senators Obama and McCain attempted to present themselves to the public as energetic, active leaders, but Obama seems to have been more successful. The physical contrast between the two men contributed to their respective images. Obama simply looked younger, more vigorous, more energetic, than the older, gray-haired McCain.

In 2012 both Governor Romney and President Obama attempted to present themselves to the public as energetic, active leaders. The physical contrast between the two men seemed to favor Romney during the first debate. During his four years as president, Barack Obama had aged. His hair was starting to turn gray. In the first debate he seemed less energetic compared to the later debates. Romney appeared slightly older than Obama, but his vigorous and energetic delivery contributed to his being perceived as an activist.

In the second debate, Obama seemed much more energetic, consistent with what the public might expect of an activist president. However, as the two men moved around the stage in the second, or town hall, debate, Romney did not back down from the president. On occasion Romney seemed to be directly challenging the president as both men approached one another, getting into one another's personal space, and the physical picture that was transmitted to viewers would suggest that both men were activists. The physical image that both men projected in the final debate suggested that both were engaged in the debate and prepared to be activist presidents.

In 2016, both Clinton and Trump spoke of their experience and successful leadership. Of course, Clinton had filled the roles of first lady, senator, and secretary of state. For Trump, it was as businessperson. In terms of Trump and leadership, Ben Voth presents an interesting argument. In general, the media were mostly hostile toward Trump. Without debating the complex issue of media bias, in terms of tone, media coverage was more negative toward Trump. According to a Harvard Shorenstein study, Trump received 77 percent negative coverage and 23 percent positive.[64] Much of the coverage was justified, according to journalists, because of some outrageous comments made by Trump and revelation of Trump's past personal behavior. However, it is also important to note that public trust in media reached an all-time low in June 2016 of just 8 percent. Such public mistrust of the media in general, and among Republicans more specifically, may well have benefited Trump in terms of perceptions of leadership.

The second image strategy that lends itself to political debating is *personification*, the effort of the candidate to personify a definite role. For example, the candidate may work to be perceived as a nice guy, an efficient manager, or a strong leader. In 2012 both President Obama and Governor Romney sought to personify themselves as economic experts who could remedy the nation's economic woes. Moreover, President Obama also sought to portray himself as the champion of the middle class and by implication suggest that Governor Romney was more interested in the wealthy.

Their responses to the very first question asked in the debates, in which moderator Lehrer asked how each man would create new jobs, indicate the nature of the persona they each sought to create. Obama initially reviewed the successes of his administration and then contrasted his perception of Romney's approach with his own approach.

> Governor Romney has a perspective that says if we cut taxes, skewed towards the wealthy, and roll back regulations, that we'll be better off. I've got a different view. I think we've got to invest in education and training. I think it's important for us to develop new sources of energy here in America, that we change our tax code to make sure that we're helping small businesses and companies that are investing here in the United States.

Throughout the debate, Obama claimed that for the past four years his economic policies had been working, although more slowly than he might have wished. His economic successes indicated his economic expertise, and his remedies for the nation's economic ills would benefit all citizens, unlike Romney, whose policies were aimed primarily at benefiting the rich.

Romney too claimed the mantle of economic expertise and denied being partial to the wealthy. Moreover, Romney suggested that Obama's personification of himself as an economic guru was simply not accurate. Rather, Obama's policies had hurt America, especially the middle class.

> My view is that we ought to provide tax relief to people in the middle class. But I'm not going to reduce the share of taxes paid by high-income people. High-income people are doing just fine in this economy. They'll do fine whether you're president or I am. The people who are having the hard time right now are middle-income Americans. Under the president's policies, middle-income Americans have been buried. They're just being crushed. Middle-income Americans have seen their income come down by $4,300. This is a—this is a tax in and of itself. I'll call it the economy tax. It's been crushing. At the same time, gasoline prices have doubled under the president. Electric rates are up. Food prices are up. Health care costs have gone up by $2,500 per family. Middle-income families are being crushed.

Romney then went on to detail his plan for the economic revival of the country. He criticized the duplication of forty-seven federal education and training programs housed in eight different federal agencies as typical federal government inefficiency and suggested that much of that money should be returned to the states, who were closer to the people and better understood the education and training needs of their citizens. He discussed the need to develop natural gas and coal both for the nation's economic benefit and for the jobs such development would create.

Throughout all three debates both men tried to personify themselves as economic experts who had the background to lead the nation forward. Obama did so primarily by claiming success in getting the recovery started over the previous four years. Romney did so primarily by citing his proven success in the private sector and his programs for the future. Moreover, Obama personified himself as a champion of the middle class and attempted to personify Romney as the champion of the wealthy. Romney too personified himself as an economic expert, relying primarily on his private-sector successes to support his claim of expertise. He claimed that the president's policies were a failure. Moreover, Romney defended himself against the president's charges that he favored the wealthy at the expense of the middle class, denying Obama's charges.

As we know, in 2016, both Trump and Clinton suffered low approval ratings, well in the mid- to low 40 percent range. Neither rated high on trust either. As a result, both attempted to demonstrate potential competence if elected president.

The final image strategy is *identification*. Debaters attempt to identify themselves with what they believe are the principal aspirations of their audience. In 2012 both candidates attempted to do this throughout the debates, although it was perhaps most apparent in the closing statements that they made in the last debate. Both men centered their final remarks on the nation's aspirations for a stronger economy, which would be characterized by less debt and less unemployment.

In addition to the nation's aspiration for a healthy economy, Obama also felt that the country aspired to have fair government policies that did not favor any single class. In addition to the nation's aspiration for a healthy economy, Romney also felt that the country aspired to strong presidential leadership that would work with the other party to advance the nation. These aspirations were evident throughout the debates, but perhaps nowhere more than in their final closing remarks to the nation, at the end of the third presidential debate.

President Obama's final remarks in the third debate well illustrated his perceptions of the nation's aspirations. He claimed that Romney favored policies that "won't create jobs, won't reduce our deficit, but will make sure that the folks at the very top don't have to play by the same rules that you do." In contrast, said the president, "I want to build on our strengths. And I've put forward a plan to make sure that we're bringing manufacturing jobs back to our shores by rewarding companies and small businesses that are investing here, not overseas." He then claimed that he would improve education and work toward energy independence, both of which would help the nation's sagging economy. Importantly, given his perception of the nation's aspirations and of Romney, the president also noted, "Yes, I want to reduce the deficit by cutting spending that we don't need but also by asking the wealthy to do a little bit more so that we can invest in things like research and technology that are the key to a 21st century economy."

Governor Romney's remarks concluding the final debate also clearly reflected his perceptions of the nation's aspirations. He divided his concluding statement into a section on the economy and a section on leadership. Representative of his observations was the statement that "there are two very different paths that the country can take. One is a path represented by the president, which at the end of four years would mean we'd have $20 trillion in debt. . . . I'll get us on track to a balanced budget." Romney went on to conclude that "the president's path will mean a continuing decline in take-home pay. I want to make sure take-home pay turns around and starts to grow. The president's path means 20 million people out of work struggling for a good job. I'll put people to work with 12 million new jobs."

In addition to his focus on the national aspiration for an improved economy, Romney also felt that the nation aspired to strong bipartisan presidential leadership that could break through the gridlock in Washington. "America's going to come back," claimed Romney, "and for that to happen, we're going to have to have a president who can work across the aisle. I was in a state where my legislature was 87 percent Democrat. I learned how to get along on the other side of the aisle. We've got to do that in Washington." Romney finished his concluding remarks by claiming that "we need strong leadership. I'd like to be that leader with your support. I'll work with you. I'll lead you in an open and honest way, and I ask for your vote."

Thus, both men throughout the debates spoke to what they perceived to be the nation's aspirations. Both candidates frequently addressed the national aspiration for an improved economy. In addition, Obama spoke to his perception that the nation aspired to a government that was even-handed in its treatment of all citizens and did not favor the wealthy. Like Obama, Romney spoke to the national aspiration for an improved economy. In addition, he spoke to his perception that the nation aspired to a strong leader who would work cooperatively with members of the other party to break the gridlock in Washington.

As you will learn in the chapter on the 2016 election, Hillary Clinton had difficulty relating to millennial women. Some questioned her feminist credentials because of how she treated the affairs of her husband and statements she made about Monica Lewinsky. What is equally interesting is how a billionaire could relate to middle-working class voters. James Ceaser and his colleagues speculate that those voters, "it turns out, resent condescending professionals much more than the super-rich, who they often admire and dream of emulating."[65]

As these examples make clear, there is a close relationship between a candidate's response to specific issues and the image that the candidate projects. Nevertheless, as the debate is in progress, the candidate should have a clear idea of an overall issue strategy or thesis to which specific answers can be related. Moreover, candidates should be cognizant of the image they may be projecting and develop appropriate strategies, such as a leadership style, personification, and identification, to create the persona they want.

## Post-Debate Strategies

Political debates are not over when the last word is uttered. Who won? Who made a grievous error? Who seemed best in control? Questions like these immediately follow the debate, and their answers are often as important as the debate itself. After all, it is what the audience perceives to have happened in the debate that is of consequence. Therefore, the well-prepared campaign will be ready to try to influence audience perceptions of the debate as soon as it concludes.

The importance of post-debate strategies was best dramatized in the second Ford-Carter debate of 1976, perhaps best remembered because President Ford seemed to be unaware of the Soviet domination of Eastern Europe. Yet, at the time that Ford made his unfortunate statement, it was barely noticed. It was not until the next day, after continual publicity of his remark, that Ford was perceived as having erred badly. Frederick T. Steeper studied this debate and concluded:

> The volunteered descriptions of the debate by the voters surveyed immediately after the debate included no mentions of Ford's statement on Eastern Europe. Not until the afternoon of the next day did such references appear, and by Thursday night they were the most frequent criticism given Ford's performance. Similarly, the panelists monitored during the debate gave no indication of an unfavorable reaction at the time they heard Ford's Eastern European remarks. The conclusion is that the preponderance of viewers of the second debate most likely were not certain of the true status of Eastern Europe, or less likely, did not consider Ford's error important. Given the amount of publicity given Ford's East European statements the next day by the news media and the concomitant change that took place it is concluded that this publicity caused the change.[66]

Most students of political debate believe that the effects often lag behind the debate itself. Frequently, audience members do not reach final judgment until they have discussed the debate with others and have observed the media reaction.[67] During these hours, when interpersonal influence and media influence are often operating, the campaign engages in the post-debate strategy of favorably influencing perceptions of the debate.

The first presidential debate of 2000 well illustrates the importance of favorably influencing public perceptions of the debate and how that perception often lags a day or so behind the debate itself. At first glance this was a close debate, with perhaps a slight edge going to Vice President Gore, who seemed more fluent and conversant with the issues. Immediately after the debate, Gore bested Bush in three of the four "instant polls" taken.[68] Press accounts stressed the clash between the two candidates while also observing that both candidates were attempting to move their parties to the center of the political spectrum.[69] However, although the first accounts portrayed a close debate with a slight edge going to Gore, the following day three stories were developing from the debate and all of them clearly favored Texas governor George W. Bush.

First, Gore had not proven to be a substantially stronger debater than Bush. Bush had challenged Gore sharply on critical issues such as tax policy, Social Security reform, prescription drugs for the elderly, education, and rebuilding the military. Moreover, he had repeatedly questioned Gore's use of statistics. The initial perceptions, fostered during the pre-debate period deliberately by the Bush camp and inadvertently by the Gore camp, were that Gore was clearly the better debater, in large part because he was so much more familiar with the issues. Hence, Gore failed to live up to expectations. He did not appear substantially more fit for the office than Bush. Bush exceeded expectations. He seemed to be approximately as well prepared and able to assume the office as Gore.

Second, Gore's statements in the debate were examined and on three occasions it appeared as though he had exaggerated his accomplishments.[70] This problem had plagued Gore throughout the campaign. By the day after the debate, the first debate was being interpreted as yet another example of Gore's propensity to exaggerate his own accomplishments. Gore's exaggerations, for many observers little more than a euphemism for lies, became the second major story to come out of the debate.

Gore's arrogant and bullying attitude was the third major story to come out of the debate. Viewers found him condescending toward Bush. As the debate progressed, Gore could be heard sighing into his microphone when Bush spoke. His facial expressions as Bush spoke also suggested to many viewers that he had little respect for his foe. Also adding to this negative impression of Gore were his constant attempts to interrupt both Bush and moderator Jim Lehrer. Gore consistently exceeded his time limits and attempted to have the last word on a topic, often in violation of the ground rules for the debate. He came across to many as simply not a very nice person.

In the twenty-four- to forty-eight-hour period that followed the debate, these three story lines dominated coverage and discussion. During that period, Bush pollster Matthew Dowd told the Bush high command that his polling indicated that viewers judged the debate a draw but they "had focused on Gore's grimace, his sighs, his mannerisms."[71] Dowd claimed that Gore was hurting himself. Similarly, Gore pollster Stan Greenberg was unhappy with Gore's performance in the first debate. He urged Gore to defend his ideas more and attack Bush less.[72]

Clearly, as these three story lines were being developed, the initial reaction to the debate as one in which Gore had won a close debate was turning around. Within little more than twenty-four to forty-eight hours the first debate was being considered a Bush triumph. Bush had exceeded expectations and seemed equal to both his opponent and the job. Gore had continued to exaggerate and had shown himself to be arrogant and bullying.

*Offering a Large, Well-Coordinated Surrogate Effort*

The principal post-debate strategy is to provide a massive and well-coordinated surrogate effort. Typically, campaigns will make available to the press a host of surrogate spokespersons who will claim their candidate won the debate. Moreover, these surrogates will be briefed in advance, so that they will all be speaking about the same few issues that their candidate used to defeat the opponent. But the surrogate efforts that have followed recent debates were not as successful as they had been in the past.[73] First, the press, having "been used" in this fashion in the past, is more resistant. Second, in recent years the debate schedule has been compressed, the second and later debates all taking place within a few days of each other. Hence, the press does not have several days or perhaps a week or more between debates in which to look back and examine a completed debate. Such a situation provides the press with an opportunity to interview party leaders and other candidate allies who serve as surrogates. When a series of three presidential debates and a vice presidential debate all take place in less than three weeks, as has happened in each campaign since 1996, the press has little time to examine a completed debate. Rather, after a day or two of examining the completed debate, the press typically starts to write about the upcoming debate.

*Using Ads to Underscore Debate Themes*

Although the use of surrogates does remain the primary post-debate strategy, a second post-debate strategy is to utilize advertising that capitalizes on the major theme and points made by a candidate during the debate. Often candidates will buy advertising time and utilize an excerpt from the debate in the commercial they run. In recent years, many campaigns have also put excerpts from the debate on the internet, making use of such venues as YouTube to in effect "advertise" their candidate's best moments in the debate.[74]

*Using Audience Members to Project a Positive View*

The use of prominent spokespersons to present a positive view of the debate and the posting of key moments on the internet are the most common post-debate strategies. They are used in all levels of campaigns. In well-financed campaigns, paid advertisements may be used to reiterate and stress a key idea made in the debate. Other strategies are less common and often depend on the circumstances and formats of the specific debate. Often, if an audience is present, campaign staff members will work to "load" the audience with partisans. Not only will they provide positive responses during the debate, but as they are interviewed later, they may well do the same thing. Community leaders known to be sympathetic to the candidate can be urged to write letters to the editors of local papers, commenting favorably upon the candidate's performance. In every instance, post-debate strategies such as the use of surrogates, internet postings, advertisements, audience members, and letters are designed to influence public perception in the crucial hours and days that immediately follow the debate.

## EFFECTS OF POLITICAL DEBATES

Any discussion of the effects of political debates must be tempered with awareness that it is difficult to draw strong conclusions about them. This difficulty
arises for several reasons. First, each debate is different. It involves different
candidates, different offices, different issues, different audiences, different press
coverage, different formats, and a host of other differences. Hence, to talk about
the specific effects of debates is virtually impossible, for no two will be identical,
nor will their effects be identical.

Second, debate effects cannot be isolated from the effects of all the other communication that voters receive during the campaign. Individuals may be exposed
to dozens of messages about the candidates on the very day of the debate. Distinguishing the effects of the debate from all the others is difficult.

Third, while there have been countless political debates in the past fifty years,
by and large researchers have only studied the presidential debates in detail.
Hence, our discussion of effects must necessarily be limited to a consideration of
the effects of presidential debates. We cannot be certain that the effects of nationally televised political debates are similar to those of the vast majority of political
debates held in campaigns for lesser offices. Most debates are not nationally televised. They are not well publicized in advance. They are not subjected to endless
speculation, examination, and evaluation both before and after the debate. Thus,
findings concerning the effects of presidential debates are not necessarily valid
for other debates. Intuitively, there may be reason to suspect a broad similarity in
the pattern of effects produced by political debates. But, empirically, McKinney
and Carlin accurately summarize existing research when they claim, "We find
that existing debate research—or, actually, the lack of such research—prevents us
from extrapolating findings from the study of presidential debates to the possible
effects or content outcomes of nonpresidential campaign debates."[75] Until additional research on nonpresidential campaign debates is conducted, our discussion
of debate effects must be confined to presidential debates.

Finally, unlike laboratory experiments, scientists cannot control political debates. Hence, those debates that have been examined are often subject to studies
that, of necessity, are prepared under less than ideal conditions, including little
planning and an inability to control fully all the variables in the study.

Despite each of the above problems, at this time there appear to be some striking findings about the effects of political debates, which are subject to revision as
debating becomes an even more widely studied communication event.

### Increased Audiences

Political debates, even at the local or state level, attract large audiences. Debates
create conflict, the essence of drama. Hence, it should not surprise us that presidential debates attract huge audiences. Similarly, we might well hypothesize that
debates attract larger audiences than virtually any other activity that takes place
during the typical campaign. While research on audiences for nonpresidential
debates is not yet widely available, the basic element of conflict exists and might
operate as it evidently does in presidential debates—to attract a large audience.

In 1960 CBS estimated that more than one hundred million people in the United States watched at least part of the Kennedy-Nixon debates.[76] Numerous other surveys also suggested that the Kennedy-Nixon debates drew an immense national audience. In fact, the debates drew the largest audience for any speaking event in history, up to that time.[77]

Similarly, every measure of audience size conducted in connection with the 1976 debates also suggests a massive audience. Most measures of the 1976 debates claim that over 70 percent of the nation watched at least part of the first Carter-Ford debate. While viewing fell off somewhat as the series of debates progressed, it never fell below 60 percent.[78]

In 1960 and again in 1976, debates between presidential candidates were novelties. However, such debates have been a feature of every election since. Moreover, debates between the vice presidential candidates have also become common. This may, in part, account for the fact that between 1980 and 2000, the audiences for national political debates diminished. Nevertheless, they attracted the largest audiences of any campaign activity.

The audience for presidential debates in 2004 rebounded. The first debate between Bush and Kerry attracted an audience of 62.4 million viewers, up 34 percent from the audience for the first Bush-Gore debates four years earlier. The second debate attracted an audience of 46.7 million. The final debate attracted an audience of 51.1 million. The total audience size for the 2004 presidential debates exceeded 160 million, in contrast to 2000 when 121 million Americans watched the Bush-Gore debates.[79]

In 2008 the debate audience grew dramatically. A total of almost 240 million viewers watched the four debates. Startlingly, it was the vice presidential debate that attracted by far the largest audience. Almost 70 million Americans watched that debate, while the highest audience for any of the presidential debates was 63 million.[80] This anomaly was a function of several factors. Typically, the first presidential debate draws the largest audience. But in 2008 that debate was held on a Friday night. Friday night is traditionally the lowest TV viewership night, especially in September when millions of Americans are attending high school football games. Additionally, no doubt many Americans wanted to watch the vice presidential debates to get what for many would be their first extended exposure to the Republican vice presidential candidate, Governor Sarah Palin. The 50 percent jump in viewership between the 2004 and 2008 debates is partially accounted for by the dramatic increase in interest in the vice presidential debate. Other factors include the nation's concern over a badly faltering economy, which was not a factor in 2004, and the fact that the nation was at war.

Additionally, the presence of the first major party black presidential candidate likely increased viewership. Moreover, the extensive voter contact efforts and get-out-the-vote efforts of both major parties may have also piqued the interest of many Americans who had rarely, if ever, been contacted by the parties in the past. Viewership for the 2012 debates was slightly higher than that for the 2008 debates. Viewership for the vice presidential debate between Vice President Joseph Biden and Congressman Paul Ryan was down by about 18.5 million, compared to viewership for the 2008 vice presidential debate. However, viewership for each of the presidential debates was higher, and the total viewership for the

2012 debates exceeded total viewership for the 2008 debates by 1.4 million view-ers.[81] Although the public seems to have become accustomed to debates between presidential candidates, those debates continue to draw by far the largest audi-ences of any campaign activity.

## Reinforce Audience Opinions

Comedian Lenny Bruce unwittingly summarized a host of research studies about the effects of political debates when he observed:

> Everybody hears what he wants to hear. Like when they were in the heat of the 1960 election campaign I was with a group who were watching the debate and all the Nixon fans were saying "Isn't he making Kennedy look like a jerk?"—and all the Kennedy fans were saying "Look at him make a jerk out of Nixon." Each group re-ally feels that their man is up there making the other man look like an idiot. So, then I realized that a candidate would have had to have been that blatant—he would have had to look at his audience right in the camera and say, "I am corrupt. I am the worst choice you could ever have for President." And even then, his followers would say, "Boy there's an honest man. It takes a big guy to admit that. That's the kind of man we should have for a President."[82]

As Bruce's comment suggests, most research has concluded that political de-bates tend to reinforce the positions of a candidate's partisans. After the 1960 debates, most researchers did not find substantial shifts of voter opinion. Rather, they found that Kennedy and Nixon partisans became more strongly committed to their candidate. As *Newsweek* reported, the debates "merely stiffened attitudes."[83]

Research since the 1960 debates tends to confirm these early findings. Examin-ing data pertinent to all the presidential debates held prior to 1987, George Gal-lup, Jr., claimed that "presidential debates in all years have tended to reinforce the convictions of voters who were already committed. They have caused few people to change their minds."[84] Similarly, the debates held since 1988 seem to have served primarily to reinforce existing attitudes.[85]

In 2012 the electorate seemed very closely divided throughout the campaign pe-riod. A consensus of public opinion polling immediately prior to the first debate suggested that President Obama was ahead of Governor Romney by 3.3 percent. At the conclusion of the debates, that same consensus of public opinion polling found that Obama's standing in the polls had fallen by 1.9 percent and Romney's standing had increased by 2.3 percent. Hence, Romney led in the polls by 0.9 per-cent. Although a limited number of voters had shifted their opinion during the period in which the debates were being held, clearly the vast majority of Ameri-cans who watched the debate had not changed their mind.[86]

The reason for this effect is explained by Sears and Chaffee, who claimed that "the information flow stimulated by debates tends to be translated by voters into evaluations that coincide with prior political dispositions. They perceive their party's candidate as having 'won' and they discuss the outcome with like-minded people." Sears and Chaffee continued, noting that at a time when the Democratic Party was substantially larger than the Republican, the net effect of the cumula-tive reinforcement stimulated by the debates probably benefited Democratic candidates.[87] Nationally, the Democratic Party is no longer substantially larger than the Republican, as it was when Sears and Chaffee first wrote. However, their reasoning remains valid. Consequently, in a very evenly divided nation, the cumulative reinforcement stimulated by the debates probably benefits Republican and Democratic candidates almost equally. The logical outgrowth of these conclusions, applied to local campaigns, would be that debates, because they tend to reinforce prior political dispositions, generally work to the advantage of the party that is dominant in the district, city, or state.

## Shift Limited Numbers of Voters

Political debates do not normally result in massive shifts of votes. As indicated above, most audience members have their existing predispositions reinforced by the debate. However, some voters may shift. In a close election, the numbers of those who shift as a consequence of debates might be decisive.

The Kennedy-Nixon debates were widely perceived at the time as having affected massive numbers of voters. President Kennedy helped foster this impression by attributing his election to the debates. Yet evidence on this point suggests that while they may have been decisive due to the extremely close nature of the election, the debates did not shift massive numbers of votes. The highest estimate of voter shift is pollster Elmo Roper's guess that four million voters, about 6 percent of the vote, changed as a consequence of the debates.[88]

However, most researchers are far more cautious. Katz and Feldman, after examining thirty-one studies of the 1960 debates, typify the conclusions of most when they write, "Did the debates really affect the final outcome? Apart from strengthening Democratic convictions about their candidate, it is very difficult to tell."[89] Evidence on the 1976 presidential debates,[90] as well as those of 1980, tends to confirm this "limited effects" paradigm.[91]

In their perceptive analysis of the effects of the 1984 presidential debates, Smith and Smith observe that although some polls reported that Walter Mondale had clearly beaten Ronald Reagan in their first debate, this victory did not translate into a shift in votes.[92] Similarly, in 1996 Clinton continually polled 51 to 53 percent of the vote during the portion of the campaign shortly before, during, and shortly after the debates. During this same period, Senator Dole remained consistently at 34 to 36 percent and Ross Perot trailed with 12 to 14 percent.[93]

The 2000 debates did give Governor George W. Bush a slight increase in his poll standings. However, as Kathleen Hall Jamieson has illustrated, that increase was not a direct consequence of the debates. Indeed, as we have seen, immediately after the debates Gore bested Bush in three of the four instant polls. Rather, Bush's increase in the polls came as the three story lines developed by the press took hold. As Jamieson points out, those who actually watched the debate remained consistent to their first impressions. Those voters who shifted their judgments in favor of Bush were, for the most part, those who had not watched the debate but rather relied on media accounts.[94]

As we have seen, in 2008 Obama gained 3.4 percent in the public opinion polls during the period of the debates. Although this is a relatively slight shift in voters, it was sufficient to turn a tight race into a decisive victory for Obama and helped scores of Democratic candidates running for other offices as well.[95] Similarly, in the very close election of 2012 a shift of a very limited number of voters was sufficient to give Governor Romney a temporary lead in the polls immediately after the debates.[96] That lead no doubt helped Romney raise money and benefited other Republican candidates, although it was ultimately more than offset by Obama's organizational prowess on Election Day. As noted above, while Hillary Clinton benefited from some modest advantage in the poll numbers, Voth suggests "that the public notion of a 'winner' in the debates was opposed to their own private notions of what was best for the nation politically. . . . In the general election phase, overly aggressive journalist moderators led to a heightened public backlash against the poll results of the debate showing Clinton winning all three debates."[97]

## Help Set Voters' Agenda

As we have discussed in chapter 4, much recent research has stressed the importance of the agenda-setting function of mass communication. In essence, this research holds that "we judge as important what the media judge as important. Media priorities become our own."[98] If the considerable body of evidence that supports the agenda-setting function of mass media is correct, then it would stand to reason that those issues stressed in mass media political debates, and mass media coverage of those debates, should also become issues of high priority for voters who watch the debates and attend to the media's coverage of them.

Swanson and Swanson offer strong evidence in support of the agenda-setting function of political debates.[99] They attempted to determine whether those issues of primary concern to voters changed as a consequence of watching political debates. Based on research done at the University of Illinois during the 1976 campaign, they concluded that "the first Ford-Carter debate exerted an agenda-setting effect on our subjects who viewed it, although that effect was tempered by enduring personal priorities of subjects."[100] As Swanson and Swanson subsequently observed, "To the extent that citizens base their voting choices on their assessment of campaign issues, this is surely an effect of some political importance."[101] The agenda-setting function of political debates seems to remain strong. However, as campaigns become more and more sophisticated and candidates attempt to work into their debates the very lines that permeate their speeches and paid advertising, it grows increasingly difficult to isolate the agenda-setting effects of political debate from the overall agenda-setting effects of media coverage of the entire campaign.

The importance of the potential agenda-setting effects of debates has been implicitly acknowledged in the format of every series of presidential debates since 1992. At least one debate in each campaign since 1992 allowed an audience of undecided voters to either question the candidates directly or write questions from which the moderator selected. Allowing voters, rather than journalists, to question the candidates is, in part, an attempt to ensure that the public's agenda is served by the debates. Nevertheless, critics of the presidential debates claim that the debates focus on narrow policy issues and never treat major systemic issues that are critical to the democratic process and that would resonate with a public that is growing increasingly disenchanted with the entire political process.[102]

## 5  Increase the Voters' Knowledge of Issues

A wide variety of studies have attempted to determine whether political debates increase the voters' knowledge of the issues. These studies seem to point to three conclusions. First, voters do seem more knowledgeable as a consequence of watching political debates. Second, debates are particularly helpful to voters in local elections. Tempering these conclusions is the final conclusion: often voters do not learn about the very issues that most concern them.

That voters clearly learn about the issues as a consequence of watching debates seems to have been well established by research.[103] Moreover, it would appear that debates serve as a more important source of information in local elections, which receive comparatively little media coverage, than for major national or statewide races. One study suggests that 80 percent of the viewers of debates between local candidates report that they had learned about the candidates by viewing the debates, whereas only 55 percent made the same claim about the presidential debates.[104] Several other studies also point to the high informational value of debates between local and statewide candidates.[105]

Although voters apparently learn about issues by watching debates, often they do not learn about the issues that most concern them. Michael Pfau has cogently argued, "A political debate ought to match—to the extent possible—the agendas of the candidates and the public." However, after studying several presidential debates, he concluded, "The journalists' questions have virtually ignored the public's agenda."[106] The problem is well illustrated in the remarks of one of the journalists who helped to set the agenda of the 1980 debates with her questions. She claimed that she "felt under enormous pressure to try forming a single question that would somehow catch the well-briefed candidates by surprise on a subject of importance."[107] More appropriately for the public, she might have attempted to ask a question dealing with those issues that were of greatest public concern. But far too often, the public's concerns are not reflected in the journalists' questions.[108]

Indeed, one critic of the 1988 debates characterized many of the questions asked in that year's presidential debates as "trite."[109] It should be recalled that in 1960, when the precedents that have since been largely followed were established, the impetus for a panel of journalists/questioners came from the candidates, not the press.[110]

Hence, for a variety of reasons, not the least of which was the intrusion of journalistic panels, the public agenda was frequently poorly served in earlier political debates. Since 1992 the Commission on Presidential Debates has attempted to accommodate this concern by including at least one debate where undecided voters ask questions. Additionally, since 1996 the traditional use of a panel of journalists has been abandoned. Rather, one journalist has served as the moderator and questioner. The use of a single moderator was designed to allow follow-up questions. Multi-journalist panels tended to skip from one topic area to the next, as each of the journalists asks a question about a different topic. The use of one questioner meant that the questioner could repeat a question and follow up on evasive answers, thus providing greater information to the public. In sum, while debates do increase the voters' knowledge of issues, particularly debates in local campaigns, their formats often prevent them from being as informative as the public might wish. The Commission on Presidential Debates has attempted to be responsive to this concern and changed the formats used at the presidential level in recent years.

## 𝒍 Modify Candidate Images

Debates apparently affect the images of candidates. In their evaluation of the impact of the 1976 debates, Hagner and Rieselbach suggest that debates affect candidate images primarily when the candidate is not well known and hence the candidate's public image is not well developed.[111] When the public is unfamiliar with the candidate, perception of the candidate's general character, personality attributes, and general competency seems to be affected by political debates and their subsequent media coverage.

Most accounts of the 1960 debates note that Kennedy, the comparative unknown, improved his image as a consequence of the debates. He was able to convey a sense of competency and familiarity with major issues, as well as a charming personality. Similarly, Sears and Chaffee summarize a number of studies of the 1976 debates and conclude that the public's image of the candidates was affected by the debates.[112]

In 2008, both major party candidates were well known. Senator John McCain had been a national figure throughout most of his years of congressional service and had made a serious run for the Republican nomination in 2000. Senator Barack Obama had far less experience, but the hotly contested Democratic primaries, especially those at the end, which came down to a series of races between Obama and Hillary Clinton, had quickly made him a highly recognizable figure. Nevertheless, some questions concerning Obama's competency lingered, as he had risen so quickly and had very little experience.

Hence, the debates offered him an opportunity to create an image of presidential competency. Most observers felt that Obama was successful in projecting an image of competence. He spoke in a strong, firm voice, directly responded to most questions he was asked, and looked straight into the camera. Relatively unknown and little experienced, it was vital for Obama to project an image of competency in these debates. Much like John Kennedy in his 1960 debates, Obama's appearance and delivery seemed to help him cross the threshold of presidential competency for most Americans. McCain's image was not as strong during the first debate, although it improved throughout the series of three presidential debates. McCain's competence was never subject to serious question, as Obama's was, largely because of his years of congressional experience. Thus, he attempted to capitalize on that experience to reinforce his presidential image largely by constant references to his diplomatic and legislative experience. Responding to question after question, McCain spoke about his visits to foreign countries, his friendships with foreign leaders, and the legislation he introduced, supported, or opposed while in Congress.

By 2012, having served four years as president, Barack Obama was well known to the public. But his challenger, Governor Romney, was not. Hence, throughout the spring and summer, Obama launched a massive negative campaign against Romney. Romney, preoccupied with the primaries and then raising money for the general election, was not effective in responding early. One longtime political reporter observed that

> Mitt Romney's fate might have been sealed over the summer, when President Obama's campaign carpet-bombed the Republican with attack ads. The commercials hammered Romney as a craven capitalist who sent jobs overseas, refused to release his tax returns and would give zillionaires like himself even heftier tax breaks at the expense of the middle-class. While demonizing Romney, the strategy also deflected attention from Obama's handling of the economy. Obama's subliminal message was stark: You may not like me much, but Romney's worse, much worse.[113]

In large part because of Obama's attacks, by the time of the first debate, Romney's image was not good. Fully 86 percent of Obama's advertising had been negative, more than in any presidential campaign in history, and it had a telling effect on the public perception of Romney.[114] Thus, for Mitt Romney, the 2012 debates offered a unique opportunity to reshape his image. He would be speaking directly to a massive audience who could judge him for themselves, not through the lens of Obama's political advertisements.

The fact that the race tightened after the first debate, and remained close until a late Obama surge, suggests that Romney was able to alter his image in the minds of some voters. He constantly spoke of his desire to create jobs and to improve life for middle-income Americans and his accomplishments as a businessman, with the Olympics, and as a governor. Moreover, on occasion he referenced his family and background. For voters lacking familiarity with Romney, and for voters whose familiarity with Romney was colored in part by countless negative ads directed at him, the debates might have served to improve Romney's image. Romney might well have come across to many in his audience during the debates as a likable, competent, well-meaning candidate.

In sum, debates can affect public perception of a candidate's image—general competency, personality attributes, and character traits. The potential for affecting image seems to be inversely related to public knowledge of the candidate. The better known the candidate, the less likely the debate will greatly affect that candidate's image. Hence, the potential for improving one's image is generally greater for the lesser-known candidate. Well-known candidates will have difficulty changing their images during debates, but they can reinforce preexisting audience perceptions of their image. Moreover, it is likely that in races for lesser offices, among lesser-known candidates, the impact of a debate on the image of the candidates is potentially great.

## ¶ Freeze the Campaign

The timing of the 1992 debates, all four of which came in a twelve-day period, and those of 1996, all three of which came in a ten-day period, emphasized a previously little-noticed effect of debates. As Dan Hahn has observed, once debates are announced, "there will be an electoral flat-line until after the debates."[115] Once debates are announced, most voters tend to harden their positions until after the debates. Partisans see no reason to consider changing until after the debates, and as we have observed earlier, the debates rarely provide them with sufficient cause to change. Undecided voters tend to reserve judgment in the days immediately preceding the debates and throughout the debates, preferring to utilize the debates in making their judgment.

The tendency to schedule debates in a short window of time—all four of the debates in both 2008 and 2012 as well as the three in 2016 were held within nineteen days—is likely to continue. This effect of debates, to largely freeze the campaign in place until their conclusion, works to the advantage of the leading candidate. It makes the leader more difficult to catch by effectively shortening the time the trailing candidates have to catch up. Presidential debates are likely to be scheduled within a short window of time both because of pressure from the leading candidate and because of the contractual considerations of the television networks, some of whom have contracts to televise sporting events such as the baseball playoffs and the Olympics during the closing weeks of the campaign.

## 𝟫 Build Confidence in U.S. Democracy

A wide variety of studies has attempted to evaluate the effects of political debates on American political institutions. Do debates result in greater confidence and support of political institutions and office holders? Do debates facilitate political socialization? While individual studies differ, and continued research will no doubt shed greater light on questions such as these, current research does offer some tentative answers.

First, as Kraus and Davis argue, debates are consistent with democratic theory, which stresses the importance of rational decision making by an informed electorate.[116] Second, as Becker, Pepper, Weiner, and Kim point out, debates provide voters with greater exposure to information about candidates, which "probably resulted in a certain degree of commitment to the election process and to the candidate selected through that process."[117] Third, as Chaffee illustrates, debates apparently have a positive impact on people's confidence in government institutions and play a positive role in political socialization or the recruitment of new members into the body politic.[118]

More recently, although pundits often speak of America's growing cynicism about its electoral system, research by Lynda Lee Kaid and others has suggested that the viewing of political debates seems to lower political cynicism.[119] Public disgust and cynicism with our political system have no doubt grown in recent years. However, McKinney and Carlin are correct when they conclude that "our democracy has been well served, that our citizenry has benefited from their leaders' willingness to meet, face to face, seeking public support."[120]

In recent presidential elections, the candidates have largely targeted their media effort at about one-third of the nation, the battleground states. Consequently, much of the nation is virtually never directly exposed to the media campaign of the candidates. Debates are virtually the only aspect of a contemporary presidential campaign to which the entire nation is now exposed. They serve as one of the few campaign experiences the entire nation has in common.

In sum, it appears that political debates contribute to voter satisfaction with the democratic process. Although much has been written about growing voter apathy, growing voter disenchantment with the political process, and growing voter skepticism about politicians, it would appear that this overall trend of disaffection with the political process is not fostered by debates. Quite the contrary, as Sidney Kraus has claimed, "televised presidential debates may be unparalleled in modern campaigning as an innovation that engages citizens in the political process."[121] Indeed, current research suggests that political debates might be a step in the direction of remedying current disaffection.

## CONCLUSIONS

In sum, it would appear that political debates have at least eight distinct effects. Typically, they attract large audiences. Second, they seem to reinforce many of the preexisting attitudes and beliefs of audience members. Third, they seem to shift a limited number of voters. Although the number of voters whose opinions are shifted by the debates is limited, it should be kept in mind that in close elections the shift of a limited number of voters might well prove crucial to the outcome. Fourth, debates help to set the political agenda. Fifth, debates contribute to the education of audience members. Voters who watch the debates apparently are more knowledgeable as a consequence of their watching. This educational benefit of debates must be tempered somewhat by the recognition that current debate formats often preclude the viewers really learning about the issues that most concern them. Sixth, debates seem to affect the images of candidates. The image of the lesser-known participant is normally affected more by a political debate. Seventh, debates tend to freeze the campaign in place until their conclusion. Finally, debates seem to contribute to the public's confidence in government institutions and leaders.

## NOTES

1. Quoted in *The Lincoln-Douglas Debates*, ed. Robert W. Johannsen (New York: Oxford University Press, 1965), 3.

2. Kathleen Hall Jamieson and David S. Birdsell note that since as early as 1788, when two future presidents, James Madison and James Monroe, debated for a seat in the new House of Representatives, debates have been a part of American election campaigns. See their *Presidential Debates: The Challenge of Creating an Informed Electorate* (New York: Oxford University Press, 1988), 34.

3. J. Jeffery Auer, "The Counterfeit Debates," in *The Great Debates: Kennedy vs. Nixon, 1960*, ed. Sidney Kraus (Bloomington: Indiana University Press, 1962), 146.

4. Ibid.

5. Auer first used this term in his essay "The Counterfeit Debates," to describe the 1960 debates. It has since been used to describe many political debates, most notably by Lloyd Bitzer and Theodore Rueter in their work *Carter vs. Ford: The Counterfeit Debates of 1976* (Madison: University of Wisconsin Press, 1980).

6. The statements in this paragraph were made by panelists Robert Flemming and Stuart Novins during the opening minutes of the first Kennedy-Nixon debate. See *The Joint Appearances of Senator John F. Kennedy and Vice-President Richard M. Nixon: Presidential Campaign of 1960* (Washington, DC: Government Printing Office, 1961), 78.

7. See Bitzer and Rueter, *Carter vs. Ford*, especially chapter 3, for an excellent analysis of the adversarial nature of the press in the 1976 debates. The adversarial nature of the press remains a characteristic feature of campaign debates. Susan A. Hellweg and Anna M. Verhoye, "A Comparative Verbal Analysis of the Two 1988 Bush-Dukakis Presidential Debates," paper presented at the Speech Communication Association, November 1989, 17–18, details the extent of adversarial questioning in the 1988 presidential debates. The single moderator format of recent years seems to have placed the moderator in a less adversarial role. Rather, with the conspicuous exception of Candy Crowley in the second presidential debate of 2012, recent moderators seem intent on being even-handed with both candidates and enforcing the time and other rules.

8. The 2012 format used in two of the three presidential debates provided the recipient of a question two minutes to answer. The other candidate then had two minutes to respond, followed by an eleven-minute discussion between the candidates on the issue. This format was followed in two of the three presidential debates. The third and the vice presidential debates provided for shorter discussion periods. For details of the 2012 presidential debate formats, see the website of the Commission on Presidential Debates at www .debates.org/index.php?page=format.

9. Formats of the presidential debates are fairly well known. For examinations of the formats used in presidential primary debates, see Susan A. Hellweg and Steven L. Phillips, "Form and Substance: A Comparative Analysis of Five Formats Used in the 1980 Presidential Debates," *Speaker and Gavel* 18 (Winter 1981): 67–76; Michael Pfau, "A Comparative Assessment of Intra-Party Debate Formats," paper presented at the Speech Communication Association Convention, Chicago, Illinois, November 1984. Examinations of debate formats at the nonpresidential level can be found in Jack Kay, "Campaign Debate Formats: At the Non-Presidential Level," paper presented at the Speech Communication Association Convention, Anaheim, California, November 1981; and Michael Pfau, "Criteria and Format to Optimize Series," paper presented at the Speech Communication Association Convention, Anaheim, California, November 1981. Ironically, Patrick Caddell noted that the 1980 presidential debate format used by Reagan and Carter, which allowed for nine to ten minutes of discussion on a single topic, was "exhaustive." See his "Memo of October 21, 1980," reprinted in Elizabeth Drew, *Portrait of an Election: The 1980 Election* (New York: Simon & Schuster, 1981), 426.

10. Ben Voth, "The Presidential Debates 2016," in *The 2016 U.S. Presidential Campaign: Political Communication and Practice*, ed. Robert E. Denton, Jr. (Cham, Switzerland: Palgrave Macmillan, 2017), 78.

11. Auer, "Counterfeit Debates," 148.

12. Perhaps the debate with the most significance for the subsequent development of political debating was the one held between the Tennessee gubernatorial candidates in 1886. For an explanation of the subsequent impact of this debate, see Herbert A. Terry and Sidney Kraus, "Legal and Political Aspects: Was Section 315 Circumvented?" in *The Great Debates: Carter vs. Ford, 1976*, ed. Sidney Kraus (Bloomington: Indiana University Press, 1979), 44–45.

13. See Jamieson and Birdsell, *Presidential Debates*, 35–36, for a discussion of this feature of nineteenth-century campaigns.

14. When debates were held, they were frequently the centerpieces of the campaigns. For an especially informative example of this, see Cal M. Logue, "Gubernatorial Campaign in Georgia in 1880," *Southern Speech Communication Journal* 40 (Fall 1974): 12–32.

15. Samuel L. Becker and Elmer W. Lower, "Broadcasting in Presidential Campaigns," in *The Great Debates: Kennedy vs. Nixon, 1960*, ed. Sidney Kraus (Bloomington: Indiana University Press, 1962), 29.

16. Quoted in Sidney Head, *Broadcasting in America* (Boston: Houghton Mifflin, 1976), 331.

17. For a full discussion of these changes, see Edward W. Chester, *Radio, Television and American Politics* (New York: Sheed and Ward, 1969), 247–65. Also see Head, *Broadcasting in America*, 330–32.

18. Chester, *Radio, Television and American Politics*, 37. Also see Becker and Lower, "Broadcasting in Presidential Campaigns," 35.

19. Chester, *Radio, Television and American Politics*, 42.

20. An excellent description of this debate can be found in Robert F. Ray, "Thomas E. Dewey: The Great Oregon Debate of 1948," in *American Public Address: Studies in Honor of Albert Craig Baird*, ed. Loren Reid (Columbia: University of Missouri Press, 1961), 245–70.

21. Lee M. Mitchell, *With the Nation Watching* (Lexington, MA: D. C. Heath, 1979), 28, claims that Moody made his suggestion while being interviewed on the CBS radio network show *The People's Platform* in July 1952. J. Leonard Reinsch, a media consultant to presidents Roosevelt and Truman, also made an early effort to get Stevenson and Eisenhower to debate. See Goodwin Berquist, "The 1976 Carter-Ford Presidential Debates," in *Rhetorical Studies of National Political Debates: 1960–1988*, ed. Robert V. Friedenberg (New York: Praeger, 1990), 29.

22. In 1952 neither man felt comfortable with the idea of televised debates. Both candidates were also advised not to debate.

23. Mitchell, *With the Nation Watching*, 30.

24. Chester, *Radio, Television and American Politics*, 133–35, provides a brief account of the stimulus that the 1960 presidential debates had on political debating.

25. For a complete and far more thorough account of this change in the equal time provisions, see Terry and Kraus, "Legal and Political Aspects," 41–49.

26. This section is based primarily on two articles by Robert Friedenberg. Full citations for all quoted material and fuller explanations of all major points can be found in those two articles. See Robert V. Friedenberg, "'We Are Present Here Today for the Purpose of Having a Joint Discussion': The Conditions Requisite for Political Debates," *Journal of the American Forensic Association* 16 (Summer 1979): 1–9; Robert V. Friedenberg, "'Selfish Interest,' or the Prerequisites for Political Debate: An Analysis of the 1980 Presidential Debate and Its Implications for Future Campaigns," *Journal of the American Forensic Association* 18 (Fall 1981): 91–98.

27. One of the rare recent exceptions was the decision by Senator Dianne Feinstein not to debate her opponent Elizabeth Emken in her successful 2012 reelection campaign. California has become a one-party state, and Feinstein was ahead in the polls by twenty-six points (57 percent to 31 percent) and had raised far more money than Emken. Hence, she faced no real pressure to debate and declined to risk making a serious error if she did so. See Martin Wisckol, "Sen. Feinstein Explains Decision Not to Debate," *Orange County Register*, October 31, 2012, accessed October 31, 2012, www.ocregister.com/articles/emken-376332-feinstein -debate.html.

28. Reagan's 1984 advisors have been quoted as claiming that "they did not think it would be politically acceptable" for the president to refuse to debate. Apparently well in command of the election, Reagan and his strategists nevertheless evidently feared the negative reaction his refusal to debate might prompt. See J. Jeffery Auer, "Presidential Debates: Public Understanding and Political Institutionalization," *Speaker and Gavel* 24 (Fall 1986): 5. Auer cites a conversation between Reagan advisors and reporter Elizabeth Drew. Similarly, see Craig Allen Smith and Kathy B. Smith, "The 1984 Reagan-Mondale Presidential Debates," in *Rhetorical Studies of National Political Debates: 1960–1988*, ed. Robert V. Friedenberg (New York: Praeger, 1990), 96.

29. On the evolution of public attitudes toward incumbent presidential debating, see Robert V. Friedenberg, "Patterns and Trends in National Political Debates: 1960–1996," in *Rhetorical Studies of National Political Debates*, ed. Robert V. Friedenberg (New York: Praeger, 1998), 62–64.

30. Although common in the United States, in many countries political debates are still a novelty. For example, the major party candidates for prime minister in Great Britain held the first political debate between such candidates in 2010.

31. Robert V. Friedenberg, "The 2000 Presidential Debates," in *The 2000 Presidential Campaign: A Communication Perspective*, ed. Robert E. Denton, Jr. (Lanham, MD: Rowman & Littlefield, 2002), 147.

32. Ben Voth, "Presidential Debates 2012," in *The 2012 Presidential Campaign: Communication Perspective*, ed. Robert E. Denton, Jr. (Lanham, MD: Rowman & Littlefield, 2014), 48.

33. Goodwin F. Berquist and James L. Golden, "Media Rhetoric, Criticism, and the Public Perception of the 1980 Presidential Debates," *Quarterly Journal of Speech* 67 (May 1981): 125–26.

34. Ibid., 127–28.

35. Gore 2000, "Bush Debate Duck," found daily throughout the spring of 2000 at www.gore2000.org.

36. Howard Kurtz, "Leaks, Rats and Blackberries," *Washington Post*, December 17, 2000, C1.

37. Jennifer Parker, "Obama, McCain Prep for Presidential Debates," ABC News, September 23, 2008, accessed May 27, 2010, abcnews.go.com/print?id=5857679.

38. For the details of this challenge, see David Jackson, "McCain Challenges Obama to Town Hall-Style Debates," *USA Today*, June 4, 2008, accessed May 27, 2010, www.usatoday.com/news/politics/election2008/2008-06-04-mccain.htm.

39. On the distinctions between the town hall and other formats, from which this paragraph draws heavily, see Eric Trager, "The Town Hall Debate Format," *Commentary*, October 7, 2008, accessed May 27, 2010, www.commentarymagazine.com/blogs/index.php/trager/35852.

40. David Plouffe, *The Audacity to Win* (New York: Viking, 2009), 352.

41. For Messina's comments, see "Debates: Obama Camp Downplays Expectations, Romney Looks for Game Changer," *Wall Street Journal*, September 22, 2012, accessed September 22, 2012, www.foxnews.com/politics/2012/09/22/debates-obama-camp.

42. *USA Today*, October 1, 2012, https://www.usatoday.com/videos/news/politics/2012/10/01/1605375.

43. Ryan is quoted in "GOP Sends Mixed Messages on Romney Debate Expectations," ABC News, September 30, 2012, accessed October 16, 2012, abcnews.go.com/Politics/gop-sends-mixed-messages-romney.

44. The Pew poll results were retrieved from *Huffington Post*, accessed October 15, 2012, www.huffingtonpost.com/2012/10/15obama-debate-poll_n_1968425.html.

45. Gibbs is quoted in Jude Sheerin, "Obama Team Raises Expectations for Debate with Romney," BBC, accessed October 16, 2012, www.bbc.co.uk/news/world-us-canada-19965927?print=true. Axelrod is quoted in "Obama, Romney Teams Upend Expectations Game Heading into Second Debate," Fox News, accessed October 16, 2012, https://www.foxnews.com/politics/obama-romney-teams-upend-expectations-game-heading-into-second-debate.

46. Monica Alba and Ali Vitali, "Hillary Clinton and Donald Trump Take Different Approaches to First 2016 Debate Prep," NBC News, accessed November 13, 2018, https://www.nbcnews.com/storyline/2016-presidential-debates/clinton-trump-take-different-approaches-first-debate-prep-n652726.

47. Ibid.

48. One of us, Friedenberg, has been involved in a variety of political debates. Also see, for examples, Dale Hardy-Short, "An Insider's View of the Constraints Affecting Geraldine Ferraro's Preparation for the 1984 Vice Presidential Debate," *Speaker and Gavel* 24 (Fall 1986): 8–22; Myles Martel, "Debate Preparations in the Reagan Camp: An Insider's View," *Speaker and Gavel* 18 (Winter 1981): 34–46; Martin Schram, *Running for President*

(New York: Pocket Books, 1977), 326–31, 348–64, 370–89; Caddell, "Memo of October 21, 1980," 410–39; Theodore White, *Making of the President 1960* (New York: Athenaeum, 1988), 335–55; Theodore Otto Windt, "The 1960 Kennedy-Nixon Presidential Debates," in *Rhetorical Studies of National Political Debates: 1960–1988*, ed. Robert V. Friedenberg (New York: Praeger, 1990), 9–10; and Judith S. Trent, "The 1984 Bush-Ferraro Vice Presidential Debate," also in *Rhetorical Studies of National Political Debates: 1960–1988*, 135–36. Most press reports of contemporary campaigns, including those cited elsewhere in this chapter involving the candidate preparation for the 2008 and 2012 debates, suggest the same practices as those utilized by earlier candidates.

49. Plouffe, *Audacity to Win*, 337.

50. Jon Ward, "Three Days in October: How the Debates Changed the Race," *Huffington Post*, accessed November 3, 2012, https://www.huffingtonpost.com/2012/11/02/three-days-in-october-how_n_2049394.html.

51. Ibid.

52. By all accounts, Ronald Reagan's preparation for his 1980 debates with John Anderson and Jimmy Carter was the most thorough in this regard. Reagan practiced in a garage converted to resemble the actual television studios used in the debates. His staff went to great lengths to simulate and anticipate his opponents, including studying tapes of prior debates involving Anderson and Carter. Eventually David Stockman, a former administrative assistant to John Anderson, based largely on his study of tapes, played both Anderson and Carter in Reagan's practices. The 1980 proliferation of candidate forums and candidate debates during the primary season meant that by the general election, at least at the presidential level, candidates had been in a variety of debates or debate-like situations and an opponent would normally have access to tapes of their prior performances.

53. This and the next paragraphs concerning the debate preparation of the 2012 candidates are based largely on the debate practice accounts found in contemporary journalist reports and the reports of participants. Among the most valuable were Glen Johnson, "John Kerry to Play Role of Mitt Romney for President Obama's Debate Prep," *Boston Globe*, June 18, 2012, accessed August 22, 2012, www.boston.com/politicalintelligence/2012/06/18john-kerry-play-role-mitt-romney-for-president-obama-debate; Deirdre Shesgreen, "Portman Reprises Role of President," *Cincinnati Enquirer*, October 3, 2012, A-1; Thomas DeFrank, "Exclusive Mitt Romney Already Prepping for First Debate with Obama Even Though It Is Still 13 Weeks Away," *New York Daily News*, July 6, 2012, accessed July 6, 2012, nydailynews.com/2012-0706/news/32569672_1_mitt-romney-veteran-debate-president-obama; Nancy Cordes and Jill Jackson, "Obama Campaign Chooses Chris Van Hollen to Play Paul Ryan in VP Debate Prep," CBS News, August 16, 2012, accessed August, 16, 2012, http://www.cbsnews.com/news/obama-campaign-chooses-chris-van-hollen-to-play-paul-ryan-in-vp-debate-prep; Ed Henry, "Paul Ryan Completes P90X-Style Debate Training Ahead of Biden Showdown," Fox News, October 11, 2012, accessed October 22, 2012, https://www.foxnews.com/politics/paul-ryan-completes-p90x-style-debate-training-ahead-of-biden-showdown.

54. Toby Harnden, "Obama 'Believed He Had BEATEN Romney' in Denver Debate—After Ignoring Advice of Top Aides on Preparation," *Daily Mail*, October 9, 2012, accessed November 1, 2012, www.dailymail.co.uk/news/article-2215173/Obama-believed-beaten-Romney-Denver-debate-ignoring-advice-aides.html?printingPage=true.

55. Ibid.

56. Zeke J. Miller, "How Hillary Clinton Is Preparing for the Debates," *Time*, August 9, 2016, accessed November 13, 2018, http://time.com/4444560/how-hillary-clinton-is-preparing-for-the-debates.

57. Philip Rucker, Robert Costa, and Anne Gearan, "Inside Debate Prep: Clinton's Careful Case vs. Trump's 'WrestleMania,'" *Washington Post*, August 27, 2016.

58. An informative account of this frequently overlooked precursor to the 1960 general election debates can be found in Goodwin F. Berquist, "The Kennedy-Humphrey Debate," *Today's Speech* 7 (September 1960): 2–3.

59. This and all subsequent quotes to the 2008 presidential debates are taken from the transcripts of the debates provided by the Commission on Presidential Debates at its internet site. For the 2008 debates, go to www.debates.org/index.php?page=2008-debate -transcript.

60. This and all subsequent quotes to the 2012 presidential debates are taken from the transcripts of the debates provided by the Commission on Presidential Debates at its internet site. For the 2012 debates, go to www.debates.org/index.php?page=2012 debate -transcript.

61. Robert O. Weiss, "The Presidential Debates in Their Political Context: The Issue-Image Interface in the 1980 Campaign," *Speaker and Gavel* 18 (Winter 1981): 22–27.

62. Ibid., 22.

63. This threefold analysis of image strategies is based on Dan Nimmo's discussion of the techniques that a political figure can use. The terminology and definitions are Nimmo's. See Dan Nimmo, *Popular Images of Politics* (Englewood Cliffs, NJ: Prentice Hall, 1974), 100–102.

64. Voth, "Presidential Debates 2016," 85.

65. James Ceaser, Andrew E. Busch, and John Pitney, *Defying the Odds: The 2016 Elections and American Politics* (Lanham, MD: Rowman & Littlefield, 2017), 72.

66. Frederick T. Steeper, "Public Response to Gerald Ford's Statements on Eastern Europe in the Second Debate," in *The Presidential Debates: Media, Electoral and Policy Perspectives*, ed. George F. Bishop, Robert G. Meadow, and Marilyn Jackson-Beeck (New York: Praeger, 1978), 101.

67. Ibid. Also see Roger Desmond and Thomas Donohue, "The Role of the 1976 Televised Presidential Debates in the Political Socialization of Adolescents," *Communication Quarterly* 29 (Fall 1981): 306–8; and George A. Barnett, "A Multi-dimensional Analysis of the 1976 Presidential Campaign," *Communication Quarterly* 29 (Summer 1981): 156–65.

68. Thomas Ferrano, "Gore Buoyed by Polls, Raises Fists in Victory," found at Excite News.com, October 4, 2000. This Reuters news service story is not archived by Excite News or Reuters, but a hard copy is available from the authors. Also see Will Lester, "Gore Fares Better in 3 of 4 Polls," which ran on the Associated Press Wire, October 4, 2000. The Associated Press does not archive old stories. A hard copy is available from the authors.

69. See, for example, Dan Balz and Terry Neal, "Gore and Bush Clash Sharply on Policy Issues," *Washington Post*, October 4, 2000, A-1.

70. Gore claimed to have visited Texas to help with federal emergency relief efforts after a series of severe brush fires. In fact, although he had visited Texas after weather-related emergencies, he had not visited on this occasion. He used as an example of a crowded and poorly equipped high school a school that was not crowded and was among the best equipped in the state of Florida. More seriously, he claimed that a Bush recommendation on getting Russia involved in Kosovo was terribly risky, when in fact that was precisely the policy that President Clinton and Secretary of State Madeleine Albright were attempting to follow.

71. Evan Thomas and *Newsweek*'s special projects team, "The Inside Story: What a Long Strange Trip," *Newsweek*, November 20, 2000, 103–4. Also see Dowd's remarks made after the campaign in Kathleen Hall Jamieson and Paul Waldman, *Electing the President, 2000: The Insider's View* (Philadelphia: University of Pennsylvania Press, 2001), 22–23.

72. Thomas et al., "Inside Story," 104.

73. Steven Brydon's study suggests that the networks were becoming sensitive to being "used" in this fashion by as early as 1988. Hence, in recent elections, the networks

have relied more heavily on their own news staffs and political or debate consultants for analysis. See Steven R. Brydon, "Spinners on Patrol: Network Coverage in the Aftermath of Presidential and Vice Presidential Debates," paper presented to the Speech Communication Association Convention, San Francisco, California, November 1989.

74. For examples of this as it was practiced in the 2008 Democratic primaries, see Allan Louden, "Drexel's Digital Divide—Post Debate Spin," accessed November 4, 2007, www .debatescoop.org/story/2007/11/2/0243/9129.

75. Mitchell S. McKinney and Diana B. Carlin, "Political Campaign Debates," in *Handbook of Political Communication Research*, ed. Lynda Lee Kaid (New York: Routledge, 2008), 226.

76. Cited in Harry P. Kerr, "The Great Debates in a New Perspective," *Today's Speech* 9 (November 1961): 11.

77. Susan A. Hellweg and Steven L. Phillips, "A Verbal and Visual Analysis of the 1980 Houston Republican Presidential Primary Debate," *Southern Speech Communication Journal* 47 (Fall 1981): 24.

78. John P. Robinson, "The Polls," in *The Great Debates: Carter vs. Ford, 1976*, ed. Sidney Kraus (Bloomington: Indiana University Press, 1979), 262–63.

79. The figures used in this paragraph are drawn from the history section of the Commission on Presidential Debates internet site, accessed November 13, 2012, www.debates .org/pages/his_2004.html.

80. These figures were retrieved from "Debates: Democracy in Action, 2008," George Washington University website, accessed June 8, 2012, www.gwu.edu/~action/2008/ chrndebs08.html.

81. The figures used in this paragraph are drawn from the history section of the Commission on Presidential Debates internet site, accessed November 13, 2012, www.debates .org/index.php?page=2012-debates.

82. Bruce is quoted in Kitty Bruce, *The Almost Unpublished Lenny Bruce* (Philadelphia: Running Press, 1984), 91.

83. "The Silent Vote," *Newsweek*, October 17, 1960, 27.

84. George Gallup, Jr., "The Impact of Presidential Debates on the Vote and Turnout," in *Presidential Debates: 1988 and Beyond*, ed. Joel L. Swerdlow (Washington, DC: Congressional Quarterly Press, 1987), 34.

85. The debates seemed to have very slight effect in 1996. Typical of many polls were the findings of the Gallup organization, which were done for several media outlets. Gallup found that during the week prior to the first debate, Clinton was favored by 52.42 percent of the voters. In the week after the last debate, Clinton was favored by 52.71 percent of the voters. In the week prior to the debates, Dole was favored by 36.85 percent of the voters. In the week after the debates, Dole was favored by 34.14 percent. See "Daily Tracking Poll," available at www.usatoday.com/elect/eq/eq/127.htm. The Gallup figures are highly consistent with those of other polling groups. See, for example, the results of the ABC News Poll, "The Data," www.politicsnow.com/news/Oct96/31/abc1031data.

86. The figures used in this paragraph represent the consensus figures used by Real-Clear Politics, the most widely quoted internet polling site in 2012. RealClear Politics utilizes all the major public opinion polls and averages them to arrive at its consensus figure. Although their statistical procedures are not perfect, the RealClear Politics consensus figures involve far more polls and samples than other sources and hence were often relied upon by both the press and political professionals in 2012. See the "RealClear Politics Poll Average," accessed November 13, 2008, www.realclearpolitics.com/epolls/2012/presi dent/us/general_election_romney_vs_obama-1171.html. The dates used for the figures mentioned in this paragraph were October 2, the day before the first debate, and October 23, the day after the last debate.

87. David O. Sears and Steven H. Chaffee, "Uses and Effects of the 1976 Debates: An Overview of Empirical Studies," in *The Great Debates: Carter vs. Ford, 1976*, ed. Sidney Kraus (Bloomington: Indiana University Press, 1979), 255.

88. Elmo Roper, "Polling Post-Mortem," *Saturday Review*, November 1960, 10–13.

89. Elihu Katz and Jacob Feldman, "The Debates in Light of Research: A Survey of Surveys," in *The Great Debates: Kennedy vs. Nixon, 1960*, ed. Sidney Kraus (Bloomington: Indiana University Press, 1962), 211.

90. Jack M. McLeod et al., "Reactions of Young and Older Voters: Expanding the Context of Effects," in *The Great Debates: Carter vs. Ford, 1976*, ed. Sidney Kraus (Bloomington: Indiana University Press, 1979), 365–66; Paul R. Hagner and Leroy N. Rieselbach, "The Impact of the 1976 Presidential Debates: Conversion or Reinforcement?" in *The Presidential Debates: Media, Electoral, and Policy Perspectives*, ed. George F. Bishop, Robert G. Meadow, and Marilyn Jackson-Beeck (New York: Praeger, 1978), 178.

91. David A. Leuthold and David C. Valentine, "How Reagan 'Won' the Cleveland Debate: Audience Predispositions and Presidential Debate 'Winners,'" *Speaker and Gavel* 18 (Winter 1981): 62.

92. Smith and Smith, "1984 Reagan-Mondale Presidential Debates," 102.

93. See "Daily Tracking Poll" and "The Data."

94. Jamieson and Waldman, *Electing the President 2000*, 5, 75.

95. If 1.7 percent of McCain's voters shifted to Obama, the effect would be to lower McCain's vote by 1.7 percent and increase that of Obama by the same 1.7 percent, resulting in the difference between them growing by 3.4 percent. Although Obama's favorability grew by 3.4 percent, it is impossible to know if his gains were entirely at McCain's expense or involved undecided voters and voters previously committed to third-party candidates as well.

96. Using the RealClear Politics figures cited in the previous section, it would appear that the 2012 debates might have contributed to the shift of approximately 2.3 percent of the vote during the period that the debates were being held. Presumably Obama's fall of 1.9 percent during the period of the debates accounts for most of Romney's increase of 2.3 percent during that same period.

97. Voth, "Presidential Debates 2016," 93.

98. Maxwell McCombs, "Agenda Setting Research: A Bibliographic Essay," *Political Communication Review* 1 (Summer 1976): 3.

99. Linda L. Swanson and David L. Swanson, "The Agenda Setting Function of the First Ford-Carter Debate," *Communication Monographs* 45 (November 1978): 347–53.

100. Ibid., 353.

101. Ibid.

102. This is one of many indictments of the current system of presidential debates leveled by George Farah. On agenda setting in the debates, see Farah, *No Debate* (New York: Seven Stories, 2004), 125–39.

103. Lee B. Becker et al., "Debates' Effects on Voter Understanding of Candidates and Issues," in *The Presidential Debates: Media, Electoral, and Policy Perspectives*, ed. George F. Bishop, Robert G. Meadow, and Marilyn Jackson-Beeck (New York: Praeger, 1978), 137–38; Steven H. Chaffee, "Presidential Debates—Are They Helpful to Voters?" *Communication Monographs* 45 (November 1978): 336; Jian Huazhu, J. Ronald Milawsky, and Rahul Biswas, "Do Televised Debates Affect Image Perception More Than Issue Knowledge? A Study of the First 1992 Presidential Debate," *Human Communication Research* 20 (March 1994): 302–32; and McKinney and Carlin, "Political Campaign Debates," 211–12.

104. Allen Lichtenstein, "Differences in Impact Between Local and National Televised Political Candidates' Debates," *Western Journal of Speech Communication* 46 (Summer 1982): 296.

105. See McKinney and Carlin, "Political Campaign Debates," 226–27.

106. Pfau, "Criteria and Format," 5–6.

107. Soma Golden, "Inside the Debate," *New York Times*, September 24, 1980, A30.

108. For an examination of the differing agenda of voters, reporters, and candidates, see Marilyn Jackson-Beeck and Robert Meadow, "The Triple Agenda of Presidential Debates," *Public Opinion Quarterly* 42 (Summer 1979): 173–80.

109. Halford Ryan, "The 1988 Bush-Dukakis Presidential Debates," in *Rhetorical Studies of National Political Debates, 1960–1992*, ed. Robert V. Friedenberg (Westport, CT: Praeger, 1994), 160.

110. Windt, "1960 Kennedy-Nixon Presidential Debates," 4.

111. Hagner and Rieselbach, "Impact of 1976 Presidential Debates," 172.

112. Sears and Chaffee, "Uses and Effects of 1976 Debates," 246–47.

113. Thomas M. DeFrank, "Obama Campaign Attack Ads Appeared Effective," *New York Daily News*, November 12, 2012, accessed November 15, 2012, articles.nydailynews .com/2012-11-07/news/34977495_1_obama-campaign-attack-ads-independent-republi can-groups-romney-aides.

114. Donovan Slack, "R.I.P. Positive Ads in 2012," *Politico*, November 4, 2012, accessed November 15, 2012, dyn.politico.com/printstory.cfm?uuid=0951FE40-4A80-42E8. Donovan also reports that 79 percent of Romney's ads were negative, but because Obama was better known, they probably did not affect the public perception of Obama as well as Obama's ads might have affected public perception of the lesser-known Romney.

115. Dan Hahn, "The 1992 Clinton-Bush-Perot Presidential Debate," in *Rhetorical Studies of National Political Debates: 1960–1992*, ed. Robert V. Friedenberg (New York: Praeger, 1994), 208.

116. Sidney Kraus and Dennis Davis, "Political Debates," in *Handbook of Political Communication*, ed. Dan Nimmo and Keith Sanders (Beverly Hills, CA: Sage, 1981), 273–98.

117. Samuel L. Becker et al., "Information Flow and the Shaping of Meanings," in *The Great Debates: Carter vs. Ford, 1976*, ed. Sidney Kraus (Bloomington: Indiana University Press, 1979), 396.

118. Chaffee, "Presidential Debates," 343–45.

119. Lynda Lee Kaid, Mitchell S. McKinney, and John C. Tedesco, *Civic Dialogue in the 1996 Presidential Campaign: Candidate, Media, and Public Voices* (Cresskill, NJ: Hampton Press), 206, cited in McKinney and Carlin, "Political Campaign Debates," 213.

120. McKinney and Carlin, "Political Campaign Debates," 203–4.

121. Sidney Kraus, *Televised Presidential Debates and Public Policy* (Hillsdale, NJ: Erlbaum, 1988), 123.

# 10

⚛

# Interpersonal Communication
# in Political Campaigns

This chapter examines the place of interpersonal communication in political campaigns. We perceive interpersonal communication to be transactional. When people communicate, they define themselves and simultaneously respond to their perceptions of the definitions being offered by others. This transactional perspective, which we share with most communication scholars, has several implications that have unusual importance for political communication.

First, interpersonal communication is contextual. Part of the context in which any communication takes place is the other person. You behave differently when you are with your parents than when you are with your employer. Each participant affects the other. Similarly, candidates behave differently when they visit with small groups of bowlers in neighborhood bowling alleys from when they visit with a few large financial contributors in someone's home. The physical setting of the two transactions, the differences in background music and noise, the differences in clothing worn by the bowlers and the contributors, the differences in the language used by the two groups, and countless other stimuli help define the bowlers and the contributors to the candidate. Simultaneously, the presence of the candidate in the bowling alley or at a contributor's home, the clothing and language of the candidate, and countless other stimuli that the candidate emits enable the bowlers and the contributors to define the candidate. As each party to the transaction shapes and refines definitions of the other, their own behavior will be affected, thus continually changing the communication context.

Second, this perspective suggests that each party to the transaction is simultaneously both a sender and a receiver of verbal and nonverbal messages. When you meet the candidate at a neighborhood coffee and criticize a local bond issue that the candidate supports, you are simultaneously watching facial expressions, observing the tightening of the candidate's fist, and noting that the candidate's face is becoming flushed. As candidates emit these communicative stimuli, they are defining themselves to you. You sense better that candidate's support for this bond issue and the irritation your criticism provokes, even though that candidate may have said nothing.

Clearly, as you observe candidates listening to your criticism, they appear affected by your statements. Similarly, as you see the candidate's face flush and fist tighten, you begin to temper your criticism. You gradually lower your voice and use more moderate language. You have been affected by this communication transaction, and so has the candidate. This is the third major implication that the transactional perspective has for political communication; that is, each participant affects and is affected by the other.

In addition to noting our transactional perspective, before beginning our discussion of interpersonal communication and political campaigning, we want to note two other characteristics of the interpersonal communication studied in this chapter. They deliberately narrow the expanse of interpersonal communication, limiting it to interpersonal communication utilized in political campaigns. First, one party to the interpersonal transactions discussed in this chapter is either a candidate or the surrogate/advocate of a candidate. The surrogate/advocate may be a formal representative of the candidate, such as a member of the campaign staff, or an informal representative, such as a voter who is not in any way affiliated with the candidate but nevertheless discusses the candidate. The final characteristic of the interpersonal transactions examined is that the overt, normally verbal, messages either directly or indirectly involve a campaign for public office.

Daniel Shea and Michael Burton argue that campaigns have moved from "old-style" to "new-style" campaigning.[1] In the old style, parties ran candidates for office. Between 1830 and 1960, campaigns were party-driven, with voter contact the function of party activists. Old-style politics involved traditional strategies of group-based appeals with traditional party messages. The goal was voter education and broad mass appeal. Today, individuals run for office. Once nominated, the candidate carries the campaign function with little else but party endorsement. With the advent of television, campaigns became personality-driven and candidate-centered. The strategies and tactics are more narrowly defined and targeted. Voter preferences are revealed through scientific research and messages are targeted to voter segments. Candidates need professionals to run their campaigns. Virtually at all levels, we have the "consultant-centered" campaigns. Richard Semiatin argues, "Campaigns are becoming more individualized and tailored to *you*, the voter."[2] For Semiatin, we are witnessing the next generation of voter targeting. "Campaigns used to be about parties and candidates. Increasingly, campaigns will be about you, the voter, or as Madison Avenue would say, the customer."[3] Methods and frequency of voter contact continue to expand. Campaigns have access to so much more than computerized voter files. Today firms are actively assessing all the collective information on voters to develop predictive modeling of voting behavior. They overlay an ever-growing list of predictive values to the large amount of individual data available on voters. They can build unique voter profiles on values, issues, past voting, media usage, age, civic work, religious affiliation, and so on. According to political consultant Bob Blaemire, "The growing amount of artificial intelligence and known individual data is a powerful combination that makes campaigns smarter."[4]

However, there still are true "citizen-politicians" at the state and local level. In essence, local and statewide politics are retail politics. This means it's about direct voter contact. It's about meeting voters, talking to voters, and shaking as many hands as possible. Naturally, the more local the race, the more retail the expectation. Direct voter contact is invaluable for several reasons. First, direct contact with a candidate makes the voter more committed to the candidate and more engaged in the campaign. Second, it allows for two-way communication and interaction where voters can express concerns and ask questions. This makes voters feel important while generating interest in the candidacy and campaign. Face-to-face contact also humanizes the candidate, allowing a more personal, firsthand observation and evaluation. Studies also show that people are more likely to vote for a candidate they meet in person, regardless of party or even issue positions.[5]

In this chapter, we discuss crucial areas of interpersonal communication in political campaigns: interpersonal communication between the candidate and voters, interpersonal communication between the candidate and potential financial contributors, interpersonal communication between voters, interpersonal communication and the mass media, interpersonal communication and the get-out-the-vote effort of campaigns, and finally, behavioral characteristics of successful interpersonal campaigners.

## INTERPERSONAL COMMUNICATION BETWEEN CANDIDATE AND VOTERS

As indicated in chapter 5, no resource is more vital to the campaign than the candidate's time. This is a finite resource. Once the time is lost, it cannot be replaced. Consequently, if candidates are spending time meeting individuals or small groups of individuals, they must be sure that there is an unusually high chance that these meetings will be productive. For candidates to spend an hour or more with two, four, or ten people and come away with nothing is a loss that cannot be recovered. More money cannot buy lost time, nor can more volunteers produce it. Hence, decisions on where candidates should spend time, and with whom, are critical.

The use of the candidate's time is especially critical in local campaigns. Over half a million public offices are filled by election.[6] Lynda Lee Kaid points out that the tendency of researchers to study highly visible national and statewide campaigns has caused us often to neglect what is the most effective channel of political persuasion in vast numbers of races—the interpersonal communication of the candidate.[7] As Kaid notes, the channels of communication available to the candidates in thousands of campaigns below the national and statewide levels are often severely limited.

There are four basic communication channels: the electronic media (in all its forms, including social media), the print media, display media (e.g., billboards, bumper stickers, pins, etc.), and personal contact. It is a most difficult task to determine the best combination of media to reach the potential audience and that which best communicates the desired theme. In addition, the factors of timing, money, and distribution are also important considerations. Candidates must decide when and where they will concentrate their communication efforts, making sure that they do not peak too soon or spend too much in areas of little consequence. In many campaigns, the geographic makeup of the district precludes the effective use of mass media such as radio and television, especially in more rural areas. Some districts may include several media markets. In contrast, large urban areas may have a single media market, but running ads is very expensive.

Television, radio, and other mass media are simply impractical for thousands of races nationally, depending on the geographic characteristics of the district and the media that serve the district. The targeting provided by mass media is often simply not narrow enough for many lower-ballot races. Additionally, messages on behalf of most local candidates, delivered through the mass media, are likely to be ignored or ineffective when those media are saturated with information concerning many major candidates running for federal and state offices. Lynda Kaid recognized more than thirty years ago that "the interplay of some or all of these limitations may create an environment in which interpersonal communication, particularly communication between the candidate and the voters, may be a crucial factor in the outcome of an election."[8] This is especially true for those for lesser offices and those in rural areas.

Given the importance of the candidate's time and given that in many races its waste cannot be offset by purchasing media time, it is essential that the candidate's interpersonal communication be utilized effectively.[9] This means that the candidate must know where to campaign. Consequently, in local races especially, the most valuable materials that a campaign can have are often the precinct analysis of recent voter statistics, such as those illustrated in chapter 7. The thoroughness of such analysis is a direct function of the amounts of money spent on obtaining them. In most states, party organizations will prepare voter statistics for candidates. Hence, even in areas where the local organization is weak, candidates should not have trouble obtaining a complete analysis of prior voting statistics for their district. Moreover, if the various party organizations do not provide an analysis of statistics, candidates can obtain the statistics themselves and perform their own analysis; all vote totals are a matter of public record and are kept on file by the appropriate election boards.

Once they have access to prior election results, particularly a precinct-by-precinct analysis, candidates can determine which precincts are essentially Republican, Democratic, or marked by a high incidence of ticket splitting. As we observed in chapter 7, the candidates should direct the campaign primarily at those precincts where the party traditionally runs well and those precincts where ticket splitting commonly takes place. Most of the candidate's interpersonal communication should take place in these precincts.

Far more than national figures, local candidates must know precisely where to spend their time. Because their constituencies are smaller, in many instances local candidates can knock on every door in their district or at least on every door in those precincts that are deemed most important. The door-to-door campaigning of candidates for major offices is most often done for media coverage, rather than for any direct impact. It allows the major candidate to appear in the media while walking through a barrio or a cornfield, presumably illustrating concern for Latinos or farmers. Local candidates will not receive media exposure of their door-to-door campaigning. Rather, their efforts will put them face to face with a significant percentage of their constituency. Interpersonal campaigning is not symbolic for the local candidate, as it is for the major candidate. Rather, it is often the major thrust of the campaign, an essential means of compensating for the lack of media exposure.

It is often difficult for an inexperienced candidate or campaign staffer to recognize the critical importance of targeting voters, even in interpersonal campaigning. Candidates and campaign staffers are frequently tempted to meet the most people, not necessarily targeted people. But just as duck hunters must go where the ducks are, regardless of where the deer or the turkeys may be, so too, candidates must go to where their targeted voters are, not simply where there are a lot of people. Candidates for lower-ballot races especially will often want to campaign at the county fair, the Little League game, the municipal pool, the factory gate, or the busy intersection. Typically, the people whom the candidate may meet in these situations are often not those targeted by the campaign. Indeed, a good deal of the candidate's precious time might well be wasted dealing with people who are not even registered to vote or not registered in their district. The candidate's interpersonal communication should always be targeted to potential voters and supporters. If this allows the campaign to utilize the candidate or other affiliated spokespersons at the factory gate or the busy street corner, fine. But campaigns, particularly local campaigns, must keep in mind that their interpersonal communication efforts must be aimed not at communicating with the most voters but rather at communicating with *targeted* voters.[10]

Although major candidates do not rely as extensively on interpersonal campaigning as do local candidates, it does often serve an important place in their campaigns. Clearly, because of the size of the constituency, major candidates, as well as many local candidates, will utilize surrogates/advocates to represent them in door-to-door canvasses of a community. The door-to-door canvass is often especially effective in the primary campaigns of major candidates. Such races typically involve substantially fewer voters than the general election. Candidates and their representatives can often reach a high percentage of those voters who are eligible to vote in the primary. George McGovern's effective use of the principles of interpersonal communication in door-to-door canvassing in small state primaries that occurred early in 1972, such as New Hampshire, Massachusetts, and Rhode Island, played a substantial role in his success that year. It has been emulated, with changes often driven by technology, in every primary season since.[11]

Campaign activities at the local level have three primary purposes. They serve the campaign by assisting in fund-raising and volunteer recruitment and by generating voter support. While the activities identified below are part of all campaigns, they are more important and of greater influence in local elections. The most typical methods of interpersonal campaigning by candidates or their representatives are special events, public appearances, dinners, coffees, and door-to-door canvasses.

## Special Events

Special events, according to Catherine Shaw, are "campaign-sponsored activities intended to raise money and support for the campaign."[12] She observes that special events actually raise little money and are very time-consuming. Because they tend to be primarily attended by supporters, such events have little to no impact on undecided or independent voters. However, the events are valuable in generating publicity, strengthening bonds among volunteers, and increasing subsequent commitment to the candidate.[13] Special events need a defined purpose such as to raise money, thank supporters, or attract endorsements. Attention to detail is critical, and promotion of events is vital to ensure a good turnout. A poorly attended event is embarrassing to the candidate and communicates a lack of candidate interest and support.[14] In essence, all the items discussed below are "special events" with unique considerations.

## Public Appearances

Candidates spend a great deal of time visiting local civic clubs and groups. Such appearances aid name recognition, credibility, and candidate legitimacy. While the candidate will deliver the basic "stump speech," there should be specific items included relevant to the purpose and goals of the organization. For example, if speaking at a local chamber of commerce meeting, one would acknowledge the work they do for the community and address issues of jobs and the economy. Local sporting events, fairs, parades, and town gatherings provide wonderful opportunities to meet local residents in a very positive and relaxed setting.

## Dinners

Especially in local campaigns, sponsored dinners are traditional and very effective means of fund-raising. Usually a restaurant will donate the dinners at cost while the campaign sells tickets for a much higher price. In local campaigns it is more common to sponsor numerous smaller and targeted dinners than to sponsor one or two very large dinners. Smaller dinners allow for more individual contact with the candidate. Often, individuals host private dinners in their homes. Usually a well-known individual from the community will host a high-end catered meal at his or her own expense with a very targeted and selective guest list. As one would expect, the ticket costs are much greater. A private dinner may well generate several thousand dollars. Well-known state or other local leaders may join in the dinner as incentive for attendance.[15]

## "Coffees"/Receptions

Keeping in mind the precinct analysis of voters, the campaign organization will arrange a schedule of coffees. The events can be as casual or formal as the hosts wish. Some hosts will keep it very informal, serving coffee, tea, soft drinks, perhaps beer. If, as might happen on occasion, the event is also to serve as a fund-raiser, the refreshments will typically be somewhat more elaborate. But these details are for hosts/hostesses to arrange. Once they have agreed to host the event, the campaign may provide them guidance, but it is, after all, their party for the candidate.[16] The primary advantage of coffees is that they can be held throughout the campaign and throughout the day ranging from midmorning to late afternoon or early evening.

The organization should arrange the coffees so that the candidate is able to meet with two groups. First, the candidate should meet with "those people residing in areas which are generally independent" and in which considerable ticket splitting takes place. Second, "coffees should be scheduled in areas where the candidate and his [or her] party can be expected to run well."[17] In these areas, coffees give "the candidate an opportunity to pay personal attention to those who are working for him [or her, and] it gives the campaign organization an opportunity to recruit new workers."

Keeping in mind our transactional viewpoint of interpersonal communication, we can readily see why campaigners seek to hold coffees and similar events that promote interpersonal transactions with neutral and friendly voters. Such events provide the candidate with much more than the opportunity simply to meet voters. They offer an opportunity to establish a relationship and to affect the other parties in the transaction. They also provide opportunities to solicit volunteers and distribute yard signs to the most loyal supporters.

In virtually any election, but perhaps more so in local elections, candidates will often meet constituents in countless small social gatherings early in the campaign. They can then follow up on the relationships initiated at these meetings by remaining in contact with short notes, letters, calls, or emails. The candidates affect people they meet this way, and subsequently those people often prove helpful to the candidates.

Conversely, candidates are also affected by interpersonal transactions such as coffees. As we have seen in chapter 2, promises made during the surfacing and primary stages of a campaign tend to be kept more than those made later. Part of the reason for this seems to be that promises made early in the campaign are frequently made in small interpersonal contexts, where the candidate is more prone to be affected by voters. Later in the campaign, crowded candidate schedules often prohibit the types of interpersonal transactions that frequently take place early in the campaign.

Candidates should never attend coffees by themselves. They should always have another person with them. The function of this other individual is to get the candidate away from the coffee gracefully if the host/hostess fails to do so. The candidate's associate, not the candidate or the host/hostess, can take the blame for rushing the candidate away if that becomes necessary. The candidates should avoid making speeches at coffees. Rather, a candidate "need give only brief informal remarks." After the candidate's brief remarks, a short question-and-answer period is appropriate.

Four rules should govern every coffee. First, the "optimum size of the gathering is twenty to thirty people." This includes the host and hostess, candidate, and those traveling with the candidate. Second, name tags should be provided for each guest. The affair is essentially social, and the candidate wants to establish a first-name relationship with the guests. One consultant who has been involved in arranging many meetings of this sort advises candidates to "obtain a list of the attendees prior to the event and become familiar with your audience."[18] The individual traveling with the candidate might also help in this regard. Third, the host or hostess should "never permit a guest to buttonhole the candidate or enter into arguments." Finally, it should always be remembered that the coffee "is an excuse for getting together, and the stress should be on easy informality and comfort."

This description of an ideal coffee clearly indicates that the simple act of being present and interacting with a number of voters is as important as, if not more than, what the candidate actually says. A well-run coffee maximizes the opportunities for fruitful interpersonal transactions. Time is devoted to establishing personal friendships. The group is small enough for the candidate to interact with everyone, and the candidate's aide as well as the host/hostess of the coffee should facilitate the candidate's interaction with everyone.

Laura Peck, vice president of a large political consulting firm, says that, in situations such as these, eye contact is essential. She tells candidates, "Give your full attention, even if for just a few seconds, to the person in front of you. If someone is anxious to meet you, you will feel positively encouraged and reinforced. Once the connection is sealed, you can then move on."[19]

Peck also stresses the importance of handshakes. She claims, "With a handshake, you touch your audience physically for the first time. This tactile presentation will be remembered." She adds, "If you wish to make the connection especially heart-felt, place your other hand on top of the handshake."[20]

Local candidates often run for administrative positions that do not involve issues of policy. The county recorder, engineer, prosecutor, and sheriff, for example, provide administrative service, but they rarely set policy. Hence, interpersonal communication opportunities, where candidates can establish relationships illustrating their concern, personality, and character, are vital. Given that many local races lack real issues between the candidates and that the candidates are relatively unknown, often the candidates who are best known in the district, who have visited the neighborhoods, who seem to make themselves available and accessible, and who have worked at establishing relationships are the candidates who most appeal to the voter.

Good campaigns can effectively arrange three coffees an evening for their candidate, several evenings a week, through the last months of the campaign. Such programs, particularly in local races, enable candidates to interact with a significant percentage of their constituency. Moreover, the candidate's presence in the neighborhood will be rapidly reported the next day over backyard fences, in beauty parlors and barbershops, markets and restaurants, as those invited to the coffee discuss their experience.

Late afternoon and early evening receptions are also very popular for more local campaigns. They generally cost less than dinners and allow for larger crowds. Like dinners and coffees, high-profile citizens serve as sponsors and cover the expenses. The general purposes, operational considerations, and candidate behaviors follow those suggested for coffees.

## Door-to-Door Canvasses

The use of small social gatherings, such as coffees, serves primarily to foster interaction between the candidate and voters. A second major form of interpersonal communication between the candidate and voters, the door-to-door canvass, typically serves several additional purposes. Like the coffees, candidates meeting voters while canvassing will be perceived as accessible and concerned, leaving a positive image with the voters they meet. Presumably, the same impressions should be left with voters who meet the candidates' representatives. As Richard Semiatin observes, "Despite being labor intensive, the most effective form of traditional voter contact is door-to-door canvassing."[21] The combination of political targeting and personal contact is an effective tactic.

Canvassing is targeting specific precincts. Using voter lists, the campaign may target voters of the same party, of the opposition party, or those identified as independent. Targeting those households of the same party is useful to motivate partisans for the candidacy. Targeting those of the opposing party and independents attempts to increase share in a specific precinct. Candidates should focus their efforts in "swing" neighborhoods. Candidates usually begin neighborhood walks in mid to late summer and continue up to Election Day. There are two types of canvassing: a "knock" and a "drop." The "knock" is simply approaching the house and speaking with one or more person of voting age. It is best if volunteers are familiar with the candidate's positions and can easily express reasons for support. The "drop" is simply leaving a brochure or doorknob flyer at the door. Drops are much less expensive than mail and cover more territory in a short time.

When utilized in major races, representatives of the candidate do the majority of the canvassing. Regardless of who is canvassing, the canvass can identify voters who are favorable, neutral, or hostile to the candidate. Depending on their attitudes, these voters can subsequently be contacted. In addition to the canvass being an excellent means of distributing information about the candidate, a conversation between the canvasser and the voter can provide information about the candidate. In addition, if the voter has a specific concern, the canvasser can arrange to have additional information sent later.[22]

If they are doing their jobs well, canvassers will follow several important principles of interpersonal communication. The instructions given to those who canvass on behalf of a candidate "will typically exhibit sensitivity to psychological principles important in interpersonal communication."[23] Instructions such as these are representative of what most campaigns will encourage:

1. Speak with enthusiasm and sincerity.
2. Be a good listener. Let the voters speak. Do not interrupt or argue.
3. Be open-minded. Whenever possible, express your agreement with the voter.
4. Family members make good surrogates. It impresses voters that the candidate's husband, wife, mother, father, or sibling came to their door. When unrelated strangers canvass, people sometimes wonder what the canvasser is getting out of it.
5. Don't knock on doors after dark.[24]

Pennsylvania state legislator Mike Hanna adds several additional guidelines that candidates should use when they are doing the canvassing. When candidates canvass themselves, Hanna advises them to dress in normal business clothing. He observes, "People will take you seriously if you look the part of a serious candidate." Additionally, he advises that candidates always end their interaction in a canvass by "explicitly" asking for the citizen's vote. Most important, Hanna observes that, when candidates are going door to door, they should avoid long conversations. "Civics lessons aside," claims Hanna, "your job is not to bring voters over to your point of view. Your objective is to show yourself at their door for a brief and shining moment and leave them with an impression that you are a nice, trustworthy person and that you care."[25]

These guidelines focus primarily on the actual canvass itself. Peck adds several suggestions that campaigns might follow to prepare for the canvass. She suggests that, prior to canvassing a neighborhood, the campaign should provide advance warning by utilizing yard signs announcing the impending canvass or sending out a mailing that lets voters know that the candidate will be visiting their neighborhood. Similarly, she recommends that candidates might ask neighborhood residents to accompany them on canvasses and brief them on the neighborhood in which the canvass is taking place.[26] Peck also suggests that the neighborhood canvass might be made into a memorable neighborhood event by creating a mini-parade. As the candidate canvasses door to door, one or more campaign vehicles with signs can accompany the candidate down the street, and several campaign volunteers wearing campaign shirts could also be on the street.[27] Canvassers who follow instructions such as these can accomplish much. They can leave literature, determine voting intentions, or question for other information that the campaign desires.[28] Additionally, when done by well-prepared canvassers, particularly the candidate and members of the candidate's family, the door-to-door canvass leaves voters with a positive feeling about the candidate that will not be readily forgotten.

In sum, interpersonal communication between the candidate and the voter is, for most people, a unique event. The details of the coffee or the door-to-door canvass meeting will no doubt fade from an individual's memory, but the fact that the candidate cared enough to come to the neighborhood or send a representative or family member and followed up the initial coffee or canvass will often remain and loom far larger in the voter's mind than the specifics of what may have been said.

## Phone Banks

Phone banks are used throughout a campaign for a variety of purposes: fund-raising, yard sign placements, solicitation of volunteers, and as part of the campaign's get-out-the-vote efforts. Partisan volunteers work between one to two hours making phone calls. Research suggests that calls made by campaign volunteers are a more effective means to encourage voter turnout than traditional prerecorded "robocalls" (those recorded by well-known politicians or celebrities).[29] A full-service phone bank has three "types" of calls: persuasion, identification, and activation. The persuasive call delivers a brief "pitch" for the candidate. Usually callers have a script to follow. An identification call attempts to obtain some basic information about the voter: favorable, undecided, major issue of concern, and so forth. Those rated as undecided may receive an additional call as Election Day nears. Activation calls urge voters to vote for the candidate of preference. Most calls are made between 7:00 and 9:00 p.m. to avoid receiver aggravation. Usually callers can complete twenty to thirty calls per hour.

## The Internet

The internet has rapidly become an essential element of all political campaigns. Although the internet is clearly not interpersonal campaigning, in some respects it approximates interpersonal campaigning to a greater degree than any other medium. The characteristic that most distinguishes the internet from other mass media and makes it most analogous to interpersonal exchanges is the fact that both parties can be sources and receivers of messages. The print, radio, and television media facilitate one-way communication only. Candidates and their staffs send messages to audiences who receive those messages. But the internet allows audience members to respond. It is this characteristic, the fact that both parties can be senders and receivers of messages, that makes the internet analogous to interpersonal communication. Equally important is the fact that social media is not about content per se, but about the building and nurturing of relationships.

John Allen Hendricks and Dan Schill argue, "Without incorporating social and digital media into a political campaign, a candidate has almost no chance of being competitive. Communicating with the electorate is vital for politicians, and to do it proficiently, candidates must go where the voters can be found—online and using social media. Particularly, social media such as Facebook, Instagram, and Twitter are the most viable social media outlets to communicate with voters."[30]

A very detailed analysis of the use of the internet and other new technologies is the focus of chapter 12. The internet is also discussed as an advertising medium in chapter 11. However, it is important to recognize here the growing personalization and social dimensions of the medium. There are numerous ways to interact with potential voters and supporters. And for younger voters, the "relationships" developed are as personal and interactive as those with peers.

One of the primary differences between the internet and other forms of media is the level of candidate involvement. To voters, the internet seems to offer an opportunity to interact directly with candidates and their principal advisors. Primarily through social media, voters can provide feedback to candidates. Other media do not offer this opportunity, which is more characteristic of interpersonal communication. However, as Laura Woolsey has observed, radio and television often involve candidates themselves communicating through the media. Hence, candidates using them should have some level of proficiency in using these media.[31] The same is true in terms of the internet. Virtually all campaigns have social media directors, and large campaigns will have a dedicated social media team. In 2016, Hillary Clinton had a staff of more than one hundred to manage and direct her digital campaign.[32] For some campaigns, more money is spent using new media than the traditional television, radio, or print.

In 2012, both presidential campaigns utilized new media to gather voter information and then create tailored and targeted messages. Also, for both campaigns, social media played an important and more prominent role in the marketing strategies of the campaigns as well.

The use of Twitter provided the narrative of both campaigns and hence the election. According to John Hendricks, "Twitter allowed the candidates to communicate directly with supporters without having to go through traditional-media gatekeepers and agenda setters."[33] Twitter as a technology is both inexpensive and immediate.

In 2011, YouTube created a political channel that allowed both candidate and campaign videos but also material created by private individuals unaffiliated with campaigns. Interestingly, both content and viewership were down from 2008 in terms of political material.[34]

Pinterest, a site that allows users to organize and share favorite things on virtually any topic or item, was the tenth most-visited website during the 2012 election. The demographic for Pinterest was primarily twenty-five- to thirty-four-year-olds. The site was only two years old when first used in the 2012 presidential election. Sixty-eight percent of the users of this site were women. Hence, the campaigns used this site to target women voters with candidate spouses sponsoring their own pages.[35]

Finally, Tumblr, another site where users can share any items or things of interest, was less used in the 2012 campaign. Of all the social media, it ranked twentieth in terms of the 2012 presidential campaign. Like Pinterest, it is also dominated by women but primarily those between eighteen and twenty-four years old.[36]

According to Hendricks and Schill, "social media radically upended the traditional campaign norms and practices in 2016." The social media environment was volatile and unpredictable. Campaigns could not control the elements, despite efforts to do so. There was also much blurring between fact and fiction, news and entertainment, and information producers and consumers. Such an environment may have benefited Donald Trump's disruptive and attacking style.[37]

In this election, the sheer volume of social media followers reached new records. Among his Facebook, Twitter, Instagram, and Reddit accounts, Trump had more than twenty-two million followers compared to Clinton's fourteen million. Trump dominated across all the platforms.[38] Clinton's campaign strategy related to social media was to "humanize" and "soften" her image.[39] Of course, Twitter was the platform of choice for Trump with more than thirteen million followers on Election Day. However, more important than the number of followers was the forwarding and retweeting of posts. He averaged over 2,000 retweets per post.[40] This alone demonstrates the value of interpersonal influence and sharing messages during a campaign. More about the usage of social media platforms in the 2016 presidential contest will be discussed in chapter 14.

## INTERPERSONAL COMMUNICATION BETWEEN THE CANDIDATE AND PROSPECTIVE FINANCIAL CONTRIBUTORS

Dan Balz argues that the 2012 presidential campaign essentially ended the public financing of campaigns in return for agreements on limits of total spending. The system was established after Watergate and lasted only twenty-five years. For the first time since 1992, neither candidate accepted public funds for the primary or general election. The demise began in 2000 when George W. Bush opted out of public financing during the primary period. John Kerry and Howard Dean did the same in 2004. Obama was the first in 2008 to decline public financing for the general election.[41] Romney followed suit in 2012 and both Hillary Clinton and Donald Trump declined public financing in 2016. With each successive presidential election, all spending records were broken.

In 2008, Obama raised an amazing $750 million for his campaign. That was more than twice what George W. Bush raised in 2004 and seven times more than Bush raised in 2000. Together, Obama and McCain spent well over $1 billion.[42]

In 2012 a total of $2.1 billion was spent by the candidates, parties, and outside groups. The Obama campaign raised $741 million, actually down from the $750 million in 2008. The Romney campaign raised a total of $473 million, considerably less than the Obama campaign. However, Super PACs and other outside groups generated a record $416 million for Romney and $142 million for Obama. The parties played a major role as well. The Republican National Committee raised $381 million, compared to $289 million for the Democratic National Committee.[43]

The Obama team continued its fund-raising dominance on the internet. They raised about $690 million digitally in 2012, up from $500 million in 2008. When including those initially generated by just email, social media, mobile, and the website, the total was $504 million.[44]

The innovation of online giving during this election was text message fund-raising. In 2006, the Federal Election Commission exempted any restrictions on internet political and fund-raising activities. According to Toner and Trainer, "The practical effect of the FEC's regulations has been that individuals, volunteers, and anyone else with access to a computer can conduct a wide range of internet activities on behalf of federal candidates—such as setting up and maintaining websites, blogging, emailing, linking, and posting videos on YouTube—without fear that the FEC will monitor or restrict their activities."[45] Interestingly, both the Romney and Obama campaigns declined to publicly disclose the amount of money generated from text messaging activities.

The 2016 presidential campaign was unprecedented in terms of campaign finance. First, it was the most expensive presidential campaign in American history, with over $7 billion spent from all sides on the election. Second, it is the first time in the modern era that a candidate was substantially outspent but still won. Finally, which has become a trend, Super PACs and other special interest groups are significantly spending more on presidential campaigns.[46]

Since the 1970s, advocates of campaign finance reform have legislatively sought to reduce the influence of wealthy contributors, encourage donations from smaller donors, and improve disclosure. The specific intent of the McCain-Feingold legislation of 2002 was to reduce the effect of large contributions. However, one of the unintended consequences of that legislation is that it gave rise to 527 groups, the precursor to today's Super PACs. The 527 group contributions came in any size from anyone who wished to contribute. But because there was no limit on the contribution size, 527 groups were typically financed primarily by a highly limited number of donors giving exceedingly large amounts of money. Political action committees may make large independent expenditures on behalf of a candidate as long as there is no contact between the PAC and the candidate's organization. Moreover, they may contribute the legally acceptable amounts to each campaign. Although PACs raise and contribute large sums of money, they often derive that money from small individual contributors. Some organizations, such as AARP, the National Education Association, and many unions, have PACs that are often financed, at least in part, out of member dues. Collectively, because of the large membership, this money can be used for large political expenditures on behalf of candidates the group supports. Thus, although PACs often make large independent expenditures on behalf of candidates they favor, their money often comes from relatively modest donations from large numbers of people.

The U.S. Supreme Court and the Federal Election Commission issued several rulings after the 2004 election that would impact the way money would be spent in the 2008 elections. In a most significant ruling, the Supreme Court decided that organized interests, unions, and corporations could indeed air ads during elections as long as they did not specifically advocate for or against a candidate.[47]

Of course, by implication, it is very clear which candidates these ads favor. The Federal Election Commission also placed restrictions on the 527 groups, treating them more like PACs. For example, if funds were going to be used to support or to defeat a specific candidate, donors were limited to contributions of $5,000. In addition, at least half of their money must be from contributions of $5,000 or less.[48]

The now infamous Supreme Court decision in 2010 in *Citizens United v. Federal Election Commission* clearly changed the dynamics of campaign fund-raising and magnified the influence of corporations, unions, and wealthy individuals. The ruling established "Super PACs" and campaign "committees" that could collect cash without sharing donor names and information. In addition, the ruling allowed for unlimited contributions from entities because any restrictions limited the constitutional speech of corporations, unions, and trade organizations.

In 2012, outside groups spent $1 billion on the contests. Three of the groups spent over a third of the total amount: American Crossroads, Crossroads GPS, and Restore Our Future. Republican-leaning groups spent an estimated $440 million and accounted for 70 percent of the total spent. In the end, estimates are that Romney's campaign and allies spent $1.2 billion, compared to just $1 billion for Obama.[49] Some of the top contributors to Obama included Microsoft, Google, and Harvard University. For Romney, the list included Goldman Sachs, Bank of America, Morgan Stanley, and JPMorgan Chase. Overall in 2012, Super PACs spent $631 million, committees and groups $401 million, and the parties a total of $252 million.[50] Thus, more than half of all the money spent in the 2012 presidential campaign came from outside groups.

The trend continued in 2016. In fact, outside groups spent 32 percent more in the 2016 race than in the 2012 election. Super PACs and nonprofit political organizations spent $1.5 billion during the 2016 campaign. There were 188 single-candidate PACs, compared to 103 in 2012. The largest nonparty outside spenders were Priorities USA Action (pro-Clinton), Right to Rise USA (pro–Jeb Bush), Senate Leadership Fund, and Senate Majority PAC. Among the largest business contributors were the National Association of Realtors PAC, National Beer Wholesalers Association PAC, AT&T, Inc. PAC, Honeywell International PAC, and National Auto Dealers Association PAC.[51]

## The Importance of Individual Contributors

As the above sections indicate, in 2012 there was an unprecedented flood of money from outside groups. The role and importance of smaller individual donations remain an important question in the future. In 2012, the Obama and Romney campaigns raised a combined total of $285 million from small donors giving less than $200 each. This accounts for about 1,425,500 individual contributions at this level. In 2016, small individual contributions of less than $200 constituted 26 percent of total funds raised for Trump,[52] compared to 19 percent for the Clinton campaign.[53]

In this context, it is still important to note that individual contributions by "regular" citizens are essential in state and local campaigns. Such contributions provide the largest portions of campaign support. However, campaign finance legislation and the growing use of the internet as a means of fund-raising should increase the contributions of individual citizens. The 2020 presidential race will provide insight into the value and scope of individual political contributions in the future.

## The Role of Attraction

People do not contribute to a political campaign unless they are attracted to the candidate. Political fund-raising is largely interpersonal in nature. Typically, the candidate, finance director, and members of the finance committee seek contributions from individuals they believe would be receptive to such an appeal. Similar in conception, although obviously less personal in execution, are direct mail and internet fund-raising. Here again, the campaign seeks contributions from individuals believed to be receptive to the candidate. Invariably, the key is to determine who would be attracted to the candidate and thus receptive to financial appeals.

Students of interpersonal communication identify at least five principles of human attraction.[54] First, we are attracted to people who are in physical proximity to us. Second, we are attracted to people who are similar to us. Third, we are attracted to people who provide us with positive feedback. Fourth, if we find ourselves in an anxiety-producing situation, we tend to have a greater need for human interaction and hence are more prone to be attracted to other people. Fifth, if we have already extended some type of supportive behavior to an individual, we are more likely to be attracted to that individual than if we had never provided such behavior. Each of these five principles of human attraction has major implications for conducting political fund-raising.

The first determinant of attraction is proximity. That is, all things being equal, the more closely two people are located, the more likely they are to be attracted to each other. Far too often, campaigns tend to neglect this simple fact. Rather than seek fiscal support from the most likely sources—people within the district—they seek financial support out of the district. Doing so creates two potential problems. First, and most serious, it rarely works. Just as charity begins at home, just as most of us contribute to our own United Way, our own church, and our own schools and colleges, most of us will be more prone to contribute to candidates who will directly affect us.

The importance of proximity is also illustrated by the guidelines both the Republican and Democratic National Committees use to determine which candidates will receive financial support. One of those guidelines is that candidates must demonstrate fund-raising ability *within* their districts. The assumption is that, if they cannot raise money among people in close proximity, they cannot raise money from anyone.[55]

The second determinant of human attraction that is of exceptional importance for political fund-raising is similarity. We are attracted to people who are similar to us. Potential donors should always be approached by people who are highly similar to them. A carefully selected and highly motivated fund-raising committee working through their own social networks (the people to whom they are most similar) and drawing on the candidate's presence when necessary is perhaps the most effective means of utilizing the concept of similarity. The key to a successful interpersonal fund-raising effort is in the selection of the individuals who will head the fund-raising effort by endorsing the candidate and seeking contributions for the candidate from their friends and associates. Political consultant Cathy Allen calls the use of these interpersonal fund-raising networks "peer pressure politics" and observes that, in selecting key fund-raisers, candidates must remember that they "are soliciting an endorsement which will translate into thousands of dollars in contributions from the endorser's peers."

She observes that the key fund-raiser in each group (Lawyers for Smith, Nurses for Smith, Environmentalists for Smith, etc.) should be a highly credible and influential member of the group—someone, in other words, whom group members will perceive favorably in large part because of their similarity.[56]

When the candidate is making the solicitation calls, the principle of similarity is still critical. Allen suggests that, immediately after establishing rapport, candidates who are phoning for contributions should explain what they have in common with the prospective donor.[57] Even if the prospective donor rejects the candidate's request for money, the candidate's response should utilize the concept of similarity. Allen suggests that, virtually regardless of the reason for the turndown ("I'm supporting someone else"; "I don't have any money right now"; "I really don't know you well"; "I want to learn about all the candidates first"), the candidate should respond with "feel, felt, found." That is, the candidate should indicate similarity to the donor by observing, "I know how you feel; I've felt that way myself, but I have found that . . ."[58] Notice that prior to directly responding to the prospective donor's rationale for refusing a donation, the candidate attempts to establish similarity by speaking about mutual feelings.

The third principle of attraction that has import for political fund-raising is that we are attracted to and respond favorably to people who like us and validate us with positive feedback. Candidates and their surrogates must keep this fact uppermost in their minds as they seek funds. This does not mean the fund-raiser must be overly compliant. If fund-raisers feel compelled to do that, then they are not dealing with equals. They should not be attempting to get donations from persons with whom they do not feel similar and equal. Rather, it means that fund-raisers must do their research. They should be able to make references to the potential contributor's family by name, and to recent accomplishments of the potential contributor's business, schools, family, and friends. In many fund-raising meetings, it is fair to say that topics such as politics, current events, and making political contributions do not take up more than two to three minutes of a ten-minute conversation. Fund-raising situations are so patently obvious that often they do not need any belaboring. Rather, such meetings stress the similarities among the candidates, their supporters, and the prospective contributors, as the candidates or their supporters attempt to provide positive feedback to the prospective contributors. Often this is done by focusing comments on the contributor's role in mutual projects of a nonpolitical nature, such as charitable, social, educational, or civic projects.

Once the similarities among the candidate, fund-raiser, and potential contributor have been established, the fund-raiser can make the pitch on behalf of the candidate, stressing the philosophical or issue similarities between the candidate and the potential contributor. If the fund-raiser has done a good job of establishing similarities, the final pitch on behalf of the candidate should convince the contributor that the question is not so much whether to give to the candidate but rather how much to give.

A fourth principle of human attraction enters into political fund-raising. Research suggests that we experience a heightened need for human attraction during moments of anxiety.[59] The competent political fund-raiser should make note of this point. As the campaign develops, the good fund-raiser will keep in mind those who might be made anxious by current events. As opponents make statements and develop their campaigns, the good fund-raiser will follow them closely, seeking to determine who might be made anxious by the opponents' statements and positions. And as current events take place and receive publicity, the well-run campaign will have the appropriate person seeking funds from the individuals most likely to be made highly anxious by these events, at the very moment that they may be causing anxiety. An interesting example will help for clarification. During the first debate between Obama and Romney, moderated by PBS's Jim Lehrer, Romney responded to things he would cut in order to balance the budget and pay for his proposed tax cuts. "I'm sorry, Jim. I'm going to stop the subsidy to PBS. I'm going to stop other things. I like PBS. I love Big Bird. I actually like you, too. But I'm not going to keep on spending money on things to borrow money from China to pay for it."[60] Throughout the evening, Big Bird and friends Oscar the Grouch, Bert, and Ernie became a major Twitter trend, leading users to post 17,000 tweets per minute. The Obama campaign created a fund-raising campaign claiming that Romney wanted to kill Big Bird in order to pay for tax cuts for the rich. The fund-raising goal was $1 million.[61]

The final basis of human attraction that warrants the attention of the political fund-raiser is the concept of supportive behavior. Research suggests that our own behavior greatly influences our perception of other people. If, for example, you perform a favor for another person, you tend to like that person better as a consequence.[62] Hence, good fund-raisers, if unsuccessful in getting what they want—large contributions—should always have backup requests. If the car dealer will not contribute any money to the Smith for City Council campaign, will the dealer at least let candidate Smith use that beautiful yellow car in the showroom for three hours during the Labor Day parade? At minimum, the car dealer can look over some of Smith's campaign literature.

The practice of consistently seeking some type of supportive behavior, minimal as it may be, has at least two beneficial effects. First, the tangible benefit requested will be honored. Candidate Smith does ride in the most attractive car in the parade. Second, now that the car dealer has provided some sort of supportive behavior to the candidate, the dealer is more likely to respond favorably to a second fund-raising appeal. Importantly, once people have made an initial contribution to the candidate, they are prone to make a second or third contribution. Effective fund-raisers are aware of the positive effect that supportive behavior has on subsequent behavior and consistently strive to obtain some type of supportive behavior from everyone they approach. As Robert Kaplan, president of one of the most successful political fund-raising firms in the country, has observed, "At its core, a successful fund-raising philosophy is based on asking, asking again and asking one more time."[63]

These principles of interpersonal communication should guide candidates and fund-raisers as they seek contributions. Moreover, they clearly have implications for other forms of fund-raising. They can help determine, for example, both the mailing list and the message content of direct mail solicitations, phone solicitations, and internet solicitations on behalf of the candidate. Ultimately, all the principal means of fund-raising involve asking for money. Whether the candidate is asking others for contributions, whether the candidate's supporters are asking their friends and associates for contributions, whether the candidate and the candidate's supporters are asking others to organize fund-raising events and sell tickets, or whether the asking takes place through direct mail, telephone appeals, or internet appeals, the principles of interpersonal communication invariably come into play.[64] In sum, candidates and fund-raisers who are skillful interpersonal communicators, clearly sensitive to and aware of the determinants of human attraction, are far more apt to achieve success than those who ignore these important variables of interpersonal communication.

## INTERPERSONAL COMMUNICATION BETWEEN VOTERS

Voters talk among themselves about politics, campaigns, and candidates. Interpersonal communication between voters is an important aspect of virtually every campaign. The process of learning about politics and our political system is referred to as "political socialization." Political socialization is a lifelong process of learning and developing social and political attitudes. Most of this process is one of social interaction with others. According to Michael Carpini, "Political socialization is a continuing process influenced by ongoing interactions with family and friends, the workplace, and significant personal and societal events, as well as through life cycle changes that affect one's contact with and relationship to the political and social world."[65] Research shows that one outcome of political socialization is the frequency of political discussion. Those who know more about and enjoy politics are more likely to discuss politics and political issues with others. Our political attitudes and behaviors are greatly influenced by our social networks and peer group pressure. Our interactions with others tend to influence candidate preference, partisan support, and issue opinions. The effect is primarily one of reinforcement. Because we tend to associate with those of similar political beliefs, attitudes, and values, our social interactions tend to support preexisting political beliefs and attitudes.

Interestingly, those who engage in discussions of politics and current events with others are also more likely to vote and participate in political campaigns.

According to Zuckerman, such conversations encourage voting, for example, by supplying information for decision making.[66] In fact, R. L. Lake and Robert Huckfeldt found that the amount of political discussion in one's social network correlates with one's level of political participation.[67] Studies also show that a few individuals play the role of "opinion leader," serving more or less as a conduit of information, interpretation, and analysis about political issues or candidates obtained primarily from the mass media. Opinion leaders exist in all social groups and economic levels.

### Importance

Interpersonal communication between voters is normally of greatest importance in those campaigns that receive little media attention. When information about the campaign and the candidates is lacking in the media, voters rely more heavily on interpersonal communication. Consequently, several types of campaigns characteristically lacking in media coverage often must rely heavily on interpersonal communication. First are campaigns for lesser offices and local offices; second are primary campaigns. L. Erwin Atwood and Keith Sanders have found that communication with other people was the most credible source of information for 32 percent of the voters in a primary election, but that it was the most credible source of information for only 12 percent of the voters in a general election.[68] Although there has been little research since the work of Atwood and Sanders on this point, and the exact figures may have changed, their basic conclusion that people learn more about primary elections from other people, where other sources of information are limited, and less about general elections, where other sources of information are more plentiful, continues to make sense. Often, as when three or more candidates seek a single office in a primary, the media coverage received by any single candidate tends to be more limited than in a general election. Moreover, the media budgets of most primary campaigns are lower than those of general elections. The reduced media coverage of individual candidates and campaigns in some primaries likely causes voters to rely more heavily on interpersonal communication in these elections than in general elections. Knowing little about a candidate, the opinion of a friend or relative may take on added importance in lower-ballot and primary elections.

Direct voter contact is especially important for congressional races. Although it may be less efficient in reaching a large number of voters, it is very effective on a per voter basis. In fact, it appears that any direct request for support tends to be effective. After the candidate, candidate family members, friends, volunteers, party, and interest group activists are all also effective in soliciting voter support. According to Burton and Shea, there are several reasons why direct voter contact is valuable. First, contact with the candidate brings the voter to a different cognitive level than other communication contacts. The voter becomes more engaged and attentive when meeting with the actual candidate. Second, direct contact allows two-way communication. Voters value the opportunity to not only meet candidates but to interact with them. Third, voter interaction humanizes the candidate. Media portrayals of campaigns are less real than face-to-face interaction. Finally, direct voter contact brings more commitment and enthusiasm to a campaign.[69] More detailed strategies and tactics of voter contact will be discussed in the next chapter.

In considering issues, most congressional candidates identify with valence issues such as good schools, strong economy, job growth, safe streets, and national security; these issues and positions possess universal agreement. Candidates avoid more controversial or wedge issues. Challengers will often make one issue the centerpiece of their campaign. Economic issues tend to drive congressional races, whether positive, such as low inflation and good jobs, or negative, such as high unemployment and increased taxes.[70]

The third group of campaigns where interpersonal communication between voters seems to play an unusually important role is those campaigns in which the constituency has a relatively high educational level. Research on this point is limited, and much of it has been done primarily on school-age populations. Nevertheless, it does tend to suggest that well-educated voters are less affected by the media, are more apt to discuss current events, and are more likely to be influenced by those discussions.[71]

## Discussion Topics

Voters discuss virtually everything that is pertinent to a campaign. However, three subjects tend to dominate their conversations. First, interpersonal communication is often the way people initially learn of a newsworthy development in the campaign. In one of the first studies to focus on how people learn about campaign events, Wayne Danielson found that knowledge of news events in a presidential campaign was most rapidly spread throughout the population by radio and interpersonal communication. Television and newspapers, according to Danielson, did not transmit knowledge of news events as rapidly.[72]

Although Danielson's findings may have since been altered by the widespread growth of television and the internet, it nevertheless seems safe to conclude that many people do frequently discuss and often first learn of news events through interaction with one another.

Second, William Kimsey and L. Erwin Atwood found that voters tend to "talk most about the things they like least about candidates."[73] Conversations between voters are not subject to libel laws, equal time laws, and other legal constraints that may affect the various mass media. Media coverage of the negative aspects of a candidate may be tempered by considerations such as these, but interpersonal communication is not.

Additionally, Kimsey and Atwood found that voters tend to use interpersonal communication selectively to reinforce their ballot decisions.[74] This finding makes good sense because of our tendency to be attracted to, and communicate primarily with, those who are similar to us. Hence, we are prone to be exposed to messages congruent with our own ideas. Moreover, we do not equally attend to all the messages we receive. We are inclined to attend selectively to those messages that conform to our existing attitudes and beliefs. Kimsey and Atwood's findings, that we use interpersonal communication selectively to reinforce prior decisions, seem to be very much in accord with our existing knowledge of interpersonal communication.

Thus, voters use interpersonal communication to deal with virtually everything that happens in a campaign. However, in contrast to other forms of campaign communication, it may be especially important as a medium of news transmission, as a medium by which negative information about a candidate is transmitted, and as a medium that serves to reinforce attitudes and beliefs.

## INTERPERSONAL COMMUNICATION AMONG VOTERS, MASS MEDIA, AND VOTING BEHAVIOR

As early as 1948, students of mass media realized the relationship and importance of interpersonal communication. John P. Robinson provides us with a critique of the relationships among voting behavior, mass media, and interpersonal communication.[75] Robinson, like prior researchers, finds that, when interpersonal communication is in conflict with media information, "interpersonal sources wield greater influence."[76] The explanation for this no doubt rests in large part on the feedback and adaptation that one voter can provide to another as they discuss politics. Mass media messages cannot adapt and react to feedback as can interpersonal communication. However, Robinson also finds that interpersonal influence attempts are not that pervasive in elections. More people seem to be exposed to media attempts to influence their votes than to interpersonal attempts to influence their votes.[77] Those people who receive media messages attempting to influence their votes but no interpersonal messages seem much more receptive to direct influence from the media.[78] Silvo Lenart argues for what he calls "an integrated model." He claims that candidates and campaigns utilize the mass media to communicate to voters but that these efforts are often affected by such interpersonal influences as the characteristics of individual voters, the one-to-one individual discussions between voters, and the group interactions that voters have.

As mentioned above, opinion leaders tend to belong to the same primary groups as family, close friends, or coworkers. The groups tend to share the same values and are of similar educational and socioeconomic backgrounds. Evidence of group influence comes from network analysis and social context research. Individuals are viewed as interdependent with others in rather homogeneous groups where members basically conform to group goals and identity through peer pressure. The interpersonal relationships provide networks of support, value reinforcement, and anchor points for political attitudes and opinions. The more cohesive the group, the greater the influence or conformity in terms of beliefs, attitudes, values, and even behavior. It is important to note that the more homogeneous the group, the higher the level of individual satisfaction as a member of the group.

The mass media influence the general "opinion climate." If interpersonal conversations overlap with media political content, then the interactions will tend to reinforce media effects. Likewise, the more cohesive the group, the more the interactions will amplify media influences. Lenart concludes, "Once a campaign is underway in the media, the entire communication process is best characterized as a dynamic interplay among media, interpersonal interactions, and opinion climate pressures."[79]

We know that television news covers elections and campaigns more through visual depictions than through their verbal statements. Scholars have shown that "image bites" when candidates are shown but not heard have grown significantly since 1990s. In contrast, "soundbites" from candidates have shrunk.[80]

Some research has focused on the impact of facial displays, gestures, and voice tone. In general, viewers can detect facial expressions of reassuring, neutral, or threatening smiles but less differentiating between felt and amused smiles.[81] Candidate facial displays influence voter perceptions of attractiveness and competence.

Evidence suggests that exposure to nonverbal information impacts voter decisions, especially those "low information" elections and less partisan voters where voting depends more on personal impressions of leadership qualities than policy or issue positions.[82] According to Delia Dumitrescu, upon reviewing nonverbal communication in politics, visuals "function as an important element of the decision-making process, particularly for those who do not possess other information."[83] Perhaps not surprising, but regrettable, there does seem to be a correlation between candidate attractiveness and electoral support and victory.[84]

Although most candidates make special efforts to facilitate interpersonal communication between themselves and voters and between themselves and financial contributors, few candidates make concrete efforts to facilitate interpersonal communication between voters that might have a favorable impact on their candidacy. However, at least one political consultant has long attempted to stimulate interpersonal communication among voters to benefit his clients. Stephen Shadegg, who advised Barry Goldwater and whose son served in Congress for sixteen years, recommends that candidates develop "social precincts" as crucial elements of their campaigns.[85] *Social precincts*, as Shadegg employs the term, are simply enthusiastic and knowledgeable supporters of the candidate. They are not members of special organizations or groups, nor are they in any way prominent in their communities. Initially, members of social precincts are recruited from among friends and associates of the candidate, and gradually the number of members is increased. Many of these people may not even know the candidate well. Members of social precincts are provided "inside" information. As the campaign progresses, they get key press releases a day in advance, and their opinion is solicited before the candidate makes a key speech. They are made to feel that they are insiders whose opinions and advice are valued by the candidate. And indeed, they are just that. By using the internet and other technology, the candidate is able to develop a large group of people who look upon the candidate as someone with whom they have a special relationship. Based on extensive experience with social precincts, Shadegg claims that, if he can enlist 3 to 5 percent of the constituency in these social precincts, he will win the election. For if 3 to 5 percent of the constituency believe they have a special interest in a candidate, Shadegg feels that, in their normal day-to-day social interactions, they will prove influential on a significantly large enough number of voters to win most elections.

Shadegg's approach is one of the few clear attempts to mobilize interpersonal communication among voters on behalf of a candidate. His success with social precincts, as well as research evidence on the relationship among voting behavior, mass communication, and interpersonal communication, speaks to the importance of interpersonal communication between voters.

## INTERPERSONAL COMMUNICATION
## AND GETTING-OUT-THE-VOTE EFFORTS

GOTV or get-out-the-vote efforts are a vital part of every campaign. Of course, every activity of a campaign is attempting to get people to favor the candidate or campaign and to vote. However, GOTV activities are specifically tailored to motivate and activate supporters to go the polls and vote. A subtle distinction, but an important one, is that GOTV is not about increasing general election turnout as much as to increase the turnout of supporters for a specific candidate or campaign. The traditional rule of GOTV efforts is to target 10 percent of the votes needed for victory. For example, if a local candidate needs 15,000 votes to generally win, then the campaign needs to target 1,500 voters to push to the polls.[86]

GOTV activities have changed in at least two rather dramatic ways in recent elections. Understanding the evolution of the change is instructive. First, GOTV activities have simply become much more critical to the success of campaigns, particularly upper-ballot campaigns such as those for the presidency and statewide offices. Second, interpersonal communication is becoming more and more widely recognized as the key to a successful effort, especially as it relates to the use of social media. As recognized earlier in the chapter, social media is all about creating, building, and maintaining relationships. Thus, direct "touching the voter" activities and the use of social media form the basis for GOTV efforts.

The 1990s witnessed a decline in ticket splitting. As has been the case since 1968, but with the exception of Bill Clinton in 1996, the GOP presidential nominee, win or lose, has won more ticket-splitting districts than the Democratic presidential nominee.[87] There have been numerous studies attempting to explain why voters choose to split their votes between congressional and presidential candidates between the two major parties. However, there is little agreement among the scholars about why voters split their tickets. Campaigns today are more concerned about independent and "swing" voters. In 2012, about 23 percent of registered voters identified themselves as "swing voters," those who are undecided or lean toward one candidate but indicate their mind could change before casting a ballot. That number is down from 33 percent in 2008.[88] Self-identified independent or non-Democrat or Republican voters continue to increase. Thirty-four percent in 2016 identified as independent and of those, the vote was split with 43 percent supporting Trump and 42 percent supporting Clinton.[89] However, the number shifts from election to election. For example, Gallup polls suggest that the number of swing voters was 27 percent in 2006.[90]

The Republican campaign in 2004 was not geared to persuading weakly committed Democratic voters and independents but was consciously designed to reinforce committed Republican voters and get them out to the polls on Election Day. Similarly, the Democratic Party's focus was primarily on voters already committed to that party. Both parties placed a premium on interpersonal contact rather than on persuasive media advertising and were successful in turning out large numbers of their voters. But the Republicans were significantly more successful at increasing their turnout than were the Democrats. President Bush won 23 percent more votes in 2004 than he did in 2000. His vote total increased from fifty million in 2000 to sixty-two million in 2004. Senator Kerry won 16 percent more votes in 2004 than did Vice President Gore in 2000. Gore won fifty-one million votes in 2000 compared to Kerry's fifty-nine million in 2004.[91] A key to the Republicans' success was their interpersonal communication with the voters, especially in their GOTV efforts.

In 2004 the Democrats built their GOTV effort on the backs of union labor and the well-funded efforts of 527 groups such as MoveOn.org. These groups relied on paid workers. They organized heavily in black neighborhoods and university towns. These were the types of communities that had exceedingly strong Democratic voting histories.

One important key to the Republican victories was the interpersonal nature of the Republican GOTV effort. "The Bush-Cheney '04 campaign was built around the concept of personal contact. Everything was geared around one human being talking to another, be it by telephone or in person."[92] Moreover, all the efforts in the weeks and months prior to the election were designed to facilitate a final seventy-two-hour GOTV effort. First, throughout the nation, for months in advance of the election, Bush-Cheney supporters were being identified. A variety of means were used to identify Republican-leaning voters. They were all interpersonal in nature: door-to-door neighborhood canvasses, millions of phone calls, and internet responses to Republican websites. As we have noted, although the internet is not explicitly interpersonal, the fact that a typical citizen can be both a sender and receiver of messages to and from the campaign gives it an interpersonal nature that is lacking in most other mass media.

For more than two years, the Bush campaign also built an organization of 1.4 million active volunteers. The size of this organization dwarfed the volunteer organizations of the past. The Democratic National Committee, by contrast, claimed the services of 223,000 volunteers.[93] Importantly, as potentially sympathetic names were amassed by the campaign, the organization followed up and prepared for their GOTV effort. These follow-ups and many initial contacts were not by paid workers, who might have little in common with those they were contacting. Rather, the Republicans tried to match their volunteers with people with whom they had something in common. The Bush campaign used existing connections to recruit volunteers, identify voters, and, perhaps most importantly, get out the vote.

The 2008 Obama campaign signaled a drastic change and innovation in GOTV. They certainly learned from the Bush campaign in 2004. Their goal was to construct a "voter builder program." What is interesting about the Obama field organization is that among the staff and volunteers, 75 percent had never been actively involved in a campaign before. Jon Carson of the Obama campaign called their office strategy the "Starbucks strategy."[94] They wanted offices literally everywhere, with massive numbers of volunteers. They utilized daily phone calls and neighborhood knocking on doors. The "interpersonal" approach was threefold. First, they wanted to get as many people registered as possible, primarily those who were not registered or who had never voted. Second, they wanted volunteers to provide personal testimony and advocacy on behalf of Obama. "The mission we were given on the persuasion side was that our volunteers would really be validators. To win these Republican states, you have to persuade people who had never voted for a Democrat before."[95] In addition, they sought "weak voting

Democrats."[96] Finally, what made a huge difference is neighbor-to-neighbor contact, with volunteers knocking on doors and soliciting support. This is a form of peer pressure never formally utilized before in a get-out-the-vote effort.

The Obama campaign even developed a formula for increasing votes by reviewing some research by the Consortium of Behavioral Scientists. The research also informed their GOTV scripts. They found, for example, that the campaign needed 389 mail contacts, 460 phone contacts, and 14 canvass contacts to yield just one additional vote![97] The campaign also learned, as suggested earlier, that it was important to match callers to respondents, and the same for door-to-door activities. For example, have veterans contact veterans and teachers approach teachers, and so forth.[98] By the end of the campaign, a CBS poll revealed that 26 percent of voters were contacted by the Obama campaign, compared to 19 percent by the McCain campaign. Most importantly, Obama received 65 percent of votes from those contacted by the campaign, compared to 47 percent of votes from those who were not contacted.[99]

In 2012, once again the Obama campaign had a far superior voter contact and thus turnout program than the Romney campaign. They stressed early voting and identifying nonregistered and "less-likely-to-vote" citizens, thus "banking" many thousands of "extra" votes before Election Day, especially in swing states.[100]

Obama's databases already knew a lot about the approximately 180 million registered voters in the United States from the past campaign. The goal was to collect intelligence about potential voters' 2012 intentions and distill that down to a series of individual-level predictions based upon voter "scores."[101] The most important of these scores, on a range from 0 to 100, assessed an individual's likelihood of supporting Barack Obama and of casting a ballot altogether.

Obama's analysts built statistical models to pull out factors that distinguished voters from nonvoters. Socioeconomic factors like income and housing type played a role in likelihood of voting of those who lived in multitenant dwellings who were generally less likely to vote. But within those households Obama's analysts went a step further. Voters living with other people who had a demonstrated history of voting were predicted to be more likely to turn out to vote. As a result, the Obama campaign's algorithms ran the numbers and predicted the likelihood that every voter in the country would cast a ballot by assigning every voter a turnout score. By their account from polling new groups of voters, the Obama campaign found that their predictions were accurate 87 percent of the time.[102]

However, in terms of specifically GOTV, it is informative to see how the Obama campaign used "person-to-person" contact on Facebook to reach more than five million voters, primarily those eighteen to twenty-nine years old. It is important to note that this vital and essential age group of voters for the Obama campaign cannot successfully be reached by phone. The campaign relied on Facebook to extend its reach by contacting potential voters who in turn would share with their friends messages and information. The Obama campaign reported that 20 percent of people asked by their friends to register and vote did so. By Election Day, about one million people had signed up for the Obama for America Facebook app. The campaign reached more than five million with seven million pieces of content.[103]

The final important innovation in 2012 in terms of GOTV became early voting. Once again, Democrats enjoyed the edge over Republicans. By Election Day,

Obama's campaign declared that Romney would need 60 percent of the vote to counter Obama's lead in early voting.[104] In the years ahead, some analysts predict that more than 50 percent of the vote will be cast before Election Day. Once again, frequency of contact to voters will aid and motivate them to get to the polls early.

The details of the use of social media will be provided in much greater detail in chapter 12. In the digital world, GOTV efforts really start with the first time someone enters a website; they are tracked and contacted routinely, not just during the last few weeks of a campaign. And, as already suggested, social media is becoming the primary tool connecting with voters, keeping them involved with the campaign and committed to vote. Thus, more traditional GOTV efforts were reduced by the Trump campaign in 2016. The Trump campaign only had 207 field offices compared to 489 for the Clinton campaign. The Clinton campaign also developed state-specific sites for all fifty states and the District of Columbia.[105] Thus, GOTV efforts are evolving and changing because of the increased importance and role of social media, as well as early voting.

It has become clear, as partisanship becomes more pronounced in our society, that fewer and fewer voters are amenable to persuasion. Consequently, to a greater degree than ever before, parties and candidates are striving to "gin up the base." That is, they are striving to get their strong supporters excited about candidates and committed to voting for those candidates. As we have seen, perhaps the most effective way of accomplishing that is through interpersonal communication.

## BEHAVIORAL CHARACTERISTICS OF SUCCESSFUL INTERPERSONAL CAMPAIGNERS

As we know from our own personal experience, some people are more interpersonally successful than others. Some people seem able to establish more and stronger interpersonal relationships than others. Clearly, that ability would be a major asset for an individual seeking elected office. Yet, until recently, little research has focused on the ways in which political candidates might behave that would enhance their interpersonal attractiveness. One team of researchers has attempted to focus on desirable interpersonal communication behavior for political candidates. Their work warrants our attention because clearly it is among the few studies that offer practical behavioral suggestions to candidates seeking to increase their interpersonal attractiveness to voters.

Timothy Stephen, Teresa M. Harrison, William Husson, and David Albert have focused their work on the interpersonal communication styles of political candidates. Specifically, in their most recent study, they have attempted to distinguish between the interpersonal behaviors of winning and losing candidates in three recent presidential elections.[106] Breaking these overall observations down, Stephen, Harrison, Husson, and Albert identify a number of behavior characteristics that are perceived in successful presidential candidates. To a greater degree:

- Winners are perceived to more frequently tell jokes and use humor than losers.
- Winners are perceived to laugh more frequently than losers.
- Winners are perceived to smile more frequently than losers.

- Winners are perceived to explain by using examples, analogies, and stories.
- Winners are perceived to make frequent and appropriate eye contact.
- Winners are perceived to be calm and relaxed in manner.

Moreover, losers are perceived to behave differently than winners. To a greater degree:

- Losers are perceived to control what gets talked about.
- Losers are perceived to dominate others in conversation.
- Losers are perceived to have loud voices.
- Losers are perceived to insist that terms be carefully defined.
- Losers are perceived to disagree frequently.
- Losers are perceived to be more likely to blame or accuse.

Stephen, Harrison, Husson, and Albert also identify a variety of interpersonal behaviors where the differences between winning and losing candidates are relatively slight. Their work is unusual because it represents an effort to identify specific interpersonal behavioral differences among candidates. To some degree, it provides candidates with explicit interpersonal communication behavioral objectives to be used throughout the campaign.

## CONCLUSIONS

In this chapter, we have found that interpersonal communication between the candidate and voters is exceptionally important in local campaigns, in campaigns where the use of media may not be feasible, and in primary campaigns. In such campaigns, the interpersonal communication between the candidate and voters through programs of informal coffees and canvasses can be extremely valuable. Moreover, we have found that political fund-raising lends itself to interpersonal communication and that current interpersonal communication research on attraction has major implications for interpersonal fund-raising by political candidates and their advocates.

Moreover, we have examined the often-neglected interpersonal communication between voters. We have seen in which campaigns such communication is most important, what voters tend to discuss among themselves, and the relationship among voting behavior, media, and interpersonal communication. Additionally, we have observed how critical get-out-the-vote efforts have become in recent years and how interpersonal communication plays a vital role in those efforts. Finally, we have observed that the perceptions of the interpersonal behavioral characteristics of winning and losing candidates differ and we have offered some of the characteristics of both winning and losing candidates.

## NOTES

1. Daniel Shea and Michael Burton, *Campaign Craft*, 4th ed. (Westport, CT: Praeger, 2006), 8–10.

2. Richard Semiatin, ed., *Campaigns on the Cutting Edge* (Washington, DC: Congressional Quarterly Press, 2008), 3.

3. Ibid.

4. Bob Blaemire, "Evolution of the Voter File," *Campaigns & Elections*, May/June 2013, 23.

5. Semiatin, *Campaigns on the Cutting Edge*, 182–83.

6. Herbert E. Alexander, *Financing Politics: Money, Elections and Political Reform* (Washington, DC: Congressional Quarterly Press, 1980), 1.

7. Lynda Lee Kaid, "The Neglected Candidate: Interpersonal Communication in Political Campaigns," *Western Journal of Speech Communication* 41 (Fall 1977): 245.

8. Ibid.

9. The following analysis of the importance of interpersonal campaigning in local political campaigns is based heavily on Robert V. Friedenberg, "Interpersonal Communication in Local Political Campaigns," *Ohio Speech Journal* 12 (1974): 19–27.

10. Shea and Burton, *Campaign Craft*, 191.

11. See L. Patrick Devlin, "The McGovern Canvass: A Study in Interpersonal Political Campaign Communication," *Central States Speech Journal* 24 (Summer 1973): 83–90, for an account of some of the McGovern techniques that have been widely copied.

12. Catherine Shaw, *The Campaign Manager*, 3rd ed. (Boulder, CO: Westview Press, 2004), 1–2.

13. Ibid., 81.

14. Ibid., 87–89.

15. Ibid., 82–83.

16. See Nancy Bocskor, "No Place Like Home," *Campaigns and Elections*, April 1998, 28–29. Bocskor stresses the fund-raising potential of coffees and similar events hosted by supporters of the candidate in their own homes.

17. This statement and all quotations in this section, unless otherwise explicitly noted, are drawn from "Coffee: The Campaign Beverage," a pamphlet issued by the Republican State Central and Executive Committee of Ohio to candidates for state and local offices. No date or place of publication is available.

18. Laura Peck, "Face to Face Campaigning: How to Work a Room," *Campaigns and Elections*, April 1996, 47.

19. Ibid.

20. Ibid.

21. Richard Semiatin, "Voter Mobilization—Into the Future," in *Campaigns on the Cutting Edge,* ed. Richard Semiatin (Washington, DC: Congressional Quarterly Press, 2008), 90.

22. See Devlin, "McGovern Canvass," 82–90, for an excellent description of a highly effective canvassing operation that served all the functions described in these paragraphs.

23. Ibid., 89.

24. These guidelines are modeled after those provided to McGovern canvassers during the 1972 presidential primaries, which have been widely copied ever since, and after the guidelines recommended by Pennsylvania Democratic state representative Mike Hanna, whose 1990 election upset with 65 percent of the vote in a district where Republicans had dominated was largely attributed to his successful utilization of door-to-door canvassing. See Devlin, "McGovern Canvass," 84–85, and Mike Hanna, "The Campaign Door Knocking Game," *Campaigns and Elections*, September 1991, 52–53.

25. Hanna, "The Campaign Door Knocking Game," 52.

26. Laura Peck, "Going Door-to-Door: 10 Tips for Success," *Campaigns and Elections*, July 1996, 45.

27. Ibid.

28. See Robert Agranoff, *Management of Election Campaigns* (Boston: Holbrook Press, 1976), 411–54, for a discussion of the many purposes of canvasses as well as illustrations of the material used in canvasses.

29. Shea and Burton, *Campaign Craft*, 195–96.

30. John Allen Hendricks and Dan Schill, "The Social Media Election of 2016," in *The 2016 US Presidential Campaign: Political Communication and Practice*, ed. Robert E. Denton, Jr. (Cham, Switzerland: Palgrave Macmillan, 2017), 121.

31. Laura Woolsey, "Web Usability: The Development and Application of a New Instrument for Objective Usability Inspection," master's thesis, Miami University, 2001, 41.

32. Hendricks and Schill, "Social Media Election of 2016," 125.

33. John Hendricks, "The New Media Campaign of 2012," in *The 2012 Presidential Campaign*, ed. Robert E. Denton, Jr. (Lanham, MD: Rowman & Littlefield, 2013), 138.

34. Ibid., 139.

35. Ibid., 139–41.

36. Ibid., 141.

37. Hendricks and Schill, "Social Media Election of 2016," 122.

38. Ibid., 125.

39. Ibid., 127.

40. Ibid., 131–32.

41. Dan Balz, *Collision 2012* (New York: Viking, 2013), 351.

42. Michael Toner, "The Impact of Federal Elections Laws on the 2008 Presidential Election," in *The Year of Obama: How Barack Obama Won the White House*, ed. Larry Sabato (New York: Longman, 2010), 149.

43. Michael Toner and Karen Trainer, "The Six-Billion-Dollar Election," in *Barack Obama and the New America*, ed. Larry J. Sabato (Lanham, MD: Rowman & Littlefield, 2013), 85–94.

44. Michael Schere, "Exclusive: Obama's 2012 Digital Fundraising Outperformed 2008," *Time*, November 15, 2012, accessed December 31, 2014, swampland.time.com/2012/11/15/exclusive-obamas-2012-digital-fundraising-outperformed-2008.

45. Toner and Trainer, "Six-Billion-Dollar Election," 96.

46. Michael Toner and Karen Trainer, "The $7 Billion Election: Emerging Campaign Finance Trends and Their Impact on the 2016 Presidential Race and Beyond," in *Trumped: The 2016 Election That Broke All the Rules*, ed. Larry J. Sabato, Kyle Kondik, and Geoffrey Skelley (Lanham, MD: Rowman & Littlefield, 2017), 181–82.

47. Marian Currinder, "Campaign Finance: Fundraising and Spending in the 2008 Elections," in *The Elections of 2008*, ed. Michael Nelson (Washington, DC: Congressional Quarterly Press, 2010), 166.

48. Ibid., 167.

49. Toner and Trainer, "Six-Billion-Dollar Election," 92.

50. Ibid.

51. Toner and Trainer, "$7 Billion Election," 181–90.

52. "Donald Trump," OpenSecrets.org, November 17, 2017, accessed November 18, 2018, https://www.opensecrets.org/pres16/candidate.php?id=N00023864.

53. "Hillary Clinton," OpenSecrets.org, November 17, 2017, accessed November 18, 2018, https://www.opensecrets.org/pres16/candidate.php?id=N00000019.

54. Many researchers have attempted to establish the major determinants of human attraction. Two of the better summaries of current research, on which this analysis is based, are Joseph Devito, *The Interpersonal Communication Book* (New York: Longman, 2003), 253–56; and Stewart L. Tubbs and Sylvia Moss, *Human Communication* (New York: Random House, 1987), 66–75.

55. This guideline is a long-standing one used by Republican and Democratic National Committee field staff to help determine which candidates are the most viable and hence warrant aid from their respective national committees.

56. Cathy Allen, "Peer Pressure Politics: Getting Your Money's Worth from Friends and Colleagues," *Campaigns and Elections*, June/July 1990, 49.

57. Cathy Allen, "How to Ask for Money," *Campaigns and Elections*, April 1998, 25.

58. Ibid., 27.

59. Tubbs and Moss, *Human Communication*, 72–73.

60. "Big Bird in the Presidential Debate: Mitt Advocating Cutting Funding for Sesame Street, PBS," *Washington Post*, October 10, 2012, accessed January 1, 2015, www.wash ingtonpost.com/politics/decision2012/big-bird-in-the-presidential-debate-mitt-romney -advocates-cutting-funding-for-sesame-street-pbs/2012/10/04/f7f280ba-0e1f-11e2-bb5e -492c0d30bff6_story.html.

61. "Does Mitt Romney Want to 'Kill' Big Bird?" *Washington Post*, October 10, 2012, accessed January 1, 2015, www.washingtonpost.com/blogs/fact-checker/post/does-mitt -romney-want-to-kill-big-bird/2012/10/09/336f9172-127c-11e2-ba83a7a396e6b2a7_blog .html.

62. William Wilmot, *Dyadic Communication: A Transactional Perspective* (Reading, MA: Addison-Wesley, 1975), 73–74.

63. Robert Kaplan, "Psychology of Silence: Raising More Money by Psyching Out Donors," *Campaigns and Elections*, November 1991, 54.

64. Ron Faucheux, "Ask and You Shall Receive," *Campaigns and Elections*, April 2005, 25.

65. Michael Carpini, "Mediating Democratic Engagement," in *Handbook of Political Communication Research*, ed. Lynda Lee Kaid (Mahwah, NJ: Lawrence Erlbaum, 2004), 410.

66. Alan Zuckerman, "Returning to the Social Logic of Politics," in *The Social Logic of Politics: Personal Networks as Contexts for Political Behavior*, ed. Alan S. Zuckerman (Philadelphia: Temple University Press, 2004), 47.

67. R. L. Lake and Robert Huckfeldt, "Social Capital, Social Networks, and Political Participation," *Political Psychology* 19 (1998): 567–83.

68. L. Erwin Atwood and Keith R. Sanders, "Information Sources and Voting in a Primary and General Election," *Journal of Broadcasting* 20 (Summer 1976): 298.

69. Shea and Burton, *Campaign Craft*, 182–83.

70. Paul Herrnson, *Congressional Elections*, 2nd ed. (Washington, DC: Congressional Quarterly Press, 1998), 172–74.

71. John P. Robinson, "Interpersonal Influence in Election Campaigns: Two-Step Flow Hypotheses," *Public Opinion Quarterly* 40 (Fall 1976): 312; and Marilyn Jackson-Beeck, "Interpersonal and Mass Communication in Children's Political Socialization," *Journalism Quarterly* 56 (Spring 1979): 53.

72. Wayne A. Danielson, "Eisenhower's February Decision: A Study of News Impact," *Journalism Quarterly* 33 (Fall 1956): 437.

73. William D. Kimsey and L. Erwin Atwood, "A Path Model of Political Cognitions and Attitudes, Communication and Voting Behavior in a Congressional Election," *Communication Monographs* 40 (August 1979): 429.

74. Ibid., 430.

75. Robinson, "Interpersonal Influence in Election Campaigns," 304–19.

76. Ibid., 315.

77. Ibid.

78. Ibid., 316.

79. Silvo Lenart, *Shaping Political Attitudes: The Impact of Interpersonal Communication and Mass Media* (Thousand Oaks, CA: Sage, 1994), 110–12.

80. Delia Dumitrescu, "Nonverbal Communication in Politics: A Review of Research Developments, 2005–2015," *American Behavioral Scientist* 60, no. 14 (2016): 1658.

81. Ibid., 1659.

82. Ibid., 1661.

83. Ibid., 1669.

84. Ibid., 1666.

85. This discussion of social precincts is based on Stephen C. Shadegg, *The New How to Win an Election* (New York: Tapplinger, 1976), 103–19.

86. Shea and Burton, *Campaign Craft*, 200.

87. Demoinesdem, "Where the Ticket-Splitters Are," December 8, 2008, accessed November 28, 2010, http://mydd.com/2008/12/8/where-the-ticket-splitters-are.

88. "Percentage of Swing Voters Declines Compared to Four Years Ago," Pew Center for Research, May 3, 2012, accessed January 2, 2014, www.pewresearch.org/daily-num ber/percentage-of-swing-voters-declines-compared-to-four-years-ago.

89. "An Examination of the 2016 Electorate, Based on Validated Voters," Pew Research Center, August 9, 2018, accessed November 18, 2018, http://www.people-press .org/2018/08/09/an-examination-of-the-2016-electorate-based-on-validated-voters.

90. Gallup, "Fewer Swing Voters 2010 Prior Midterm Years," accessed November 26, 2010, www.gallup.com/poll/144065/fewer-swing-voters-2010-prior-midterm-years.aspx.

91. Michael Barone, "American Politics in the Networking Era," *National Journal*, February 25, 2005.

92. Adam Carrington and James Kresge, "In the Midst of History: The Ground Game in Ohio." *On Principle* 13, no. 1 (April 2005).

93. Barone, "American Politics," 2.

94. Kathleen Hall Jamieson, *Electing the President, 2008* (Philadelphia: University of Pennsylvania Press, 2009), 43, 251–62.

95. Ibid., 44.

96. Ibid., 45.

97. Ibid., 156.

98. Ibid., 156.

99. Ibid., 157.

100. Larry J. Sabato, "The Obama Encore That Broke Some Rules," in *Barack Obama and the New America*, ed. Larry J. Sabato (Lanham, MD: Rowman & Littlefield, 2013), 9.

101. Sasha Issenberg, "Why Obama Is Better at Getting Out the Vote," *Slate*, November 5, 2012, accessed January 2, 2015, www.slate.com/articles/news_and_politics/victory_ lab/2012/11/obama_s_get_out_the_vote_effort_why_it_s_better_than_romney_s.html.

102. Ibid.

103. Nick Judd, "Obama's Targeted GOTV on Facebook Reached 5 Million Voters, Goff Says," Techpresident.com, November 30, 2012, accessed January 2, 2015, techpresident .com/news/23202/obamas-targeted-gotv-facebook-reached-5-million-voters-goff-says.

104. Toner and Trainer, "Six-Billion-Dollar Election."

105. Susan Milligan, "The Fight on the Ground," *US News*, October 14, 2016, accessed November 18, 2018, https://www.usnews.com/news/the-report/articles/2016-10-14/ donald-trump-abandons-the-ground-game.

106. Timothy Stephen, Teresa M. Harrison, William Husson, and David Albert, "Interpersonal Communication Styles of Political Candidates: Predicting Winning and Losing Candidates in Three U.S. Presidential Elections," in *Presidential Candidate Images*, ed. Kenneth L. Hacker (Lanham, MD: Rowman & Littlefield, 2004), 177–96.

# 11

❦

# Advertising in
# Political Campaigns

There are four basic channels of campaign communication. They include electronic media, print media, display media (e.g., billboards), and personal contact. The greatest challenge is to determine the best combination of media to reach the potential audience and that which best communicates campaign themes. In addition, the factors of timing, money, and distribution are critical considerations. Candidates must decide when, where, and how much they will concentrate their communication efforts, making sure the campaign does not peak too soon or spend too much in areas of little consequence or electoral support.

Advertising is an essential and major element of all campaigns whether local, regional, statewide, or national in scope. Although there are numerous specific advertising formats and strategies, there are four basic political advertising messages. There are positive messages designed to promote the positive personal characteristics and attributes of a candidate. Elements of leadership, character, and experience are highlighted within the context of traditional values and those of the "American Dream." Negative messages are specifically designed to attack the opponent. They tend to focus on the personal weaknesses, voting record, or public pronouncements of the candidate. Comparative messages are still designed to attack the opponent but tend to focus on issue positions. Comparative messages give the impression of providing two sides or positions of an issue, but the resulting comparisons clearly favor the candidate sponsoring the ad. Finally, there are response messages designed to directly answer opponent charges, allegations, and attacks.

Many campaigns are waged essentially through advertising, primarily over radio and television. These campaigns tend to be high-profile races, such as those for national and statewide office. In many urban areas, lower races such as those for city offices are also waged heavily using radio and television. However, in lower-level races, where budgets preclude the extensive use of radio and television or where local demographic conditions make it impractical, other forms of advertising remain dominant. Moreover, even high-profile media campaigns cannot forsake the more traditional, often pre–electronic media means of campaigning and advertising. If they do so, they run a serious risk of incurring consequences that so badly damage their efforts, even a highly effective media campaign cannot win the election.

Four thoughts should always be kept in mind when considering the uses of political advertising: (1) that political advertising is enormously costly, not only in dollars but also in time and effort; (2) that as appealing as television commercials may be, rarely can a campaign be waged successfully by relying exclusively on television; (3) that advertising media are simply vehicles for conveying the images and ideas of candidates, and it is the images and ideas, not the size and placement of the commercial buy, that ultimately are of the most consequence; and (4) all campaigns from national down to the most local must utilize new and social media. Today, such media are essential in terms of message targeting, fundraising, and GOTV efforts. The remainder of this chapter focuses first on factors that affect the selection and use of various advertising media available to political campaigners. A much more detailed discussion of the growing influence and role of social media in campaigns will be explored in chapter 12. Second, we consider what have become key figures in many contemporary campaigns—professional political consultants—with emphasis on those who specialize in media.

## DEVELOPING A MASTER PLAN FOR POLITICAL ADVERTISING

The array of advertising media that has been used in political campaigns is staggering. A partial listing includes brochures, newsletters, questionnaires, letters, billboards, yard signs, bumper stickers, newspaper advertisements, magazine advertisements, buttons, pencils, banner ads, faxes, internet home pages, social media ads, tweets, videos, and, of course, radio and television commercials. Indeed, the list is endless. Political campaigners have used virtually every technological advance in communication to facilitate getting their messages to the public. However, almost every campaigner pays homage to the adage that the good campaign dominates the dominant media. If the dominant medium in the school board election is yard signs, the good campaign will have the best and the most yard signs. If the dominant medium in the congressional race is television, the good campaign will have the best and the most television commercials.

Among the first responsibilities of any campaign is to develop a master plan that should include a section on expected advertising. Typically, such a plan should be developed fifteen to eighteen months before Election Day[1] and should serve to coordinate all the paid media activities of the campaign. Not only must all the paid media activities of the campaign be coordinated with one another, but the paid media component of the campaign must also be coordinated with other components of the campaign, including the overall strategy and targeting, the budget and fund-raising, and the earned media.[2] Obviously occasions will arise when events make it necessary to deviate from the overall plan. However, well-run campaigns plan their media activities early and then stick as closely as possible to their overall blueprint, adjusting as events make it necessary.

Before the launch of a campaign, much of a digital strategy should be in place prior to any public hint or announcement of a campaign.[3] Months before any announcement, the campaign needs to establish Twitter and Facebook accounts to start building and expanding social media contacts.

The campaign should also purchase domain names. Again, these should be purchased before any hints of a campaign. You don't want to be in the position to purchase a name at an exorbitant fee once the campaign begins. Also, you don't want your opponent to establish a related site that will post attack and negative information. It is important to purchase at the beginning every combination of the candidate's first and last names possible, including all nicknames. One should also even purchase domains of misspellings of the candidate's name. Consultant Laura Packard recommends using the candidate's full name in the domain. This helps with recognition by search engines. Having established a domain well in advance of announcing one's candidacy, most newspaper articles and blog posts will include the campaign website in their copy, thus further optimizing search engine access.

Packard recommends several operational tasks for campaigns to perform to maximize a successful web presence. She highly recommends that campaigns get professional headshots and photos for the website and social media profiles. It is also important to get professional help with all graphics and logos. Creative elements should be consistent across all media. In terms of the site itself, at a minimum a simple "splash page" on the website should give some information about the candidate and have a donate option, email sign-up (for followers and to recruit volunteers), and social media links. Finally, the announcement email and the press release should be written and ready to send to contacts. The day of the announcement, everything should go live.

The advantages of planning cannot be overestimated. Decisions that are made as the campaign is beginning tend to be made more dispassionately and are typically based on greater objectivity, thought, and research. Decisions made impulsively in response to campaign events are typically subject to less thought, less research, and less analysis, and hence are prone to be less successful.

The many advantages of planning can be best illustrated by an example. Let us imagine that we are involved in planning a congressional primary race. Our candidate is only moderately known in the district. However, our opponent is also known only moderately in the district. They are vying for the nomination to succeed a popular incumbent who is retiring after twenty-four years in Congress. We will imagine that our candidate is a university professor who has served on local school boards and subsequently was elected mayor of a small college town of twenty-one thousand within the district, a position she currently holds. She is also highly active in supporting the arts and has been a longtime supporter of the local symphony orchestra. Our opponent is a young lawyer who has just completed his second term in the state House of Representatives, representing a district of about eighty thousand, located in the suburbs of a large city. His district comprises about one-fourth of the congressional district; the town in which our candidate serves as mayor comprises only about 6 percent of the district. Another 25 percent of the district is composed of suburbs, such as the one our opponent has represented, and about half the district is rural, although the rural area includes several towns of about fifteen thousand to twenty-five thousand, such as the one our candidate has served as mayor. For the sake of illustration, we will imagine that traditionally candidates wait until January before announcing their candidacy for the May 1 primary.

Using the surfacing period during the summer of the year preceding the election, we draft our first master plan. We decide to run a series of radio and television commercials for ten days immediately after declaring candidacy in January. Moreover, we decide to take out large advertisements in the three daily papers that serve the district and in each of the district's ten highest-circulation weekly papers in the week immediately following our candidate's announcement. Our advertising master plan then calls for three direct mail efforts in February and March. The first two mailings (in February) are to target groups that may be expected to be highly supportive of the candidate. We might imagine a master plan that calls for a mailing on February 12 to individuals concerned with education, such as members of teacher groups, PTAs, and similar organizations. The master plan then calls for a mailing on February 25 to members of a variety of groups concerned with culture and music, such as season-ticket purchasers to local theater groups, symphonies, and ballets. The master plan we develop further calls for a mailing on March 25 to all voters eligible to participate in the primary. In addition to mailings, we develop a master plan that calls for the distribution of five hundred yard signs during the first two weeks of March and a major push to distribute five hundred yard signs on each of the last two weekends of March.

Since the primary election is scheduled for May 1, we decide that our radio advertising should start on April 1, doubling in quantity every ten days. That is, for every commercial run between April 1 and 10, two radio commercials will be run between April 11 and 20. For every commercial run between April 11 and 20, two radio commercials will be run between April 20 and May 1. Moreover, we decide to use a second and final round of television commercials to start on April 1, and their number is to double on April 21.

Additionally, the master plan calls for running large advertisements in each of the three daily papers and in each of the ten largest weekly papers in the district during the last phase of the campaign. Advertisements will be placed on each of the last three days in the three dailies and in each of the last two editions for the ten weekly papers. Finally, the master plan calls for a final mailing to all eligible voters to be sent on April 25, to be received by voters within three days of the election.

Notice what developing this relatively simple advertising plan has forced us to do and how it impacts on and governs much of the rest of the campaign. The first advantage to developing this plan early is that it forces us to identify our basic goal in the campaign. In this example, we have one basic goal: acquiring name recognition as a prominent member of our party. Since this is a primary, there may not be major differences between the candidates. Moreover, since the incumbent of our party has won this congressional seat for the last twenty-four years, securing the party nomination may in itself be the critical step necessary for our candidate's ultimate election. In most campaigns, the first advantage to developing an initial advertising program is that it forces the campaign to develop and prioritize its overall objectives or goals for the campaign.

Since our goal is recognition, we have decided to campaign vigorously from the moment of our announcement. If we are going to use newspapers, radio, and television all in the first weeks of the campaign, as our plan calls for, then clearly, we need money early in the campaign. Our master plan for advertising must be coordinated with our fund-raising. For example, if we cannot raise money for ten days' worth of radio and television at the outset of the campaign, what can we do? Perhaps we should curtail the radio and television and use yard signs earlier in the campaign. Yard signs, however, may call for considerable use of volunteers. Yards have to be solicited; signs have to be made and distributed. We can estimate the cost of producing commercials and buying time. We can estimate the number of volunteers needed to produce and place yard signs. The second advantage to planning our advertising campaign early is that it forces us to work closely with those involved in fund-raising and volunteer efforts, making sure the entire campaign is well coordinated.

In this example, we may conclude that, since name recognition is clearly an early problem for us, we are best served, given our limited initial finances, by using radio, billboards, and yard signs early in the campaign. These forms of media can all be used effectively to help establish early name recognition. Moreover, they are typically less expensive than newspaper advertisements and television commercials. Hopefully, early in the campaign when we are laying out our positions, we may be able to supplement advertising with free media, such as stories in newspapers and stories and interviews on local radio and television shows. Later, when we have more money, and when we may need to communicate more than our name and party, billboards and yard signs will be of little help. Using them in March, as we originally planned, may not make as much sense as using them earlier, which also enables us to save money for newspaper and television advertisements that we might need later in the campaign to explain our positions. Moreover, if we use yard signs early, it forces our volunteer coordinators to amass a large number of volunteers early, and those people may be vital to our later efforts to put out a variety of mailings and mount a strong get-out-the-vote effort. Thus, as we plan early, we are able to refine our advertising program in those ways that best enable us to blend the efforts of all elements of the campaign.

Additionally, as we begin to recognize our financial problems, we may choose to divert a greater effort in that area. We may be forced to have our candidate spend a greater percentage of her time on fund-raising. We may have to develop extra fund-raising activities. Regardless of our situation, by giving ourselves ample time to plan, we can make the most of whatever resources we have available to us. Among the factors that our advance media planning should consider are the following:

- relative costs in dollars of available media
- relative costs in candidate time/volunteer effort or other campaign resources of available media
- ability of media to target specific audiences
- ability of various media to accomplish specific goals of advertising
- sequential development of advertising
- coordinating advertising with the remainder of the campaign

We can best understand many of these factors by examining the various media that campaigners can choose to employ.

## BASIC CONSIDERATIONS IN THE SELECTION OF POLITICAL ADVERTISING MEDIA

Political campaigns make use of eight types of advertising media: display graphics, brochures, direct mail, telephone, print, radio, television, and the internet. Each of these options has virtues, and each has liabilities. Planning, to evaluate those virtues and liabilities in relation to the factors listed above, facilitates a skillfully developed campaign advertising program. Hence, this discussion focuses on each of the eight types of advertising media in relation to the factors that must be considered as the campaign's advertising program is developed.

### Display Graphics

Display advertising, also called graphic advertising, most commonly includes such items as billboards, posters, yard signs, bumper stickers, and buttons. Such advertising has been a part of American campaigning virtually from our nation's inception. As technology has changed, so, too, has display advertising. For example, campaign buttons were virtually unknown until the late nineteenth century. But by 1896, the celluloid button process had been patented, and in the 1896 campaigns of William McKinley and William Jennings Bryan, buttons assumed their place in the arsenal of the campaign persuader. In the 1920s, technological changes allowed for the lithographed production of buttons on tin. This process did not allow for the elaborate artwork and use of photographs that celluloid buttons did, but it brought the cost of buttons down dramatically.[4]

Display advertising can be instrumental in helping (1) create and reinforce name recognition, (2) give a very quick impression of the candidate, (3) serve as a reminder medium when other campaign activity is limited, such as between a primary and the outset of the general election period, and (4) reach markets that other media cannot reach, such as rural areas.[5] If these are among the goals of the advertising campaign, and often early in the campaign they are, the use of display advertising should be considered. Such advertising normally carries an exceedingly brief message, often not more than the candidate's name or the name and a brief slogan.

Every presidential campaign tries to encapsulate its message in the campaign slogan. A good slogan crystallizes what the campaign is trying to say and provides direction for messaging. Al Ries, longtime advertising guru, argues that not all slogans are created equal.[6] Some slogans are one-sided and some slogans are two-sided. A two-sided slogan is like a two-sided knife. It cuts both ways. It says something positive about your brand and something negative about the competition. For example, Romney's 2012 slogan of "Believe in America" is a one-sided slogan. It says something positive about Romney, but nothing about Obama. His slogan is fine for those already supporting Romney and believing that Obama is an apologist for American values. According to Ries, in contrast, Obama's "forward" slogan was two-sided. This slogan implies that Republicans want to go back to the policies that failed in the past. It also claims that while the economy is still shaky, Obama needs more time to "finish the job." Donald Trump's slogan of 2016, "Make America Great Again," was two-sided. It called for a dramatic return to an America of the past in terms of "greatness" in values, economy, health care, less crime, and so on. The slogan also implies that America, currently, was not great and deficient in many ways. Hillary Clinton's slogan, "Stronger Together," was more positive and inclusive without any negative connotations.

Display graphics, the format of which does not allow for an extended message, can serve two additional important, yet often overlooked, functions. They are particularly useful in reinforcing partisans who are already committed to the candidate. When distributed at campaign meetings, rallies, and similar activities, they often enhance the spirit of the staff and volunteers, serving as a visible link between the candidate and the worker. Indeed, many campaigns will purchase a few hundred pins, bumper stickers, or yard signs, simply to keep up the morale of the staff. One candidate with whom the authors are acquainted complained so much about his lack of yard signs that the campaign manager assigned a volunteer to post fifty yard signs on the mile and a half route that the candidate took into his headquarters every morning, and then to check once a week to replace any signs that had come down. The manager reported an immediate improvement in the candidate's outlook and performance! On occasion, the cost for a small amount of display / graphic advertising is well worth the improved staff and volunteer morale that it provides.

Finally, if handled well, display graphics can be used to impress voters with the candidate's strength and help to create a bandwagon effect. For example, most consultants would advise that yard signs or bumper stickers not be given out in a small trickle, a few every day. Rather, a well-coordinated effort should be made to distribute a massive number of them simultaneously. So, for example, on September 9 there are virtually no yard signs in the district. All of a sudden, on September 10, there seems to be one on every block. Although there is not a sign on every block, the startlingly sudden appearance of many signs multiplies their effectiveness, making the casual voter highly aware of them and often suggesting to that voter that the candidate must have a large organization behind him to get up so many signs so quickly. Putting up massive numbers of yard signs all at once makes their impact far stronger, suggests massive support for the candidate, and helps create a bandwagon effect among casual voters. A similar effect can be achieved by distributing bumper stickers throughout the district all at once. Many campaigns will post volunteers in every high school football field parking lot one Friday night in early October, and in that fashion, they distribute thousands of bumper stickers simultaneously. The same effect can be achieved by using shopping mall parking lots.

In recent years, the quantity and variety of display graphic advertising in political campaigns have diminished. This is a direct function of cost. As recently as twenty-five years ago, it was not uncommon for a voter to be able to walk into the campaign office of a candidate and be given pins, bumper stickers, and similar materials, not only of that candidate but also of other candidates of the same party. Today, voters seeking such material are often asked to leave a contribution for every button or bumper sticker they take.

Display graphics are expensive, in terms of dollars as well as time and effort. Costs vary from community to community, although national suppliers that specialize in campaign materials tend to be exceedingly competitive. The cost for one thousand 2.25-inch celluloid buttons that allow the use of photographs, other elaborate artwork, and a variety of colors will be about $500, or fifty cents each, from most national suppliers. Most suppliers offer quantity discounts for orders of twenty-five hundred, five thousand, or more, which will bring the price per button down. Large-quantity orders, well over one thousand, will reduce the costs by about twenty cents per button.[7] In recent years, many campaigns have saved on the cost of buttons by utilizing adhesive lapel stickers. These stickers will adhere to clothing, serving the same name recognition function as a button. Unlike a button, though, they cannot be readily reused from day to day. The current cost for 2.5-inch round lapel stickers, utilizing one color on a solid contrasting background, is $300 per thousand, about thirty cents each. Most suppliers will offer substantial discounts for volume purchases, bringing the costs down to approximately ten cents for each label when five thousand labels are ordered and six cents each for twenty-five thousand labels. Additionally, some suppliers will offer reduced rates for labels if they are purchased simultaneously with buttons.[8]

In addition to buttons or stickers, perhaps the most popular small form of display graphic is the bumper sticker. They function as "mini-billboards" providing an inexpensive way to build name recognition and impressions of candidate momentum. They also, when associated with specific individuals, serve as a personal endorsement of a campaign. The current cost for a thousand of the simplest, standard 3-by-11-inch bumper stickers, one color printed on a standard background color, is about $500, or fifty cents each. Most vendors offer a substantial discount for volume. Five thousand of the same bumper stickers will cost about $2,000, which brings the cost down to forty cents each.[9]

A wide variety of other smaller forms of display graphics have been used by campaigns. They include such products as emery boards, car litter bags, pocket combs, pens, pencils, and balloons—always with the candidate's name prominently displayed. Prices for these smaller forms of display advertising vary, but most can be obtained for between $500 and $1,000 per thousand.[10]

Larger forms of display advertising such as billboards and yard signs are also costly. The costs of billboards vary greatly depending upon size, location, printed or digital, and number of signs in a package. In larger cities, the price can range from $3,000 to over $15,000 per month. If a campaign wishes to maximize the number of "views" in high-traffic areas, the costs could easily exceed $20,000. Purchases to cover more of a market or for longer durations of time will typically be discounted.

Yard signs are also costly. Their price will vary depending on such factors as the size and quality of the material used. However, because they are designed to remain outside, and must be weather resistant, many campaigns are opting to use corrugated plastic yard signs. The current cost for one thousand professionally printed corrugated plastic yard signs, measuring a standard 18-by-24-inch size, using one-color printing on a standard background color with the same copy and color on both sides, ranges from about $2,000 to $3,000 from national suppliers (wire stakes separate).[11] It should be remembered that typically some expenses will be incurred in transporting and erecting yard signs throughout the district.

Increasingly, polyethylene bags or sleeves have replaced or supplemented the materials used by thousands of campaigns for their yard signs. These signs are printed on a heavy-duty polyethylene plastic bag or sleeve that fits over a wire frame, provided and included in the cost. Patriot Signage, the leading supplier of this alternative to traditional yard signs, prices a 26-by-16-inch sign utilizing one color plus white at $2,280 per thousand and $3,880 for four color, including the metal frames over which the bag or sleeve is spread. As with the suppliers of most display graphics, purchases in larger quantity will result in substantial price reductions.[12]

## Brochures

A basic, generic brochure is the fundamental piece of campaign advertising for local races. It is the introductory piece, and perhaps the only piece, of campaign literature. It usually provides a brief biography with several photos and a list of key issues of the campaign. Brochures are very versatile and can be used in direct mail and handed out at neighborhood walks and at all campaign activities.[13] In terms of brochure copy, one should keep to one major idea/issue/theme per paragraph, use short sentences, use bullet points when possible, and divide the text into sections.[14] The primary color and design should be consistent with all printed materials. Photos should include one of the candidate, "action" shots, and the candidate interacting with various or key constituent groups. The content should provide a clear overview of the qualifications of the candidate, issue positions, and motivation for citizen support.

## Direct Mail

In this day of new technology and instant messaging, many would think direct mail or "snail mail" advertising would not be effective. However, today as never before, mail allows for more precise targeting and more unique creativity and fills the gap in the increasing difficulty in reaching people through more traditional media. Although rather self-serving, the United States Postal Service commissioned a voter survey on the effectiveness and attitudes about the use of direct mail in political campaigns. The survey was focused on Virginia's gubernatorial race in 2017. Among the results of the survey, 68 percent of surveyed voters ranked direct mail among the three most credible forms of political advertising. Nearly half of voters in the survey indicated that the political direct mail received influenced their voting decision. A look behind the numbers reveals that Millennials were the most likely to read the mail at 76 percent, compared to just 45 percent of Gen Xers and 38 percent of Baby Boomers. Also interesting in terms of Millennials, nearly 60 percent indicated that the mail read caused them to go to the internet to learn more about the candidates.[15]

Romney and the Republican National Committee spent more than $100 million on mail costs, compared to $70 million for the Obama campaign in 2012.[16] In fact, in the 2014 campaigns, party committees and outside groups spent $150 million on political direct mail.[17] The 2016 presidential campaign doubled that number, spending $301 million in direct mail.[18] Direct mail advertising provides campaigns with one enormous advantage that cannot be readily duplicated by any other form of political advertising. It allows the campaign to be highly selective in targeting audiences. The wise use of radio and television commercials or of newspaper and magazine advertisements also allows for some degree of targeting. However, direct mail allows the campaign to target an audience more precisely than virtually any other form of advertising. The only comparable media, in terms of precise targeting, is the telephone.

With bigger computer files and commercial databases, messages can be individualized in ways never possible before. The opportunities of targeting are almost limitless. Likewise, innovation in printing technologies allows for personalization as well as attention-getting creative content.

Unlike many other forms of campaign communication, direct mail can be considered "high-interest, low-backlash communication."[19] That is, a direct mail piece can be tailored to reflect the interests of a specific constituency. For example, the candidate's views on reestablishing the draft might be featured in a mailing sent to a large section of the district near a university, where many residents are young. However, the candidate's views on Social Security can be featured in a mailing sent to an immediately adjacent retirement community in the district where the residents are older. Such mailings focus on topics of high interest to the recipients. The more specific and tailored the message, the more effective the piece. In addition, they create low backlash. If the candidate spoke about reestablishing the draft or Social Security on radio or television, or in the print media, it is possible that many viewers or readers would have little interest in the topic of the ad and hence react negatively to the candidate for boring them by failing to address their concerns. By using direct mail to target audiences, the likelihood of high recipient interest is increased and the risk of backlash is largely eliminated.

Not only does direct mail allow for precise targeting of audiences, but it also allows for an extended message. It is a vehicle that enables candidates to fully express themselves on a given issue. It is not uncommon for candidates to use letters and mailings that run four or more pages in length to treat one specific issue or a group of closely related issues. For example, a candidate may wish to fully explain her position on real estate taxes. To do so might require considerable radio and television time or considerable newspaper space, and hence be extremely expensive. However, by using a mailing piece directed at property owners, the candidate can explain her position more fully than would be possible by using other media, to an audience of individuals targeted precisely because of their interest in property taxes. The candidate might actually save money because her direct mail is targeted more narrowly, and she will not be paying for audience members who might not be affected by her comments on property taxes.

Because it allows for precise targeting and because it can be used to convey a long message, political campaigns have used direct mail both to persuade voters and to raise money from contributors. In the 1970s, direct mail became the principal means of fund-raising for a variety of candidates, most notably George McGovern, who harnessed the direct mail team of Morris Dees and Tom Collins to find approximately 250,000 supporters who financed his presidential campaign largely by responding to his repeated direct mail solicitations.[20] Since that time, fund-raising is the primary function of direct mail in political campaigns. Professionals use emotion and motivational techniques to increase contributions. They know, for example, that voters are more likely to give if the letter specifies how the funds will be used. Participation devices increase interest and thus many mailings include opinion surveys or sample ballots. In addition, suggested contribution amounts tend to start with the largest amount, such as $500, $250, $100, or $50. Professionals also know that direct mail donors are more committed to the candidate and are likely to contribute again in subsequent mailings.

Many specialists in the use of direct mail suggest that it is most effective in raising funds among older voters and hence is best suited to use with contributor lists that are oriented toward older voters.[21] Indeed, recent research suggests that the person who responds to direct mail is at least fifty-five years old.[22] In contrast, in recent years, the internet has often been mentioned as a medium that is unusually well suited to raising funds among younger voters.[23] Although direct mail is an expensive way of raising funds, with 60 to 70 percent of every dollar collected often going to offset the cost of the mailing, it has been the principal means of fund-raising for many candidates.[24] Although direct mail's fund-raising use may be declining, in part as a consequence of the use of the internet for this purpose, it nevertheless remains a valuable tool for conveying both persuasive messages and fund-raising appeals to voters.

The dollar costs of direct mail are difficult to assess because mail pieces can be as simple as a photocopied flyer or as elaborate as a multicolor, multipage letter and brochure with pictures produced on high-quality stock. There are also considerations of postage, design, printing, and distribution lists of names. The largest expense, of course, is postage. Mailing lists charge per thousand names and the price varies depending on the number of criteria desired. There are direct mail vendors that will do all the processing, labeling, addressing, presorting, and delivery of mail drop. As with most display graphics, quantity orders yield considerable discounts. Keep in mind that while costs for the mailing piece itself normally diminish as the number of pieces purchased increases, the larger the mailing, the larger the costs of postage and the larger the costs in the use of volunteer time or payment to a direct mail house that arranges the mailing.

By controlling the costs of the individual mail piece itself, as well as the size of the mailing, the cost of direct mail can generally be managed to conform to the campaign's needs, enabling most campaigns to use mailings. Direct mailings are the major form of campaign advertising in many lower-level races. Often, the advertisements that the lower-level campaign might use in newspapers or on radio and television are likely to be lost in the large number of political advertisements that flood those media in the weeks before election. Moreover, often the costs of purchasing sufficient radio or television time, or newspaper space, are simply beyond the ability of small local campaigns. Direct mail, which can be made to fit most campaign budgets, can be targeted to specific voter blocs, and allows candidates to explain themselves thoroughly, is often critical in lower-level races. Direct mail tends to work best for both fund-raising and general advertising purposes if the campaign expects a low voter turnout, if the district or geographic area is not part of a major media market, or if the race is "down-ballot" in an expensive media market. Also, in general, campaigns normally send about 20 percent of direct mail where the candidate is the strongest or weakest and about 80 percent in swing areas.[25]

Finally, direct mail is used to attack or "hit" opponents. Larry Sabato refers to direct mail as "the poisoned pen of politics."[26] The "hit" is based upon opposition research and the "hits" may be on the opponent's poor attendance record, certain key votes, over-budget spending, lack of effectiveness, and so forth. The attacks should be direct, simple, and clear. Actually, attack direct mail is most effective a week before the election. This reduces time for the opponent to challenge or respond. In fact, some of the most negative direct mail pieces arrive the Saturday before the Tuesday election.

Indeed, while most laypersons think of television as the principal medium of political campaigns, more money is actually spent on direct mail than on any other campaign medium. When every race from the bottom of the ballot to the top is counted, and when all the expenses involved in direct mailings (including list rentals, database management, labeling, printing, and of course postage) are included, political candidates and their committees spent more money on direct mail than on any other advertising medium, with the exception of contemporary presidential races. As with any form of campaign communication, some principles have proven successful in the use of direct mail. Hal Malchow, creative director of The November Group, a well-respected political direct mail firm, has suggested a variety of guidelines for designing direct mail. Among them are:

- *Give the voter a reason to read your mailing.* Begin the mail piece in a dramatic and compelling way. The opening panel of the mail piece should attract attention with a dramatic headline or an interesting photograph.
- *Localize your message.* Because direct mail facilitates very precise targeting, it should be used accordingly. If a neighborhood in your district is concerned about a school issue or a proposed highway, be sure that the mail sent to that community reflects your interest in their concern and does not ignore local issues in favor of simply treating issues of more general concern throughout your constituency.
- *Use the twenty-second test.* Malchow claims that the average voter will give a mail piece between twenty and sixty seconds. "They will look at the cover, the headlines, the pictures and often the captions under the photographs. But few people will actually read your literature." Consequently, "to be effective, you have to tell your story in a 20-second glance. Can someone in 20 seconds read the headlines, look at the pictures and maybe read the captions and come away with the basic points of your message? If not, you have not designed a good piece of campaign literature."
- *Use a letter shop.* Malchow is an advocate of using a professional mailing organization. He claims, "We all want to save money, but don't be a dunce. A letter shop is cheaper than pizza and beer for your volunteers." Malchow has found that, for two to five cents per piece, a letter shop will automatically label your pieces, sort and bag the mail, and fully prepare it for the post office in a manner that qualifies for full postal discounts for presorted

mail. He claims that "even the poorest campaign should avoid" hand labeling and sorting third-class mail. He finds such a task to be both so difficult
and so time-consuming that the costs of having it done professionally are
well worth the expense.[27]

Since 75 percent of all direct mail is not opened, Malchow and others focus not
only on the content of the direct mail piece, but also on the envelope. Malchow has
suggested not even utilizing an envelope. To save money, and more importantly
to gain attention, he recommends using oversized postcards, unusual shapes, and
folded pieces that bear no resemblance to a letter or traditional campaign brochure.[28] Other direct mail specialists focus on using the envelope itself to attract
attention. Todd Meredith, co-owner of the Direct Mail Marketing Group, who has
worked on behalf of forty members of Congress, claims that varying envelope
color and size are the most basic ways of gaining voter attention.[29]

With new technologies and the internet, some observers speculate that direct
mail may be a dying medium. However, Liz Chadderdon disagrees. "This new
generation that's all about Facebook now, will they be Facebooking at 40? If they
are, that will obviously change the way we communicate with them. Right now,
I may have five email addresses, but if you want to catch me, I still get my bills
in one place. So, we're not dying yet. And it seems like every time I turn around
there's another mail firm out there. I don't feel that way about media and polling."[30] For Steven Stenberg, the future challenges for direct mail are no different
from those of other past media. "There are certainly challenges with younger voters as it pertains to direct mail, but TV has that same problem."[31]

**Telephone Contact Services**

The telephone became a tool of political campaigns in the 1960s. Calling voters
was primarily a volunteer operation. Robocalls, automated political phone calls,
started in the mid-1970s. Recorded messages by celebrities became routine and
are still used today as "get-out-the-vote" efforts.[32]

Growing sophistication in the application of computer technology to campaigning has resulted not only in the growth of direct mail but also in the growth
of telephone contact services. Companies providing such services, in many instances, will work from voter lists that they have prepared and will sell or lease to
candidates, as well as from lists that the campaign itself provides. Campaigns will
use telephone contact for a variety of purposes. Most commonly, it will be used to
deliver persuasive messages, raise money, and get out the vote on Election Day.

According to Walter and Anne Clinton, there is usually close coordination between direct mail efforts and phone efforts in three distinct phases. The first is a
sensitizing phase where voters get a short and direct phone call asking for support
and advising them to be on the lookout for something coming in the mail. Within
a day or so, the voter receives a piece of direct mail from the campaign. The second phase, identification, occurs about two months before the election. The goal
of this phase is to identify those who favor the candidate or are leaning toward
voting for the candidate. The phone call identifies the campaign and proceeds to
ask several questions, including: Do you support the candidate? If so, why? And if

not, why? This information allows for the creation of a specific and tailored piece of direct mail personalized for the voter. One week to ten days out, the phone call targets voters by specific issues to commit support for the candidate as well as to motivate the person to actually vote. For example, the call may target senior citizens with a message of support for Social Security. The final phase is to get out the vote, where identified supporters are called at least twice within a couple of days of the election. The call is straightforward, not so much asking for support, but urging the individual to go to the polls.[33]

When persuasion is the goal, voters can be targeted by demographic characteristics, and a persuasive message can be scripted for members of each group being called. Similarly, fund-raising solicitations can also be narrowly targeted and a precise script developed to use with various types of potential contributors. Telephone contact, like direct mail, allows for precise targeting. On Election Day, telephones are an essential part of the final get-out-the-vote efforts. As the day progresses, voters previously identified as supportive can be contacted to remind them, and if necessary help them, to get to the polls.

Telephone contact firms will provide several services to a campaign. First, they will often script the phone conversation. Second, they will provide professionally trained callers to actually make the calls. Third, they will provide state-of-the-art equipment to facilitate efficient use of the phone. Predictive dialing systems, used by most major national telephone contact services, which utilize sophisticated dialing equipment and computer software, can provide the campaign with major savings in time and cost. Typically, by filtering out all busy signals, answering machines, disconnected lines, and other useless responses, such systems allow the campaign to deliver as many as thirty to forty messages of ninety seconds in length each hour from each phone being used. Noncomputerized phone banks will average about fifteen calls per phone, per hour, of the same length. Moreover, these systems can reduce the per-call cost of reaching voters by 30 percent or more, often bringing the costs down to under a dollar a call for persuasive messages and as little as thirty-five cents or less for Election Day get-out-the-vote calls. In addition, a sustained effort can reach a large number of voters. With good equipment, a fifty-line phone bank, using a ninety-second script, operating three hours an evening, can place approximately five thousand calls per night.[34]

Since 2006, an innovation was introduced to set up "telephone town halls" with a candidate and literally thousands of participants by telephone. The participants can be targeted by geography, demographic criteria, or issue concerns. Campaigns quickly discovered that participants are more likely to contribute to the campaign. This service allows a candidate to "meet" and "interact" with many more potential voters than doing so in person.

The Telephone Consumer Protection Act of 1991 provides guidelines regulating phone contact with the public. In general, there are certain hours when calls cannot be made, and they may not use autodialers or recorded messages that result in costs to the receiver. However, there are several exceptions; businesses are allowed to call customers where there is an established relationship, and calls can be made by nonprofit organizations and for noncommercial purposes, which include polling and political campaigns. Thus, it is legal for campaigns to call voters on landline phones using those annoying autodialers or "robocalls" (with prerecorded messages). Interestingly, it is not legal for campaigns to contact individuals by their cell phones "without prior express consent." However, campaigns have several techniques to get voters to share cell phone numbers. In addition, if one uses a cell phone number as the contact number when registering to vote, that number can be called by campaigns.[35]

Caller ID, answering machines, and, of course, cell phones make it harder for campaigns to get the attention of voters. Campaigns continue to develop tactics and techniques to meet these challenges. Thus, despite all the new technologies, there is still a very important role for phones in political campaigns.

## Print Advertising

Print advertisements in newspapers and magazines have been a part of American campaigns from our nation's inception.[36] Newspaper and magazine advertisements, the two types of print advertisements on which this section focuses, offer political advertisers several advantages. First, they provide for timeliness. Not only can the campaign plan well in advance to determine precisely when it wants an advertisement to run, but normally the campaign can make changes, both in the advertisement content and in the advertisement size, relatively quickly. Consequently, utilizing the daily paper may be an effective means of quickly countering an opposition argument. Newspapers also offer the broadest reach of mass media, providing exposure to a wide range of readers. Certainly, in local elections, newspaper advertising costs less per thousand readers than television, radio, and direct mail. Also, newspapers offer a variety of ad sizes, thus allowing many cost options. In terms of creativity, newspapers offer flexibility in ad content, placement, and design.

Unlike television, radio, or cable, ad space is always available. Newspapers do not run out of inventory (all ads are laid out first, then the news content; in effect, the length of newspapers is dictated not by all the news worthy to print, but by the number of ads). It should also be noted that newspaper readers are voters. Typically, nine out of ten newspaper readers cast ballots in presidential elections. Even in off-year elections, daily newspaper readers outvote other media observers. In addition, the people believe newspapers to be more believable and authentic than other media.[37]

Typically, if advertisement space has been purchased in advance, the copy can be changed on short notice in most metropolitan dailies. Additionally, a new advertisement can be purchased on short notice.[38] Since skilled writers can normally produce a political advertisement extremely quickly, the daily paper is an efficient means of responding to opponents. Radio commercials offer a similar advantage, but television is normally not as advantageous. Although television stations can accommodate changes in commercials, it normally takes a greater effort to produce a television commercial than to produce a newspaper or radio spot, making it more difficult for the candidate to respond rapidly through television. This is not to say that television commercials cannot be changed, for frequently they are. However, typically, the process is either slower or entails more hardship on the campaign.[39]

Newspapers and magazine advertisements also offer the opportunity for candidates to express themselves more fully than do most other types of paid advertising. Candidates can present a considerable amount of material about themselves in a full-page or even a half- or quarter-page advertisement. Speaking at the normal rate of speed, a sixty-second radio or television commercial forces the campaign to reduce its message to one hundred and fifty words or less.[40] By adjusting the size of both the advertisement and the type used in the advertisement, candidates can easily present a print message that is three times longer or more and still create a physically appealing advertisement. If the message being sent is complex and needs considerable explanation, newspapers and magazines are often exceptionally good vehicles for getting the message to voters.

There are several rather standard formats used in newspaper ads. Perhaps the most used format mimics a news story layout or an opinion column. The candidate's photo is prominent with a bold headline and copy alongside. The campaign slogan is bold and in a different font, and each ad usually focuses on just one issue. This format allows for standardization while allowing for rotation among numerous issues and topics.

Next in popularity in newspaper ads are testimonial or endorsement ads. A list of prominent citizens and social and business leaders is an effective way to gain support among those who are less familiar with one's campaign or the candidates.

Just as in television advertising, ad placement is also an important consideration. The ad will gain attention from very different people if it appears in the sports section compared to the business section. Campaigns target newspaper ads by section based on considerations of potential readers, usually by occupation, interests, and even gender.[41]

The liabilities of print advertising involve targeting and cost. It is frequently difficult to target specific audiences with newspaper and magazine advertisements. However, in recent years targeting messages to specific magazine and newspaper audiences has become easier. Many larger daily papers that have readerships located in large geographical areas have special sections or editions that are used in the appropriate geographic area. For example, the daily newspapers in Cincinnati, Ohio, have special northern Kentucky editions. While the paper is largely the same, the northern Kentucky editions focus the local news coverage more heavily on northern Kentucky than on Ohio. These editions are distributed to Kentucky subscribers and used on newsstands in Kentucky, facilitating some geographical targeting. The use of special editions aimed at specific geographic segments of the market has become commonplace for many larger metropolitan newspapers.

Smaller newspapers, because their circulation is limited, may also lend themselves to targeting. Candidates running for offices that include the entire voting populations of smaller towns may do well to advertise in the weekly papers that service most smaller communities or suburban communities. Candidates who have targeted a specific religious, ethnic, or occupational group might also do well to consider advertising in the smaller, often weekly, newspapers that are aimed at these audiences.

Additionally, today many magazine advertisements can be bought on a regional or even a zip code basis. This type of magazine purchase facilitates rather precise targeting. For example, a congressional candidate might choose to advertise in a special interest magazine that is read heavily by a group the campaign has targeted. Moreover, the candidate can limit the purchase to subscribers who live in those zip codes within the congressional district.

An additional advantage to this type of purchase is that it may give a local, regional, or statewide candidate additional stature to be associated with a national publication. The degree to which specific magazines can accommodate this type of advertising varies, as of course does price. In recent years, primarily as a function of the growth of computerization within the newspaper and magazine industry, the use of magazines and newspapers for targeted audiences has become more feasible. However, they are still considered "mass media" and cannot be focused as narrowly as direct mail.

Of course, today newspapers are moving online, offering digital editions and more localized information. News aggregators such as *Drudge Report*, *Huffington Post*, or *Daily Beast* have become major sources of political news and hence ads. There will be much more discussion about digital advertising in the next chapter.

## Radio

Radio is often an underestimated vehicle for political advertisements, especially in local and rural races. There are more radio stations than ever before, including new online and satellite options. Next to direct mail, radio provides the best opportunities for targeting messages based upon demographic and psychographic variables. The wide variety of radio stations found in most areas tends to segment the audience and provides campaigns with the means to target some audiences. In addition, the production costs are the least expensive of all media, and radio ads allow the most flexibility and immediacy in terms of timing, scheduling, and presentation.[42]

For much of the first half of the twentieth century, radio was ranked with the print media as the dominant media of political advertising. However, beginning in the 1950s, radio was utilized less and less frequently. The 1952 presidential campaign between General Dwight David Eisenhower and Governor Adlai Stevenson was the last national campaign in which expenditures on radio advertising were roughly equal to those on television.[43] Since 1952, television has superseded radio as the dominant electronic media.

Radio is always on across America. Ninety-three percent of Americans listen to AM/FM radio, which is higher than those who watch television (88 percent), use a smartphone (83 percent), or use a PC (50 percent). Radio reaches 95 percent of Millennials each month, 97 percent of Generation X, and 98 percent of Baby Boomers.[44] Country is the top radio format at 13 percent of listeners, followed by the News/Talk format with 12 percent.[45]

Radio retains an important place in the arsenal of political advertising weapons available to candidates for at least three reasons. First, radio lends itself to advertisements that can vary greatly in length, and hence can serve a variety of functions. Second, radio can be targeted. Third, radio is not perceived as an expensive medium. Today, radio is considered a "hyper-local" medium focusing on serving the local communities with news, information, advertising, and programming.

Radio commercials can be bought in a variety of time lengths, ranging from ten or fifteen seconds, through the more common thirty- and sixty-second spots, to longer time slots, such as five minutes, fifteen minutes, or half an hour. Consequently, radio can serve a variety of functions. For example, a fifteen-second spot might consist of nothing more than a brief jingle in which the candidate's name is repeated several times. Constant use of this jingle can quickly help to establish name recognition. Since 80 percent of radio users are using it to hear music, jingles are often suggested as especially appropriate for use on radio.[46] Designing a jingle that fits the overall format of the station on which it is being played can enhance the effect of political jingles. A jingle that sounds like music from the 1950s and 1960s might, for example, be used effectively on an oldies station.

Traditional thirty- and sixty-second radio advertisements might be used for jingles and other commercials to establish name recognition, but they can also provide some insight into the candidate and the candidate's beliefs. A five-minute commercial allows the candidate to present a reasonably complete analysis of one or perhaps more questions. Purchasing such time slots on television is often either costly or impractical.

Radio can be targeted because certain stations tend to attract certain demographic groups. Easy listening stations, religious stations, foreign-language stations, hard rock stations, news talk stations, and oldies stations all appeal to different demographic groups. Radio gives the campaign an opportunity to target specific audiences and prepare messages aimed at those audiences. It is impossible to say whether radio allows for better targeting than, for example, newspapers and magazines. Every campaign has to evaluate the available media and the audiences it wishes to target. Nevertheless, in many communities, radio can be used to reach targeted audiences and often lends itself to this use better than many other forms of advertising.

Most political campaigns seek to advertise during drive times—5:00 to 9:00 a.m. and 2:00 to 6:00 p.m.—when commuters on their way to and from work help create the largest radio audiences. Clearly, differences in audience size and audience demographics between radio stations will influence their attractiveness to political advertisers.

As evident in the next section, in some areas the cost of a single television commercial on a local nightly news program may be the equivalent of a week's worth of drive-time radio advertising on a highly rated station, or two weeks or more of drive-time advertising on a station that may not attract a broad audience but that appeals to a group targeted by the campaign.

It is very important to note the drastically changing landscape of radio. The advent of digital devices, tablets, internet radio, and satellite radio is leading to decreased listening to local or traditional radio. However, these technological advances have led to a proliferation of new radio outlets, increasing opportunities to reach very specific audiences. The amount of money spent on digital political advertising has expanded twenty-fold since 2010, according to research firm Borrell Associates. Pandora has information about the age, gender, and zip code of its users. Tim Westergren, the company's cofounder, has said that it can tell with 90 percent accuracy whether a specific Pandora listener is a Republican, Independent, or Democrat based on his or her activity on the network.[47] SiriusXM, America's only satellite radio provider, had over thirty-three million subscribers in 2018.[48] Pandora, the largest digital-only audio provider, has over thirty-two million users.

In terms of political campaigns, it is essential to note the increasing role of news/talk radio. Although country music is the nation's leading radio format, news/talk radio is second in afternoons and evenings. The audience is older (fifty-five and above), primarily male, overall well educated, and above the national mean in terms of income. Not surprisingly, these listeners are voters and their online usage is primarily seeking news and information. Finally, the listeners are more politically conservative in general; however, a very large segment of the audience considers themselves independent voters.[49]

Radio is particularly popular among political advertisers who are campaigning in rural areas and those who are campaigning for lesser offices. Rural areas may be reliant on papers from larger nearby cities or on more urban areas for television. Advertising in the larger papers or on television forces the campaign to purchase an audience that cannot vote in its election. This is often simply not cost-effective for the rural election. Utilizing the small-town paper provides an appropriate audience, but that audience can only be addressed once per week. Hence, many rural campaigns find local small-town radio stations an attractive option to include in their media mix. Similarly, lower-level elections, often poorly financed and often covering a smaller geographical area than that served by television stations and large-circulation metropolitan area papers, find radio a viable option.

Indeed, radio stations in some areas have been forced to put a limit on the number of political commercials they will accept. Such limits are often necessary because the demands of political advertisers during the few weeks preceding the election are often so great that stations could not accommodate their normal advertisers and honor their long-term advertising contracts to those advertisers if they accepted all the political commercials that campaigns wish to air.

Although radio has many virtues as a vehicle for political commercials, it also has drawbacks. Chief among them is the fact that, among all the major forms of media, radio demands the least amount of attention. Most radio is listened to by individuals simultaneously engaged in other activities. Consequently, campaigns are paying for audiences that are not giving them full attention.

## Television

Television, in all its forms, is still the dominant medium of political advertising. The Pew Center found that 91 percent of adults seek political information in any given week, with 24 percent identifying cable news and social media followed by local television at 14 percent, news websites and apps at 13 percent, radio at 11 percent, network news at 10 percent, and late-night comedy shows tied with local newspapers at 3 percent. Pew also discovered that candidates' social media profiles on Facebook and Twitter were the most popular sources of political content.[50] Thus, well over one-third of adults utilize television as the primary source of political information.

Television also serves to stimulate political discussion. One study by Engagement Labs sponsored by TVB, the trade association of America's local broadcast television industry, found that citizens engage in six daily conversations about news. Sixty-five percent of Americans are most likely to share news from local television, followed by 45 percent from social media. Thus, not surprisingly, research found that television still most affects political conversations with 55 percent, followed by online media at 24 percent. While trust in media in general is on the decline, Engagement Labs found that 85 percent of Americans trust news from local broadcast television, compared to just 44 percent from online sources and just 28 percent from social media. Given the experiences of the 2016 elections, 64 percent of Americans find fake news most prevalent on social media.[51]

Television offers the political advertiser a variety of advantages. First, it is the only advertising medium that appeals to two of our senses—seeing and hearing. Television advertising is a powerful combination of the visual and audible. Consequently, television is able to convey more in a short time, and typically it has a greater impact on the viewer, who is getting "twice the message."

Second, of all the mass media, television is often able to produce the largest audiences. The viewership for a popular show often far exceeds the readership for the largest circulation papers in a community. If the candidate seeks widespread exposure, television is unmatched as an advertising medium. However, many television programs attract audiences that are politically apathetic, thus somewhat diminishing their value. Because news programs tend to attract audiences that are attentive to current events and more prone to vote, political advertisers normally seek to place their advertisements on news programs and other shows such as *60 Minutes, Prime Time Live, Dateline, Today, Good Morning America,* and local newscasts that attract individuals with an interest in current events.

Somewhat related to the fact that television can provide a large audience is the third advantage of television: in our media-oriented society, television lends a degree of credibility. Imagine how seriously a presidential candidate would be taken if he or she never used television. Indeed, this was one of the problems that Jesse Jackson faced in 1984. In part because his campaign did not make extensive use of television, he was not viewed as a viable candidate. Candidates running for lesser offices have also recognized the legitimacy that television confers on a candidate. Today, in many areas, it is not uncommon to see television commercials on behalf of candidates for every federal and statewide office and for many local offices such as mayor, city council member, county prosecutor, judge, or sheriff. Candidates for offices that voters have come to associate with television commercials run a real risk of losing credibility if they do not include television in their media mix.

A final advantage of television is that it does allow for some degree of targeting. As indicated earlier, certain shows tend to attract audiences composed of individuals who are concerned with current events and are apt to vote. Other shows attract audiences that are heavily weighted toward a given demographic group that the campaign may have targeted. For example, *Monday Night Football* is more prone to attract a heavily male audience, while *General Hospital* is more likely to attract a heavily female audience. Even local news shows often attract audiences with different demographic makeups, often depending on the nature of the anchorpersons and the way the news is presented.

In sum, television has become the dominant media of political advertising for a variety of reasons. Because it allows the viewer to use two senses, it is often able to convey more than other media. Television can provide wide exposure, helping unknown candidates become known rapidly. Moreover, it lends a sense of credibility to candidates and allows for some degree of targeting. However, like all political media, television is not without its liabilities.

The most obvious disadvantage of television is the enormous expense associated with it. For the growing number of campaigns that utilize television, it almost invariably is the principal expense that these campaigns incur. Many campaigns budget 75 to 80 percent of their advertising money for television. Thus, in many states it has become impossible to be a serious candidate for the U.S. Senate without the prospect of raising nearly $20 million and in many congressional districts $1 million or more.

The 2012 election was the most expensive presidential election in the nation's history, with the Obama and Romney campaigns spending over $1 billion in advertising. In total, 474 unique ads aired during the 2012 presidential campaign.[52] Thus, the 2012 contest set a record for the number of ads created and aired and dollars spent on advertising. The 2016 presidential election was unique in many ways; however, perhaps most significantly, the spending on televised advertising *did not* exceed the 2012 contest. Less spending to television for advertising also meant fewer total ads. For example, between September 16, 2016, and October 13, 2016, there were 117,000 ads aired by all groups, compared to 256,000 in 2012.[53] Televised advertising during the 2016 presidential election will be discussed further in chapter 14.

A second difficulty with television is one that is a function of geography. In many parts of the nation, targeting with television is difficult and candidates may be forced to pay for audiences that cannot vote in their elections. For example, the media markets served by stations in such cities as St. Louis, Kansas City, Philadelphia, New York City, Louisville, Washington, D.C., and Boston, to name just a few, are composed of residents of more than one state. Thus, candidates running for any local office, and even state offices, are forced to pay for audiences who cannot participate in their election. While this problem also exists for other media serving communities such as these, the expenses of television heighten the problem.

A third potential problem with television is that many candidates do not project well using television. Although some candidates like President Ronald Reagan, Senator Jesse Helms, and former Arizona congressman J. D. Hayworth entered politics after first working in radio and television, and others such as former Florida congressman Joe Scarborough and former Cincinnati mayor Jerry Springer had such an affinity for television that when they left elected office they became television personalities, many candidates are not comfortable with television. This does not by any means preclude the use of television, but it does mean that a realistic assessment of the candidate's abilities must be made, and if the candidate is found wanting, the campaign may have to change its advertising strategy.[54]

The use of cable television also allows political figures to capitalize on the power of television as a medium, while providing better targeting than can typically be done through network and local affiliate programming. Cable allows for narrowcasting messages for specific audiences. Much of the programming and content is designed to attract the interests of specific or narrowly defined groups. Now, with literally hundreds of stations and even more programming, messages can be tailored to niche audiences. For example, ESPN is good to target young men, BET for African Americans and Latinos, Lifetime for women, and so on. The availability of national advertising on the cable networks, local advertising on cable networks and local cable shows, and even regional advertising on "cable interconnects," which link cable systems into regional networks, facilitates voter targeting by geography as well. Campaigns also tend to buy ads during or near newscasts. Those who view news programs are voters. It should also be noted that cable advertising is very affordable for any campaign at any level. Even community access cable is a good value, and viewers are community leaders, activists, and voters as well.[55]

Today, satellite TV providers can offer direct access to specific households. Essentially, one family might see a specific campaign ad during a program and the neighbor will not, even with both households watching the same program. During 2012, Obama's campaign targeted women on channels such as Food Network and Lifetime and men on ESPN. The Obama campaign also identified zip codes surrounding tire-manufacturing facilities in Ohio and ran cable ads noting Obama's efforts to block tire imports from China.[56]

As recently as the 1988 and 1990 election cycles, political campaigns made little use of cable television. But as the industry grew, so too did its attractiveness to political candidates. By 1992, cable billings to political campaigns totaled $4.5 million. By 1996, some estimates suggest that 36 percent of political media budgets was spent on cable, and 80 percent of all congressional candidates used cable.[57]

Since 2012, cable has become an important element of ad placement. In 2016, broadcast television advertising was down 20 percent from 2012 while cable witnessed a 52 percent increase in advertising spending from 2012.[58] Many cable companies such as Comcast, Cox, and Time Warner, for example, have employed political data and analytics firms to demonstrate voter targeting opportunities for campaigns. Such firms can provide all types of information about program viewers beyond whether they are likely to vote or are Democrats or Republicans to such characteristics as likely gun owners, hunters, relative income, and so on. Cable outlets can insert ads by zip codes for specific programs. Such targeting expands the placement of ads beyond news programs to such networks as Food Channel or HGTV, for example. The top three networks for the number of spots are Fox News, CNN, and ESPN.[59]

In sum, the enormous costs of television advertising are driving political campaigners to seek the most bang for their buck. Consequently, political campaigns, seeking to harness the power of television with better ability to target and reduce costs, now utilize alternatives to the traditional over-the-air television advertisements—most notably, placement on the internet and cable television. Just as with any other advertising medium, television offers political candidates both advantages and disadvantages. Television commercials often have a strong impact on viewers who must utilize two of their senses as they attend to the commercials. Television can also provide a massive audience for the campaign's messages, contribute to the candidate's credibility, and allow for limited targeting. However, the costs of television are extremely high, especially in many races where candidates find themselves paying for audiences that cannot participate in the election. Moreover, many candidates do not perform well on television. All these factors must be weighed as the campaign develops its own unique media mix.

## The Internet

In chapter 12 we will focus in detail on digital strategies and social media in campaigns. Here we provide just a brief overview of the history and early use of the internet and campaign websites.

In reality, alternative media enhances the impact of television advertising. There is "interactivity" between television advertising and new media. Ads on television can "drive" people to campaign websites. In addition, with today's "smart devices," ads can be sent directly to individuals, allowing for the most targeting of messages.[60]

It was the 1992 Clinton presidential campaign that first used the internet. It was limited to email, discussion groups, and listserv distribution of basic campaign information.[61] In 1993, Ted Kennedy became the first U.S. senator to have a website, while in 1994, Dianne Feinstein established the first candidate website.[62] Although the number of candidate websites increased in 1994, the dominant presence on the web was primarily nonprofit organizations and special-interest groups. By 1996, both major parties had websites, as did about half of Senate candidates and 15 percent of House candidates.[63] In 1998, Jesse Ventura won the governorship of Minnesota, and observers, as well as Ventura staff, claimed that he could not have done so without his effective use of the internet. Political online advertising also started in 1998, in a New York gubernatorial race between Peter Vallone and George Pataki.[64] Moreover, by the late 1990s, a website was more of a campaign necessity than a campaign novelty. Although candidates for a wide variety of reasons used the internet during the 2000 and 2002 election cycles, 2004 was a watershed year in terms of internet political impact and influence. Nearly one hundred million citizens used the internet for political information, nearly fifty million discussed the election by email, thirteen million made a contribution online, and 52 percent of voters indicated that information obtained from the internet influenced their vote.[65] The first time online advertising was used in a presidential campaign was in 2004; however, it was less than 1 percent of the amount spent on television.[66]

For the first time during the midterm elections of 2006, the internet ranked among the top sources of campaign information. Thirty-one percent of Americans went online for candidate and campaign information. Social media also played a major role, with comments by candidates George Allen and Conrad Burns exposed on YouTube likely costing the Republicans control of the Senate.[67]

However, as already noted, the 2008 presidential bid by Barack Obama changed forever the use of the internet and Web 2.0 in campaigns. Without question, the Obama campaign utilized new media, providing the blueprint for future campaigns.

The internet not only provides candidates a means of dispensing information directly to the public, but also provides a means to develop a frequency of individual contact and connect with potential voters. Digital ads zero in on individuals by matching a campaign's voter profile with "cookies" on the user's computer put there by commercial advertisers. There are also numerous video ads on sites such as YouTube, Hulu, and other individual content sites. Again, more will be discussed in chapter 12.

The implications of this are considerable. The internet is a high-return, low-cost means of dispersing information. Campaigns can establish an internet presence for a very modest amount, compared to the costs of many other forms of advertising. As a consequence, it can be utilized by even poorly funded campaigns.

According to Owen, 10 percent of the presidential campaign budgets in 2012 were spent for online ads, up from 3 percent in 2008. The magnitude at the time was simply astounding. Starting in January, the Obama campaign delivered more than eight hundred million paid displayed ads per month.[68] However, in 2016 over one billion dollars was spent on digital advertising, a 789 percent increase from 2012.[69] In short, political internet sites serve a variety of functions. They serve to:

1. provide information to voters about the candidate,
2. raise money,
3. provide information to voters about candidate views on policy issues,
4. provide political information and news about the campaign,
5. communicate with supporters and endorsing groups,
6. provide election information to voters (polling place, registration information, etc.),
7. recruit campaign volunteers,
8. provide information and news about the community,
9. seek voter opinion on issues,
10. attack the opposition, and
11. generate news coverage with specific internet ads.

Candidate sites are not the only places on the internet where users can get political information. Virtually every major news organization in the nation has a website. Moreover, there are political news sites that are not affiliated with any candidate or party. During the 2012 presidential campaign, the internet was the main source of campaign news for 39 percent of the electorate. Social networking sites like Facebook and Google Plus were the primary source of campaign information for 19 percent of Americans, and Twitter for 3 percent. The top websites were Yahoo News, Google News, CNN, local news sources, MSNBC, and Fox.[70]

As already noted in this chapter, cable news was the primary source for political information at 24 percent, followed by social media and local television both at 14 percent, and news websites and apps at 13 percent.[71] The top websites were Google, Facebook, and YouTube.

The most common features of campaign websites include biography, issue positions, campaign news, links to other sites, donation information, contact information (in addition to email), volunteer sign-up, photos of campaign events, and campaign calendar.[72] In sum, the use of the internet as an advertising medium by political candidates has come of age and is now a mainstay of advertising strategy. Internet sites are vital advertising tools for every campaign. As you will discover in the next chapter, with the ever-continuing innovation with new technologies, candidates will develop increasingly sophisticated ways of using them to communicate with voters.

## MAKING TELEVISION ADS

The steps in making a political ad are generally research and ad concept, ad creation, ad testing, and final production and launching of the ad. The research may well rely upon survey data, targeting analysis, and interviews with key constituent groups or focus groups. Based upon the information gathered, the campaign will decide what message they wish to communicate about the candidate or issues for a specific targeted audience. In creating an ad, the production team will focus on visuals, music, and copy. Some may be rather straightforward while others may have a comic or artistic flair. While the next step, ad testing, is expensive and time consuming, it is an important step to ensure that the ad generates the desired effects. Based upon the test results, the ad is produced. The launch is usually well orchestrated with press conferences, press releases, and social media posts on all types of websites such as YouTube. Reporters are encouraged to write about the ads. This is one way the campaign can benefit from free media coverage.[73]

## TARGETING OF TELEVISION ADS

From the early days of political television advertising until 2000, most campaigns placed ads targeted to very broad audiences by shows, but mostly by the time of day. For example, daytime ads on television were aimed at women, primetime evening for both men and women. By 2000, audience profiles of those watching specific programming became more available. Campaigns could actually sort audiences, among other variables, by which programs were watched by more Democrats or Republicans. This information added another level for targeting ads. According to Fowler and her colleagues, since 2012, not only have the viewing habits and characteristics of program viewers expanded; detailed information became available for campaigns to learn which types of voters watched specific programs. In 2016, satellite programming allowed for campaigns to target specific households with specific viewing habits and characteristics. Campaign access to both public and private data allows for extensive microtargeting based on a host of variables and geographical considerations.[74]

It is not surprising that most television ads are shown on national and local news programs, comprising about 60 percent of all ads. While the placement of ads on news programming for congressional and gubernatorial races has remained about the same, those for presidential campaigns have declined on newscasts. What is unique about local news viewers is that they closely match the partisan divide of the country in terms of those who identify as Democrats or Republicans, and over half who identify as Independents.[75]

There is an interesting partisan divide in general television viewing. Overall, Democrats watch television more than Republicans across the entire day except for primetime, where self-identified members of both parties watch at the same rate. While still less than Democrats, Republicans watch more television in early morning because of local news programming. Thus, both parties place ads in early morning and primetime, followed by late-night news programming.[76]

## CAMPAIGN ADVERTISING STRATEGIES

The circumstances of the campaign normally dictate the use of one of four basic patterns in the purchase of radio and television time. Since radio and television constitute a major portion of the advertising of most campaigns, the strategies used for purchasing radio and television time typically characterize the entire campaign's advertising strategy. Studies indicate that congressional candidates spend about 40 percent of their budget on advertising and presidential campaigns as much as 60 percent of their budget.[77] Time buyers aim at reaching targeted voters the maximum number of times the campaign budget allows. To do so, they utilize the standard audience measure, gross rating points. A gross rating point represents 1 percent of the TV viewing audience. Theoretically, a purchase of one hundred points means that the entire TV audience will see the commercial once. Since most consultants estimate that a commercial needs to be seen at least five to seven times a week before it makes an impression, a purchase of five hundred points is considered "saturation."[78]

According to Darrell West, candidates have basically four major considerations relating to buying advertising time. Each is strategic in nature. First, campaigns must decide how many issues to emphasize. Historically, campaigns usually stick to just a few basic themes and issues as well as a limited number of spots. More recently, using a larger number of ads allows for appealing to more specific voting groups. However, the danger with too many themes and issues is in losing focus or rationale for the preference of the candidate and confusing media in terms of coverage. Second, campaigns must determine the timing and frequency of attack ads. Virtually all campaigns have an attack phase, but the use of attack ads influences candidate favorability, image, and potential votes of key constituent groups. Third, campaigns must decide how frequently to air specific ads. The trick is in airing an ad enough to break through the "media clutter," generating awareness and leaving voters able to recall key message points associated with the candidate. Finally, campaigns must determine the right mix of ad placement among all the media options and outlets, such as network or cable, news programs or prime-time programs, daytime or evening programming. Increasingly, most ads, even in presidential campaigns, are targeted to local markets with cable inserts.[79]

Buying backward from Election Day, campaigns will seek purchases of at least five hundred points. In markets where costs are low and perhaps where a large number of highly targeted voters can be expected to see the advertisements, or in exceedingly well-financed campaigns, it is not unheard of for a campaign to purchase twenty-five hundred points in the last weeks of the campaign, thus providing that theoretically voters will see the commercial twenty-five times. Computerization of such things as program schedules, demographic audience data, and pricing information has facilitated increased sophistication in the purchasing of airtime.[80]

The purchase of commercial time reflects a campaign's overall strategy. With some differences that are reflected in the unique virtues of each form of media, the basic radio and television strategy is often commonly extended to the use of display graphics, direct mail, and print media. In this section, we briefly examine several of the most common basic advertising strategies and four specifically utilized by political campaigns.[81]

## Media Concentration and Media Dispersion

Media concentration and media dispersion are two very basic and common approaches to media placement. At the heart of each approach is the frequency of running ads and the breadth of media selected. The media concentration approach uses fewer media categories and greater frequency of (and spending on) ads. This approach may build name recognition very quickly, reinforce image concerns, or rebut issue attacks.

In contrast, the media dispersion approach uses many more platforms and multiple media categories. This approach naturally reaches larger segments of potential voters. Campaign messages extend beyond just supporters. They help reinforcement of issue positions and candidate image. This approach works best for incumbents or those who have high name recognition.

## Continuity Scheduling, Flight Scheduling, and Pulse Scheduling

As the name implies, continuity scheduling of ads is basically running the same number of ads every month. The goal is to keep "top mind awareness" of a candidate or issue. In essence, early in a campaign such a scheduling establishes a minimal presence, usually running bio ads.

Flight scheduling is running heavy advertising for a specific period and absent others. This type of scheduling makes sense in the commercial world where some products are in demand for limited times, such as in summer or getting ready for the Christmas holiday season. This approach has little benefit from a political perspective unless a candidate is running for reelection unopposed. In this situation, the candidate may just spend funds several weeks out from the general election.

In many ways, pulse scheduling is a combination of the above methods. While there is consistent advertising over time, during some weeks or months there are noticeably more ads. This approach is certainly more the general norm. As you can imagine, factors such as incumbency, primaries, poll position, budget, and so forth all influence the scheduling of ads. In 2012, from a macro perspective, one could notice two contrasting approaches to the scheduling of ads. The Obama campaign viewed the race as a seven-month campaign, whereas the Romney campaign viewed the race as an intense three-month sprint to Election Day. As a result, the Obama campaign started running ads early and then ever increasingly toward the end of the campaign. The Romney campaign, in an attempt to save money, waited until the Republican convention to start a concentrated heavy flight scheduling of ads.[82]

## The Spurt Strategy

The "spurt strategy" is similar to the pulse strategy tailored to political scheduling. Candidates who are not well known at the outset of the campaign often use this approach. The strategy is to "spurt" early in the campaign, often four to six months before the election, purchasing a large amount of radio and television time for one to two weeks. The use of radio and television is often supplemented with an early round of newspaper advertisements and an early effort at distributing a large number of yard signs, bumper stickers, buttons, and other display graphics. The point of this early spurt is to build name recognition and help establish the candidate as a credible contender for the office.

The campaign, having now utilized a reasonable amount of its resources early, then typically eliminates or drastically reduces its use of radio and television for an extended period. During this period, the campaign may well focus on the internet and direct mail efforts, often using these media both to target specific audiences for persuasive messages and to help raise funds to replenish the monies spent on the early spurt deemed necessary to establish name recognition. Moreover, the campaign may do a considerable amount of neighborhood canvassing, leaving literature throughout the district.

Finally, the campaign makes a last spurt, purchasing considerable radio and television time from the morning of the election backward as far as it can, hopefully at least a week. As with the original spurt, the final radio and television spurt is accompanied by other media.

The point of this strategy is to allow the candidate to open strongly and close strongly. While all candidates seek to close strongly, those who start at a disadvantage often utilize the spurt strategy to get them into the race. The candidate who starts out with little name recognition typically has many problems. The initial spurt in advertising spending will hopefully create a spurt in the candidate's standing in the polls, enhance the candidate's credibility, facilitate greater fundraising, encourage more people to volunteer support, and, in sum, simply get the campaign moving.

### The Fast Finish Strategy

This strategy goes by a variety of names, including the Silky Sullivan strategy, the Miracle Braves strategy, or the '51 Giants strategy. Just as Silky Sullivan, the famous California-bred racehorse, and those famous baseball teams started very slowly, only to close with a rush and win, some candidates choose to start slowly and close with a rush, expecting to win on Election Day.

Typically, this strategy is implemented by buying a complete schedule of radio and television advertisements for the last portion of the pre-election period. Buying backward from Election Day, the campaign purchases a complete schedule of radio and television time for as many days as it can afford, normally at least a week, and further back if it can afford it. Then, depending on what the campaign can afford, still buying backward, the campaign gradually diminishes the number of commercials it purchases each day. The effect of this type of purchase is that voters see the campaign starting very slowly, with a scattering of commercials. Gradually, the advertising increases until voters are completely saturated in the week immediately preceding the election. Similarly, other media efforts are intensified as the election draws closer.

Most campaigns will use some variation of this strategy. Clearly, candidates want their messages to have the greatest impact and feel that this is best achieved by surrounding the voter with their message in the days immediately preceding the election. Candidates who start from a position of strength find this strategy particularly appealing, since they often feel that their initial strength allows them to husband their resources until near the end of the campaign. By then, concentrating their advertising in a limited time, they can purchase so much airtime in the last days of the campaign that they are confident that voters cannot miss their messages.

### The Really Big Show Strategy

This strategy is designed to capitalize on free news coverage. Named after the expression frequently used by 1950s and 1960s television variety show host Ed Sullivan to describe his program, this strategy is built around several major events that are scheduled periodically throughout the campaign. For example, in a congressional race, the candidate holds a press conference and immediately follows it up with several speeches making a major accusation about the shortcomings of her opponent. Second, the candidate has a debate with her opponent. Third, a major national figure comes to town to speak on behalf of the candidate. Each of these three occurrences is a major event in the campaign. Moreover, the candidate has considerable control over their timing.

Using the "really big show" strategy, the candidate will focus her advertising around those events that are likely to receive considerable free media coverage on the news. She will increase her paid advertising at the time of the press conference and speeches, reinforcing through advertising what she is saying in the conference and speeches. She will increase her advertising at the time of the debate, reinforcing positions she takes in the debate or perhaps using cinema verité and testimonial commercials to emphasize how effective she was in the debate and reinforce the points she made during the debate. She will increase her advertising immediately preceding, during, and after the visit by the major national figure, better linking herself to that figure and basking in that figure's prominence and credibility.

By increasing her advertising at the time she is naturally receiving greater free coverage in the news, the candidate turns a campaign event into a "really big show." Often, because of the proximity in timing between the news coverage and the commercials, and depending on how her advertisements are handled, the paid media blends with the free news coverage in the mind of the voter. Candidates using this strategy will generally ensure that at least one major event takes place within a few days of the election so that they can combine elements of this approach with the fast finish strategy. Moreover, this strategy can also be blended with the spurt approach by coordinating the early media effort with an important campaign event.

### The Cruise Control Strategy

This strategy is particularly appealing for candidates who are clearly ahead and are striving to maintain their lead. This is basically the continuous media pattern. Just as the cruise control of a car allows the driver to drive at a steady speed, this approach calls for the campaign to advertise at a steady rate. The campaign makes what the media industry calls a "flat buy," purchasing a constant number of commercials each day during the stages of the campaign when media will be used.

Often this strategy is combined with the fast finish approach, so that the campaign makes a flat buy for several weeks or even a month or more prior to the last week or two of the campaign, when it then increases its advertising. This strategy allows the candidate who is ahead to remain constantly visible for a long period of time and then finish strongly.

In sum, the overall advertising strategies of political campaigns can be characterized by the way they purchase radio and television time. Most campaigns utilize one of four approaches or some combination of them. Although factors such as the availability of funds, poll results, and the strategies of opponents may force modifications, part of the initial campaign plan should be to develop an overall advertising strategy.

## MEDIA AND OTHER TYPES OF POLITICAL CONSULTANTS

There have always been political advisors or consultants to campaigns since the founding of the nation. While political consultants provide a variety of services to their candidates, most of those services are advertising and media related. Hence, we will conclude this chapter on the practices of political advertising by briefly examining the rise and growth of political consulting and the functions of political consultants.

### History of Political Consulting

Virtually every political candidate, from George Washington's day forward, has turned to a group of advisors for advice on getting elected and often for advice on governing. Perhaps the most outstanding of America's early political consultants was John Beckley, a close personal friend and key political advisor to Thomas Jefferson. During Jefferson's bids for the presidency, Beckley wrote campaign material, arranged for its distribution in key states, and organized a speaker's bureau on behalf of Jefferson.[83]

Throughout the nineteenth and early twentieth centuries, the growth of political parties, improvements in communication and transportation technology, and the need to deal with rapidly growing constituencies all contributed to the professionalization of political campaigning. The presidential campaigns of 1828, 1840, and 1896 were especially notable for advances in political campaigning and served as precursors to the consultant-driven campaigns of today.[84]

However, it was not until the 1920s, when Calvin Coolidge turned to Edward Bernays, that political figures began to seek the advice of individuals with extensive backgrounds and expertise in advertising, public relations, and polling. Few political figures listened to Bernays, a public relations counselor who was far ahead of his time in advising candidates to make better use of the media and polling. Nevertheless, his ideas foreshadowed much of what political campaigning has become at the outset of the twenty-first century.[85]

In 1934, Californians Clem Whitaker and his wife, Leona Baxter, founded the public relations firm of Whitaker and Baxter, which from its inception took on political clients, normally California Republicans. In that year, the firm helped defeat the popular writer Upton Sinclair, the Democratic candidate for governor. From that point on, political candidates sought their services. Whitaker and Baxter were a pioneering firm, and although they eventually diversified to handle a wide variety of accounts, they were still helping candidates as late as 1967, when they handled Shirley Temple's unsuccessful congressional race.[86]

Jason Johnson identifies four eras in the development of the political consulting industry.[87] The "personal era" occurred from about 1950 to 1970. During this period, social science methodologies were applied to political campaigns. Public polling was evolving and being used in national elections. Campaign staff members began to expand to include individuals with special skills. It was between 1970 and 1980 with the "professionalization" of the industry that the American Association of Political Consultants was formed and campaigns hired staff in polling, marketing, advertising, and strategic messaging. Johnson calls the decade of 1980 to 1990 the "party downfall era." The first and still published trade publication, *Campaigns and Elections*, was started; it analyzed and shared campaign strategies and tactics. Political parties reduced their role in managing and running campaigns. Individual candidates formed their own campaign staff with increasing numbers and specialists. Between 1990 and 2000, some political consultants gained "celebrity status." They became pundits on news programs, wrote books, and gained notoriety as they were credited for "winning" campaigns. Documentaries were often made of campaigns where managers and staff were stars. Perhaps the most notable example is the film *The War Room* featuring consultants George Stephanopoulos, James Carville, and Dick Morris of the 1992 Bill Clinton campaign. The "modern era" of the evolution of the political consulting industry is the decade of 2000 to 2010. Campaigns at all levels utilized specialists and relied on social science and marketing research.

In 1952, television was first used as an advertising medium in a presidential campaign. The 1952 campaigns of both General Dwight David Eisenhower and Illinois governor Adlai Stevenson made use of television. Although both candidates had reservations about television, both campaigns secured the services of advertising agencies to help produce television commercials and serve in a variety of other functions.[88] The fact that media consultants, whether in the employ of political consulting firms or advertising agencies, were in politics to stay was evident in 1956 when Stevenson again challenged Eisenhower. Accepting the Democratic nomination, Stevenson decried the use of mass media advertising techniques, claiming that "the idea that you can merchandise candidates for high office like breakfast cereal—that you can gather votes like box tops—is, I think, the ultimate indignity in the democratic process." Yet, Stevenson made this very remark from a platform that had been redesigned by an advertising agency, to a national convention whose activities were being orchestrated in no small part by that same agency, for the benefit of the television audience.[89]

By the 1960s, campaigns were being waged more and more in the media, and political consultants were becoming more and more conspicuous in the conduct of those campaigns. Stuart Spencer, Bill Roberts, David Garth, Tony Schwartz, and a host of other consultants began to bring high technology to political campaigning throughout the 1960s.

In recent years, two factors have combined to make political consultants essential players in virtually every major political campaign. First, getting elected has become a perpetual job. Thus, helping candidates has become a perpetual job. In the past it was difficult to work as a political consultant, simply because, during nonelection years, the political consultant had no clients.

But the 1970s witnessed the advent of the perpetual candidate.[90] In the footsteps of the perpetual candidate has come the perpetual political consultant. As Burdett Loomis has incisively illustrated, since 1974, a "new breed" of politicians has encouraged the growth of administrative staffs, subcommittee and committee staffs, campaign staffs, a variety of political caucuses and their staffs, a variety of task forces and their staffs, a host of party organizations and their staffs, as well as the expansion of lobby groups and the dramatic growth of political action committees. Although the surge of these enterprises is perhaps most evident in Washington, it is also apparent in virtually every state capital as well. Political consultants can work on a campaign, which today might well start eighteen months to two years prior to the election, and when the campaign ends, they can move to another campaign or to an organization such as those mentioned above, which utilize many of the skills of political consultants. As soon as the next campaign opening is available, they can then move to that opening, with very little "down" time.

In addition to the increased opportunities for employment of those with the skills of political consultants, political consulting itself has now become a full-time job for many consultants. As more and more campaigns are able to afford consultants, campaigns that once would not have used consultants are today often doing so. In sum, since the 1970s political consulting has become a viable career for many individuals.

The rapid growth of the political consulting profession is a consequence of a variety of changes in our political system during the last decades of the twentieth century. From the standpoint of candidates, political consultants provide two big advantages over a candidate's own campaign staff and the efforts of party professionals. First, they provide a bigger bang for the buck, a greater return on the money spent in the campaign. Consultants are specialists in designing media messages and ensuring that those messages are transmitted most effectively. Whether it is a consultant who specializes in setting up phone banks, coaching political debaters, or producing television advertisements, consultants provide the campaign with a better return on its dollars. Second, political consultants provide campaigns with public opinion polling designed and executed specifically to help the campaign locate voters and prepare messages for those voters. Hence, the consulting profession has grown rapidly in the past three decades because it has provided candidates with highly desired services.[91]

Moreover, the growth of political consulting services has made the field one in which growing numbers of people are able to make a living. The top 150 consulting firms grossed more than $500 million nationally from the 2011–2012 electoral season.[92] The "elite" political consultants, a group of about fifty firms, have focused most of their efforts on statewide races. Working for presidential candidates, while potentially bringing prestige to a firm, is risky from a business standpoint. Only two of perhaps ten or more candidates will make it through the primaries. A consulting firm whose clients lose primaries has little to boast about when it seeks additional clients. Moreover, a presidential campaign is so demanding that a consulting firm handling one normally must sacrifice other candidates or neglect them. Hence, a firm that opts to work for a presidential candidate typically turns away business during the primary season and may find itself lacking clients for the general election if its candidate loses the primaries.[93] Although overhead and expenses for consulting are high, for a growing number of people, political consulting has become a viable way to make a living.[94] It should be remembered, however, that as with the time of any professional—plumber, electrician, lawyer, or doctor—the time of political consultants is limited. Most consultants avoid taking on more than four or five races simultaneously.[95] Hence, political consulting is no longer the province of enthusiastic amateurs, perhaps occasionally taking leaves from their other positions to help the candidate of their choice. While that type of individual is still a feature of some campaigns and may provide valuable services, today political consulting is a fast-growing profession.

Although this discussion has focused on the economic aspects of consulting, because it was not until the field became an economically viable one that people could enter it on a full-time basis, virtually everyone involved in political consulting will note that monetary rewards are a secondary motivation. The primary motivation of most consultants is to have an impact on the political process. Most consultants have strong political beliefs. They work for like-minded candidates. And, invariably, consultants will claim that the most satisfying aspect of their job is to "win one you're not supposed to win."[96]

## Functions of Political Consultants

Political consultants can provide candidates with virtually any service necessary in the conduct of a campaign, including help in targeting voters, establishing a precinct organization, setting up and utilizing phone banks, polling the electorate, preparing and utilizing direct mail, preparing and using radio and television commercials, writing and preparing to deliver a speech, preparing for a debate, mounting a fund-raising campaign, and establishing and utilizing a website. A full-service political consulting firm can provide clients with virtually all these services, although it may well specialize in a more limited number. Smaller firms will limit their work to providing a group of related services. It would be impossible to discuss all the services provided by consulting firms in the remainder of this chapter.[97] Rather, we will briefly focus on four services that are directly related to the campaign's efforts to communicate through advertising.

### Writers

The preparation and communication of messages are at the heart of any campaign. Hence, virtually all consultants are involved in some form of writing. In the chapter on public speaking, we discussed political speechwriting. Consultants who specialize in writing can often handle virtually all the advertising writing chores in the campaign: radio and television scripts, press releases, and copy for all printed materials such as brochures, mail pieces, or newspaper and magazine advertisements. There are techniques unique to writing each of these types of advertisements well, and often in larger campaigns different individuals will handle each. In small and midsized campaigns, the writer who often also serves as the press secretary and speechwriter is generally involved in the preparation of scripts for commercials.

### Speech Coaches

One of the basic services frequently provided at the schools for candidates run by the Republican and Democratic Party organizations is speech coaching. Many consulting firms will coach candidates in public speaking and, if necessary, in debate. Most speech coaches would agree with Democratic consultant Michael Sheehan, who has worked with President Clinton and former Texas governor Ann Richards, among others, when he describes his job by claiming, "I bring out their [the candidates'] strengths; I try to bring out the best qualities in candidates that they already have."[98] Republican Roger Ailes, who coached both Ronald Reagan and George H. W. Bush for many of their major addresses and debates, was among the best-known consultants to have specialized in coaching candidates for speeches and debates. Based on his experiences, Ailes had identified what he called the ten most common communication problems. Depending on the individual candidate's strengths and weaknesses, speech coaches will normally work to help the candidate overcome one or more of the following problems Ailes identified:

1. Lack of initial rapport with listeners
2. Stiffness or woodenness in use of the body
3. Presentation of material is intellectually oriented, forgetting to involve the audience emotionally
4. Speaker seems uncomfortable because of fear of failure
5. Poor use of eye contact and facial expression
6. Lack of humor
7. Speech direction and intent unclear due to improper preparation
8. Inability to use silence for impact
9. Lack of energy, causing inappropriate pitch pattern, speech rate, and volume
10. Use of boring language and lack of interesting material[99]

### Direct Mail Specialists

Preparing direct mail pieces, and in many instances providing the lists of individuals to whom such pieces are sent, has become a critical political consulting specialty. Such firms are typically involved in utilizing direct mail both for voter persuasion and for fund-raising. Perhaps the best-known early consultant to specialize in direct mail was Richard Viguerie; his story is highly illustrative of how direct mail specialists operate.

In 1960–1961, Viguerie worked in the Houston campaign offices of Texas senator John Tower. Soon after, he was employed by Young Americans for Freedom (YAF), a group of conservative young people, and was placed in charge of the organization's fund-raising. Recalling his early experiences, Viguerie states: "I'm basically a pretty shy person and I did not feel comfortable asking for money directly. So, I began writing letters instead, and they seemed to work. So, I wrote more and more letters and before many months, direct mail was my whole focus—for fundraising, subscriptions for *The New Guard* [a YAF publication], YAF membership, everything."[100]

Quickly recognizing the power of direct mail, Viguerie used the most obvious means to begin to develop a mailing list. After the 1964 election, he simply copied the names and addresses of those who had given $50 or more to the Goldwater campaign from the contributor records that, by law, were on file with the clerk of the House of Representatives. This effort provided him with over twelve thousand names, which became his first mailing list.[101] Direct mail consultants like Viguerie are continually building their lists, adding new names after each campaign in which they are involved. The use of sophisticated computers and printers enables them to handle thousands of pieces of mail quickly and further enables them to tailor lists to the geographic and demographic needs of a client.

Political consultants who specialize in direct mail typically provide two services for their clients. First, they can help in designing and producing the actual mail pieces. Second, they can create lists of individuals to whom such pieces should be sent. This second service is highly valuable for major national campaigns and other larger races.

However, in smaller races, often the candidate and campaign staff can develop a good mailing list, based on their associates, the lists of other candidates who have run in the same area, or the lists of the local party. Candidates who contract to utilize the lists of consulting firms must be certain that the lists are likely to be of help to them and almost invariably will want to supplement those lists. One of the principal ways in which direct mail firms increase the size and value of their lists is by constantly adding names from the campaigns in which they work.

### Specialists in Television Commercial Production and Placement

Because of the large expense involved and the technical expertise necessary, today few campaigns will attempt to produce and air television commercials without the advice of political consultants who specialize in such work. Some campaigns will supplement the efforts of such consultants by also employing local advertising agencies familiar with local media. Nevertheless, political media consultants have come to dominate the business of producing and buying time for televised campaign commercials.

Clearly, the candidate and campaign staff must make the final decisions. Typically, the campaign staff, the polling firm, and the television consultants will all work closely together, with the campaign having the final authority. Aware of the issues in their particular campaign, the campaign will certainly be receptive to the advice of consultants, but they must make the final decisions on what they want to accomplish with the commercials. Well-financed campaigns test ads in focus groups and never air the ones that don't work. At one time the standard approach was to begin the campaign with biographical ads and continue with issue ads, followed by endorsement and attack ads, before ending with inspirational commercials, in the belief that voters want something positive as they enter the voting booth.[102] While all these types of ads are still utilized in contemporary campaigns, there is really no longer a standard approach or sequencing of the ads. Moreover, use of attack or negative ads, or "comparison" ads in which the candidate or her ideas is contrasted to the opponent or the opponent's ideas, has grown to dominate many recent campaigns.

Political consultants can help in a variety of ways. They can suggest types of commercials that can implement the candidate's goals. They may be able to point out how other campaigns successfully, or unsuccessfully, handled similar problems. They are aware of what approaches are working or failing in other parts of the country and hence might or might not work in the relevant region. Depending on their background, they will help script and produce the commercial, utilizing their skills in every phase of production, including casting, shooting, and editing. Well-financed campaigns can use focus groups and electronic advertising-testing techniques to monitor voter responses to individual sentences, phrases, and split-second visual images contained within the ad; through this process some commercials are rejected and others are improved before they are finally accepted for broadcast. In many campaigns, the consultant takes personal control over creating the commercials.

The consulting firm will also purchase airtime. A good firm knows the demographics of the local media market, is experienced in dealing with the local media, and is familiar with the candidate's strategy. Using all this information, it purchases airtime to maximize the impact of the candidate's messages among those voters whom the campaign has targeted. While consultants are often paid a percentage of the cost of the television time they purchase and hence have self-interest in purchasing larger quantities of time, it is hard to deny that traditional viewing habits have been changed by technology and that voter indifference to politics is widespread.

### Summary

Clearly, campaigns can make use of a wide variety of political consultants. In this section, we have treated the types of consultants we feel impact most directly on political advertising. It is significant to note that, although we have not treated such consulting specialties as the public opinion pollster, the fund-raising specialist, the precinct organizer, or the database manager, it could well be argued that even these consultants impact on political communication and political advertising. We would not dispute that argument in the least, for it gives further credence to the principal thesis of this book—that communication is at the heart of political campaigning.

### CONCLUSIONS

This chapter has illustrated some of the practical concerns that must be confronted when using political advertising. We have first noted the importance of planning in the development of the campaign's use of political advertising. Second, we have examined the eight principal advertising media used in political campaigns: display graphics, brochures, direct mail, telephone, print, radio, television, and the internet. We have illustrated the virtues and liabilities of each medium for political advertising. Third, we have examined the four principal overall advertising strategies commonly utilized in political campaigns: spurt, fast finish, really big show, and cruise control. Fourth, we have discussed political consultants, who have, largely because of their mastery of advertising media, become key players in contemporary political campaigns. We have considered the history of political consulting in the past three decades. Moreover, we have examined the functions of those political consultants who are most directly concerned with communication and advertising: writers, speech coaches, direct mail specialists, and television specialists.

## NOTES

1. Frank Luntz, "Preparing Your Campaign Playbook," *Campaigns and Elections*, July 1991, 40–46.

2. For valuable insight into the components of a campaign plan, see Ron Faucheux, "Writing Your Campaign Plan," *Campaigns and Elections*, April 2004, 26–29.

3. All the information and suggestions discussed about developing a digital strategy are based upon Laura Packard, "Ready, Set, Launch," *Campaigns and Elections*, March/April 2014, 34–37.

4. Smithsonian Institution, National Museum of American History, "Campaign Buttons" (Washington, DC: Smithsonian Institution, 1989). This small flyer on the history of campaign buttons is included with a variety of reproductions of campaign materials available through the Smithsonian.

5. The four functions discussed in this paragraph are mentioned primarily as the functions of billboard advertising by Craig Varoga of Varoga and Rice, a California consulting firm. However, virtually all display graphics serve one or more of these functions. See Craig Varoga, "Hiring Fundraisers, Using Billboards," *Campaigns and Elections*, May 2001, 69.

6. Al Ries, "'Forward' Easily Beats 'Believe in America,'" *Ad Age*, November 7, 2012, accessed January 4, 2015, adage.com/article/campaign-trail/obama-s-slogan-cut-mitt -romney-s-chances/238179.

7. The figures in this paragraph are drawn from the online catalogs of several suppliers. They include Signelect and the Button King, accessed November 23, 2018, at www .signelect.com/buttons.htm and www.thebuttonking.com/magento/index.php/badges/ adhesive-name-badges.html.

8. Ibid.

9. Ibid.

10. Ibid.

11. These figures are drawn from the online catalog of Signelect.com, accessed November 23, 2018, www.signelect.com/18x24_yard_signs.htm.

12. The cost figure used in this paragraph comes from the online catalog of Patriot Signage, accessed November 26, 2018, https://www.patriotsigns.com/political-poly-bag.

13. Catherine Shaw, *The Campaign Manager*, 3rd ed. (Boulder, CO: Westview Press, 2004), 21–22.

14. "Tips for Creating a Great Campaign Brochure," Online Candidate, accessed January 7, 2015, www.onlinecandidate.com/articles/tips-for-creating-a-great-campaign-brochure.

15. Elena Neely, "New Research Reveals Direct Mail to Be Most Credible Form of Media Outreach among Voters," *Campaigns and Elections*, January 31, 2018, accessed July 12, 2018, https://www.campaignsandelections.com/campaign-insider/new-research-re veals-direct-mail-to-be-most-credible-form-of-media-outreach-among-voters.

16. Dan Eggen, "Direct Mail Still a Force in Campaigns," *Washington Post*, October 12, 2012, accessed January 7, 2015, www.washingtonpost.com/politics/decision2012/direct-mail-still-a-force-in-campaigns/2012/10/12/24f6f830-0bf9-11e2-bb5e-492c0d30bff6_story.html.

17. Victoria Belknap, "Campaigns Look to More Cost-Effective Direct Mail Options," *Campaigns and Elections*, October 20, 2014, accessed January 7, 2015, www.campaignsandelections.com/campaign-insider/2342/campaigns-look-to-more-cost-effective-direct-mail-options.

18. Kate Kaye, "Data-Driven Targeting Creates Huge 2016 Political Ad Shift," *Ad Age*, January 3, 2017, accessed November 23, 2018, https://adage.com/article/media/2016-political-broadcast-tv-spend-20-cable-52/307346.

19. Direct mail has often been called a "high interest, low backlash communications vehicle" in campaign seminars conducted by the Republican National Committee and in the literature that the committee has produced for candidates and their staffs. See, for example, Republican National Committee, *Campaign Seminars: Campaign Graphics, Direct Mail and Outdoor Advertising* (Washington, DC: Republican National Committee, n.d.), 5.

20. See Richard Viguerie, *The New Right: We're Ready to Lead* (Falls Church, VA: Viguerie Company, 1980), 125–26. Viguerie, the principal direct mail fundraiser of the conservative movement throughout the 1960s and 1970s, credits the McGovern campaign with making political figures aware of the enormous potential of direct mail as a medium of political fund-raising.

21. Ron Kanfer, "Direct to the Bank," *Campaigns and Elections*, July 1991, 22. Kanfer is president of Response Dynamics, Inc., a political direct mail fund-raising firm.

22. Todd Meredith, "Open the Envelope: Getting People to Look at the Direct Mail They Receive," *Campaigns and Elections*, December 2004/January 2005, 27. Todd Meredith is co-owner of the Direct Mail Marketing Group and has worked with more than forty members of Congress.

23. Joe Trippi notes that fully one-fourth of the contributors to Howard Dean's campaign were under thirty years old and claims that "this is an amazing number, given that we are living in an age when political involvement among young people is at a historic low." See Joe Trippi, *The Revolution Will Not Be Televised: Democracy, the Internet, and the Overthrow of Everything* (New York: Regan Books, 2004), 190.

24. See both Kanfer, "Direct to the Bank," 24, and Viguerie, *The New Right*, 124. Viguerie argues that in the 1960–1980 era direct mail fund-raising was exceptionally useful for underdog, non-establishment candidates, much as Trippi has more recently argued that the internet is exceptionally useful for underdog, non-establishment candidates.

25. William Bike, *Winning Political Campaigns*, 2nd ed. (Juneau: Denali Press, 2001), 3.

26. Larry Sabato, *The Rise of the Political Consultants* (New York: Basic Books, 1981), 220.

27. Hal Malchow, "10 Ways to Design In-House Voter Mail That Works," *Campaigns and Elections*, June/July 1990, 50–51. The cost figures that Malchow mentions in connection with the services of a letter shop have gone up slightly since he first wrote. However, so, too, have the costs of everything, including beer and pizza, so his point that such shops are a bargain likely remains true.

28. Ibid, 50.

29. Meredith, "Open the Envelope," 77.

30. "Shop Talk," *Campaigns and Elections*, May 27, 2009, accessed December 28, 2010, www.campaignsandelections.com/campaign-insider/345.

31. Ibid.

32. Dennis W. Johnson, *Democracy for Hire: A History of American Political Consulting* (New York: Oxford University Press, 2017), 234.

33. Walter Clinton and Anne Clinton, "Telephone and Direct Mail," in *The Manship School Guide to Political Communication*, ed. David Perlmutter (Baton Rouge: Louisiana State University Press, 1999), 137–46.

34. For good overviews of telephone contact services, see Roger S. Conrad, "Winning Votes on the Information Super Highway," *Campaigns and Elections*, July 1994, 22–25, 52–54; Robert V. Friedenberg, *Communication Consultants in Political Campaigns: Ballot Box Warriors* (Westport, CT: Praeger, 1997), 112–18. On the cost of voter contact services, Friedenberg provides representative figures for the 1996 election cycle; the reader can obtain current costs by contacting the firms directly. Most major firms are listed under "Telephone Contact Services" in the Political Pages Directory, a section of the *Campaigns and Elections* website, at https://www.campaignsandelections.com/politicalpages.

35. "Is It Legal for Political Campaigns to Call Your Cellphone?" CTIA BLOG, accessed January 11, 2015, blog.ctia.org/2012/02/08/is-it-legal-for-political-campaigns-to-call-you-on-your-cellphone.

36. Newspaper advertisements played a role in the nation's earliest elections. See Robert J. Dinkin, *Campaigning in America: A History of Election Practices* (Westport, CT: Greenwood, 1989), 3–4, 14–16. Also see Kathleen Hall Jamieson, *Packaging the Presidency: A History and Criticism of Presidential Campaign Advertising* (New York: Oxford University Press, 1984), 5.

37. Daniel Shea and Michael Burton, *Campaign Craft*, 4th ed. (Westport, CT: Praeger, 2006), 172.

38. This information was provided by Shawn Savage of the *Cincinnati Enquirer* advertising sales department. Phone interview with Robert V. Friedenberg, April 26, 2002.

39. Typical of many major market stations, in the Cincinnati market most television stations must be provided the television commercial by noon of the workday prior to when it will first air.

40. Studies have repeatedly indicated that Americans usually speak at a rate of between 120 and 150 words per minute. See Stephen E. Lucas, *The Art of Public Speaking* (New York: Random House, 2004), 300.

41. Shaw, *Campaign Manager*, 213–26.

42. Bike, *Winning Political Campaigns*, 8.

43. Dinkin, *Campaigning in America*, 167.

44. "Radio Facts and Figures," News Generation, accessed November 24, 2018, https://www.newsgeneration.com/broadcast-resources/radio-facts-and-figures.

45. "Audio Today 2018." Nielsen Company, April 2018, accessed November 24, 2018, https://americanradiohistory.com/Archive-Arbitron/Radio-Today-State-of-the-Media/Nielsen-Audio-Today-Report-2018-April.pdf.

46. Curtis Green, "A Good Radio Jingle Goes a Long Way," *Campaigns and Elections*, April 2005, 37–38.

47. Joshua Brustein, "Pandora Knows How to Cash In on Nasty Politics," *Bloomberg Businessweek*, July 24, 2014, accessed January 13, 2015, www.businessweek.com/articles/2014-07-24/pandora-knows-how-to-cash-in-on-nasty-politics.

48. "Number of Sirius XM Holdings' Subscribers," Statista, 2018, accessed November 24, 2018, https://www.statista.com/statistics/252812/number-of-sirius-xms-subscribers.

49. Michael O'Shea, "Who listens to talk radio and radio shows these days (2017)? Disproportionately people of lower intelligence?" March 7, 2017, https://www.quora.com/Who-listens-to-talk-radio-and-radio-shows-these-days-2017-Disproportionately-people-of-lower-intelligence.

50. Dan Schill and John Allen Hendricks, *The Presidency and Social Media* (New York: Routledge, 2018), xvii.

51. Steve Lanzano, "Marketing to Voters: Media's Influence on Word of Mouth," *Campaigns and Elections*, June 14, 2018, accessed July 12, 2018, https://campaignsandelections.com/campaign-insider/marketing-to-voters-media-s-inflence-on-word-of-mouth.

52. John Tedesco and Scott Dunn, "Political Advertising in the 2012 US Presidential Campaign," in *The 2012 Presidential Campaign: A Communication Perspective*, ed. Robert E. Denton, Jr. (Lanham, MD: Rowman & Littlefield, 2013).

53. Scott Dunn and John C. Tedesco, "Political Advertising in the 2016 Presidential Election" in *The 2016 US Presidential Campaign*, ed. Robert E. Denton, Jr. (Cham, Switzerland: Palgrave Macmillan, 2017), 100.

54. Typically, the change will be to a form of commercial that does not require the candidate to be on the camera. One of the most successful such adjustments was engineered by New York governor Nelson Rockefeller's 1966 reelection campaign managers. At the outset of the campaign, Rockefeller had several major political liabilities; moreover, his deep, gravelly bass voice was not appealing. These factors caused his management team to conclude that putting him on television was counterproductive. Instead, they produced a series of advertisements featuring a puppet fish that focused on his many accomplishments as governor. Later in the campaign, when his standing had increased, Rockefeller appeared in his own advertisements. See Edwin Diamond and Stephen Bates, *The Spot: The Rise of Political Advertising on Television* (Cambridge, MA: MIT Press, 1984), 318–19, for an account of this campaign.

55. Bike, *Winning Political Campaigns*, 5–6.

56. "Obama 2012: President's Ad Team Used Cable TV to Outplay Mitt Romney," *Huffington Post*, March 7, 2013, accessed January 19, 2015, www.huffingtonpost.com/2013/01/05/obama-2012_n_2414955.html.

57. The 36 percent estimate was made by Robin Roberts of National Media, Inc., one of the largest Republican media consulting firms, in an interview with Robert Friedenberg, Alexandria, Virginia, January 17, 1997. The 80 percent estimate was made by Online Fortune of Creative Cable TV in an interview with Robert Friedenberg, Washington, DC, January 16, 1997.

58. Kaye, "Data-Driven Targeting."

59. Kate Kaye, "Data Drives Political Advertisers to Buy More Cable TV Than Ever," *Ad Age*, February 23, 2016, accessed November 27, 2018, https://adage.com/article/campaign-trail/data-drives-political-advertisers-buy-cable-tv/302793.

60. Tad Devine, "Paid Media—in an Era of Revolutionary Change," in *Campaigns on the Cutting Edge*, ed. Richard Semiatin (Washington, DC: Congressional Quarterly Press, 2008), 28.

61. Kristen Foot and Steven Schneider, *Web Campaigning* (Cambridge, MA: MIT Press, 2006), 8.

62. Laura Woolsey, "Web Usability: The Development and Application of a New Instrument for Objective Usability Inspection," master's thesis, Miami University, 2001, 40.

63. Foot and Schneider, *Web Campaigning*, 8.

64. Johnson, *Democracy for Hire*, 337.

65. Andrew Williams and John Tedesco, "Introduction," in *The Internet Election*, ed. Andrew Williams and John Tedesco (Lanham, MD: Rowman & Littlefield, 2006), 1.

66. Johnson, *Democracy for Hire*, 337.

67. Morley Winograd and Michael Hais, *Millennial Makeover: MySpace, YouTube, and the Future of American Politics* (New Brunswick, NJ: Rutgers University Press, 2008), 166.

68. Diana Owen, "Voters to the Sidelines: Old and New Media in the 2012 Election," in *Barack Obama and the New America*, ed. Larry Sabato (Lanham, MD: Rowman & Littlefield, 2013), 111.

69. Kaye, "Data-Driven Targeting."

70. "In Changing News Landscape, Even Television Is Vulnerable," Pew Research Center, September 27, 2012, accessed January 13, 2014, www.people-press.org/files/legacy-pdf/2012%20News%20Consumption%20Report.pdf.

71. Schill and Hendricks, *Presidency and Social Media*, xvii.

72. Winograd and Hais, *Millennial Makeover*, 158.

73. Erika Fowler, Michael Franz, and Travis Ridout, *Political Advertising in the United States* (Boulder, CO: Westview Press, 2016), 75–81.

74. Ibid., 97–98.

75. Ibid., 103.

76. Ibid., 106.

77. Darrell West, *Air Wars*, 5th ed. (Washington, DC: Congressional Quarterly Press, 2010), 27.

78. Stephen D. Hull, "Understanding Political Media Buying," WinningCampaigns.org, accessed January 2, 2011, www.winningcampaigns.org/Winning-Campaigns-Archive-Articles/Understanding-Political-Media-Buying.html.

79. West, *Air Wars*, 26–27.

80. The explanation of buying found in this paragraph is based on Jerry Hagstrom, *Political Consulting: A Guide for Reporters and Citizens* (New York: Freedom Forum, 1992), 22–23.

81. These strategies are adapted and in some cases renamed from those presented in Republican National Committee, *Campaign Seminars*, 21–22.

82. Paul Steinhauser, "Different Strategies in Campaign Ad Battle," CNN, August 24, 2012, accessed January 23, 2015, politicalticker.blogs.cnn.com/2012/08/24/different-strategies-in-campaign-ad-battle.

83. The best readily available source of information on Beckley is Nobel E. Cunningham, Jr., "John Beckley: An Early American Party Manager," *William and Mary Quarterly* 13 (January 1956): 40–52.

84. See Friedenberg, *Communication Consultants in Political Campaigns*, 2–15, for an overview of the growth of political consulting during the nineteenth and early twentieth centuries. For details on the 1840 campaign, also see the prologue in Robert V. Friedenberg, *Notable Speeches in Contemporary Presidential Campaigns* (Westport, CT: Praeger, 2002).

85. On Bernays, see Friedenberg, *Communication Consultants in Political Campaigns*, 16–17; Sidney Blumenthal, *The Permanent Campaign: Inside the World of Elite Political Operatives* (Boston: Beacon, 1980), 11–26; and for the last interview Bernays gave prior to his death, see chapter 1 of Stuart Ewen, *PR! The Social History of Spin* (New York: Basic Books, 1996).

86. Blumenthal, *Permanent Campaign*, 143–47.

87. Jason Johnson, *Political Consultants and Campaigns: One Day Sale* (Boulder, CO: Westview Press, 2012), 2–9.

88. On Eisenhower's and Stevenson's television consultants in 1952, see Friedenberg, *Communication Consultants in Political Campaigns*, 153–56; and chapter 2 of Jamieson, *Packaging the Presidency*.

89. For a brief discussion of the rise of political advertising and media influence on the 1956 campaign, which includes the quotation from Stevenson, see Stan Le Roy Wilson, *Mass Media/Mass Culture* (New York: Random House, 1989), 309.

90. In his remarkably incisive study, Burdett Loomis claims that the huge freshman class of "Watergate" congressmen elected in 1974 changed the face of American politics by combining ambition and entrepreneurship to work perpetually at acquiring resources to guarantee their reelection and to push their favorite policies. Since 1974, the "new breed" politician, Loomis argues, approaches Congress as an enterprise and seeks to develop a group of personnel resources, such as those discussed in this paragraph, that can be relied on to further the politicians' own election and policy aspirations. See Burdett Loomis, *The New American Politician: Ambition, Entrepreneurship, and the Changing Face of Political*

*Life* (New York: Basic Books, 1988), 1–52, 181–208. This paragraph is based largely on the analysis of Charles Press and Kenneth Verburg, *American Politics and Journalists* (Glenview, IL: Scott, Foresman, 1988), 155–56.

91. This paragraph is based largely on the analysis of Charles Press and Kenneth Verburg, *American Politics and Journalists* (Glenview, IL: Scott, Foresman, 1988), 155–56.

92. "Political Consultants Rake It In, $466 Million and Counting in 2012 Cycle," huffingtonpost.com, June 8, 2012, accessed January 24, 2015, www.huffingtonpost.com/2012/06/05/political-consultants-2012-campaign-big-money_n_1570157.html.

93. Hagstrom, *Political Consulting*, 6.

94. Larger political consulting firms that contract to handle a variety of races during a single election period are normally headed by one or more individuals with exceptional reputations. These individuals serve as "magnets" to attract clients. Often, they are heavily involved in the formulation of basic strategies and subsequently turn much of the work over to their associates and/or the local campaign staff to implement, returning periodically to help the candidate with major events such as filming commercials or preparing for a debate. Like any business, the consulting firm must judge the often considerable costs of doing business (e.g., labor, materials, travel, etc.) when establishing fees.

95. Most consultants recognize that, if they spread themselves too thin, they run the risk of being involved in losing races, hence jeopardizing future employment. Additionally, today most candidates, expecting their consultants to provide them with considerable time and service, avoid those who have already committed to a large number of other races. The exceptions to this rule are polling consultants who can deal with many campaigns at once.

96. This sentiment is constantly voiced when consultants are asked about the satisfaction of their job. It has come up in virtually every consultant interview Friedenberg conducted for material used in this chapter and related writings.

97. Perhaps the best way to get a sense of the wide variety of political consulting services now available to candidates is to simply examine a few recent editions of *Campaigns and Elections*, the "trade paper" of the industry. *Campaigns and Elections* publishes a special edition each winter, normally the March edition, called *The Political Pages*, which is a directory of political consulting firms organized by consulting specialty. The 2010 edition of *The Political Pages*, which is in effect the March 2010 issue of *Campaigns and Elections*, is organized around sixty-four campaign consulting specialties and twenty-one public affairs and grassroots lobbying specialties.

98. Morgan Stewart, "Michael Sheehan: Coaching Clinton," *Campaigns and Elections*, June/July 1993, 54.

99. Roger Ailes, *You Are the Message: Secrets of the Master Communicators* (Homewood, IL: Dow Jones–Irwin, 1988), 9.

100. Viguerie, *The New Right*, 26.

101. Ibid., 26–27.

102. Hagstrom, *Political Consulting*, 14.

# 12

❧

# Political Campaigning in the Age of the Internet and the Growing Influence of Social Media

As society and technology change, so do the ways politicians campaign and govern. The medium does impact the message in terms of types of appeal, verbal style, and modes of delivery.[1] During the Revolution, pamphlets and newspapers provided highly partisan statements of political philosophy. The United States also has a rich history of political oratory. Public speaking was the main avenue of political success and public popularity. Politicians were expected to make frequent and long orations. The political gatherings were festive events with banners, bands, and even fireworks.

After the Civil War, public speeches became shorter, more direct, pragmatic, and concise.[2] During this same time frame, the number of newspaper and magazine articles increased, although they also became much shorter in length. In both print and oral discourse, the focus was on utility of message and sharing of information.

Radio dramatically changed the nature of political discourse, campaigns, and governing. The 1924 Democratic convention was broadcast to more than five million Americans who had radio receivers. President Calvin Coolidge gave the first State of the Union address on radio. During the 1928 presidential campaign, Herbert Hoover made eight national radio addresses. In fact, radio was the dominant medium for politics until 1952, after the invention of television. During this period, radio introduced talk shows and "news reports" and imposed time constraints upon speakers for message presentation. From a campaign perspective, radio allowed for the crossing of ethnic and geographic boundaries. Politicians were careful not to say one thing in one part of the country and something else in another. Members of the press became filters and interpreters of political information.[3] Also during the 1920s, both political parties used newsreels and silent films to target specific audiences.

As with radio, television drastically transformed the form and content of political discourse and campaigns. Television became a major player in American politics in 1952 with the broadcast of the party conventions and the first political ads. The medium brought the candidates and leaders into the intimacy of our living rooms. Television provided the illusion of private, intimate, and interpersonal exchanges. Kathleen Jamieson argues that television demanded a "new eloquence," one in which candidates and presidents adopt a personal and revealing style that engages the audience in conversation.[4] This meant shorter speeches, a more conversational tone, and self-disclosure in political discourse. This sense of "intimacy" allows the audience to feel as if they truly know the politician, and the frequent "conversations" result in feelings of friendship and trust.[5]

Without question, the wave of new communication technology has impacted the creation, collection, and dissemination of information. In addition, the new media enhances citizen issue understanding and political engagement. Over a decade ago, Bruce Gronbeck recognized that we were transitioning from candidate-centered campaigns to citizen-centered campaigns.[6] Citizen-centered campaigns encourage more political participation and a wide variety of ways to participate. For Gronbeck, this transition was "a paradigm shift in American politicking," moving from "mediated communication" to "electric communication."[7]

By 2012, the role and impact of the internet and social media had become a central part of any national campaign. Digital campaign teams now number in the hundreds. Somewhat prophetic, Hajj Flemings of Blackenterprise.com proclaimed, "It is no question that social media is changing everything and possibly predicting who will become the forty-fifth president of the United States."[8] According to John Hendricks, social media platforms allow candidates to bypass traditional media as well as issues or themes they may desire to ignore.[9] The 2016 election of Donald Trump demonstrated the power of social media. Social media provide an increasingly important and essential outlet for campaigns.

## HISTORICAL OVERVIEW OF CAMPAIGNS AND NEW COMMUNICATION TECHNOLOGIES

One needs to go back to the late 1970s to trace the impact of new technologies. The first online bulletin board systems developed were "usenet" groups organized around topics of interest of members. Email became routine in the mid- to late 1980s. It was in 1991 that the World Wide Web made its debut. In the early days of the internet, campaigns established websites functioning as "virtual billboards," offering material that would traditionally be printed as leaflets. By the end of the 1990s, search engines, portals, and e-commerce sites were common.[10] In the decade of the 1990s, new campaign technologies included computerized interactive telephone calls. The segmentation of cable audiences continued with nearly one hundred channel offerings. Satellites were used for distance media interviews and conferences. Video press releases were created for local media, and video mail was targeted to specific constituent groups or geographic areas. The decade of the 2000s presented a paradigm shift in the use of digital communication technologies. Interactivity with voters and frequency of contact became the mainstay of the use of social media in campaigns. Online social networking will continue to alter the political campaign landscape in the future.

The 1992 Clinton presidential campaign was the first to extensively use the internet. However, it was limited to email, discussion groups, and listserv distribution of information.[11] During the Clinton administration, the largest expansion of the internet resulted from a two-trillion-dollar investment in its infrastructure and the establishment of the Office of Electronic Publishing and Public Access Electronic Mail.[12] Although the number of candidate websites increased in 1994, the dominant presence on the web was nonprofit organizations and special interest groups. Most of the sites were informational rather than partisan. A good example was the site Project VoteSmart, which contained candidate profiles, voting records, political philosophies, and histories. Candidate websites were rather crude compared to e-commerce and online gaming sites at the time.[13] By 1996, both major parties had websites, as did about half of Senate candidates and 15 percent of House candidates.[14] There was some interactivity on the websites, limited to audio greetings or video postcards.[15] However, more significantly, all the major news networks and organizations had a large online presence with expanded coverage of the election. Network sites included video, news reports, and poll results throughout the election period.[16] According to Stromer-Galley, digital media strategies were more experimental in the 2000 presidential campaign. There were campaign staff dedicated to digital media. Campaigns began to recognize that they could mobilize strong supporters, raise large amounts of money, and begin to build databases of email addresses to target voters.[17] By 2000, websites could accept donations and provide a daily calendar of events and photos. In fact, John McCain made headlines by raising more than $7 million online.[18] Opposition groups and third parties utilized websites to mobilize supporters. However, observers argued that the internet had little impact in influencing voters. Websites served more as echo chambers where like-minded individuals and partisans were doing most of the interaction. From a persuasion perspective, the web functioned best at attitude- and candidate-preference reinforcement.[19]

In terms of internet impact and influence, 2004 was a watershed year. Nearly one hundred million citizens used the internet for political information, nearly fifty million discussed the election by email, thirteen million made a contribution online, and 52 percent of voters indicated that information obtained from the internet influenced their vote.[20] The paradigm shift in the 2004 campaign was represented by the insurgent campaigns of Democratic candidates Howard Dean and Wesley Clark. There was the most interactivity online during this election cycle. It provided a platform for the underdogs to gain attention and compete with major party candidates during the primary period.[21] Wiese and Gronbeck argue that there were six major developments in "cyberpolitics" that emerged during the 2004 presidential election: the introduction of network software and theory to online campaign strategy, the move to expand database functions to enhance email and wireless uses, the incorporation of coproduction features to increase citizen participation for online campaigns, the entrenchment of web video and web advertising for online messages, the evolution of candidate websites into a standard genre of web text, and the introduction of blogs.[22] The latter element was huge. The traffic on some sites and blogs surpassed viewers on major television news network coverage of the campaign. Specialized software and databases allowed email targeting of voters with personalized messages. At the very least, by 2004, the internet had become an essential part of American politics and campaigns.

For the first time during the midterm elections of 2006, the internet ranked among the top sources of campaign information. Thirty-one percent of Americans went online for candidate and campaign information.[23] Social media also played a major role in the midterm elections. The YouTube exposure of campaign comments by George Allen and Conrad Burns cost Republicans control of the Senate.

Democratic campaigns embraced new media and demonstrated a better understanding of how to use the technology. During this election cycle, the Democratic National Committee spent $7.4 million on web-oriented campaigning, compared with just $600,000 by the Republican National Committee.[24,]

Without question, the 2008 presidential bid by Barack Obama changed forever the use of the internet and Web 2.0 in campaigns. The Obama campaign utilized new media, providing the blueprint for future campaigns. Political scientists Jody Baumgartner and Jonathan Morris call Obama "America's first Internet President."[25]

In 2008, the Barack Obama campaign took full advantage of digital communication technologies to provide a greater role for citizens in the daily campaign activities. The campaign's digital media strategies were a major factor in obtaining the nomination over Hillary Clinton. Campaign messages resonated and activated young voters and the wide variety of digital technologies allowed supporters to participate daily in the campaign. In raising far more money than John McCain, the Obama campaign was able to spend sufficient money on digital media. Finally, it must be recognized that the Obama campaign invested in some of the nation's youngest and brightest stars in new media. They understood the potential and mechanics of social media and digital technologies like no other presidential campaign in history.[26] In fact, the Obama campaign spent $25 million on new media in 2008.[27] The Obama campaign had ten times more online staff than the McCain campaign. In fact, Obama added online communications as a separate and equal element of his campaign team and strategy.[28] Obama's digital campaign staff numbered 750, compared to just 87 for Romney.[29] In addition, the Obama campaign posted four times more content than Romney and utilized twice as many social media platforms.[30]

With a clear blueprint established for campaigns, the uniqueness of the 2012 contest was in using data and analytics to make strategic decisions. The data-driven strategies allowed for targeting and activating voters as never before. Citizens were the targets and active participants in getting people to become interested, loyal voters. Campaigns built unique applications for platforms such as Facebook, YouTube, Oracle, and Narwhal. According to Stromer-Galley, "By 2012, the Obama campaign had found a practice that proved remarkably effective: team-based organizing, mostly done offline, in neighborhoods, especially in swing states, controlling the message in a hierarchical, top-down fashion, orchestrating supporters to move with the campaign as a single entity: citizens enveloped with the campaign, the perfect agents to deploy in service of electing the candidate."[31]

In 2016, Hillary Clinton and her supporters ran about 75 percent of the presidential TV spots, while Donald Trump invested early in digital, spending $8 million in July compared with Clinton's $130,000. Overall, Republicans outspent Democrats on digital platforms by a margin of about two to one.[32] John Podesta said this about the Clinton campaign's ad strategy: "Our campaign didn't do enough persuasion through social media channels. I think we relied overwhelmingly on television to do persuasion and used social media largely to talk to our own supporters and our activists. And, in retrospect, when those channels are flooded with information that's coming from dubious sources, you've got to be able to talk to people and get your message across in those areas that people are looking at . . . that's something I feel strongly about."[33] There will be more discussion of the use of social media in the 2016 presidential campaign in chapter 14.

## SOCIAL MEDIA IN CAMPAIGNS

With each increasing wave of new communication technologies, platforms, and apps, there are new ways to target and communicate with people. Loren Merchan recognizes that today we live in "a multi-screen world. . . . Recent history demonstrates that not only does it no longer make sense to spend all your money on just one screen, but that each screen needs to be utilized in the right way. Campaigns that primarily run ads through traditional media channels have no chance of reaching some of their voters on a regular basis, if they're reached at all."[34]

It is also important to recognize the importance of social media in terms of gathering political information and as a source of news. Sixty-eight percent of Americans say they occasionally get news on social media, nearly 50 percent often and sometimes. However, 57 percent of those expect what they find to be "largely inaccurate." Surprisingly, only 11 percent think the news from social media is biased or too political, 10 percent that the news is low quality, and 8 percent are concerned about the way people behave. Perhaps not surprisingly, self-identified Republicans are more negative about the information than Democrats. Seventy-two percent expect what they see to be inaccurate, compared to just 46 percent of Democrats. Consumers of news on social media like its convenience (21 percent), interacting with people (8 percent), the speed (7 percent), and its being up to date (6 percent). Finally, 36 percent of news consumers on social media think it helps them better understand current events, while only 15 percent think it made them more confused about current events.[35]

The Pew Research Center finds Facebook still the most commonly used website for news with 43 percent, followed by YouTube with 21 percent and Twitter with 12 percent. Eight percent or fewer identify the social networks of Instagram, LinkedIn, or Snapchat. In terms of exposure to news, 67 percent of Facebook users, 71 percent of Twitter users, and 73 percent of Reddit users are exposed to news. The full implications of such usage are revealed by age and education of the users. Seventy-five percent of Snapchat users are eighteen to twenty-nine years of age. Users of the sites LinkedIn, Twitter, and Reddit tend to have at least bachelor's degrees (61 percent, 46 percent, and 41 percent). These sites serve as "pathways" to news and sites with the most news-focused users.[36]

Facebook no longer dominates among American teenagers. Fifty-one percent say they use Facebook, whereas 85 percent use YouTube, 72 percent Instagram, 69 percent Snapchat, 32 percent Twitter, 9 percent Tumblr, and 7 percent Reddit. Ninety-five percent of today's youth have a smartphone providing constant online access.[37]

There are several motives people express for using social media:[38]

- Convenience, the ability to easily access information quickly.
- Entertainment, search information for amusement, curiosity, or relaxation.
- Self-expression; allows for sharing opinions.
- Guidance, information influences decision making.
- Information seeking, means of keeping informed, access to up-to-date information.
- Social utility; by accessing information assists in social interaction and discussions with others.

Jason Gainous and Kevin Wagner argue that social media has had a profound impact on politics by primarily shifting "who controls information, who consumes information, and how that information is distributed."[39] Social media changes the political learning process in two ways. First, consumers of information select content that agrees with their beliefs, attitudes, and values, thus avoiding conflicting information or ideas. Second, there are so many outlets and sources of information that special interests and political parties can shape and direct the content as they wish.[40] As a result, social media has changed the media landscape and structure of political communication. Where political actors can tailor and target messages directly to receivers, the content is not moderated for accuracy or tempered by review as is often the case with more traditional media.[41] It is important to note that "truthful" and "objective" information and opinion abounds on social media, but users are the ones who self-select the information, thus dictating exposure. They argue that social media stimulates and activates citizen political participation while also contributing to political polarization and more extreme political attitudes and issue positions.[42]

Certainly, new digital technologies of today allow for more contacts, interactions, and associations with political campaigns and candidates than in the past. The digital environment shifted the role of citizens from one of "passive" receiver of messages to "instruments" to work on behalf of campaigns, to share messages, enthusiasm, and support for candidates.[43] As noted by Stromer-Galley, with each election cycle, campaigns moved from "having voters not *passively* watching political ads as they would have in the 1980s and earlier, but by getting them out and *actively* talking neighbor to neighbor, calling undecided voters in a nearby state, or sharing on Facebook enthusiasm for a new campaign-generated YouTube video."[44] Indeed, a study by Warner and his colleagues revealed that when people received news shared by a friend via social media, they trusted it more than news reported from other sources.[45]

Stephanie Martin and Andrea Terry argue that social media and the online environment have indeed transformed how campaign messages are constructed and disseminated. They conclude that today's presidential campaign communications "will become fragmented, necessitating progressively simple and repetitive posts."[46] As a result, this creates "a superfluity of messages from candidates and their campaigns."[47]

The research of Kenneth Moffett and Laurie Rice demonstrates that issue priorities of younger voters do push them to engage in online forms of participation.

Issues that move them to participation vary from election to election.[48] In 2012 the issues that motivated student online participation were same-sex marriage, immigration, and education.[49] Also, Moffett and Rice found that higher levels of online news and blog reading were also correlated to higher levels of civic activity. Not surprisingly, strong partisans and political science majors also have higher levels of civic engagement.[50] Interestingly, "friending" or "joining" online does lead to higher levels of offline political engagement.[51] Moffett and Rice conclude that "As the internet and mobile usage of children and teenagers make clear, each new cohort of college students for the foreseeable future will face a technological advantage . . . when campaigns use online tools to offer opportunities for involvement, a sizeable portion of young adults respond."[52]

## SOCIAL MEDIA AND DIGITAL STRATEGIES

The internet, broadly defined, offers numerous "tools" and opportunities for campaigns to reach specific audiences. Granted, some trend toward younger audiences, but with each election cycle, more middle-aged and older people are using the internet. Gainous and Wagner define social media as "a broad and growing portion of the Internet that is designed as a platform which allows users, and groups of users, to create and exchange content, often in an interactive or collaborative fashion."[53]

John Palfrey and Urs Gasser refer to those born after 1980 as "digital natives."[54] They have grown up with the ever-evolving new technologies. They argue that this generation of youth is very different. Virtually every aspect of their lives is mediated by digital technology. Most of the digital natives live their lives without distinguishing between online and offline. They have a unique identity and are constantly connected.

According to Loren Merchan, it is never too early to start campaign messaging. It's important to get your message out first and often. Thus, securing a digital team early is essential. "Having a team ready before launch means they can take advantage of, amplify, and guide earned media for awareness, persuasion, and acquisition when the candidate announces."[55] Digital activities are flexible, affordable, and relevant; "digital can help maintain a presence with target audiences in key environments (like when they're sharing opinions on social media, searching for something on Google, or reading a related news article) at a much lower cost. . . . The data that can be pulled and used from digital channels can help craft and deliver the most persuasive message possible."[56]

Obviously, the priority is to develop a good website, an email list, and a distribution system, and get the social media channels ready. Then the campaign adds the "bells and whistles" of tweeting, blogging, and posting YouTube videos. The more sophisticated campaigns will develop social networking sites. According to Baumgartner and Morris, social networking websites construct a public profile within a "bounded system"; articulate a list of others who share commonalities of beliefs, attitudes, or values; and "view and traverse" lists of connections within the system.[57] The assumption is that internet users are not easily categorized. They skim many topics and hit many sites. The key is to target "persuasive" messages for the right niche. In addition to geographic and demographic targeting, the internet also allows targeting ads by key words or phrases. If someone is searching a specific word, a related ad is triggered. If someone searches for "fuel-efficient cars," for example, a candidate ad presenting a plan to lower gas prices would appear. Thus, campaigns create their own keyword lists. If a campaign wanted to reach farmers, keywords might include, "feed stores," "farm supply," or "tractors," for example. The result is advertising across thousands of websites.[58]

Candidate websites have a communication role or function that changes throughout the course of a campaign. Early in a campaign, the primary function is to communicate with activists and the press. As the campaign progresses, one hopes to "push" undecided voters to the site so they may learn more about issues and candidates.[59] In her research, Terri Towner found that using visuals on social media content influences users' feelings about the candidate. In fact, she argues that "infographics and photos posted on social media matter more than text and video."[60] A good website can accomplish several things for a campaign. A website is an important way to raise funds, connect with specific constituent groups, organize campaign events, and register voters.[61]

Foot and Schneider identify three basic web techniques significant to electoral campaigning. Coproduction is the joint generation of content or objects that may appear across websites. Convergence is coordinating online and offline activities through organizations, actions, and media. Linking is the most common technique, leading the user to other websites and postings.[62] A great web campaign, for Foot and Schneider, informs, involves, connects, and mobilizes supporters.[63] They also argue that "the necessary strategic, rhetorical, structural, and aesthetic choices in Web production are made within the context of the campaign as a socio-technical organization."[64] The most common features of campaign websites include biography, issue positions, campaign news, links to other sites, donation information, contact information (in addition to email), volunteer sign-up, photos of campaign events, and a campaign calendar.[65]

In 2012, the Obama website was used to gather and compile personal information from those who accessed the page. Before being allowed to access content, one had to provide an email address and postal zip code. Of course, visitors were encouraged to donate money and the site provided opportunities to engage with other voters. The campaign website also provided links to twenty distinct groups providing policy positions. Groups included demographic ones such as African Americans and Asian Americans as well as interest groups such as sportsmen, small business owners, and so on. Finally, the Obama site provided thirteen opportunities to "connect" with his campaign: Facebook, Flickr, Google+, Instagram, Mobile App, Pinterest, RSS, SMS, Spotify, Storify, Tumblr, Twitter, and YouTube.[66]

Romney's website was very similar in content to Obama's website. He also requested personal information, invited visitors to donate money, provided opportunities for participation, and provided dedicated links to specific demographic and interest groups. Romney's opportunities to "connect" with the campaign by social media were more limited: Facebook, Twitter, Google+, Flickr, Spotify, Tumblr, and YouTube.[67]

Political online advertising started in 1998, in a New York gubernatorial race between Peter Vallone and George Pataki. It wasn't until 2004 that online advertising was used in a presidential campaign. However, the advertising was less than 1 percent of the amount spent on television. Four years later, online advertising was equally modest.[68]

Usually, digital advertising begins very early in a campaign to help build name recognition and to build lists. The early digital ads will be a mix of search ads on the candidate's name, Facebook ads "geotargeted" at election areas, and "voter-file-targeted" content ads (banner or video ads) placed automatically on various websites.[69] Merchan notes that starting television ads early and continuously requires large amounts of money. Digital ads can "help maintain a presence with target audiences in key environments (like when they're sharing opinions on social media, searching for something on Google, or reading a related news article) at a much lower cost."[70] It is also very expensive to create and run multiple versions of ads on television. Digital advertising provides the flexibility to test multiple versions of an ad and hone messages for specific and different audiences.

Digital advertising in 2016 broke the billion-dollar mark for the first time. Nearly $1.4 billion was spent on video ads, mobile, email, and social media, representing a 789 percent increase over the 2012 presidential campaign. However, it only represented 14 percent of the total ad spending in 2016.[71] Interestingly, Republicans outspent Democrats by two to one. The Clinton campaign and supporters ran 75 percent of ads on television while the Trump campaign invested early in digital efforts.

While the role and usage of social media in the 2016 presidential campaign will be discussed in greater detail in chapter 14, it is useful to take a quick review of the history and role of new communication technologies, platforms, and social media in general.

## Blogs

Less than two decades ago, the word *blog*—a contraction of *web* and *log*, now a verb in its own right—did not exist. At the most basic level, a blog is a "frequently updated Website consisting of dated entries arranged in reverse chronological order so the most recent post appears first."[72] Today there are literally millions of blogs and billions of blog posts written each day worldwide.[73] In fact, the total number of blogs just on Tumblr, Squarespace, and Wordpress is nearly five hundred million. According to Wordpress, there are seventy-six million posts published each month, with over four hundred million people viewing over twenty-two billion blog pages each month.[74]

Blogging came into existence in 1999 when Pyra Labs offered free software designed for blogging. This software was user-friendly and provided easy updating of websites.[75] In 2000 there were thousands of blogs, in 2004 there were an estimated 4.3 million, and by 2008 there were nearly 150 million blogs, with approximately 120,000 new blogs started each day.[76] In 2012, there were an estimated 31 million bloggers in the United States.[77]

However, it is important to note that political blogs constitute a very tiny portion of the blogosphere. Most blogs deal with food, family life, health, sports, entertainment, and technology. In fact, leading up to the 2012 election in the blogosphere, 10 percent of the topics of stories were on government, 9 percent on campaign and politics, and 5 percent on U.S. foreign affairs. Thus, 24 percent of the dialogue on blogs was devoted to public policy and campaign issues.[78]

Jill Rettberg argues that blogs have become the closest thing to citizen journalism.[79] Blogs do influence policy in several ways. They may follow the traditional route of blog to media to public to policymaker. Blogs may also bypass the media and general public targeting and activate citizens as part of grassroots lobbying efforts of policymakers. According to Richard Davis, "The blogosphere has joined in a transactional relationship with others that allows it to occasionally affect agendas as well as the actions of other agenda seekers, the press, and the public. That association with these players offers blogs an opportunity to be part of agenda setting."[80] Blogs often function to amplify media coverage, may become an echo chamber for media stories for citizen activation, and provide more detailed information and issue discussion. Blogs are also more quickly able to respond to events than even traditional media.[81] In terms of campaigns, blogs allow campaigns to bypass traditional media to reach a specific audience. They also help candidates win, especially in lower-level races. Bloggers have also helped to recruit challengers. Blogs provide talking points to activists on issues and campaigns. Finally, bloggers expose and embarrass candidates.[82] It should be noted that political blog audiences are unique. They are more likely to be male and older than internet users in general. They are also well educated, affluent, and more politically engaged than other users.[83]

## Web 2.0

Web 2.0 is considered the second wave of the internet, marked by the dot-com bust in the fall of 2001. It marks the age of social media and technology. Web 2.0 is instantaneous, interactive, and personal. As noted, the new technology generated a new online political environment. It allows connections with supporters on a more personal basis. The use of technology allows new ways of creating, collaborating, editing, and sharing user-generated content. More specifically, social networking sites such as Facebook and MySpace allow campaigns to target younger voters and increasingly older voters as well, to stay connected in a variety of ways throughout a campaign.[84]

## Facebook

Facebook was launched in 2004 by Mark Zuckerberg, a Harvard University student, with the help of friends Dustin Moskowitz and Chris Hughes. By 2006, the site was open to anyone with an email address. Facebook first entered electoral politics in 2006 with "Election Pulse," a section containing profiles of candidates running for federal or gubernatorial office. By 2008, 75 percent of eighteen-to-twenty-four-year-olds had some form of profile on a social networking site.[85] At the basic level, campaigns use Facebook as another channel to publish information about the campaign. The advantage is that supporters can view updates via Facebook without having to check the website every day. Posting photos and videos also enhances interest. Facebook also allows targeting geographic locations with ads. "Facebook is an open megaphone to your community."[86]

In 2008, Obama had more than two million "friends" on Facebook, compared to McCain's 600,000. Of course, both political parties not only had their own Facebook sites but also started "parody" ones about the opposition as well.[87] The Obama campaign actually had the help of Chris Hughes, one of the founders of Facebook. He was tasked to create an online social network, my.barackobama. com. The site allowed visitors to create personal profiles and blogs, share information with others, organize events, and solicit donations. By midsummer 2008, the site had more than 900,000 subscribers. By the end of the campaign, there were two million profiles created, 200,000 offline events planned, 35,000 groups formed, 400,000 blogs posted, and 30 million dollars raised.[88] The site also monitored discussions, allowing the campaign to respond personally to comments or questions. Supporters were invited to create their own sites and customize them with features from iTunes and Mobile Me. The size, functions, and scope of the Obama campaign site, as noted, were simply historic.

The 2012 presidential campaign was another innovative year in terms of using Facebook. According to Ryan Cohn, "Whether through advertising, search, messaging or community development, these two Presidential campaigns are pioneering the use of social media unlike ever before."[89] The Obama campaign placed ads in the newsfeed of Facebook users in battleground states. They used sidebar ads as well.[90] The Romney campaign used a special tool where sponsored links would appear in a drop-down menu related to the searches being conducted. For example, if terms "Barack Obama" or "Joe Biden" were searched, the first "sponsored" link would direct users to Romney and Paul Ryan pages. According to John Allen Hendricks, there was parity in the use of Facebook between the campaigns.[91]

As you will learn in chapter 14, Facebook was an essential part of Trump's 2016 presidential campaign. The data collected by users of the platform provided the most "granular" levels of analysis and targeting of voters. In fact, the platform actually offered its help and data to various political campaigns. Trump led Clinton in terms of followers, with 12.2 million to Clinton's 8.2 million.[92] It should also be noted that the Trump campaign utilized "Facebook Live" more than did the Clinton campaign.

## YouTube

The social media platform YouTube continues to grow in terms of political influence. Today, YouTube has become the medium of "gotcha journalism." It started with the video of then-senator George Allen of Virginia. At a rally in 2006, Allen pointed to a man in the crowd: "This fellow here, over here with the yellow shirt, Macaca, or whatever his name is, he's with my opponent. He's following us around everywhere. And it's just great." He later said to him, "Welcome to the real America." The term *Macaca* was interpreted as a racial slur. The video was posted on YouTube. News organizations picked up the video, and it dominated news coverage throughout the remainder of the campaign. At the very least, the episode demonstrated the potential impact of a "candid camera moment."[93]

In 2008, candidates used YouTube to attack opponents, introduce response ads, and encourage less-than-flattering "creative" works posted about opponents or flattering works supporting a campaign. Independent groups also developed specific content for the medium. The Obama campaign had nine staff members who contributed to video productions, including an Emmy winner and former CNN journalist. Many of the videos enjoyed millions of hits.[94] YouTube also participated in a presidential debate. Voters used the website to ask questions of the candidates. More than two thousand people submitted videos. There were mixed reviews about the value of the debate primarily because of the nature, type, and presentation of some of the questions.[95] Larry Powell notes, "Before the 2008 election had started, reporters were using e-mail to gather information and scouring the Internet for information to use in their stories. With the 2008 campaign, videos on YouTube became fodder for the mainstream media."[96]

In 2011, YouTube created a separate "politics" channel dedicated to content produced by both candidates and others with a political perspective. While still a strong presence, the impact in 2012 was less than in 2008, which had notable viral videos such as the "Obama Girl." Nevertheless, by the end of the campaign, the unique YouTube channel had 74,533 subscribers with more than ten million video views.[97] As was the case in 2008, the Obama campaign enjoyed more subscribers and viewership. Obama's channel had more than 250,000 subscribers and more than 260 million video views, compared to Romney's 27,633 subscribers and 30 million video views.[98]

YouTube was a major source of campaign material in 2016 with over four billion views of candidate videos viewed in the last eight months and over one billion in the final month.[99] Both campaigns enjoyed equal usage and viewership. The platform carried traditional ads, late-night comedy clips, various commentary videos, and live events, to name just a few.

Thus, YouTube as a website not only is entertaining but also demonstrates the power of individual voters to influence an election. Posted material may be viewed by millions, be picked up by the news media, and generate public discussion.

## MySpace

MySpace was created in 2003. Early on, it served as a free alternative to "Friendster," a fee-based service. The use of MySpace did not generate headlines or controversy during the 2008 presidential campaign. Like the other tools of social media, it just provided another way to connect and interact with supporters. MySpace entered politics in 2007 by creating "Impact Channel," where users could read candidate blogs and view pictures or video of candidates, but more importantly, users could add their favorite candidates to their friends lists. Obama had nearly 850,000 "friends" on MySpace.[100]

Actually, between 2005 to 2008, Myspace was the most visited social network. Its greatest influence was over music and pop culture. It started losing visitors in 2008, primarily because of Facebook, and its influence diminished. Since 2008, its focus is on music and gaming. However, in 2012 both candidates had a MySpace page. As with all the social media outlets, the Obama campaign was dominant with more than 110 million members by the time of the election.

There was a data breach in early 2016 of 360 million accounts that found their way into the "dark web." While still "not dead," it is less viable now than in the past.[101] Like other outlets, MySpace allows people to share their thoughts openly and freely.

## Mobile Devices

Cell phones have been around since 1973, and the first "smartphone" came on the scene in 1993. The campaign potential of the cell phone was realized with the introduction of the business-friendly Blackberry in 2002, which offered organizing, paging, calendar, and email functions. Apple's iPhone was released in 2007, just prior to the presidential election.[102]

According to Jenn Mackay, it was with Obama in the 2008 presidential campaign that cell phones became "a powerhouse of political proportions." "The popularity of Web 2.0, the growing sophistication of handheld devices, and the merger between social networking and the mobile internet changed the dynamic of this campaign and campaigns of the future."[103] The Obama campaign offered a free iPhone application, allowing supporters to organize personal contacts by battleground states, receive automatic updates, and access campaign videos and photos. The campaign also had specific phone wallpapers and ringtones designed for supporters.[104]

Of course, today the use of mobile devices as part of any message strategy is routine. In 2012, both campaigns had unique media apps. Romney's app was designed to reveal his vice presidential choice for the ticket. In order to receive the notification, users had to provide the campaign an email address, phone number, and zip code. The app sent users to the main campaign website with solicitations for a donation and provided the opportunity to share opinions of the selection. With Obama's app, supporters could organize campaign events.[105]

Other mobile strategies include conducting surveys, pushing reminders of voter registration or absentee ballots, inviting people to local campaign events, promoting down-ballot candidates on a zip code basis, and all types of "get-out-the-vote" efforts. Mobile devices today, of course, provide total access to all platforms and have become a major "carrier" of political campaign information, strategy, and tactics.

## Text Messaging

Text messaging was first used by Democratic candidate Howard Dean's nomination campaign in 2004. The campaign provided regular event updates. Mackay reports that a study of the 2006 elections found that 26 percent of those surveyed claimed text messaging with a campaign increased the likelihood of voting.[106] In 2008, campaigns used text messaging in several ways. Some messages were displayed at rallies on a large screen for all to see. Primarily, text messaging allowed campaigns to create an active contact list of supporters. Most important was the frequency of contact. Campaigns could also send thank-you messages and other related comments on a regular basis.

As with the other tools of the new communication media, Obama used text messaging more than any other campaign. His campaign built a very large database of supporters and made frequent contact to keep them engaged and committed to the campaign. The campaign even encouraged supporters to send questions, comments, or ideas to the campaign. Personal appeals for volunteer help were sent in key precincts during primary election days. Their database could be sorted by area code, zip code, and other demographic information. There was even a great deal of media attention and buzz surrounding Obama's announcement of his vice presidential choice via text messaging. Those who had signed up were promised they would learn of his nominee before anyone else. It is estimated that the announcement went electronically to nearly three million people.[107]

By 2012, text messaging was routine. It provides campaigns with the ability to inform citizens about specific issues related to a campaign and raise donations continuously, but equally importantly, it can direct voters to polling places. As part of the Obama 2012 mobile app, those with GPS-enabled devices, if they opted in, allowed the campaign to track their locations. The campaign could target messages to voters in certain areas. Text message strategies were used to interact with voters at events and build their mobile database. At every campaign event, attendees were encouraged to enter a short code, 62262 (which spelled "Obama"), and opt in for future text messages.

Text messaging is a relatively cheap and easy way to keep in touch with supporters with key messages. It provides a 24/7 environment. More and more campaigns are relying on texting as a tool for getting out the vote. A text can remind people to vote, can include links to polling locations, confirm if person has voted, and so on. For example, in the four days leading up to the 2017 Virginia gubernatorial election, Democrat Ralph Northam's campaign sent 1.4 million texts.[108]

## Twitter

Twitter was first introduced in 2006 and is used by individuals posting personal impressions, news outlets covering live events, companies advertising products, and organizations sharing information. Twitter provides a broad network of connections and real-time insights. Originally, users posted short messages of 140 characters to "followers," who may also "retweet" or forward messages to their friends or followers. Now the limit is 280.

There are more than three hundred million monthly active users of Twitter nationwide.[109] For campaigns, it's another way to "touch" supporters. The primary function of Twitter is "authentic personal communication."[110] From a campaign perspective, it's about writing a speech in 280 characters. There are several reasons for candidates and elected officials to use Twitter. Perhaps the main and most important one is that Twitter allows for candidates and officials to communicate directly with a mass audience. Second, it allows for candidates to avoid relying upon media or news media to get out their message. Twitter can also mobilize supporters for action. Parmelee and Bichard claim that the use of Twitter gave rise to the Tea Party mobilizing individuals to form a movement. Another great advantage of the use of Twitter is speed. One can instantaneously respond to events. Finally, Twitter allows politicians to communicate and influence audiences much larger than could be reached through traditional media.[111]

Frederic Solop cautions that candidates should avoid tweets of "pointless babble." Rather, they should be substantive, on an issue or relating to a newsworthy event. They should also have a link to the campaign website. Even the Twitter handle should be carefully assigned. Candidates should have short tags included in messages to tap into communities who are searching for information about the topic of discussion. Twitter may also allow campaigns to listen to supporters. Campaigns can monitor responses, note those who respond, and address specific inquiries.[112] Campaign use of Twitter is cost efficient and a way to get messages out to supporters, avoiding traditional media and gatekeepers.

Interestingly, those who identify themselves as politically conservative took to the use of Twitter more quickly than those who identify themselves as politically liberal.[113] Additionally, followers who are strong liberals or strong conservatives are most likely to avoid receiving tweets from folks with whom they disagree. Thus, those of strong ideological perspectives only follow those with whom they agree.[114]

Parmelee and Bichard found that political tweets influence subsequent word-of-mouth communication from followers. In addition, political tweets influence the actions of followers in terms of looking for more information on a subject, retweeting messages, contributing to campaigns, or signing a petition.[115] The research of Parmelee and Bichard revealed nine elements that make political tweets more likely to be read and acted upon: clarity; a call to action; personal relevance; professional usefulness; containing links and hashtags; including a political counterpoint; humor; interactivity; and outrageousness.[116]

Obama generated his first tweet on April 29, 2007. In total, the Obama campaign produced 262 tweets during the presidential campaign of 2008. Early in the campaign, the focus of the tweets was on Obama's issue positions, such as his opposition to the Iraq war and our dependency on foreign oil. The campaign used Twitter primarily to announce where Obama was at any moment. The second primary use was to continually direct people to the campaign website. A significant number of tweets also provided notice of live event streaming on the website.[117] Interestingly, even as president, Obama continued to post tweets. They primarily ask followers to support various policy initiatives, such as health care in 2010.

In 2012, Obama had nearly twenty-two million followers, compared to just about two million for Romney. Across the campaign, Obama had 7,500 tweets to Romney's 1,300. Interestingly, Romney's tweets were retweeted and shared more often than those of Obama.[118]

Trump forever changed the presidential campaigns by use of Twitter in 2016. Trump opened his Twitter account in 2009, announcing a forthcoming appearance on the *Late Show with David Letterman*. After he announced his candidacy for the presidency, the number of his followers grew to over thirteen million. It became his instrument to speak directly to his supporters and largely bypass the traditional press.[119] They had to rely on and report his tweets, thus shaping and influencing his coverage in the media.[120] Some studies suggest that the tweets of the candidates influenced newspaper coverage on the economy, employment, foreign policy, and taxes.[121] Thus, candidates influenced the issues covered by the media. From the convention to election day, the Trump campaign sent over thirty thousand tweets, compared to just seven thousand for the Clinton campaign.[122]

In terms of Trump's tweets, Katherine Haenschen and colleagues argue that what was unique was Trump's willingness to break the norms of what a candidate should or should not say. By using a personal and authentic style of communication, Trump was able to gain a great deal of attention and connect with his followers.[123] Haenschen and colleagues report that Trump's tweets were less professional, self-focused, more negative, and tended to attack his opponents.[124]

## Pinterest

Pinterest, introduced in 2010, was first used in the 2012 presidential campaign. Pinterest functions as a "virtual pinboard" where users share favorite things and items. Like on Twitter, Pinterest users can share or "re-pin" items. Pinterest users are primarily women between twenty-five and thirty-four years old.[125]

Both campaigns had Pinterest pages. However, because Pinterest users were primarily women, Michelle Obama and Ann Romney had their own Pinterest pages as well. Michelle Obama had 45,000 Pinterest followers, compared to Ann Romney's 14,000. In comparison, President Obama had nearly 36,000 Pinterest followers and Mitt Romney just over 2,000.[126]

The use of Pinterest was less than influential. However, as in the past two elections, the women's vote was critical to the election. The use of Pinterest, by sharing favorite items and things, humanizes the candidates and their spouses.

In 2016, there were thousands of political and campaign images and posts by parties, interest groups, and campaigns. As you will see, virtually all the social media platforms became the repository for posts by Russians attempting to influence our elections. It is not that Russian operatives directly posted items; however, users would bookmark the items on their online boards. And this is not just the case for newer platforms. Disinformation spread on Google, Facebook, Twitter, and other platforms.

## Tumblr

David Karp and Marco Arment developed the Tumblr website in 2007. What made it unique is that visitors could like other people's posts and incorporate them into their own postings. Today, the platform is a "microblogging" social networking site. Visitors can post multimedia and other content in the form of short blogs. It has about five hundred million monthly visitors.

By election time in 2012, Tumblr had eighty million blogs and thirty-five million posts.[127] However, because Tumblr does not provide follower counts, it is impossible to judge its effectiveness. Nevertheless, as a platform, all campaigns will include the site as part of their social media strategy. This is true also for 2016. However, it is now revealed that there were twenty-one Tumblr accounts with connections to Russia's attempt to interfere in the 2016 presidential election. "The names of the accounts showed bizarre attempts at concocting slang terms, apparently in an effort to appear authentically African-American, like 'Ghetta Blasta,' 'Hustle In A Trap,' and 'Swag In The Rain.' Those users uniformly pushed mostly relatable memes about being black in America, then filtered in invitations to protests by IRA [Internet Research Agency] groups like Blacktivist, along with conspiracy theories about Hillary Clinton."[128]

## Reddit

Reddit was started in 2005 by Alexis Ohanian and Steve Huffman, both in their twenties. Initially, visitors would share links with a description and vote for them. The posts are ranked and shown on the site. In 2008, Reddit.com became an open source software. Today, Reddit is one of the largest social media sites. It routinely receives more than a billion page views on a monthly basis. According to the Pew Center, only about 4 percent of American adults use Reddit. However, those who use the platform are news oriented. Seventy percent seek news from the platform and nearly half indicate that they "learn[ed] about the election in the past week." Participants tend to be male (71 percent), between eighteen and twenty-nine years of age (59 percent), and conservative (53 percent).[129] It has a reputation as "unruly and sometimes extreme." Certainly, posts about opponents or issues tend to be rude, crude, and often offensive. Thus, this platform attracts a specific subset of online participants.[130]

In 2012, the platform was just gaining notice and younger users participated in the "Barack Obama in 2012" community. The platform became an outlet for a substantial group of Trump supporters in 2016. According to John Herrman, the outlet allowed Trump to "amplify his pronouncements" where supporters share links, photos, and arguments with family and friends. One Reddit community called "The Donald" had nearly 100,000 subscribers. The "Bernie Sanders Reddit" community was controlled by the actual campaign.[131] As with other platforms, there were Russian "online agitators" on Reddit during the 2016 presidential campaign. Content from IRA-backed websites like "BlackMattersUs.com" received thousands upvotes on subreddits like "r/The_Donald" and "r/HillaryForPrison."[132]

## Snapchat

Evan Spiegel created Snapchat in 2012. Snapchat "is a one-to-one and group messaging app that lets users send photo, video, and text messages that disappear after several seconds." Nearly 200 million people use Snapchat every day. The platform also allows stories (content that stays for twenty-four hours), memories (saved photos to share later) and "stickers." The platform is primarily used by millennials, twelve to twenty-four years old.[133] Users would post items from live campaign events. The postings were spontaneous and informal. Both Trump and Clinton purchased Snap Ads, ten-second videos that would capture an event, location, or "fun" moment.[134] It will be interesting to see if its use increases during the 2020 presidential campaign.

## Instagram

Instagram was released in 2010 and within a year reached over one million users; by the end of 2011 it achieved more than ten million. In 2012 Facebook bought the company for one billion dollars. Today it is a photo and video-sharing social networking service.[135]

In 2016, both campaigns used Instagram. Trump had 1,300 posts with 4.5 million followers, compared to Clinton with 835 posts with 4.2 million followers.

Common to both campaigns were shared personal stories, pictures of family, and informal shots at campaign rallies. Hendricks and Schill note that Trump actually broke campaign norms during the primaries by posting attack style videos. These videos were also posted on other platforms.[136]

## Email

The first national political campaign to extensively use email was John McCain's 2000 Republican presidential nomination race. The use of "VirtualSprockets" software allowed the campaign to send different emails to a single person or thousands of voters. McCain also used email to organize nearly 150,000 volunteers and to raise funds; his email fund-raising was most successful, breaking records for the time.[137] In 2004, Howard Dean's campaign for the Democratic nomination followed McCain's lead in using email.[138] According to Brandon Waite, email performs four strategic tasks for political campaigns. First, it allows targeted messages to specific types of voters by issue or demographic variables. Second, email provides a cheap way to solicit funds and donations. Third, it is a way to recruit volunteers for campaign activities. Finally, it is a tool to activate supporters to get them to the polls on Election Day.[139]

Not surprisingly, email was a central part of the 2008 Obama campaign. Long before the primary season, the campaign established email lists in each state. The campaign website encouraged supporters to sign up to receive candidate emails. As already mentioned, Obama even made his vice presidential announcement by email and text message. By Election Day, the Obama campaign had collected thirteen million addresses.[140] The campaign developed an elaborate email marketing strategy. Messaging was based on supporter interests, demographic characteristics, and donor level. Every email also provided an opportunity to contribute to the campaign, even in amounts less than twenty dollars.[141] Through email, the Obama campaign developed short-term and long-term message themes. The daily emails reinforced the major points made by the candidate on the campaign trail. Subject lines of emails were personalized to the receiver. The campaign even sent emails to supporters from members of the staff attempting to make recipients feel they were part of the "inner circle."[142]

In 2012 the Obama campaign increased its email efforts, raising $700 million. A research team of about twenty continuously tested various appeals, language, and offers. They tested multiple drafts and formats. By the end of the campaign, they had eighteen or so writers working ten-hour days. The top three most successful subject lines in terms of fund-raising:[143]

- No. 1: "I will be outspent" brought in $2,540,866.
- No. 2: "Some scary numbers" got $1,941,379 in donations.
- No. 3: "If you believe in what we're doing . . ." pulled in $911,806.

Just as email is routine today, it has become essential to fund-raising, campaign messaging, and get-out-the-vote efforts. Email is still "king" and can accomplish multiple tasks.

## CONCLUSIONS

Historically, with each new communication technology, politicians are quick to adapt and use the technology to their advantage. Such is certainly the case with the internet, social media, and countless apps and platforms. We are now fully in the digital age. Everyone has a voice and shares views in ways never witnessed in history. According to Foot and Schneider, the future of the web in politics will be in the way campaigns engage in the practices of involving potential voters and connecting with them on an individual basis. They anticipate greater convergence between online and offline activities. "Campaigns will increasingly use calendaring features and reservation systems to attract audiences and crowds to significant events. Location-aware technology, such as GPS-enabled cell phones, will be used by campaign organizations to assemble small groups of highly committed supporters on short notice at events sponsored by other actors, such as state fairs, sporting events, etc."[144] Melissa Smith argues that in the future, websites will be *the* foundation of a campaign. Web presence will require dedicated financial and staffing resources. "One thing that is abundantly clear is that current and future candidates will need to make an investment in online technology and people."[145] Social media has become an important and essential part of any electoral effort. Each advancement allows for the microtargeting of undecided voters by finding and connecting them with like-minded supporters. Campaigns are already coproducing materials for supporters by providing templates, graphics, logos, or documents, for example, to individuals interested in creating supportive websites and social media postings and voter participation.

Mackay predicts that whatever the most recent handheld technology is will be the prominent campaign tool in the future. Such devices provide instant contact 24/7 with voters. Naturally, there will be many new gadgets and technologies introduced that we cannot now imagine. Google and other commercial sites will continue to expand web-based services that may be tailored to political campaigns. She also speculates that it is probably safe to say that local races will increasingly use contemporary technologies as well.[146] And, perhaps somewhat alarming, social media and other platforms and technologies are excited to share their information, analytics, and data with campaigns—of course, for the right price. Certainly, we learned in 2016 and even more recently, large web operations filter and censor information, raising concerns about freedom of speech and censorship across platforms.

It should have become obvious that the Obama campaigns of 2008 and 2012 set the standard for fully incorporated new media technologies. The Obama campaign literally utilized every new available technology, too many to mention in detail: Dashboard, Instagram, Reddit AMA, Square, Foursquare, and Google+ Hangouts,[147] to name a few. New media provide engagement but also much personal information, allowing for the personalization of messages and appeals.

The simple fact is that today the opportunity to engage, to present ideas and information to millions, exists for virtually anyone with the desire to do so. There is no question that more people engage in electronic discussions and viewing. However, have the new technologies translated into more direct political involvement? Have they made us more democratic? Better informed? Have they resulted in better candidates and leaders? In terms of campaigns, the web has the potential to encourage civic deliberation and participation. But a word of caution is needed. Most of the civic sites may do well during campaigns but end after the election. In addition, most of the sites are dominated by commercial interests and run by politicians and other professionals. And, like more traditional media, they are more and more biased and ideological.

Stromer-Galley challenges the notion that the use of digital communication technologies in political campaigns enhances democracy. Certainly, such technologies provide the potential to involve, connect, and inform citizens. However, campaigns do not use them in such a way. The intent of campaigns *is not* to engage citizens as "coequal partners." Instead, the purpose of campaigns is to win elections. In essence, her argument is that the way campaigns use digital communication technologies is to benefit the candidate, not to enhance democracy.[148]

Social media condenses news and information in easily accessible formats; however, some scholars argue that the users actually receive little information or substantive knowledge about topics or issues. The treatment is superficial and contains more opinion than fact.[149] In terms of the 2016 presidential race, Schill and Hendricks conclude:

> Yes, communication technologies expanded the availability and reach of information, introduced new voices into the public sphere and empowered citizens, and allowed political outsiders to more easily fundraise and engage, but they also allowed for the spreading of fake news, rewarded harsh and extreme political rhetoric and lessened democratic institutions.[150]

Thus, political content and discussions on social media favor emotion rather than content, tend to be less respectful and civil, reinforce existing views rather than challenge them, and serve to easily disseminate inaccurate information.[151]

We should not forget that in a democracy, citizen knowledge and participation are critical. More political campaign communication does not ensure better communication and understanding. More technology alone does not guarantee more effective communication. Sadly, despite all the new communication technologies, citizen political awareness, knowledge, and understanding continue to decline. The question for political communication scholars is whether the new technologies cultivate civic responsibility and initiative or simply become highly sophisticated tools of social manipulation.

## NOTES

1. Barnet Baskerville, *The People's Voice* (Lexington: University of Kentucky Press, 1979), 4.

2. See, for instance, Walter Dill Scott, *Influencing Men in Business* (New York: Ronald Press Company, 1911).

3. Samuel Becker and Edward Lower, "Broadcasting in Presidential Campaigns," in *The Great Debates: Carter vs. Ford, 1976,* ed. Sidney Kraus (Bloomington: Indiana University Press, 1979), 22.

4. Kathleen Hall Jamieson, *Eloquence in an Electronic Age* (New York: Oxford University Press, 1988), 166.

5. Robert E. Denton, Jr., *The Primetime Presidency of Ronald Reagan* (New York: Praeger, 1988), 84.

6. Bruce E. Gronbeck, "The Web, Campaign 07–08, and Engaged Citizens," in *The 2008 Presidential Campaign*, ed. Robert E. Denton, Jr. (Lanham, MD: Rowman & Littlefield, 2009), 229.

7. Ibid.

8. John Allen Hendricks, "The New Media Campaign of 2012," in *The 2012 Presidential Campaign: A Communication Perspective*, ed. Robert E. Denton, Jr. (Lanham, MD: Rowman & Littlefield, 2004), 134.

9. Ibid., 149.

10. John Palfrey and Urs Gasser, *Born Digital* (New York: Basic Books, 2008), 2–3.

11. Kristen Foot and Steven Schneider, *Web Campaigning* (Cambridge, MA: MIT Press, 2006), 8.

12. Gronbeck, "The Web, Campaign 07–08, and Engaged Citizens," 230–31.

13. Danielle Wiese and Bruce E. Gronbeck, "Campaign 2004 Developments in Cyberpolitics," in *The 2004 Presidential Campaign: A Communication Perspective*, ed. Robert E. Denton, Jr. (Lanham, MD: Rowman & Littlefield, 2005), 218.

14. Foot and Schneider, *Web Campaigning*, 8.

15. Jennifer Stromer-Galley, *Presidential Campaigning in the Internet Age* (New York: Oxford University Press, 2014), 40.

16. Robert Friedenberg, *Communication Consultants in Political Campaigns* (Westport, CT: Praeger, 1997), 218.

17. Stromer-Galley, *Presidential Campaigning*, 69.

18. Palfrey and Gasser, *Born Digital*, 260–61.

19. Wiese and Gronbeck, "Campaign 2004 Developments in Cyberpolitics," 220.

20. Andrew Williams and John Tedesco, "Introduction," in *The Internet Election*, ed. Andrew Williams and John Tedesco (Lanham, MD: Rowman & Littlefield, 2006), 1.

21. Stromer-Galey, *Presidential Campaigning*, 102.

22. Wiese and Gronbeck, "Campaign 2004 Developments in Cyberpolitics," 220.

23. Morley Winograd and Michael Hais, *Millennial Makeover: MySpace, YouTube, and the Future of American Politics* (New Brunswick, NJ: Rutgers University Press, 2008), 166.

24. Ibid., 175.

25. Jody Baumgartner and Jonathan Morris, "Who Wants to Be My Friend? Obama, Youth, and Social Networks in the 2008 Campaign," in *Communicator-in-Chief: How Barack Obama Used New Media Technology to Win the White House*, ed. John Allen Hendricks and Robert E. Denton, Jr. (Lanham, MD: Lexington Books, 2010), 51.

26. Stromer-Galley, *Presidential Campaigning*, 138–39.

27. John Rowley, "New Media, Like Jazz, Requires Fundamentals," *Campaigns & Elections*, April 2010, 50.

28. Baumgartner and Morris, "Who Wants to Be My Friend?" 56.

29. Hendricks, "New Media Campaign of 2012," 134–35.

30. Ibid.

31. Stromer-Galley, *Presidential Campaigning*, 170.

32. Loren Merchan, "On Digital Strategy, Too Many Campaigns Still Don't Get it," *Campaigns & Elections*, August 3, 2018, accessed November 27, 2018, https://www.campaignsandelections.com/campaign-insider/on-digital-strategy-too-many-campaigns-still-don-t-get-it.

33. Ibid.

34. Merchan, "On Digital Strategy."

35. Katerina Matsa, "News Use Across Social Media Platforms 2018," Pew Research Center, September 10, 2018, accessed November 24, 2018, http://www.journalism .org/2018/09/10/news-use-across-social-media-platforms-2018.

36. Ibid.

37. "Teens, Social Media & Technology 2018," Pew Research Center, May 31, 2018, accessed June 14, 2018, http://www.pewinternet.org/2018/05/31/teens-social-media -technology-2018.

38. Jason Gainous and Kevin Wagner, *Tweeting to Power: The Social Media Revolution in American Politics* (New York: Oxford University Press, 2014).

39. Ibid., 1.

40. Ibid.

41. Ibid, 152.

42. Ibid., 15.

43. Stromer-Galley, *Presidential Campaigning*, 12–13.

44. Ibid., 174.

45. Benjamin Warner, Molly Hardy, Freddie Jennings, and Josh Bramlett, "The Effects of Political Social Media Use on Efficacy and Cynicism in the 2016 Presidential Election," in *The Presidency and Social Media*, ed. Dan Schill and John Allen Hendricks (New York: Routledge, 2018), 107.

46. Stephanie Martin and Andrea Terry, "Social Media Candidate Attack and Hillary Clinton's Failed Narrative in the 2016 Presidential Campaign," in *The 2016 American Presidential Campaign and the News*, ed. Jim A. Kuypers (Lanham, MD: Lexington Books, 2018), 137.

47. Ibid.

48. Kenneth Moffett and Laurie Rice, *Web 2.0 and the Political Mobilization of College Students* (Lanham, MD: Lexington Books, 2016), 34.

49. Ibid., 35.

50. Ibid., 49.

51. Ibid., 100.

52. Ibid., 140.

53. Gainous and Wagner, *Tweeting to Power*, 2.

54. Palfrey and Gasser, *Born Digital*, 1.

55. Merchan, "On Digital Strategy."

56. Ibid.

57. Baumgartner and Morris, "Who Wants to Be My Friend?" 52.

58. Josh Koster, "Long-Tail Nanotargeting," *Campaigns & Elections*, February 2009, 24, 26.

59. Foot and Schneider, *Web Campaigning*, 167.

60. Terri Towner, "The Infographic Election," in Dan Schill and John Allen Hendricks, *The Presidency and Social Media* (New York: Routledge, 2018), 251.

61. Jason Johnson, *Political Consultants and Campaigns: One Day Sale* (Boulder, CO: Westview Press, 2012), 197.

62. Foot and Schneider, *Web Campaigning*, 35.

63. Ibid., 46.

64. Ibid., 167.

65. Ibid., 158.

66. Hendricks, "New Media Campaign of 2012," 141–42.

67. Ibid., 142.

68. Dennis W. Johnson, *Democracy for Hire: A History of American Political Consulting* (New York: Oxford University Press, 2017), 337.

69. Colin Delany, "Three Things Digital That Campaigns Should Do Right Now," *Campaigns & Elections*, February 28, 2018, accessed July 12, 2018, https://www.campaigns

andelections.com/campaign-insider/three-things-digital-that-campaigns-should-do -right-now.

70. Merchan, "On Digital Strategy."

71. Kate Kaye, "Data-Driven Targeting Creates Huge 2016 Political Ad Shift," *Ad Age*, January 3, 2017, accessed November 23, 2018, https://adage.com/article/media/2016 -political-broadcast-tv-spend-20-cable-52/307346.

72. Jill Rettberg, *Blogging* (Malden, MA: Polity Press, 2008), 19.

73. "Blog Posts Written Today," Worldometers, December 3, 2018, accessed December 3, 2018, http://www.worldometers.info/blogs.

74. "How Many Blogs Are There in the World?" MediaKix, September 2017, accessed December 3, 2018, http://mediakix.com/2017/09/how-many-blogs-are-there-in-the -world/#gs.SJIG_Zw.

75. Richard Davis, *Typing Politics: The Role of Blogs in American Politics* (New York: Oxford Press, 2009), 3–4.

76. Ibid., 4.

77. Jeff Bullas, "Blogging Statistics, Facts and Figures in 2012—Infographic," jeffbullas .com, accessed March 6, 2015, www.jeffbullas.com/2012/08/02/blogging-statistics-facts -and-figures-in-2012-infographic.

78. "The Year on Blogs and Twitter," Pew Research Center, December 21, 2011, accessed March 5, 2015, www.journalism.org/2011/12/21/year-blogs-and-twitter.

79. Rettberg, *Blogging*, 84.

80. Davis, *Typing Politics*, 178.

81. Ibid., 179–80.

82. Ibid., 26.

83. Ibid., 164.

84. Jenn Mackay, "Gadgets, Gismos, and the Web 2.0 Election," in *Communicator-in-Chief: How Barack Obama Used New Media Technology to Win the White House*, ed. John Allen Hendricks and Robert E. Denton, Jr. (Lanham, MD: Lexington Books, 2010), 24.

85. Baumgartner and Morris, "Who Wants to Be My Friend?" 54.

86. Steve Pearson and Ford O'Connell, "Eyes Front, Facebook Forward," *Campaigns & Elections*, June 2010, 14.

87. Mackay, "Gadgets, Gismos, and the Web 2.0 Election," 26.

88. Frederic Solop, "'RT @BarackObama We Just Made History': Twitter and the 2008 Presidential Election," in *Communicator-in-Chief: How Barack Obama Used New Media Technology to Win the White House*, ed. John Allen Hendricks and Robert E. Denton, Jr. (Lanham, MD: Lexington Books, 2010), 37.

89. Ryan Cohn, "Who Is Winning the Presidential Election on Facebook? Obama or Romney?" SocialFresh.com, October 22, 2012, accessed March 5, 2015, socialfresh.com/ Obama-vs-romney-facebook-strategy.

90. Hendricks, "New Media Campaign of 2012," 137.

91. Ibid.

92. John Allen Hendricks and Dan Schill, "The Social Media Election of 2016," in *The 2016 US Presidential Campaign: Political Communication and Practice*, ed. Robert E. Denton, Jr. (Cham, Switzerland: Palgrave Macmillan, 2017), 129.

93. Larry Powell, "Obama and Obama Girl: YouTube, Viral Videos, and the 2008 Presidential Campaign," in *Communicator-in-Chief: How Barack Obama Used New Media Technology to Win the White House*, ed. John Allen Hendricks and Robert E. Denton, Jr. (Lanham, MD: Lexington Books, 2010), 86.

94. Mackay, "Gadgets, Gismos, and the Web 2.0 Election," 27.

95. Powell, "Obama and Obama Girl," 91.

96. Ibid., 96.

97. Hendricks, "New Media Campaign of 2012," 139.

98. Ibid.

99. Hendricks and Schill, "Social Media Election of 2016," 138.

100. Baumgartner and Morris, "Who Wants to Be My Friend?" 54.

101. Elise Moreau, "Is Myspace Dead?' Lifewire, November 26, 2018, accessed December 3, 2018, https://www.lifewire.com/is-myspace-dead-3486012.

102. Mackay, "Gadgets, Gismos, and the Web 2.0 Election," 20.

103. Ibid., 19.

104. Ibid., 22.

105. Hendricks, "New Media Campaign of 2012," 136.

106. Mackay, "Gadgets, Gismos, and the Web 2.0 Election," 21.

107. Ibid., 22.

108. Michael Pope, "The Campaigns of the Future May Rely Increasingly on Text Messaging," WVTF-FM, November 29, 2017, accessed July 11, 2018, http://wvtf.org/post/campaigns-future-may-rely-increasingly-text-messaging.

109. "Number of Monthly Active Twitter Users Worldwide," Statista, September 2018, accessed December 5, 2018, https://www.statista.com/statistics/282087/number-of-monthly-active-twitter-users.

110. Solop, "'RT @BarackObama We Just Made History,'" 40.

111. John Parmelee and Shannon Bichard, *Politics and the Twitter Revolution* (Lanham, MD: Lexington Books, 2012), 11–19.

112. Solop, "'RT @BarackObama We Just Made History,'" 14–15.

113. Parmelee and Bichard, *Politics and the Twitter Revolution*, 13.

114. Ibid., 137.

115. Ibid., 104.

116. Ibid., 105.

117. Solop, "'RT @BarackObama We Just Made History,'" 41.

118. Hendricks, "New Media Campaign of 2012," 138.

119. Katherine Haenschen, Michael Horning, and Jim A. Kuypers, "Donald J. Trump's Use of Twitter in the 2016 Campaign," in *The 2016 American Presidential Campaign and the News*, ed. Jim A. Kuypers (Lanham, MD: Lexington Books, 2018), 55.

120. Ibid., 56.

121. Ibid., 58.

122. Ibid., 56.

123. Ibid., 70.

124. Ibid., 59.

125. Hendricks, "New Media Campaign of 2012," 140.

126. Ibid.

127. Ibid.

128. Ben Collins and Josh Russell, "Russians Used Reddit and Tumblr to Troll the 2016 Election," Daily Beast, March 1, 2018, accessed December 5, 2018, https://www.thedaily-beast.com/russians-used-reddit-and-tumblr-to-troll-the-2016-election.

129. Michael Barthel, "How the 2016 Presidential Campaign Is Being Discussed on Reddit," Pew Center, May 2016, accessed December 5, 2018, http://www.pewresearch.org/fact-tank/2016/05/26/how-the-2016-presidential-campaign-is-being-discussed-on-reddit.

130. John Herrman, "Donald Trump Finds Support in Reddit's Unruly Corners," *New York Times*, April 8, 2018, accessed December 5, 2018, https://www.nytimes.com/2016/04/09/business/media/in-reddits-unruly-corners-trump-finds-support.html.

131. Ibid.

132. Collins and Russell, "Russians Used Reddit and Tumblr."

133. Sophia Bernazzani, "A Brief History of Snapchat," Hubspot, August 2016, accessed December 5, 2018, https://blog.hubspot.com/marketing/history-of-snapchat.

134. Hendricks and Schill, "Social Media Election of 2016," 137.

135. Ben Woods, "Instagram—A Brief History," The Next Web, June 21, 2013, accessed December 7, 2018, https://thenextweb.com/magazine/2013/06/21/instagram-a-brief-history.

136. Hendricks and Schill, "Social Media Election of 2016," 139.

137. Brandon Waite, "Email and Electoral Fortunes: Obama's Campaign Internet Insurgency," in *Communicator-in-Chief: How Barack Obama Used New Media Technology to Win the White House*, ed. John Allen Hendricks and Robert E. Denton, Jr. (Lanham, MD: Lexington Books, 2010), 105.

138. Ibid., 107.

139. Ibid., 105.

140. Ibid., 108.

141. Ibid., 108–9.

142. Ibid., 110, 114.

143. Joshua Green, "The Science Behind Those Obama Campaign E-mails," Bloomberg Business, November 29, 2012, accessed March 9, 2015, www.bloomberg.com/bw/articles/2012-11-29/the-science-behind-those-obama-campaign-e-mails.

144. Foot and Schneider, *Web Campaigning*, 206.

145. Melissa Smith, "Political Campaigns in the Twenty-first Century: Implications of New Media Technology," in *Communicator-in-Chief: How Barack Obama Used New Media Technology to Win the White House*, ed. John Allen Hendricks and Robert E. Denton, Jr. (Lanham, MD: Lexington Books, 2010), 152.

146. Mackay, "Gadgets, Gismos, and the Web 2.0 Election," 29, 31.

147. Google+ is shutting down as of April 2, 2019.

148. Stromer-Galley, *Presidential Campaigning*, 2–3.

149. Dan Schill and John Allen Hendricks, *The Presidency and Social Media* (New York: Routledge, 2018), 28.

150. Ibid., 29.

151. Ibid., 30.

# 13

⟨⟩

# Journalism in Contemporary Political Campaigns

## *From Information to Fake News*

Sadly, for decades, public trust of the media has continued to decline. Trust in television press has suffered the greatest decline, from about 20 percent of Americans who have a very high trust in television news to now just single digits.[1] In the 1970s, public trust in the press was in the 80-plus percentage range. By 2004 it had declined to a low point of 56 percent.[2] A recent Gallup poll sponsored by the Knight Foundation reports that 39 percent of Americans believe that the news they see on television, read in newspapers, or hear on radio is misinformation. Also according to Gallup, 32 percent of Americans say that media organizations are careful to separate fact from opinion, down from 58 percent in 1984.[3] In fact, trust in the press is at its lowest level in the history of polling.[4]

In addition to media trust, perceptions of media bias continue to rise. Forty-five percent see a great deal of political bias in news coverage, up from 25 percent in 1989, and a majority cannot even identify a news source that reports the news objectively.[5] Numerous surveys and self-reporting of journalists' ideological views and party affiliations lean left and favor Democrats fourteen to one.[6]

The lack of trust is not just with traditional news media and organizations. Sixty-six percent of Americans believe the news on social media is also misinformation.[7] Today as never before, there is a great deal of hoaxes, misinformation, and inaccurate content flowing across digital platforms. Today's digital environment presents new challenges for news organizations that are already facing economic, technological, political, and social pressures.[8] The simple fact is, among the general public there is high distrust of the news media and information across media and platforms.

In this chapter we review the historic and transforming role of the news media in covering political campaigns. Especially since the 2000 presidential campaign and the rise of cable news outlets, the role of the press has become an issue amid charges of bias and misinformation. The growth of partisan and social media has also created challenges in covering and reporting on national and now even on state elections. We also explore the general media coverage of the 2016 presidential campaign and the rise of what is now called "fake news." The chapter concludes with some basic tips on how to potentially identify questionable news stories, social media posts, and websites.

## THE TRANSITION OF AMERICAN JOURNALISM

The Standard Model of Professional Journalism "includes the disciplines of accuracy, disinterestedness in reporting, independence from the people and organizations reported upon or affected by the report, a mode of presentation sometimes called objective or neutral, and the clear labeling of what is fact and what is opinion."[9] According to Walter Lippmann in the 1930s, a journalist should "confront the facts with a mind and with a heart that had no hidden entanglements."[10] Some argue that being objective is a process of gathering facts and information fairly and then representing them as they exist. For others, objectivity in reporting requires providing multiple points of view on issues and presentations.[11]

There have been several changes in the practice of journalism since the Revolution and founding of the nation. Over the years, American news media transformed from partisan press to professional, objective, fact-based journalism into now, for some critics, a biased and liberal press.[12] According to Jim Kuypers, in the 1960s American journalism began leaning to the ideological left, followed by issue-oriented activism by journalists, resulting today in a partisan press. For Kuypers, the difference in today's partisan press from that of the Jacksonian era is that today journalists "operate behind a veil of objectivity. They present opinion under the guise of an objective journalism."[13]

In the 1950s, conservatives felt that they were underrepresented in the major newsrooms in America. Conservatives launched the publication of *National Review* and *Human Events* in an attempt to bring some balance. Vice President Spiro Agnew, in his now famous 1969 speech in Des Moines, Iowa, proclaimed that a "small and unelected elite" had a profound power influencing American public opinion without any checks or regards to fairness. Ronald Reagan noted his differences with the perceived bias of the press during his presidency. In 1987 the Media Research Center was formed, seeking to demonstrate media bias and expose patterns of slanted and ideological coverage of the news. Rush Limbaugh soon followed and in 1996 the Fox News Channel joined the airwaves. Every subsequent Republican president has publicly noted the inherent bias of the mainstream and then cable media.[14]

As recently as the 1970s, households had only six or seven channels to choose from for entertainment and news. In some remote areas, households were lucky to have three channel options of networks. By 2010, over 90 percent of homes had access to cable or satellite television, routinely providing over 130 channels.[15] The hope was that the cable news channels and options would provide even more access to all types of news, information, and viewpoints. However, over the years, as Kevin Arceneaux and Martin Johnson observe, "cable news outlets have become purveyors of pitched, partisan discourse."[16]

For years, the primary objective of news was to inform the public. Within the last couple of decades, the objective of news has apparently become to persuade viewers to specific issue positions and political or ideological attitudes. Matthew Levendusky defines partisan media as presenting facts in such a way as to support a specific conclusion. Stories are framed and slanted toward particular political agendas. "News is not an end in and of itself, but rather, the news is a vehicle to advancing a particular point of view."[17] Studies have shown that indeed, partisan news can influence attitudes and even voter choice.[18] Thus, partisan media leads to bolstering and reinforcement of preexisting beliefs, attitudes, and values. Kevin Arceneaux and Martin Johnson argue that not only does partisan media reinforce existing views, they actually motivate viewers to maintain the existing views, becoming even more resistant to counterinformation or viewpoints.[19] The resulting inclination of news viewers to select corresponding partisan channels may well create a public that views the world from their own point of view, resulting in more polarized and extreme political attitudes.[20] In addition, Levendusky speculates that because partisan media is so critical of "the opposition," consumers come to have less respect for the opposition and become less willing to compromise. Thus, members of the opposition are untrustworthy and merit ridicule.[21] Arceneaux and Johnson conclude that cable news and opinion shows gave rise to an "increasingly polarized presentation of political information and in-your-face, vituperative commentary."[22]

Ironically, those who watch partisan news are better informed about politics than the general population. Some speculate that because of the high political knowledge of such viewers, they seek related analysis and perspectives on the news.[23] In reviewing the research of the effects of partisan media, Levendusky concludes that "partisan media can increase viewers' attitudinal polarization, decrease affect for the opposition, and diminish support for bipartisanship and compromise."[24]

While America certainly had partisan media in the eighteenth and nineteenth centuries, today's partisan press is very different. Now we have the twenty-four-hour news cycle where stories' influence and impact are immediate and there are countless, nearly limitless sources of information. We live in a very different media environment than earlier times when there were fewer outlets of news and it took much longer to travel across the nation.[25]

## THE 2016 PRESIDENTIAL ELECTION AND THE RISE OF FAKE NEWS

The presidential election of 2016 generated a new catchphrase, "fake news." According to Diana Owen, one of the hallmarks of the 2016 campaign was "the amount of misinformation, misleading stories, and boldface lies that were propagated."[26] James Ceaser and colleagues view fake news as "deliberately falsified or distorted online stories that go viral within political communities of the left and right."[27] The preponderance of misinformation originated on social media platforms. Items "liked," "shared," and "retweeted" generated the "fake news" phenomenon.[28] Highly partisan websites published questionable material of speculation, rumors, and innuendos. Websites would release fabricated, half-truthful, speculative, and sensational stories that would sometimes be reported by cable and other journalists. Many of the sites, such as *Infowars*, *The Rightest*, or *National*

*Report*, were designed to look like legitimate news sites or political blogs.[29] These websites received money based upon "hits," thus the more sensational the stories, the more "hits" for the sites. The stories and material were "true" enough to appeal to the readers, fitting their ideological and political preferences. The so-called fake news reached millions of people during the campaign. And the "fake news" was reposted and mentioned on legitimate sites such as Facebook or Snapchat and others. Examples of "fake news" widely reported include: Pope Francis had endorsed Trump, Clinton had sold weapons to ISIS, an FBI agent was found dead after participating in leaking Clinton emails, protesters at Trump rallies were being paid thousands by the Clinton campaign, Clinton was at the center of a pedophile ring linked to Anthony Weiner's (husband of Clinton close aide Huma Abedin) alleged inappropriate emails to a minor, to name just a few.[30]

Social media encourages a "minute-by-minute" coverage of the campaign. Social media sources also exaggerate the sensational, the unusual, and the wacky relative to more traditional coverage of issues and events. Social media coverage seldom encourages the in-depth coverage and analysis of traditional media. Likewise, Ceaser and his colleagues argue that today's new media environment creates echo chambers with outlets catering to narrow and specific political parties, ideologies, or issue perspectives. Facebook has algorithms that provide news stories that complement the political views of the reader.[31] Political discussions and exposure are with sources of "like mind." Thus, individual beliefs, values, and prejudices are reinforced and seldom challenged. They argue this environment allowed for the growth of "fake news." They report a survey where virtually 90 percent of both Clinton and Trump supporters believed conspiracies involving the other candidate basically at face value.[32]

According to Dartmouth political scientist Brendan Nyhan, this was "the most consequential election for political journalism in my lifetime."[33] For Nyhan, if "truth" is the standard, then a more aggressive approach, as noted at the beginning of this chapter, was well justified. However, it appeared that news organizations were more open and comfortable with expressing biases. Rich Lowry, editor of *National Review*, believes "going forward news organizations may become less apologetic about those biases. It could be a step to a British-style journalism that's a little more partisan and wears its biases on its sleeve."[34] Ron Schiller, former NPR chief, argues, "There's a newfound toughness, a pugilist form that reporters have been embracing."[35] Yes, Trump was the catalyst for this shift. However, the question is whether or not it is here to stay. Certainly, in the early stages of the Trump presidency, it appears to be the case.

According to Abe Aamidor, there are two broad categories of definitions of "fake news." One is based on simply made-up stuff, events or quotes that never happened, items reported from totally "phony" websites, and so on. This category includes stories that are "provably false yet seem to be believed by millions of people."[36] The other broad category includes those who view biased reporting, out-of-context quotes, the use of anonymous sources, or even stories that are not "newsworthy" but are reported to damage a candidate, person, or cause.[37] Misinformation or fake news encompasses three notions: intentional deception, low-quality information, and hyperpartisan news.[38] However, for Aamidor, the most problematic issue for Americans and our electoral process is the general lack of trust in the news media. As he views it, "a free press is critical to a functioning democracy and if people don't trust the press then our democracy will suffer."[39]

Craig Silverman argues, "Lies spread much farther than the truth, and news organizations play a powerful role in making this happen. News websites dedicate far more time and resources to propagating questionable and often false claims than they do working to verify and/or debunk viral content and online rumors. Rather than acting as a source of accurate information, online media frequently promote misinformation in an attempt to drive traffic and social engagement."[40] Some critics, such as Paul Mihailidis and Samantha Viotty, claim that we now live in a "post-fact culture" where "we are left with a world that is hostile toward any claim of expertise and that is increasingly framed by a kind of postmodern relativism."[41]

Today, the fact is that it only takes a few hundred dollars to buy literally thousands of social media accounts or millions of email addresses. Virtually anyone can hire "writers" to develop "content" that may spread a message or ideology to millions. Technology today allows microtargeting individuals where fake news stories or hyperpartisan ones are distributed by bots. As Janna Anderson explains, "the internet's continuous growth and accelerating innovation allow more people and artificial intelligence to create and instantly spread manipulative narratives."[42] Jan Schaffer, executive director of J-Lab, laments, "there are so many people seeking to disseminate fake news and produce fake videos in which officials appear to be talking that it will be impossible to shut them all down. Twitter and Facebook and other social media players could play a stronger role. Only a few national news organizations will be trusted sources—if they can manage to survive."[43]

In the wake of the 2016 presidential election, many media outlets and critics claimed that one of the reasons Clinton lost to Trump was that many websites published false and damaging stories about Clinton. Post-election, Facebook and Google committed to fact-check stories to mitigate the proliferation of "fake news." Of course, such "fact-checking" could lead to censorship and manipulating differences of opinion. For some, ultimately the "truth" will prevail, especially if citizens were more diligent about their sources of information and of sufficient knowledge to recognize questionable material. Few, it is assumed, favor government controlling or dictating what is fake or not. Thomas Jefferson wrote in a letter to Elbridge Gerry, fellow member at the Constitutional Convention, "I am . . . for freedom of the press, and against all violations of the Constitution to silence by force and not by reason the complaints or criticisms, just or unjust, of our citizens against the conduct of their agents."[44]

Brian Cute, longtime internet executive, posits, "I am not optimistic that humans will collectively develop the type of rigorous habits that can positively impact the fake news environment. Humans have to become more effective consumers of information for the environment to improve. That means they have to be active and effective 'editors' of the information they consume. And that means they have to be active and effective editors of the information they *share* on the internet, because poorly researched information feeds the fake news cycle."[45] Tiffany Shlain, filmmaker and founder of the Webby Award, concurs: "I am concerned that as artificial intelligences advance, distinguishing between what is written by a human and what is generated by a bot will become more difficult."[46]

Dylan Byers argues that, because of Trump, "The traditional model of 'he said, she said' journalism, in which news reports simply put both sides of a story against one another, was thrown out the window in favor of a more aggressive journalism that sought to prioritize accuracy over balance."[47] However, for many Americans, especially those on the right, this shift was viewed as media bias.

Beyond the stories of the candidacy of Hillary Clinton, the victory of Donald Trump, and the unprecedented role of social media in 2016, as noted, is the impact and transformation of American journalism. Noted media scholar Diana Owen characterizes the 2016 presidential campaign as the demarcation of "the era of post-truth news." Alarming to Owen is the fact that press legitimacy was "being challenged by an alternative media universe where Twitter rants and fake news hijack the political agenda obscuring the important issues of the day."[48] While many acknowledge that Trump, with his countless tweets and campaign rally comments, provided plenty of fodder for criticism by the media covering the campaign, many individuals believed that the media in general turned his remarks into a very negative caricature of him and thus of his supporters. In many supporters' minds, the media characterizations became personal. For example, some argued that the media should not characterize Black Lives Matter supporters by extremist members, nor should the same occur for Trump supporters.

In an unprecedented action, the *New York Times* executive editor, Dean Baquet, and publisher Arthur Sulzberger, printed a post-election letter vowing to "rededicate ourselves to the fundamental mission of *Times* journalism. That is to report America and the world honestly, without fear or favor, striving always to understand and reflect all political perspectives and life experiences." However, they also claimed that their coverage was accurate and fair.[49]

Throughout the 2016 presidential campaign, Trump attacked the press for being biased, dishonest, and sloppy and claimed that the news media were in "collusion" to get Hillary Clinton elected. Trump shouted the claims at every event, constantly in interviews and in tweets. The public's respect and esteem for the media declined over the course of the campaign. Post-election, the media had the lowest credibility rating on record at the time: just 18 percent of Americans had "a lot of trust" in the news media. In addition, two-thirds of Americans thought the mainstream media was full of "fake news."[50]

Just after the election, Jim Rutenberg of the *New York Times* characterized the Trump victory as "a 'Dewey Defeats Truman' Lesson for the Digital Age."[51] He noted that "the news media by and large missed what was happening all around it, and it was the story of a lifetime. The numbers weren't just a poor guide for election night—they were an off-ramp away from what was actually happening."[52] For him, the missed prediction of a Trump victory was more than an error in polling. "It was a failure to capture the boiling anger of a large portion of the American electorate that feels left behind by a selective recovery, betrayed by trade deals that they see as threats to their jobs and disrespected by establishment Washington, Wall Street and the mainstream media."[53] Rutenberg concludes that the election made "clear that something was fundamentally broken in journalism, which has been unable to keep up with the antiestablishment mood that is turning the world upside down."[54] However, Will Rahn of CBS News was less charitable. "We were all tacitly or explicitly #WithHer, which has led to a certain anguish in the face of Donald Trump's victory. More than that and more importantly, we also missed the story, after having spent months mocking the people who had a better sense of what was going on. . . . This is all symptomatic of modern journalism's great moral and intellectual failing: its unbearable smugness."[55]

As typical in recent presidential contests, the horse race between the candidates dominated the coverage consisting of 42 percent, followed by scandals and controversies with 17 percent, and only 10 percent focusing on policy issues.[56] According to the Tyndall Report, the three major evening news networks devoted just thirty-two minutes to issue coverage in the 2016 general election. For ABC, the issue was terrorism for eight minutes; for NBC issues of terrorism, LBGT issues, and foreign policy for eight minutes; and CBS the issues of foreign policy, terrorism, immigration, policing, and the Environmental Protection Agency for a total of sixteen minutes. In previous presidential elections, coverage surpassed two hundred minutes. However, during the primary season, the networks spent 333 minutes focusing on Donald Trump. Clinton's emails garnered one hundred minutes of coverage from the networks.[57]

Overall, both candidates received highly negative coverage, with 66 percent for Clinton and a record-high 77 percent for Trump. Even when issues were discussed, 84 percent of the coverage criticized candidate positions. During the general campaign, Trump received 15 percent more coverage than Clinton, mostly of outrageous or provocative statements or behaviors at rallies. In addition, Trump surrogates received more airtime than Clinton surrogates.[58]

Trump was given a huge amount of time on the cable networks. They would cover his rallies in full. The networks also allowed him to phone in his interviews. This allowed him to hit multiple shows within minutes, flooding the airwaves; he could avoid questions he did not like or provide glib answers. Even unedited, he got by with misleading statements or what some would call actual falsehoods without interruption or clarification.[59] In addition, according to Owen, cable news coverage of the campaigns provided hours of panels of highly partisan commentators who argued over every tweet, and single lines from speeches uttered at rallies, while largely ignoring more substantive issues and policies. "In-depth reporting was supplanted by a steady flow of sensational factoids, many of which were derived from candidates' and their surrogates' communications. To suit their format, cable news organizations repackaged legacy journalists' detailed analyses as superficial 'breaking news' snippets devoid of context or factual nuances."[60]

Matt Gertz argues that although the coverage became increasingly negative for Trump, the media was holding a rather low bar for his campaign, believing the public would not favor his candidacy. Thus, most, if not all, of the media did not practice deep investigative reporting. There was no need, after all; most in the media openly questioned how folks could fall for Trump as president. Gertz concludes, "editors and executives at major media outlets failed in their responsibility to present to their audience the full picture of the election in proper context, instead providing disproportionate scrutiny to relatively minor Clinton 'scandals' in a way that ultimately resulted in a skewed picture of the election."[61] In the end, "the political press was unable to adapt its methods and practices to a dramatically different election season."[62]

## CONCLUSIONS

It is now evident that American journalism is in transition in terms of election coverage as well as general coverage of elected and government officials. There is real tension between the issues of free speech and censorship. That tension will continue to grow as government and platforms grapple with how to monitor, censor, and even delete questionable content. Such disputes are bound to enter the court system for adjudication. The distinction between "news" and "opinion" has become blurred as what is "news" versus "entertainment."

In terms of social media and the internet, the genie is out of the bottle. However, there is a wide range of things one can do to attempt to avoid fake news. In general, one needs to know problematic sites that are usually fake or biased. There are various compiled lists of questionable news sites. One is Media Bias/ Fact Check, which identifies questionable sources of news and information. One can also learn to recognize problematic elements of news articles that alert suspicion, such as strange URLs, very provocative or inflammatory headlines, references to outdated information, general lack of identifying sources of information or quotes, the use of poor grammar, or the use of pictures or quotes without proper citations or identifications. If a story is based upon other news stories, locate the original source of the information and compare the content. In order to be exposed to a wide range of credible news sources, disable Google's personalized search function and use such sites as AllSides news service, which provides multiple perspectives.[63]

The International Consortium of Investigative Journalists provides several easy suggestions in spotting fake news.[64] For them, clues include that if a story is too crazy to be true, then don't trust it. If other well-known news organizations are not reporting the same story, then the news item is probably fake. Does the news item pass the "CRAAP" test?

- Currency (when was it published?)
- Relevance (is it created for the right audience?)
- Authority (who wrote it?)
- Accuracy (is the evidence backed up with data?)
- Purpose (why was this material created and is there an underlying bias?)

They also suggest that before you forward an item, reflect upon its content, do a quick search for validation of content, and subscribe to trustworthy, quality journalism outlets as a daily reading of news and headlines for information.

The good news is that programmers and computer professionals are designing apps and downloads that can verify stories or information in a matter of minutes. The availability of such applications is increasing in number and popularity. However, today as never before, it is up to the individual citizen to ensure becoming informed on issues, to view multiple sources of information and perspectives, and to ensure proper vetting of information. This is a tall order, but the quality of our democracy and polity depends upon our due diligence and obligations as citizens. The last chapter of this book provides an overview of citizen responsibilities as a contributing member of a democracy.

# NOTES

1. Ben Voth, "Journalistic Hegemony of 'Blue Privilege,'" in *The 2016 American Presidential Campaign and the News*, ed. Jim A. Kuypers (Lanham, MD: Lexington Books, 2018), 205.

2. Jack Fuller, *What Is Happening to News?* (Chicago: University of Chicago Press, 2010), 87.

3. "Americans See More News Bias; Most Can't Name Neutral Source," Gallup, January 17, 2018, accessed July 11, 2018, https://news.gallup.com/poll/225755/americans-news-bias-name-neutral-source.aspx.

4. "News Coverage of the 2016 General Election," Shorenstein Center, January 7, 2018, accessed July 11, 2018, https://shorensteincenter.org/news-coverage-2016-general-election.

5. "Americans See More News Bias."

6. Voth, "Journalistic Hegemony," 205.

7. "Americans' Views of Misinformation in the News and How to Counteract It," Knight Foundation, June 20, 2018, accessed June 23, 2018, https://knightfoundation.org/reports/americans-views-of-misinformation-in-the-news-and-how-to-counteract-it.

8. Paul Mihailidis and Samantha Viotty, "Spreadable Spectacle in Digital Culture: Civic Expression, Fake News, and the Role of Media Literacies in 'Post-Fact' Society," *American Behavioral Scientist* 61, no. 4 (2017): 447.

9. Fuller, *What Is Happening to News?*, 12.

10. Michael Horning, "The Pundit Problem," in *The 2016 American Presidential Campaign and the News*, ed. Jim A. Kuypers (Lanham, MD: Lexington Books, 2018), 79.

11. Ibid.

12. Jim A. Kuypers, *Partisan Journalism* (Lanham, MD: Rowman & Littlefield, 2014), 6.

13. Ibid.

14. Tim Alberta, "The Deep Roots of Trump's War on the Press," *Politico*, April 26, 2018, accessed July 11, 2018, https://www.politico.com/magazine/story/2018/04/26/the-deep-roots-trumps-war-on-the-press-218105.

15. Kevin Arceneaux and Martin Johnson, *Changing Minds or Changing Channels?* (Chicago: University of Chicago Press, 2013), 2.

16. Ibid., 3.

17. Matthew Levendusky, *How Partisan Media Polarize America* (Chicago: University of Chicago Press, 2013), 8.

18. Ibid., 18.

19. Arceneaux and Johnson, *Changing Minds or Changing Channels?*, 10.

20. Ibid., 4.

21. Levendusky, *How Partisan Media Polarize America*, 4.

22. Arceneaux and Johnson, *Changing Minds or Changing Channels?*, 166.

23. Levendusky, *How Partisan Media Polarize America*, 9.

24. Ibid., 111.

25. Ibid., 157.

26. Diana Owen, "Twitter Rants, Press Bashing, and Fake News," in *Trumped: The 2016 Election That Broke All the Rules*, ed. Larry J. Sabato, Kyle Kondik, and Geoffrey Skelley (Lanham, MD: Rowman & Littlefield, 2017), 175.

27. James Ceaser, Andrew E. Busch, and John J. Pitney, Jr., *Defying the Odds: The 2016 Elections and American Politics* (Lanham, MD: Rowman & Littlefield, 2017), 23.

28. John Allen Hendricks and Dan Schill, "The Social Media Election of 2016," in *The 2016 US Presidential Campaign: Political Communication and Practice*, ed. Robert E. Denton, Jr. (Cham, Switzerland: Palgrave Macmillan, 2017), 130–31.

29. Owen, "Twitter Rants," 176.

30. Ibid., 176–77.

31. Ceaser, Busch, and Pitney, *Defying the Odds*, 179.

32. Ibid., 23.

33. Dylan Byers, "How Donald Trump Changed Political Journalism," Money.CNN.com, November 2, 2016, accessed November 15, 2016, http://money.cnn.com/2016/11/01/media/political-journalism-2016/index.html?iid=Lead.

34. Ibid.

35. Ibid.

36. Abe Aamidor, "Fact or Fiction: Defining Fake News during the 2016 U.S. Presidential Election," in *The 2016 American Presidential Campaign and the News*, ed. Jim A. Kuypers (Lanham, MD: Lexington Books, 2018), 12.

37. Ibid., 13.

38. Janna Anderson, "The Future of Truth and Misinformation Online," Pew Research Center, October 19, 2017, accessed December 27, 2017, http://www.pewinternet.org/2017/10/19/the-future-of-truth-and-misinformation-online.

39. Aamidor, "Fact or Fiction," 23.

40. Mihailidis and Viotty, "Spreadable Spectacle in Digital Culture."

41. Ibid., 448.

42. Anderson, "The Future of Truth."

43. Ibid.

44. Jarrett Stepman, "The History of Fake News in the United States," Daily Signal, January 3, 2018, accessed July 11, 2018, https://www.dailysignal.com/2018/01/01/the-history-of-fake-news-in-the-united-states.

45. Anderson, "The Future of Truth."

46. Ibid.

47. Byers, "How Donald Trump Changed Political Journalism."

48. Owen, "Twitter Rants," 177.

49. Liz Spayd, "One Thing Voters Agree On: Better Campaign Coverage Was Needed," *New York Times*, November 19, 2016, accessed May 24, 2017, https://www.nytimes.com/2016/11/20/public-editor/one-thing-voters-agree-on-better-campaign-coverage-was-needed.html.

50. Jim A. Kuypers, "The 2016 Presidential Campaign, the News, and the Republic," in *The 2016 American Presidential Campaign and the News*, ed. Jim A. Kuypers (Lanham, MD: Lexington Books, 2018), 2.

51. Jim Rutenberg, "A 'Dewey Defeats Truman' Lesson for the Digital Age," *New York Times*, November 9, 2016, accessed March 2, 2017, https://www.nytimes.com/2016/11/09/business/media/media-trump-clinton.html.

52. Ibid.

53. Ibid.

54. Ibid.

55. Will Rahn, "Commentary: The Unbearable Smugness of the Press," CBS News, November 10, 2016, accessed February 2, 2017, http://www.cbsnews.com/news/commentary-the-unbearable-smugness-of-the-press-presidential-election-2016.

56. Owen, "Twitter Rants," 169.

57. "Study Confirms Network Evening Newscasts Have Abandoned Policy Coverage for 2016 Campaign," Media Matters, October 26, 2016, accessed May 24, 2017, https://www.mediamatters.org/print/739016.

58. Owen, "Twitter Rants," 170.

59. Matt Gertz, "Election Post-Mortem: 2016 Broke Political Journalism," National Memo, December 30, 2017, accessed February 2, 3017, http://www.nationalmemo.com/2016-broke-political-journalism.

60. Owen, "Twitter Rants," 169.

61. Gertz, "Election Post-Mortem."

62. Ibid.

63. "Real vs. Fake News: Detecting Lies, Hoaxes and Clickbait," Columbia College, February 13, 2018, accessed August 23, 2018, https://columbiacollege-ca.libguides.com/fake_news.

64. "Six Tips for How to Spot (and Stop) Fake News," International Consortium of Investigative Journalists, October 3, 2017, accessed August 23, 2018, https://www.icij.org/blog/2017/10/six-tips-spot-fake-news.

# 14

❧

# Political Campaign Communication in the 2016 Presidential Election

Scholars of presidential campaigns note that every campaign is unique and historic, especially in terms of candidates, issues, strategies, and elements of the strategic environment. However, to characterize the 2016 presidential election as historic is an understatement indeed. The election was certainly unique in the modern era of political campaigns. Many campaign conventions, norms, and expectations were thrown out the window. Scholars, pundits, and certainly veteran journalists were continually confounded by candidate performances, campaign events, and strategies. Without exaggeration, Donald Trump pulled off one of the greatest political feats in modern history. Pundits and scholars will continue to study and analyze this election in the coming years. Many argue that the impact of this campaign will not only affect elections in the future but also the nature of the contemporary practice of journalism and no less notions of participatory democracy.

On Election Day, Donald Trump put together the winning coalition of non-college-educated, working-class, and nonurban voters, who turned out in record numbers.[1] Especially in critical Midwest battleground states, the disaffected wanted change. In the immediate aftermath of the election, there was the meme of Trump's victory based on hateful, racist, xenophobic, misogynistic, and homophobic attitudes of his supporters. Others made the assertion that the election was not based on issues; rather, it was based on personalities. Seldom have we had two candidates running for office with such high disapproval ratings and perceptions of ethical misgivings. Some observers claim the election was not based on issues; however, I would offer some caution. Those voting for Trump, as revealed in exit polls, were indeed motivated to vote based upon issues:

- Fifty-six percent of voters who saw the Supreme Court nominations as "the most important factor" supported Trump.
- Sixty-four percent of voters who thought immigration was the "most important issue" voted for Trump, as did 86 percent of those who want a wall built on the U.S.-Mexico border.

- Eighty-three percent of voters who felt Obamacare "went too far" supported Trump.
- Fifty-seven percent of those who viewed terrorism as the top issue backed Trump, as did 85 percent of those who thought the fight against ISIS was going "very badly."
- Seventy-three percent of voters who felt the "government [is] doing too much" went for Trump.

Exit polls also revealed that most voters expected Clinton to continue the policies of President Obama. For some, the election represented a referendum on the Obama administration; for others it was a rejection of establishment candidates, norms, and "business as usual."

After the election, the focus of discussion was equally on how Clinton lost what was a virtual certainty of election. Explanations included Clinton as a poor candidate, the campaign ignoring the Rust Belt battleground states, and FBI director James Comey's surprise announcement of reopening the private server investigation and the thousands of leaked emails from her secretary of state tenure, to name only a few. In hindsight, tactical errors of the Clinton campaign were noted. In the end, although she won the popular vote, Hillary Clinton underperformed among young people, minorities, and the white working class. She also underperformed in the thirteen swing states where Obama won rather easily, yet Trump won by 1.8 percent.[2] Finally, what we also learned is that voters deciding within the last week of the election went for Trump.

Another factor that must be noted is that the 2016 presidential election was one of the most polarized elections in contemporary history along the lines of ideology, party, income, gender, and age. For more than a year prior to the election, national anger and frustration grew to historic levels. Polls revealed that the public was frustrated with the direction of the nation and with the institutions of government. Americans, especially those in the middle class, blue-collar workers, and minorities, were downright angry. Not since the 1990s have we witnessed such general anger and political fragmentation. An argument can be made that the general frustration may well explain the candidacies of Donald Trump and Bernie Sanders.

As observers of campaigns, one could not help but note a rather dramatic shift in tone and aggressiveness in media coverage during the campaign. Trump's relationship with the media during and after the campaign may well have changed the nature of American political journalism.[3] Journalists were aggressive, challenging, contextualizing, fact checking, and even editorializing more than in the past because of Trump's confrontational style and often sweeping generalizations, or even what some would label falsehoods. As a result, especially for Trump supporters, the "mainstream media" appeared biased, hostile, liberal, and as advocates for Clinton. More will be discussed on the transformative nature of media coverage and consequences of the 2016 presidential campaign later in this chapter.

The purpose of this chapter is to provide a brief overview and general summary of some of the variables of political campaign communication in the 2016 presidential campaign. Topic areas mirror many of those in the primary text, including candidate surfacing, the primaries, the conventions, the debates, advertising, social media, journalism and fake news, and issues of gender.

## CANDIDATE SURFACING PHASE

According to Craig Allen Smith, Republicans and Democrats approached the primaries with very different issue concerns.[4] Republicans were very dissatisfied with government in general, followed by the economy and immigration. For Democrats, the primary concerns were the economy, unemployment, and gridlock in government. Polls also revealed major differences between the parties on issues of national security, the federal deficit, race relations, and terrorism, to name a few.[5]

Republicans started with seventeen candidates expressing interest and the Democrats with five. According to Smith, during the candidate-surfacing phase of a campaign, critical considerations include ability in fund-raising, obtaining major endorsements, the nature of media coverage, rankings in national polls, and success in the all-important Iowa caucuses.[6] Hillary Clinton clearly dominated the surfacing stage of the campaign, followed rather closely by Bernie Sanders. Among the Republicans, it was much more complicated, and various candidates had strengths and weaknesses across all the five elements of the surfacing phase of the campaign. The dominant candidates to emerge were Donald Trump, Marco Rubio, and Ted Cruz, while Jeb Bush, Ben Carson, and John Kasich committed to compete in the primary season.

## THE PRIMARIES

Perhaps no candidate was better positioned to receive the nomination than Hillary Clinton. In addition to being the former first lady, Clinton had served as senator from New York and secretary of state. Yet as the primary season began, many claimed that over the years she became one of the "elites," a multimillionaire with an elaborate lifestyle. She was a grandmother in her late sixties with rumors of health concerns. Bill Clinton's past followed her as she tried to appeal to a younger generation. Hillary had her own potential scandals, with questions of the Clinton Foundation and her use of a private server as secretary of state. For some Democrats, there was simply "Clinton fatigue," a time for new leadership, new ideas, and generational change.[7]

Although even older than Clinton, Bernie Sanders provided new and "progressive" ideas about issues, policy, and the role of government in American lives. A self-proclaimed socialist and longtime Independent, Sanders advocated for tax increases on the wealthy, greater government services across the board, and equally important, he voted against the Iraq war. He grew a following among the most liberal and younger members of the party. He appeared "authentic" and spoke with conviction. Throughout the early primary season, Sanders focused on the economy and political reform. While moving to the left as well, Clinton aggressively pursued the African American vote, embracing the Black Lives Matter movement. Clinton inched toward the nomination with major victories on Super Tuesday. Sanders's supporters vowed to continue to the convention. As Ceaser and his colleagues observe, "Bernie Sanders lost the nomination but won the party."[8] According to polls, Sanders enjoyed a higher favorability rating than Clinton.

Republicans had a wealth of promising potential candidates from which to select a nominee: governors, senators, businesspeople, and even a noted surgeon. There was ethnic and ideological diversity represented among the contenders. Republicans controlled the federal House and Senate, and many state legislative bodies. Initially, few politicians, pundits, or political operatives took the candidacy of Donald Trump seriously. However, soon it became clear that he was developing a devoted following. To many, he tapped into their anger and frustration.

Many Republican primary voters liked his boldness, aggressiveness, and "tell it like it is" approach to issues. They especially liked his attacks upon the media and Washington culture, and the call for change across the board. Other candidates found it difficult to gain free airtime; Trump dominated the news cycle. Media attacks as well as those of opponents during debates actually backfired, providing motivation for stronger support among Trump devotees. One by one, Trump prevailed in the primaries. No controversy or attack slowed his momentum. Although splitting the vote in the primaries among the contenders, Trump won the Republican vote. Ceaser and his colleagues attribute his success to the fact that "he jumped out to an early lead, consolidated it while his opponents were busy fighting among themselves, and held on despite late advances by others."[9] In the end, Trump won twenty-seven of the forty-two state contests. Although victorious, as the conventions approached Trump's task was to unite the party and provide a rationale for his candidacy.

For the primaries, Republicans enjoyed a record number of primary voters and the second highest number of primary voters for the Democrats.[10] In total, more than sixty million citizens participated in the presidential primaries. Part of the reason is that 2016 was the first election in eight years without an incumbent. There was high interest in both parties. In addition, the two high-profile and historic candidacies of Hillary Clinton and Donald Trump clearly added excitement and "drama" to the nomination process.

On the Republican side, Trump dominated the media coverage, receiving over $2 billion in "free media" coverage. As a candidate, he moved from less than 5 percent support among Republicans to more than 30 percent support by the beginning of primary voting.[11] Trump dominated the primaries, winning seventeen of the twenty-one primaries. Bernie Sanders in the Democratic nomination race enjoyed enthusiastic supporters; however, Hillary Clinton dominated the two-person race, receiving four million more votes and commitments from the "super delegates" heading for the convention. According to Rhodes Cook, the turnout profiles of the

primary season did provide clues to the pending fall election. The Trump campaign brought in new Republican voters across key demographic groups. In addition, his campaign outperformed Democrat rivals in key battleground states such as Florida,

Iowa, Michigan, North Carolina, Ohio, and Wisconsin. Thus, according to Cook, Trump's success in these battleground states served as a harbinger for the fall election.[12]

## THE CONVENTIONS

Given the nature of the primaries on both sides, there was much interest and excitement in anticipation of the party conventions. There were widespread expectations of drama, especially with the Republicans. Nominating conventions serve as the transition from the primary campaign to the general election. From a communication perspective, conventions "reaffirm and celebrate the democratic selection of candidates, thereby legitimizing both the process and the nominees. The conventions also create a communication moment through which the political parties set aside the divisions evident in the primary campaign and establish party unity, commitment, and excitement for the general election. Finally the conventions afford the candidate a platform to introduce and elaborate campaign issues and messages in a highly controlled, choreographed, and scripted production."[13] The parties create a narrative of American core beliefs, attitudes, and values. They share a vision of the nation and the path forward.

In the aftermath of the primaries, the national mood was still one of frustration and anxiety for the future direction of the country. In addition, both parties confronted internal splits within party loyalists. On the Republican side, there was speculation of a possible "brokered" convention. For Democrats, the challenge was to reassure Sanders's wing of the party that Clinton would honor some of his campaign's issue positions and causes. As Rachel Holloway notes, "Both candidates faced significant rhetorical challenges as they prepared for the nominating conventions."[14]

### The Republicans

The Republican convention was first, and the theme was the now infamous "Make America Great Again." Each evening had a subtheme: Monday was "Make America Safe Again," Tuesday "Make America Work Again," Wednesday "Make America First Again," and Thursday "Make America One Again." Some opponents would not attend, nor former presidents George H. W. Bush or George W. Bush, nor former nominees John McCain or Mitt Romney, nor numerous elected House representatives and senators. From an operational perspective, the convention lacked clear organization and campaign messaging. To make matters more difficult, there was a floor fight led by the "Never Trump" leaders to avert Trump's nomination. Collectively, Republican speakers presented a dangerous world—America under attack both internationally and domestically, all the result of the "Obama/Clinton" years in office.[15]

Members of Trump's family attempted to portray a "softer" image of Trump. Trump's wife, Melania, shared her story as an immigrant to this country and spoke at length of Trump's positive personal attributes of "caring," "fairness," and "kindness." While she made a very good effort, she was criticized for passages of similarity to Michelle Obama's 2008 Democratic Convention address. His son, Donald Trump, Jr., spoke of his father's business successes and commitment to blue-collar workers. Son Eric Trump followed suit and detailed how his father would bring jobs and better health care for working families.[16]

Some of Trump's opponents did speak in support of Trump: Chris Christie, Ben Carson, Scott Walker, Marco Rubio, and Rick Perry. However, all eyes were on Ted Cruz. While allowed to speak, he had not provided any indication of endorsement. Cruz focused on conservative values and his agenda for the country. In the middle of his address, Trump entered the convention center with cameras focused. Cruz concluded with a call to action but did not formally endorse Trump. Cruz left the stage to a resounding chorus of boos.[17] Vice presidential nominee Mike Pence provided a more traditional address, articulating Republican values, a conservative agenda, and the rationale for supporting Trump. There were a diverse group of speakers in favor of Trump, mostly focusing on his personal values and agenda. Daughter Ivanka Trump introduced her father, characterizing him as an "outsider," "fighter," person of "compassion," and one who hires the best people for jobs. In essence, her father was simply the best person for the job and task of "Making America Great Again."[18]

Trump's acceptance speech was more than an hour long, and according to Jim Kuypers, the speech conformed to the general norms and expectations of a nomination acceptance speech.[19] The nation was in "crisis." Trump provided a litany of domestic and international problems. To change America required a drastic change in leadership. As an outsider, he alone could fix the economy, strengthen our position in the world, tackle terrorism and destroy ISIS, and protect our borders. Trump concluded:

> I am your voice. So, to every parent who dreams for their child, and every child who dreams for their future, I say these words to you tonight: I am with you, and I will fight for you, and I will win for you! To all Americans tonight, in all our cities and towns, I make this promise: We will make America strong again! We will make America proud again! We will make America safe again! And we will make America great again![20]

## The Democrats

As with the Republicans, there was a last-minute effort by Sanders's diehard supporters to challenge Clinton's nomination on the floor of the convention. To make matters worse, just days before the convention over twenty thousand Democratic National Committee emails were released showing clear bias in favor of Clinton's nomination. This resulted in a change of leadership at the DNC. Despite protests, it was clear that Clinton would proceed to win the nomination.

The theme of the Democratic Convention was "Stronger Together." According to Holloway, unlike the Republican Convention, the Democratic Convention was well organized, scripted, and choreographed with targeted messages and crafted videos that praised Clinton's achievements and future promises.[21] Every message was counter to Trump's statements, character, issue positions, and prescribed policies, often using clips of his own words during the primary campaign. Each evening hosted a diverse group of speakers and testimonials praising Clinton and attacking Trump. The first night featured speeches by Michelle Obama and

Elizabeth Warren, with a video tribute to Bernie Sanders, who took to the podium to endorse Clinton. The message was one of recognizing the life work of Clinton in public service and party unity. On the second night, it was Sanders who made a motion to accept Clinton's nomination by acclamation.[22]

Throughout the convention, speakers included celebrities, noted political leaders, and representatives from key special interest groups and organizations such as Planned Parenthood Federation of America and the Mothers of the Movement from Blacks Lives Matter. There were speakers representing every major voting bloc, including military veterans who could attest to her fitness as the potential commander in chief.[23] The keynote speaker for the convention was former president Bill Clinton. As expected, he provided a firsthand account of their life together and her many fine attributes. Interestingly, he directly addressed the notion that she was an ultimate insider, who had been around too long on the political scene. He acknowledged:

> So, people say, well, we need to change. She's been around a long time, she sure has, and she's sure been worth every single year she's put into making people's lives better. I can tell you this. If you were sitting where I'm sitting and you heard what I have heard at every dinner conversation, every lunch conversation, on every long walk, you would say this woman has never been satisfied with the status quo in anything. She always wants to move the ball forward. That is just who she is.[24]

Other notable speakers included Vice President Joe Biden and President Barack Obama, as well as vice presidential nominee Tim Kaine.[25] Like Trump, Clinton relied upon her daughter, Chelsea Clinton, to share the more personal side of her role as mother and lessons learned in the face of crisis and defeat. Her mother was a "champion," "fighter," and "hero."[26]

In Clinton's acceptance speech, she contrasted her vision of America with the negative one of Trump. She portrayed Trump as polarizing, divisive, and of the wrong temperament for the presidency. Clinton provided in great detail how she would address economic, social, and foreign policy issues.[27]

For Jim Kuypers, both campaigns achieved the goals of an acceptance address. "Both closed their respective primary contests; both lauded their respective political parties; both transitioned their respective campaigns to the general election. Certainly, both candidates attacked the opposition and acclaimed their own positions and parties."[28] However, from the public perspective, the Democratic Convention was more successful than the Republican Convention. More Democrats were "more favorable" toward Clinton's candidacy in the aftermath of the convention.[29] There was a clear difference in tone and vision between the two conventions. However, both conventions acknowledged the anger and frustration of Americans across the board. And both conventions offered a candidate who would be a change agent. As Holloway observes, "Both candidates were described as pragmatic problem solvers who would 'have the back' of those who were forgotten or left behind. Both parties promised a leader who recognized and valued the 'common person.' Both campaigns promised to restore the American Dream, to focus on building a country that would benefit all Americans, especially those who felt the government no longer worked to support their well-being. Both candidates said creating a better world for future generations was a primary motivation of their campaigns."[30] In the end, Holloway argues that the nominating conventions actually "reaffirmed a deep concern among the American people, distrust in government."[31] As a result, neither candidate received a significant "convention bounce" in the polls, and both "entered the general election only slightly better off than when the convention began."[32]

## THE DEBATES

As the general campaign began, both candidates had among the lowest approval ratings in the history of contemporary presidential campaigns, both well under 50 percent. There was great anticipation for the pending debates between Trump and Clinton. Indeed, more than eighty-one million tuned in to the first debate, establishing a historical record of viewers. The average audience across the three debates surpassed seventy-three million. Collectively, polls reveal that the debates were an "important factor" for 82 percent of voters. Historically, research shows that 7 percent of undecided voters select candidate preference based upon debate performance.[33]

According to Ben Voth, even the primary debates generated historic audiences, especially among the Republicans.[34] The first primary debate actually provided the first time the general public could witness Trump in exchanges with opponents and not in a "protected" environment as on the campaign trail. The first primary debate also provided a glimpse of how Trump would handle adversarial questions and personal attacks. The main headlines following the first debate focused on Trump with his attack on moderator Megyn Kelly and his refusal to take the pledge to support the winner of the nomination process. Republicans engaged in a total of eleven debates. With each debate, the field of candidates shrank and Trump became less defensive and more focused on message and issues. However, he was the target of opponents and moderators.[35]

Each of the debates with Clinton provided "high drama" and key moments of exchanges that generated headlines and material for campaigns and pundits alike. While there is not space to provide a detailed synopsis of the debates, Ben Voth noticed several interesting findings from his analyses:

- During the debate period, Trump received historic negative media coverage in tone compared to generally favorable coverage for Clinton.
- Interestingly, both Trump and Clinton received about equal amounts of speaking time across the debates (moderators consumed about 15 percent of all speaking time).
- There were several noted incidents of collusion between the Clinton campaign and the moderators. Donna Brazile of CNN leaked questions to Clinton's campaign prior to one primary debate, and Matt Lauer deferred to Clinton's request not to ask a question about the email scandal.
- Moderators became more active in the debates, playing the role of "fact checker," especially with Trump. Moderators challenged, corrected, and interrupted Trump during the debates 106 times, compared to Clinton's 44 times. In fact, moderators took 50 percent more time during the debates than

in 2012. Thus, not only did we witness a new degree of activism by the moderators, they clearly focused on Trump more than on Clinton.

- Despite the viewership and "rough-and-tumble" nature of the debates, neither candidate received huge bumps in the polls. There is some evidence that Trump might have benefited slightly from the exchanges.[36]

Polls did indicate that Clinton "won" the three debates, although each contained some "magic moments" of exchanges. However, the third debate was Trump's best in terms of overall performance. He showed more discipline, stayed on his message points, and was effective in challenging and attacking Clinton.[37]

In the end, the debates did not appear to generate major shifts of support between the candidates. Trump met expectations of "being Trump," and moderators were criticized for being biased toward Clinton. However, the debate performances reinforced commitment to the individual candidates.

## ADVERTISING

According to Scott Dunn and John Tedesco, political advertising is a candidate-controlled medium that allows campaigns to present positive messages about their candidates, to attack issue stances and opponent images, or to respond to the attacks made by the opposition. Most specifically, television advertising is a form of communication that allows candidates to create and disseminate messages without journalistic gatekeeping or direct interpretation.[38] Research shows that political advertising reinforces attitudes of base voters and may well sway low-information voters. As with virtually every other feature or characteristic of the 2016 presidential campaign, television advertising was also unique and historic. Televised spending and the total number of ads were down from the previous campaign. During the general campaign season, 117,000 ads aired, compared to 256,000 during the 2012 presidential campaign.[39] Because Trump received so much "free media," he stated, "You know, I go around, I make speeches. I talk to reporters. I don't even need commercials, if you want to know the truth."[40]

In terms of outside interests or "Super PAC" ads, over $1.5 billion was spent during the presidential campaign, up from about $1 billion in 2012. Three times more of the allocation was spent in favor of Clinton than for Trump. Compare these numbers to $338 million in 2008.[41]

Overall, Dunn and Tedesco found that the ads in 2016 were primarily negative and image focused, with few ads focused on issues. Both candidates tended to rely upon comparative ads to convince the public that the candidate of the sponsor of the ad was the least objectionable alternative.[42] Lynn Vavreck found that 75 percent of Clinton's appeals in ads were about character traits, with only 9 percent focusing on jobs and the economy.[43] Clinton ads attempted to argue that Trump was clearly unfit for office primarily because of his temperament and lack of experience. Any positive Clinton ads focused on her record working for families and children. Clinton used several strategies in her ads. The predominant one was using Trump's own words from campaign events and media interviews to demonstrate his unfitness for office. His language, characterizations of immigrants and opponents, impersonations, references to specific individuals such as Senator McCain, and grandiose boasts portrayed Trump as a bad role model, bully, and bigot. A second strategy was to use anti-Trump quotes and comments by Republicans, from well-known leaders such as Mitt Romney to testimonials from ordinary citizens. Finally, as mentioned above, the Clinton campaign used comparative ads to contrast Trump's lack of experience and questions of temperament compared to her "proven" qualities of leadership, experience, and empathy.[44]

The Trump campaign relied even more heavily on negative and comparative ads. The primary strategy for Trump's ads was focused on allegations of Clinton's corruption, which clearly would make her unfit to be president. Most of the ads focused on words from FBI director James Comey, the many revelations from the leaked emails, and Clinton's contradictory statements about the email server. Ads also raised questions about Clinton's "fortitude, strength, or stamina." As with the Clinton campaign, the Trump campaign also used the strategy of using Clinton's own words to question her veracity and judgment.

They especially put her comments characterizing Trump supporters as "the basket of deplorables" to good use. The campaign also used comparative ads to attack Clinton. In addition, several ads compared the differing visions of America between the candidates and Trump's experience in the private sector versus Clinton's experience in government. Collectively, the Trump campaign ads portrayed Clinton as a corrupt career politician.[45] Interestingly, about a third of Trump's appeal in ads was focused on economic issues of jobs, taxes, and trade.[46]

As will be discussed next, there were other media outlets for message dissemination. However, in terms of television advertising, the messages were highly negative, attempting to get people to vote "against" the other candidate rather than "for" either of them. As Dunn and Tedesco conclude from their analysis of the ads, "More ambivalent voters would have had a hard time discerning any compelling reason to vote for either candidate based on the campaign advertising (although they would have found plenty of reason to vote *against* both candidates)."[47]

## SOCIAL MEDIA

Social media, broadly defined, has transformed electoral politics, especially at the national level. In fact, John Allen Hendricks and Dan Schill argue that "political campaigns today *are* social media campaigns."[48] Social media, of course, allows candidates to speak directly, without filter, to voters. And the access is staggering. According to the Pew Research Center, 86 percent of Americans use the internet, and among those, 80 percent use Facebook, 32 percent Instagram, 31 percent Pinterest, and 24 percent Twitter.[49] In addition, 75 percent of Americans own a smartphone.[50] During the 2016 campaign, 65 percent of voters sought news of the campaign from digital sources.[51] For Hendricks and Schill, the unprecedented use of social media in the 2016 presidential campaign led to unpredictability, disruption, and the blurring of political discourse.[52] Tweets would generate headlines, some Facebook posts would advocate "hate" and "violence," and rumors and dubious posts were treated as factual and accurate journalism. Often during the campaign, according to Diana Owen, "Social media fed the cable news media beast and drowned out legacy news journalism."[53]

For campaigns, social media provides two primary functions. First, social media campaigns can solidify and activate the candidate's base or core constituencies. Second, as discovered during the 2016 election, the use of social media can drive media coverage and stories of the campaigns.[54] The Clinton campaign used digital outlets to focus on solidifying her base targeted to women, young voters, and minorities. In contrast, Trump would use social media to attack opponents as well as the press, generating content that dominated news coverage almost daily.

These innovations to campaign communication, for good or bad, naturally fit Donald Trump. He saw the value of personal appeals and access to very distinct groups and voters without filters. Clinton's use of social media was to create "warm and fuzzy" images or as a key element of get-out-the-vote efforts. Trump, in contrast, used social media for highly personal statements, immediate reactions, and personal engagement with supporters.[55]

In terms of numbers, Trump enjoyed twenty-two million followers on his Facebook, Twitter, Instagram, and Reddit accounts, compared to Clinton's fourteen million. It is worthy to note that these numbers far surpass the daily viewership on cable network news outlets, including leader Fox News.[56] The networks and cable outlets simply could not keep up or muster the audience, hence the influence of social media. The success of Trump on social media was, as noted above, one reason the Trump campaign spent so little and found little need to spend large sums of money on paid advertising. In fact, campaign social media generated $3.4 million in free media coverage for Trump and only $1.4 million for the Clinton campaign.[57]

The Clinton campaign had a staff of over one hundred assigned to its digital team, responsible for all the content development, production, and execution of posts and advertising.[58] As already noted, the team wanted content to be highly favorable to Clinton and inspirational. The goal was to humanize Clinton with references to her roles as mother, wife, and grandparent. Clinton's podcasts attempted to make her more personable and open. The Clinton campaign also used social media to attack Trump. The analysis of political communication scholar Jennifer Stromer-Galley found that the Clinton campaign posted three times more messages on issues than the Trump campaign. They also tended to provide facts backing any claims. In contrast, Trump used more personal posts with broad generalizations or more generic claims with little factual evidence.[59]

For the Trump campaign, son-in-law Jared Kushner led the social media efforts and the general campaign advertising strategy. Hendricks and Schill note that the campaign also relied heavily on "big data" to make message content and targeting decisions. The information also identified which issues and messages to target for different regions of the nation. Interestingly, the data also influenced decisions of travel, fund-raising, and speech topics.[60]

When considering platforms, Twitter was the dominant medium of choice for Trump. He also enjoyed the most "likes" and "retweets" during the campaign. Trump and/or his campaign posted more than three thousand tweets, with some estimates that one in eight were personal insults.[61] By Election Day, Trump had over thirteen million followers, compared to Clinton's ten million. In addition,

Trump supporters were most likely to "retweet," thus extending his reach and influence with potential voters.[62]

Although only 4 percent of Americans use Reddit, the social media outlet that allows users to vote on content, 70 percent of users get news from the site. Users are younger and male. On this platform, Bernie Sanders was the most discussed candidate with comments (165,000), followed by Clinton (85,000) and Trump (73,000).[63] Snapchat, a relatively new platform, was also popular among younger Americans ages eighteen to thirty-four. This medium provided the opportunity to reach the younger and millennial youth. Pictures and story content disappear after twenty-four hours. Users would post items from live campaign events. The postings were spontaneous and informal. Both Trump and Clinton purchased Snap Ads, ten-second videos that would capture an event, location, or "fun" moment.[64]

Both campaigns also used Instagram on a major scale. Trump had 1,300 posts with 4.5 million followers, compared to Clinton with 835 posts and 4.2 million followers. Both campaigns shared personal stories, pictures of family, and informal shots at campaign rallies. Hendricks and Schill note that Trump actually broke campaign norms during the primaries by posting attack-style videos. These videos were also posted on other platforms.[65]

YouTube was a major source of campaign material. Over four billion views of candidate videos occurred in the last eight months of the campaign, and well over one billion in the final month.[66] Both campaigns were virtually equal in usage and viewership. The ads were most effective, with three ranking among YouTube's top ten most watched ads in its history.[67] According to Hendricks and Schill, in addition to more traditional ads, the most common videos were late-night comedy clips, commentary videos, news clips, debate exchanges, live events, and parody clips.[68]

Finally, Facebook was not only an essential part of the social media campaign for Trump and Clinton; political action committees and special interest groups used it as well. The platform even solicited campaigns offering special tools and capabilities.[69] The data collected on users of the platform allowed campaigns to "pinpoint individual voters at the most granular of levels and tailor messages to voters based on the issues and appeals that will be most likely to resonate with each individual voter."[70] On this platform, Trump, once again, led in followers with 12.2 million to Clinton's 8.2 million. For Trump, the Facebook appeals generated over $250 million in contributions. The Trump campaign also utilized the Facebook Live function significantly more than the Clinton campaign. On all aspects of Facebook, the Trump campaign dominated.[71]

## JOURNALISM AND THE 2016 PRESIDENTIAL CAMPAIGN

As noted in great detail in chapter 13, there was a major transition in the reporting and coverage of the 2016 presidential campaign. While it largely reflected the national polarization and fragmentation of political views and values generally, media hostility and sources of misinformation prevailed. This was true for both Hillary Clinton and Donald Trump. Clearly, the coverage of the campaigns has damaged the practice and profession of journalism in the United States. In the post-election era, controversy about the tone, coverage, and truthfulness of the media continues. And sadly, most Americans continue to "live" in news bubbles where information reinforces existing beliefs, attitudes, and values. One cannot examine the factors, context, and dynamics of the 2016 presidential campaign without noting the role of the news media.

## THE ISSUE OF GENDER

According to virtually all political observers and pundits, Hillary Clinton was going to be elected the first woman president of the United States. Despite the surprisingly challenging primary season, the election was hers to lose. As noted in the introduction, Trump managed a historic election upset. In the aftermath of the election, women had voted in overwhelming numbers for Clinton; however, non-college-educated women voted for Trump two to one, and he won evangelical white women by double digits. Exit polls also revealed that many women who voted for Clinton did so with some ambivalence. Younger, "third wave feminists" stayed home compared to previous elections.[72]

There was no question that gender would be an issue in the presidential campaign, not unlike it was in the 2008 contest with the nomination fight between Obama and Clinton and with Sarah Palin as the Republican vice presidential candidate. A great deal of research recognizes many challenges for women in American electoral politics, ranging from feminine versus masculine traits, level of perceived aggressiveness, management skills, role of emotion, and even dress, to name a few. During the campaign, as anticipated, there were some "gendered" issues raised about Clinton: comments about her hairstyles, pantsuits, and fashion choices, shrill voice, and her shouting and screaming her lines at rallies.[73] A Rasmussen poll in 2016 reported that 78 percent of men and 79 percent of women could vote for a woman for president, but only 4 percent would vote for a woman *because* the candidate was female.[74]

Unlike the 2008 campaign where Clinton downplayed her gender and the historic nature of the potential of a woman president, in 2016 she used her gender as a strategic appeal. In terms of women, Clinton was quick to note the historic importance of the election of a woman president. Second, she reminded voters of her "feminist" credentials, and finally she addressed issues and positions most important to women voters, such as education, health care, gun control, equal pay, women's choice, and more. An interesting tactic that evolved was Clinton talking about her role as mother and now grandmother. Such discussions and appeals allowed her be perceived as more personable and warm.[75]

What became apparent during the primary season was that younger, millennial women were not enamored with her candidacy and felt no obligation to support Clinton because of her gender. The younger women viewed Clinton's feminism as more traditional, outdated, and limited. She lacked concern for women of color and lower socioeconomic class, and issues of social and economic justice. To this generation of feminists, her appeal was more concerned with women's empowerment. In addition, many younger women questioned her authenticity as a feminist because her entire career was based on her husband, Bill Clinton.[76]

To make matters worse, as the younger women became familiar with the Monica Lewinsky scandal, they questioned her comments about and treatment of women who came forward accusing Bill Clinton of sexual assault. Of course, Trump entered the debate accusing Clinton of being a hypocrite in terms of defending her husband. According to him, she was actually "an enabler."[77] Any time the Clinton campaign would call Trump a sexist, supporters of Trump would claim she was using the "woman's card." Throughout the campaign, Clinton did try to appeal to millennials, relying upon surrogates such as actor Lena Dunham (creator and star of HBO's *Girls*) and singer Demi Lovato, who would introduce her at rallies.[78]

Issues of gender were actually equal or more central to the Trump campaign. During the primary period, Trump made headlines with attacks on former Fox anchor Megyn Kelly, opponent Carly Fiorina, and Ted Cruz's wife, Heidi. In addition, he vowed to "punish" women who have abortions if they are made illegal and defended his campaign manager, who was accused of shoving a female reporter. During the primary season, Clinton enjoyed a twenty-point advantage over Trump with women voters. Among Republican women, he garnered half of their support. However, for those women who did support him, they largely discounted criticisms, saying he was not politically correct, not a professional politician, and that he treats men and women equally and even hires more women in his companies than men. Nevertheless, the "gender gap" problem followed Trump throughout the primary season.[79]

The myriad issues of gender, broadly defined, continued during the general campaign season. Gender, as a topic and related issues, dominated media coverage and political commentary, and also was addressed by the candidates. The 2016 presidential election evolved as the most "gendered" presidential campaign in American history. For Clinton, it was because she occupied a historic moment. However, for Trump, some argued that he made gender an issue strategically and by design. Julie Sedivy argued that Trump proudly displayed his masculinity. He continually displayed his "maleness" in statements and actions.[80] At rallies, Trump encouraged the chant "Lock her up," and said that she didn't have a "presidential look" or the needed "stamina" to do the job. He raised questions of her health and state of mind.

The debates also displayed issues of gender both directly and indirectly. Trump was accused of "chauvinistic bullying" during the debates. For example, in the first debate, Trump made a total of seventy-three interruptions, including seizing the floor from Clinton three times. Clinton made only five interruptions throughout the debate.[81] During the debate there was a "magic moment" when Clinton directly attacked Trump for his treatment of women by using the example of former Miss Universe Alicia Machado, whom he called "Ms. Piggy" and "Ms. Housekeeping." For several days after the debate, Trump had to defend his comments and others considered demeaning toward women. Trump defenders noted his lack of direct attack on Clinton in response during the debate, that Clinton took money from countries that stoned and imprisoned women, and that she was a "phony feminist" for defending the behavior of her husband, Bill Clinton.[82]

Of course, one cannot discuss gender and the campaign without noting the *Access Hollywood* tape where Trump was very crass and even suggested an act of sexual assault. Trump apologized and described the exchange as "locker room" talk. General outrage was expressed universally, but among Republican women, 73 percent indicated that they would still support him. The rationale was that issues and candidate positions were more important in the election.[83]

In response to the "gender gap," Trump hired Kellyanne Conway, a long-time Republican strategist and pollster. At all rallies Trump reiterated his love, support, and respect for women and addressed women's issues and concerns directly. Conway is credited with softening his rhetoric, keeping him more focused and disciplined in terms of messaging. She also encouraged his appeal to black voters to demonstrate that he was not a bigot. In addition, Conway was a great media spokesperson for Trump. As a successful woman and mother of four young children, she could attack Clinton and demonstrate that she understood the issues of concern for all women.[84]

In the final weeks of the campaign, both candidates made overt appeals for the women's vote. The Clinton campaign made several ads targeted to women using Trump's own words to reflect his "true" attitudes toward women and related issues. The Trump campaign used ads featuring his daughter Ivanka, a mother of three herself, calling for laws to help women in the workplace. The Trump campaign emphasized the issues of health and education more than the Clinton campaign, especially in the final days of the campaign.[85]

The "gender gap" in voting emerged in the 1980s. Married white women and white evangelical women favored Republicans, whereas minority and younger women favored Democrats. The "gap" went from the low double digits by the mid-1980s to the low twenties by 2000 forward. Many pundits predicted a record high in the size of the gender gap for 2016.[86] However, that would not be the case. Clinton received 54 percent to Trump's 42 percent of the women's vote. Upon further analysis, Trump received 53 percent of the white women's vote, 62 percent of white non-college-educated women's vote, 45 percent of white college-educated women's vote, and 89 percent of Republican women's vote. In fact, Clinton got 1 percent less of the women's vote than Barack Obama in 2012.[87] In the end, Trump performed as most contemporary Republican presidential candidates. Perhaps issues and life experiences mean more than gender when it comes to voting. Certainly, in terms of gender, identity politics did not play the role anticipated by the Clinton campaign.

Issues of gender were certainly an important part of the 2016 presidential campaign for both Clinton and Trump. No doubt women in record numbers voted against Trump, and those who voted for Clinton reveal some degree of misgiving. There were the expected gender characterizations and portrayals that hamper most women candidates for any office. However, it was unexpected reactions of the "third wave" feminist and younger women voters who largely rejected the notion of a first woman president as justification for voting for Clinton. In addition, who would have guessed the multitude of questionable sexist statements and behaviors of Trump in a presidential campaign? In her concession speech, Clinton did hold out hope and optimism that indeed a woman would become president sooner rather than later. "And to all the women, and especially the young women, who put their faith in this campaign and in me, I want you to know that nothing has made me prouder than to be your champion. Now, I know we have still not shattered that highest and hardest glass ceiling, but some day someone will and hopefully sooner than we might think right now."[88]

## CONCLUSIONS

As noted in the introduction to this chapter, thousands of volumes and millions of pages will be written about the 2016 presidential campaign. Discussions about the 2020 campaign have already begun. Concerns about the role of the media continue, and it has become clear that Trump will be our first "Twitter president." And issues of gender will continue to be of concern, with several women's names being mentioned as running for the presidency in 2020. While traditional elements of campaign communication were evident and played major roles in the election, newer elements of social media and journalistic practices transformed the political campaign landscape in America.

Campaigns, as noted in the preface of *Political Campaign Communication: Principles and Practice,* are indeed a communication phenomenon. They represent in many ways our national conversations on issues, policies, and government. Campaigns are also highly complex and sophisticated communication events. This chapter provided a very brief overview of some of the communication elements, strategies, and tactics of the 2016 presidential campaign.

## NOTES

1. Much of this discussion is based on introductory material in Robert E. Denton, Jr., "Preface," in *The 2016 US Presidential Campaign: Political Communication and Practice,* ed. Robert E. Denton, Jr. (Cham, Switzerland: Palgrave Macmillan, 2017), vii–x.

2. "56 Interesting Facts about the 2016 Election," Cook Political Report, December 16, 2012, accessed December 20, 2016, http://cookpolitical.com/story/10201.

3. Dylan Byers, "How Donald Trump Changed Political Journalism," Money.CNN.com, November 2, 2016, accessed November 15, 2016, http://money.cnn.com/2016/11/01/media/political-journalism-2016/index.html?iid=Lead.

4. Craig Allen Smith, "Setting the Stage: Three Dimensions of Surfacing for 2016," in *The 2016 US Presidential Campaign: Political Communication and Practice,* ed. Robert E. Denton, Jr. (Cham, Switzerland: Palgrave Macmillan, 2017), 3–25.

5. Ibid., 12–13.

6. Ibid., 15–20.

7. James Ceaser, Andrew E. Busch, and John J. Pitney, Jr., *Defying the Odds: The 2016 Elections and American Politics* (Lanham, MD: Rowman & Littlefield, 2017), 43–46.

8. Ibid., 59.

9. Ibid., 94.

10. Rhodes Cook, "Presidential Primaries: A Hit at the Ballot Box," in *Trumped: The 2016 Election That Broke All the Rules,* ed. Larry Sabato, Kyle Kondik, and Geoffrey Skelley (Lanham, MD: Rowman & Littlefield, 2017), 83.

11. Ibid., 85.

12. Ibid., 90.

13. Judith Trent, Robert Friedenberg, and Robert E. Denton, Jr., *Political Campaign Communication: Principles and Practices,* 8th ed. (Lanham, MD: Rowman & Littlefield, 2016), 34–45.

14. Rachel L. Holloway, "Midnight in America: The Political Conventions in 2016," in *The 2016 US Presidential Campaign: Political Communication and Practice,* ed. Robert E. Denton, Jr. (Cham, Switzerland: Palgrave Macmillan, 2017), 30.

15. Ibid., 30–33.

16. Ibid., 34–37.

17. Ibid., 38.

18. Ibid., 41–44.

19. Jim A. Kuypers, "The Presidential Nomination Acceptance Speeches of Donald J. Trump and Hillary Clinton," in *Political Campaign Communication: Theory, Method, and Practice*, ed. Robert E. Denton, Jr. (Lanham, MD: Rowman & Littlefield, 2017), 143.

20. "Donald Trump, Republican Presidential Candidate, Delivers Remarks at the 2016 Republican National Convention," *Federal News Service*, July 21, 2016, accessed June 16, 2017 from Lexis/Nexis Academic database.

21. Holloway, "Midnight in America," 48.

22. Ibid., 48–49.

23. Ibid., 52–53.

24. "Bill Clinton Delivers Remarks at the 2016 Democratic National Convention," *Federal News Service*, July 26, 2016, accessed June 16, 2017 from Lexis/Nexis Academic database.

25. Holloway, "Midnight in America," 54–58.

26. Ibid., 61–62.

27. Ibid., 61–64.

28. Kuypers, "Presidential Nomination Acceptance Speeches," 161–62.

29. Holloway, "Midnight in America," 64.

30. Ibid., 65.

31. Ibid., 66.

32. Ibid., 67.

33. Ben Voth, "The Presidential Debates 2016," in *The 2016 US Presidential Campaign: Political Communication and Practice*, ed. Robert E. Denton, Jr. (Cham, Switzerland: Palgrave Macmillan, 2017), 78–79.

34. Ibid., 81.

35. Ibid., 81–82.

36. Ibid., 80–94.

37. Ceaser, Busch, and Pitney, *Defying the Odds*, 112.

38. Scott Dunn and John C. Tedesco, "Political Advertising in the 2016 Presidential Election," in *The 2016 US Presidential Campaign: Political Communication and Practice*, ed. Robert E. Denton, Jr. (Cham, Switzerland: Palgrave Macmillan, 2017), 99–100.

39. Ibid., 100.

40. Ibid.

41. Michael E. Toner and Karen E. Trainer, "The $7 Billion Election," in *Trumped: The 2016 Election That Broke All the Rules*, ed. Larry J. Sabato, Kyle Kondik, and Geoffrey Skelley (Lanham, MD: Rowman & Littlefield, 2017), 186.

42. Dunn and Tedesco, "Political Advertising in the 2016 Presidential Election," 108.

43. Lynn Vavreck, "Why This Election Was Not about the Issues," *New York Times*, November 23, 2016, accessed June 22, 2017, https://www.nytimes.com/2016/11/23/upshot/this-election-was-not-about-the-issues-blame-the-candidates.html.

44. Dunn and Tedesco, "Political Advertising in the 2016 Presidential Election," 103–10.

45. Ibid., 110–15.

46. Vavreck, "Why This Election Was Not about the Issues."

47. Dunn and Tedesco, "Political Advertising in the 2016 Presidential Election," 115.

48. John Allen Hendricks and Dan Schill, "The Social Media Election of 2016," in *The 2016 US Presidential Campaign: Political Communication and Practice*, ed. Robert E. Denton, Jr. (Cham, Switzerland: Palgrave Macmillan, 2017).

49. Shannon Greenwood, Andrew Perrin, and Maeve Duggan, "Social Media Update 2016: Facebook Usage and Engagement Is on the Rise, While Adoption of Other Platforms

Holds Steady," Pew Research Center, November 11, 2016, http://www.pewinternet .org/2016/11/11/social-media-update-2016.

50. Keely Lockhart, "Watch: Why Social Media Is Donald Trump's Most Powerful Weapon," *[London] Telegraph*, September 22, 2016, http://www.telegraph.co.uk/ news/2016/09/22/watch-why-social-media-is-donald-trumps-most-powerful-weapon/.

51. Diana Owen, "Twitter Rants, Press Bashing, and Fake News," in *Trumped: The 2016 Election That Broke All the Rules*, ed. Larry J. Sabato, Kyle Kondik, and Geoffrey Skelley (Lanham, MD: Rowman & Littlefield, 2017), 172.

52. Hendricks and Schill, "Social Media Election of 2016," 122.

53. Owen, "Twitter Rants," 167.

54. Ibid., 173.

55. Hendricks and Schill, "Social Media Election of 2016," 122–23.

56. Ibid., 124.

57. Darren Samuelsohn, "Trump's Twitter Army: New Data Show the GOP Nominee's Followers Are Exactly What the Dems Hoped They Weren't—Reliable Voters," *Politico*, June 15, 2016, https://www.politico.com/story/2016/06/trumps-twitter-army-224345.

58. Hendricks and Schill, "Social Media Election of 2016," 125–29.

59. Jennifer Stromer-Galley, "In the Age of Social Media, Voters Still Need Journalists," U.S. Election Analysis 2016, http://www.electionanalysis2016.us/us-election-analysis 2016/section-6-internet/in-the-age-of-social-media-voters-still-need-journalists.

60. Hendricks and Schill, "Social Media Election of 2016," 129.

61. Ibid., 134.

62. Ibid., 131.

63. Ibid., 136.

64. Ibid., 137.

65. Ibid., 139.

66. Ibid., 138.

67. Ibid.

68. Ibid.

69. Ibid., 140.

70. Ibid.

71. Ibid., 141.

72. Robert E. Denton, Jr., "Issues of Gender in the 2016 Presidential Campaign," in *The 2016 US Presidential Campaign: Political Communication and Practice*, ed. Robert E. Denton, Jr. (Cham, Switzerland: Palgrave Macmillan, 2017), 179–80.

73. See ibid., 180–81.

74. "Should Women Vote First for Women?" Rasmussen Reports, February 11, 2016, accessed July 2, 2017, http://www.rasmussenreports.com/public_content/politics/ general_politics/february_2016/should_women_vote_first_for_women.

75. Denton, "Issues of Gender in the 2016 Presidential Campaign," 182.

76. Ibid., 182–84.

77. Amy Chozick, "'90s Scandals Threaten to Erode Hillary Clinton's Strength with Women," *New York Times*, January 20, 2016, accessed January 20, 2016, https://www .nytimes.com/2016/01/21/us/politics/90s-scandals-threaten-to-erode-hillary-clintons -strength-with-women.html.

78. Denton, "Issues of Gender in the 2016 Presidential Campaign," 184.

79. Ibid., 189–90.

80. Julie Sedivy, "Donald Trump Talks Like a Woman," *Politico*, October 25, 2016, accessed October 26, 2016, http://www.politico.com/magazine/story/2016/10/trump -feminine-speaking-style-214391.

81. Ben Schreckinger and Daniel Strauss, "Did Trump Come Off as Sexist?" *Politico*, September 27, 2016, accessed September 27, 2016, http://www.politico.com/story/2016/09/trump-women-sexism-debate-clinton-228759.

82. Ibid.

83. Clare Malone, "For Many GOP Women, Party Loyalty Trumps Personal Affront," FiveThirtyEight.com, October 14, 2016, accessed October 15, 2016, http://fivethirtyeight.com/features/for-many-gop-women-party-loyalty-trumps-personal-affront.

84. Ibid.

85. Philip Rucker, "Trump Has a Challenge with White Women: 'You Just Want to Smack Him,'" *Washington Post*, October 1, 2016, accessed October 2, 2016, https://www.washingtonpost.com/politics/trump-has-a-challenge-with-white-women-you-just-want-to-smack-him/2016/10/01/df08f9ee-875b-11e6-a3ef-f35afb41797f_story.html?utm_term=.b24677b65c3e.

86. Geoffrey Skelley, "Venus vs. Mars: A Record-Setting Gender Gap?" Sabato's Crystal Ball, July 7, 2016, accessed July 13, 2016, http://www.centerforpolitics.org/crystalball/articles/venus-vs-mars-a-record-setting-gender-gap.

87. Susan Page, "For Clinton, Sisterhood Is Powerful—and Trump Helps," *USA Today*, July 11, 2016, accessed July 12, 2016, http://www.usatoday.com/story/news/politics/elections/2016/07/10/hillary-clinton-women-voters/86793244.

88. "Hillary Clinton's Concession Speech (full text)," CNN, November 9, 2016, http://www.cnn.com/2016/11/09/politics/hillary-clinton-concession-speech.

# Index

# About the Authors

**Robert E. Denton, Jr.,** holds the W. Thomas Rice Chair of Leadership Studies in the Pamplin College of Business and is professor in the Department of Communication at Virginia Tech. He served as the founding director of the Rice Center for Leader Development from 1996 to 2007. He currently serves as Head of the Department of Communication since 2009, a position he also held from 1988 until 1996. He has degrees in political science and communication from Wake Forest University and Purdue University. In addition to numerous articles, essays, and book chapters, he is author, coauthor, or editor of thirty books, several in multiple editions. The most recent titles include *Studies of Communication in the 2016 Presidential Campaign* (2018), *The 2016 Presidential Campaign: Political Communication and Practice* (2017), and *Social Fragmentation and the Decline of American Democracy: The End of the Social Contract* (with Ben Voth, 2017).

**Judith S. Trent** is professor emerita of communication at the University of Cincinnati. She is the author of numerous books, book chapters, and journal articles, most recently including "The Early Presidential Campaign of 2012 and the Grand Old Party 'Wannabees': Surfacing Still Counts," in *Studies of Communication in the 2012 Presidential Campaign* (Robert E. Denton, Jr., ed.; 2014); "The Early Presidential Campaign of 2008: The Good, the Historical, but Rarely the Bad," in *The 2008 Presidential Campaign: A Communication Perspective* (Robert E. Denton, Jr., ed.; 2009); and "Political Communication: A Flourishing Field of Study and Scholarship," in *From 20th Century Beginnings to 21st Century Advances* (with Robert V. Friedenberg; James W. Chesebro, ed.; 2009). She has also served as editor of the books *Included in Communication: Learning Climates That Cultivate Racial and Ethnic Diversity* (2002) and *Communication: Views from the Helm for the 21st Century* (1998). She has written and spoken widely on the subject of political campaign communication and is a frequent commentator and analyst on political campaigns and candidates for the ABC, NBC, and CBS television affiliates in Cincinnati, as well as Ohio/Cincinnati newspapers. She won the 2009 Achievement Award from the

Western Michigan University College of Arts and Sciences and in 1997 she served as the president of the National Communication Association.

**Robert V. Friedenberg** is professor emeritus of communication at Miami (Ohio) University. He is the author of numerous books, book chapters, and articles, including "The 2004 Presidential Debate" in *The 2004 Presidential Campaign: A Communication Perspective* (Robert E. Denton, Jr., ed.; 2005). He is the author of *Notable Speeches in Contemporary Presidential Campaigns* (2002), *Communication Consultants in Political Campaigns: Ballot Box Warriors* (1997), and *Theodore Roosevelt and the Rhetoric of Militant Decency* (1989). He is the editor of *Rhetorical Studies of National Political Debates—1996* (1997) and *Rhetorical Studies of National Political Debates: 1960–1992* (1994). In 1989, he received the Outstanding Book of the Year Award from the Religious Speech Communication Association for *"Hear O Israel": The History of American Jewish Preaching, 1654–1970*. He has served as a communication consultant for the Republican National Committee and has been involved in more than seventy political campaigns.